Comparative Digital Copyright Law

Comparative Digital Copyright Law
Textbook

Péter Mezei - Dóra Hajdú - Luis Javier Capote-Pérez - Jie Qin

Published by:

Vandeplas Publishing, LLC – August 2020

801 International Parkway, 5th Floor
Lake Mary, FL. 32746
USA

www.vandeplaspublishing.com

ISBN: 978-1-60042-514-1

COMPARATIVE DIGITAL COPYRIGHT LAW

Textbook

Péter Mezei
Dóra Hajdú
Luis Javier Capote-Pérez
Jie Qin

Table of contents

How to Use the Book? An Introduction

When the first copyright statute was signed by *Stuart Anne*, Queen of England, in 1709, nobody expected that this fresh field of law will develop into such an economically and socially important one by the 21st century. The *Statute of Anne* tried to reach consensus between the interests of printers/booksellers and the authors. Three hundred years later stakeholders also include other creators (e.g. painters, sculpturers), neighbouring rightsholders (e.g. sound recording producers, radio and television companies, performers), *sui generis* rights holders (e.g. database producers in the European Union), platforms (most importantly streaming service providers) and the society (users, cultural organisations and the like). The task of legislators and judges in striking the balance of interests seems to be extremely hard these days. Authors were originally granted protection against illegal reproduction, translation and distribution of their works. Nowadays the list of their exclusive rights is much longer than ever before (including moral rights as well). In order to maintain a fair balance of these rights and the interests of the users, various limitations and exceptions apply, e.g. free uses, collective rights management, territorial and term restrictions.

The broadening of copyright norms has been due to different factors since the appearance of Gutenberg's printing press in the middle of the 15th century. These factors include technological innovation as well as the constant changes of rightsholders' and society's needs and interests. While the pace of development in the first two centuries of copyright law was quite slow, legislation and case law have expanded with an enormous speed in the last half century.

This book introduces some of the most recent and relevant examples of the economic, social and legal disputes related to digital copyright law. The list of the "hot topics" is purposefully selective. This selection was to comply with the needs of a course offered for Hungarian and international law students in various countries. With the help of the book students can get familiarized with the most important features of the digital copyright law of the European Union, the United States of America and the People's Republic of China, and will gather the knowledge how to handle similar copyright problems during their future career.

All chapters discuss the selected problems through the comparative analysis of case law from multiple jurisdictions. The cases are edited where necessary, leaving only the most important elements of the – sometimes really long – judgments for discussion and debate. Decisions might be analysed through two converging approaches. The lecturers of the course might prefer to use either the American "*IRAC*" method or a revised version of the traditional French method of "*fiche d'arrêt*".

The term *IRAC* is the abbreviation of the process through which the case is dissected into four parts. "I" is for issue, "R" is for the rules, "A" is for the arguments and finally "C" is for conclusion. The *issue* includes all the relevant facts of the case. The correct understanding of these facts is a must for any further analysis of the decisions. This requires the accurate knowledge of both basic legal definitions and – in case of digital copyright disputes – the skill to understand technological features of the relevant uses. *Rules* include both statutes (and other regulations) and precedents. Referring to former court decisions has become general both in the Anglo-Saxon countries (like the United States and the United Kingdom) and in the case law of the Court of Justice of the European Union. *Arguments* cover both the statements and evidences of parties and the reasoning used by judges in reaching the conclusion. (These statements and evidences might only be indirectly deducted from the rulings.) Law students are the lawyers of the future and they might face similar legal troubles during their career. It is important for students to understand these arguments. Studying how parties succeeded or failed to win a case is extremely useful to improve students' personal skills of argumentation. Similarly, learning how judges reach a specific conclusion is inevitable to acquire the ability to predict future court decisions. Finally, *conclusion* is the heart of the judgments: material facts, binding rules and relevant arguments mixed into sentences that sum up precisely how the judge solves the debate. The *IRAC* process is not *per se* "within" (or written by) the decisions. This methodology shall be used during classroom education.

"*Fiche d'arrêt*" means an abstract of the given judgement. This traditional French method requires the answer of five questions. Like in the *IRAC* method, the first step is the *identification* and selection of the relevant facts of the case. The separation of the relevant and the irrelevant elements implies a prequalification of the material facts. This step is highly important while reading a complex case with several legal questions: usually diverse facts are related to every question. Mentioning *previous procedures* is the second part of the analysis. In the case law of the Court of Justice of European Union, the questions referred for a preliminary ruling by the national court fit in that part of the analysis. (The detailed discussion of the trial court rulings by the U.S. Circuit Courts plays the same role.) *Arguments* of the parties cover the third main part of the abstract. Distinguishing the arguments of the parties and arguments of the judge is the hardest part of the analysis. Sometimes the former ones do not appear in the case. Following these three warm-up questions, the analysis continues with two further tasks. Students have to *find the legal problem(s)*, in other words they have to raise the precise question(s) that the court shall answer. Speaking of the case law of the European Union, this step seems easy: the referring national court has already asked the questions. However, it might be necessary to rephrase them with the own words of the student in order to profoundly understand the legal problem.

The final phase is to determine the arguments of the court and the *conclusion* to answer the separate questions.

This textbook adds three further ways to support studying. Each case is followed by a "*Think it over*" section that tries to call attention to substantial questions related to the discussed topics. While there might be plenty of questions related to each court ruling, we have limited ourselves to raise maximum four or five questions. "*Further case law*" and "*Recommended readings*" sections, in accordance with their names, provide further tips for enthusiastic students what to read to broaden their knowledge in the given field. (Again, these recommendations are only a humble selection of the massive amounts of available resources.) As the book will be used in various countries, the editors collected cases and academic papers to cover various jurisdictions. Finally, the book includes a chapter titled "*Test Your Knowledge*". Here, the authors have included a few essay questions that were assigned to participants of their courses on digital copyright law. Students shall not forget that a proper answer to the essay question might require further research. You can find relevant resources for that purpose in the respective "*Further case law*" and "*Recommended readings*" sections.

The authors of this book are convinced that participants of the planned course will get familiarized with the practice-oriented, analytical aspects of copyright hot topics. The comparative legal aspect allows the students to understand the major differences of the various legal systems in order to study or criticize the different legal solutions. This approach will help the students to use European, American, Chinese and international copyright law rules in their future career at law firms or at courts, and to undertake independent research on the subject, using both traditional and Internet resources.

Admittedly, the book does not include the full analysis of the cases. That is always reserved for the classroom education and consultation with the students. Nevertheless, the concept of the book and the methodology used by the authors is introduced through the discussion of Case C-360/13 of the Court of Justice of the European Union, below.

PUBLIC RELATIONS CONSULTANTS ASSOCIATION LTD V. THE NEWSPAPER LICENSING AGENCY LTD AND OTHERS

Case C-360/13 - Judgment of the Court (Fourth Chamber), 5 June 2014 [ECLI:EU:C:2014:1195]

Background of the case

The ordinary use of the Internet involves the creation of temporary copies at several stages. Copies are created during transmission in Internet routers and proxy servers. Where an end-user watches a webpage on his computer, without downloading the exact content, the technical processes involved requires the temporary copying on screen and in the Internet cache memory of the hard disk. In computing, a cache is a hardware or software component that stores data so future requests for that data can be served faster. Data stored in a cache might be the result of an earlier computation or the duplication of data stored elsewhere.

The screen copy is an essential part of the technology involved. No webpages can be viewed without a screen copy. It will remain on screen until the user moves away from the webpage. The function of the Internet cache is somewhat more complex. It is a universal feature of current Internet browsing technology. It would be possible to design browsing software without an Internet cache, but in the present state of technology, the result would be that the Internet would be unable to cope with the traffic and would not function properly. The cache may be deliberately cleared by the end-user, but otherwise other material will overwrite it after an interval. Such period of time might depend on the capacity of the user's computer and the volume and timing of the user's Internet usage.

Discussion

The case introduces an important question about the application of copyright law to the technical process involved in viewing copyright material on the Internet. The capacity of the Internet cache might be modified by altering the browser settings on the user's computer. Deleted material can sometimes be retrieved by special software or specialised technicians. However, this is not the ordinary use of the Internet; the important point is that in none of these cases does the end-user set out to make a copy of the webpages unless he or she chooses to download it or print it out. The object is to view if the material and the copies temporarily retained on the screen or the Internet cache are merely an incidental consequence of the use of a computer to do that. The question, for the Supreme Court of the United Kingdom in the instant case, was whether those copies are infringing ones unless licensed by the rightsholders.

Public Relations Consultants Association Limited (PRC) is a professional association of public relations professionals. PRC monitors news coverage on behalf of its clients. One way of doing this is to use online monitoring of search services. Newspaper Licensing Agency (NLA) is an organization licensing media monitoring services that crawl the web and offer paid-for services based on their filtered results. The majority of media monitoring agencies signed up for the new web licence but not Meltwater. Meltwater argued that no license was required by its clients for this purpose, and in conjunction with PRC referred the case to the Copyright Tribunal.

The case is about the services provided to members of PRC by Meltwater. This group uses automated software programmes to create an index of words appearing on newspaper websites. Meltwater's customers provide search terms of interest to them, and Meltwater produces a monitoring report listing the results of a search of the index for those keywords. For each search hit, the monitoring report will present the opening words of the article, the keyword together with several words on either side of it, and a hyperlink – in the form of a reproduction of the headline – which enables the user to access the article on the relevant source website. It should, however, be noted that if that website has a paywall, the link will not enable the user to avoid it. The user will have to pay to access the material behind the paywall on the same terms as anyone else. Meltwater sends the monitoring report to the customer by email or the customers accesses it on Meltwater's website.

Central question

Meltwater's service involves the transmission of the monitoring report by e-mail. The e-mail copy is not temporary. It is stored on the recipient's hard drive until the end-user chooses to delete it. The question is whether customers would need a licence to receive the service if the monitoring report were made available only on the website. If the user downloads the report, there is a copy that will infringe the newspaper's copyright unless the customer is licensed. But what if the user merely views the material on the website? The Copyright Tribunal and the Court of Appeals held that a licence is also needed in that scenario. The problem affects, however, millions of non-commercial users of the Internet who may be incurring civil liability by viewing copyright material on the Internet without the authority of the rights owner.

Legal context

Section 28A Copyright, Designs and Patents Act 1988:

"Making of temporary copies

Copyright in a literary work, other than a computer program or a database, or in a dramatic, musical or artistic work, the typographical arrangement of a published edition, a sound recording or a film, is not infringed by the making of a temporary copy which is transient or incidental, which is an integral and essential part of a technological process and the sole purpose of which is to enable—

(a) a transmission of the work in a network between third parties by an intermediary; or

(b) a lawful use of the work;

and which has no independent economic significance."

This rule implements Article 5 of the Directive 2001/29/EC of 22 May 2001 on the harmonisation of certain aspects of copyright and related rights in the information society (InfoSoc Directive). The InfoSoc Directive introduces the possibility of some exceptions to the exclusive copyright to allow certain acts of temporary reproduction, in the name of the new electronic environment. According to the InfoSoc Directive:

"Recital (31) A fair balance of rights and interests between the different categories of rightholders, as well as between the different categories of rightholders and users of protected subject-matter must be safeguarded. The existing exceptions and limitations to the rights as set out by the Member States have to be reassessed in the light of the new electronic environment. Existing differences in the exceptions and limitations to certain restricted acts have direct negative effects on the functioning of the internal market of copyright and related rights. Such differences could well become more pronounced in view of the further development of transborder exploitation of works and cross-border activities. In order to ensure the proper functioning of the internal market, such exceptions and limitations should be defined more harmoniously. The degree of their harmonisation should be based on their impact on the smooth functioning of the internal market."

"Recital (33) The exclusive right of reproduction should be subject to an exception to allow certain acts of temporary reproduction, which are transient or incidental reproductions, forming an integral and essential part of a technological process and carried out for the sole purpose of enabling either efficient transmission in a network between third parties by an intermediary, or a lawful use of a work or other subject-matter to be made. The acts of reproduction concerned should have no separate economic value on their own. To the extent that they meet these conditions, this exception should include acts which enable browsing as well as acts of caching to take place, including those which enable transmission systems to function efficiently, provided that the intermediary does not modify the information and does not interfere with the lawful use of technology, widely recognised and used by industry, to obtain data on the use of the information. A use should be considered lawful where it is authorised by the rightholder or not restricted by law."

"Article 5
Exceptions and limitations

1. Temporary acts of reproduction referred to in Article 2, which are transient or incidental [and] an integral and essential part of a technological process and whose sole purpose is to enable:

(a) a transmission in a network between third parties by an intermediary, or

(b) a lawful use of a work or other subject-matter to be made, and which have no independent economic significance, shall be exempted from the reproduction right provided for in Article 2.

5. The exceptions and limitations provided for in paragraphs 1, 2, 3 and 4 shall only be applied in certain special cases which do not conflict with a normal exploitation of the work or other subject-matter and do not unreasonably prejudice the legitimate interests of the rightholder."

Decision

The Copyright Tribunal decided that Meltwater's customers needed a licence both to receive the monitoring reports by e-mail and to access them on Meltwater's website. The Court of Appeals confirmed this ruling, as the acts of reproduction took place following voluntary human process of accessing Meltwater's webpage. The Supreme Court decided to halt the case and ask the Court of Justice of the European Union for a preliminary ruling. The Supreme Court claimed that the issue had a transnational dimension and the application of copyright law to Internet uses has important implications for many millions of people across the EU. The tensions stemming from the case should be resolved in a manner which will apply uniformly in the EU. Thus, the Supreme Court requested quidance on Article 5.1 of the InfoSoc Directive. More precisely, whether the requirements of the InfoSoc Directive are satisfied in circumstances where:

- an end-user views a webpage without downloading, printing or otherwise setting out to make a copy of it;
- copies of that webpage are automatically made on screen and in the Internet "cache" on the end-user's hard disk;
- the creation of those copies is indispensable to the technical processes involved in correct and efficient Internet browsing;
- the screen copy remains on screen until the end-user moves away from the relevant web-page, when it is automatically deleted by the normal operation of the computer;
- the cached copy remains in the cache until it is overwritten by other material as the end-user views further webpages, when it is automatically deleted by the normal operation of the computer; and
- the copies are retained for no longer than the ordinary processes associated with Internet use referred to circumstances fourth and fifth.

The CJEU concluded that the conditions for the exceptions of Article 5.1 to 5.5 must be interpreted strictly, because they are derogations from the general rule, according to which the rightsholder shall authorize any reproduction of the protected subject matters. At the same time, exemptions provided in those articles shall allow and ensure the development and operation of new technologies, and safeguard a fair balance between the rights and interests of rightsholders and of users of protected works who wish to avail themselves of those technologies.

The CJEU stressed that the act of reproduction must be *temporary.* On-screen copies are deleted when the Internet user moves away from the website viewed. Cached copies are automatically replaced by other content after a certain time, depending on the capacity of the cache and on the extent and frequency of Internet usage. Thus, it must be held that those copies satisfy the condition of being temporary.

The act of reproduction shall also be an *integral part of a technological process*. In the instant case on-screen copies and the cached copies are created and deleted by the technological process used for viewing websites, with the result that they were made entirely in the context of that process. It is irrelevant that the process in question is activated by the Internet user and that it is terminated by a temporary act of reproduction such as the on-screen copy. There is no preclusion of the technological process from involving human intervention and from being activated or completed manually. In sum, the CJEU concluded that on-screen copies and cached copies are integral parts of the technological process described in the case.

The act of reproduction shall also be an *essential part of a technological process*. In the present case cached copies facilitate browsing on the Internet, since without these copies, the Internet would be unable to cope with current volumes of data transmitted online. The on-screen copies are required in the process of viewing websites on computers to function correctly and efficiently. Thus, the CJEU held that on-screen copies and cached copies are essential parts of the technological process described in the case.

Furthermore, the act of reproduction must be either transient or incidental. An act might be *transient*, if its duration is limited to what is necessary for that process to work properly. It is understood that that process must be automated inasmuch as it deleted such an act automatically, without human intervention, once its function of enabling the completion of such a process has ended. The requirement of automatic deletion does not preclude such a deletion from being preceded by human intervention directed at terminating the use of the technological process. An act of reproduction does not lose its transient nature merely because the deletion by the system of the copy generated is preceded by the intervention of the end-user designed to terminate the technological process concerned. On-screen copies remain in existence strictly during the time needed for the proper functioning of the technological process used for viewing the website concerned. Consequently, on-screen copies are transient.

An act of reproduction might be *incidental* if it neither exists independently of, nor has a purpose independent of the technological process of which it forms part. On-screen copies are automatically deleted by the computer at the moment when the Internet user moves away from the website concerned and, therefore, at the moment when there is a termination of the technological process used for viewing that site.

In compliance with Article 5.5 of the InfoSoc Directive, temporarys act of reproduction (like any other limitations and exceptions) shall remain certain special cases which do not conflict with a normal exploitation of the work and do not unreasonably prejudice the legitimate interests of the rightsholders. On-screen copies and cache copies are created only for the purpose of viewing websites. Those copies make it possible for Internet users to access works displayed on websites without the authorization of the copyright holders, but do not unreasonably prejudice the legitimate interests of those right holders. The works are made available to Internet users by the publishers of the websites, those publishers being required to obtain authorization from the copyright holders concerned, since that making available constitutes a communication to the public. The legitimate interests of rightsholders concerned are thus properly safeguarded.

Consequently, the CJEU answered that Article 5 of Directive 2001/29 must be interpreted as meaning that the on-screen copies and the cached copies made by an end-user in the course of viewing a website satisfy the conditions that those copies must be temporary, that they must be transient or incidental in nature and that they must constitute an integral and essential part of a technological process, as well as the conditions laid down in Article 5.5 of that Directive, and that they may therefore be made without the authorization of the copyright holders.

THINK IT OVER!

1. What do you think about the argument exposed in the case that should the viewing of copyright material on a webpage remain unlicenced, the copyright owner would be exposed to a *large-scale piracy that would be difficult to detect or prevent?* What do you think about *requiring all users to compensate rightsholders for the mere accessing of copyrighted materials?*

2. Meltwater was also sued in the United States. There, Associated Press sued Meltwater for infringing its copyrights by clipping and sharing news items. Meltwater argued that it shall be excused from liability under the fair use doctrine. The New York Southern District Court held that the copying by the defendant was not exempted under the fair use doctrine and Meltwater infringed the copyright of Associated Press. *What are the similarities of the two cases and the judgements? What relevant differences exist in the copyright norms of the United States and the European Union? What can be the consequences of different decisions in similar cases in a globalised market?*

3. *Can it be treated illegal to make periodical copies of all data stored on the end-user's hard drive on a backup system (e.g. in the cloud)?*

Further Case Law

Case C-5/08 - Infopaq International A/S v. Danske Dagblades Forening, Judgement of the Court (Fourth Chamber), 16 July 2009 [ECLI:EU:C:2009:465]

Case C-110/15 - Microsoft Mobile Sales International Oy and others vs Ministerio per I beni e le attività culturali, Judgment of the Court (Second Chamber), 22 September 2016 [ECLI:EU:C:2016:717]

Case C-527/15 - Stichting Brein vs Jack Frederik Wullens, Judgment of the Court (Second Chamber), 26 April 2017 [ECLI:EU:C:2017:300]

Associated Press v. Meltwater U. S. Holdings, Inc., et. al, 931 *F.Supp.2d* 537 (2013)

Recommended readings

In English

Martin Kretschmer: Digital Copyright: the End of an Era, *European Intellectual Property Review,* Issue 8/2003, p. 333-341

Lucie Guibault: Why Cherry-Picking Never Leads to Harmonisation: the Case of the Limitations on Copyright under Directive 2001/29/EC, *JIPITEC,* Issue 2/2010, p. 55-66.

Dylan J. Quinn: Associated Press v. Meltwater: Are Courts Being Fair to News Aggregators?, *Minnesota Journal of Law, Science & Technology,* Issue 2/2014, p. 1189-1219

Steven James: And Breathe ... You can Continue Browsing the Internet, as the CJEU Hands Down its Decision in PRCA v NLA (Meltwater), *Computer and Telecommunications Law Review,* Issue 6/2014, p. 169-171.

Paul Joseph - Adam Cusworth: Meltwater: Liability for Internet Browsing, *Journal of Intellectual Property Law and Practice,* Issue 11/2014, p. 885-887.

Michael Hart: The Legality of Internet Browsing in the Digital Age, *European Intellectual Property Review,* Issue 10/2014, p. 630-639.

Rosalind Jane Schonwald: Associated Press v. Meltwater US Holdings, Inc.: Fair Use, a Changing News Industry, and the Influence of Judicial Discretion and Custom, *Berkeley Technology Law Journal,* 2014, p. 799-836.

Irini Stamatoudi: *'Linking' and 'Browsing' in the Light of the EU Court of Justice's Case Law.* In: Tana Pistorius (Ed.): Intellectual Property Perspectives on the Regulation of New Technologies, Edward Elgar, Cheltenham, 2018, p. 179-207.

In French

Laure Marino: Arrêt Meltwater: du soleil et du surf (sur Internet), *Revue de jurisprudence sociale,* 2014, p. 27.

In German

Jochen Marly: Bildschirmkopien, Cache-Kopien und Streaming als urheberrechtliche Herausforderungen, *Europäische Zeitschrift für Wirtschaftsrecht,* Heft 16/2014, p. 616-619.

Michel M. Walter: Internet-Browsing - Bildschirm- und Cache-Kopien, *MR-Int: Internationale Rundschau zum Medienrecht, IP- & IT-Recht,* Heft 1/2015, p. 17.

In Spanish

Núria Gallart: Reflexiones ante la transposición de la Directiva 2001/29/CE, relativa a los derechos de autor en la sociedad de la información, *PH,* boletín 38, 2002, p. 244-246.

Ramón Casas Vallés: *La transposición de la Directiva 2001/29/CE en España* (artículo en línea), UOC, 2004 (http://www.uoc.edu/dt/esp/casas1204.pdf)

Juan Francisco Ortega Díaz: "Las excepciones de cita e ilustración en el entorno tradicional y digital. A propósito de la Directiva 2001/29/CE, de 22 de mayo, relativa a la adaptación de los derechos de autor y derechos afines en la sociedad de la información, *Revista de Propiedad Intelectual,* 19, 2005, p. 71-98.

Rodrigo Bercovitz Rodríguez-Cano: "Más sobre la excepción de copia privada", *Revista Doctrinal Aranzadi Civil-Mercantil,* n° 3/2015, parte comentario

~~~

Some people deserve special acknowledgment for their constructive contribution to this volume. *Dr. Mark Hyland,* Lecturer, College of Business, Technological University Dublin, Ireland has supported us with valuable data on the UK's case law on website blocking. *Emircan Karabuga* and *Usman Ghaffar,* master students of the Technical University of Dresden's IP LLM program – who have spent a full semester in Szeged, Hungary to expand their knowledge on comparative IP law – have provided proofreading help to us. A handful of Chinese master level students deserve appreciation as well. *Xiao Baiyang, Xu Zongyu, He Shuqin, Liu Kui, Li Yuhang, Shen Haolan, Yang Yulong, He Lujun* and *Luo Jie* have actively participated in the selection, translation, abridgement and analysis of the Chinese cases included in this book. From them, *Xiao Baiyang* deserves a special acknowledgement. He has acted as the main coordinator of the Chinese group of students, and provided inevitable extra information during the final editing process.
~~~

Chapter I
Protection of Computer Programs

Bezpečnostní softwarová asociace - Svaz softwarové ochrany v Ministerstvo kultury
Case C-393/09 - Judgment of the Court (Third Chamber), 22 December 2010 [ECLI:EU:C:2010:816]

(...) Legal context

International law

3 Under Article 10(1) of the Agreement on Trade-Related Aspects of Intellectual Property Rights, which constitutes Annex 1C to the Agreement establishing the World Trade Organisation, signed in Marrakech on 15 April 1994 and approved by Council Decision 94/800/EC of 22 December 1994 concerning the conclusion on behalf of the European Community, as regards matters within its competence, of the agreements reached in the Uruguay Round multilateral negotiations (1986-1994) (OJ 1994 L 336, p. 1; 'the TRIPs Agreement'):
'Computer programs, whether expressed in source code or in object code, will be protected as literary works pursuant to the Berne Convention [(Paris Act of 24 July 1971), as amended on 28 September 1979 ('the Berne Convention')].'

European Union legislation

Directive 91/250

4 The 7th, 10th and 11th recitals in the preamble to Directive 91/250 read as follows:
'Whereas, for the purpose of this Directive, the term 'computer program' shall include programs in any form, including those which are incorporated into hardware; whereas this term also includes preparatory design work leading to the development of a computer program provided that the nature of the preparatory work is such that a computer program can result from it at a later stage;
(...)

Whereas the function of a computer program is to communicate and work together with other components of a computer system and with users and, for this purpose, a logical and, where appropriate, physical interconnection and interaction is required to permit all elements of software and hardware to work with other software and hardware and with users in all the ways in which they are intended to function;

Whereas the parts of the program which provide for such interconnection and interaction between elements of software and hardware are generally known as "interfaces".'

5 Article 1 of Directive 91/250 provides:

'*1. In accordance with the provisions of this Directive, Member States shall protect computer programs, by copyright, as literary works within the meaning of the Berne Convention for the Protection of Literary and Artistic Works. For the purposes of this Directive, the term "computer programs" shall include their preparatory design material.*

2. Protection in accordance with this Directive shall apply to the expression in any form of a computer program. Ideas and principles which underlie any element of a computer program, including those which underlie its interfaces, are not protected by copyright under this Directive.

3. A computer program shall be protected if it is original in the sense that it is the author's own intellectual creation. No other criteria shall be applied to determine its eligibility for protection.'

Directive 2001/29

6 The 9th and 10th recitals in the preamble to Directive 2001/29 state:

'*Any harmonisation of copyright and related rights must take as a basis a high level of protection, since such rights are crucial to intellectual creation. Their protection helps to ensure the maintenance and development of creativity in the interests of authors, performers, producers, consumers, culture, industry and the public at large. Intellectual property has therefore been recognised as an integral part of property.*

If authors or performers are to continue their creative and artistic work, they have to receive an appropriate reward for the use of their work, as must producers in order to be able to finance this work. The investment required to produce products such as phonograms, films or multimedia products, and services such as "on-demand" services, is considerable. Adequate legal protection of intellectual property rights is necessary in order to guarantee the availability of such a reward and provide the opportunity for satisfactory returns on this investment.'

7 The 20th and 23rd recitals in the preamble to Directive 2001/29 state:

'*This Directive is based on principles and rules already laid down in the Directives currently in force in this area, in particular [Directive 91/250], and it develops those principles and rules and places them in the context of the information society. The provisions of this Directive should be without prejudice to the provisions of those Directives, unless otherwise provided in this Directive.*

(...)

This Directive should harmonise further the author's right of communication to the public. This right should be understood in a broad sense covering all communication to the public not present at the place where the communication originates. This right should cover any such transmission or retransmission of a work to the public by wire or wireless means, including broadcasting. This right should not cover any other acts.'

8 Article 1 of Directive 2001/29 provides:
'1. This Directive concerns the legal protection of copyright and related rights in the framework of the internal market, with particular emphasis on the information society.
2. Except in the cases referred to in Article 11, this Directive shall leave intact and shall in no way affect existing Community provisions relating to:
(a) the legal protection of computer programs; (...)'

9 Under Article 2(a) of Directive 2001/29:
'Member States shall provide for the exclusive right to authorise or prohibit direct or indirect, temporary or permanent reproduction by any means and in any form, in whole or in part:
(a) for authors, of their works.'

10 Article 3(1) of Directive 2001/29 provides:
'Member States shall provide authors with the exclusive right to authorise or prohibit any communication to the public of their works, by wire or wireless means, including the making available to the public of their works in such a way that members of the public may access them from a place and at a time individually chosen by them.'

National legislation

11 Directive 91/250 was transposed into the Czech legal order by Law No 121/2000 on copyright and related rights and the amendment of various laws (zákon č. 121/2000 o právu autorském, o právech souvisejících s právem autorským a o změně některých zákonů) of 7 April 2000 ('the Copyright Law').

12 By virtue of Article 2(1) of that Law, copyright covers all literary works or other artistic work created by its author, which may be expressed in any objectively perceptible form, including electronic, permanent or temporary, without regard to its scope, purpose or meaning.

13 Article 2(2) of that Law states that a computer program is also regarded as a work if it is original, in that it is an intellectual creation of its author.

14 In accordance with Article 65 of that Law:

'1. Computer programs, without regard to the form of their expression, including the preparatory elements of their conception, are protected as literary works.

2. The ideas and principles on which all elements of a computer program are based, including whose which are the basis of its connection to another program, are not protected under this Law.'

The dispute in the main proceedings and the questions referred for a preliminary ruling

15 On 9 April 2001, BSA, as an association, applied to the Ministerstvo kultury for authorisation for the collective administration of copyrights to computer programs, under Paragraph 98 of the Copyright Law. BSA defined the extent of those rights in a letter dated 12 June 2001.

16 That application was refused, and the administrative action brought against that refusal was dismissed. BSA then brought a legal action against those decisions before the Vrchní soud v Praze (High Court, Prague).

17 Following the setting aside of those two rejection decisions by the Nejvyšší správní soud (Supreme Administrative Court), to which the case was referred, on 14 April 2004 the Ministerstvo kultury adopted a fresh decision by which it again dismissed BSA's application. BSA therefore brought an administrative appeal before the Ministerstvo kultury, which annulled that rejection decision.

18 On 27 January 2005, the Ministerstvo kultury adopted a new decision, by which it rejected BSA's application yet again on the ground, firstly, in particular, that the Copyright Law protects only the object code and the source code of a computer program, but not the result of the display of the program on the computer screen, since the graphic user interface was protected only against unfair competition. Secondly, it stated that the collective administration of computer programs was indeed possible in theory, but that mandatory collective administration was not an option and that voluntary collective administration served no purpose.

19 BSA lodged an appeal against that decision, which was dismissed on 6 June 2005 by a decision of the Ministerstvo kultury. The association then challenged the latter decision before the Městský Soud v Praze (Regional Court, Prague). In its action, BSA submitted that the definition of a computer program in Paragraph 2(2) of the Copyright Law also covers the

user interface. In its submission, a computer program can be perceived at the level both of the source or object code and of the method of communication (communication interface).

20 The Městský soud v Praze having dismissed its action, BSA appealed on a point of law before the Nejvyšší správní soud. BSA takes the view that a computer program is used when it is shown in a display on user screens and that, consequently, such use must be protected by copyright.

21 As regards the interpretation of the provisions of Directives 91/250 and 2001/29, the Nejvyšší správní soud decided to stay the proceedings and refer the following questions to the Court for a preliminary ruling:

'1. Should Article 1(2) of [Directive 91/250] be interpreted as meaning that, for the purposes of the copyright protection of a computer program as a work under that directive, the phrase 'the expression in any form of a computer program' also includes the graphic user interface of the computer programme or part thereof?

2. If the answer to the first question is in the affirmative, does television broadcasting, whereby the public is enabled to have sensory perception of the graphic user interface of a computer program or part thereof, albeit without the possibility of actively exercising control over that program, constitute making a work or part thereof available to the public within the meaning of Article 3(1) of [Directive 2001/29]?'

(...)

Consideration of the questions referred

The first question

28 By its first question, the national court asks, in essence, whether the graphic user interface of a computer program is a form of expression of that program within the meaning of Article 1(2) of Directive 91/250 and is thus protected by copyright as a computer program under that directive.

29 Directive 91/250 does not define the notion of 'expression in any form of a computer program'.

30 In those circumstances, that notion must be defined having regard to the wording and context of Article 1(2) of Directive 91/250, where the reference to it is to be found and in the light of both the overall objectives of that directive and international law.

31 In accordance with Article 1(1) of Directive 91/250, computer programs are protected by copyright as literary works within the meaning of the Berne Convention. Article 1(2) thereof extends that protection to the expression in any form of a computer program.

32 The first sentence of the seventh recital in the preamble to Directive 91/250 states that, for the purposes of that directive, the term 'computer program' shall include programs in any form, including those which are incorporated into hardware.

33 In that regard, reference must be made to Article 10(1) of the TRIPS Agreement, which provides that computer programs, whether expressed in source code or in object code, will be protected as literary works pursuant to the Berne Convention.

34 It follows that the source code and the object code of a computer program are forms of expression thereof which, consequently, are entitled to be protected by copyright as computer programs, by virtue of Article 1(2) of Directive 91/250.

35 Accordingly, the object of the protection conferred by that directive is the expression in any form of a computer program which permits reproduction in different computer languages, such as the source code and the object code.

36 It is also appropriate to highlight the second sentence of the seventh recital in the preamble to Directive 91/250, in accordance with which the term 'computer program' also includes preparatory design work leading to the development of a computer program provided that the nature of the preparatory work is such that a computer program can result from it at a later stage.

37 Thus, the object of protection under Directive 91/250 includes the forms of expression of a computer program and the preparatory design work capable of leading, respectively, to the reproduction or the subsequent creation of such a program.

38 As the Advocate General states in Point 61 of his Opinion, any form of expression of a computer program must be protected from the moment when its reproduction would engender the reproduction of the computer program itself, thus enabling the computer to perform its task.

39 In accordance with the 10th and 11th recitals in the preamble to Directive 91/250, interfaces are parts of a computer program which provide for interconnection and interaction of

elements of software and hardware with other software and hardware and with users in all the ways in which they are intended to function.

40 In particular, the graphic user interface is an interaction interface which enables communication between the computer program and the user.

41 In those circumstances, the graphic user interface does not enable the reproduction of that computer program, but merely constitutes one element of that program by means of which users make use of the features of that program.

42 It follows that that interface does not constitute a form of expression of a computer program within the meaning of Article 1(2) of Directive 91/250 and that, consequently, it cannot be protected specifically by copyright in computer programs by virtue of that directive.

43 Nevertheless, even if the national court has limited its question to the interpretation of Article 1(2) of Directive 91/250, such a situation does not prevent the Court from providing the national court with all the elements of interpretation of European Union law which may enable it to rule on the case before it, whether or not reference is made thereto in the question referred.

44 In that regard, it is appropriate to ascertain whether the graphic user interface of a computer program can be protected by the ordinary law of copyright by virtue of Directive 2001/29.

45 The Court has held that copyright within the meaning of Directive 2001/29 is liable to apply only in relation to a subject-matter which is original in the sense that it is its author's own intellectual creation.

46 Consequently, the graphic user interface can, as a work, be protected by copyright if it is its author's own intellectual creation.

47 It is for the national court to ascertain whether that is the case in the dispute before it.

48 When making that assessment, the national court must take account, inter alia, of the specific arrangement or configuration of all the components which form part of the graphic user interface in order to determine which meet the criterion of originality. In that regard, that criterion cannot be met by components of the graphic user interface which are differentiated only by their technical function.

49 As the Advocate General states in Points 75 and 76 of his Opinion, where the expression of those components is dictated by their technical function, the criterion of originality is not met, since the different methods of implementing an idea are so limited that the idea and the expression become indissociable.

50 In such a situation, the components of a graphic user interface do not permit the author to express his creativity in an original manner and achieve a result which is an intellectual creation of that author.

51 In the light of the foregoing considerations, the answer to the first question referred is that a graphic user interface is not a form of expression of that program within the meaning of Article 1(2) of Directive 91/250 and thus is not protected by copyright as a computer program under that directive. Nevertheless, such an interface can be protected by copyright as a work by Directive 2001/29 if that interface is its author's own intellectual creation.

The second question

52 By its second question, the national court asks, in essence, whether television broadcasting of a graphic user interface constitutes communication to the public of a work protected by copyright within the meaning of Article 3(1) of Directive 2001/29.

53 In accordance with that article, Member States are to provide authors with the exclusive right to authorise or prohibit any communication to the public of their works, by wire or wireless means, including the making available to the public of their works in such a way that members of the public may access them from a place and at a time individually chosen by them.

54 It follows from the 23rd recital in the preamble to Directive 2001/29 that 'communication to the public' must be interpreted broadly. Such an interpretation is moreover essential to achieve the principal objective of that directive, which, as can be seen from its 9th and 10th recitals, is to establish a high level of protection of, inter alia, authors, allowing them to obtain an appropriate reward for the use of their works, in particular on the occasion of communication to the public.

55 It follows that, in principle, television broadcasting of a work is a communication to the public which its author has the exclusive right to authorise or prohibit.

56 In addition, it is apparent from paragraph 46 of the present judgment that the graphic user interface can be its author's own intellectual creation.

57 Nevertheless, if, in the context of television broadcasting of a programme, a graphic user interface is displayed, television viewers receive a communication of that graphic user interface solely in a passive manner, without the possibility of intervening. They cannot use the feature of that interface which consists in enabling interaction between the computer program and the user. Having regard to the fact that, by television broadcasting, the graphic user interface is not communicated to the public in such a way that individuals can have access to the essential element characterising the interface, that is to say, interaction with the user, there is no communication to the public of the graphic user interface within the meaning of Article 3(1) of Directive 2001/29.

58 Consequently, the answer to the second question referred is that television broadcasting of a graphic user interface does not constitute communication to the public of a work protected by copyright within the meaning of Article 3(1) of Directive 2001/29. (...)

THINK IT OVER!

1. The user interface is the space where interactions between humans and machines occur. The goal of this interaction is to allow effective operation and control of the machine from the human end, whilst the machine simultaneously feeds back information that aids the operators' decision-making process. Examples of this broad concept of user interfaces include the interactive aspects of computer operating systems, hand tools, heavy machinery operator controls, and process controls. The design considerations applicable when creating user interfaces are related to or involve such disciplines as ergonomics and psychology. The graphical user interface (GUI) is a form of user interface that allows users to interact with electronic devices through graphical icons and audio indicator such as primary notation, instead of text-based user interfaces, typed command labels or text navigation. These interfaces were introduced in reaction to the perceived steep learning curve of command-line interfaces, which require commands to be typed on a computer keyboard. Actions are usually performed through direct manipulation of the graphical elements. Beyond computers, they are used in many portable devices.

2. *What do you think about the concept of "originality" exposed in the case as a requirement to extend copyright protection to computer program interfaces? Is a general concept of originality under EU law a good idea?* For your consideration, the CJEU aims to interpret the concept of originality in a uniform way. Preliminary rulings in varying factual situations involving different subject matters (e.g. literary texts, photographs, taste of a cheese, designs of clothes) have confirmed the existence of a uniform concept of originality. *Isn't it a better idea to develop different concepts (or levels) of originality for different subject matters?*

3. *What if an interactive system/platform allows individuals not only to passively view a GUI, but also interactively use the graphic interface of a computer program? Should there be any need for licensing such activities under copyright law?*

4. *Should we consider gameplays uploaded into social networks like YouTube as activities that allow a passive watching à la carte of videogame GUIs?*

Further Case Law

Case C-5/08 - Infopaq International A/S v. Danske Dagblades Forening, Judgement of the Court (Fourth Chamber), 16 July 2009 [ECLI:EU:C:2009:465]

Case C-360/13 - Public Relations Consultants Association Ltd v The Newspaper Licensing Agency Ltd and Others, Judgment of the Court (Fourth Chamber), 5 June 2014 [ECLI:EU:C:2014:1195]

SzJSzT-19/13 - Számítógépi program jogi védelme. In: *Iparjogvédelmi és Szerzői Jogi Szemle*, 2014/4. szám, p. 248-257.

SzJSzT-27/13 - Számítógépi program jogi védelme. In: *Iparjogvédelmi és Szerzői Jogi Szemle*, 2014/4. szám, p. 258-264.

Recommended readings

In English

Leigh J. Smith: Whether Copyright Protects the Graphic User Interface of a Computer Program: Bezpečnostní softwarová asociace - Svaz softwarové ochrany contre Ministerstvo kultury (C-393/09), *Computer and Telecommunications Law Review*, Issue 3/2011, p. 70-72.

Noam Shemtov: *Software and Graphical User Interfaces*. In: Tanya Aplin (Ed.): *Research Handbook on Intellectual Property and Digital Technologies*, Edward Elgar, Cheltenham, 2020, p. 2-10.

In French

Lionel Costes: Protection des interfaces graphiques des logiciels: la position de la CJUE, *Droit de l'immatériel: informatique, médias, communication*, 2011, n° 68, p. 30-31.

Hubert Bitan: L'interface graphique d'un logiciel constitue une oeuvre autonome distincte du logiciel, *Droit de l'immatériel: informatique, médias, communication*, 2011, n° 70, p. 13-19.

In German

Jochen Marly: Der Urheberrechtsschutz grafischer Benutzeroberflächen von Computerprogrammen, *Gewerblicher Rechtsschutz und Urheberrecht*, Heft 3/2011, p. 204-208.

In Spanish

Enrique Fernández Masiá: *La protección internacional de los programas de ordenador*, tesis doctoral leída en la Universidad de Castilla-La Mancha, 1996.

Manuel Heredero Higueras: La protección de los programas de ordenador en el proyecto de Ley de Propiedad Intelectual, *Revista Crítica de Derecho Inmobiliario,* año nº 63, nº 581, 1987, p. 1021-1044.
L. Fernando Ramos Simón: Protección versus accesibilidad de la información digital, *Hipertext. net,* nº 2, 2004.
Fernando Ramos Suárez: Protección de los derechos de autor en Internet, *Cuadernos de Documentación Multimedia,* vol. 9, año 2000, p. 75-79.

In Hungarian
Pogácsás Anett: A számítógépi program szerzői jogi védelméről - Számítógépi programok grafikus felhasználói felületének és annak televíziós sugárzásának szerzői jogi megítélése, *Jogesetek Magyarázata,* 2011/1. szám, p. 59-65.
Békés Gergely: *Szoftverek szerzői jogi védelme a gyakorlatban.* In: Legeza Dénes (Szerk.): A szerzői jog gyakoralti kérdései - Válogatás a Szerzői Jogi Szakértő Testület szakvéleményeiből (2010-2013) efennállásának 130. évfordulója alkalmából, Szellemi Tulajdon Nemzeti Hivatala, Budapest, 2014: p. 150-163.

SAS INSTITUTE INC. V WORLD PROGRAMMING LTD.

Case C-406/10 - Judgment of the Court (Grand Chamber), 2 May 2012 [ECLI:EU:C:2012:259]

(...) **Legal context**

International legislation

3 Article 2(1) of the Convention for the Protection of Literary and Artistic Works, signed at Berne on 9 September 1886 (Paris Act of 24 July 1971), as amended on 28 September 1979 ('the Berne Convention') provides:
'The expression "literary and artistic works" shall include every production in the literary (...) domain, whatever may be the mode or form of its expression (...)'

4 Article 9 of the Agreement on Trade-Related Aspects of Intellectual Property Rights ('the TRIPs Agreement'), as set out in Annex 1C to the Marrakech Agreement establishing the World Trade Organisation, which was approved by Council Decision 94/800/EC of 22 December 1994 concerning the conclusion on behalf of the European Community, as regards matters within its competence, of the agreements reached in the Uruguay Round multilateral negotiations (1986-1994) (OJ 1994 L 336, p. 1), provides:

'1. Members shall comply with Articles 1 through 21 of the [Berne Convention] and the Appendix thereto (...)
2. Copyright protection shall extend to expressions and not to ideas, procedures, methods of operation or mathematical concepts as such.'

5 Article 10(1) of the TRIPs Agreement provides:
'Computer programs, whether in source or object code, shall be protected as literary works under the [Berne Convention].'

6 Article 2 of the World Intellectual Property Organisation (WIPO) Copyright Treaty, adopted in Geneva on 20 December 1996, which entered into force, as regards the European Union, on 14 March 2010 (OJ 2010 L 32, p. 1), is worded as follows:
'Copyright protection extends to expressions and not to ideas, procedures, methods of operation or mathematical concepts as such.'

7 Article 4 of that treaty provides as follows:
'Computer programs are protected as literary works within the meaning of Article 2 of the Berne Convention. Such protection applies to computer programs, whatever may be the mode or form of their expression.'

European Union legislation

Directive 91/250

8 The 3rd, 7th, 8th, 14th, 15th, 17th, 18th, 21st and 23rd recitals in the preamble to Directive 91/250 provide:
'(3) (...) computer programs are playing an increasingly important role in a broad range of industries and computer program technology can accordingly be considered as being of fundamental importance for the Community's industrial development;
(...)
(7) (...) for the purpose of this Directive, the term "computer program" shall include programs in any form, including those which are incorporated into hardware; ... this term also includes preparatory design work leading to the development of a computer program, provided that the nature of the preparatory work is such that a computer program can result from it at a later stage;
(8) (...) in respect of the criteria to be applied in determining whether or not a computer program is an original work, no tests as to the qualitative or aesthetic merits of the program should be applied;
(...)

(14) (...) in accordance with [the principle that only the expression of a computer program is protected by copyright], to the extent that logic, algorithms and programming languages comprise ideas and principles, those ideas and principles are not protected under this Directive;
(15) (...) in accordance with the legislation and jurisprudence of the Member States and the international copyright conventions, the expression of those ideas and principles is to be protected by copyright;

(...)

(17) (...) the exclusive rights of the author to prevent the unauthorised reproduction of his work have to be subject to a limited exception in the case of a computer program to allow the reproduction technically necessary for the use of that program by the lawful acquirer; ... this means that the acts of loading and running necessary for the use of a copy of a program which has been lawfully acquired, and the act of correction of its errors, may not be prohibited by contract; ... in the absence of specific contractual provisions, including when a copy of the program has been sold, any other act necessary for the use of the copy of a program may be performed in accordance with its intended purpose by a lawful acquirer of that copy;
(18) (...) a person having a right to use a computer program should not be prevented from performing acts necessary to observe, study or test the functioning of the program, provided that these acts do not infringe the copyright in the program;

(...)

(21) (...) it has therefore to be considered that, in these limited circumstances only, performance of the acts of reproduction and translation by or on behalf of a person having a right to use a copy of the program is legitimate and compatible with fair practice and must therefore be deemed not to require the authorisation of the rightholder;

(...)

(23) (...) such an exception to the author's exclusive rights may not be used in a way which prejudices the legitimate interests of the rightholder or which conflicts with a normal exploitation of the program'.

9 Under the heading 'Object of protection', Article 1 of Directive 91/250 provides:
'1. In accordance with the provisions of this Directive, Member States shall protect computer programs, by copyright, as literary works within the meaning of the Berne Convention for the Protection of Literary and Artistic Works. For the purposes of this Directive, the term "computer programs" shall include their preparatory design material.
2. Protection in accordance with this Directive shall apply to the expression in any form of a computer program. Ideas and principles which underlie any element of a computer program, including those which underlie its interfaces, are not protected by copyright under this Directive.
3. A computer program shall be protected if it is original in the sense that it is the author's own intellectual creation. No other criteria shall be applied to determine its eligibility for protection.'

10 Paragraphs (a) and (b) of Article 4 of that directive, headed 'Restricted Acts', provide:
'Subject to the provisions of Articles 5 and 6, the exclusive rights of the rightholder, within the meaning of Article 2, shall include the right to do or to authorise:
(a) the permanent or temporary reproduction of a computer program by any means and in any form, in part or in whole. In so far as loading, displaying, running, transmission or storage of the computer program necessitate such reproduction, such acts shall be subject to authorisation by the rightholder;
(b) the translation, adaptation, arrangement and any other alteration of a computer program and the reproduction of the results thereof, without prejudice to the rights of the person who alters the program'.

11 Article 5 of Directive 91/250, which provides for exceptions to the restricted acts, reads as follows:
'1. In the absence of specific contractual provisions, the acts referred to in Article 4(a) and (b) shall not require authorisation by the rightholder where they are necessary for the use of the computer program by the lawful acquirer in accordance with its intended purpose, including for error correction.

(...)

3. The person having a right to use a copy of a computer program shall be entitled, without the authorisation of the rightholder, to observe, study or test the functioning of the program in order to determine the ideas and principles which underlie any element of the program if he does so while performing any of the acts of loading, displaying, running, transmitting or storing the program which he is entitled to do.'

12 Article 6 of that directive, relating to decompilation, states:
'1. The authorisation of the rightholder shall not be required where reproduction of the code and translation of its form within the meaning of Article 4(a) and (b) are indispensable to obtain the information necessary to achieve the interoperability of an independently created computer program with other programs, provided that the following conditions are met:

(a) these acts are performed by the licensee or by another person having a right to use a copy of a program, or on their behalf by a person authorised to do so;

(b) the information necessary to achieve interoperability has not previously been readily available to the persons referred to in subparagraph (a);

and

(c) these acts are confined to the parts of the original program which are necessary to achieve interoperability.

2. The provisions of paragraph 1 shall not permit the information obtained through its application:

(a) to be used for goals other than to achieve the interoperability of the independently created computer program;

(b) to be given to others, except when necessary for the interoperability of the independently created computer program; or

(c) to be used for the development, production or marketing of a computer program substantially similar in its expression, or for any other act which infringes copyright.

3. In accordance with the provisions of the Berne Convention for the Protection of Literary and Artistic Works, the provisions of this Article may not be interpreted in such a way as to allow its application to be used in a manner which unreasonably prejudices the rightholder's legitimate interests or conflicts with a normal exploitation of the computer program.'

13 Pursuant to Article 9 of Directive 91/250, the provisions of that directive are without prejudice to any other legal provisions such as those concerning patent rights, trade marks, unfair competition, trade secrets, protection of semi-conductor products or the law of contract. Any contractual provisions that are contrary to Article 6 or to the exceptions provided for in Article 5(2) and (3) of Directive 91/250 are null and void.

Directive 2001/29

14 According to recital 20 in the preamble to Directive 2001/29, that directive is based on principles and rules already laid down in the directives currently in force in this area, inter alia Directive 91/250. Directive 2001/29 develops those principles and rules and places them in the context of the information society.

15 Article 1 of Directive 2001/29 provides:

'1. This Directive concerns the legal protection of copyright and related rights in the framework of the internal market, with particular emphasis on the information society.

2. Except in the cases referred to in Article 11, this Directive shall leave intact and shall in no way affect existing Community provisions relating to:

(a) the legal protection of computer programs;

16 Article 2(a) of Directive 2001/29 states:

'Member States shall provide for the exclusive right to authorise or prohibit direct or indirect, temporary or permanent reproduction by any means and in any form, in whole or in part:

(a) for authors, of their works (...)'.

National legislation

17 Directives 91/250 and 2001/29 were transposed into national law by the Copyright, Designs and Patents Act 1988, as amended by the Copyright (Computer Programs) Regulations 1992 and by the Copyright and Related Rights Regulations 2003 ('the 1988 Act').

18 Section 1(1)(a) of the 1988 Act provides that copyright is a property right which subsists in original literary, dramatic, musical or artistic works. According to section 3(1)(a) to (d) of the Act, 'literary work' means any work, other than a dramatic or musical work, which is written, spoken or sung, and includes a table or compilation other than a database, a computer program, preparatory design material for a computer program, and a database.

19 Section 16(1)(a) of the 1988 Act provides that the owner of the copyright in a work has the exclusive right to copy the work.

20 According to section 16(3)(a) and (b) of the 1988 Act, restrictions imposed by copyright in respect of acts performed on a work apply in relation to the work as a whole or any substantial part of it, either directly or indirectly.

21 Under section 17(2) of the 1988 Act, copying in relation to a literary, dramatic, musical or artistic work means reproducing the work in any material form. This includes storing the work in any medium by electronic means.

22 Section 50BA(1) of the 1988 Act states that it is not an infringement of copyright for a lawful user of a copy of a computer program to observe, study or test the functioning of the program in order to determine the ideas and principles which underlie any element of the program if he does so while performing any of the acts of loading, displaying, running, transmitting or storing the program which he is entitled to do. Section 50BA(2) of the Act states that, where an act is permitted under subsection (1), it is irrelevant whether or not there exists any term or condition in an agreement which purports to prohibit or restrict the act in question.

The dispute in the main proceedings and the questions referred for a preliminary ruling

23 SAS Institute is a developer of analytical software. It has developed an integrated set of computer programs over a period of 35 years which enables users to carry out a wide range of data processing and analysis tasks, in particular, statistical analysis ('the SAS System').

The core component of the SAS System, called 'Base SAS', enables users to write and run their own application programs in order to adapt the SAS System to work with their data (Scripts). Such Scripts are written in a language which is peculiar to the SAS System ('the SAS Language').

24 WPL perceived that there was a market demand for alternative software capable of executing application programs written in the SAS Language. WPL therefore produced the 'World Programming System', designed to emulate the SAS components as closely as possible in that, with a few minor exceptions, it attempted to ensure that the same inputs would produce the same outputs. This would enable users of the SAS System to run the Scripts which they have developed for use with the SAS System on the 'World Programming System'.

25 The High Court of Justice of England and Wales, Chancery Division, points out that it is not established that, in order to do so, WPL had access to the source code of the SAS components, copied any of the text of that source code or copied any of the structural design of the source code.

26 The High Court also points out that two previous courts have held, in the context of separate proceedings, that it is not an infringement of the copyright in the source code of a computer program for a competitor of the copyright owner to study how the program functions and then to write its own program to emulate that functionality.

27 SAS Institute, disputing that approach, has brought an action before the referring court. Its principal claims are that WPL:

- copied the manuals for the SAS System published by SAS Institute when creating the 'World Programming System', thereby infringing SAS Institute's copyright in those manuals;
- in so doing, indirectly copied the computer programs comprising the SAS components, thereby infringing its copyright in those components;
- used a version of the SAS system known as the 'Learning Edition', in breach of the terms of the licence relating to that version and of the commitments made under that licence, and in breach of SAS Institute's copyright in that version; and
- infringed the copyright in the manuals for the SAS System by creating its own manual.

28 In those circumstances, the High Court of Justice of England and Wales, Chancery Division, decided to stay the proceedings and to refer the following questions to the Court of Justice for a preliminary ruling:

'(1) Where a computer program ("the First Program") is protected by copyright as a literary work, is Article 1(2) [of Directive 91/250] to be interpreted as meaning that it is not an infringement of the copyright in the First Program for a competitor of the rightholder without access to the source code of the First Program, either directly or via a process such as decompilation of the object code, to create another program ("the Second Program") which replicates the functions of the First Program?

(2) Is the answer to Question 1 affected by any of the following factors:

(a) the nature and/or extent of the functionality of the First Program;

(b) the nature and/or extent of the skill, judgment and labour which has been expended by the author of the First Program in devising the functionality of the First Program;

(c) the level of detail to which the functionality of the First Program has been reproduced in the Second Program;

(d) if the source code for the Second Program reproduces aspects of the source code of the First Program to an extent which goes beyond that which was strictly necessary in order to produce the same functionality as the First Program?

(3) Where the First Program interprets and executes application programs written by users of the First Program in a programming language devised by the author of the First Program which comprises keywords devised or selected by the author of the First Program and a syntax devised by the author of the First Program, is Article 1(2) [of Directive 91/250] to be interpreted as meaning that it is not an infringement of the copyright in the First Program for the Second Program to be written so as to interpret and execute such application programs using the same keywords and the same syntax?

(4) Where the First Program reads from and writes to data files in a particular format devised by the author of the First Program, is Article 1(2) [of Directive 91/250] to be interpreted as meaning that it is not an infringement of the copyright in the First Program for the Second Program to be written so as to read from and write to data files in the same format?

(5) Does it make any difference to the answer to Questions 1, 3 and 4 if the author of the Second Program created the Second Program by:

(a) observing, studying and testing the functioning of the First Program; or

(b) reading a manual created and published by the author of the First Program which describes the functions of the First Program ("the Manual"); or

(c) both (a) and (b)?

(6) Where a person has the right to use a copy of the First Program under a licence, is Article 5(3) [of Directive 91/250] to be interpreted as meaning that the licensee is entitled, without the authorisation of the rightholder, to perform acts of loading, running and storing the program in order to observe, test or study the functioning of the First Program so as to determine the ideas and principles which underlie any element of the program, if the licence permits the licensee to perform acts of loading, running and storing the First Program when using it for the particular purpose

permitted by the licence, but the acts done in order to observe, study or test the First Program extend outside the scope of the purpose permitted by the licence?

(7) Is Article 5(3) [of Directive 91/250] to be interpreted as meaning that acts of observing, testing or studying of the functioning of the First Program are to be regarded as being done in order to determine the ideas or principles which underlie any element of the First Program where they are done:

(a) to ascertain the way in which the First Program functions, in particular details which are not described in the Manual, for the purpose of writing the Second Program in the manner referred to in Question 1 above;

(b) to ascertain how the First Program interprets and executes statements written in the programming language which it interprets and executes (see Question 3 above);

(c) to ascertain the formats of data files which are written to or read by the First Program (see Question 4 above);

(d) to compare the performance of the Second Program with the First Program for the purpose of investigating reasons why their performances differ and to improve the performance of the Second Program;

(e) to conduct parallel tests of the First Program and the Second Program in order to compare their outputs in the course of developing the Second Program, in particular by running the same test scripts through both the First Program and the Second Program;

(f) to ascertain the output of the log file generated by the First Program in order to produce a log file which is identical or similar in appearance;

(g) to cause the First Program to output data (in fact, data correlating zip codes to States of the [United States of America] for the purpose of ascertaining whether or not it corresponds with official databases of such data, and if it does not so correspond, to program the Second Program so that it will respond in the same way as the First Program to the same input data.

(8) Where the Manual is protected by copyright as a literary work, is Article 2(a) [of Directive 2001/29] to be interpreted as meaning that it is an infringement of the copyright in the Manual for the author of the Second Program to reproduce or substantially reproduce in the Second Program any of the following matters described in the Manual:

(a) the selection of statistical operations which have been implemented in the First Program;

(b) the mathematical formulae used in the Manual to describe those operations;

(c) the particular commands or combinations of commands by which those operations may be invoked;

(d) the options which the author of the First Program has provided in respect of various commands;

(e) the keywords and syntax recognised by the First Program;

(f) the defaults which the author of the First Program has chosen to implement in the event that a particular command or option is not specified by the user;

(g) the number of iterations which the First Program will perform in certain circumstances?

(9) Is Article 2(a) [of Directive 2001/29] to be interpreted as meaning that it is an infringement of the copyright in the Manual for the author of the Second Program to reproduce or substantially reproduce in a manual describing the Second Program the keywords and syntax recognised by the First Program?'

Consideration of the questions referred

Questions 1 to 5

29 By these questions, the national court asks, in essence, whether Article 1(2) of Directive 91/250 must be interpreted as meaning that the functionality of a computer program and the programming language and the format of data files used in a computer program in order to exploit certain of its functions constitute a form of expression of that program and may, as such, be protected by copyright in computer programs for the purposes of that directive.

30 In accordance with Article 1(1) of Directive 91/250, computer programs are protected by copyright as literary works within the meaning of the Berne Convention.

31 Article 1(2) of Directive 91/250 extends that protection to the expression in any form of a computer program. That provision states, however, that the ideas and principles which underlie any element of a computer program, including those which underlie its interfaces, are not protected by copyright under that directive.

32 The 14th recital in the preamble to Directive 91/250 confirms, in this respect, that, in accordance with the principle that only the expression of a computer program is protected by copyright, to the extent that logic, algorithms and programming languages comprise ideas and principles, those ideas and principles are not protected under that directive. The 15th recital in the preamble to Directive 91/250 states that, in accordance with the legislation and jurisprudence of the Member States and the international copyright conventions, the expression of those ideas and principles is to be protected by copyright.

33 With respect to international law, both Article 2 of the WIPO Copyright Treaty and Article 9(2) of the TRIPs Agreement provide that copyright protection extends to expressions and not to ideas, procedures, methods of operation or mathematical concepts as such.

34 Article 10(1) of the TRIPs Agreement provides that computer programs, whether in source or object code, are to be protected as literary works under the Berne Convention.

35 In a judgment delivered after the reference for a preliminary ruling had been lodged in the present case, the Court interpreted Article 1(2) of Directive 91/250 as meaning that the object of the protection conferred by that directive is the expression in any form of a computer program, such as the source code and the object code, which permits reproduction in different computer languages.

36 In accordance with the second phrase of the seventh recital in the preamble to Directive 91/250, the term 'computer program' also includes preparatory design work leading to the development of a computer program, provided that the nature of the preparatory work is such that a computer program can result from it at a later stage.

37 Thus, the object of protection under Directive 91/250 includes the forms of expression of a computer program and the preparatory design work capable of leading, respectively, to the reproduction or the subsequent creation of such a program.

38 From this the Court concluded that the source code and the object code of a computer program are forms of expression thereof which, consequently, are entitled to be protected by copyright as computer programs, by virtue of Article 1(2) of Directive 91/250. On the other hand, as regards the graphic user interface, the Court held that such an interface does not enable the reproduction of the computer program, but merely constitutes one element of that program by means of which users make use of the features of that program.

39 On the basis of those considerations, it must be stated that, with regard to the elements of a computer program which are the subject of Questions 1 to 5, neither the functionality of a computer program nor the programming language and the format of data files used in a computer program in order to exploit certain of its functions constitute a form of expression of that program for the purposes of Article 1(2) of Directive 91/250.

40 As the Advocate General states in point 57 of his Opinion, to accept that the functionality of a computer program can be protected by copyright would amount to making it possible to monopolise ideas, to the detriment of technological progress and industrial development.

41 Moreover, point 3.7 of the explanatory memorandum to the Proposal for Directive 91/250 [COM(88) 816] states that the main advantage of protecting computer programs by copyright is that such protection covers only the individual expression of the work and thus leaves other authors the desired latitude to create similar or even identical programs provided that they refrain from copying.

42 With respect to the programming language and the format of data files used in a computer program to interpret and execute application programs written by users and to read and write data in a specific format of data files, these are elements of that program by means of which users exploit certain functions of that program.

43 In that context, it should be made clear that, if a third party were to procure the part of the source code or the object code relating to the programming language or to the format of data files used in a computer program, and if that party were to create, with the aid of that code, similar elements in its own computer program, that conduct would be liable to constitute partial reproduction within the meaning of Article 4(a) of Directive 91/250.

44 As is, however, apparent from the order for reference, WPL did not have access to the source code of SAS Institute's program and did not carry out any decompilation of the object code of that program. By means of observing, studying and testing the behaviour of SAS Institute's program, WPL reproduced the functionality of that program by using the same programming language and the same format of data files.

45 The Court also points out that the finding made in paragraph 39 of the present judgment cannot affect the possibility that the SAS language and the format of SAS Institute's data files might be protected, as works, by copyright under Directive 2001/29 if they are their author's own intellectual creation.

46 Consequently, the answer to Questions 1 to 5 is that Article 1(2) of Directive 91/250 must be interpreted as meaning that neither the functionality of a computer program nor the programming language and the format of data files used in a computer program in order to exploit certain of its functions constitute a form of expression of that program and, as such, are not protected by copyright in computer programs for the purposes of that directive.

Questions 6 and 7

47 By these questions, the national court asks, in essence, whether Article 5(3) of Directive 91/250 must be interpreted as meaning that a person who has obtained a copy of a computer program under a licence is entitled, without the authorisation of the owner of the copyright in that program, to observe, study or test the functioning of that program in order to determine the ideas and principles which underlie any element of the program, in the case where that person carries out acts covered by that licence with a purpose that goes beyond the framework established by the licence.

48 In the main proceedings, it is apparent from the order for reference that WPL lawfully purchased copies of the Learning Edition of SAS Institute's program, which were supplied under a 'click-through' licence which required the purchaser to accept the terms of the licence before being permitted to access the software. The terms of that licence restricted the licence to non-production purposes. According to the national court, WPL used the various copies of the Learning Edition of SAS Institute's program to perform acts which fall outside the scope of the licence in question.

49 Consequently, the national court raises the question as to whether the purpose of the study or observation of the functioning of a computer program has an effect on whether the person who has obtained the licence may invoke the exception set out in Article 5(3) of Directive 91/250.

50 The Court observes that, from the wording of that provision, it is clear, first, that a licensee is entitled to observe, study or test the functioning of a computer program in order to determine the ideas and principles which underlie any element of the program.

51 In this respect, Article 5(3) of Directive 91/250 seeks to ensure that the ideas and principles which underlie any element of a computer program are not protected by the owner of the copyright by means of a licensing agreement.

52 That provision is therefore consistent with the basic principle laid down in Article 1(2) of Directive 91/250, pursuant to which protection in accordance with that directive applies to the expression in any form of a computer program and ideas and principles which underlie any element of a computer program are not protected by copyright under that directive.

53 Article 9(1) of Directive 91/250 adds, moreover, that any contractual provisions contrary to the exceptions provided for in Article 5(2) and (3) of that directive are null and void.

54 Second, under Article 5(3) of Directive 91/250, a licensee is entitled to determine the ideas and principles which underlie any element of the computer program if he does so while performing any of the acts of loading, displaying, running, transmitting or storing that program which he is entitled to do.

55 It follows that the determination of those ideas and principles may be carried out within the framework of the acts permitted by the licence.

56 In addition, the 18th recital in the preamble to Directive 91/250 states that a person having a right to use a computer program should not be prevented from performing acts necessary to observe, study or test the functioning of the program, provided that these acts do not infringe the copyright in that program.

57 As the Advocate General states in point 95 of his Opinion, the acts in question are those referred to in Article 4(a) and (b) of Directive 91/250, which sets out the exclusive rights of the rightholder to do or to authorise, and those referred to in Article 5(1) thereof, relating to the acts necessary for the use of the computer program by the lawful acquirer in accordance with its intended purpose, including for error correction.

58 In that latter regard, the 17th recital in the preamble to Directive 91/250 states that the acts of loading and running necessary for that use may not be prohibited by contract.

59 Consequently, the owner of the copyright in a computer program may not prevent, by relying on the licensing agreement, the person who has obtained that licence from determining the ideas and principles which underlie all the elements of that program in the case where that person carries out acts which that licence permits him to perform and the acts of loading and running necessary for the use of the computer program, and on condition that that person does not infringe the exclusive rights of the owner in that program.

60 As regards that latter condition, Article 6(2)(c) of Directive 91/250 relating to decompilation states that decompilation does not permit the information obtained through its application to be used for the development, production or marketing of a computer program substantially similar in its expression, or for any other act which infringes copyright.

61 It must therefore be held that the copyright in a computer program cannot be infringed where, as in the present case, the lawful acquirer of the licence did not have access to the source code of the computer program to which that licence relates, but merely studied, observed and tested that program in order to reproduce its functionality in a second program.

62 In those circumstances, the answer to Questions 6 and 7 is that Article 5(3) of Directive 91/250 must be interpreted as meaning that a person who has obtained a copy of a computer program under a licence is entitled, without the authorisation of the owner of the copyright, to observe, study or test the functioning of that program so as to determine the ideas and principles which underlie any element of the program, in the case where that person carries out acts covered by that licence and acts of loading and running necessary

for the use of the computer program, and on condition that that person does not infringe the exclusive rights of the owner of the copyright in that program.

Questions 8 and 9

63 By these questions, the national court asks, in essence, whether Article 2(a) of Directive 2001/29 must be interpreted as meaning that the reproduction, in a computer program or a user manual for that program, of certain elements described in the user manual for another computer program protected by copyright constitutes an infringement of that right in the latter manual.

64 It is apparent from the order for reference that the user manual for SAS Institute's computer program is a protected literary work for the purposes of Directive 2001/29.

65 The Court has already held that the various parts of a work enjoy protection under Article 2(a) of Directive 2001/29, provided that they contain some of the elements which are the expression of the intellectual creation of the author of the work.

66 In the present case, the keywords, syntax, commands and combinations of commands, options, defaults and iterations consist of words, figures or mathematical concepts which, considered in isolation, are not, as such, an intellectual creation of the author of the computer program.

67 It is only through the choice, sequence and combination of those words, figures or mathematical concepts that the author may express his creativity in an original manner and achieve a result, namely the user manual for the computer program, which is an intellectual creation.

68 It is for the national court to ascertain whether the reproduction of those elements constitutes the reproduction of the expression of the intellectual creation of the author of the user manual for the computer program at issue in the main proceedings.

69 In this respect, the examination, in the light of Directive 2001/29, of the reproduction of those elements of the user manual for a computer program must be the same with respect to the creation of the user manual for a second program as it is with respect to the creation of that second program.

70 Consequently, in the light of the foregoing considerations, the answer to Questions 8 and 9 is that Article 2(a) of Directive 2001/29 must be interpreted as meaning that the reproduction, in a computer program or a user manual for that program, of certain elements described in the user manual for another computer program protected by copyright is capable of constituting an infringement of the copyright in the latter manual if – this being a matter for the national court to ascertain – that reproduction constitutes the expression of the intellectual creation of the author of the user manual for the computer program protected by copyright. (...)

THINK IT OVER!

1. The software market and the competition between program developers introduces an interesting controversy about limits of licenses and the extensions of their acquisitions, when there are objectives of studying and testing, with the final one of creating alternatives that could provide similar functionalities to those provided by the program whom license was acquired previously. This controversy is one aspect of the classic discussion about the juridical status of software programs.

2. SAS Institute sued WPL in the United States as well. There the Fourth Circuit awarded plaintiff $79.1 million in damages. The court ruled that WPL had engaged in unfair and deceptive trade practices. Especially, as it had misrepresented its intentions in order to obtain the license to the software, and violated the contract granted, which only allowed for non-commercial use; and that it had infringed on the copyright of its manual by copying portions of it into its own manual. On the other hand, the ruling said that WPL had not infringed on the copyright of SAS's software. *What are the similarities and the differences between the resolutions of the CJEU and the Fourth Circuit? What do you think about the concept of "misrepresented intentions"?*

Further Case Law

Case C-5/08 - Infopaq International A/S v. Danske Dagblades Forening, Judgement of the Court (Fourth Chamber), 16 July 2009 [ECLI:EU:C:2009:465]

Case C-393/09 - Bezpečnostní softwarová asociace - Svaz softwarové ochrany v. Ministerstvo kultury, Judgement of the Court (Third Chamber), 22 December 2010 [ECLI:EU:C:2010:816]

Case C-360/13 - Public Relations Consultants Association Ltd v. The Newspaper Licensing Agency Ltd and Others, Judgment of the Court (Fourth Chamber), 5 June 2014 [ECLI:EU:C:2014:1195]

SAS Institute, Inc. v. World Programming Limited, 874 *F.3d* 370 (2017).

Recommended readings

In English

Ed Barker - Iona Harding: Copyright, the ideas/expression dichotomy and harmonization: digging deeper into SAS, *Journal of Intellectual Property Law and Practice,* Issue 9/2012, p. 673-679.

David Nickless: Functionality of a computer program and programming language cannot be protected by copyright under the Software Directive, *Journal of Intellectual Property Law and Practice,* Issue 10/2012, p. 709-711.

Robert Onslow - Isabel Jamal: Copyright Infringement and Software Emulation: SAS Inc v World Programming Ltd, *European Intellectual Property Review,* Issue 6/2013, p. 352-356.

Noam Shemtov: *Software and Graphical User Interfaces.* In: Tanya Aplin (Ed.): *Research Handbook on Intellectual Property and Digital Technologies,* Edward Elgar, Cheltenham, 2020, p. 2-10.

Richard Arnold: *Copyright in Software: Functionality.* In: Tanya Aplin (Ed.): *Research Handbook on Intellectual Property and Digital Technologies,* Edward Elgar, Cheltenham, 2020, p. 26-43.

In Spanish

Manuel Heredero Higueras: La protección de los programas de ordenador en el proyecto de Ley de Propiedad Intelectual, *Revista Crítica de Derecho Inmobiliario,* año nº 63, nº 581, 1987, p. 1021-1044.

Enrique Fernández Masiá: *La protección internacional de los programas de ordenador,* tesis doctoral leída en la Universidad de Castilla-La Mancha, 1996

In French

Marlène Trézéguet: Absence de protection des fonctionnalités et du langage de programmation d'un logiciel, *Droit de l'immatériel: informatique, médias, communication,* 2012, nº 78, p. 21-22.

Lionel Costes: Protection par le droit d'auteur des programmes d'ordinateur: les précisions de la CJUE, *Droit de l'immatériel: informatique, médias, communication,* 2012, nº 82, p. 20-21.

Céline Castets-Renard: Limitations du droit d'auteur européen portant sur les logiciels, *Droit de l'immatériel: informatique, médias, communication,* 2012, nº 83, p. 6-10.

In German

Gerald Spindler: Grenzen des Softwareschutzes, *Computer und Recht,* Heft 7/2012, p. 417-422.

Thomas Heymann: EuGH: Kein Urheberrechtsschutz für Programmiersprache und Funktionalitäten eines Computerprogramms, *Computer und Recht,* Heft 7/2012, p. 431-433.

Jochen Marly: Der Schutzgegenstand des urheberrechtlichen Softwareschutzes, *Gewerblicher Rechtsschutz und Urheberrecht,* Heft 8/2012, p. 773-779.

In Hungarian

Békés Gergely: *Szoftverek szerzői jogi védelme a gyakorlatban.* In: Legeza Dénes (Szerk.): A szerzői jog gyakoralti kérdései - Válogatás a Szerzői Jogi Szakértő Testület szakvéleményeiből (2010-2013) efennállásának 130. évfordulója alkalmából, Szellemi Tulajdon Nemzeti Hivatala, Budapest, 2014: p. 150-163.

NINTENDO CO. LTD AND OTHERS V. PC BOX SRL AND 9NET SRL

Case C-355/12 - Judgment of the Court (Fourth Chamber), 23 January 2014 [ECLI:EU:C:2014:25]

(...) Legal context

International law

3 In the words of Article 2(1) of the Convention for the Protection of Literary and Artistic Works, signed at Berne on 9 September 1886 (Paris Act of 24 July 1971), as amended on 28 September 1979 ('the Berne Convention'):

'The expression "literary and artistic works" shall include every production in the literary, scientific and artistic domain, whatever may be the mode or form of its expression (...)'

European Union law

Directive 2001/29

4 Recitals 9 and 47 to 50 in the preamble to Directive 2001/29 state:

'(9) Any harmonisation of copyright and related rights must take as a basis a high level of protection, since such rights are crucial to intellectual creation. (...)

(...)

(47) Technological development will allow rightholders to make use of technological measures designed to prevent or restrict acts not authorised by the rightholders of any copyright, rights related to copyright or the sui generis right in databases. The danger, however, exists that illegal activities might be carried out in order to enable or facilitate the circumvention of the technical protection provided by these measures. In order to avoid fragmented legal approaches that could potentially hinder the functioning of the internal market, there is a need to provide for harmonised legal protection against circumvention of effective technological measures and against provision of devices and products or services to this effect.

(48) Such legal protection should be provided in respect of technological measures that effectively restrict acts not authorised by the rightholders of any copyright, rights related to copyright or the sui generis right in databases without, however, preventing the normal operation of electronic equipment and its technological development. Such legal protection implies no obligation to design devices, products, components or services to correspond to technological measures, so long as such device, product, component or service does not otherwise fall under the prohibition of Article 6. Such legal protection should respect proportionality and should not prohibit those devices or activities which have a commercially significant purpose or use other than to circumvent the technical protection. In particular, this protection should not hinder research into cryptography.
(49) The legal protection of technological measures is without prejudice to the application of any national provisions which may prohibit the private possession of devices, products or components for the circumvention of technological measures.
(50) Such a harmonised legal protection does not affect the specific provisions on protection provided for by [Directive 2009/24/EC of the European Parliament and of the Council of 23 April 2009 on the legal protection of computer programs (OJ 2009 L 111, p.16)]. In particular, it should not apply to the protection of technological measures used in connection with computer programs, which is exclusively addressed in that Directive. It should neither inhibit nor prevent the development or use of any means of circumventing a technological measure that is necessary to enable acts to be undertaken in accordance with the terms of Article 5(3) or Article 6 of Directive [2009/24]. Articles 5 and 6 of that Directive exclusively determine exceptions to the exclusive rights applicable to computer programs.'

5 Article 1 of Directive 2001/29 provides that:
'1. This Directive concerns the legal protection of copyright and related rights in the framework of the internal market, with particular emphasis on the information society.
2. Except in the cases referred to in Article 11, this Directive shall leave intact and shall in no way affect existing Community provisions relating to:
(a) the legal protection of computer programs; (...)'

6 Article 6(1) to (3) of Directive 2004/113 provide that:
'1. Member States shall provide adequate legal protection against the circumvention of any effective technological measures, which the person concerned carries out in the knowledge, or with reasonable grounds to know, that he or she is pursuing that objective.
2. Member States shall provide adequate legal protection against the manufacture, import, distribution, sale, rental, advertisement for sale or rental, or possession for commercial purposes of devices, products or components or the provision of services which:
(a) are promoted, advertised or marketed for the purpose of circumvention of, or
(b) have only a limited commercially significant purpose or use other than to circumvent, or

(c) are primarily designed, produced, adapted or performed for the purpose of enabling or facilitating the circumvention of, any effective technological measures.
3. For the purposes of this Directive, the expression "technological measures" means any technology, device or component that, in the normal course of its operation, is designed to prevent or restrict acts, in respect of works or other subject-matter, which are not authorised by the rightholder of any copyright or any right related to copyright as provided for by law or the sui generis right provided for in Chapter III of Directive 96/9/EC [of the European Parliament and of the Council of 11 March 1996 on the legal protection of databases (OJ 1996 L 77, p. 20)]. Technological measures shall be deemed "effective" where the use of a protected work or other subject-matter is controlled by the rightholders through application of an access control or protection process, such as encryption, scrambling or other transformation of the work or other subject-matter or a copy control mechanism, which achieves the protection objective.'

Directive 2009/24

7 Article 1(1) of Directive 2009/24 is worded as follows:
'In accordance with the provisions of this Directive, Member States shall protect computer programs, by copyright, as literary works within the meaning of the Berne Convention for the Protection of Literary and Artistic Works. For the purposes of this Directive, the term "computer programs" shall include their preparatory design material.'

Italian law

8 Article 102c of Law No 633 on the protection of copyright and other rights relating to its exercise (legge n° 633 – Protezione del diritto d'autore e di altri diritti connessi al suo esercizio) of 22 April 1941 (GURI No 166 of 16 July 1941), as amended by Legislative Decree No 68, transposing directive 2001/29/EC of the European Parliament and of the Council of 22 May 2001 on the harmonisation of certain aspects of copyright and related rights in the information society (decreto legislativo n. 68 – Attuazione della direttiva 2001/29/CE sull'armonizzazione di taluni aspetti del diritto d'autore e dei diritti connessi nella società dell'informazione), of 9 April 2003 (Ordinary Supplement to GURI No 87, of 14 April 2003), provides that:
'1. Rightholders of any copyright or of any related right as well as of the right under Article 102bis (3) [concerning databases], may apply to protected works or objects effective technological protection measures, including any technology, device or component that, in the normal course of its operation, is designed to prevent or restrict acts which are not authorised by the rightholders.
2. Technological protection measures shall be deemed effective where the use of the protected work or object is controlled by the rightholders through the application of an access control or protection

process, such as encryption, scrambling or other transformation of the work or the protected work, or if that use is limited by a copy control mechanism which achieves the objective of protection.

3. The present article shall not affect the application of the provisions concerning computer programs referred to in Title 1, Chapter IV, Part VI.'

The dispute in the main proceedings and the questions referred for a preliminary ruling

9 The Nintendo undertakings, members of a group which creates and produces videogames, market two types of products for those games, namely portable systems, 'DS' consoles and fixed console videogame systems, 'Wii' consoles.

10 The Nintendo undertakings have adopted technological measures, namely a recognition system installed in the consoles, and the encrypted code of the physical housing system onto which the videogames which are protected by copyright are registered. Those measures have the effect of preventing the use of illegal copies of videogames. Games lacking a code cannot be launched on either of the two types of equipment marketed by the Nintendo undertakings.

11 It is also apparent from the order for reference that those technological measures prevent use on the consoles of programs, games and, generally, multimedia content not from Nintendo.

12 The Nintendo undertakings have observed the existence of PC Box equipment which, once installed on the console, circumvent the protection system present on the hardware and enable illegal use of videogames.

13 Considering that the principal purpose of the PC Box equipment was to circumvent and to avoid the technological protection measures of Nintendo games, the Nintendo undertakings brought proceedings against PC Box and 9Net before the Tribunale di Milano.

14 PC Box markets original Nintendo consoles together with additional software consisting of certain applications from independent manufacturers, 'homebrews' created specifically to be used in such consoles and the use of which requires the prior installation of PC Box equipment which deactivates the installed device which constitutes the technological protection measure.

15 In the opinion of PC Box, the actual purpose pursued by the Nintendo undertakings is to prevent use of independent software which does not constitute an illegal copy of videogames,

but which is intended to enable MP3 files, movies and videos to be read on consoles, in order to fully use those consoles.

16 The referring court considers that the protection of videogames cannot be reduced to that provided for computer programs. Indeed, although videogames take their functionality from a computer program, they begin and progress following a narrated predetermined route by the authors of those games in a way to make a group of images and sounds appear together with some conceptual autonomy.

17 That court queries whether the implementation of technological protection measures such as those at issue in the main proceedings used by Nintendo exceeds what is provided for that purpose by Article 6 of Directive 2001/29, such as interpreted in the light of recital 48 in the preamble to that directive.

18 In those circumstances, the Tribunale di Milano decided to stay the proceedings and to refer the following questions to the Court of Justice for a preliminary ruling:

'(1) Must Article 6 of [Directive 2001/29] be interpreted, including in the light of recital 48 [thereof], as meaning that the protection of technological protection measures attaching to copyright-protected works or other subject matter may also extend to a system, produced and marketed by the same undertaking, in which a device is installed in the hardware which is capable of recognising on a separate housing mechanism containing the protected works (videogames produced by the same undertaking as well as by third parties, proprietors of the protected works) a recognition code, in the absence of which the works in question cannot be visualised or used in conjunction with that system, the equipment in question thus incorporating a system which is not interoperable with complementary equipment or products other than those of the undertaking which produces the system itself?

(2) Should it be necessary to consider whether or not the use of a product or component whose purpose is to circumvent a technological protection measure predominates over other commercially important purposes or uses, may Article 6 of [Directive 2001/29] be interpreted, including in the light of recital 48 [thereof], as meaning that the national court must adopt criteria in assessing that question which give prominence to the particular intended use attributed by the rightholder to the product in which the protected content is inserted or, in the alternative or in addition, criteria of a quantative nature relating to the extent of the uses under comparison, or criteria of a qualitative nature, that is, relating to the nature and importance of the uses themselves?'

Consideration of the questions referred

19 By its questions, which it is appropriate to examine together, the referring court asks, in essence, in the first place, whether Directive 2001/29 must be interpreted as meaning that the concept of an 'effective technological measure', for the purposes of Article 6(3) of that directive, is capable of covering technological measures comprising, principally, equipping not only the housing system containing the protected work, such as the videogame, with a recognition device in order to protect it against acts which are not authorised by the holder of any copyright, but also portable equipment or consoles intended to ensure access to those games and their use.

20 In the second place, that court asks the Court of Justice, in essence, according to which criteria the scope of legal protection against circumventing technological protection measures within the meaning of Article 6 of Directive 2001/29 should be assessed. In particular, that court seeks to ascertain in that regard whether, first, the particular intended use attributed by the rightholder to the product in which the protected content is inserted, such as the Nintendo consoles, and, second, the scope, the nature and the importance of the use of devices, products or components capable of circumventing those effective technological measures, such as PC Box equipment, are relevant.

21 In that regard, first of all it must be noted that Directive 2001/29 concerns, as is apparent inter alia from Article 1(1) thereof, the legal protection of copyright and related rights, including, for authors, exclusive rights to their works. As for works such as computer programs, they are protected by copyright provided that they are original, that is that they are their author's own intellectual creation.

22 As regards the parts of a work, it should be borne in mind that there is nothing in Directive 2001/29 indicating that those parts are to be treated any differently from the work as a whole. It follows that they are protected by copyright since, as such, they share the originality of the whole work.

23 That finding is not weakened by the fact that Directive 2009/24 constitutes a *lex specialis* in relation to Directive 2001/29. In accordance with Article 1(1) thereof, the protection offered by Directive 2009/24 is limited to computer programs. As is apparent from the order for reference, videogames, such as those at issue in the main proceedings, constitute complex matter comprising not only a computer program but also graphic and sound elements, which, although encrypted in computer language, have a unique creative value which cannot be reduced to that encryption. In so far as the parts of a videogame, in this case, the

graphic and sound elements, are part of its originality, they are protected, together with the entire work, by copyright in the context of the system established by Directive 2001/29.

24 As regards Article 6 of Directive 2001/29, it is important to note that it requires the Member States to provide adequate legal protection against the circumvention of any effective 'technological measure' which is defined, in paragraph 3, as any technology, device or component that, in the normal course of its operation, is designed to prevent or restrict acts, in respect of works or other subject-matter, which are not authorised by the rightholder of any copyright or any right related to copyright as provided for by law or the *sui generis* right provided for in Chapter III of Directive 96/9.

25 Those acts constitute, as is apparent from Articles 2 to 4 of Directive 2001/29, the reproduction, the communication to the public of works and making them available to the public, and the distribution of the original or copies of works. The legal protection referred to in Article 6 of that directive applies only in the light of protecting that rightholder against acts which require his authorisation.

26 In that regard, it must be stated, in the first place, that there is nothing in that directive to suggest that Article 6(3) thereof does not refer to technological measures such as those at issue in the main proceedings, which are partly incorporated in the physical housing systems of games and partly in consoles which requires interaction between them.

27 Indeed, as the Advocate General noted in point 43 of her Opinion, it is apparent from that provision that the concept of 'effective technological measures' is defined broadly and includes application of an access control or protection process, such as encryption, scrambling or other transformation of the work or other subject-matter or a copy control mechanism. Such a definition, moreover, complies with the principal objective of Directive 2001/29 which, as is apparent from recital 9 thereof, is to establish a high level of protection in favour, in particular, of authors, which is crucial to intellectual creation.

28 In those circumstances, it must be considered that technological measures such as those at issue in the case in the main proceedings, which are partly incorporated in the physical housing of videogames and partly in consoles and which require interaction between them, fall within the concept of 'effective technological measures' within the meaning of Article 6(3) of Directive 2001/29 if their objective is to prevent or to limit acts adversely affecting the rights of the holder protected by them.

29 In the second place, it is necessary to examine according to which criteria the scope of legal protection against circumventing technological protection measures within the meaning of Article 6 of Directive 2001/29 should be assessed.

30 As the Advocate General noted in points 53 to 63 of her Opinion, the examination of that question requires that account be taken of the fact that legal protection against acts not authorised by the rightholder of any copyright must respect the principle of proportionality, in accordance with Article 6(2) of Directive 2001/29, interpreted in the light of recital 48 thereof, and should not prohibit devices or activities which have a commercially significant purpose or use other than to circumvent the technical protection.

31 Accordingly, that legal protection is granted only with regard to technological measures which pursue the objective of preventing or eliminating, as regards works, acts not authorised by the rightholder of copyright referred to in paragraph 25 of the present judgment. Those measures must be suitable for achieving that objective and must not go beyond what is necessary for this purpose.

32 In those circumstances, it is necessary to examine whether other measures or measures which are not installed in consoles could have caused less interference with the activities of third parties not requiring authorisation by the rightholder of copyright or fewer limitations to those activities, while still providing comparable protection of that rightholder's rights.

33 Accordingly, it is relevant to take account, inter alia, of the relative costs of different types of technological measures, of technological and practical aspects of their implementation, and of a comparison of the effectiveness of those different types of technological measures as regards the protection of rightholder's rights, that effectiveness however not having to be absolute.

34 The assessment of the scope of the legal protection at issue would not have to be carried out, as the Advocate General noted at point 67 of her Opinion, by reference to the particular use of consoles, as envisaged by the copyright holder. It would, however, have to take account of the criteria laid down, as regards the devices, products or components capable of circumventing the protection of effective technological measures, in Article 6(2) of Directive 2001/29.

35 More specifically, that provision requires the Member States to provide adequate legal protection against those devices, products or components which have the purpose of

circumventing that protection of effective technological measures which have only a limited commercially significant purpose or use other than to circumvent that protection, or are primarily designed, produced, adapted or performed for the purpose of enabling or facilitating that circumvention.

36 In that regard, with a view to examining the purpose of those devices, products or components, the evidence of actual use which is made of them by third parties will, in the light of the circumstances at issue, be particularly relevant. The referring court may, in particular, examine how often PC Box's devices are in fact used in order to allow unauthorised copies of Nintendo and Nintendo-licensed games to be used on Nintendo consoles and how often that equipment is used for purposes which do not infringe copyright in Nintendo and Nintendo-licensed games.

37 In the light of the foregoing, the answer to the questions referred is that Directive 2001/29 must be interpreted as meaning that the concept of an 'effective technological measure', for the purposes of Article 6(3) of that directive, is capable of covering technological measures comprising, principally, equipping not only the housing system containing the protected work, such as the videogame, with a recognition device in order to protect it against acts which are not authorised by the holder of any copyright, but also portable equipment or consoles intended to ensure access to those games and their use.

38 It is for the national court to determine whether other measures or measures which are not installed in consoles could cause less interference with the activities of third parties or limitations to those activities, while still providing comparable protection of the rightholder's rights. Accordingly, it is relevant to take account, inter alia, of the relative costs of different types of technological measures, of technological and practical aspects of their implementation, and of a comparison of the effectiveness of those different types of technological measures as regards the protection of the rightholder's rights, that effectiveness however not having to be absolute. That court must also examine the purpose of devices, products or components, which are capable of circumventing those technological measures. In that regard, the evidence of use which third parties actually make of them will, in the light of the circumstances at issue, be particularly relevant. The national court may, in particular, examine how often those devices, products or components are in fact used in disregard of copyright and how often they are used for purposes which do not infringe copyright. (...)

THINK IT OVER!

1. The selling of devices that could circumvent measures introduced in video-consoles and video games leads to a discussion about the copyright protection of video games as a combination of computer program, images, sounds and interactive stories. There is another controversial matter here. *How can we guarantee a balance between the interests of various stakeholders related to technological measures to protect copyright in consoles and games on the one hand and software and hardware devices that allow users to install other programs and multimedia contents from independent producers on the other hand? Are Nintendo's technological measures to prevent the use of illegal copies of programs going beyond this purpose, if they also prevent the use of other software and multimedia contents legally acquired by the users and players of the consoles?*

2. *How could we define the concept of "often" in order to determine, whether devices as those marketed by PC Box are used against or with due respect to copyright norms?*

3. *Can we talk about "purposes of devices capable of circumventing technological measures" or should we analyse the specific use of each consumer who owns the given device? Does "possibility" mean "inevitability"?*

4. The *Nintendo* ruling has an indirect effect on the future of the digital exhaustion hype. The *UsedSoft* decision will be discussed below (see page 419). In short, this ruling's conclusion was that the distribution right of computer programs exhausts in case the program was originally offered for "sale" via an online platform. Such ratio might be effectively overruled by the *Nintendo* decision with respect to computer programs that combine "mere" computer codes with other subject matters (e.g. "pure" literary works or – in case of computer games mainly – musical or audiovisual contents) that are harmonized under the InfoSoc-Directive rather than the Software Directive. The *Nintendo* decision stresses that in case of software that combine various subject matter, the guiding European source of interpretation is the InfoSoc-Directive that speaks against digital exhaustion, rather than the Software Directive that is silent (or unclear) on this matter.

Further Case Law

Case C-5/08 - Infopaq International A/S v. Danske Dagblades Forening, Judgement of the Court (Fourth Chamber), 16 July 2009 [ECLI:EU:C:2009:465]

Case C-128/11 - UsedSoft GmbH v. Oracle International Corp, Judgement of the Court (Grand Chamber), 3 July 2012 [ECLI:EU:C:2012:407]

Case C-527/15 - Stichting Brein v. Jack Frederick Wullems, Judgement of the Court (Second Chamber), 26 April 2017 [ECLI:EU:C:2017:300]

Recommended readings

In English

Heather Newton - Andrew Moir - Rachel Montagnon: CJEU Increases Burden on Manufacturers of Games Consoles to Prove the Unlawfulness of Devices Circumventing Technological Protection Measures and that Their TPMs Are Proportionate, *Journal of Intellectual Property Law and Practice*, Issue 6/2014, p. 456-458.

Tito Rendas: Lex Specialis(sima): Videogames and Technological Protection Measures in EU Copyright Law, *European Intellectual Property Review*, Issue 1/2015, p. 39-45.

In French

Costes, Lionel: Précisions de la CJUE sur l'utilisation de mesures techniques de protection, *Droit de l'immatériel: informatique, médias, communication*, 2014, n° 101, p. 27-28.

Alexandre Cassart; Cruquenaire, Alexandre: Arrêt «Nintendo»: quelle protection pour les mesures techniques?, *Journal de droit européen*, 2014, n° 209, p. 201-202.

Benoît Galopin: Affaire Nintendo: la CJUE précise les conditions de protection des mesures techniques, *Droit de l'immatériel: informatique, médias, communication*, 2014, n° 102, p. 58-63.

In German

Michel M. Walter: Technische Schutzmaßnahmen - Nintendo-Spielkonsole, *MR-Int: Internationale Rundschau zum Medienrecht, IP- & IT-Recht*, Heft 3/2014, p. 77-78.

Claas Oehler: EuGH: Umgehung des Schutzsystems für eine Videospielkonsole, *Multimedia und Recht*, Heft 6/2014, p. 403-405.

In Spanish

F. J. Donaire Villa - A. J. Planells de la Maza: *La protección jurídica de los derechos de autor de los creadores de videojuegos. 'Statu quo', perspectivas y desafíos*, Fundación Arte y Derecho, Trama Editorial, Madrid, 2012

S. F. Álvarez Cabrera - K. Y. Reyes Hernández: Protección jurídica de los videojuegos a través del derecho de autor», *Opinión jurídica*, 31/2017, p. 155-174. (https://doi.org/10.22395/ojum.v16n31a7)

APPLE COMPUTER, INC. V. FRANKLIN COMPUTER CORPORATION

714 *F.2d* 1240 (1983)

OPINION OF THE COURT
SLOVITER, Circuit Judge.

(...) II. FACTS AND PROCEDURAL HISTORY

Apple, one of the computer industry leaders, manufactures and markets personal computers (microcomputers), related peripheral equipment such as disk drives (peripherals), and computer programs (software). It presently manufactures Apple II computers and distributes over 150 programs. Apple has sold over 400,000 Apple II computers, employs approximately 3,000 people, and had annual sales of $335,000,000 for fiscal year 1981. One of the byproducts of Apple's success is the independent development by third parties of numerous computer programs which are designed to run on the Apple II computer.

Franklin, the defendant below, manufactures and sells the ACE 100 personal computer and at the time of the hearing employed about 75 people and had sold fewer than 1,000 computers. The ACE 100 was designed to be "Apple compatible," so that peripheral equipment and software developed for use with the Apple II computer could be used in conjunction with the ACE 100. Franklin's copying of Apple's operating system computer programs in an effort to achieve such compatibility precipitated this suit.

Like all computers both the Apple II and ACE 100 have a central processing unit (CPU) which is the integrated circuit that executes programs. In lay terms, the CPU does the work it is instructed to do. Those instructions are contained on computer programs.

There are three levels of computer language in which computer programs may be written. High level language, such as the commonly used BASIC or FORTRAN, uses English words and symbols, and is relatively easy to learn and understand (e.g., "GO TO 40" tells the computer to skip intervening steps and go to the step at line 40). A somewhat lower level language is assembly language, which consists of alphanumeric labels (e.g., "ADC" means "add with carry"). Statements in high level language, and apparently also statements in assembly language, are referred to as written in "source code." The third, or lowest level computer language, is machine language, a binary language using two symbols, 0 and 1, to indicate an open or closed switch (e.g., "01101001" means, to the Apple, add two numbers and save the result). Statements in machine language are referred to as written in "object code."

The CPU can only follow instructions written in object code. However, programs are usually written in source code which is more intelligible to humans. Programs written in source code can be converted or translated by a "compiler" program into object code for use by the computer. Programs are generally distributed only in their object code version stored on a memory device.

A computer program can be stored or fixed on a variety of memory devices, two of which are of particular relevance for this case. The ROM (Read Only Memory) is an internal permanent memory device consisting of a semi-conductor "chip" which is incorporated into the circuitry of the computer. A program in object code is embedded on a ROM before it is incorporated in the computer. Information stored on a ROM can only be read, not erased or rewritten. The ACE 100 apparently contains EPROMS (Erasable Programmable Read Only Memory) on which the stored information can be erased and the chip reprogrammed, but the district court found that for purposes of this proceeding, the difference between ROMs and EPROMs is inconsequential. The other device used for storing the programs at issue is a diskette or "floppy disk", an auxiliary memory device consisting of a flexible magnetic disk resembling a phonograph record, which can be inserted into the computer and from which data or instructions can be read.

Computer programs can be categorized by function as either application programs or operating system programs. Application programs usually perform a specific task for the computer user, such as word processing, checkbook balancing, or playing a game. In contrast, operating system programs generally manage the internal functions of the computer or facilitate use of application programs. The parties agree that the fourteen computer programs at issue in this suit are operating system programs. (...)

III. THE DISTRICT COURT OPINION

In its opinion, the district court referred to the four factors to be considered on request for a preliminary injunction: a reasonable probability of success on the merits; irreparable injury; the improbability of harm to other interested persons; and the public interest. The court stated it based its denial of the motion on the first two factors. The court held Apple had not made the requisite showing of likelihood of success on the merits because it "concluded that there is some doubt as to the copyrightability of the programs described in this litigation." It also stated that "Apple is better suited to withstand whatever injury it might sustain during litigation than is Franklin to withstand the effects of a preliminary injunction" because an injunction would have a "devastating effect" on Franklin's business, apparently concluding on that basis that Apple had failed to show irreparable harm.

It is difficult to discern precisely why the district court questioned the copyrightability of the programs at issue since there is no finding, statement, or holding on which we can focus which clearly sets forth the district court's view. Throughout the opinion the district court referred to the "complexity of the question presented by the present case", and the "baffling" problem at issue.

The opinion expresses a series of generalized concerns which may have led the court to its ultimate conclusion, and which the parties and amici treat as holdings. The district court referred to the requirement under the Copyright Act of finding "original works of authorship", and seems to have found that there was a sufficient "modicum of creativity" to satisfy the statutory requirement of an "original work". The court was less clear as to whether the creation of a computer program by a programmer satisfied the requirement of "works of authorship", and whether an operating system program in "binary code or one represented either in a ROM or by micro-switches" was an "expression" which could be copyrighted as distinguished from an "idea" which could not be.

Again, although we cannot point to a specific holding, running throughout the district court opinion is the suggestion that programs in object code and ROMs may not be copyrightable. Thus, for example, in a series of discursive footnotes, the district court stated that it found "persuasive" a district court opinion "holding that object code in ROM is not copyright protected", described an opinion reaching a contrary conclusion as containing "rather terse analysis [which] provides little guidance", and stated that "Congressional intent regarding the copyrightability of object codes and ROMs is not clear", and that even among members of the industry it was not clear that the copyright law protects works "like those in suit that are ROM-based".

We read the district court opinion as presenting the following legal issues: (1) whether copyright can exist in a computer program expressed in object code, (2) whether copyright can exist in a computer program embedded on a ROM, (3) whether copyright can exist in an operating system program, and (4) whether independent irreparable harm must be shown for a preliminary injunction in copyright infringement actions.

IV. DISCUSSION

A. Copyrightability of a Computer Program Expressed in Object Code

Certain statements by the district court suggest that programs expressed in object code, as distinguished from source code, may not be the proper subject of copyright. We find no basis in the statute for any such concern. Furthermore, our decision in *Williams Electronics, Inc. v. Artic International, Inc.*, laid to rest many of the doubts expressed by the district court.

In 1976, after considerable study, Congress enacted a new copyright law to replace that which had governed since 1909. Under the law, two primary requirements must be satisfied in order for a work to constitute copyrightable subject matter – it must be an "original wor [k] of authorship" and must be "fixed in [a] tangible medium of expression." 17 U.S.C. § 102(a). The statute provides:

> "(a) Copyright protection subsists, in accordance with this title, in original works of authorship fixed in any tangible medium of expression, now known or later developed, from which they can be perceived, reproduced, or otherwise communicated, either directly or with the aid of a machine or device."

The statute enumerates seven categories under "works of authorship" including "literary works", defined as follows:

> "'Literary works' are works, other than audiovisual works, expressed in words, numbers, or other verbal or numerical symbols or indicia, regardless of the nature of the material objects, such as books, periodicals, manuscripts, phonorecords, film, tapes, disks, or cards, in which they are embodied."

A work is "fixed" in a tangible medium of expression when:

> "its embodiment in a copy or phonorecord, by or under the authority of the author, is sufficiently permanent or stable to permit it to be perceived, reproduced, or otherwise communicated for a period of more than transitory duration. A work consisting of sounds, images, or both, that are being transmitted, is 'fixed' for purposes of this title if a fixation of the work is being made simultaneously with its transmission."

Although section 102(a) does not expressly list computer programs as works of authorship, the legislative history suggests that programs were considered copyrightable as literary works. Because a Commission on New Technological Uses ("CONTU") had been created by Congress to study, inter alia, computer uses of copyrighted works, Congress enacted a status quo provision, section 117, in the 1976 Act concerning such computer uses pending the CONTU report and recommendations.

The CONTU Final Report recommended that the copyright law be amended, inter alia, "to make it explicit that computer programs, to the extent that they embody an author's original creation, are proper subject matter of copyright." CONTU recommended two changes relevant here: that section 117, the status quo provision, be repealed and replaced with a section limiting exclusive rights in computer programs so as "to ensure that rightful possessors of copies of computer programs may use or adapt these copies for their use," and that a definition of computer program be added to section 101. Congress adopted both changes. The revisions embodied CONTU's recommendations to clarify the law of copyright of computer software.

The 1980 amendments added a definition of a computer program:

> "A 'computer program' is a set of statements or instructions to be used directly or indirectly in a computer in order to bring about a certain result."

The amendments also substituted a new section 117 which provides that "it is not an infringement for the owner of a copy of a computer program to make or authorize the making of another copy or adaptation of that computer program" when necessary to "the utilization of the computer program" or "for archival purposes only." The parties agree that this section is not implicated in the instant lawsuit. The language of the provision, however, by carving out an exception to the normal proscriptions against copying, clearly indicates that programs are copyrightable and are otherwise afforded copyright protection.

We considered the issue of copyright protection for a computer program in *Williams Electronics, Inc. v. Artic International, Inc.*, and concluded that "the copyrightability of computer programs is firmly established after the 1980 amendment to the Copyright Act." At issue in *Williams* were not only two audiovisual copyrights to the "attract" and "play" modes of a video game, but also the computer program which was expressed in object code embodied in ROM and which controlled the sights and sounds of the game. Defendant there had argued "that when the issue is the copyright on a computer program, a distinction must be drawn between the 'source code' version of a computer program, which ... can be afforded copyright protection, and the 'object code' stage, which ... cannot be so protected," an argument we rejected.

The district court here questioned whether copyright was to be limited to works "designed to be 'read' by a human reader [as distinguished from] read by an expert with a microscope and patience". The suggestion that copyrightability depends on a communicative function to individuals stems from the early decision of White-Smith Music Publishing Co. v. Apollo Co., 209 U.S. 1 (1908), which held a piano roll was not a copy of the musical composition because it was not in a form others, except perhaps for a very expert few, could perceive. However, it is clear from the language of the 1976 Act and its legislative history that it was intended to obliterate distinctions engendered by *White-Smith.*

Under the statute, copyright extends to works in any tangible means of expression "*from which they can be perceived,* reproduced, or otherwise communicated, either directly or *with the aid of a machine or device.*" Further, the definition of "computer program" adopted by Congress in the 1980 amendments is "sets of statements or instructions to be used *directly or indirectly* in a computer in order to bring about a certain result." As source code instructions must be translated into object code before the computer can act upon them, only instructions expressed in object code can be used "directly" by the computer. This definition was adopted following the CONTU Report in which the majority clearly took the position that object codes are proper subjects of copyright. The majority's conclusion was reached although confronted by a dissent based upon the theory that the "machine-control phase" of a program is not directed at a human audience.

The defendant in *Williams* had also argued that a copyrightable work "must be intelligible to human beings and must be intended as a medium of communication to human beings". We reiterate the statement we made in *Williams* when we rejected that argument: "[t]he answer to defendant's contention is in the words of the statute itself."

The district court also expressed uncertainty as to whether a computer program in object code could be classified as a "literary work." However, the category of "literary works", one of the seven copyrightable categories, is not confined to literature in the nature of Hemingway's *For Whom the Bell Tolls.* The definition of "literary works" in section 101 includes expression not only in words but also "numbers, or other ... numerical symbols or indicia", thereby expanding the common usage of "literary works." Thus a computer program, whether in object code or source code, is a "literary work" and is protected from unauthorized copying, whether from its object or source code version.

B. Copyrightability of a Computer Program Embedded on a ROM

Just as the district court's suggestion of a distinction between source code and object code was rejected by our opinion in *Williams* issued three days after the district court opinion, so also was its suggestion that embodiment of a computer program on a ROM, as distinguished from in a traditional writing, detracts from its copyrightability. In *Williams* we rejected the argument that "a computer program is not infringed when the program is loaded into electronic memory devices (ROMs) and used to control the activity of machines." Defendant there had argued that there can be no copyright protection for the ROMs because they are utilitarian objects or machine parts. We held that the statutory requirement of "fixation", the manner in which the issue arises, is satisfied through the embodiment of the expression in the ROM devices. Therefore we reaffirm that a computer program in object code embedded in a ROM chip is an appropriate subject of copyright.

C. Copyrightability of Computer Operating System Programs

We turn to the heart of Franklin's position on appeal which is that computer operating system programs, as distinguished from application programs, are not the proper subject of copyright "regardless of the language or medium in which they are fixed." Apple suggests that this issue too is foreclosed by our *Williams* decision because some portion of the program at issue there was in effect an operating system program. Franklin is correct that this was not an issue raised by the parties in *Williams* and it was not considered by the court. Thus we consider it as a matter of first impression.

Franklin contends that operating system programs are *per se* excluded from copyright protection under the express terms of section 102(b) of the Copyright Act, and under the precedent and underlying principles of Baker v. Selden, 101 U.S. 99 (1879). These separate grounds have substantial analytic overlap.

In *Baker v. Selden,* plaintiff's testator held a copyright on a book explaining a bookkeeping system which included blank forms with ruled lines and headings designed for use with that system. Plaintiff sued for copyright infringement on the basis of defendant's publication of a book containing a different arrangement of the columns and different headings, but which used a similar plan so far as results were concerned. The Court, in reversing the decree for the plaintiff, concluded that blank account-books were not the subject of copyright and that "the mere copyright of Selden's book did not confer upon him the exclusive right to make and use account-books, ruled and arranged as designated by him and described and illustrated in said book." The Court stated that copyright of the books did not give the plaintiff the exclusive right to use the system explained in the books, noting, for example, that "copyright of a work on mathematical science cannot give to the author an exclusive right to the methods of operation which he propounds."

Franklin reads *Baker v. Selden* as "stand[ing] for several fundamental principles, each presenting ... an insuperable obstacle to the copyrightability of Apple's operating systems." It states:

> "*First, Baker* teaches that use of a system itself does not infringe a copyright on the description of the system. *Second, Baker* enunciates the rule that copyright does not extend to purely utilitarian works. *Finally, Baker* emphasizes that the copyright laws may not be used to obtain and hold a monopoly over an idea. In so doing, *Baker* highlights the principal difference between the copyright and patent laws – a difference that is highly pertinent in this case."

Section 102(b) of the Copyright Act, the other ground on which Franklin relies, appeared first in the 1976 version, long after the decision in *Baker v. Selden.* It provides:

> "In no case does copyright protection for an original work of authorship extend to any idea, procedure, process, system, method of operation, concept, principle, or discovery, regardless of the form in which it is described, explained, illustrated, or embodied in such work."

It is apparent that section 102(b) codifies a substantial part of the holding and dictum of *Baker v. Selden.*

We turn to consider the two principal points of Franklin's argument.

1. "Process", "System" or "Method of Operation"

Franklin argues that an operating system program is either a "process", "system", or "method of operation" and hence uncopyrightable. Franklin correctly notes that underlying section 102(b) and many of the statements for which *Baker v. Selden* is cited is the distinction which must be made between property subject to the patent law, which protects discoveries, and that subject to copyright law, which protects the writings describing such discoveries. However, Franklin's argument misapplies that distinction in this case. Apple does not seek to copyright the method which instructs the computer to perform its operating functions but only the instructions themselves. The method would be protected, if at all, by the patent law, an issue as yet unresolved.

Franklin's attack on operating system programs as "methods" or "processes" seems inconsistent with its concession that application programs are an appropriate subject of copyright. Both types of programs instruct the computer to do something. Therefore, it should make no difference for purposes of section 102(b) whether these instructions tell the computer to help prepare an income tax return (the task of an application program) or to translate a high level language program from source code into its binary language object code form (the task of an operating system program such as "Applesoft". Since it is only the instructions which are protected, a "process" is no more involved because the instructions in an operating system program may be used to activate the operation of the computer than it would be if instructions were written in ordinary English in a manual which described the necessary steps to activate an intricate complicated machine. There is, therefore, no reason to afford any less copyright protection to the instructions in an operating system program than to the instructions in an application program.

Franklin's argument, receptively treated by the district court, that an operating system program is part of a machine mistakenly focuses on the physical characteristics of the instructions. But the medium is not the message. We have already considered and rejected aspects of this contention in the discussion of object code and ROM. The mere fact that the operating system program may be etched on a ROM does not make the program either a machine, part of a machine or its equivalent. Furthermore, as one of Franklin's witnesses testified, an operating system does not have to be permanently in the machine in ROM, but it may be on some other medium, such as a diskette or magnetic tape, where it could be readily transferred into the temporary memory space of the computer. In fact, some of the operating systems at issue were on diskette. As the CONTU majority stated,

> "Programs should no more be considered machine parts than videotapes should be considered parts of projectors or phonorecords parts of sound reproduction equipment.... That the words of a program are used ultimately in the implementation of a process should in no way affect their copyrightability."

Franklin also argues that the operating systems cannot be copyrighted because they are "purely utilitarian works" and that Apple is seeking to block the use of the art embodied in its operating systems. This argument stems from the following dictum in *Baker v. Selden:*

> "The very object of publishing a book on science or the useful arts is to communicate to the world the useful knowledge which it contains. But this object would be frustrated if the knowledge could not be used without incurring the guilt of piracy of the book. And where the art it teaches cannot be used without employing the methods and diagrams used to illustrate the book, or such as are similar to them, such methods and diagrams are to be considered as necessary incidents to the art, and given therewith to the public; not given for the purpose of publication in other works explanatory of the art, but for the purpose of practical application."

We cannot accept the expansive reading given to this language by some courts. In this respect we agree with the views expressed by Professor Nimmer in his treatise.

Although a literal construction of this language could support Franklin's reading that precludes copyrightability if the copyright work is put to a utilitarian use, that interpretation has been rejected by a later Supreme Court decision. In Mazer v. Stein, 347 U.S. 201 (1954), the Court stated: "We find nothing in the copyright statute to support the argument that the intended use or use in industry of an article eligible for copyright bars or invalidates its registration. We do not read such a limitation into the copyright law." The CONTU majority also rejected the expansive view some courts have given *Baker v. Selden,* and stated, "That the words of a program are used ultimately in the implementation of a process should in no way affect their copyrightability." It referred to "copyright practice past and present, which recognizes copyright protection for a work of authorship regardless of the uses to which it may be put." The Commission continued: "The copyright status of the written rules for a game *or a system for the operation of a machine* is unaffected by the fact that those rules direct the actions of those who play the game or *carry out the process.*" As we previously noted, we can consider the CONTU Report as accepted by Congress since Congress wrote into the law the majority's recommendations almost verbatim.

Perhaps the most convincing item leading us to reject Franklin's argument is that the statutory definition of a computer program as a set of instructions to be used in a computer in order to bring about a certain result, makes no distinction between application programs and operating programs. Franklin can point to no decision which adopts the distinction it seeks to make. In the one other reported case to have considered it, the court reached the same conclusion which we do, *i.e.* that an operating system program is not *per se* precluded from copyright. It stated, "There is nothing in any of the statutory terms which suggest a different result for different types of computer programs based upon the function they serve within the machine." Other courts have also upheld the copyrightability of operating programs without discussion of this issue.

2. Idea/Expression Dichotomy

Franklin's other challenge to copyright of operating system programs relies on the line which is drawn between ideas and their expression. *Baker v. Selden* remains a benchmark in the law of copyright for the reading given it in *Mazer v. Stein, supra,* where the Court stated, "Unlike a patent, a copyright gives no exclusive right to the art disclosed; protection is given only to the expression of the idea – not the idea itself."

The expression/idea dichotomy is now expressly recognized in section 102(b) which precludes copyright for "any idea." This provision was not intended to enlarge or contract the scope of copyright protection but "to restate ... that the basic dichotomy between expression and idea remains unchanged." The legislative history indicates that section 102(b) was intended "to make clear that the expression adopted by the programmer is the copyrightable element in a computer program, and that the actual processes or methods embodied in the program are not within the scope of the copyright law."

Many of the courts which have sought to draw the line between an idea and expression have found difficulty in articulating where it falls. We believe that in the context before us, a program for an operating system, the line must be a pragmatic one, which also keeps in consideration "the preservation of the balance between competition and protection reflected in the patent and copyright laws". As we stated in *Franklin Mint Corp. v. National Wildlife Art Exchange, Inc.*, "[u] nlike a patent, a copyright protects originality rather than novelty or invention." (...)

We adopt the suggestion in the above language and thus focus on whether the idea is capable of various modes of expression. If other programs can be written or created which perform the same function as an Apple's operating system program, then that program is an expression of the idea and hence copyrightable. In essence, this inquiry is no different than that made to determine whether the expression and idea have merged, which has been stated to occur where there are no or few other ways of expressing a particular idea.

The district court made no findings as to whether some or all of Apple's operating programs represent the only means of expression of the idea underlying them. Although there seems to be a concession by Franklin that at least some of the programs can be rewritten, we do not believe that the record on that issue is so clear that it can be decided at the appellate level. Therefore, if the issue is pressed on remand, the necessary finding can be made at that time.

Franklin claims that whether or not the programs can be rewritten, there are a limited "number of ways to arrange operating systems to enable a computer to run the vast body of Apple-compatible software". This claim has no pertinence to either the idea/expression dichotomy or merger. The idea which may merge with the expression, thus making the copyright unavailable, is the idea which is the subject of the expression. The idea of one of the operating system programs is, for example, how to translate source code into object code. If other methods of expressing that idea are not foreclosed as a practical matter, then there is no merger. Franklin may wish to achieve total compatibility with independently developed application programs written for the Apple II, but that is a commercial and competitive objective which does not enter into the somewhat metaphysical issue of whether particular ideas and expressions have merged.

In summary, Franklin's contentions that operating system programs are *per se* not copyrightable is unpersuasive. The other courts before whom this issue has been raised have rejected the distinction. Neither the CONTU majority nor Congress made a distinction between operating and application programs. We believe that the 1980 amendments reflect Congress' receptivity to new technology and its desire to encourage, through the copyright laws, continued imagination and creativity in computer programming. Since we believe that the district court's decision on the preliminary injunction was, to a large part, influenced by an erroneous view of the availability of copyright for operating system programs and unnecessary concerns about object code and ROMs, we must reverse the denial of the preliminary injunction and remand for reconsideration.

D. Irreparable Harm

The district court, without any extended discussion, found that Apple had not made the requisite showing of irreparable harm, stating "Apple is better suited to withstand whatever injury it might sustain during litigation than is Franklin to withstand the effects of a preliminary injunction." In so ruling, the district court failed to consider the prevailing view that a showing of a prima facie case of copyright infringement or reasonable likelihood of success on the merits raises a presumption of irreparable harm. A copyright plaintiff who makes out a prima facie case of infringement is entitled to a preliminary injunction without a detailed showing of irreparable harm.

The CONTU Final Report recognized that "[t]he cost of developing computer programs is far greater than the cost of their duplication." Apple introduced substantial evidence of the considerable time and money it had invested in the development of the computer programs in suit. Thus even without the presumption of irreparable harm generally applied in copyright infringement cases, the jeopardy to Apple's investment and competitive position caused by Franklin's wholesale copying of many of its key operating programs would satisfy the requirement of irreparable harm needed to support a preliminary injunction.

In *Kontes Glass Co. v. Lab Glass, Inc.*, this court appeared to adopt an inverse relationship approach to the irreparable harm issue, suggesting that the strength of the required showing of irreparable injury varies inversely with the strength of plaintiff's showing of a likelihood of success on the merits. In *Kontes*, we were not presented with a case in which copyrighted material central to the essence of plaintiff's operations was concededly copied, as we are here. We believe the *Kontes* approach is best suited to those cases where the injury from copying can be fairly considered minimal, limited or conjectural. In those circumstances it provides flexibility in applying the equitable remedy of preliminary injunctions through evaluation of the irreparable harm factor. Normally, however, the public interest underlying the copyright law requires a presumption of irreparable harm, as long as there is, as here, adequate evidence of the expenditure of significant time, effort and money directed to the production of the copyrighted material. Otherwise, the rationale for protecting copyright, that of encouraging creativity, would be undermined. As Judge Broderick stated in *Klitzner Industries, Inc. v. H.K. James & Co.*:

> "Since Congress has elected to grant certain exclusive rights to the owner of a copyright in a protected work, it is virtually axiomatic that the public interest can only be served by upholding copyright protections and, correspondingly, preventing the misappropriation of the skills, creative energies, and resources which are invested in the protected work."

Nor can we accept the district court's explanation which stressed the "devastating effect" of a preliminary injunction on Franklin's business. If that were the correct standard, then a knowing infringer would be permitted to construct its business around its infringement, a result we cannot condone. The size of the infringer should not be determinative of the copyright holder's ability to get prompt judicial redress. (...)

V.

For the reasons set forth in this opinion, **WE WILL REVERSE THE DENIAL OF THE PRELIMINARY INJUNCTION AND REMAND TO THE DISTRICT COURT FOR FURTHER PROCEEDINGS IN ACCORDANCE HEREWITH.**

THINK IT OVER!

1. The case is one of the earliest rulings on the protectability of computer programs under copyright law. The ruling heavily builds on CONTU's final recommendations that software shall be eligible for protection as a literary work under §102 of the USCA. This view has been ultimately confirmed by a myriad of decisions. Importantly, in *Atari Games v. Oman*, the D.C. Circuit has ruled that computer programs might be copyrightable "if the requisite level of creativity is met by either the individual screens or the relationship of each screen to the others and/or the accompanying sound effects". (Atari Games v. Oman, p. 244.) The question that computer programs are eligible for copyright protection is settled now. *Is copyright law the right way to protect computer programs?*

2. Originality is one of the most important prerequisites of copyright protection. It is, however, not the only one. A great amount of cases dealt with another notable prerequisite of protection, namely the fixation requirement (see §102 of the U.S. Copyright Act). In Stern Electronics v. Kaufman, 669 *F.2d* 852 (1982), the Second Circuit had to answer the question whether audiovisual images generated by a video game are fixed in a tangible medium of expression? The court answered positively, and concluded that the storage of data in the read only memory (ROM) chips necessarily means fixation. Shortly thereafter, the Seventh Circuit ruled in Midway Manufacturing Co. v. Artic International, Inc., 704 *F.2d* 1009 (1983), that the participation of the player in the game (namely, shooting at and destroying "alien enemies") does not prevent the fixation of audiovisual images, as the shape of aliens, what they look like, and how they move are fixed in the computer's memory.

Further Case Law

Kontes Glass Co. v. Lab Glass, Inc., 373 *F.2d* 319 (1967)

Stern Electronics v. Kaufman, 669 *F.2d* 852 (1982)

Williams Electronics, Inc. v. Artic International, Inc., 685 *F.2d* 870 (1982)

Midway Manufacturing Co. v. Artic International, Inc., 704 *F.2d* 1009 (1983)

Computer Associates International, Inc. v. Altai, Inc., 982 *F.2d* 693 (1992)

Atari Games Corporation v. Oman, 979 *F.2d* 242 (1992)

Recommended readings

In English

National Commission on New Technological Uses of Copyrighted Works (CONTU), Final Report on the National Commission on New Technological Uses of Copyrighted Works. In: *Computer Law Journal*, 1981, p. 53-104. [CONTU Report]

Paul Goldstein: *Copyright's Highway - From Gutenberg to the Celestial Jukebox*, Revised Edition, Stanford University Press, Stanford, 2003, p. 190-197.

COMPUTER ASSOCIATES INTERNATIONAL, INC. V. ALTAI, INC.

982 *F.2d* 693 (1992)

Opinion

WALKER, Circuit Judge:

(...) BACKGROUND (...)

I. COMPUTER PROGRAM DESIGN

Certain elementary facts concerning the nature of computer programs are vital to the following discussion. The Copyright Act defines a computer program as "a set of statements or instructions to be used directly or indirectly in a computer in order to bring about a certain result." In writing these directions, the programmer works "from the general to the specific."

The first step in this procedure is to identify a program's ultimate function or purpose. An example of such an ultimate purpose might be the creation and maintenance of a business ledger. Once this goal has been achieved, a programmer breaks down or "decomposes" the program's ultimate function into "simpler constituent problems or 'subtasks,'" which are also known as subroutines or modules. In the context of a business ledger program, a module or subroutine might be responsible for the task of updating a list of outstanding accounts receivable. Sometimes, depending upon the complexity of its task, a subroutine may be broken down further into sub-subroutines.

Having sufficiently decomposed the program's ultimate function into its component elements, a programmer will then arrange the subroutines or modules into what are known as organizational or flow charts. Flow charts map the interactions between modules that achieve the program's end goal.

In order to accomplish these intra-program interactions, a programmer must carefully design each module's parameter list. A parameter list, according to the expert appointed and fully credited by the district court, Dr. Randall Davis, is "the information sent to and received from a subroutine." The term "parameter list" refers to the form in which information is passed between modules (e.g. for accounts receivable, the designated time frame and particular customer identifying number) and the information's actual content (e.g. 8/91–7/92; customer No. 3). With respect to form, interacting modules must share similar parameter lists so that they are capable of exchanging information.

"The functions of the modules in a program together with each module's relationships to other modules constitute the 'structure' of the program." Additionally, the term structure may include the category of modules referred to as "macros." A macro is a single instruction that initiates a sequence of operations or module interactions within the program. Very often the user will accompany a macro with an instruction from the parameter list to refine the instruction (e.g. current total of accounts receivable (macro), but limited to those for 8/91 to 7/92 from customer No. 3 (parameters)).

In fashioning the structure, a programmer will normally attempt to maximize the program's speed, efficiency, as well as simplicity for user operation, while taking into consideration certain externalities such as the memory constraints of the computer upon which the program will be run. "This stage of program design often requires the most time and investment."

Once each necessary module has been identified, designed, and its relationship to the other modules has been laid out conceptually, the resulting program structure must be embodied in a written language that the computer can read. This process is called "coding," and requires two steps. First, the programmer must transpose the program's structural blue-print into a source code. This step has been described as "comparable to the novelist fleshing out the broad outline of his plot by crafting from words and sentences the paragraphs that convey the ideas." The source code may be written in any one of several computer languages, such as COBAL, FORTRAN, BASIC, EDL, etc., depending upon the type of computer for which the program is intended. Once the source code has been completed, the second step is to translate or "compile" it into object code. Object code is the binary language comprised of zeros and ones through which the computer directly receives its instructions.

After the coding is finished, the programmer will run the program on the computer in order to find and correct any logical and syntactical errors. This is known as "debugging" and, once done, the program is complete.

II. FACTS

CA is a Delaware corporation, with its principal place of business in Garden City, New York. Altai is a Texas corporation, doing business primarily in Arlington, Texas. Both companies are in the computer software industry – designing, developing and marketing various types of computer programs.

The subject of this litigation originates with one of CA's marketed programs entitled CA-SCHEDULER. CA-SCHEDULER is a job scheduling program designed for IBM mainframe computers. Its primary functions are straightforward: to create a schedule specifying when the computer should run various tasks, and then to control the computer as it executes the schedule. CA-SCHEDULER contains a sub-program entitled ADAPTER, also developed by CA. ADAPTER is not an independently marketed product of CA; it is a wholly integrated component of CA-SCHEDULER and has no capacity for independent use.

Nevertheless, ADAPTER plays an extremely important role. It is an "operating system compatibility component," which means, roughly speaking, it serves as a translator. An "operating system" is itself a program that manages the resources of the computer, allocating those resources to other programs as needed. The IBM System 370 family of computers, for which CA-SCHEDULER was created, is, depending upon the computer's size, designed to contain one of three operating systems: DOS/VSE, MVS, or CMS. As the district court noted, the general rule is that "a program written for one operating system, e.g., DOS/VSE, will not, without modification, run under another operating system such as MVS." ADAPTER's function is to translate the language of a given program into the particular language that the computer's own operating system can understand.

The district court succinctly outlined the manner in which ADAPTER works within the context of the larger program. In order to enable CA–SCHEDULER to function on different operating systems, CA divided the CA–SCHEDULER into two components:

- a first component that contains only the task-specific portions of the program, independent of all operating system issues, and

- a second component that contains all the interconnections between the first component and the operating system.

In a program constructed in this way, whenever the first, task-specific, component needs to ask the operating system for some resource through a "system call", it calls the second component instead of calling the operating system directly.

The second component serves as an "interface" or "compatibility component" between the task-specific portion of the program and the operating system. It receives the request from the first component and translates it into the appropriate system call that will be recognized by whatever operating system is installed on the computer, *e.g.*, DOS/VSE, MVS, or CMS. Since the first, task-specific component calls the adapter component rather than the operating system, the first component need not be customized to use any specific operating system. The second, interface, component insures that all the system calls are performed properly for the particular operating system in use.

ADAPTER serves as the second, "common system interface" component referred to above.

A program like ADAPTER, which allows a computer user to change or use multiple operating systems while maintaining the same software, is highly desirable. It saves the user the costs, both in time and money, that otherwise would be expended in purchasing new programs, modifying existing systems to run them, and gaining familiarity with their operation. The benefits run both ways. The increased compatibility afforded by an ADAPTER-like component, and its resulting popularity among consumers, makes whatever software in which it is incorporated significantly more marketable.

Starting in 1982, Altai began marketing its own job scheduling program entitled ZEKE. The original version of ZEKE was designed for use in conjunction with a VSE operating system. By late 1983, in response to customer demand, Altai decided to rewrite ZEKE so that it could be run in conjunction with an MVS operating system.

At that time, James P. Williams ("Williams"), then an employee of Altai and now its President, approached Claude F. Arney, III ("Arney"), a computer programmer who worked for CA. Williams and Arney were longstanding friends, and had in fact been co-workers at CA for some time before Williams left CA to work for Altai's predecessor. Williams wanted to recruit Arney to assist Altai in designing an MVS version of ZEKE.

At the time he first spoke with Arney, Williams was aware of both the CA–SCHEDULER and ADAPTER programs. However, Williams was not involved in their development and had never seen the codes of either program. When he asked Arney to come work for Altai, Williams did not know that ADAPTER was a component of CA–SCHEDULER.

Arney, on the other hand, was intimately familiar with various aspects of ADAPTER. While working for CA, he helped improve the VSE version of ADAPTER, and was permitted to take home a copy of ADAPTER'S source code. This apparently developed into an irresistible habit, for when Arney left CA to work for Altai in January, 1984, he took with him copies of the source code for both the VSE and MVS versions of ADAPTER. He did this in knowing violation of the CA employee agreements that he had signed.

Once at Altai, Arney and Williams discussed design possibilities for adapting ZEKE to run on MVS operating systems. Williams, who had created the VSE version of ZEKE, thought that approximately 30% of his original program would have to be modified in order to accommodate MVS. Arney persuaded Williams that the best way to make the needed modifications was to introduce a "common system interface" component into ZEKE. He did not tell Williams that his idea stemmed from his familiarity with ADAPTER. They decided to name this new component-program OSCAR.

Arney went to work creating OSCAR at Altai's offices using the ADAPTER source code. The district court accepted Williams' testimony that no one at Altai, with the exception of Arney, affirmatively knew that Arney had the ADAPTER code, or that he was using it to create OSCAR/VSE. However, during this time period, Williams' office was adjacent to Arney's. Williams testified that he and Arney "conversed quite frequently" while Arney was "investigating the source code of ZEKE" and that Arney was in his office "a number of times daily, asking questions." In three months, Arney successfully completed the OSCAR/VSE project. In an additional month he developed an OSCAR/MVS version. When the dust finally settled, Arney had copied approximately 30% of OSCAR's code from CA's ADAPTER program.

The first generation of OSCAR programs was known as OSCAR 3.4. From 1985 to August 1988, Altai used OSCAR 3.4 in its ZEKE product, as well as in programs entitled ZACK and ZEBB. In late July 1988, CA first learned that Altai may have appropriated parts of ADAPTER. After confirming its suspicions, CA secured copyrights on its 2.1 and 7.0 versions of CA-SCHEDULER. CA then brought this copyright and trade secret misappropriation action against Altai.

Apparently, it was upon receipt of the summons and complaint that Altai first learned that Arney had copied much of the OSCAR code from ADAPTER. After Arney confirmed to Williams that CA's accusations of copying were true, Williams immediately set out to survey the damage. Without ever looking at the ADAPTER code himself, Williams learned from Arney exactly which sections of code Arney had taken from ADAPTER.

Upon advice of counsel, Williams initiated OSCAR's rewrite. The project's goal was to save as much of OSCAR 3.4 as legitimately could be used, and to excise those portions which had been copied from ADAPTER. Arney was entirely excluded from the process, and his copy of the ADAPTER code was locked away. Williams put eight other programmers on the project, none of whom had been involved in any way in the development of OSCAR 3.4. Williams provided the programmers with a description of the ZEKE operating system services so that they could rewrite the appropriate code. The rewrite project took about six months to complete and was finished in mid-November 1989. The resulting program was entitled OSCAR 3.5.

From that point on, Altai shipped only OSCAR 3.5 to its new customers. Altai also shipped OSCAR 3.5 as a "free upgrade" to all customers that had previously purchased OSCAR 3.4. While Altai and Williams acted responsibly to correct Arney's literal copying of the ADAPTER program, copyright infringement had occurred.

After CA originally instituted this action in the United States District Court for the District of New Jersey, the parties stipulated its transfer in March, 1989, to the Eastern District of New York where it was assigned to Judge Jacob Mishler. On October 26, 1989, Judge Mishler transferred the case to Judge Pratt who was sitting in the district court by designation. Judge Pratt conducted a six day trial from March 28 through April 6, 1990. He entered judgment on August 12, 1991, and this appeal followed.

DISCUSSION (...)

I. COPYRIGHT INFRINGEMENT

In any suit for copyright infringement, the plaintiff must establish its ownership of a valid copyright, and that the defendant copied the copyrighted work. The plaintiff may prove defendant's copying either by direct evidence or, as is most often the case, by showing that (1) the defendant had access to the plaintiff's copyrighted work and (2) that defendant's work is substantially similar to the plaintiff's copyrightable material.

For the purpose of analysis, the district court assumed that Altai had access to the ADAPTER code when creating OSCAR 3.5. Thus, in determining whether Altai had unlawfully copied protected aspects of CA's ADAPTER, the district court narrowed its focus of inquiry to ascertaining whether Altai's OSCAR 3.5 was substantially similar to ADAPTER. Because we approve Judge Pratt's conclusions regarding substantial similarity, our analysis will proceed along the same assumption.

As a general matter, and to varying degrees, copyright protection extends beyond a literary work's strictly textual form to its non-literal components. As we have said, "[i]t is of course essential to any protection of literary property ... that the right cannot be limited literally to the text, else a plagiarist would escape by immaterial variations." Thus, where "the fundamental essence or structure of one work is duplicated in another," courts have found copyright infringement. This black letter proposition is the springboard for our discussion.

A. *Copyright Protection for the Non-literal Elements of Computer Programs*

It is now well settled that the literal elements of computer programs, i.e., their source and object codes, are the subject of copyright protection. Here, as noted earlier, Altai admits having copied approximately 30% of the OSCAR 3.4 program from CA's ADAPTER source code, and does not challenge the district court's related finding of infringement.

In this case, the hotly contested issues surround OSCAR 3.5. As recounted above, OSCAR 3.5 is the product of Altai's carefully orchestrated rewrite of OSCAR 3.4. After the purge, none of the ADAPTER source code remained in the 3.5 version; thus, Altai made sure that the literal elements of its revamped OSCAR program were no longer substantially similar to the literal elements of CA's ADAPTER.

According to CA, the district court erroneously concluded that Altai's OSCAR 3.5 was not substantially similar to its own ADAPTER program. CA argues that this occurred because the district court "committed legal error in analyzing [its] claims of copyright infringement by failing to find that copyright protects expression contained in the non-literal elements of computer software." We disagree.

CA argues that, despite Altai's rewrite of the OSCAR code, the resulting program remained substantially similar to the *structure* of its ADAPTER program. As discussed above, a program's structure includes its non-literal components such as general flow charts as well as the more specific organization of inter-modular relationships, parameter lists, and macros. In addition to these aspects, CA contends that OSCAR 3.5 is also substantially similar to ADAPTER with respect to the list of services that both ADAPTER and OSCAR obtain from their respective operating systems. We must decide whether and to what extent these elements of computer programs are protected by copyright law.

The statutory terrain in this area has been well explored. The Copyright Act affords protection to "original works of authorship fixed in any tangible medium of expression...." This broad category of protected "works" includes "literary works," which are defined by the Act as

> "works, other than audiovisual works, expressed in words, numbers, or other verbal or numerical symbols or indicia, regardless of the nature of the material objects, such as books, periodicals, manuscripts, phonorecords, film tapes, disks, or cards, in which they are embodied."

While computer programs are not specifically listed as part of the above statutory definition, the legislative history leaves no doubt that Congress intended them to be considered literary works.

The syllogism that follows from the foregoing premises is a powerful one: if the non-literal structures of literary works are protected by copyright; and if computer programs are literary works, as we are told by the legislature; then the non-literal structures of computer programs are protected by copyright. We have no reservation in joining the company of those courts that have already ascribed to this logic. However, that conclusion does not end our analysis. We must determine the scope of copyright protection that extends to a computer program's non-literal structure.

As a caveat, we note that our decision here does not control infringement actions regarding categorically distinct works, such as certain types of screen displays. These items represent products of computer programs, rather than the programs themselves, and fall under the copyright rubric of audiovisual works. If a computer audiovisual display is copyrighted separately as an audiovisual work, apart from the literary work that generates it (i.e., the program), the display may be protectable regardless of the underlying program's copyright status. Of course, the copyright protection that these displays enjoy extends only so far as their expression is protectable. In this case, however, we are concerned not with a program's display, but the program itself, and then with only its non-literal components. In considering the copyrightability of these components, we must refer to venerable doctrines of copyright law.

1) Idea vs. Expression Dichotomy

It is a fundamental principle of copyright law that a copyright does not protect an idea, but only the expression of the idea. This axiom of common law has been incorporated into the governing statute. Section 102(b) of the Act provides:

> "In no case does copyright protection for an original work of authorship extend to any idea, procedure, process, system, method of operation, concept, principle, or discovery, regardless of the form in which it is described, explained, illustrated, or embodied in such work."

Congress made no special exception for computer programs. To the contrary, the legislative history explicitly states that copyright protects computer programs only "to the extent that they incorporate authorship in programmer's expression of original ideas, as distinguished from the ideas themselves."

Similarly, the National Commission on New Technological Uses of Copyrighted Works ("CONTU") established by Congress to survey the issues generated by the interrelationship of advancing technology and copyright law, recommended, *inter alia,* that the 1976 Copyright Act "be amended ... to make it explicit that computer programs, to the extent that they embody the author's original creation, are proper subject matter for copyright." To that end, Congress adopted CONTU's suggestions and amended the Copyright Act by adding, among other things, a provision to 17 U.S.C. § 101 which defined the term "computer program." CONTU also "concluded that the idea-expression distinction should be used to determine which aspects of computer programs are copyrightable."

Drawing the line between idea and expression is a tricky business. Judge Learned Hand noted that "[n]obody has ever been able to fix that boundary, and nobody ever can." Thirty years later his convictions remained firm. "Obviously, no principle can be stated as to when an imitator has gone beyond copying the 'idea,' and has borrowed its 'expression,' " Judge Hand concluded. "Decisions must therefore inevitably be *ad hoc.*"

The essentially utilitarian nature of a computer program further complicates the task of distilling its idea from its expression. In order to describe both computational processes and abstract ideas, its content "combines creative and technical expression." The variations of expression found in purely creative compositions, as opposed to those contained in utilitarian works, are not directed towards practical application. For example, a narration of Humpty Dumpty's demise, which would clearly be a creative composition, does not serve the same ends as, say, a recipe for scrambled eggs – which is a more process oriented text. Thus, compared to aesthetic works, computer programs hover even more closely to the elusive boundary line described in §102(b).

The doctrinal starting point in analyses of utilitarian works, is the seminal case of Baker v. Selden, 101 U.S. 99 (1879). In *Baker*, the Supreme Court faced the question of "whether the exclusive property in a system of bookkeeping can be claimed, under the law of copyright, by means of a book in which that system is explained?" Selden had copyrighted a book that expounded a particular method of bookkeeping. The book contained lined pages with headings intended to illustrate the manner in which the system operated. Baker's accounting publication included ledger sheets that employed "substantially the same ruled lines and headings...." Selden's testator sued Baker for copyright infringement on the theory that the ledger sheets were protected by Selden's copyright.

The Supreme Court found nothing copyrightable in Selden's bookkeeping system, and rejected his infringement claim regarding the ledger sheets. The Court held that:

> "The fact that the art described in the book by illustrations of lines and figures which are reproduced in practice in the application of the art, makes no difference. Those illustrations are the mere language employed by the author to convey his ideas more clearly. Had he used words of description instead of diagrams (which merely stand in the place of words), there could not be the slightest doubt that others, applying the art to practical use, might lawfully draw the lines and diagrams which were in the author's mind, and which he thus described by words in his book.

The copyright of a work on mathematical science cannot give to the author an exclusive right to the methods of operation which he propounds, or to the diagrams which he employs to explain them, so as to prevent an engineer from using them whenever occasion requires."

To the extent that an accounting text and a computer program are both "a set of statements or instructions ... to bring about a certain result," they are roughly analogous. In the former case, the processes are ultimately conducted by human agency; in the latter, by electronic means. In either case, as already stated, the processes themselves are not protectable. But the holding in *Baker* goes farther. The Court concluded that those aspects of a work, which "must necessarily be used as incident to" the idea, system or process that the work describes, are also not copyrightable. Selden's ledger sheets, therefore, enjoyed no copyright protection because they were "necessary incidents to" the system of accounting that he described. From this reasoning, we conclude that those elements of a computer program that are necessarily incidental to its function are similarly unprotectable.

While *Baker v. Selden* provides a sound analytical foundation, it offers scant guidance on how to separate idea or process from expression, and moreover, on how to further distinguish protectable expression from that expression which "must necessarily be used as incident to" the work's underlying concept. In the context of computer programs, the Third Circuit's noted decision in *Whelan* has, thus far, been the most thoughtful attempt to accomplish these ends.

The court in *Whelan* faced substantially the same problem as is presented by this case. There, the defendant was accused of making off with the non-literal structure of the plaintiff's copyrighted dental lab management program, and employing it to create its own competitive version. In assessing whether there had been an infringement, the court had to determine which aspects of the programs involved were ideas, and which were expression. In separating the two, the court settled upon the following conceptual approach:

> "[T]he line between idea and expression may be drawn with reference to the end sought to be achieved by the work in question. In other words, *the purpose or function of a utilitarian work would be the work's idea, and everything that is not necessary to that purpose or function would be part of the expression of the idea....* Where there are various means of achieving the desired purpose, then the particular means chosen is not necessary to the purpose; hence, there is expression, not idea."

The "idea" of the program at issue in *Whelan* was identified by the court as simply "the efficient management of a dental laboratory."

So far, in the courts, the *Whelan* rule has received a mixed reception. While some decisions have adopted its reasoning, others have rejected it.

Whelan has fared even more poorly in the academic community, where its standard for distinguishing idea from expression has been widely criticized for being conceptually overbroad. The leading commentator in the field has stated that "[t]he crucial flaw in [*Whelan* 's] reasoning is that it assumes that only one 'idea,' in copyright law terms, underlies any computer program, and that once a separable idea can be identified, everything else must be expression." This criticism focuses not upon the program's ultimate purpose but upon the reality of its structural design. As we have already noted, a computer program's ultimate function or purpose is the composite result of interacting subroutines. Since each subroutine is itself a program, and thus, may be said to have its own "idea," *Whelan* 's general formulation that a program's overall purpose equates with the program's idea is descriptively inadequate.

Accordingly, we think that Judge Pratt wisely declined to follow *Whelan*. In addition to noting the weakness in the *Whelan* definition of "program-idea," mentioned above, Judge Pratt found that *Whelan*'s synonymous use of the terms "structure, sequence, and organization," demonstrated a flawed understanding of a computer program's method of operation. Rightly, the district court found *Whelan* 's rationale suspect because it is so closely tied to what can now be seen – with the passage of time – as the opinion's somewhat outdated appreciation of computer science.

2) Substantial Similarity Test for Computer Program Structure: Abstraction – Filtration – Comparison

We think that *Whelan*'s approach to separating idea from expression in computer programs relies too heavily on metaphysical distinctions and does not place enough emphasis on practical considerations. As the cases that we shall discuss demonstrate, a satisfactory answer to this problem cannot be reached by resorting, *a priori,* to philosophical first principals.

As discussed herein, we think that district courts would be well-advised to undertake a three-step procedure, based on the abstractions test utilized by the district court, in order to determine whether the non-literal elements of two or more computer programs are substantially similar. This approach breaks no new ground; rather, it draws on such familiar copyright doctrines as merger, *scenes a faire,* and public domain. In taking this approach, however, we are cognizant that computer technology is a dynamic field which can quickly outpace judicial decisionmaking. Thus, in cases where the technology in question does not allow for a literal application of the procedure we outline below, our opinion should not be read to foreclose the district courts of our circuit from utilizing a modified version.

In ascertaining substantial similarity under this approach, a court would first break down the allegedly infringed program into its constituent structural parts. Then, by examining each of these parts for such things as incorporated ideas, expression that is necessarily incidental to those ideas, and elements that are taken from the public domain, a court would then be able to sift out all non-protectable material. Left with a kernel, or possible kernels, of creative expression after following this process of elimination, the court's last step would be to compare this material with the structure of an allegedly infringing program. The result of this comparison will determine whether the protectable elements of the programs at issue are substantially similar so as to warrant a finding of infringement. It will be helpful to elaborate a bit further.

Step One: Abstraction

As the district court appreciated, the theoretic framework for analyzing substantial similarity expounded by Learned Hand in the *Nichols* case is helpful in the present context. In *Nichols,* we enunciated what has now become known as the "abstractions" test for separating idea from expression:

> "Upon any work ... a great number of patterns of increasing generality will fit equally well, as more and more of the incident is left out. The last may perhaps be no more than the most general statement of what the [work] is about, and at times might consist only of its title; but there is a point in this series of abstractions where they are no longer protected, since otherwise the

> [author] could prevent the use of his 'ideas', to which, apart from their expression, his property is never extended."

While the abstractions test was originally applied in relation to literary works such as novels and plays, it is adaptable to computer programs. In contrast to the *Whelan* approach, the abstractions test "implicitly recognizes that any given work may consist of a mixture of numerous ideas and expressions."

As applied to computer programs, the abstractions test will comprise the first step in the examination for substantial similarity. Initially, in a manner that resembles reverse engineering on a theoretical plane, a court should dissect the allegedly copied program's structure and isolate each level of abstraction contained within it. This process begins with the code and ends with an articulation of the program's ultimate function. Along the way, it is necessary essentially to retrace and map each of the designer's steps – in the opposite order in which they were taken during the program's creation.

As an anatomical guide to this procedure, the following description is helpful:

> "At the lowest level of abstraction, a computer program may be thought of in its entirety as a set of individual instructions organized into a hierarchy of modules. At a higher level of abstraction, the instructions in the lowest-level modules may be replaced conceptually by the functions of those modules. At progressively higher levels of abstraction, the functions of higher-level modules conceptually replace the implementations of those modules in terms of lower-level modules and instructions, until finally, one is left with nothing but the ultimate function of the program.... A program has structure at every level of abstraction at which it is viewed. At low levels of abstraction, a program's structure may be quite complex; at the highest level it is trivial."

Step Two: Filtration

Once the program's abstraction levels have been discovered, the substantial similarity inquiry moves from the conceptual to the concrete. Professor Nimmer suggests, and we endorse, a "successive filtering method" for separating protectable expression from non-protectable material. This process entails examining the structural components at each level of abstraction to determine whether their particular inclusion at that level was "idea" or was dictated by considerations of efficiency, so as to be necessarily incidental to that idea; required by factors external to the program itself; or taken from the public domain and hence is nonprotectable expression. The structure of any given program may reflect some, all, or none of these considerations. Each case requires its own fact specific investigation.

Strictly speaking, this filtration serves "the purpose of defining the scope of plaintiff's copyright." By applying well developed doctrines of copyright law, it may ultimately leave behind a "core of protectable material." Further explication of this second step may be helpful.

(a) Elements Dictated by Efficiency

The portion of *Baker v. Selden,* discussed earlier, which denies copyright protection to expression necessarily incidental to the idea being expressed, appears to be the cornerstone for what has developed into the doctrine of merger. The doctrine's underlying principle is that "[w]hen there is essentially only one way to express an idea, the idea and its expression are inseparable and copyright is no bar to copying that expression." Under these circumstances, the expression is said to have "merged" with the idea itself. In order not to confer a monopoly of the idea upon the copyright owner, such expression should not be protected.

CONTU recognized the applicability of the merger doctrine to computer programs. In its report to Congress it stated that:

> "[C]opyrighted language may be copied without infringing when there is but a limited number of ways to express a given idea.... In the computer context, this means that when specific instructions, even though previously copyrighted, are the only and essential means of accomplishing a given task, their later use by another will not amount to infringement."

While this statement directly concerns only the application of merger to program code, that is, the textual aspect of the program, it reasonably suggests that the doctrine fits comfortably within the general context of computer programs.

Furthermore, when one considers the fact that programmers generally strive to create programs "that meet the user's needs in the most efficient manner," the applicability of the merger doctrine to computer programs becomes compelling. In the context of computer program design, the concept of efficiency is akin to deriving the most concise logical proof or formulating the most succinct mathematical computation. Thus, the more efficient a set of modules are, the more closely they approximate the idea or process embodied in that particular aspect of the program's structure.

While, hypothetically, there might be a myriad of ways in which a programmer may effectuate certain functions within a program, – i.e., express the idea embodied in a given subroutine – efficiency concerns may so narrow the practical range of choice as to make only one or two forms of expression workable options. Of course, not all program structure is informed by efficiency concerns. It follows that in order to determine whether the merger doctrine precludes copyright protection to an aspect of a program's structure that is so oriented, a court must inquire "whether the use of *this particular set* of modules is necessary efficiently to implement that part of the program's process" being implemented. If the answer is yes, then the expression represented by the programmer's choice of a specific module or group of modules has merged with their underlying idea and is unprotected.

Another justification for linking structural economy with the application of the merger doctrine stems from a program's essentially utilitarian nature and the competitive forces that exist in the software marketplace. Working in tandem, these factors give rise to a problem of proof which merger helps to eliminate.

Efficiency is an industry-wide goal. Since, as we have already noted, there may be only a limited number of efficient implementations for any given program task, it is quite possible that multiple programmers, working independently, will design the identical method employed in the allegedly infringed work. Of course, if this is the case, there is no copyright infringement.

Under these circumstances, the fact that two programs contain the same efficient structure may as likely lead to an inference of independent creation as it does to one of copying. Thus, since evidence of similarly efficient structure is not particularly probative of copying, it should be disregarded in the overall substantial similarity analysis.

We find support for applying the merger doctrine in cases that have already addressed the question of substantial similarity in the context of computer program structure. Most recently, in *Lotus Dev. Corp.*, the district court had before it a claim of copyright infringement relating to the structure of a computer spreadsheet program. The court observed that "the basic spreadsheet screen display that resembles a rotated 'L' ..., if not present in every expression of such a program, is present in most expressions." Similarly, the court found that "an essential detail present in most if not all expressions of an electronic spreadsheet – is the designation of a particular key that, when pressed, will invoke the menu command system." Applying the merger doctrine, the court denied copyright protection to both program elements.

In *Manufacturers Technologies, Inc. v. Cams, Inc.*, the infringement claims stemmed from various alleged program similarities "as indicated in their screen displays." Stressing efficiency concerns in the context of a merger analysis, the court determined that the program's method of allowing the user to navigate within the screen displays was not protectable because, in part, "the process or manner of navigating internally on any specific screen displays ... is limited in the number of ways it may be simply achieved to facilitate user comfort."

The court also found that expression contained in various screen displays (in the form of alphabetical and numerical columns) was not the proper subject of copyright protection because it was "necessarily incident to the idea[s]" embodied in the displays.

We agree with the approach taken in these decisions, and conclude that application of the merger doctrine in this setting is an effective way to eliminate non-protectable expression contained in computer programs.

(b) Elements Dictated By External Factors

We have stated that where "it is virtually impossible to write about a particular historical era or fictional theme without employing certain 'stock' or standard literary devices," such expression is not copyrightable. For example, the *Hoehling* case was an infringement suit stemming from several works on the Hindenberg disaster. There we concluded that similarities in representations of German beer halls, scenes depicting German greetings such as "Heil Hitler," or the singing of certain German songs would not lead to a finding of infringement because they were " 'indispensable, or at least standard, in the treatment of' " life in Nazi Germany. This is known as the *scenes a faire* doctrine, and like "merger," it has its analogous application to computer programs.

Professor Nimmer points out that "in many instances it is virtually impossible to write a program to perform particular functions in a specific computing environment without employing standard techniques." This is a result of the fact that a programmer's freedom of design choice is often circumscribed by extrinsic considerations such as (1) the mechanical specifications of the computer on which a particular program is intended to run; (2) compatibility requirements of other programs with which a program is designed to operate in conjunction; (3) computer manufacturers' design standards; (4) demands of the industry being serviced; and (5) widely accepted programming practices within the computer industry.

Courts have already considered some of these factors in denying copyright protection to various elements of computer programs. In the *Plains Cotton* case, the Fifth Circuit refused to reverse the district court's denial of a preliminary injunction against an alleged program infringer because, in part, "many of the similarities between the ... programs [were] dictated by the externalities of the cotton market."

In *Manufacturers Technologies,* the district court noted that the program's method of screen navigation "is influenced by the type of hardware that the software is designed to be used on." Because, in part, "the functioning of the hardware package impact[ed] and constrain[ed] the type of navigational tools used in plaintiff's screen displays," the court denied copyright protection to that aspect of the program.

Finally, the district court in *Q-Co Industries* rested its holding on what, perhaps, most closely approximates a traditional *scenes a faire* rationale. There, the court denied copyright protection to four program modules employed in a teleprompter program. This decision was ultimately based upon the court's finding that "the same modules would be an inherent part of any prompting program."

Building upon this existing case law, we conclude that a court must also examine the structural content of an allegedly infringed program for elements that might have been dictated by external factors.

(c) Elements Taken from the Public Domain

Closely related to the non-protectability of *scenes a faire,* is material found in the public domain. Such material is free for the taking and cannot be appropriated by a single author even though it is included in a copyrighted work. We see no reason to make an exception to this rule for elements of a computer program that have entered the public domain by virtue of freely accessible program exchanges and the like. Thus, a court must also filter out this material from the allegedly infringed program before it makes the final inquiry in its substantial similarity analysis.

Step Three: Comparison

The third and final step of the test for substantial similarity that we believe appropriate for non-literal program components entails a comparison. Once a court has sifted out all elements of the allegedly infringed program which are "ideas" or are dictated by efficiency or external factors, or taken from the public domain, there may remain a core of protectable expression. In terms of a work's copyright value, this is the golden nugget. At this point, the court's substantial similarity inquiry focuses on whether the defendant copied any aspect of this protected expression, as well as an assessment of the copied portion's relative importance with respect to the plaintiff's overall program.

3) Policy Considerations

We are satisfied that the three step approach we have just outlined not only comports with, but advances the constitutional policies underlying the Copyright Act. Since any method that tries to distinguish idea from expression ultimately impacts on the scope of copyright protection afforded to a particular type of work, "the line [it draws] must be a pragmatic one, which also keeps in consideration 'the preservation of the balance between competition and protection....'"

CA and some *amici* argue against the type of approach that we have set forth on the grounds that it will be a disincentive for future computer program research and development. At bottom, they claim that if programmers are not guaranteed broad copyright protection for their work, they will not invest the extensive time, energy and funds required to design and improve program structures. While they have a point, their argument cannot carry the day. The interest of the copyright law is not in simply conferring a monopoly on industrious persons, but in advancing the public welfare through rewarding artistic creativity, in a manner that permits the free use and development of non-protectable ideas and processes.

In this respect, our conclusion is informed by Justice Stewart's concise discussion of the principles that correctly govern the adaptation of the copyright law to new circumstances. In *Twentieth Century Music Corp. v. Aiken,* he wrote:

> "The limited scope of the copyright holder's statutory monopoly, like the limited copyright duration required by the Constitution, reflects a balance of competing claims upon the public interest: Creative work is to be encouraged and rewarded, but private motivation must ultimately serve the cause of promoting broad public availability of literature, music, and the other arts.

The immediate effect of our copyright law is to secure a fair return for an 'author's' creative labor. But the ultimate aim is, by this incentive, to stimulate artistic creativity for the general public good.... When technological change has rendered its literal terms ambiguous, the Copyright Act must be construed in light of this basic purpose."

Recently, the Supreme Court has emphatically reiterated that "[t]he primary objective of copyright is not to reward the *labor* of authors...." While the *Feist* decision deals primarily with the copyrightability of purely factual compilations, its underlying tenets apply to much of the work involved in computer programming. *Feist* put to rest the "sweat of the brow" doctrine in copyright law. The rationale of that doctrine "was that copyright was a reward for the hard work that went into compiling facts." The Court flatly rejected this justification for extending copyright protection, noting that it "eschewed the most fundamental axiom of copyright law – that no one may copyright facts or ideas."

Feist teaches that substantial effort alone cannot confer copyright status on an otherwise uncopyrightable work. As we have discussed, despite the fact that significant labor and expense often goes into computer program flow-charting and debugging, that process does not always result in inherently protectable expression. Thus, *Feist* implicitly undercuts the *Whelan* rationale, "which allow[ed] copyright protection beyond the literal computer code ... [in order to] provide the proper incentive for programmers by protecting their most valuable efforts...." We note that *Whelan* was decided prior to *Feist* when the "sweat of the brow" doctrine still had vitality. In view of the Supreme Court's recent holding, however, we must reject the legal basis of CA's disincentive argument.

Furthermore, we are unpersuaded that the test we approve today will lead to the dire consequences for the computer program industry that plaintiff and some *amici* predict. To the contrary, serious students of the industry have been highly critical of the sweeping scope of copyright protection engendered by the *Whelan* rule, in that it "enables first comers to 'lock up' basic programming techniques as implemented in programs to perform particular tasks."

To be frank, the exact contours of copyright protection for non-literal program structure are not completely clear. We trust that as future cases are decided, those limits will become better defined. Indeed, it may well be that the Copyright Act serves as a relatively weak barrier against public access to the theoretical interstices behind a program's source and object codes. This results from the hybrid nature of a computer program, which, while it is literary expression, is also a highly functional, utilitarian component in the larger process of computing.

Generally, we think that copyright registration – with its indiscriminating availability – is not ideally suited to deal with the highly dynamic technology of computer science. Thus far, many of the decisions in this area reflect the courts' attempt to fit the proverbial square peg in a round hole. The district court, and at least one commentator have suggested that patent registration, with its exacting up-front novelty and non-obviousness requirements, might be the more appropriate rubric of protection for intellectual property of this kind. In any event, now that more than 12 years have passed since CONTU issued its final report, the resolution of this specific issue could benefit from further legislative investigation – perhaps a CONTU II.

In the meantime, Congress has made clear that computer programs are literary works entitled to copyright protection. Of course, we shall abide by these instructions, but in so doing we must not impair the overall integrity of copyright law. While incentive based arguments in favor of broad copyright protection are perhaps attractive from a pure policy perspective, ultimately, they have a corrosive effect on certain fundamental tenets of copyright doctrine. If the test we have outlined results in narrowing the scope of protection, as we expect it will, that result flows from applying, in accordance with Congressional intent, long-standing principles of copyright law to computer programs. Of course, our decision is also informed by our concern that these fundamental principles remain undistorted.

B. *The District Court Decision*

We turn now to our review of the district court's decision in this particular case. At the outset, we must address CA's claim that the district court erred by relying too heavily on the court appointed expert's "personal opinions on the factual and legal issues before the court.

1) Use of Expert Evidence in Determining Substantial Similarity Between Computer Programs

Pursuant to Fed.R.Evid. 706, and with the consent of both Altai and CA, Judge Pratt appointed and relied upon Dr. Randall Davis of the Massachusetts Institute of Technology as the court's own expert witness on the issue of substantial similarity. Dr. Davis submitted a comprehensive written report that analyzed the various aspects of the computer programs at issue and evaluated the parties' expert evidence. At trial, Dr. Davis was extensively cross-examined by both CA and Altai.

The well-established general rule in this circuit has been to limit the use of expert opinion in determining whether works at issue are substantially similar. As a threshold matter, expert testimony may be used to assist the fact finder in ascertaining whether the defendant had copied any part of the plaintiff's work. To this end, "the two works are to be compared in their entirety ... [and] in making such comparison resort may properly be made to expert analysis...."

However, once some amount of copying has been established, it remains solely for the trier of fact to determine whether the copying was "illicit," that is to say, whether the "defendant took from plaintiff's works so much of what is pleasing to [lay observers] who comprise the audience for whom such [works are] composed, that defendant wrongfully appropriated something which belongs to the plaintiff." Since the test for illicit copying is based upon the response of ordinary lay observers, expert testimony is thus "irrelevant" and not permitted. We have subsequently described this method of inquiry as "merely an alternative way of formulating the issue of substantial similarity."

Historically, *Arnstein*'s ordinary observer standard had its roots in "an attempt to apply the 'reasonable person' doctrine as found in other areas of the law to copyright." That approach may well have served its purpose when the material under scrutiny was limited to art forms readily comprehensible and generally familiar to the average lay person. However, in considering the extension of the rule to the present case, we are reminded of Holmes' admonition that, "[t]he life of the law has not been logic: it has been experience."

Thus, in deciding the limits to which expert opinion may be employed in ascertaining the substantial similarity of computer programs, we cannot disregard the highly complicated and technical subject matter at the heart of these claims. Rather, we recognize the reality that computer programs are likely to be somewhat impenetrable by lay observers – whether they be judges or juries – and, thus, seem to fall outside the category of works contemplated by those who engineered the *Arnstein* test. As Judge Pratt correctly observed:

> "In the context of computer programs, many of the familiar tests of similarity prove to be inadequate, for they were developed historically in the context of artistic and literary, rather than utilitarian, works."

In making its finding on substantial similarity with respect to computer programs, we believe that the trier of fact need not be limited by the strictures of its own lay perspective. Rather, we leave it to the discretion of the district court to decide to what extent, if any, expert opinion, regarding the highly technical nature of computer programs, is warranted in a given case.

In so holding, we do not intend to disturb the traditional role of lay observers in judging substantial similarity in copyright cases that involve the aesthetic arts, such as music, visual works or literature.

In this case, Dr. Davis' opinion was instrumental in dismantling the intricacies of computer science so that the court could formulate and apply an appropriate rule of law. While Dr. Davis' report and testimony undoubtedly shed valuable light on the subject matter of the litigation,

Judge Pratt remained, in the final analysis, the trier of fact. The district court's use of the expert's assistance, in the context of this case, was entirely appropriate.

2) Evidentiary Analysis

The district court had to determine whether Altai's OSCAR 3.5 program was substantially similar to CA's ADAPTER. We note that Judge Pratt's method of analysis effectively served as a road map for our own, with one exception – Judge Pratt filtered out the non-copyrightable aspects of OSCAR 3.5 rather than those found in ADAPTER, the allegedly infringed program. We think that our approach – i.e., filtering out the unprotected aspects of an allegedly infringed program and then comparing the end product to the structure of the suspect program – is preferable, and therefore believe that district courts should proceed in this manner in future cases.

We opt for this strategy because, in some cases, the defendant's program structure might contain protectable expression and/or other elements that are not found in the plaintiff's program. Since it is extraneous to the allegedly copied work, this material would have no bearing on any potential substantial similarity between the two programs. Thus, its filtration would be wasteful and unnecessarily time consuming. Furthermore, by focusing the analysis on the infringing rather than on the infringed material, a court may mistakenly place too little emphasis on a quantitatively small misappropriation which is, in reality, a qualitatively vital aspect of the plaintiff's protectable expression.

The fact that the district court's analysis proceeded in the reverse order, however, had no material impact on the outcome of this case. Since Judge Pratt determined that OSCAR effectively contained no protectable expression whatsoever, the most serious charge that can be levelled against him is that he was overly thorough in his examination.

The district court took the first step in the analysis set forth in this opinion when it separated the program by levels of abstraction. The district court stated:

> "As applied to computer software programs, this abstractions test would progress in order of "increasing generality" from object code, to source code, to parameter lists, to services required, to general outline. In discussing the particular similarities, therefore, we shall focus on these levels."

While the facts of a different case might require that a district court draw a more particularized blueprint of a program's overall structure, this description is a workable one for the case at hand.

Moving to the district court's evaluation of OSCAR 3.5's structural components, we agree with Judge Pratt's systematic exclusion of non-protectable expression. With respect to code, the district court observed that after the rewrite of OSCAR 3.4 to OSCAR 3.5, "there remained virtually no lines of code that were identical to ADAPTER." Accordingly, the court found that the code "present[ed] no similarity at all."

Next, Judge Pratt addressed the issue of similarity between the two programs' parameter lists and macros. He concluded that, viewing the conflicting evidence most favorably to CA, it demonstrated that "only a few of the lists and macros were similar to protected elements in ADAPTER; the others were either in the public domain or dictated by the functional demands of the program." As discussed above, functional elements and elements taken from the public domain do not qualify for copyright protection. With respect to the few remaining parameter lists and macros, the district court could reasonably conclude that they did not warrant a finding of infringement given their relative contribution to the overall program. In any event, the district court reasonably found that, for lack of persuasive evidence, CA failed to meet its burden of proof on whether the macros and parameter lists at issue were substantially similar.

The district court also found that the overlap exhibited between the list of services required for both ADAPTER and OSCAR 3.5 was "determined by the demands of the operating system and of the applications program to which it [was] to be linked through ADAPTER or OSCAR...". In other words, this aspect of the program's structure was dictated by the nature of other programs with which it was designed to interact and, thus, is not protected by copyright.

Finally, in his infringement analysis, Judge Pratt accorded no weight to the similarities between the two programs' organizational charts, "because [the charts were] so simple and obvious to anyone exposed to the operation of the program[s]." CA argues that the district court's action in this regard "is not consistent with copyright law" – that "obvious" expression is protected, and that the district court erroneously failed to realize this. However, to say that elements of a work are "obvious," in the manner in which the district court used the word, is to say that they "follow naturally from the work's theme rather than from the author's creativity." This is but one formulation of the *scenes a faire* doctrine, which we have already endorsed as a means of weeding out unprotectable expression.

CA argues, at some length, that many of the district court's factual conclusions regarding the creative nature of its program's components are simply wrong. Of course, we are limited in our review of factual findings to setting aside only those that we determine are clearly erroneous. Upon a thorough review of the voluminous record in this case, which is comprised of conflicting testimony and other highly technical evidence, we discern no error on the part of Judge Pratt, let alone clear error.

Since we accept Judge Pratt's factual conclusions and the results of his legal analysis, we affirm his denial of CA's copyright infringement claim based upon OSCAR 3.5. We emphasize that, like all copyright infringement cases, those that involve computer programs are highly fact specific. The amount of protection due structural elements, in any given case, will vary according to the protectable expression found to exist within the program at issue. (...)

Accordingly, **WE AFFIRM THE JUDGMENT OF THE DISTRICT COURT IN PART; VACATE IN PART; AND REMAND FOR FURTHER PROCEEDINGS.** (...)

THINK IT OVER!

Prior to this ruling, US federal courts have settled that copyright law can protect computer programs. As seen above, *Apple Computer v. Franklin Computer* concluded that literal elements of program code are eligible for federal copyright protection in the USA. *Computer Associates v. Altai* focused on whether and to what extent the US Copyright Act covers non-literal elements of program code, e.g. the structure, sequence and organization of the program. The Second Circuit's "*abstraction-filtration-comparison test*" is some kind of (digital) reinvention of copyright principles of merger, scenes a faire, and the public domain in a software law environment. The court first determined what formed a constituent (material) part of the allegedly infringed program. Second, the court filtered out any non-protected elements, e.g. elements with a limited number of ways it can be expressed and thus incidental to the idea (mirroring the idea of merger), standard techniques (representing scenes a faire), and design elements that belong to the public domain. The abstraction-filtration-comparison test has been followed by the US courts in the vast majority of post-Altai cases focusing on the protection of non-literal elements. Such non-literal elements include a software's programming language, functional user interface, or its clever algorithm. (Compare to the ruling in *Google v. Oracle* on the protectability of application programming interface at page 86.)

Further Case Law

Apple Computer, Inc. v. Formula International, Inc., 562 *F. Supp.* 775 (1983)

Apple Computer, Inc. v. Franklin Computer Corporation, 714 *F.2d* 1240 (1983)

Whelan Associates, Inc. v. Jaslow Dental Laboratry, Inc., 797 *F.2d* 1222 (1986)

Manufacturers Technologies, Inc. v. Cams, Inc., 706 *F.Supp.* 984 (1989)

Lotus Dev. Corp. v. Paperback Software International, 740 *F.Supp.* 37 (1990)

Lexmark International, Inc. v. Static Control Components, Inc., 387 *F.3d* 522 (2004)

Oracle America, Inc. v. Google Inc., 750 *F.3d* 1339 (2014)

Recommended readings

In English

National Commission on New Technological Uses of Copyrighted Works (CONTU), Final Report on the National Commission on New Technological Uses of Copyrighted Works. In: *Computer Law Journal*, 1981, p. 53-104. [CONTU Report]

Mark T. Kretschmer: Copyright Protection For Software Architecture: Just Say No!, *Columbia Business Law Review*, 1988, p. 823-853.

Peter G. Spivack: Does Form Follow Function? The Idea/Expression Dichotomy in Copyright Protection of Computer Software, *U.C.L.A. Law Review*, 1988, p. 723-778.

Peter S. Menell: An Analysis of the Scope of Copyright Protection for Application Programs, *Stanford Law Review*, 1989, p. 1045-1104.

Steven R. Englund: Idea, Process, or Protected Expression?: Determining the Scope of Copyright Protection of the Structure of Computer Programs, *Michigan Law Review*, 1990, p. 866-909.

Dennis Karjala: Recent United States and International Developments in Software Protection: Part I, *European Intellectual Property Review*, Issue 1/1994, p. 13-20.

Dennis Karjala: Recent United States and International Developments in Software Protection: Part II, *European Intellectual Property Review*, Issue 2/1994, p. 58-66.

Pamela Samuelson: Why Copyright Law Excludes Systems and Processes from the Scope of Its Protection, *Texas Law Review*, 2007, p. 1921-1977.

ORACLE AMERICA, INC. V. GOOGLE INC.

750 *F.3d* 1339 (2014)

Opinion
O'MALLEY, Circuit Judge.

(…) BACKGROUND

A. The Technology

Sun Microsystems, Inc. ("Sun") developed the Java "platform" for computer programming and released it in 1996. The aim was to relieve programmers from the burden of writing different versions of their computer programs for different operating systems or devices. "The Java platform, through the use of a virtual machine, enable[d] software developers to write programs that [we]re able to run on different types of computer hardware without having to rewrite them for each different type." With Java, a software programmer could "write once, run anywhere."

The Java virtual machine ("JVM") plays a central role in the overall Java platform. The Java programming language itself – which includes words, symbols, and other units, together with syntax rules for using them to create instructions – is the language in which a Java programmer writes source code, the version of a program that is "in a human-readable language." For the instructions to be executed, they must be converted (or compiled) into binary machine code (object code) consisting of 0s and 1s understandable by the particular computing device. In the Java system, "source code is first converted into 'bytecode,' an intermediate form, before it is then converted into binary machine code by the Java virtual machine" that has been designed for that device. The Java platform includes the "Java development kit (JDK), javac compiler, tools and utilities, runtime programs, class libraries (API packages), and the Java virtual machine."

Sun wrote a number of ready-to-use Java programs to perform common computer functions and organized those programs into groups it called "packages." These packages, which are the application programming interfaces at issue in this appeal, allow programmers to use the pre-written code to build certain functions into their own programs, rather than write their own code to perform those functions from scratch. They are shortcuts. Sun called the code for a specific operation (function) a "method." It defined "classes" so that each class consists of specified methods plus variables and other elements on which the methods operate. To organize the classes for users, then, it grouped classes (along with certain related "interfaces") into "packages." The parties have not disputed the district court's analogy: Oracle's collection of API packages is like a library, each package is like a bookshelf in the library, each class is like a book on the shelf, and each method is like a how-to chapter in a book.

The original Java Standard Edition Platform ("Java SE") included "eight packages of pre-written programs." The district court found, and Oracle concedes to some extent, that three of those packages – java.lang, java.io, and java.util – were "core" packages, meaning that programmers using the Java language had to use them "in order to make any worthwhile use of the language." By 2008, the Java platform had more than 6,000 methods making up more than 600 classes grouped into 166 API packages. There are 37 Java API packages at issue in this appeal, three of which are the core packages identified by the district court. These packages contain thousands of individual elements, including classes, subclasses, methods, and interfaces.

Every package consists of two types of source code – what the parties call (1) declaring code; and (2) implementing code. Declaring code is the expression that identifies the prewritten function and is sometimes referred to as the "declaration" or "header." As the district court explained, the "main point is that this header line of code introduces the method body and specifies very precisely the inputs, name and other functionality." The expressions used by the programmer from the declaring code command the computer to execute the associated implementing code, which gives the computer the step-by-step instructions for carrying out the declared function.

To use the district court's example, one of the Java API packages at issue is "java.lang." Within that package is a class called "math," and within "math" there are several methods, including one that is designed to find the larger of two numbers: "max." The declaration for the "max" method, as defined for integers, is: "public static int max(int x, int y)," where the word "public" means that the method is generally accessible, "static" means that no specific instance of the class is needed to call the method, the first "int" indicates that the method returns an integer, and "int x" and "int y" are the two numbers (inputs) being compared. A programmer calls the "max" method by typing the name of the method stated in the declaring code and providing unique inputs for the variables "x" and "y." The expressions used command the computer to execute the implementing code that carries out the operation of returning the larger number.

Although Oracle owns the copyright on Java SE and the API packages, it offers three different licenses to those who want to make use of them. The first is the General Public License, which is free of charge and provides that the licensee can use the packages – both the declaring and implementing code – but must "contribute back" its innovations to the public. This arrangement is referred to as an "open source" license. The second option is the Specification License, which provides that the licensee can use the declaring code and organization of Oracle's API packages but must write its own implementing code. The third option is the Commercial License, which is for businesses that "want to use and customize the full Java code in their commercial products and keep their code secret." Oracle offers the Commercial License in exchange for royalties. To maintain Java's "write once, run anywhere" motto, the Specification and Commercial Licenses require that the licensees' programs pass certain tests to ensure compatibility with the Java platform.

The testimony at trial also revealed that Sun was licensing a derivative version of the Java platform for use on mobile devices: the Java Micro Edition ("Java ME"). Oracle licensed Java ME for use on feature phones and smartphones. Sun/Oracle has never successfully developed its own smartphone platform using Java.

B. Google's Accused Product: Android

The accused product is Android, a software platform that was designed for mobile devices and competes with Java in that market. Google acquired Android, Inc. in 2005 as part of a plan to develop a smartphone platform. Later that same year, Google and Sun began discussing the possibility of Google "taking a license to use and to adapt the entire Java platform for mobile devices." They also discussed a "possible co-development partnership deal with Sun under which Java technology would become an open-source part of the Android platform, adapted for mobile devices." The parties negotiated for months but were unable to reach an agreement. The point of contention between the parties was Google's refusal to make the implementation of its programs compatible with the Java virtual machine or interoperable with other Java programs.

Because Sun/Oracle found that position to be anathema to the "write once, run anywhere" philosophy, it did not grant Google a license to use the Java API packages.

When the parties' negotiations reached an impasse, Google decided to use the Java programming language to design its own virtual machine – the Dalvik virtual machine ("Dalvik VM") – and "to write its own implementations for the functions in the Java API that were key to mobile devices." Google developed the Android platform, which grew to include 168 API packages – 37 of which correspond to the Java API packages at issue in this appeal.

With respect to the 37 packages at issue, "Google believed Java application programmers would want to find the same 37 sets of functionalities in the new Android system callable by the same names as used in Java." To achieve this result, Google copied the declaring source code from the 37 Java API packages verbatim, inserting that code into parts of its Android software. In doing so, Google copied the elaborately organized taxonomy of all the names of methods, classes, interfaces, and packages – the "overall system of organized names – covering 37 packages, with over six hundred classes, with over six thousand methods." The parties and district court referred to this taxonomy of expressions as the "structure, sequence, and organization" or "SSO" of the 37 packages. It is undisputed, however, that Google wrote its own implementing code, except with respect to: (1) the rangeCheck function, which consisted of nine lines of code; and (2) eight decompiled security files.

As to rangeCheck, the court found that the Sun engineer who wrote it later worked for Google and contributed two files he created containing the rangeCheck function – "Timsort.java" and "ComparableTimsort" – to the Android platform. In doing so, the nine-line rangeCheck function was copied directly into Android. As to the eight decompiled files, the district court found that they were copied and used as test files but "never found their way into Android or any handset."

Google released the Android platform in 2007, and the first Android phones went on sale the following year. Although it is undisputed that certain Android software contains copies of the 37 API packages' declaring code at issue, neither the district court nor the parties specify in which programs those copies appear. Oracle indicated at oral argument, however, that all Android phones contain copies of the accused portions of the Android software. Android smartphones "rapidly grew in popularity and now comprise a large share of the United States market." Google provides the Android platform free of charge to smartphone manufacturers and receives revenue when customers use particular functions on the Android phone. Although Android uses the Java programming language, it is undisputed that Android is not generally Java compatible. As Oracle explains, "Google ultimately designed Android to be *incompatible* with the Java platform, so that apps written for one will not work on the other." (...)

DISCUSSION

I. ORACLE'S APPEAL (...)

A. Copyrightability

The Copyright Act provides protection to "original works of authorship fixed in any tangible medium of expression," including "literary works." It is undisputed that computer programs – defined in the Copyright Act as "a set of statements or instructions to be used directly or indirectly in a computer in order to bring about a certain result," – can be subject to copyright protection as "literary works." Indeed, the legislative history explains that "literary works" includes "computer programs to the extent that they incorporate authorship in the programmer's expression of original ideas, as distinguished from the ideas themselves."

By statute, a work must be "original" to qualify for copyright protection. This "originality requirement is not particularly stringent," however. "Original, as the term is used in copyright, means only that the work was independently created by the author (as opposed to copied from other works), and that it possesses at least some minimal degree of creativity."

Copyright protection extends only to the expression of an idea – not to the underlying idea itself. This distinction – commonly referred to as the "idea/expression dichotomy" – is codified in Section 102(b) of the Copyright Act, which provides:

> "In no case does copyright protection for an original work of authorship extend to any idea, procedure, process, system, method of operation, concept, principle, or discovery, regardless of the form in which it is described, explained, illustrated, or embodied in such work."

The idea/expression dichotomy traces back to the Supreme Court's decision in Baker v. Selden, 101 U.S. 99 (1879). In *Baker,* the plaintiff Selden wrote and obtained copyrights on a series of books setting out a new system of bookkeeping. The books included an introductory essay explaining the system and blank forms with ruled lines and headings designed for use with that system. Baker published account books employing a system with similar forms, and Selden filed suit alleging copyright infringement. According to Selden, the "ruled lines and headings, given to illustrate the system, are a part of the book" and "no one can make or use similar ruled lines and headings, or ruled lines and headings made and arranged on substantially the same system, without violating the copyright."

The Supreme Court framed the issue on appeal in *Baker* as "whether the exclusive property in a system of book-keeping can be claimed, under the law of copyright, by means of a book in which that system is explained." In reversing the circuit court's decision, the Court concluded that the "copyright of a book on book-keeping cannot secure the exclusive right to make, sell, and use account-books prepared upon the plan set forth in such book." Likewise, the "copyright of a work on mathematical science cannot give to the author an exclusive right to the methods of operation which he propounds." The Court found that, although the copyright protects the way Selden "explained and described a peculiar system of book-keeping," it does not prevent others from using the system described therein. The Court further indicated that, if it is necessary to use the forms Selden included in his books to make use of the accounting system, that use would not amount to copyright infringement.

Courts routinely cite *Baker* as the source of several principles incorporated into Section 102(b) that relate to this appeal, including that: (1) copyright protection extends only to expression, not to ideas, systems, or processes; and (2) "those elements of a computer program that are necessarily incidental to its function are ... unprotectable."

It is well established that copyright protection can extend to both literal and non-literal elements of a computer program. The literal elements of a computer program are the source code and object code. Courts have defined source code as "the spelled-out program commands that humans can read." Object code refers to "the binary language comprised of zeros and ones through which the computer directly receives its instructions." Both source and object code "are consistently held protected by a copyright on the program." Google nowhere disputes that premise.

The non-literal components of a computer program include, among other things, the program's sequence, structure, and organization, as well as the program's user interface. As discussed below, whether the non-literal elements of a program "are protected depends on whether, on the particular facts of each case, the component in question qualifies as an expression of an idea, or an idea itself."

In this case, Oracle claims copyright protection with respect to both: (1) literal elements of its API packages – the 7,000 lines of declaring source code; and (2) non-literal elements – the structure, sequence, and organization of each of the 37 Java API packages.

The distinction between literal and non-literal aspects of a computer program is separate from the distinction between literal and non-literal copying. "Literal" copying is verbatim copying of original expression. "Non-literal" copying is "paraphrased or loosely paraphrased rather than word for word." Here, Google concedes that it copied the declaring code verbatim. Oracle explains that the lines of declaring code "embody the structure of each [API] package, just as the chapter titles and topic sentences represent the structure of a novel." As Oracle explains, when Google copied the declaring code in these packages "it also copied the 'sequence and organization' of the packages (i.e., the three-dimensional structure with all the chutes and ladders)" employed by Sun/Oracle in the packages. Oracle also argues that the nonliteral elements of the API packages – the structure, sequence, and organization that led naturally to the implementing code Google created – are entitled to protection. Oracle does not assert "literal" copying of the entire SSO, but, rather, that Google literally copied the declaring code and then paraphrased the remainder of the SSO by writing its own implementing code. It therefore asserts non-literal copying with respect to the entirety of the SSO.

At this stage, it is undisputed that the declaring code and the structure and organization of the Java API packages are original. The testimony at trial revealed that designing the Java API packages was a creative process and that the Sun/Oracle developers had a vast range of options for the structure and organization. In its copyrightability decision, the district court specifically found that the API packages are both creative and original, and Google concedes on appeal that the originality requirements are met. The court found, however, that neither the declaring code nor the SSO was entitled to copyright protection under the Copyright Act.

Although the parties agree that Oracle's API packages meet the originality requirement under Section 102(a), they disagree as to the proper interpretation and application of Section 102(b). For its part, Google suggests that there is a two-step copyrightability analysis, wherein Section 102(a) grants copyright protection to original works, while Section 102(b) takes it away if the work has a functional component. To the contrary, however, Congress emphasized that Section 102(b) "in no way enlarges or contracts the scope of copyright protection" and that its "purpose is to restate ... that the basic dichotomy between expression and idea remains unchanged." "Section 102(b) does not extinguish the protection accorded a particular expression of an idea merely because that expression is embodied in a method of operation." Section 102(a) and 102(b) are to be considered collectively so that certain expressions are subject to greater scrutiny. In assessing copyrightability, the district court is required to ferret out apparent expressive aspects of a work and then separate protectable expression from "unprotectable ideas, facts, processes, and methods of operation."

Of course, as with many things, in defining this task, the devil is in the details. Circuit courts have struggled with, and disagree over, the tests to be employed when attempting to draw the line between what is protectable expression and what is not. When assessing whether the non-literal elements of a computer program constitute protectable expression, the Ninth Circuit has endorsed an "abstraction-filtration-comparison" test formulated by the Second Circuit and expressly adopted by several other circuits. This test rejects the notion that anything that performs a function is necessarily uncopyrightable. And it also rejects as flawed the *Whelan* assumption that, once any separable idea can be identified in a computer program everything else must be protectable expression, on grounds that more than one idea may be embodied in any particular program.

Thus, this test eschews bright line approaches and requires a more nuanced assessment of the particular program at issue in order to determine what expression is protectable and infringed. As the Second Circuit explains, this test has three steps. In the abstraction step, the court "first break[s] down the allegedly infringed program into its constituent structural parts." In the filtration step, the court "sift[s] out all non-protectable material," including ideas and "expression that is necessarily incidental to those ideas." In the final step, the court compares the remaining creative expression with the allegedly infringing program.

In the second step, the court is first to assess whether the expression is original to the programmer or author. The court must then determine whether the particular inclusion of any level of abstraction is dictated by considerations of efficiency, required by factors already external to the program itself, or taken from the public domain – all of which would render the expression unprotectable. These conclusions are to be informed by traditional copyright principles of originality, merger, and scenes a faire.

In all circuits, it is clear that the first step is part of the copyrightability analysis and that the third is an infringement question. It is at the second step of this analysis where the circuits are in less accord. Some treat all aspects of this second step as part of the copyrightability analysis, while others divide questions of originality from the other inquiries, treating the former as a question of copyrightability and the latter as part of the infringement inquiry. We need not assess the wisdom of these respective views because there is no doubt on which side of this circuit split the Ninth Circuit falls.

In the Ninth Circuit, while questions regarding originality are considered questions of copyrightability, concepts of merger and scenes a faire are affirmative defenses to claims of infringement. The Ninth Circuit has acknowledged that "there is some disagreement among courts as to whether these two doctrines figure into the issue of copyrightability or are more properly defenses to infringement." It, nonetheless, has made clear that, in that circuit, these concepts are to be treated as defenses to infringement.

With these principles in mind, we turn to the trial court's analysis and judgment and to Oracle's objections thereto. While the trial court mentioned the abstraction-filtration-comparison test when describing the development of relevant law, it did not purport to actually apply that test. Instead, it moved directly to application of familiar principles of copyright law when assessing the copyrightability of the declaring code and interpreted Section 102(b) to preclude copyrightability for any functional element "essential for interoperability" "regardless of its form."

Oracle asserts that all of the trial court's conclusions regarding copyrightability are erroneous. Oracle argues that its Java API packages are entitled to protection under the Copyright Act because they are expressive and could have been written and organized in any number of ways to achieve the same functions. Specifically, Oracle argues that the district court erred when it: (1) concluded that each line of declaring code is uncopyrightable because the idea and expression have merged; (2) found the declaring code uncopyrightable because it employs short phrases; (3) found all aspects of the SSO devoid of protection as a "method of operation" under 17 U.S.C. § 102(b); and (4) invoked Google's "interoperability" concerns in the copyrightability analysis. For the reasons explained below, we agree with Oracle on each point.

1. Declaring Source Code

First, Oracle argues that the district court erred in concluding that each line of declaring source code is completely unprotected under the merger and short phrases doctrines. Google responds that Oracle waived its right to assert copyrightability based on the 7,000 lines of declaring code by failing "to object to instructions and a verdict form that effectively eliminated that theory from the case." Even if not waived, moreover, Google argues that, because there is only one way to write the names and declarations, the merger doctrine bars copyright protection.

We find that Oracle did not waive arguments based on Google's literal copying of the declaring code. Prior to trial, both parties informed the court that Oracle's copyright infringement claims included the declarations of the API elements in the Android class library source code.

While Google is correct that the jury instructions and verdict form focused on the structure and organization of the packages, we agree with Oracle that there was no need for the jury to address copying of the declaring code because Google conceded that it copied it verbatim. Indeed, the district court specifically instructed the jury that "Google agrees that it uses the same names and declarations" in Android.

That the district court addressed the declaring code in its post-jury verdict copyrightability decision further confirms that the verbatim copying of declaring code remained in the case. The court explained that the "identical lines" that Google copied into Android "are those lines that specify the names, parameters and functionality of the methods and classes, lines called 'declarations' or 'headers.'" The court specifically found that the declaring code was not entitled to copyright protection under the merger and short phrases doctrines. We address each in turn.

a. Merger

The merger doctrine functions as an exception to the idea/expression dichotomy. It provides that, when there are a limited number of ways to express an idea, the idea is said to "merge" with its expression, and the expression becomes unprotected. As noted, the Ninth Circuit treats this concept as an affirmative defense to infringement. Accordingly, it appears that the district court's merger analysis is irrelevant to the question of whether Oracle's API packages are copyrightable in the first instance. Regardless of when the analysis occurs, we conclude that merger does not apply on the record before us.

Under the merger doctrine, a court will not protect a copyrighted work from infringement if the idea contained therein can be expressed in only one way. For computer programs, "this means that when specific [parts of the code], even though previously copyrighted, are the only and essential means of accomplishing a given task, their later use by another will not amount to infringement." We have recognized, however, applying Ninth Circuit law, that the "unique arrangement of computer program expression ... does not merge with the process so long as alternate expressions are available."

In *Atari,* for example, Nintendo designed a program – the 10NES – to prevent its video game system from accepting unauthorized game cartridges. Nintendo "chose arbitrary programming instructions and arranged them in a unique sequence to create a purely arbitrary data stream" which "serves as the key to unlock the NES." Because Nintendo produced expert testimony "showing a multitude of different ways to generate a data stream which unlocks the NES console," we concluded that Nintendo's specific choice of code did not merge with the process.

Here, the district court found that, "no matter how creative or imaginative a Java method specification may be, the entire world is entitled to use the same method specification (inputs, outputs, parameters) so long as the line-by-line implementations are different." In its analysis, the court identified the method declaration as the idea and found that the implementation is the expression. The court explained that, under the rules of Java, a programmer must use the identical "declaration or method header lines" to "declare a method specifying the *same* functionality." Because the district court found that there was only one way to write the declaring code for each of the Java packages, it concluded that "the merger doctrine bars anyone from claiming exclusive copyright ownership" of it. Accordingly, the court held there could be "no copyright violation in using the identical declarations."

Google agrees with the district court that the implementing code is the expression entitled to protection – not the declaring code. Indeed, at oral argument, counsel for Google explained that, "it is not our position that none of Java is copyrightable. Obviously, Google spent two and a half years ... to write from scratch all of the implementing code." Because it is undisputed that Google wrote its own implementing code, the copyrightability of the precise language of that code is not at issue on appeal. Instead, our focus is on the declaring code and structure of the API packages.

On appeal, Oracle argues that the district court: (1) misapplied the merger doctrine; and (2) failed to focus its analysis on the options available to the original author. We agree with Oracle on both points. First, we agree that merger cannot bar copyright protection for any lines of declaring source code unless Sun/Oracle had only one way, or a limited number of ways, to write them. The evidence showed that Oracle had "unlimited options as to the selection and arrangement of the 7000 lines Google copied." Using the district court's "java.lang.Math.max" example, Oracle explains that the developers could have called it any number of things, including "Math. maximum" or "Arith.larger." This was not a situation where Oracle was selecting among preordained names and phrases to create its packages. As the district court recognized, moreover, "the Android method and class names could have been different from the names of their counterparts in Java and still have worked."

We further find that the district court erred in focusing its merger analysis on the options available to Google at the time of copying. It is well-established that copyrightability and the scope of protectable activity are to be evaluated at the time of creation, not at the time of infringement. The focus is, therefore, on the options that were available to Sun/Oracle at the time it created the API packages. Of course, once Sun/Oracle created "java.lang.Math.max," programmers who want to use that particular package have to call it by that name. But, as the court acknowledged, nothing prevented Google from writing its own declaring code, along with its own implementing code, to achieve the same result. In such circumstances, the chosen expression simply does not merge with the idea being expressed.

It seems possible that the merger doctrine, when properly analyzed, would exclude the three packages identified by the district court as core packages from the scope of actionable infringing conduct. This would be so if the Java authors, at the time these packages were created, had only a limited number of ways to express the methods and classes therein if they wanted to write in the Java language. In that instance, the idea may well be merged with the expression in these three packages. Google did not present its merger argument in this way below and does not do so here, however. Indeed, Google does not try to differentiate among the packages for purposes of its copyrightability analysis and does not appeal the infringement verdict as to the packages. For these reasons, we reject the trial court's merger analysis.

b. Short Phrases

The district court also found that Oracle's declaring code consists of uncopyrightable short phrases. Specifically, the court concluded that, "while the Android method and class names could have been different from the names of their counterparts in Java and still have worked, copyright protection never extends to names or short phrases as a matter of law."

The district court is correct that "[w]ords and short phrases such as names, titles, and slogans" are not subject to copyright protection. The court failed to recognize, however, that the relevant question for copyrightability purposes is not whether the work at issue contains short phrases – as literary works often do – but, rather, whether those phrases are creative. And, by dissecting the individual lines of declaring code at issue into short phrases, the district court further failed to recognize that an original combination of elements can be copyrightable.

By analogy, the opening of Charles Dickens' *A Tale of Two Cities* is nothing but a string of short phrases. Yet no one could contend that this portion of Dickens' work is unworthy of copyright protection because it can be broken into those shorter constituent components. The question is not whether a short phrase or series of short phrases can be extracted from the work, but whether the manner in which they are used or strung together exhibits creativity.

Although the district court apparently focused on individual lines of code, Oracle is not seeking copyright protection for a specific short phrase or word. Instead, the portion of declaring code at issue is 7,000 lines, and Google's own "Java guru" conceded that there can be "creativity and artistry even in a single method declaration." Because Oracle "exercised creativity in the selection and arrangement" of the method declarations when it created the API packages and wrote the relevant declaring code, they contain protectable expression that is entitled to copyright protection. Accordingly, we conclude that the district court erred in applying the short phrases doctrine to find the declaring code not copyrightable.

c. Scenes a Faire

The scenes a faire doctrine, which is related to the merger doctrine, operates to bar certain otherwise creative expression from copyright protection. It provides that "expressive elements of a work of authorship are not entitled to protection against infringement if they are standard, stock, or common to a topic, or if they necessarily follow from a common theme or setting." Under this doctrine, "when certain commonplace expressions are indispensable and naturally associated with the treatment of a given idea, those expressions are treated like ideas and therefore [are] not protected by copyright." In the computer context, "the scene a faire doctrine denies protection to program elements that are dictated by external factors such as 'the mechanical specifications of the computer on which a particular program is intended to run' or 'widely accepted programming practices within the computer industry.'"

The trial court rejected Google's reliance on the scenes a faire doctrine. It did so in a footnote, finding that Google had failed to present evidence to support the claim that either the grouping of methods within the classes or the code chosen for them "would be so expected and customary as to be permissible under the scenes a faire doctrine." Specifically, the trial court found that "it is impossible to say on this record that *all* of the classes and their contents are typical of such classes and, on this record, this order rejects Google's global argument based on *scenes a faire.*"

On appeal, Google refers to scenes a faire concepts briefly, as do some amici, apparently contending that, because programmers have become accustomed to and comfortable using the groupings in the Java API packages, those groupings are so commonplace as to be indispensable to the expression of an acceptable programming platform. As such, the argument goes, they are so associated with the "idea" of what the packages are accomplishing that they should be treated as ideas rather than expression.

Google cannot rely on the scenes a faire doctrine as an alternative ground upon which we might affirm the copyrightability judgment of the district court. This is so for several reasons. First, as noted, like merger, in the Ninth Circuit, the scenes a faire doctrine is a component of the infringement analysis. "[S]imilarity of expression, whether literal or non-literal, which necessarily results from the fact that the common idea is only capable of expression in more or less stereotyped form, will preclude a finding of actionable similarity." Thus, the expression is not excluded from copyright protection; it is just that certain copying is forgiven as a necessary incident of *any* expression of the underlying idea.

Second, Google has not objected to the trial court's conclusion that Google failed to make a sufficient factual record to support its contention that the groupings and code chosen for the 37 Java API packages were driven by external factors or premised on features that were either commonplace or essential to the idea being expressed. Google provides no record citations indicating that such a showing was made and does not contend that the trial court erred when it expressly found it was not. Indeed, Google does not even make this argument with respect to the core packages.

Finally, Google's reliance on the doctrine below and the amici reference to it here are premised on a fundamental misunderstanding of the doctrine. Like merger, the focus of the scenes a faire doctrine is on the circumstances presented to the creator, not the copier. The court's analytical focus must be upon the external factors that dictated Sun's selection of classes, methods, and code – not upon what Google encountered at the time it chose to copy those groupings and that code. "[T]he scenes a faire doctrine identifies and excludes from protection against infringement expression whose creation 'flowed naturally from considerations external to the author's creativity.'" It is this showing the trial court found Google failed to make, and Google cites to nothing in the record which indicates otherwise.

For these reasons, the trial court was correct to conclude that the scenes a faire doctrine does not affect the copyrightability of either the declaring code in, or the SSO of, the Java API packages at issue.

2. The Structure, Sequence, and Organization of the API Packages

The district court found that the SSO of the Java API packages is creative and original, but nevertheless held that it is a "system or method of operation ... and, therefore, cannot be copyrighted" under 17 U.S.C. § 102(b). In reaching this conclusion, the district court seems to have relied upon language contained in a First Circuit decision: Lotus Development Corp. v. Borland International, Inc.

In *Lotus,* it was undisputed that the defendant copied the menu command hierarchy and interface from Lotus 1–2–3, a computer spreadsheet program "that enables users to perform accounting functions electronically on a computer." The menu command hierarchy referred to a series of commands – such as "Copy," "Print," and "Quit" – which were arranged into more than 50 menus and submenus. Although the defendant did not copy any Lotus source code, it copied the menu command hierarchy into its rival program. The question before the court was "whether a computer menu command hierarchy is copyrightable subject matter."

Although it accepted the district court's finding that Lotus developers made some expressive choices in selecting and arranging the command terms, the First Circuit found that the command hierarchy was not copyrightable because, among other things, it was a "method of operation" under Section 102(b). In reaching this conclusion, the court defined a "method of operation" as "the means by which a person operates something, whether it be a car, a food processor, or a computer." Because the Lotus menu command hierarchy provided "the means by which users control and operate Lotus 1–2–3," it was deemed unprotectable. For example, if users wanted to copy material, they would use the "Copy" command and the command terms would tell the computer what to do. According to the *Lotus* court, the "fact that Lotus developers could have designed the Lotus menu command hierarchy differently is immaterial to the question of whether it is a 'method of operation.'" The court further indicated that, "[i]f specific words are essential to operating something, then they are part of a 'method of operation' and, as such, are unprotectable."

On appeal, Oracle argues that the district court's reliance on *Lotus* is misplaced because it is distinguishable on its facts and is inconsistent with Ninth Circuit law. We agree. First, while the defendant in *Lotus* did not copy any of the underlying code, Google concedes that it copied portions of Oracle's declaring source code verbatim. Second, the *Lotus* court found that the commands at issue there (copy, print, etc.) were not creative, but it is undisputed here that the declaring code and the structure and organization of the API packages are both creative and original. Finally, while the court in *Lotus* found the commands at issue were "essential to operating" the system, it is undisputed that – other than perhaps as to the three core packages – Google did not need to copy the structure, sequence, and organization of the Java API packages to write programs in the Java language.

More importantly, however, the Ninth Circuit has not adopted the court's "method of operation" reasoning in *Lotus,* and we conclude that it is inconsistent with binding precedent. Specifically, we find that *Lotus* is inconsistent with Ninth Circuit case law recognizing that the structure, sequence, and organization of a computer program is eligible for copyright protection where it qualifies as an expression of an idea, rather than the idea itself. And, while the court in *Lotus* held "that expression that is part of a 'method of operation' cannot be copyrighted," this court – applying Ninth Circuit law – reached the exact opposite conclusion, finding that copyright protects "the expression of [a] process or method".

We find, moreover, that the hard and fast rule set down in *Lotus* and employed by the district court here – i.e., that elements which perform a function can never be copyrightable – is at odds with the Ninth Circuit's endorsement of the abstraction-filtration-comparison analysis discussed earlier. As the Tenth Circuit concluded in expressly rejecting the *Lotus* "method of operation" analysis, in favor of the Second Circuit's abstraction-filtration-comparison test, "although an element of a work may be characterized as a method of operation, that element may nevertheless contain expression that is eligible for copyright protection." Specifically, the court found that Section 102(b) "does not extinguish the protection accorded a particular expression of an idea merely because that expression is embodied in a method of operation at a higher level of abstraction."

Other courts agree that components of a program that can be characterized as a "method of operation" may nevertheless be copyrightable. For example, the Third Circuit rejected a defendant's argument that operating system programs are "per se" uncopyrightable because an operating system is a "method of operation" for a computer. The court distinguished between the "method which instructs the computer to perform its operating functions" and "the instructions themselves," and found that the instructions were copyrightable. In its analysis, the court noted: "[t]hat the words of a program are used ultimately in the implementation of a process should in no way affect their copyrightability." The court focused "on whether the idea is capable of various modes of expression" and indicated that, "[i]f other programs can be written or created which perform the same function as [i]n Apple's operating system program, then that program is an expression of the idea and hence copyrightable." Notably, no other circuit has adopted the First Circuit's "method of operation" analysis.

Courts have likewise found that classifying a work as a "system" does not preclude copyright for the particular expression of that system.

Here, the district court recognized that the SSO "resembles a taxonomy," but found that "it is nevertheless a command structure, a system or method of operation – a long hierarchy of over six thousand commands to carry out pre-assigned functions." In other words, the court concluded that, although the SSO is expressive, it is not copyrightable because it is also functional. The problem with the district court's approach is that computer programs are by definition functional – they are all designed to accomplish some task. Indeed, the statutory definition of "computer program" acknowledges that they function "to bring about a certain result." If we were to accept the district court's suggestion that a computer program is uncopyrightable simply because it "carr[ies] out pre-assigned functions," no computer program is protectable. That result contradicts Congress's express intent to provide copyright protection to computer programs, as well as binding Ninth Circuit case law finding computer programs copyrightable, despite their utilitarian or functional purpose. Though the trial court did add the caveat that it "does not hold that the structure, sequence and organization of all computer programs may be stolen," it is hard to see how its method of operation analysis could lead to any other conclusion.

While it does not appear that the Ninth Circuit has addressed the precise issue, we conclude that a set of commands to instruct a computer to carry out desired operations may contain expression that is eligible for copyright protection. We agree with Oracle that, under Ninth Circuit law, an original work – even one that serves a function – is entitled to copyright protection as long as the author had multiple ways to express the underlying idea. Section 102(b) does not, as Google seems to suggest, automatically deny copyright protection to elements of a computer program that are functional. Instead, as noted, Section 102(b) codifies the idea/expression dichotomy and the legislative history confirms that, among other things, Section 102(b) was "intended to make clear that the expression adopted by the programmer is the copyrightable element in a computer program." Therefore, even if an element directs a computer to perform operations, the court must nevertheless determine whether it contains any separable expression entitled to protection.

On appeal, Oracle does not – and concedes that it cannot – claim copyright in the idea of organizing functions of a computer program or in the "package-class-method" organizational structure in the abstract. Instead, Oracle claims copyright protection only in its *particular* way of naming and organizing each of the 37 Java API packages. Oracle recognizes, for example, that it "cannot copyright the idea of programs that open an internet connection," but "it can copyright the precise strings of code used to do so, at least so long as 'other language is available' to achieve the same function." Thus, Oracle concedes that Google and others could employ the Java language – much like anyone could employ the English language to write a paragraph without violating the copyrights of other English language writers. And, that Google may employ the "package-class-method" structure much like authors can employ the same rules of grammar chosen by other authors without fear of infringement. What Oracle contends is that, beyond that point, Google, like any author, is not permitted to employ the precise phrasing or precise structure chosen by Oracle to flesh out the substance of its packages – the details and arrangement of the prose.

As the district court acknowledged, Google could have structured Android differently and could have chosen different ways to express and implement the functionality that it copied. Specifically, the court found that "the very same functionality could have been offered in Android without duplicating the exact command structure used in Java." The court further explained that Google could have offered the same functions in Android by "rearranging the various methods under different groupings among the various classes and packages." The evidence showed, moreover, that Google designed many of its own API packages from scratch, and, thus, could have designed its own corresponding 37 API packages if it wanted to do so.

Given the court's findings that the SSO is original and creative, and that the declaring code could have been written and organized in any number of ways and still have achieved the same functions, we conclude that Section 102(b) does not bar the packages from copyright protection just because they also perform functions.

3. Google's Interoperability Arguments are Irrelevant to Copyrightability

Oracle also argues that the district court erred in invoking interoperability in its copyrightability analysis. Specifically, Oracle argues that Google's interoperability arguments are only relevant, if at all, to fair use – not to the question of whether the API packages are copyrightable. We agree.

In characterizing the SSO of the Java API packages as a "method of operation," the district court explained that "[d]uplication of the command structure is necessary for interoperability." The court found that, "[i]n order for at least some of [the pre-Android Java] code to run on Android, Google was required to provide the same java.package.Class.method( ) command system using the same names with the same 'taxonomy' and with the same functional specifications." And, the court concluded that "Google replicated what was necessary to achieve a degree of interoperability – but no more, taking care, as said before, to provide its own implementations." In reaching this conclusion, the court relied primarily on two Ninth Circuit decisions: Sega Enterprises v. Accolade, Inc., and Sony Computer Entertainment, Inc. v. Connectix, Corp.

Both *Sega* and *Sony* are fair use cases in which copyrightability was addressed only tangentially. In *Sega,* for example, Sega manufactured a video game console and game cartridges that contained hidden functional program elements necessary to achieve compatibility with the console. Defendant Accolade: (1) reverse-engineered Sega's video game programs to discover the requirements for compatibility; and (2) created its own games for the Sega console. As part of the reverse-engineering process, Accolade made intermediate copies of object code from Sega's console. Although the court recognized that the intermediate copying of computer code may infringe Sega's copyright, it concluded that "disassembly of copyrighted object code is, as a matter of law, a fair use of the copyrighted work if such disassembly provides the only means of access to those elements of the code that are not protected by copyright and the copier has a legitimate reason for seeking such access." The court agreed with Accolade that its copying was necessary to examine the unprotected functional aspects of the program. And, because Accolade had a legitimate interest in making its cartridges compatible with Sega's console, the court found that Accolade's intermediate copying was fair use.

Likewise, in *Sony,* the Ninth Circuit found that the defendant's reverse engineering and intermediate copying of Sony's copyrighted software program "was a fair use for the purpose of gaining access to the unprotected elements of Sony's software." The court explained that Sony's software program contained unprotected functional elements and that the defendant could only access those elements through reverse engineering. The defendant used that information to create a software program that let consumers play games designed for Sony's PlayStation console on their computers. Notably, the defendant's software program did not contain any of Sony's copyrighted material.

The district court characterized Sony and Sega as "close analogies" to this case. According to the court, both decisions "held that interface procedures that were necessary to duplicate in order to achieve interoperability were functional aspects not copyrightable under Section 102(b). "The district court's reliance on *Sega* and *Sony* in the copyrightability context is misplaced, however.

As noted, both cases were focused on fair use, not copyrightability. In *Sega,* for example, the only question was whether Accolade's intermediate copying was fair use. The court never addressed the question of whether Sega's software code, which had functional elements, also contained separable creative expression entitled to protection. Likewise, although the court in *Sony* determined that Sony's computer program had functional elements, it never addressed whether it also had expressive elements. *Sega* and *Sony* are also factually distinguishable because the defendants in those cases made intermediate copies to understand the functional aspects of the copyrighted works and then created new products. This is not a case where Google reverse-engineered Oracle's Java packages to gain access to unprotected functional elements contained therein. As the former Register of Copyrights of the United States pointed out in his brief amicus curiae, "[h]ad Google reverse engineered the programming packages to figure out the ideas and functionality of the original, and then created its own structure and its own literal code, Oracle would have no remedy under copyright whatsoever." Instead, Google chose to copy both the declaring code and the overall SSO of the 37 Java API packages at issue.

We disagree with Google's suggestion that *Sony* and *Sega* created an "interoperability exception" to copyrightability. Although both cases recognized that the software programs at issue there contained unprotected functional elements, a determination that some elements are unprotected is not the same as saying that the entire work loses copyright protection. To accept Google's reading would contradict Ninth Circuit case law recognizing that both the literal and non-literal components of a software program are eligible for copyright protection. And it would ignore the fact that the Ninth Circuit endorsed the abstraction-filtration-comparison inquiry in *Sega* itself.

As previously discussed, a court must examine the software program to determine whether it contains creative expression that can be separated from the underlying function. In doing so, the court filters out the elements of the program that are "ideas" as well as elements that are "dictated by considerations of efficiency, so as to be necessarily incidental to that idea; required by factors external to the program itself."

To determine "whether certain aspects of an allegedly infringed software are not protected by copyright law, the focus is on external factors that influenced the choice of the creator of the infringed product." The Second Circuit, for example, has noted that programmers are often constrained in their design choices by "extrinsic considerations" including "the mechanical specifications of the computer on which a particular program is intended to run" and "compatibility requirements of other programs with which a program is designed to operate in conjunction." The Ninth Circuit has likewise recognized that: (1) computer programs "contain many logical, structural, and visual display elements that are dictated by ... external factors such as compatibility requirements and industry demands"; and (2) "[i]n some circumstances, even the exact set of commands used by the programmer is deemed functional rather than creative for purposes of copyright."

Because copyrightability is focused on the choices available to the plaintiff at the time the computer program was created, the relevant compatibility inquiry asks whether the plaintiff's choices were dictated by a need to ensure that its program worked with existing third-party programs. Whether a defendant later seeks to make its program interoperable with the plaintiff's program has no bearing on whether the software the plaintiff created had any design limitations dictated by external factors. Stated differently, the focus is on the compatibility needs and programming choices of the party claiming copyright protection – not the choices the defendant made to achieve compatibility with the plaintiff's program. Consistent with this approach, courts have recognized that, once the plaintiff creates a copyrightable work, a defendant's desire "to achieve total compatibility ... is a commercial and competitive objective which does not enter into the ... issue of whether particular ideas and expressions have merged."

Given this precedent, we conclude that the district court erred in focusing its interoperability analysis on Google's desires for its Android software. Whether Google's software is "interoperable" in some sense with any aspect of the Java platform (although as Google concedes, certainly not with the JVM) has no bearing on the threshold question of whether Oracle's software is copyrightable. It is the interoperability and other needs of Oracle – not those of Google – that apply in the copyrightability context, and there is no evidence that when Oracle created the Java API packages at issue it did so to meet compatibility requirements of other pre-existing programs.

Google maintains on appeal that its use of the "Java class and method names and declarations was 'the only and essential means' of achieving a degree of interoperability with existing programs written in the [Java language]." Indeed, given the record evidence that Google designed Android so that it would *not* be compatible with the Java platform, or the JVM specifically, we find Google's interoperability argument confusing. While Google repeatedly cites to the district court's finding that Google had to copy the packages so that an app written in Java could run on Android, it cites to no evidence in the record that any such app exists and points to no Java apps that either pre-dated or post-dated Android that could run on the Android platform. The compatibility Google sought to foster was not with Oracle's Java platform or with the JVM central to that platform. Instead, Google wanted to capitalize on the fact that software developers were already trained and experienced in using the Java API packages at issue. The district court agreed, finding that, as to the 37 Java API packages, "Google believed Java application programmers would want to find the same 37 sets of functionalities in the new Android system callable by the same names as used in Java." Google's interest was in accelerating its development process by "leverag[ing] Java for its existing base of developers." Although this competitive objective might be relevant to the fair use inquiry, we conclude that it is irrelevant to the copyrightability of Oracle's declaring code and organization of the API packages.

Finally, to the extent Google suggests that it was entitled to copy the Java API packages because they had become the effective industry standard, we are unpersuaded. Google cites no authority for its suggestion that copyrighted works lose protection when they become popular, and we have found none. In fact, the Ninth Circuit has rejected the argument that a work that later becomes the industry standard is uncopyrightable. Google was free to develop its own API packages and to "lobby" programmers to adopt them. Instead, it chose to copy Oracle's declaring code and the SSO to capitalize on the preexisting community of programmers who were accustomed to using the Java API packages. That desire has nothing to do with copyrightability. For these reasons, we find that Google's industry standard argument has no bearing on the copyrightability of Oracle's work.

(...) CONCLUSION

For the foregoing reasons, we conclude that the declaring code and the structure, sequence, and organization of the 37 Java API packages at issue are entitled to copyright protection. We therefore reverse the district court's copyrightability determination with instructions to reinstate the jury's infringement verdict. (...)

AFFIRMED-IN-PART, REVERSED-IN-PART, AND REMANDED.

THINK IT OVER!

1. The protection of non-literal elements of computer programs has been in the focus of US case law for decades. A (final) ruling favouring Oracle can not only adversely effect the future of programming, but it might lead to never-ending tensions regarding past developments, especially since the functionality of APIs are significantly used by third parties (ranging from platforms to non-profit libraries) to provide for the interoperatbility of different programs and/or systems. Indeed, any such decision might also lead to the increase of copyright trolling where some companies acquire software rights solely for the purpose to sue companies that have built their software/system on a given API. In sum, interoperability as such might be at stake. The divergence of various software/systems might not only chill software innovation, but could have serious lock-in effects (where end-users will be technologically restricted – more precisely demotivated – in switching between software/platforms). *In your opinion, is the Court of Appeals ruling the correct one?*

2. Although parties discussed in details, whether the fair use doctrine applies to the case, the Federal Circuit concluded that "this is not a case in which the record contains sufficient factual findings upon which we could base a de novo assessment of Google's affirmative defense of fair use. Accordingly, we remand this question to the district court for further proceedings. On remand, the district court should revisit and revise its jury instructions on fair use consistent with this opinion so as to provide the jury with a clear and appropriate picture of the fair use defense." (*Oracle v. Google*, p. 1377.) Importantly, Google successfully petitioned to the Supreme Court to hear the case in the 2019 term. The Supreme Court granted the writ of certiorari in November 2019 (docket no. 18-956). The case will continue to focus on both the copyright eligibility of APIs and the fair use of interfaces by Google. The Supreme Court planned to hear the case on March 24, 2020, but the oral argument was postponed due to the COVID-19 epidemic, and it was rescheduled for the October Term 2020..

3. Google aimed to convince the court that patent protection is more suitable for protecting software interfaces. As the Federal Circuit noted, "Google argues that '[a]fter *Sega,* developers could no longer hope to protect [software] interfaces by copyright ... *Sega* signaled that the only reliable means for protecting the functional requirements for achieving interoperability was by patenting them.'" (*Oracle v. Google*, p. 1380.) The Federal Circuit did not follow Google's argument. Indeed, "[i]mportantly for our purposes, the Supreme Court has made clear that '[n]either the Copyright Statute nor any other says that because a thing is patentable it may not be copyrighted.' Mazer v. Stein, 347 *U.S.* 201, 217 (1954). (...) Until either the Supreme Court or Congress tells us otherwise, we are bound to respect the Ninth Circuit's decision to afford software programs protection under the copyright laws. We thus decline any invitation to declare that protection of software programs should be the domain of patent law, and only patent law." (*Oracle v. Google*, p. 1380-1381.) *Do you agree with the Federal Circuit's conclusion regarding the possible overlap of patent and copyright protection?*

Further Case Law

Atari Games Corp. v. Nintendo of America, 975 *F.2d* 832 (1992)

Sega Enterprises Ltd. v. Accolade, Inc., 977 *F.2d* 1510 (1992)

Computer Associates International, Inc. v. Altai, Inc., 982 *F.2d* 693 (1992)

Lotus Development Corp. v. Borland International, Inc., 49 *F.3d* 807 (1995)

Sony Computer Entertainment, Inc. v. Connectix, Corp., 203 *F.3d* 596 (2000)

Swirsky v. Carey, 376 *F.3d* 841 (2004)

Recommended readings

In English

Lothar Determann - David Nimmer: Software Copyright's Oracle from the Cloud, *Berkeley Technology Law Journal*, Spring 2015, p. 161-211.

Christopher J. Geissler: Oracle America, Inc. v. Google Inc., 750 F.3d 1339 (Fed. Cir. 2014), Cert. Denied: Ideas, Methods, and Expression - Whose Innovation is Protected?, *Catholic University Journal of Law & Technology*, December 2015, p. 261-271.

Deba Alam: Oracle America, Inc. v. Google, Inc.: The Battle Over APIs Continues, *DePaul Journal of Art, Technology & Intellectual Property Law*, Fall 2015, p. 39-53.

Peter S. Menell: API Copyrightability Bleak House: Unraveling and Repairing the Oracle v. Google Jurisdictional Mess, *Berkeley Technology Law Journal*, 2016, p. 1515-1595.

Michael R. Mazzella III - R. Harrison Dilday: Oracle America, Inc. v. Google Inc.: Copyrightability of Application Programming Interfaces and a Fair Use Defense, *Georgetown Law Technology Review*, 2016, p. 62-71.

Fred von Lohmann: The New Wave: Copyright and Software Interfaces in the Wake of Oracle v. Google, *Harvard Journal of Law & Technology*, Spring 2018, p. 517-533.

Ralph Oman: Computer Software as Copyrightable Subject Matter: Oracle v. Google, Legislative Intent, and the Scope of Rights in Digital Works, *Harvard Journal of Law & Technology*, Spring 2018, p. 639-652.

Noam Shemtov: *Software and Graphical User Interfaces.* In: Tanya Aplin (Ed.): *Research Handbook on Intellectual Property and Digital Technologies*, Edward Elgar, Cheltenham, 2020, p. 2-10.

BEIJING JINGDIAO TECHNOLOGY CO., LTD., V. SHANGHAI NAIKAI ELECTRONIC TECHNOLOGY CO., LTD.

(2006) Shanghai Higher People's Court Civil (IP tribunal) Final No. 110 Civil Judgment

The plaintiff, in order to develope an engraving system, obtained the copyright of the software named JDPaint engraving software V4.0 (hereinafter referred to as JDPaint) on October 16, 2001. The operation of the system required the JDPaint software to generate a data file in Eng format. The control software running on the numerical controlling computer received the data file and turned it into processing instructions. The software could only be used on the CNC engraving machine produced by the plaintiff and was not intended to be put on commercial sale. However, the defendant developed a program called Ncstudio to read/decipher the encrypted Eng format data file generated by JDPaint software. The plaintiff believed that the defendant circumvented or destroyed the technical measures taken by the plaintiff to protect the encryption method of Eng format; developed and sold the CNC system capable of reading the Eng format data file; and hence committed a copyright infringement.

Rules

Copyright Law of the People's Republic of China (2010 Amendment)

Article 48 Anyone who commits any of the following acts of infringement shall bear civil liability for such remedies as ceasing the infringing act, eliminating the effects of the act, making an apology or paying damages, depending on the circumstances' and may, in addition, be subjected by a copyright administration department to such administrative penalties as ceasing the infringing act, confiscating unlawful income from the act, confiscating and destroying infringing reproductions and imposing a fine; where the circumstances are serious, the copyright administration department may also confiscate the materials, tools, and equipment mainly used for making the infringing reproductions; and if the act constitutes a crime, the infringer shall be prosecuted for his criminal liability:

(...)

(6) intentionally circumventing or destroying the technological measures taken by a right holder for protecting the copyright or copyright-related rights in his work, sound recording or video recording, without the permission of the copyright owner, or the owner of the copyright-related rights, unless otherwise provided in law or in administrative regulations;

Regulation on Computers Software Protection (2013 Revision)

Article 2 For the purposes of these Regulations, the term "computer software" (hereinafter referred to as "software") means computer programs and relevant documents.

Article 3 For the purposes of these Regulations, the following definitions apply:

(1) "computer program" means a coded instruction sequence which may be executed by devices with information processing capabilities such as computers, or a symbolic instruction sequence or symbolic statement sequence which may be automatically converted into a coded instruction sequence for the purpose of obtaining certain expected results; the source program and object program of a computer program shall be deemed as one and the same work;

Article 24 Unless otherwise provided for in the Copyright Law of the People's Republic of China, these Regulations or other laws and administrative regulations, without the consent of the software copyright owner, any of the following infringing actions shall make the infringer liable to a civil penalty such as ceasing the infringement, eliminating the impact, making an apology, compensating for the losses, and a copyright administrative department may, if the public interest is also harmed, order the infringer to cease the infringing action, confiscate the infringer's illegal gains, confiscate and destroy the infringing reproduction(s), and impose a fine; or may also, in the event of a serious case, confiscate the materials, tools, equipment, etc. that are mainly used in producing the infringing reproduction(s); or subject the infringer to criminal liability, if the infringement violates the criminal law:

(...)

(2) Distributing, renting, or disseminating via an information network a copyright owner's software to the public.

Analysis

The Shanghai Higher People's Court held that, in accordance with the relevant provisions of the Copyright Law and the Computer Software Protection Regulation, the plaintiff/appellant improperly claimed that cracking the Eng format file falls within the scope of Article 24(3) of the Computer Software Protection Regulation. Therefore the Shanghai Higher People's Court dismissed the appeal and upheld the original judgment.

The Court held that it is not a technical measure for the engraving company to encrypt data format files.

First, from a technical point of view, the function of the Eng format file generated by JDPaint is to complete the data exchange. If the Eng format was not used, other format would be used to complete the data exchange. Therefore, the basic function of the Eng format file is not to encrypt the JDPaint software.

Second, the purpose of the use of the Eng format by the plaintiff/appellant was not to protect the software copyright through technical means, but to establish and consolidate the binding relationship between the JDPaint software and its engraving machine. Hence, the defendant's act of cracking the Eng format file did not aim to deliberately avoid or destroy the technical measure of the copyright owner.

THINK IT OVER!

What are the differences between technical measures and technical bundling? Technical measures might include defensive technical measures to prevent others from infringing, as well as offensive technical measures that can cause damage to the infringer. Since the legal protection of technical measures should be limited to preventing others from illegally accessing, browsing or copying others' copyrighted works, the technical measures protected by the Copyright Act should be limited to measures of defensive nature. "Effective" is a relative term. In Chinese copyright law, a technical protection measure is effective, if it is capable to limit avoiding or cracking the measure under normal circumstances. No protection measure shall provide for an absolute protection. *Technical bundling* combines various products into a whole, and forecloses splitting the whole into separated. At present, tied sales mainly regulated by Anti-unfair Competition Law in China. The law aims to prevent tied sales from disrupting market order and restricting others from competing on the market. In *Jingdiao v. Naikai,* reading the format file required the use of plaintiff's software. This represented a typical tied sale.

Recommended readings

In Chinese (bibliographic data translated to English)

Huang Wushuang - Li Jinfu: Revisiting Beijing Jingdiao v. Shanghai Naikai for Computer Copyright Software Infringement: A Reasonable Latitude of Technical Protection Measures and Reverse Engineering, *Electronics Intellectual Property*, Issue 10/2007, p. 58-62.

Ding Wenlian - Shi Lei: Understanding and Reference on Beijing Jingdiao v. Shanghai Naikai for Computer Copyright Software Infringement: The Data Format Outputted by Computer Software is Not Technical Protection Measures Which Stipulated by Copyright Law, *People's Judicature*, Issue 26/2016, p. 21-25.

Chapter II
Communication to the Public in the Internet Age

ITV BROADCASTING LTD. V. TVCATCHUP LTD.

Case C-607/11 - Judgment of the Court (Fourth Chamber), 7 March 2013 [ECLI:EU:C:2013:147]

(...) Legal context

European Union law

3 Recitals 23 and 27 in the preamble to Directive 2001/29 state:
'(23) This Directive should harmonise further the author's right of communication to the public. This right should be understood in a broad sense covering all communication to the public not present at the place where the communication originates. This right should cover any such transmission or retransmission of a work to the public by wire or wireless means, including broadcasting. This right should not cover any other acts.
(27) The mere provision of physical facilities for enabling or making a communication does not in itself amount to communication within the meaning of this Directive.'

4 Article 3 of that directive, entitled 'Right of communication to the public of works and right of making available to the public other subject-matter', provides:
'1. Member States shall provide authors with the exclusive right to authorise or prohibit any communication to the public of their works, by wire or wireless means, including the making available to the public of their works in such a way that members of the public may access them from a place and at a time individually chosen by them.
3. The rights referred to in paragraphs 1 and 2 shall not be exhausted by any act of communication to the public or making available to the public as set out in this Article.'

5 Article 2 of Council Directive 93/83/EEC of 27 September 1993 on the coordination of certain rules concerning copyright and rights related to copyright applicable to satellite broadcasting and cable retransmission (OJ 1993 L 248, p. 15) provides:

'Member States shall provide an exclusive right for the author to authorise the communication to the public by satellite of copyright works ...'.

6 Article 8(1) of that directive states:

'Member States shall ensure that when programmes from other Member States are retransmitted by cable in their territory the applicable copyright and related rights are observed and that such retransmission takes place on the basis of individual or collective contractual agreements between copyright owners, holders of related rights and cable operators.'

English law

7 Section 20 of the Copyright, Designs and Patents Act 1988, in the version applicable to the facts in the main proceedings, entitled 'Infringement by communication to the public', provides:

'1. The communication to the public of the work is an act restricted by the copyright in –

(a) a literary, dramatic, musical or artistic work,

(b) a sound recording or film, or

(c) a broadcast.

2. References in this Part to communication to the public are to communication to the public by electronic transmission, and in relation to a work include –

(a) the broadcasting of the work;

(b) the making available to the public of the work by electronic transmission in such a way that members of the public may access it from a place and at a time individually chosen by them.'

The dispute in the main proceedings and the questions referred for a preliminary ruling

8 The claimants in the main proceedings are commercial television broadcasters who own copyright under national law in the television broadcasts themselves and in films and other items which are included in their broadcasts. They are funded by advertising carried in their broadcasts.

9 TVC offers an internet television broadcasting service. The service permits its users to receive, via the internet, 'live' streams of free-to-air television broadcasts, including television broadcasts transmitted by the claimants in the main proceedings.

10 TVC ensures that those using its service can obtain access only to content which they are already legally entitled to watch in the United Kingdom by virtue of their television licence. The terms to which users must agree thus include the possession of a valid TV licence and a restriction of use of TVC services to the United Kingdom. The TVC website has the facility to authenticate the user's location and to refuse access where the conditions imposed on users are not satisfied.

11 The TVC service is funded by advertising. Audiovisual advertising is shown before the user is able to view the live stream. The advertisements already contained in the original broadcasts are left unchanged and sent to the user as part of the stream. There is also 'in-skin' advertising, which appears on the user's computer or other equipment.

12 For its activities, TVC uses four groups of servers, namely, (i) acquisition, (ii) encoding, (iii) origin and (iv) edge servers.

13 The input signals used by TVC are the normal terrestrial and satellite broadcast signals transmitted by the claimants in the main proceedings. The signals are captured via an aerial and then passed to the acquisition servers, which extract individual video streams from the received signal without altering them. The encoding servers then convert the incoming streams into a different compression standard. Next, the origin servers prepare streams of video for sending over the internet in a variety of formats. Beyond that point, the channels offered by TVC are processed further only if at least one TVC subscriber has requested that channel. If there is no request for a given channel, the signal is discarded.

14 Edge servers connect with a user's computer or mobile telephone using the internet. When an edge server receives a request for a channel from a user, then, unless it is already streaming that channel to a different user, the edge server connects to the origin server which streams that channel. The software on the edge server creates a separate stream for each user who requests a channel through it. An individual packet of data leaving the edge server is thus addressed to an individual user, not to a class of users.

15 The streams provided by the edge servers can be in a variety of different formats. The formats used are: Adobe Flash streams (for computers), HTTP streams (for Apple mobile devices) and RTSP streams (for Android and Blackberry mobile telephones).

16 The claimants in the main proceedings instituted proceedings against TVC before the High Court of Justice (England and Wales) (Chancery Division) for breach of their copyright in their broadcasts and films, alleging, inter alia, that there is a communication of the works

to the public prohibited by section 20 of the Copyright, Designs and Patents Act 1988, in the version applicable to the facts in the main proceedings, and by Article 3(1) of Directive 2001/29.

17 The High Court takes the view that it is not clear from the judgments in Case C-306/05 *SGAE* and in Joined Cases C-431/09 and C-432/09 *Airfield NV and Canal Digitaal* whether there is a 'communication to the public' within the meaning of Article 3(1) of Directive 2001/29 in the case where an organisation such as TVC, in full knowledge of the consequences of its acts and in order to attract an audience to its own transmissions and advertisements, streams over the internet broadcasts to members of the public who would have been entitled to access the original broadcast signal using their own television sets or laptops in their own homes.

18 In those circumstances the High Court of Justice (England and Wales) (Chancery Division) decided to stay the proceedings and to refer the following questions to the Court for a preliminary ruling:

'*1. Does the right to authorise or prohibit a "communication to the public of their works by wire or wireless means" in Article 3(1) of [Directive 2001/29] extend to a case where:*

(a) Authors authorise the inclusion of their works in a terrestrial free-to-air television broadcast which is intended for reception either throughout the territory of a Member State or within a geographical area within a Member State;

(b) A third party ([that is to say,] an organisation other than the original broadcaster) provides a service whereby individual subscribers within the intended area of reception of the broadcast who could lawfully receive the broadcast on a television receiver in their own homes may log on to the third party's server and receive the content of the broadcast by means of an internet stream?

2. Does it make any difference to the answer to the above question if:

(a) The third party's server allows only a "one-to-one" connection for each subscriber whereby each individual subscriber establishes his or her own internet connection to the server and every data packet sent by the server onto the internet is addressed to only one individual subscriber?

(b) The third party's service is funded by advertising which is presented "pre-roll" ([that is to say,] during the period of time after a subscriber logs on but before he or she begins to receive the broadcast content) or "in-skin" ([that is to say,] within the frame of the viewing software which displays the received programme on the subscriber's viewing device but outside the programme picture) but the original advertisements contained within the broadcast are presented to the subscriber at the point where they are inserted in the programme by the broadcaster?

(c) The intervening organisation is:

(i) providing an alternative service to that of the original broadcaster, thereby acting in direct competition with the original broadcaster for viewers; or

(ii) acting in direct competition with the original broadcaster for advertising revenues?'

Consideration of the questions referred

Question 1 and Question 2(a)

19 By Question 1 and Question 2(a), the referring court asks, in essence, whether the concept of 'communication to the public', within the meaning of Article 3(1) of Directive 2001/29, must be interpreted as meaning that it covers a retransmission of the works included in a terrestrial television broadcast:

- where the retransmission is made by an organisation other than the original broadcaster,
- by means of an internet stream made available to the subscribers of that other organisation who may receive the retransmission by logging on to its server,
- on the assumption that those subscribers are within the area of reception of the terrestrial television broadcast and may lawfully receive the broadcast on a television receiver.

20 First of all, it is to be noted that the principal objective of Directive 2001/29 is to establish a high level of protection of authors, allowing them to obtain an appropriate reward for the use of their works, including on the occasion of communication to the public. It follows that 'communication to the public' must be interpreted broadly, as recital 23 in the preamble to the directive indeed expressly states.

21 In the first place, it is necessary to determine the meaning of the concept of 'communication' and reply to the question whether the activity at issue in the main proceedings comes within its scope.

22 In that connection, the Court notes that Directive 2001/29 does not define the concept of 'communication' exhaustively. Thus, the meaning and scope of that concept must be defined in the light of the context in which it occurs and also in the light of the objective referred to in paragraph 20 above.

23 It follows, in particular, from recital 23 in the preamble to Directive 2001/29 that the author's right of communication to the public covers any transmission or retransmission of a work to the public not present at the place where the communication originates, by wire or wireless means, including broadcasting. In addition, it is apparent from Article 3(3)

of that directive that authorising the inclusion of protected works in a communication to the public does not exhaust the right to authorise or prohibit other communications of those works to the public.

24 If follows that, by regulating the situations in which a given work is put to multiple use, the European Union legislature intended that each transmission or retransmission of a work which uses a specific technical means must, as a rule, be individually authorised by the author of the work in question.

25 Those findings are, moreover, supported by Articles 2 and 8 of Directive 93/83, which require fresh authorisation for a simultaneous, unaltered and unabridged retransmission by satellite or cable of an initial transmission of television or radio programmes containing protected works, even though those programmes may already be received in their catchment area by other technical means, such as by wireless means or terrestrial networks.

26 Given that the making of works available through the retransmission of a terrestrial television broadcast over the internet uses a specific technical means different from that of the original communication, that retransmission must be considered to be a 'communication' within the meaning of Article 3(1) of Directive 2001/29. Consequently, such a retransmission cannot be exempt from authorisation by the authors of the retransmitted works when these are communicated to the public.

27 That conclusion cannot be undermined by TVC's objection that the making of the works available over the internet, as was done in the case in the main proceedings, is merely a technical means to ensure or improve reception of the terrestrial television broadcast in its catchment area.

28 Admittedly, it follows from the case-law of the Court that a mere technical means to ensure or improve reception of the original transmission in its catchment area does not constitute a 'communication' within the meaning of Article 3(1) of Directive 2001/29.

29 Thus, the intervention of such a technical means must be limited to maintaining or improving the quality of the reception of a pre-existing transmission and cannot be used for any other transmission.

30 In the present case, however, the intervention by TVC consists in a transmission of the protected works at issue which is different from that of the broadcasting organisation concerned. TVC's intervention is in no way intended to maintain or improve the quality of the

transmission by that other broadcasting organisation. In those circumstances, that intervention cannot be considered to be a mere technical means within the meaning specified in paragraph 28 above.

31 In the second place, in order to be categorised as a 'communication to the public' within the meaning of Article 3(1) of Directive 2001/29, the protected works must also in fact be communicated to a 'public'.

32 In that connection, it follows from the case-law of the Court that the term 'public' in Article 3(1) of Directive 2001/29 refers to an indeterminate number of potential recipients and implies, moreover, a fairly large number of persons.

33 As regards that last criterion specifically, the cumulative effect of making the works available to potential recipients should be taken into account. In that connection, it is in particular relevant to ascertain the number of persons who have access to the same work at the same time and successively.

34 In that context, it is irrelevant whether the potential recipients access the communicated works through a one-to-one connection. That technique does not prevent a large number of persons having access to the same work at the same time.

35 In the present case, it should be noted that the retransmission of the works over the internet at issue in the main proceedings is aimed at all persons resident in the United Kingdom who have an internet connection and who claim to hold a television licence in that State. Those people may access the protected works at the same time, in the context of the 'live streaming' of television programmes on the internet.

36 Thus, the retransmission in question is aimed at an indeterminate number of potential recipients and implies a large number of persons. Consequently, it must be held that, by the retransmission in question, the protected works are indeed communicated to a 'public' within the meaning of Article 3(1) of Directive 2001/29.

37 However, TVC contends that the retransmission at issue in the main proceedings does not satisfy the requirement that there must be a new public, which is none the less necessary within the meaning of the judgments in *SGAE*, *Football Association Premier League and Others*, and *Airfield and Canal Digitaal*. The recipients of the retransmission effected by TVC are, it submits, entitled to follow the televised broadcast, identical in content, using their own television sets.

38 In that connection, it should be noted that the situations examined in the cases which gave rise to the abovementioned judgments differ clearly from the situation at issue in the case in the main proceedings. In those cases, the Court examined situations in which an operator had made accessible, by its deliberate intervention, a broadcast containing protected works to a new public which was not considered by the authors concerned when they authorised the broadcast in question.

39 By contrast, the main proceedings in the present case concern the transmission of works included in a terrestrial broadcast and the making available of those works over the internet. As is apparent from paragraphs 24 to 26 above, each of those two transmissions must be authorised individually and separately by the authors concerned given that each is made under specific technical conditions, using a different means of transmission for the protected works, and each is intended for a public. In those circumstances, it is no longer necessary to examine below the requirement that there must be a new public, which is relevant only in the situations on which the Court of Justice had to rule in the cases giving rise to the judgments in *SGAE, Football Association Premier League and Others* and *Airfield and Canal Digitaal*.

40 In the light of the foregoing, the answer to Question 1 and Question 2(a) is that the concept of 'communication to the public', within the meaning of Article 3(1) of Directive 2001/29, must be interpreted as meaning that it covers a retransmission of the works included in a terrestrial television broadcast

- where the retransmission is made by an organisation other than the original broadcaster,
- by means of an internet stream made available to the subscribers of that other organisation who may receive that retransmission by logging on to its server,
- even though those subscribers are within the area of reception of that terrestrial television broadcast and may lawfully receive the broadcast on a television receiver.

Question 2(b)

41 By Question 2(b), the referring court asks, in essence, whether the answer to Question 1 is influenced by the fact that a retransmission, such as that at issue in the main proceedings, is funded by advertising and is therefore of a profit-making nature.

42 In that connection, the Court has indeed held that it is not irrelevant that a 'communication' within the meaning of Article 3(1) of Directive 2001/29 is of a profit-making nature.

However, it has acknowledged that a profit-making nature is not necessarily an essential condition for the existence of a communication to the public.

43 Consequently, a profit-making nature does not determine conclusively whether a retransmission, such as that at issue in the main proceedings, is to be categorised as a 'communication' within the meaning of Article 3(1) of Directive 2001/29.

44 The answer to Question 2(b) is therefore that the answer to Question 1 is not influenced by the fact that a retransmission, such as that at issue in the main proceedings, is funded by advertising and is therefore of a profit-making nature.

Question 2(c)

45 By Question 2(c), the referring court asks in, essence, whether the answer to Question 1 is influenced by the fact that a retransmission, such as that at issue in the main proceedings, is made by an organisation which is acting in direct competition with the original broadcaster.

46 In that connection, it suffices to note that it follows neither from Directive 2001/29 nor from the case-law of the Court that a competitive relationship between the organisations making real-time broadcasts of works protected by copyright or subsequent retransmissions of those works is relevant for the purpose of categorising a transmission as a 'communication to the public' within the meaning of Article 3(1) of Directive 2001/29.

47 Consequently, the answer to Question 2(c) is that the answer to Question 1 is not influenced by the fact that a retransmission, such as that at issue in the main proceedings, is made by an organisation which is acting in direct competition with the original broadcaster. (...)

THINK IT OVER!

1. In this case, the CJEU reaffirmed that public means an indeterminate and the same time a fairly large number of users. In *Rafael Hoteles*, the CJEU found that successive users of hotel rooms form publicity. *TVCatchup* clarified how the concept of public works in an Internet environment. There the CJEU noted that "it is irrelevant whether the potential recipients access the communicated works through a one-to-one connection" (para. 34). In sum, the CJEU correctly pointed out that the *making available of protected subject matter via the Internet necessarily allows an indeterminate and fairly large number of individuals to access the same material,* even if through "one-to-one connections".

2. According to para. 39 of the ruling, "the transmission of works included in a terrestrial broadcast and the making available of those works over the internet (...) must be authorised individually and separately by the authors concerned given that each is made under specific technical conditions, using a different means of transmission for the protected works, and each is intended for a public." Recalling Article 11bis(1)(ii) of the Berne Convention, no such requirement forms a part of the concept of communication to the public under international copyright law. Indeed, *the "theory of specific technical means"* seems to work well only as long as the use relates to the making available of television signals via the Internet, since communication of TV signals and their making available via the Internet is done necessarily under different technological conditions. The stretching of the boundaries of the right of communication to the public with the theory of specific technical means turned to be fatal in cases, where the initial and the secondary uses were equally conducted via the Internet. Compare to the *Svensson* and the following rulings of the CJEU on linking.

Further Case Law

Case C-306/05 - Sociedad General de Autores y Editores de España (SGAE) v. Rafael Hoteles, S.A., Judgement of the Court (Third Chamber), 7 December 2006 [ECLI:EU:C:2006:764]

Case C-466/12 - Nils Svensson and Others v. Retriever Sverige AB, Judgment of the Court (Fourth Chamber), 13 February 2014 [ECLI:EU:C:2014:76]

Case C-279/13 - C More Entertainment AB v. Linus Sandberg, Judgment of the Court (Ninth Chamber), 26 March 2015 [ECLI:EU:C:2015:199]

Recommended readings

In English

Simon Baggs - Sunniva Hansson: What's the Catch? The CJEU Judgment in ITV v TVCatchup, *European Intellectual Property Review*, Issue 6/2013, p. 363-365.

Iona Silverman - Yindi Gesinde: ITV v TV CatchUp: the saga continues…, *European Intellectual Property Review*, Issue 9/2016, p. 580-584.

Makeen Fouad Makeen: *Video Streaming and the Communication to the Public Right in the United States and European Union.* In: Tanya Aplin (Ed.): *Research Handbook on Intellectual Property and Digital Technologies*, Edward Elgar, Cheltenham, 2020, p. 246-275.

In French

Lionel Costes - Laure Lalot: Retransmission d'oeuvres télévisuelles en ligne: les précisions de la CJUE, *Droit de l'immatériel: informatique, médias, communication*, 2013, n° 92, p. 18.

Céline Castets-Renard: L'interprétation autonome et systémique du droit d'auteur européen par la CJUE: et maintenant?, *Droit de l'immatériel: informatique, médias, communication*, 2013, n° 93, p. 10-15.

In German

Lars Maritzen - Felicitas Rieger: EuGH: Livestreaming von Fernsehsendungen - ITV Broadcasting, *Multimedia und Recht*, Heft 7/2013, p. 461-463.

Michel M. Walter: Weiterleitung von Fernsehsendungen im Internet - Online-Streaming, *MR-Int: Internationale Rundschau zum Medienrecht, IP- & IT-Recht*, Heft 1/2013, p. 23-24.

NILS SVENSSON AND OTHERS V. RETRIEVER SVERIGE AB

Case C-466/12 - Judgment of the Court (Fourth Chamber), 13 February 2014 [ECLI:EU:C:2014:76]

(…) Legal context

International law

The WIPO Copyright Treaty

3 The World Intellectual Property Organisation (WIPO) adopted the WIPO Copyright Treaty ('the WIPO Copyright Treaty') in Geneva on 20 December 1996. It was approved on behalf of the European Community by Council Decision 2000/278/EC of 16 March 2000.

4 Article 1(4) of the WIPO Copyright Treaty provides that the contracting parties are to comply with Articles 1 to 21 of the Convention for the Protection of Literary and Artistic Works, signed at Berne on 9 September 1886 (Paris Act of 24 July 1971), as amended on 28 September 1979 ('the Berne Convention').

The Berne Convention

5 Article 20 of the Berne Convention, entitled 'Special Agreements Among Countries of the Union', states:
'The Governments of the countries of the Union reserve the right to enter into special agreements among themselves, in so far as such agreements grant to authors more extensive rights than those granted by the Convention, or contain other provisions not contrary to this Convention. The provisions of existing agreements which satisfy these conditions shall remain applicable.'

European Union law

6 Recitals 1, 4, 6, 7, 9 and 19 in the preamble to Directive 2001/29 state:
'(1) The Treaty provides for the establishment of an internal market and the institution of a system ensuring that competition in the internal market is not distorted. Harmonisation of the laws of the Member States on copyright and related rights contributes to the achievement of these objectives.
(4) A harmonised legal framework on copyright and related rights, through increased legal certainty and while providing for a high level of protection of intellectual property, will foster substantial investment in creativity and innovation, including network infrastructure, and lead in turn to growth and increased competitiveness of European industry, both in the area of content provision and information technology and more generally across a wide range of industrial and cultural sectors.
(6) Without harmonisation at Community level, legislative activities at national level which have already been initiated in a number of Member States in order to respond to the technological challenges might result in significant differences in protection and thereby in restrictions on the free movement of services and products incorporating, or based on, intellectual property, leading to a refragmentation of the internal market and legislative inconsistency. The impact of such legislative differences and uncertainties will become more significant with the further development of the information society, which has already greatly increased transborder exploitation of intellectual property. This development will and should further increase. Significant legal differences and uncertainties in protection may hinder economies of scale for new products and services containing copyright and related rights.
(7) The Community legal framework for the protection of copyright and related rights must, therefore, also be adapted and supplemented as far as is necessary for the smooth functioning of the

internal market. To that end, those national provisions on copyright and related rights which vary considerably from one Member State to another or which cause legal uncertainties hindering the smooth functioning of the internal market and the proper development of the information society in Europe should be adjusted, and inconsistent national responses to the technological developments should be avoided, whilst differences not adversely affecting the functioning of the internal market need not be removed or prevented.

(9) Any harmonisation of copyright and related rights must take as a basis a high level of protection, since such rights are crucial to intellectual creation. Their protection helps to ensure the maintenance and development of creativity in the interests of authors, performers, producers, consumers, culture, industry and the public at large. (...)

(19) The moral rights of rightholders should be exercised according to the legislation of the Member States and the provisions of the Berne Convention (...)[,] the WIPO Copyright Treaty and of the WIPO Performances and Phonograms Treaty.'

7 Article 3 of Directive 2001/29 provides:

'1. Member States shall provide authors with the exclusive right to authorise or prohibit any communication to the public of their works, by wire or wireless means, including the making available to the public of their works in such a way that members of the public may access them from a place and at a time individually chosen by them.

3. The rights referred to in paragraphs 1 and 2 shall not be exhausted by any act of communication to the public or making available to the public as set out in this Article.'

The dispute in the main proceedings and the questions referred for a preliminary ruling

8 The applicants in the main proceedings, all journalists, wrote press articles that were published in the Göteborgs-Posten newspaper and on the Göteborgs-Posten website. Retriever Sverige operates a website that provides its clients, according to their needs, with lists of clickable Internet links to articles published by other websites. It is common ground between the parties that those articles were freely accessible on the Göteborgs-Posten newspaper site. According to the applicants in the main proceedings, if a client clicks on one of those links, it is not apparent to him that he has been redirected to another site in order to access the work in which he is interested. By contrast, according to Retriever Sverige, it is clear to the client that, when he clicks on one of those links, he is redirected to another site.

9 The applicants in the main proceedings brought an action against Retriever Sverige before the Stockholms tingsrätt (Stockholm District Court) in order to obtain compensation on the

ground that that company had made use, without their authorisation, of certain articles by them, by making them available to its clients.

10 By judgment of 11 June 2010, the Stockholms tingsrätt rejected their application. The applicants in the main proceedings then brought an appeal against that judgment before the Svea hovrätt (Svea Court of Appeal).

11 Before that court, the applicants in the main proceedings claimed, inter alia, that Retriever Sverige had infringed their exclusive right to make their respective works available to the public, in that as a result of the services offered on its website, Retriever Sverige's clients had access to the applicants' works.

12 Retriever Sverige contends, in defence, that the provision of lists of Internet links to works communicated to the public on other websites does not constitute an act liable to affect the copyright in those works. Retriever Sverige also contends that it did not carry out any transmission of any protected work; its action is limited to indicating to its clients the websites on which the works that are of interest to them are to be found.

13 In those circumstances, the Svea hovrätt decided to stay the proceedings and to refer the following questions to the Court of Justice for a preliminary ruling:

'(1) If anyone other than the holder of copyright in a certain work supplies a clickable link to the work on his website, does that constitute communication to the public within the meaning of Article 3(1) of Directive [2001/29]?

(2) Is the assessment under question 1 affected if the work to which the link refers is on a website on the Internet which can be accessed by anyone without restrictions or if access is restricted in some way?

(3) When making the assessment under question 1, should any distinction be drawn between a case where the work, after the user has clicked on the link, is shown on another website and one where the work, after the user has clicked on the link, is shown in such a way as to give the impression that it is appearing on the same website?

(4) Is it possible for a Member State to give wider protection to authors' exclusive right by enabling communication to the public to cover a greater range of acts than provided for in Article 3(1) of Directive 2001/29?'

Consideration of the questions referred

The first three questions

14 By its first three questions, which it is appropriate to examine together, the referring court asks, in essence, whether Article 3(1) of Directive 2001/29 must be interpreted as meaning that the provision, on a website, of clickable links to protected works available on another website constitutes an act of communication to the public as referred to in that provision, where, on that other site, the works concerned are freely accessible.

15 In this connection, it follows from Article 3(1) of Directive 2001/29 that every act of communication of a work to the public has to be authorised by the copyright holder.

16 It is thus apparent from that provision that the concept of communication to the public includes two cumulative criteria, namely, an 'act of communication' of a work and the communication of that work to a 'public'.

17 As regards the first of those criteria, that is, the existence of an 'act of communication', this must be construed broadly, in order to ensure, in accordance with, inter alia, recitals 4 and 9 in the preamble to Directive 2001/29, a high level of protection for copyright holders.

18 In the circumstances of this case, it must be observed that the provision, on a website, of clickable links to protected works published without any access restrictions on another site, affords users of the first site direct access to those works.

19 As is apparent from Article 3(1) of Directive 2001/29, for there to be an 'act of communication', it is sufficient, in particular, that a work is made available to a public in such a way that the persons forming that public may access it, irrespective of whether they avail themselves of that opportunity.

20 It follows that, in circumstances such as those in the case in the main proceedings, the provision of clickable links to protected works must be considered to be 'making available' and, therefore, an 'act of communication', within the meaning of that provision.

21 So far as concerns the second of the abovementioned criteria, that is, that the protected work must in fact be communicated to a 'public', it follows from Article 3(1) of Directive 2001/29 that, by the term 'public', that provision refers to an indeterminate number of potential recipients and implies, moreover, a fairly large number of persons.

22 An act of communication such as that made by the manager of a website by means of clickable links is aimed at all potential users of the site managed by that person, that is to say, an indeterminate and fairly large number of recipients.

23 In those circumstances, it must be held that the manager is making a communication to a public.

24 None the less, according to settled case-law, in order to be covered by the concept of "communication to the public", within the meaning of Article 3(1) of Directive 2001/29, a communication, such as that at issue in the main proceedings, concerning the same works as those covered by the initial communication and made, as in the case of the initial communication, on the Internet, and therefore by the same technical means, must also be directed at a new public, that is to say, at a public that was not taken into account by the copyright holders when they authorised the initial communication to the public.

25 In the circumstances of this case, it must be observed that making available the works concerned by means of a clickable link, such as that in the main proceedings, does not lead to the works in question being communicated to a new public.

26 The public targeted by the initial communication consisted of all potential visitors to the site concerned, since, given that access to the works on that site was not subject to any restrictive measures, all Internet users could therefore have free access to them.

27 In those circumstances, it must be held that, where all the users of another site to whom the works at issue have been communicated by means of a clickable link could access those works directly on the site on which they were initially communicated, without the involvement of the manager of that other site, the users of the site managed by the latter must be deemed to be potential recipients of the initial communication and, therefore, as being part of the public taken into account by the copyright holders when they authorised the initial communication.

28 Therefore, since there is no new public, the authorisation of the copyright holders is not required for a communication to the public such as that in the main proceedings.

29 Such a finding cannot be called in question were the referring court to find, although this is not clear from the documents before the Court, that when Internet users click on the link at issue, the work appears in such a way as to give the impression that it is appearing on the site on which that link is found, whereas in fact that work comes from another site.

30 That additional circumstance in no way alters the conclusion that the provision on a site of a clickable link to a protected work published and freely accessible on another site has the effect of making that work available to users of the first site and that it therefore constitutes a communication to the public. However, since there is no new public, the authorisation of the copyright holders is in any event not required for such a communication to the public.

31 On the other hand, where a clickable link makes it possible for users of the site on which that link appears to circumvent restrictions put in place by the site on which the protected work appears in order to restrict public access to that work to the latter site's subscribers only, and the link accordingly constitutes an intervention without which those users would not be able to access the works transmitted, all those users must be deemed to be a new public, which was not taken into account by the copyright holders when they authorised the initial communication, and accordingly the holders' authorisation is required for such a communication to the public. This is the case, in particular, where the work is no longer available to the public on the site on which it was initially communicated or where it is henceforth available on that site only to a restricted public, while being accessible on another Internet site without the copyright holders' authorisation.

32 In those circumstances, the answer to the first three questions referred is that Article 3(1) of Directive 2001/29 must be interpreted as meaning that the provision on a website of clickable links to works freely available on another website does not constitute an act of communication to the public, as referred to in that provision.

The fourth question

33 By its fourth question, the referring court asks, in essence, whether Article 3(1) of Directive 2001/29 must be interpreted as precluding a Member State from giving wider protection to copyright holders by laying down that the concept of communication to the public includes a wider range of activities than those referred to in that provision.

34 In this connection, it is apparent, in particular, from recitals 1, 6 and 7 in the preamble to Directive 2001/29 that the objectives of the directive are, inter alia, to remedy the legislative differences and legal uncertainty that exist in relation to copyright protection. Acceptance of the proposition that a Member State may give wider protection to copyright holders by laying down that the concept of communication to the public also includes activities other than those referred to in Article 3(1) of Directive 2001/29 would have the effect of creating legislative differences and thus, for third parties, legal uncertainty.

35 Consequently, the objective pursued by Directive 2001/29 would inevitably be undermined if the concept of communication to the public were to be construed in different Member States as including a wider range of activities than those referred to in Article 3(1) of that directive.

36 It is true that recital 7 in the preamble to the directive indicates that the directive does not have the objective of removing or preventing differences that do not adversely affect the functioning of the internal market. Nevertheless, it must be observed that, if the Member States were to be afforded the possibility of laying down that the concept of communication to the public includes a wider range of activities than those referred to in Article 3(1) of the directive, the functioning of the internal market would be bound to be adversely affected.

37 It follows that Article 3(1) of Directive 2001/29 cannot be construed as allowing Member States to give wider protection to copyright holders by laying down that the concept of communication to the public includes a wider range of activities than those referred to in that provision.

38 Such a conclusion is not affected by the fact, highlighted by the applicants in the main proceedings in their written observations, that Article 20 of the Berne Convention stipulates that the signatory countries may enter into 'special agreements' among themselves with a view to granting copyright holders more extensive rights than those laid down in that Convention.

39 In this connection, suffice it to recall that, when an agreement allows, but does not require, a Member State to adopt a measure which appears to be contrary to Union law, the Member State must refrain from adopting such a measure.

40 Since the objective of Directive 2001/29 would inevitably be undermined if the concept of communication to the public were construed as including a wider range of activities than those referred to in Article 3(1) of that directive, a Member State must refrain from exercising the right granted to it by Article 20 of the Berne Convention.

41 Therefore, the answer to the fourth question is that Article 3(1) of Directive 2001/29 must be interpreted as precluding a Member State from giving wider protection to copyright holders by laying down that the concept of communication to the public includes a wider range of activities than those referred to in that provision. (...)

THINK IT OVER!

1. What is the substantial difference between communication to the public and making available to the public? Art. 3(1) of the InfoSoc-Directive declares every wire or wireless means of public transmission of protected subject matter as communication to the public, whilst making available to the public means that "members of the public may access [protected subject matter] from a place and at a time individually chosen by them". The European Copyright Society has stressed in its analysis of the *Svensson* case that "hyperlinks do not transmit a work, (to which they link) they merely provide the viewer with information as to the location of a page that the user can choose to access or not. There is thus no communication of the work. " Conversely, ALAI has noted that "'making available' as set out in WCT article 8 necessarily encompasses not only the actual transmission of a work to members of the public, but especially the *offering* to the public of the work for individualized streaming or downloading, not merely the receipt of the stream or download". *Which position is correct regarding linking?*

2. Following the CJEU's arguments in the Svensson case (compare to para. 26) *would it make any difference if the relevant protected subject matter was originally made available to the public by a third party without proper authorization by the rightholder?* The automatic response would probably be a clear "yes". See, however, the CJEU's order in the *BestWater* case, where the judges sidestepped this material issue. It is nevertheless important to know that at least three domestic courts (in Germany, the UK and Poland) have refused to follow the latter *BestWater* interpretation. In *GS Media*, the CJEU finally discussed the legality of the source of linking. See at page 133.

3. In *TVCatchup* the CJEU has noted that "by regulating the situations in which a given work is put to multiple use, the European Union legislature intended that each transmission or retransmission of a work which uses a specific technical means must, as a rule, be individually authorised by the author of the work in question. Those findings are, moreover, supported by Articles 2 and 8 of Directive 93/83, which require fresh authorisation for a simultaneous, unaltered and unabridged retransmission by satellite or cable of an initial transmission of television or radio programmes containing protected works, even though those programmes may already be received in their catchment area by other technical means, such as by wireless means or terrestrial networks. Given that the making of works available through the retransmission of a terrestrial television broadcast over the internet uses a specific technical means different from that of the original communication, that retransmission must be considered to be a 'communication' within the meaning of Article 3(1) of Directive 2001/29. Consequently, such a retransmission cannot be exempt from authorisation by the authors of the retransmitted works when these are communicated to the public." (Case C-607/11, paras. 24-26.) Some notable commentators have pointed to the flawless nature of CJEU's argumentation. As Ficsor noted:

"Article 11*bis*(1)(ii) of the Berne Convention provides for an exclusive right not only for retransmission by cable but also for rebroadcasting which means retransmission by wireless means; that is, by the same 'specific means' as what is used for broadcasting. There is no difference from the viewpoint of the applicability of this component of the right of communication to the public under its above-mentioned broad concept depending on the question of whether the subsequent communication is made by different technical means (in the case of Article 11bis(1)(ii), by wire) or by the same (in that case, by wireless means). This shows in an unequivocal manner that the 'specific technical means' theory is in conflict with international copyright norms and the EU rules implementing them; there is no element of those norms and rules or of their 'preparatory work' that would support it."
What are the dangers of the theory of "specific technical means" with respect to linking?

Further Case Law

BGH 17.7.2003 (I ZR 259/00) - Paperboy. In: *Gewerblicher Rechtsschutz und Urheberrecht*, Heft 11/2003, p. 958-963.

Case C-607/11 - ITV Broadcasting Ltd. and Others v. TVCatchup Ltd., Judgment of the Court (Fourth Chamber), 7 March 2013 [ECLI:EU:C:2013:147]

Case C-348/13 - BestWater International GmbH v. Michael Mebes and Stefan Potsch, Judgment of the Court (Ninth Chamber), 21 October 2014 [ECLI:EU:C:2014:2315]

Paramount Home Entertainment v. British Sky Broadcasting [2014] *EWHC* 937 (Ch)

Sądu Apelacyjnego w Warszawie, z dnia 7 maja 2014 r., I ACa 1663/13

BGH 9.7.2015 (I ZR 46/12) - Keine öffentliche Wiedergabe durch „Framing" - Die Realität II, *Gewerblicher Rechtsschutz und Urheberrecht*, Heft 2/2016, p. 171-176.

Case C-160/15 - GS Media BV v Sanoma Media Netherlands BV and Others, Judgment of the Court (Second Chamber), 8 September 2016 [ECLI:EU:C:2016:644]

BGH 21.9.2017 (I ZR 11/16) - Vorschaubilder III. In: *Gewerblicher Rechtsschutz und Urheberrecht*, Heft 2/2018, p. 178-189.

Warner Music UK Ltd., et al. v. TuneIn Inc. [2019] *EWHC* 2923 (Ch), 1 November 2019

Recommended readings

In English

Lionel Bently et al.: *The Reference to the CJEU in Case C-466/12 Svensson*, Legal Studies Research Paper Series, Paper No. 6/2013 (http://papers.ssrn.com/sol3/papers.cfm?abstract_id=2220326)

Jeremy de Beer - Mira Burri: Transatlantic Copyright Comparisons: Making Available via Hyperlinks in the European Union and Canada, *European Intellectual Property Review*, Issue 2/2014, p. 95-105.

Association Littéraire et Artistique Internationale: Report and Opinion on the Making Available and Communication to the Public in the Internet Environment - Focus on Linking Techniques on the Internet, *European Intellectual Property Review*, Issue 3/2014, p. 149-155.

Mihály J. Ficsor: Svensson: honest attempt at establishing due balance concerning the use of hyperlinks - spoiled by the erroneous „new public" theory, *Copyright See-Saw*, May 5, 2014 (http://www.copyrightseesaw.net/archive/?sw_10_item=63)

Andrew Moir - Rachel Montagnon - Heather Newton: Communication to the Public: the CJEU Finds Linking to Material Already "Freely Available" Cannot be Restricted by Copyright Owners: Nils Svensson and Others v. Retriever Sverige AB (C-466/12), *European Intellectual Property Review*, Issue 6/2014, p. 399-400.

Péter Mezei: Enter the Matrix: the Effects of the CJEU's Case Law on Linking and Beyond, *Journal of Intellectual Property Law & Practice*, Issue 10/2016, p. 778-794.

Christina Angelopoulos: Hyperlinks and Copyright Infringement, *The Cambridge Law Journal*, Issue 1/2017, p. 32-35.

Pauline McBride: The "New Public" Criterion after Svensson: The (Ir)relevance of Website Terms and Conditions, *Intellectual Property Quarterly*, Issue 3/2017, p. 262-285.

João Pedro Quintais: Untangling the Hyperlinking Web: In Search of the Online Right of Communication to the Public, *The Journal of World Intellectual Property*, Issue 5/2018, p. 385-420.

Irini Stamatoudi: *'Linking' and 'Browsing' in the Light of the EU Court of Justice's Case Law.* In: Tana Pistorius (Ed.): Intellectual Property Perspectives on the Regulation of New Technologies, Edward Elgar, Cheltenham, 2018, p. 179-207.

Jane Ginsburg - Alain Strowel: *Copyright Liability for Hyperlinking.* In: Tanya Aplin (Ed.): *Research Handbook on Intellectual Property and Digital Technologies*, Edward Elgar, Cheltenham, 2020, p. 217-245.

In French

Emmanuel Derieux: Lien hypertexte et droit d'auteur, *Droit de l'immatériel: informatique, médias, communication*, 2014, n° 102, p. 9-12.

Claude-Étienne Armingaud - Olivia Roche: Arrêts Bluetouff et Svensson: les contenus sur internet se conjuguent à l'imparfait du subjonctif, *Droit de l'immatériel: informatique, médias, communication*, 2014, n° 103, p. 9-14.
Lorette Dubois - Florence Gaullier: Les liens hypertextes après l'arrêt Svensson: quelles conséquences pratiques?, *Droit de l'immatériel: informatique, médias, communication*, 2014, n° 109, p. 57-63.
Sarah Dormont: La liberté de créer un lien hypertexte. Commentaire de l'arrêt CJUE, 13 février 2014, Svensson c/ Retriever Sverige AB, *Propriétés intellectuelles*, 2014, n° 52, p. 234-241.
Philippe Mouron: Les services d'enregistrement numérique, entre le droit de communication au public et l'exception de copie privée, *Droit de l'immatériel: informatique, médias, communication*, 2018, n° 148, p. 9-13.

In German
Michel M. Walter: Unionsrechtliche Relevanz von Hyperlinks, *Medien und Recht*, Heft 1/2014, p. 30-32.
Gregor Völtz: Das Kriterium der „neuen Öffentlichkeit" im Urheberrecht, *Computer und Recht*, Heft 11/2014, p. 721-726.

In Spanish
Aurelio López-Tarruella : La reforma del sistema de los derechos de autor en la Unión Europea. Estado de la cuestión, *Revista La Propiedad Inmaterial*, 22, julio-diciembre 2016 (https://ssrn.com/abstract=2900286)
Pablo Ramírez Silva: Los enlaces en Europa - El asunto Svensson (I): replica a la opinión de la European Copyright Society, *InDret*, vol. 2, 2013 (https://ssrn.com/abstract=2260216)

In Hungarian
Tóth Péter Benjamin: *Jogi felelősség hiperlink alkalmazásakor*, 2002: p. 1-34. (http://www.artisjus.hu/_userfiles/file/szerzoijogrol/hiperlink.pdf)
Mezei Péter: A linkelés szerzői jogi vonatkozásai - négyszögletes dugó a hatszögletű lyukba?, *Infokommunikáció és Jog*, 2015. március (61. szám), p. 30-39.
Szalay Klára - Polyák Gábor: Hírérték - hír, érték: A híraggregáció jogi megítélése a szerzői jog és a hírpiaci változások tükrében, *Magyar Jog*, 2018/12. szám, p. 679-689.

Case C-160/15 - Judgment of the Court (Second Chamber), 8 September 2016 [ECLI:EU:C:2016:644]

(...) Legal context

3 Recitals 3, 4, 9, 10, 23 and 31 of Directive 2001/29 state:

'(3) The proposed harmonisation will help to implement the four freedoms of the internal market and relates to compliance with the fundamental principles of law and especially of property, including intellectual property, and freedom of expression and the public interest.

(4) A harmonised legal framework on copyright and related rights, through increased legal certainty and while providing for a high level of protection of intellectual property, will foster substantial investment in creativity and innovation, including network infrastructure, and lead in turn to growth and increased competitiveness of European industry, both in the area of content provision and information technology and more generally across a wide range of industrial and cultural sectors.

(...)

(9) Any harmonisation of copyright and related rights must take as a basis a high level of protection, since such rights are crucial to intellectual creation. Their protection helps to ensure the maintenance and development of creativity in the interests of authors, performers, producers, consumers, culture, industry and the public at large. (...)

(10) If authors or performers are to continue their creative and artistic work, they have to receive an appropriate reward for the use of their work, as must producers in order to be able to finance this work. (...) Adequate legal protection of intellectual property rights is necessary in order to guarantee the availability of such a reward and provide the opportunity for satisfactory returns on this investment.

(...)

(23) This Directive should harmonise further the author's right of communication to the public. This right should be understood in a broad sense covering all communication to the public not present at the place where the communication originates.

(...)

(31) A fair balance of rights and interests between the different categories of rightholders, as well as between the different categories of rightholders and users of protected subject-matter must be safeguarded. The existing exceptions and limitations to the rights as set out by the Member States have to be reassessed in the light of the new electronic environment.'

4 Article 3 of that directive provides:

'1. Member States shall provide authors with the exclusive right to authorise or prohibit any communication to the public of their works, by wire or wireless means, including the making available to the public of their works in such a way that members of the public may access them from a place and at a time individually chosen by them.

(...)

3. The rights referred to in paragraphs 1 and 2 shall not be exhausted by any act of communication to the public or making available to the public as set out in this Article.'

5 According to Article 5(3) and (5) of that directive:

'3. Member States may provide for exceptions or limitations to the rights provided for in Articles 2 and 3 in the following cases:

(...)

c) reproduction by the press, communication to the public or making available of published articles on current economic, political or religious topics or of broadcast works or other subject-matter of the same character, in cases where such use is not expressly reserved, and as long as the source, including the author's name, is indicated, or use of works or other subject-matter in connection with the reporting of current events, to the extent justified by the informatory purpose and as long as the source, including the author's name, is indicated, unless this turns out to be impossible;

(...)

5. The exceptions and limitations provided for in paragraphs 1, 2, 3 and 4 shall only be applied in certain special cases which do not conflict with a normal exploitation of the work or other subject-matter and do not unreasonably prejudice the legitimate interests of the rightholder.'

The dispute in the main proceedings and the questions referred for a preliminary ruling

6 At the request of Sanoma, which is the publisher of Playboy magazine, on 13 and 14 October 2011 the photographer, Mr C. Hermès, took the photos at issue, which were to be published in the December 2011 edition of that magazine. In that context, Mr Hermès granted Sanoma authorisation, on an exclusive basis, to publish those photos. He also granted Sanoma authorisation to exercise the rights and powers arising from his copyright.

7 GS Media operates the website GeenStijl, which includes, according to information provided by that website, 'news, scandalous revelations and investigative journalism with lighthearted items and wacky nonsense' and which is viewed daily by more than 230 000 visitors, making it one of the 10 most visited websites in the area of news in the Netherlands.

8 On 26 October 2011, the editors of the GeenStijl website received a message from a person using a pseudonym, which included a hyperlink to an electronic file hosted on the website Filefactory.com ('the Filefactory website'), located in Australia and dedicated to data storage. That electronic file contained the photos at issue.

9 On the same day, Sanoma asked GS Media's parent company to prevent the photos at issue being published on the GeenStijl website.

10 On 27 October 2011, an article relating to those photos of Ms Dekker, entitled '...! Nude photos of ... [Ms] Dekker', was published on the GeenStijl website, which included part of one of the photos at issue, and which ended with the following words: 'And now the link with the pics you've been waiting for.' By clicking on a hyperlink accompanying that text, users were directed to the Filefactory website, on which another hyperlink allowed them to download 11 electronic files each containing one of those photos.

11 On the same day, Sanoma sent GS Media's parent company an email demanding that it confirm that the hyperlink to the photos at issue had been removed from the GeenStijl website. GS Media failed to respond to that demand.

12 However, at Sanoma's request, the photos at issue appearing on the Filefactory website were removed.

13 By letter of 7 November 2011, counsel for Sanoma and Others demanded that GS Media remove from the GeenStijl website the article of 27 October 2011, including the hyperlink, the photographs it contained and the reactions of users published on the same page of that website.

14 On the same day, an article about the dispute between GS Media and Sanoma and Others about the photos at issue was published on the GeenStijl website. That article ended with the following sentence: 'Update: Not yet seen the nude pics of [Ms. Dekker]? They are HERE.' That announcement was, once again, accompanied by a hyperlink to access the website Imageshack.us where one or more of the relevant photographs could be viewed. The operator of that website, however, also subsequently complied with Sanoma's request to remove them.

15 A third article, entitled 'Bye Bye Wave Wave Playboy', again contained a hyperlink to the photos at issue, appeared on 17 November 2011 on the GeenStijl website. Forum users of that website then posted new links to other websites where the photos at issue could be viewed.

16 In December 2011, the photos at issue were published in *Playboy* magazine.

17 Sanoma and Others brought an action before the rechtbank Amsterdam (Amsterdam District Court, Netherlands), claiming, in particular, that by posting hyperlinks and a cutout of one of the photos at issue on the GeenStijl website, GS Media had infringed Mr Hermès' copyright and acted unlawfully towards Sanoma and Others. The rechtbank Amsterdam (Amsterdam District Court) largely upheld that action.

18 The Gerechtshof Amsterdam (Amsterdam Court of Appeal, the Netherlands) set aside that decision, finding that, by posting the hyperlinks on the GeenStijl website, GS Media had not infringed Mr Hermès' copyright, since the photos at issue had already been made public before they were posted on the Filefactory website. In contrast, it found that, by posting those links, GS Media acted unlawfully toward Sanoma and Others, as visitors to that website accordingly were encouraged to view the photos at issue which were illegally posted on the Filefactory website. Without those hyperlinks, those photos would not have been easy to find. In addition, the Gerechtshof Amsterdam (Amsterdam Court of Appeal) held that, by posting a cutout of one of the photos at issue on the GeenStijl website, GS Media had infringed Mr Hermès' copyright.

19 GS Media brought an appeal against that judgment before the referring court, the Hoge Raad der Nederlanden (Supreme Court of the Netherlands).

20 Sanoma and Others brought a cross-appeal, in which they refer in particular to the judgment of *Svensson and Others*, claiming that the fact of making a hyperlink available to internet users to a website on which a work has been posted without the consent of the latter's copyright holder constitutes a communication to the public. Sanoma and Others submit, moreover, that access to the photos at issue on the Filefactory website was protected by restrictions within the meaning of that judgment which internet users could circumvent through the intervention of GS Media and its GeenStijl website, so that those photos have been made available to a wider public than the public which would normally have accessed those photos on the Filefactory website.

21 In the context of examining that cross-appeal, the referring court considers that it cannot be inferred with sufficient certainty either from the judgment of *Svensson and Others* or from the order of *BestWater* whether there is a 'communication to the public' if the work has in fact previously been published, but without the consent of the copyright holder.

22 On the one hand, it follows from that case-law of the Court that it must be established whether the intervention at issue enables a public to be reached which cannot be considered to have been included in the public for which the rightholder had previously given his consent, which is consistent with his exclusive right to exploit the work. On the other hand, if a work is already available on the internet for the general public, posting a hyperlink to the website on which the work is already posted will result in virtually no new public being reached. Furthermore, the fact that there are many works on the internet that have been communicated to the public without the rightholder's consent must also be taken into account. For the operator of a website it will not always be easy to check, if he intends to post a hyperlink to a website on which a work appears, that the rightholder has consented to the earlier posting of that work.

23 The referring court further observes, moreover, that the cross-appeal also raises the question of the conditions that must be met if they are to constitute 'restrictions' within the meaning of the judgment of *Svensson and Others*. That court points out, in that regard, that the photos at issue were not impossible to find on the internet before GS Media posted the hyperlink on the GeenStijl website, without however being easy to find, so the fact of posting that link on its site greatly facilitated access to those photos.

24 In those circumstances, the Hoge Raad der Nederlanden (Supreme Court of the Netherlands) decided to stay the proceedings and to refer the following questions to the Court of Justice for a preliminary ruling:

'1. *(a) If anyone other than the copyright holder refers by means of a hyperlink on a website controlled by him to a website which is managed by a third party and is accessible to the general internet public, on which the work has been made available without the consent of the rightholder, does that constitute a "communication to the public" within the meaning of Article 3(1) of Directive 2001/29?*

(b) Does it make any difference if the work was also not previously communicated, with the rightholder's consent, to the public in some other way?

(c) Is it important whether the 'hyperlinker' is or ought to be aware of the lack of consent by the rightholder for the placement of the work on the third party's website mentioned in 1(a) above and, as the case may be, of the fact that the work has also not previously been communicated, with the rightholder's consent, to the public in some other way?

2. *(a) If Question 1 is answered in the negative: If the answer to question 1(a) is in the negative: in that case, is there, or could there be deemed to be, a communication to the public if the website to which the hyperlink refers, and thus the work, is indeed findable for the general internet public, but not easily so, with the result that the publication of the hyperlink greatly facilitates the finding of the work?*

(b) In answering question 2(a), is it important whether the "hyperlinker" is or ought to be aware of the fact that the website to which the hyperlink refers is not easily findable by the general internet public?
3. Are there other circumstances which should be taken into account when answering the question whether there is deemed to be a communication to the public if, by means of a hyperlink, access is provided to a work which has not previously been communicated to the public with the consent of the rightholder?'

Consideration of the questions referred

25 By its three questions, which should be examined together, the referring court asks, in essence, whether, and in what possible circumstances, the fact of posting, on a website, a hyperlink to protected works, freely available on another website without the consent of the copyright holder, constitutes a 'communication to the public' within the meaning of Article 3(1) of Directive 2001/29.

26 In that context, it raises the question of the relevance of the fact that the works in question have not yet been published in another way with the consent of that rightholder, that providing those hyperlinks makes it much easier to find those works, given that the website on which they are available is not easily findable by the general internet public, and that whoever posts those links knew or ought to have been aware of those facts and the fact that that rightholder did not consent to the publication of the works in question on that latter website.

27 It follows from Article 3(1) of Directive 2001/29 that Member States are to provide authors with the exclusive right to authorise or prohibit any communication to the public of their works, by wire or wireless means, including the making available to the public of their works in such a way that members of the public may access them from a place and at a time individually chosen by them.

28 Under that provision, authors thus have a right which is preventive in nature and allows them to intervene, between possible users of their work and the communication to the public which such users might contemplate making, in order to prohibit such use.

29 As Article 3(1) of Directive 2001/29 does not define the concept of 'communication to the public', its meaning and its scope must be determined in light of the objectives pursued by that directive and of the context in which the provision being interpreted is set.

30 In that regard, it should be borne in mind that it follows from recitals 9 and 10 of Directive 2001/29 that the latter's objective is to establish a high level of protection of authors, allowing them to obtain an appropriate reward for the use of their works, including on the occasion of communication to the public. It follows that 'communication to the public' must be interpreted broadly, as recital 23 of the directive indeed expressly states.

31 At the same time, it follows from recitals 3 and 31 of Directive 2001/29 that the harmonisation effected by it is to maintain, in particular in the electronic environment, a fair balance between, on one hand, the interests of copyright holders and related rights in protecting their intellectual property rights, safeguarded by Article 17(2) of the Charter of Fundamental Rights of the European Union ('the Charter') and, on the other, the protection of the interests and fundamental rights of users of protected objects, in particular their freedom of expression and of information, safeguarded by Article 11 of the Charter, and of the general interest.

32 As the Court has previously held, the concept of 'communication to the public' includes two cumulative criteria, namely, an 'act of communication' of a work and the communication of that work to a 'public'.

33 The Court has, moreover, specified that the concept of 'communication to the public' requires an individual assessment.

34 For the purposes of such an assessment, account has to be taken of several complementary criteria, which are not autonomous and are interdependent. Since those criteria may, in different situations, be present to widely varying degrees, they must be applied both individually and in their interaction with one another.

35 Of those criteria, the Court emphasised, in the first place, the indispensable role played by the user and the deliberate nature of its intervention. The user makes an act of communication when it intervenes, in full knowledge of the consequences of its action, to give access to a protected work to its customers, and does so, in particular, where, in the absence of that intervention, its customers would not, in principle, be able to enjoy the broadcast work.

36 In the second place, it specified that the concept of the 'public' refers to an indeterminate number of potential viewers and implies, moreover, a fairly large number of people.

37 Moreover, it is settled case-law of the Court that, to be categorised as a 'communication to the public', a protected work must be communicated using specific technical means,

different from those previously used or, failing that, to a 'new public', that is to say, to a public that was not already taken into account by the copyright holders when they authorised the initial communication to the public of their work.

38 In the third place, the Court has held that it is relevant that a 'communication', within the meaning of Article 3(1) of Directive 2001/29, is of a profit-making nature.

39 It is in the light, in particular, of those criteria that it is to be assessed whether, in a situation such as that at issue in the main proceedings, the fact of posting, on a website, a hyperlink to protected works, which are freely available on another website without the consent of the copyright holder, constitutes a 'communication to the public' within the meaning of Article 3(1) of Directive 2001/29.

40 In that regard, it should be recalled that, in the judgment of *Svensson and Others*, the Court interpreted Article 3(1) of Directive 2001/29 as meaning that posting hyperlinks on a website to works freely available on another website does not constitute a 'communication to the public' as covered by that provision. That interpretation was also adopted in the order of *BestWater International* about such links using the technique known as 'transclusion' ('framing').

41 However, it follows from the reasoning of those decisions that, by them, the Court intended to refer only to the posting of hyperlinks to works which have been made freely available on another website with the consent of the rightholder, the Court having concluded that there was no communication to the public on the ground that the act of communication in question was not made to a new public.

42 In that context, it noted that, given that the hyperlink and the website to which it refers give access to the protected work using the same technical means, namely the internet, such a link must be directed to a new public. Where that is not the case, in particular, due to the fact that the work is already freely available to all internet users on another website with the authorisation of the copyright holders, that act cannot be categorised as a 'communication to the public' within the meaning of Article 3(1) of Directive 2001/29. Indeed, as soon as and as long as that work is freely available on the website to which the hyperlink allows access, it must be considered that, where the copyright holders of that work have consented to such a communication, they have included all internet users as the public.

43 Accordingly, it cannot be inferred either from the judgment of *Svensson and Others* or from the order of *BestWater International* that posting, on a website, hyperlinks to protected

works which have been made freely available on another website, but without the consent of the copyright holders of those works, would be excluded, as a matter of principle, from the concept of 'communication to the public' within the meaning of Article 3(1) of Directive 2001/29. Rather, those decisions confirm the importance of such consent under that provision, as the latter specifically provides that every act of communication of a work to the public is to be authorised by the copyright holder.

44 GS Media, the German, Portuguese and Slovak Governments and the European Commission claim, however, that the fact of automatically categorising all posting of such links to works published on other websites as 'communication to the public', since the copyright holders of those works have not consented to that publication on the internet, would have highly restrictive consequences for freedom of expression and of information and would not be consistent with the right balance which Directive 2001/29 seeks to establish between that freedom and the public interest on the one hand, and the interests of copyright holders in an effective protection of their intellectual property, on the other.

45 In that regard, it should be noted that the internet is in fact of particular importance to freedom of expression and of information, safeguarded by Article 11 of the Charter, and that hyperlinks contribute to its sound operation as well as to the exchange of opinions and information in that network characterised by the availability of immense amounts of information.

46 Furthermore, it may be difficult, in particular for individuals who wish to post such links, to ascertain whether website to which those links are expected to lead, provides access to works which are protected and, if necessary, whether the copyright holders of those works have consented to their posting on the internet. Such ascertaining is all the more difficult where those rights have been the subject of sub-licenses. Moreover, the content of a website to which a hyperlink enables access may be changed after the creation of that link, including the protected works, without the person who created that link necessarily being aware of it.

47 For the purposes of the individualised assessment of the existence of a 'communication to the public' within the meaning of Article 3(1) of Directive 2001/29, it is accordingly necessary, when the posting of a hyperlink to a work freely available on another website is carried out by a person who, in so doing, does not pursue a profit, to take account of the fact that that person does not know and cannot reasonably know, that that work had been published on the internet without the consent of the copyright holder.

48 Indeed, such a person, by making that work available to the public by providing other internet users with direct access to it does not, as a general rule, intervene in full knowledge of the consequences of his conduct in order to give customers access to a work illegally posted on the internet. In addition, where the work in question was already available with unrestricted access on the website to which the hyperlink provides access, all internet users could, in principle, already have access to it even the absence of that intervention.

49 In contrast, where it is established that such a person knew or ought to have known that the hyperlink he posted provides access to a work illegally placed on the internet, for example owing to the fact that he was notified thereof by the copyright holders, it is necessary to consider that the provision of that link constitutes a 'communication to the public' within the meaning of Article 3(1) of Directive 2001/29.

50 The same applies in the event that that link allows users of the website on which it is posted to circumvent the restrictions taken by the site where the protected work is posted in order to restrict the public's access to its own subscribers, the posting of such a link then constituting a deliberate intervention without which those users could not benefit from the works broadcast.

51 Furthermore, when the posting of hyperlinks is carried out for profit, it can be expected that the person who posted such a link carries out the necessary checks to ensure that the work concerned is not illegally published on the website to which those hyperlinks lead, so that it must be presumed that that posting has occurred with the full knowledge of the protected nature of that work and the possible lack of consent to publication on the internet by the copyright holder. In such circumstances, and in so far as that rebuttable presumption is not rebutted, the act of posting a hyperlink to a work which was illegally placed on the internet constitutes a 'communication to the public' within the meaning of Article 3(1) of Directive 2001/29.

52 However, if there is no new public, there will be no communication to the 'public' within the meaning of that provision in the event that, referred to in paragraphs 40 to 42 of the present judgment, the works to which those hyperlinks allow access have been made freely available on another website with the consent of the rightholder.

53 Such an interpretation of Article 3(1) of Directive 2001/29 provides the high level of protection for authors sought by that directive. Indeed, under that directive and within the limits set by Article 5(3) thereof, copyright holders may act not only against the initial publication of their work on a website, but also against any person posting for profit a hyperlink to the

work illegally published on that website and, under the conditions set out in paragraphs 49 and 50 of the present judgment, against persons having posted such links without pursuing financial gain. In that regard, it should in particular be noted that those rightholders, in all cases, have the possibility of informing such persons of the illegal nature of the publication of their work on the internet and of taking action against them if they refuse to remove that link, and those persons may not rely upon one of the exceptions listed in Article 5(3).

54 As regards the case in the main proceedings, it is undisputed that GS Media operates the GeenStijl website and that it provided the hyperlinks to the files containing the photos at issue, hosted on the Filefactory website, for profit. It is also undisputed that Sanoma had not authorised the publication of those photos on the internet. Moreover, it appears to follow from the presentation of the facts, as they result from the order for reference, that GS Media was aware of that latter fact and that it cannot therefore rebut the presumption that the posting of those links occurred in full knowledge of the illegal nature of that publication. In those circumstances, it appears that, subject to the checks to be made by the referring court, by posting those links, GS Media effected a 'communication to the public', within the meaning of Article 3(1) of Directive 2001/29, and it is unnecessary to assess in that context the other circumstances referred to by that court, referred to in paragraph 26 of the present judgment.

55 Having regard to the foregoing considerations, the answer to the questions raised is that Article 3(1) of Directive 2001/29 must be interpreted as meaning that, in order to establish whether the fact of posting, on a website, hyperlinks to protected works, which are freely available on another website without the consent of the copyright holder, constitutes a 'communication to the public' within the meaning of that provision, it is to be determined whether those links are provided without the pursuit of financial gain by a person who did not know or could not reasonably have known the illegal nature of the publication of those works on that other website or whether, on the contrary, those links are provided for such a purpose, a situation in which that knowledge must be presumed. (...)

THINK IT OVER!

1. In *Svensson*, the CJEU discussed whether copyright protected journal articles that were lawfully published on Göteborgs Posten's website can be hyperlinked. In *BestWater*, the CJEU sidestepped the important fact that the video embedded by the defendant was unlawfully uploaded to YouTube. In *GS Media*, the CJEU could not further evade discussing the issue of the lawfulness of the protected subject matter (here photographs). The Court tried to provide a balanced answer by differentiating between non-profit and for-profit uses, and concluded that the subjective knowledge of the user is relevant in determining his liability. The introduction of such a concept of subjective liability into European copyright law received open criticism among scholars. This is mainly because liability has generally been objective in the copyright systems of the EU Member States. (Knowledge can be relevant when it comes to damages.)

2. The CJEU's arguments have been refuted by the German Federal Supreme Court (BGH) in the *Vorschaubilder III* case. The BGH argued that the preliminary ruling of the CJEU in *GS Media does not apply to Google Images because of the particular importance of search services for the functioning of the Internet.*

3. In April 2017, as a next step in the European linking saga, the CJEU concluded in *Stichting Brein v. Jack Frederik Wullens* (the *Filmspeler* case) that the selling of set-top boxes with pre-installed add-ons that automatically directed end users to websites through which unlawful materials were accessible constituted communication to the public. *Is this kind of interpretation in line with the original purposes of the right of communication to the public, or does the Filmspeler ruling stretch this right?*

Further Case Law

BGH 17.7.2003 (I ZR 259/00) - Paperboy. In: *Gewerblicher Rechtsschutz und Urheberrecht*, Heft 11/2003, p. 958-963.

Case C-466/12 - Nils Svensson and Others v. Retriever Sverige AB, Judgment of the Court (Fourth Chamber), 13 February 2014 [ECLI:EU:C:2014:76]

Case C-348/13 - BestWater International GmbH v. Michael Mebes and Stefan Potsch, Judgment of the Court (Ninth Chamber), 21 October 2014 [ECLI:EU:C:2014:2315]

Case C-527/15 - Stichting Brein v. Jack Frederik Wullens, Judgment of the Court (Second Chamber), 26 April 2017 [ECLI:EU:C:2017:300]

BGH 21.9.2017 (I ZR 11/16) - Vorschaubilder III. In: *Gewerblicher Rechtsschutz und Urheberrecht*, Heft 2/2018, p. 178-189.

Recommended readings

In English

Jörg Wimmers - Malek Barudi - Adam Rendle: The CJEU's Communication to the Public: Better Check Before Placing a Hyperlink?, *Computer Law Review International*, Issue 5/2016, p. 129-133.

Emma Linklater: Oh Boy, Playboy: Profit-making Motive and Knowledge of the Illegality of Unauthorised Content Make Hyperlinking a Communication to the Public, *European Law Reporter*, Issue 5/2016, p. 208-212.

Bianca Hanuz: Linking to unauthorized content after the CJEU GS Media decision, *Gewerblicher Rechtsschutz und Urheberrecht Internationaler Teil*, Issue 2/2017, p. 97-98.

Birgit Clark - Julia Dickenson: Theseus and the Labyrinth? An Overview of "Communication to the Public" under EU Copyright Law: After Reha Training and GS Media Where are we Now and Where do we Go from Here?, *European Intellectual Property Review*, Issue 5/2017, p. 265-278.

Eleonora Rosati: GS Media and its Implications for the Construction of the Right of Communication to the Public Within EU Copyright Architecture, *Common Market Law Review*, Issue 4/2017, p. 1221-1242.

Irini Stamatoudi: *'Linking' and 'Browsing' in the Light of the EU Court of Justice's Case Law.* In: Tana Pistorius (Ed.): Intellectual Property Perspectives on the Regulation of New Technologies, Edward Elgar, Cheltenham, 2018, p. 179-207.

Eleonora Rosati: *Linking and Copyright: Easier at Last? First National Applications of the CJEU GS Media Judgment.* In: Tatiana-Eleni Synodinou - Philippe Jougleux - Christiana Markou - Thalia Prastitou (Ed.): *EU Internet Law in the Digital Era - Regulation and Enforcement*, Springer, Cham, 2020, p. 61-78.

Jane Ginsburg - Alain Strowel: *Copyright Liability for Hyperlinking.* In: Tanya Aplin (Ed.): *Research Handbook on Intellectual Property and Digital Technologies*, Edward Elgar, Cheltenham, 2020, p. 217-245.

In French

Lionel Costes: Liens hypertextes renvoyant à des contenus protégés par le droit d'auteur et acte de «comunication au public», *Droit de l'immatériel: informatique, médias, communication*, 2016 Juin n° 127, p. 13-14.

Fabienne Gazin: Les liens hypertexte renvoyant vers des sites permettant le téléchargement d'oeuvres protégées constituent-il des actes de communication au public? Position mesurée du juge..., *Europe*, 2016 Novembre Comm. n° 11, p. 38.

Laure Marino: Liens hypertexte et droit d'auteur : à la rencontre de la troisième voie, *La Semaine Juridique - édition générale*, 2016 n° 46, p. 2090-2092.

In German

Ole Jani - Frederik Leenen: Paradigmenwechsel bei Links und Framings, *Neue juristische Wochenschrift*, Heft 43/2016 p. 3135-3138.

Caroline Volkmann: Verlinkung & Haftung: Bedeutet die EuGH-Trilogie das Aus für die Informationsfreiheit und den Meinungsaustausch im Internet?, *Computer und Recht*, Heft 1/2017, p. 36-43.

Angela Hildebrand: Die Bedeutung der EuGH-Urteile »ACI Adam« und »GS Media« für die deutsche Privatkopieschranke, *Zeitschrift für Urheber- und Medienrecht*, Heft 1/2017, p. 16-23.

Michel M. Walter: Öffentliche Wiedergabe und Hyperlinking, *MR-Int: Internationale Rundschau zum Medienrecht, IP- & IT-Recht*, Heft 1/2017, p. 27-29.

In Hungarian

Grad-Gyenge Anikó: A jogsértésért való felelősség vagy a nyilvánossághoz közvetítési jog új határai, *Iparjogvédelmi és Szerzői Jogi Szemle*, 2017/5. szám, p. 7-14.

Ferge Zsigmond: Médialejátszók és online megosztóplatformok, avagy hogyan értelmezte az Európai Bíróság a nyilvánossághoz közvetítés fogalmát a Stichting Brein, szerzői jogok jogosultjainak érdekeit védő alapítvány kontra Jack Frederik Wullems-, valamint a Ziggo BV és XS4ALL Internet BV-ügyben hozott ítéletében, *Iparjogvédelmi és Szerzői Jogi Szemle*, 2017/5. szám, p. 15-46.

STICHTING BREIN V. JACK FREDERIK WULLEMS

Case C-527/15 - Judgment of the Court (Second Chamber), 26 April 2017 [ECLI:EU:C:2017:300]

(...) Legal context

EU law

3 Recitals 9, 10, 23, 27 and 33 of Directive 2001/29 state:

'(9) Any harmonisation of copyright and related rights must take as a basis a high level of protection, since such rights are crucial to intellectual creation. Their protection helps to ensure the maintenance and development of creativity in the interests of authors, performers, producers, consumers, culture, industry and the public at large. Intellectual property has therefore been recognised as an integral part of property.

(10) If authors or performers are to continue their creative and artistic work, they have to receive an appropriate reward for the use of their work, as must producers in order to be able to finance this work. The investment required to produce products such as phonograms, films or multimedia

products, and services such as "on-demand" services, is considerable. Adequate legal protection of intellectual property rights is necessary in order to guarantee the availability of such a reward and provide the opportunity for satisfactory returns on this investment.

(...)

(23) This Directive should harmonise further the author's right of communication to the public. This right should be understood in a broad sense covering all communication to the public not present at the place where the communication originates. This right should cover any such transmission or retransmission of a work to the public by wire or wireless means, including broadcasting. This right should not cover any other acts.

(...)

(27) The mere provision of physical facilities for enabling or making a communication does not in itself amount to communication within the meaning of this Directive.

(...)

(33) The exclusive right of reproduction should be subject to an exception to allow certain acts of temporary reproduction, which are transient or incidental reproductions, forming an integral and essential part of a technological process and carried out for the sole purpose of enabling either efficient transmission in a network between third parties by an intermediary, or a lawful use of a work or other subject matter to be made. The acts of reproduction concerned should have no separate economic value on their own. To the extent that they meet these conditions, this exception should include acts which enable browsing as well as acts of caching to take place, including those which enable transmission systems to function efficiently, provided that the intermediary does not modify the information and does not interfere with the lawful use of technology, widely recognised and used by industry, to obtain data on the use of the information. A use should be considered lawful where it is authorised by the rightholder or not restricted by law.'

4 Article 2 of Directive 2001/29, entitled 'Reproduction right', reads as follows:
'Member States shall provide for the exclusive right to authorise or prohibit direct or indirect, temporary or permanent reproduction by any means and in any form, in whole or in part:

(a) for authors, of their works;

(b) for performers, of fixations of their performances;

(c) for phonogram producers, of their phonograms;

(d) for the producers of the first fixations of films, in respect of the original and copies of their films;

(e) for broadcasting organisations, of fixations of their broadcasts, whether these broadcasts are transmitted by wire or over the air, including by cable or satellite.'

5 Article 3 of that directive, entitled 'Right of communication to the public of works and right of making available to the public other subject matter', states:

'1. Member States shall provide authors with the exclusive right to authorise or prohibit any communication to the public of their works, by wire or wireless means, including the making available to the public of their works in such a way that members of the public may access them from a place and at a time individually chosen by them.
2. Member States shall provide for the exclusive right to authorise or prohibit the making available to the public, by wire or wireless means, in such a way that members of the public may access them from a place and at a time individually chosen by them:
(a) for performers, of fixations of their performances;
(b) for phonogram producers, of their phonograms;
(c) for the producers of the first fixations of films, in respect of the original and copies of their films;
(d) for broadcasting organisations, of fixations of their broadcasts, whether these broadcasts are transmitted by wire or over the air, including by cable or satellite.

3. The rights referred to in paragraphs 1 and 2 shall not be exhausted by any act of communication to the public or making available to the public as set out in this Article.'

6 Article 5(1) and (5) of that directive provides:
'1. Temporary acts of reproduction referred to in Article 2, which are transient or incidental [and] an integral and essential part of a technological process and whose sole purpose is to enable:
(a) a transmission in a network between third parties by an intermediary, or
(b) a lawful use of a work or other subject matter to be made, and which have no independent economic significance, shall be exempted from the reproduction right provided for in Article 2.
(...)

5. The exceptions and limitations provided for in paragraphs 1, 2, 3 and 4 shall only be applied in certain special cases which do not conflict with a normal exploitation of the work or other subject matter and do not unreasonably prejudice the legitimate interests of the rightholder.'

Netherlands law

7 Article 1 of the Auteurswet (Netherlands Law on copyright, 'the Law on copyright') provides:
'Copyright is the exclusive right of the author of a literary, scientific or artistic work or his successors in title, to publish it and to reproduce it, subject to the limitations laid down by law.'

8 Article 12 of the Law on copyright is worded as follows:
'1. Publication of a literary, scientific or artistic work shall include:
1° the publication of a reproduction of the work, in full or in part;'

9 Article 13a of that law provides:

'Reproduction of a literary, scientific or artistic work shall not include a temporary act of reproduction which is transient or incidental, and an integral and essential part of a technological process and whose sole purpose is to enable

(a) the transmission in a network between third parties by an intermediary, or

(b) the lawful use of a work, and which has no independent economic significance.'

10 Article 2 of the Wet op de Naburige Rechten (Law on neighbouring rights) provides:

'1. A performer shall have the exclusive right to authorise one or more of the following acts:

(...)

d. the broadcast, repeat broadcast, making available to the public or any other form of communication of a performance, a recording of a performance or a reproduction thereof.'

11 Article 6 of the Law on neighbouring rights provides:

'1. A phonogram producer shall have the exclusive right to authorise:

(...)

c. the broadcast, repeat broadcast, making available to the public or other form of publication of a phonogram manufactured by him or a reproduction thereof.'

12 Article 7a of the Law on neighbouring rights is worded as follows:

'1. The producer of the first fixations of films shall have the exclusive right to authorise:

(...)

c. the making available to the public of the first fixation of a film or a reproduction thereof.'

13 Article 8 of the Law on neighbouring rights provides:

'A broadcasting organisation shall have the exclusive right to authorise one or more of the following acts:

(...)

e. the making available to the public of recordings of programmes or reproductions thereof or any other form of publication thereof, whatever the technical facilities used for that purpose.'

The dispute in the main proceedings and the questions referred for a preliminary ruling

14 Stichting Brein is a Netherlands foundation for the protection of the interests of copyright holders.

15 Mr Wullems sells, on a number of internet sites, including his own site www.filmspeler.nl, various models of a multimedia player. That player, sold under the name 'filmspeler', is a device which acts as a medium between, on the one hand, a source of visual and/or sound data and, on the other hand, a television screen.

16 On that player, Mr Wullems installed an open source software, which makes it possible to play files through a user-friendly interface via structured menus, and integrated into it, without alteration, add-ons available on the internet, created by third parties, some of which specifically link to websites on which protected works are made available to internet users without the consent of the copyright holders.

17 Those add-ons contain links which, when they are activated by the remote control of the multimedia player, connect to streaming websites operated by third parties, some of which give access to digital content with the authorisation of the copyright holders, whilst others give access to such content without their consent. In particular, the add-ons' function is to retrieve the desired content from streaming websites and make it start playing, with a simple click, on the multimedia player sold by Mr Wullems connected to a television screen.

18 As is clear from the order for reference, Mr Wullems advertised the 'filmspeler' multimedia player, stating that it made it possible, in particular, to watch on a television screen, freely and easily, audiovisual material available on the internet without the consent of the copyright holders.

19 On 22 May 2014 Stichting Brein asked Mr Wullems to stop selling the multimedia player. On 1 July 2014, it brought an action against Mr Wullems before the referring court seeking an order that, in essence, he stop selling multimedia players such as 'filmspeler' and offering hyperlinks that give users illegal access to protected works.

20 Before the referring court, Stichting Brein submitted that, by marketing the 'filmspeler' multimedia player, Mr Wullems made a 'communication to the public', in breach of Articles 1 and 12 of the Law on copyright and Articles 2, 6, 7a and 8 of the Law on neighbouring rights. Those provisions must, it submitted, be interpreted in the light of Article 3 of Directive 2001/29, which they transpose into the Netherlands law. The referring court considers, in that regard, that the case-law of the Court does not make it possible to answer with certainty the question of whether there is a communication to the public in circumstances such as those at issue in the main proceedings.

21 In addition, before the referring court, Mr Wullems submitted that streaming broadcasts of works protected by copyright from an illegal source was covered by the exception listed in Article 13a of the Law on copyright, which must be interpreted in the light of Article 5(1) of Directive 2001/29, which it transposes into Netherlands law. According to the referring court, the Court has not yet given a ruling on the meaning of the requirement of a 'lawful use' within the meaning of Article 5(1)(b) of Directive 2001/29.

22 In those circumstances, the Rechtbank Midden-Nederland (District Court, Midden-Nederland, Netherlands) decided to stay the proceedings and to refer the following questions to the Court of Justice for a preliminary ruling:

'(1) Must Article 3(1) of Directive 2001/29 be interpreted as meaning that there is "a communication to the public" within the meaning of that provision, when someone sells a product (multimedia player) in which he has installed add-ons containing hyperlinks to websites on which copyright-protected works, such as films, series and live broadcasts are made directly accessible, without the authorisation of the right holders?

(2) Does it make any difference

– whether the copyright-protected works as a whole have not previously been published on the internet or have only been published through subscriptions with the authorisation of the right holder?

– whether the add-ons containing hyperlinks to websites on which copyright-protected works are made directly accessible without the authorisation of the right holders are freely available and can also be installed in the multimedia player by the users themselves?

– whether the websites and thus the copyright-protected works made accessible thereon – without the authorisation of the right holders – can also be accessed by the public without the multimedia player?

(3) Should Article 5 of Directive 2001/29 be interpreted as meaning that there is no "lawful use" within the meaning of Article 5(1)(b) of that directive if a temporary reproduction is made by an end user during the streaming of a copyright-protected work from a third-party website where that copyright-protected work is offered without the authorisation of the right holder(s)?

(4) If the answer to the third question is in the negative, is the making of a temporary reproduction by an end user during the streaming of a copyright-protected work from a website where that copyright-protected work is offered without the authorisation of the right holder(s) then contrary to the "three-step test" referred to in Article 5(5) of Directive 2001/29?'

Consideration of the questions referred

The first and second questions

23 By its first and second questions, which should be examined together, the referring court asks, in essence, whether the concept of 'communication to the public', within the meaning of Article 3(1) of Directive 2001/29, must be interpreted as covering the sale of a multimedia player, such as that at issue in the main proceedings, on which there are pre-installed add-ons, available on the internet, containing hyperlinks to websites – that are freely accessible to the public – on which copyright-protected works have been made available to the public without the consent of the right holders.

24 It follows from Article 3(1) of Directive 2001/29 that Member States are to provide authors with the exclusive right to authorise or prohibit any communication to the public of their works, by wire or wireless means, including the making available to the public of their works in such a way that members of the public may access them from a place and at a time individually chosen by them.

25 Under that provision, authors thus have a right which is preventive in nature and allows them to intervene between possible users of their work and the communication to the public which such users might contemplate making, in order to prohibit such communication.

26 As Article 3(1) of Directive 2001/29 does not define the concept of 'communication to the public', its meaning and its scope must be determined in light of the objectives pursued by that directive and the context in which the provision being interpreted is set.

27 In that regard, it should be borne in mind that it follows from recitals 9 and 10 of Directive 2001/29 that the latter's objective is to establish a high level of protection for authors, allowing them to obtain an appropriate reward for the use of their works, including on the occasion of communication to the public. It follows that 'communication to the public' must be interpreted broadly, as recital 23 of the directive indeed expressly states.

28 The Court has also specified that the concept of 'communication to the public', within the meaning of Article 3(1) of Directive 2001/29, requires an individual assessment.

29 It is clear from Article 3(1) of Directive 2001/29 that the concept of 'communication to the public' includes two cumulative criteria, namely an 'act of communication' of a work and the communication of that work to a 'public'.

30 In order to determine whether a user is making a communication to the public within the meaning of Article 3(1) of Directive 2001/29 it is necessary to take into account several complementary criteria, which are not autonomous and are interdependent. Consequently, those criteria must be applied both individually and in their interaction with one another, since they may, in different situations, be present to widely varying degrees.

31 Amongst those criteria, the Court has emphasised, above all, the essential role played by the user. The user makes an act of communication when he intervenes, in full knowledge of the consequences of his action, to give access to a protected work to his customers and does so, in particular, where, in the absence of that intervention, his customers would not, in principle, be able to enjoy the broadcast work.

32 Next, it has specified that the concept of the 'public' refers to an indeterminate number of potential viewers and implies, moreover, a fairly large number of people.

33 The Court has also noted that, according to a settled line of case-law, to be categorised as a 'communication to the public', a protected work must be communicated using specific technical means, different from those previously used or, failing that, to a 'new public', that is to say, to a public that was not already taken into account by the copyright holders when they authorised the initial communication to the public of their work.

34 Finally, the Court has underlined, on many occasions, that the profit-making nature of a communication, within the meaning of Article 3(1) of Directive 2001/29, is not irrelevant.

35 As regards, in the first place, the question of whether the sale of a multimedia player, such as that at issue in the main proceedings, is an 'act of communication', within the meaning of Article 3(1) of Directive 2001/29, it must be noted, as recital 23 of Directive 2001/29 states, that the author's right of communication to the public, provided for in Article 3(1), covers any transmission or retransmission of a work to the public by wire or wireless means, including broadcasting.

36 Furthermore, as is apparent from Article 3(1) of Directive 2001/29, for there to be an 'act of communication', it is sufficient, in particular, that a work is made available to a public in such a way that the persons forming that public may access it, irrespective of whether they avail themselves of that opportunity.

37 The Court has already held, in that regard, that the provision, on a website, of clickable links to protected works published without any access restrictions on another site, affords users of the first site direct access to those works.

38 That is also the case for the sale of a multimedia player, such as that at issue in the main proceedings.

39 It is true, as recital 27 of Directive 2001/29 states, that the mere provision of physical facilities for enabling or making a communication does not in itself amount to 'communication' within the meaning of that directive.

40 The Court has nevertheless held, in that respect, as regards the provision of television sets in hotel rooms, that while the 'mere provision of physical facilities' does not as such amount to a communication to the public within the meaning of Directive 2001/29, it remains the case that that facility may make public access to broadcast works technically possible. Therefore, if, by means of television sets thus installed, the hotel distributes the signal to customers staying in its rooms, then communication to the public takes place, irrespective of the technique used to transmit the signal.

41 In the same way, it must be held that the present case does not concern a situation of the 'mere' provision of physical facilities for enabling or making a communication. As the Advocate General noted in paragraphs 53 and 54 of his opinion, Mr Wullems, with full knowledge of the consequences of his conduct, pre-installs onto the 'filmspeler' multimedia player that he markets add-ons that specifically enable purchasers to have access to protected works published – without the consent of the copyright holders of those works – on streaming websites and enable those purchasers to watch those works on their television screens. That intervention enabling a direct link to be established between websites broadcasting counterfeit works and purchasers of the multimedia player, without which the purchasers would find it difficult to benefit from those protected works, is quite different from the mere provision of physical facilities, referred to in recital 27 of Directive 2001/29. In that regard, it is clear from the observations presented to the Court that the streaming websites at issue in the main proceedings are not readily identifiable by the public and the majority of them change frequently.

42 Consequently, it must be held that the provision of a multimedia player such as that at issue in the main proceedings enables, in view of the add-ons pre-installed on it, access via structured menus to links that those add-ons which, when activated by the remote control of that multimedia player, offer its users direct access to protected works without the

consent of the copyright holders and must be regarded as an act of communication within the meaning of Article 3(1) of Directive 2001/29.

43 In the second place, in order to be categorised as a 'communication to the public' within the meaning of Article 3(1) of Directive 2001/29, the protected works must also in fact be communicated to a 'public'.

44 In that regard, the Court has stated, first, that the concept of 'public' encompasses a certain *de minimis* threshold, which excludes from the concept groups of persons which are too small, or insignificant. Second, in order to determine that number, the cumulative effect of making the works available to potential recipients should be taken into account. Thus, it is relevant to know not only how many persons have access to the same work at the same time, but also how many of them have access to it in succession.

45 In the present case, it must be observed that, according to the referring court, the 'filmspeler' multimedia player has been purchased by a fairly large number of people. Furthermore, the communication at issue in the main proceedings covers all persons who could potentially acquire that media player and have an internet connection. Those people may access the protected works at the same time, in the context of the streaming of the works at issue on the internet. Thus, that communication is aimed at an indeterminate number of potential recipients and involves a large number of persons.

46 It follows that, by the communication in question, the protected works are indeed communicated to a 'public' within the meaning of Article 3(1) of Directive 2001/29.

47 Furthermore, as regards whether the works were communicated to a 'new' public, within the meaning of the case-law cited in paragraph 33 above, it should be noted that the Court, in its judgment of 13 February 2014, *Svensson and Others* and in its order of 21 October 2014, *BestWater International*, held that such a public is a public which was not taken into account by the copyright holders when they authorised the initial communication. In its judgment of 8 September 2016, *GS Media*, the Court observed that those decisions confirmed the importance of the consent of the holder of the copyright in protected works that have been made freely available on a website, having regard to Article 3(1) of Directive 2001/29 which specifically provides that every act of communication of a work to the public must be authorised by the copyright holder.

48 It is clear from the judgments referred to in the previous paragraph that posting hyperlinks on a website to a protected work which has been made freely available on another website

with the consent of copyright holders of that work does not constitute a 'communication to the public' within the meaning of Article 3(1) of Directive 2001/29. In that regard, the Court held that as soon as and as long as that work is freely available on the website to which the hyperlink allows access, it must be considered that, where the copyright holders of that work have consented to such a communication, they have included all internet users as the public, such that the communication in question is not made to a new public. However, the same finding cannot be deduced from those judgments failing such an authorisation.

49 The Court therefore held, first of all, that where it is established that such a person knew or ought to have known that the hyperlink he posted provides access to a work illegally placed on the internet, the provision of that link constitutes a 'communication to the public' within the meaning of Article 3(1) of Directive 2001/29. The Court added, next, that the same applies in the event that that link allows users of the website on which it is posted to circumvent the restrictions taken by the site where the protected work is posted in order to restrict the public's access to its own subscribers, the posting of such a link then constituting a deliberate intervention without which those users could not benefit from the works broadcast. Finally, the Court stated that, when the posting of hyperlinks is carried out for profit, it can be expected that the person posting such a link carries out the necessary checks to ensure that the work concerned is not illegally published on the website to which those hyperlinks lead, so that it must be presumed that that posting has occurred with the full knowledge of the protected nature of that work and the possible lack of consent to publication on the internet by the copyright holder. In such circumstances, and in so far as that rebuttable presumption is not rebutted, the act of posting a hyperlink to a work which was illegally published on the internet constitutes a 'communication to the public' within the meaning of Article 3(1) of Directive 2001/29.

50 In the present case, it is common ground that the sale of the 'filmerspeler' multimedia player was made in full knowledge of the fact that the add-ons containing hyperlinks pre-installed on that player gave access to works published illegally on the internet. As was noted in paragraph 18 above, the advertising of that multimedia player specifically stated that it made it possible, in particular, to watch on a television screen, freely and easily, audiovisual material available on the internet without the consent of the copyright holders.

51 In addition, it cannot be disputed that the multimedia player is supplied with a view to making a profit, the price for the multimedia player being paid in particular to obtain direct access to protected works available on streaming websites without the consent of the copyright holders. As the Portuguese Government has pointed out, the main attraction of such

a multimedia player for potential purchasers lies precisely in the fact that add-ons are pre-installed on it which enable users to gain access to sites on which copyright-protected films are made available without the consent of the copyright holders.

52 Therefore, it is necessary to hold that the sale of such a multimedia player constitutes a 'communication to the public', within the meaning of Article 3(1) of Directive 2001/29.

53 In the light of the foregoing considerations, the answer to the first and second questions referred is that the concept of 'communication to the public', within the meaning of Article 3(1) of Directive 2001/29, must be interpreted as covering the sale of a multimedia player, such as that at issue in the main proceedings, on which there are pre-installed add-ons, available on the internet, containing hyperlinks to websites — that are freely accessible to the public — on which copyright-protected works have been made available without the consent of the right holders.

The third and fourth questions

(...) Substance

59 By its third and fourth questions, which should be examined together, the referring court asks, in essence, whether the provisions of Article 5(1) and (5) of Directive 2001/29 must be interpreted as meaning that acts of temporary reproduction, on an multimedia player such as that at issue in the main proceedings, of a copyright protected work obtained by streaming from a website belonging to a third party offering that work without the consent of the copyright holder satisfies the conditions set out in those provisions.

60 Under Article 5(1) of Directive 2001/29, an act of reproduction may be exempted from the reproduction right provided for in Article 2 thereof only if it satisfies five conditions, that is, where

– *the act is temporary;*
– *it is transient or incidental;*
– *it is an integral and essential part of a technological process;*
– *the sole purpose of that process is to enable a transmission in a network between third parties by an intermediary or a lawful use of a work or protected subject matter; and*
– *that act does not have any independent economic significance.*

61 First of all, it must be borne in mind that those conditions are cumulative in the sense that non-compliance with any one of them will lead to the act of reproduction not being

exempted, pursuant to Article 5(1) of Directive 2001/29, from the reproduction right provided for in Article 2 of that directive.

62 Furthermore, it is clear from the case-law of the Court that the conditions set out above must be interpreted strictly because Article 5(1) of Directive 2001/29 is a derogation from the general rule established by that directive that the copyright holder must authorise any reproduction of his protected work.

63 That is all the more so given that the exemption must be interpreted in the light of Article 5(5) of Directive 2001/29, under which that exemption is to be applied only in certain special cases which do not conflict with a normal exploitation of the work or other subject matter and do not unreasonably prejudice the legitimate interests of the right holder.

64 As regards the condition that the sole purpose of the process in question is to enable the transmission in a network between third parties by an intermediary or a lawful use of a work or protected subject matter, the referring court observes that the acts of reproduction at issue in the main proceedings do not seek to enable such a transmission. It is necessary therefore to examine whether those acts have the sole purpose of enabling a lawful use of a work or protected subject matter.

65 In that respect, as is apparent from recital 33 of Directive 2001/29, a use should be considered lawful where it is authorised by the right holder or where it is not restricted by the applicable legislation.

66 Since the use of the works at issue was not, in the case in the main proceedings, authorised by the copyright holders, it is necessary to assess whether the aim of the acts in question is to enable a use of the works that is not restricted by the applicable legislation. That assessment must take account, as recalled in paragraph 63 above, of the fact that the exemption referred to Article 5 of Directive 2001/29 only applies in certain special cases that do not conflict with a normal exploitation of the work and do not unreasonably prejudice the legitimate interests of the right holder.

67 In its judgment of 4 October 2011, *Football Association Premier League and Others*, the Court held that, from the television viewers' standpoint, the ephemeral acts of reproduction at issue in that case, which enabled the proper functioning of the satellite decoder and the television screen, enabled the broadcasts containing protected works to be received. The Court held, in that regard, that the mere reception of those broadcasts in itself – that is to say, the picking up of the broadcasts and their visual display in a private circle – did not

reveal an act restricted by the relevant legislation and such reception was to be considered lawful in the case of broadcasts from a Member State when brought about by means of a foreign decoding device. The Court concluded that the sole purpose of the acts of reproduction at issue was to enable a 'lawful use' of the works within the meaning of Article 5(1)(b) of Directive 2001/29.

68 Similarly, in its order of 17 January 2012, *Infopaq International*, the Court held that the drafting of a summary of newspaper articles, even though it was not authorised by the holders of the copyright over these articles, was not restricted by the applicable legislation with the result that the use at issue could not be considered to be unlawful.

69 By contrast, in circumstances such as those at issue in the main proceedings, and having regard, in particular, to the content of the advertising of the multimedia player at issue mentioned in paragraph 18 above and the fact, noted in paragraph 51 above, that the main attraction of that player for potential purchasers is the pre-installation of the add-ons concerned, it must be held that it is, as a rule, deliberately and in full knowledge of the circumstances that the purchaser of such a player accesses a free and unauthorised offer of protected works.

70 It must also be held that, as a rule, temporary acts of reproduction, on a multimedia player such as that at issue in the main proceedings, of copyright-protected works obtained from streaming websites belonging to third parties offering those works without the consent of the copyright holders are such as to adversely affect the normal exploitation of those works and causes unreasonable prejudice to the legitimate interests of the right holder, because, as the Advocate General observed in points 78 and 79 of his opinion, that practice would usually result in a diminution of lawful transactions relating to the protected works, which would cause unreasonable prejudice to copyright holders.

71 It follows that those acts do not satisfy the conditions set out in Article 5(1) and (5) of Directive 2001/29.

72 In the light of all the foregoing considerations, the answer to the third and fourth questions referred is that Article 5(1) and (5) of Directive 2001/29 must be interpreted as meaning that acts of temporary reproduction, on an multimedia player, such as that at issue in the main proceedings, of a copyright-protected work obtained by streaming from a website belonging to a third party offering that work without the consent of the copyright holder does not satisfy the conditions set out in those provisions. (...)

THINK IT OVER!

1. An important factor that led the CJEU in concluding that the sale of multimedia players infringed the right of communication to the public was that the defendant advertised the multimedia player's capability to access copyright protected without any permission. *What if Mr. Wullems has not used this kind of advertisement?* Furthermore, the multimedia players were sold with pre-installed add-ons (and hyperlinks directing users to protected subject matter). *What if the products have not not been sold with add-ons but only with the potential to install add-ons later by the users themselves?*

2. Some argue that those multimedia players should be prohibited in general as they are designed and commercialized with the sole objective to violate copyrights. *Would not is be necessary to formulate some kind of "staple article of commerce" doctrine in Europe in order to safeguard technological innovation?*

3. In a very similar case, the Canadian Federal Court concluded that the pre-loaded set-top boxes "marketed, sold and programmed by the Defendants enable consumers to obtain unauthorized access to content for which the Plaintiffs own the copyright. This is not a case where the *Defendants* merely serve as the conduit, as was argued by Mr. Wesley. Rather, they *deliberately encourage consumers and potential clients to circumvent authorized ways of accessing content* – say, by a cable subscription or by streaming content from the Plaintiffs' websites – *both in the manner in which they promote their business, and by offering tutorials in how to add and use applications which rely on illegally obtained content.* The statutory defence provided in paragraph 2.4(1)(b) of the *Copyright Act* does not apply to the Defendants who go above and beyond selling a simple 'means of telecommunication'. They also engage in acts related to the content of the infringed communications (...). Consumers can consequently stream or download the Plaintiffs' programs and store them on their device without authorization from the Plaintiffs. This constitutes *prima facie* copyright infringement pursuant to section 27 of the *Copyright Act.*" (iTVBox.net, para. 22.) In another decision, the Canadian Federal Court of Appeals (FCA) has confirmed the applicability of the above opinion to a case where the defendant deliberately set up a website (TVAddons.ag) to link to illegal materials. Indeed, the FCA has distinguished add-ons from search engines (like Google). According to the FCA, "[w]hile Google is an indiscriminate search engine that returns results based on relevance, as determined by an algorithm, infringing add-ons target predetermined infringing content in a manner that is user-friendly and reliable. (...) Using add-ons, however, takes one to the infringing content much more directly, effortlessly and safely." (Bell Canada v. Adam Lackman, para. 20.)

Further Case Law

Case C-306/05 - Sociedad General de Autores y Editores de España (SGAE) v. Rafael Hoteles, S.A., Judgement of the Court (Third Chamber), 7 December 2006 [ECLI:EU:C:2006:764]

Case C-5/08 - Infopaq International A/S v. Danske Dagblades Forening, Judgement of the Court (Fourth Chamber), 16 July 2009 [ECLI:EU:C:2009:465]

Case C-466/12 - Svenson and others v. Retriever Sverige AB, Judgement of the Court (Fourth Chamber), 13 February 2014 [ECLI:EU:C:2014:76]

Case C-360/13 - Public Relations Consultants Association Ltd v. The Newspaper Licensing Agency Ltd and Others, Judgment of the Court (Fourth Chamber), 5 June 2014, [ECLI:EU:C:2014:1195]

Bell Canada v. 1326030 Ontario Inc. (iTVBox.net) [2016] *FC* 612

Bell Canada et al. v. Adam Lackman dba TVADDONS.AG [2018] *FCA* 42. In: *Computer Law Review International*, Issue 2/2018, p. 53-58.

Recommended readings

In English

John Groom - Iona Silverman - Birgit Clark: Still lost in the labyrinth? CJEU rules in Filmspeler that pre-loading a set-top box with links to a pirate site is a communication to the public, *European Intellectual Property Review*, Issue 9/2017, p. 591-594.
Irini Stamatoudi: *'Linking' and 'Browsing' in the Light of the EU Court of Justice's Case Law*. In: Tana Pistorius (Ed.): Intellectual Property Perspectives on the Regulation of New Technologies, Edward Elgar, Cheltenham, 2018, p. 179-207.

In French

Chomiac De Sas - Pierre Xavier: La vente de lecteurs multimédia qualifiée de «communication au public», *Droit de l'immatériel: informatique, médias, communication*, 2017, n° 138, p. 19-24.
Guillaume Busseuil: Fourniture de liens hypertextes et vente d'un matériel multimédia: une nouvelle déclinaison de la notion de «communication au public», *Droit de l'immatériel: informatique, médias, communication*, 2017, n° 139, p. 8-10.
Edouard Treppoz: Droit européen de la propriété intellectuelle, *Revue trimestrielle de droit européen*, 2017, n°4, p. 864-868.

In German

Michel M. Walter: Verkauf multimedialer Medienabspieler - Streaming und Rechtmäßigkeit der Quelle, *MR-Int: Internationale Rundschau zum Medienrecht, IP- & IT-Recht*, Heft 1/2017, p. 40-41.
Arne Neubauer - Martin Soppe: „Öffentliche Wiedergabe" bei Verkauf eines multimedialen Medienabspielers, *Gewerblicher Rechtsschutz und Urheberrecht*, Heft 6/2017, p. 615-616.
Jutta Stender-Vorwachs - Hans Steege: EuGH: Streaming von Filmen ohne Zustimmung des Rechtsinhabers, *Multimedia und Recht*, Heft 7/2017, p. 465-466.
Louisa Specht: Der Verkauf technischer Gerätschaften zur Ermöglichung des Streamings - Eine Urheberrechtsverletzung? Besprechung des Urteils EuGH ZUM 2017, 587 - Stichting Brein/ Wullems, *Zeitschrift für Urheber- und Medienrecht*, Heft 7/2017, p. 582-586.

In Spanish

Raquel Xalabarder: Copyright y derecho de autor: ¿convergencia internacional en un mundo digital?, *IDP. Revista de Internet, Derecho y Política,* 2005, p. 2-6.

In Hungarian

Ferge Zsigmond: Médialejátszók és online megosztóplatformok, avagy hogyan értelmezte az Európai Bíróság a nyilvánossághoz közvetítés fogalmát a Stichting Brein, szerzői jogok jogosultjainak érdekeit védő alapítvány kontra Jack Frederik Wullems-, valamint a Ziggo BV és XS4ALL Internet BV-ügyben hozott ítéletében, *Iparjogvédelmi és Szerzői Jogi Szemle*, 2017/5. szám, p. 15-46.
Petrik Bence Ferenc: Filmspeler döntés: a nyilvánossághoz közvetítés jogának értelmezésével lép fel ismét az Európai Unió Bírósága az internetes kalózkodás ellen, *Infokommunikáció és jog*, 2017. augusztus (68. szám), p. 50-53.

THE CARTOON NETWORK, LLLP V. CSC HOLDINGS, INC.

536 *F.3d* 121 (2nd Cir. 2008)

WALKER, JR., Circuit Judge

BACKGROUND

Today's television viewers increasingly use digital video recorders ("DVRs") instead of video cassette recorders ("VCRs") to record television programs and play them back later at their convenience. DVRs generally store recorded programming on an internal hard drive rather than a cassette. But, as this case demonstrates, the generic term "DVR" actually refers to a growing number of different devices and systems. Companies like TiVo sell a stand-alone DVR device that is typically connected to a user's cable box and television much like a VCR. Many cable companies also lease to their subscribers "set-top storage DVRs," which combine many of the functions of a standard cable box and a stand-alone DVR in a single device.

In March 2006, Cablevision, an operator of cable television systems, announced the advent of its new "Remote Storage DVR System." As designed, the RS-DVR allows Cablevision customers who do not have a stand-alone DVR to record cable programming on central hard drives housed and maintained by Cablevision at a "remote" location. RS-DVR customers may then receive playback of those programs through their home television sets, using only a remote control and a standard cable box equipped with the RS-DVR software. Cablevision notified its content providers, including plaintiffs, of its plans to offer RS-DVR, but it did not seek any license from them to operate or sell the RS-DVR.

Plaintiffs, which hold the copyrights to numerous movies and television programs, sued Cablevision for declaratory and injunctive relief. They alleged that Cablevision's proposed operation of the RS-DVR would directly infringe their exclusive rights to both reproduce and publicly perform their copyrighted works. Critically for our analysis here, plaintiffs alleged theories only of direct infringement, not contributory infringement, and defendants waived any defense based on fair use.

Ultimately, the United States District Court for the Southern District of New York (Denny Chin, Judge), awarded summary judgment to the plaintiffs and enjoined Cablevision from operating the RS-DVR system without licenses from its content providers.

I. Operation of the RS-DVR System

Cable companies like Cablevision aggregate television programming from a wide variety of "content providers" – the various broadcast and cable channels that produce or provide individual programs – and transmit those programs into the homes of their subscribers via coaxial cable. At the outset of the transmission process, Cablevision gathers the content of the various television channels into a single stream of data. Generally, this stream is processed and transmitted to Cablevision's customers in real time. Thus, if a Cartoon Network program is scheduled to air Monday night at 8pm, Cartoon Network transmits that program's data to Cablevision and other cable companies nationwide at that time, and the cable companies immediately re-transmit the data to customers who subscribe to that channel.

Under the new RS-DVR, this single stream of data is split into two streams. The first is routed immediately to customers as before. The second stream flows into a device called the Broadband Media Router ("BMR"), which buffers the data stream, reformats it, and sends it to the "Arroyo Server," which consists, in relevant part, of two data buffers and a number of high-capacity hard disks. The entire stream of data moves to the first buffer (the "primary ingest buffer"), at which point the server automatically inquires as to whether any customers want to record any of that programming. If a customer has requested a particular program, the data for that program move from the primary buffer into a secondary buffer, and then onto a portion of one of the hard disks allocated to that customer. As new data flow into the primary buffer, they overwrite a corresponding quantity of data already on the buffer. The primary ingest buffer holds no more than 0.1 seconds of each channel's programming at any moment. Thus, every tenth of a second, the data residing on this buffer are automatically erased and replaced. The data buffer in the BMR holds no more than 1.2 seconds of programming at any time. While buffering occurs at other points in the operation of the RS-DVR, only the BMR buffer and the primary ingest buffer are utilized absent any request from an individual subscriber.

(...) To the customer, however, the processes of recording and playback on the RS-DVR are similar to that of a standard set-top DVR. Using a remote control, the customer can record programming by selecting a program in advance from an on-screen guide, or by pressing the record button while viewing a given program. A customer cannot, however, record the earlier portion of a program once it has begun. To begin playback, the customer selects the show from an on-screen list of previously recorded programs. The principal difference in operation is that, instead of sending signals from the remote to an on-set box, the viewer sends signals from the remote, through the cable, to the Arroyo Server at Cablevision's central facility. In this respect, RS-DVR more closely resembles a VOD service, whereby a cable subscriber uses his remote and cable box to request transmission of content, such as a movie, stored on computers at the cable company's facility. But unlike a VOD service, RS-DVR users can only play content that they previously requested to be recorded. ...

II. The District Court's Decision

In the district court, plaintiffs successfully argued that Cablevision's proposed system would directly infringe their copyrights in three ways. First, by briefly storing data in the primary ingest buffer and other data buffers integral to the function of the RS-DVR, Cablevision would make copies of protected works and thereby directly infringe plaintiffs' exclusive right of reproduction under the Copyright Act. Second, by copying programs onto the Arroyo Server hard disks (the "playback copies"), Cablevision would again directly infringe the reproduction right. And third, by transmitting the data from the Arroyo Server hard disks to its RS-DVR customers in response to a "playback" request, Cablevision would directly infringe plaintiffs' exclusive right of public performance. Agreeing with all three arguments, the district court awarded summary declaratory judgment to plaintiffs and enjoined Cablevision from operating the RS-DVR system without obtaining licenses from the plaintiff copyright holders. (...)

DISCUSSION

(...) "Section 106 of the Copyright Act grants copyright holders a bundle of exclusive rights..." This case implicates two of those rights: the right "to reproduce the copyrighted work in copies," and the right "to perform the copyrighted work publicly." 17 U.S.C. §106(1), (4). As discussed above, the district court found that Cablevision infringed the first right by 1) buffering the data from its programming stream and 2) copying content onto the Arroyo Server hard disks to enable playback of a program requested by an RS-DVR customer. In addition, the district court found that Cablevision would infringe the public performance right by transmitting a program to an RS-DVR customer in response to that customer's playback request. We address each of these three allegedly infringing acts in turn.

I. The Buffer Data

It is undisputed that Cablevision, not any customer or other entity, takes the content from one stream of programming, after the split, and stores it, one small piece at a time, in the BMR buffer and the primary ingest buffer. As a result, the information is buffered before any customer requests a recording, and would be buffered even if no such request were made. The question is whether, by buffering the data that make up a given work, Cablevision "reproduce[s]" that work "in copies," 17 U.S.C. §106(1), and thereby infringes the copyright holder's reproduction right.

"Copies," as defined in the Copyright Act, "are material objects ... in which a work is fixed by any method ... and from which the work can be ... reproduced." §101. The Act also provides that a work is "'fixed' in a tangible medium of expression when its embodiment ... is sufficiently permanent or stable to permit it to be ... reproduced ... for a period of more than transitory duration." Id. We believe that this language plainly imposes two distinct but related requirements: the work must be embodied in a medium, i.e., placed in a medium such that it can be perceived, reproduced, etc., from that medium (the "embodiment requirement"), and it must remain thus embodied "for a period of more than transitory duration" (the "duration requirement"). Unless both requirements are met, the work is not "fixed" in the buffer, and, as a result, the buffer data is not a "copy" of the original work whose data is buffered.

The district court mistakenly limited its analysis primarily to the embodiment requirement. As a result of this error, once it determined that the buffer data was "[c]learly ... capable of being reproduced," i.e., that the work was embodied in the buffer, the district court concluded that the work was therefore "fixed" in the buffer, and that a copy had thus been made. In doing so, it relied on a line of cases beginning with MAI Systems Corp. v. Peak Computer Inc., 991 F.2d 511 (9th Cir. 1993).

The district court's reliance on cases like MAI Systems is misplaced. In general, those cases conclude that an alleged copy is fixed without addressing the duration requirement; it does not follow, however, that those cases assume, much less establish, that such a requirement does not exist. Indeed, the duration requirement, by itself, was not at issue in MAI Systems and its progeny. As a result, they do not speak to the issues squarely before us here: If a work is only "embodied" in a medium for a period of transitory duration, can it be "fixed" in that medium, and thus a copy? And what constitutes a period "of more than transitory duration"?

Accordingly, we construe MAI Systems and its progeny as holding that loading a program into a computer's RAM can result in copying that program. We do not read MAI Systems as holding that, as a matter of law, loading a program into a form of RAM always results in copying. Such a holding would read the "transitory duration" language out of the definition, and we do not believe our sister circuit would dismiss this statutory language without even discussing it.

In sum, no case law or other authority dissuades us from concluding that the definition of "fixed" imposes both an embodiment requirement and a duration requirement. We now turn to whether, in this case, those requirements are met by the buffer data.

Cablevision does not seriously dispute that copyrighted works are "embodied" in the buffer. The result might be different if only a single second of a much longer work was placed in the buffer in isolation. In such a situation, it might be reasonable to conclude that only a minuscule portion of a work, rather than "a work" was embodied in the buffer. Here, however, where every second of an entire work is placed, one second at a time, in the buffer, we conclude that the work is embodied in the buffer.

Does any such embodiment last "for a period of more than transitory duration"? No bit of data remains in any buffer for more than a fleeting 1.2 seconds. And unlike the data in cases like MAI Systems, which remained embodied in the computer's RAM memory until the user turned the computer off, each bit of data here is rapidly and automatically overwritten as soon as it is processed. While our inquiry is necessarily fact-specific, and other factors not present here may alter the duration analysis significantly, these facts strongly suggest that the works in this case are embodied in the buffer for only a "transitory" period, thus failing the duration requirement.

II. Direct Liability for Creating the Playback Copies

In most copyright disputes, the allegedly infringing act and the identity of the infringer are never in doubt. These cases turn on whether the conduct in question does, in fact, infringe the plaintiff's copyright. In this case, however, the core of the dispute is over the authorship of the infringing conduct. After an RS-DVR subscriber selects a program to record, and that program airs, a copy of the program – a copyrighted work – resides on the hard disks of Cablevision's Arroyo Server, its creation unauthorized by the copyright holder. The question is who made this copy. If it is Cablevision, plaintiffs' theory of direct infringement succeeds; if it is the customer, plaintiffs' theory fails because Cablevision would then face, at most, secondary liability, a theory of liability expressly disavowed by plaintiffs. ...

When there is a dispute as to the author of an allegedly infringing instance of reproduction, [the earlier cases] ... direct our attention to the volitional conduct that causes the copy to be made. There are only two instances of volitional conduct in this case: Cablevision's conduct in designing, housing, and maintaining a system that exists only to produce a copy, and a customer's conduct in ordering that system to produce a copy of a specific program. In the case of a VCR, it seems clear – and we know of no case holding otherwise – that the operator of the VCR, the person who actually presses the button to make the recording, supplies the necessary element of volition, not the person who manufactures, maintains, or, if distinct from the operator, owns the machine. We do not believe that an RS-DVR customer is sufficiently distinguishable from a VCR user to impose liability as a direct infringer on a different party for copies that are made automatically upon that customer's command. ...

The district court found Cablevision analogous to a copy shop that makes course packs for college professors. In the leading case involving such a shop, for example, "[t]he professor [gave] the copyshop the materials of which the coursepack [was] to be made up, and the copyshop [did] the rest." There did not appear to be any serious dispute in that case that the shop itself was directly liable for reproducing copyrighted works. The district court here found that Cablevision, like this copy shop, would be "doing" the copying, albeit "at the customer's behest."

But because volitional conduct is an important element of direct liability, the district court's analogy is flawed. In determining who actually "makes" a copy, a significant difference exists between making a request to a human employee, who then volitionally operates the copying system to make the copy, and issuing a command directly to a system, which automatically obeys commands and engages in no volitional conduct. ... Here, by selling access to a system that automatically produces copies on command, Cablevision more closely resembles a store proprietor who charges customers to use a photocopier on his premises, and it seems incorrect to say, without more, that such a proprietor "makes" any copies when his machines are actually operated by his customers.

III. Transmission of RS-DVR Playback

Plaintiffs' final theory is that Cablevision will violate the Copyright Act by engaging in unauthorized public performances of their works through the playback of the RS-DVR copies. The Act grants a copyright owner the exclusive right, "in the case of ... motion pictures and other audiovisual works, to perform the copyrighted work publicly." 17 U.S.C. §106(4).

§101, the definitional section of the Act, explains that

[t]o perform or display a work "publicly" means (1) to perform or display it at a place open to the public or at any place where a substantial number of persons outside of a normal circle of a family and its social acquaintances is gathered; or (2) to transmit or otherwise communicate a performance or display of the work to a place specified by clause (1) or to the public, by means of any device or process, whether the members of the public capable of receiving the performance or display receive it in the same place or in separate places and at the same time or at different times.

The parties agree that this case does not implicate clause (1). Accordingly, we ask whether these facts satisfy the second, "transmit clause" of the public performance definition: Does Cablevision "transmit ... a performance ... of the work ... to the public"? No one disputes that the RS-DVR playback results in the transmission of a performance of a work – the transmission from the Arroyo Server to the customer's television set. Cablevision contends that (1) the RS-DVR customer, rather than Cablevision, does the transmitting and thus the performing and (2) the transmission is not "to the public" under the transmit clause.

As to Cablevision's first argument, we note that our conclusion in Part II that the customer, not Cablevision, "does" the copying does not dictate a parallel conclusion that the customer, and not Cablevision, "performs" the copyrighted work. The definitions that delineate the contours of the reproduction and public performance rights vary in significant ways. For example, the statute defines the verb "perform" and the noun "copies," but not the verbs "reproduce" or "copy." We need not address Cablevision's first argument further because, even if we assume that Cablevision makes the transmission when an RS-DVR playback occurs, we find that the RS-DVR playback, as described here, does not involve the transmission of a performance "to the public."

The statute itself does not expressly define the term "performance" or the phrase "to the public." It does explain that a transmission may be "to the public ... whether the members of the public capable of receiving the performance ... receive it in the same place or in separate places and at the same time or at different times." This plain language instructs us that, in determining whether a transmission is "to the public," it is of no moment that the potential recipients of the transmission are in different places, or that they may receive the transmission at different times. The implication from this same language, however, is that it is relevant, in determining whether a transmission is made to the public, to discern who is "capable of receiving" the performance being transmitted. The fact that the statute says "capable of receiving the performance," instead of "capable of receiving the transmission," underscores the fact that a transmission of a performance is itself a performance.

From the foregoing, it is evident that the transmit clause directs us to examine who precisely is "capable of receiving" a particular transmission of a performance. Cablevision argues that, because each RS-DVR transmission is made using a single unique copy of a work, made by an individual subscriber, one that can be decoded exclusively by that subscriber's cable box, only one subscriber is capable of receiving any given RS-DVR transmission. This argument accords with the language of the transmit clause, which, as described above, directs us to consider the potential audience of a given transmission. We are unpersuaded by the district court's reasoning and the plaintiffs' arguments that we should consider a larger potential audience in determining whether a transmission is "to the public."

The district court, in deciding whether the RS-DVR playback of a program to a particular customer is "to the public," apparently considered all of Cablevision's customers who subscribe to the channel airing that program and all of Cablevision's RS-DVR subscribers who request a copy of that program. Thus, it concluded that the RS-DVR playbacks constituted public performances because "Cablevision would transmit the same program to members of the public, who may receive the performance at different times, depending on whether they view the program in real time or at a later time as an RS-DVR playback." In essence, the district court suggested that, in considering whether a transmission is "to the public," we consider not the potential audience of a particular transmission, but the potential audience of the underlying work (i.e., "the program") whose content is being transmitted.

We cannot reconcile the district court's approach with the language of the transmit clause. That clause speaks of people capable of receiving a particular "transmission" or "performance," and not of the potential audience of a particular "work." Indeed, such an approach would render the "to the public" language surplusage. Doubtless the potential audience for every copyrighted audiovisual work is the general public. As a result, any transmission of the content of a copyrighted work would constitute a public performance under the district court's interpretation. But the transmit clause obviously contemplates the existence of non-public transmissions; if it did not, Congress would have stopped drafting that clause after "performance." ...

Although the transmit clause is not a model of clarity, we believe that when Congress speaks of transmitting a performance to the public, it refers to the performance created by the act of transmission. Thus, HBO transmits its own performance of a work when it transmits to Cablevision, and Cablevision transmits its own performance of the same work when it retransmits the feed from HBO.

Furthermore, we believe it would be inconsistent with our own transmit clause jurisprudence to consider the potential audience of an upstream transmission by a third party when determining whether a defendant's own subsequent transmission of a performance is "to the public."

In sum, none of the arguments advanced by plaintiffs or the district court alters our conclusion that, under the transmit clause, we must examine the potential audience of a given transmission by an alleged infringer to determine whether that transmission is "to the public." And because the RS-DVR system, as designed, only makes transmissions to one subscriber using a copy made by that subscriber, we believe that the universe of people capable of receiving an RS-DVR transmission is the single subscriber whose self-made copy is used to create that transmission.

Plaintiffs contend that it is "wholly irrelevant, in determining the existence of a public performance, whether 'unique' copies of the same work are used to make the transmissions." But plaintiffs cite no authority for this contention. And our analysis of the transmit clause suggests that, in general, any factor that limits the potential audience of a transmission is relevant.

Furthermore, no transmission of an audiovisual work can be made, we assume, without using a copy of that work: to transmit a performance of a movie, for example, the transmitter generally must obtain a copy of that movie. As a result, in the context of movies, television programs, and other audiovisual works, the right of reproduction can reinforce and protect the right of public performance. If the owner of a copyright believes he is injured by a particular transmission of a performance of his work, he may be able to seek redress not only for the infringing transmission, but also for the underlying copying that facilitated the transmission. Given this interplay between the various rights in this context, it seems quite consistent with the Act to treat a transmission made using Copy A as distinct from one made using Copy B, just as we would treat a transmission made by Cablevision as distinct from an otherwise identical transmission made by Comcast. Both factors – the identity of the transmitter and the source material of the transmission – limit the potential audience of a transmission in this case and are therefore germane in determining whether that transmission is made "to the public."

Indeed, we believe that Columbia Pictures Industries, Inc. v. Redd Horne, Inc., 749 *F.2d* 154 (3rd Cir. 1984), relied on by both plaintiffs and the district court, supports our decision to accord significance to the existence and use of distinct copies in our transmit clause analysis. In that case, defendant operated a video rental store, Maxwell's, which also housed a number of small private booths containing seats and a television. Patrons would select a film, enter the booth, and close the door. An employee would then load a copy of the requested movie into a bank of VCRs at the front of the store and push play, thereby transmitting the content of the tape to the television in the viewing booth.

The Third Circuit found that defendants' conduct constituted a public performance under both clauses of the statutory definition. In concluding that Maxwell's violated the transmit clause, that court explicitly relied on the fact that defendants showed the same copy of a work seriatim to its clientele, and it quoted a treatise emphasizing the same fact:

> Professor Nimmer's examination of this definition is particularly pertinent: "if the same copy ... of a given work is repeatedly played (i.e., 'performed') by different members of the public, albeit at different times, this constitutes a 'public' performance." Although Maxwell's has only one copy of each film, it shows each copy repeatedly to different members of the public. This constitutes a public performance.

Unfortunately, neither the Redd Horne court nor Prof. Nimmer explicitly explains why the use of a distinct copy affects the transmit clause inquiry. But our independent analysis confirms the soundness of their intuition: the use of a unique copy may limit the potential audience of a transmission and is therefore relevant to whether that transmission is made "to the public." Plaintiffs' unsupported arguments to the contrary are unavailing.

Given that each RS-DVR transmission is made to a given subscriber using a copy made by that subscriber, we conclude that such a transmission is not "to the public," without analyzing the contours of that phrase in great detail. No authority cited by the parties or the district court persuades us to the contrary.

In sum, we find that the transmit clause directs us to identify the potential audience of a given transmission, i.e., the persons "capable of receiving" it, to determine whether that transmission is made "to the public." Because each RS-DVR playback transmission is made to a single subscriber using a single unique copy produced by that subscriber, we conclude that such transmissions are not performances "to the public," and therefore do not infringe any exclusive right of public performance. We base this decision on the application of undisputed facts; thus, Cablevision is entitled to summary judgment on this point.

This holding, we must emphasize, does not generally permit content delivery networks to avoid all copyright liability by making copies of each item of content and associating one unique copy with each subscriber to the network, or by giving their subscribers the capacity to make their own individual copies. We do not address whether such a network operator would be able to escape any other form of copyright liability, such as liability for unauthorized reproductions or liability for contributory infringement.

In sum, because we find, on undisputed facts, that Cablevision's proposed RS-DVR system would not directly infringe plaintiffs' exclusive rights to reproduce and publicly perform their copyrighted works, we grant summary judgment in favor of Cablevision with respect to both rights.

THINK IT OVER!

1. A decade after the *Cablevision* decision, the Second Circuit summarized the importance of this ruling as well as the introduction of volitional conduct requirement as follows: "Section 106 of the Copyright Act gives copyright holders an exclusive bundle of rights, including the right 'to reproduce the copyrighted work in copies,' and the right to 'display the copyrighted work publicly.' The Copyright Act makes parties who infringe on those rights liable for damages, regardless of whether they had knowledge that the content was infringing. In other words, the Copyright Act is a strict liability regime. The advent of the internet posed a problem for this regime, however, since applying strict liability to infringing content posted online meant that websites could be held liable for infringing content posted by their users based solely on the existence of the website – an outcome that could be unfair. In response, beginning in the mid-1990s, courts began to read into the Copyright Act an implicit requirement that for a service provider to be liable for direct infringement, it must have taken some affirmative, volitional step to infringe. The doctrine posits that to hold a service provider liable for direct copyright infringement that infringement must have resulted from the provider's own volitional conduct." (*BWP Media v. Polyvore*, p. 47.)

2. *How different would be the outcome of the case, if Cablevision* would provide a VOD ("video-on-demand") service, where the service provider would record and store all available content on its central server without any request from its subscribers, and *would provide access to these fixed copies on a temporary basis?* For Hungarian students: compare this issue to the *Expert opinion No. 31/07/1* of the Hungarian Coypright Expert Board, where the panel differentiated between multiple types of VOD services, depending upon the service provider's active contrubution to the recording of TV-shows or its passive supply of digital services ("personal video recorder" or PVR service; "network PVR service" and "time-shifting"). The panel finally concluded that the recording of television signal via an IPTV service is lawful as long as the end-user fully controls the recording.

3. The Cablevision court excluded the treatment of the copies made in the primary ingest buffer and the data buffer in the BMR as fixations. *How would EU copyright law treat these copies?* Compare to Art. 5(1) of the InfoSoc-Directive on temporary acts of reproduction, and compare to the *Meltwater* ruling of the CJEU. (See at page 3.)

4. *Is the Cablevision decision wholly or partially applicable to copies made by the users in the cloud?* In *Hotfile*, the trial court found the service provider liable under contributory liability for direct infringements committed by the users of Hotfile's "cyberlocker" (file-hosting) service.

Further Case Law

SzJSzT 31/07/1 – "IPTV szolgáltatás szerzői jogi megítélése". In: *Iparjogvédelmi és Szerzői Jogi Szemle*, 2008/1. szám, p. 166-178.

Perfect 10, Inc., v. Rapidshare A.G., et al., 09-CV-2596 H (WMC), US District Court for the Southern District of California (2010)

Disney Enterprises, Inc. et al., v. Hotfile Corp. et al., 2013 *WL* 6336286 (2013)

BWP Media USA Inc., et al. v. Polyvore, Inc., 922 *F.3d* 42 (2019)

Case C-360/13 - Public Relations Consultants Association Ltd v. The Newspaper Licensing Agency Ltd and Others, Judgment of the Court (Fourth Chamber), 5 June 2014, ECLI:EU:C:2014:1195

Associated Press v. Meltwater U. S. Holdings, Inc., et. al, 931 *F.Supp.2d* 537 (2013)

Recommended readings

In English

Vivian I. Kim: The Public Performance Right in the Digital Age: Cartoon Network LP v. CSC Holdings, Inc., *Berkeley Technology Law Journal*, 2009: p. 263-297.

Jeffrey Malkan: The Public Performance Problem in Cartoon Network LP v. CSC Holdings, Inc., *Oregon Law Review*, 2010: p. 505-555.

Irene M. Pla: This Picture is Coming Fuzzy: Cartoon Network v. CSC Holdings Blurs the Line Between Direct and Secondary Coypright Infringement, *AIPLA Quarterly Journal*, Winter 2010, p. 85-111.

Ross Drath: Hotfile, Megaupload, and the Future of Copyright on the Internet: What Can Cyberlockers Tell Us about DMCA Reform?, *John Marshall Review of Intellectual Property Law*, 2012: p. 220-231.

Carrie Bodner: Master Copies, Unique Copies and Volitional Conduct: Cartoon Network's Implications for the Liability of Cyber Lockers, *Columbia Journal of Law & the Arts*, Spring 2013, p. 491-525.

Ernesto Omar Falcon: The Value of Cablevision and its Implications on International Copyright Law and the Internet, *Pacific McGeorge Global Business & Development Law Journal*, 2015: p. 303-329.

Makeen Fouad Makeen: *Video Streaming and the Communication to the Public Right in the United States and European Union.* In: Tanya Aplin (Ed.): *Research Handbook on Intellectual Property and Digital Technologies*, Edward Elgar, Cheltenham, 2020, p. 246-275.

In Spanish

Vv. Aa.: Copyright y derecho de autor: ¿convergencia internacional en un mundo digital?, *Revista de Internet, Derecho y Política,* número monográfico, 2005 (http://www.uoc.edu/idp/1/dt/esp/monografico.pdf)

In Hungarian

Mezei Péter - Németh László: A Direct Download Link (DDL) szolgáltatás szerzői jogi megítélése, *Infokommunikáció és Jog*, 2009/5. szám, p. 179-186.

Mezei Péter: Tisztul a kép a RapidShare körül? A DDL szolgáltatók felelősségének a korlátozása, *Infokommunikáció és Jog*, 2010/6. szám, p. 187-191.

Faludi Gábor - Grad-Gyenge Anikó: A cloud computing-alapú szolgáltatások szerzői jogi megítéléséről, *Infokommunikáció és Jog*, 2012/3. szám, p. 105-108.

Mezei Péter: Egyedül a sötétben - a DDL szolgáltatók felelősségének aktuális fejleményei, *Infokommunikáció és Jog*, 2014/1. szám, p. 29-38.

FLAVA WORKS, INC., V. MARQUES RONDALE GUNTER

689 *F.3d* 754 (2012)

POSNER, Circuit Judge,

Opinion

(...) Flava specializes in the production and distribution of videos of black men engaged in homosexual acts. Although some people would disapprove of such a service, there is no suggestion that it is illegal; and anyway the prevailing view is that even illegality is not a bar to copyrightability. As pointed out in the Jartech case, "obscenity is a community standard which may vary to the extent that controls thereof may be dropped by a state altogether. Acceptance of an obscenity defense would fragment copyright enforcement, protecting registered materials in a certain community, while, in effect, authorizing pirating in another locale." (...)

The websites that host them are behind a "pay wall"; that is, access to them (except for previews) is available only upon payment of a fee in advance. The user must agree not to copy, transmit, sell, etc. the video, although Flava's terms of use permit the user to download it to his computer for his "personal, noncommercial use" – only.

Enter myVidster, an online service engaged in what is called "social bookmarking" – enabling individuals who have similar tastes to point one another (and actually provide one another access) to online materials that cater to those tastes, by bookmarking materials on the social-bookmarking service's website. We need to describe how this works.

Patrons of myVidster find videos on the Internet, and if they want to make them available to other patrons of myVidster (who apparently can be anyone – as far as we can discern from the record all content on myVidster is publicly accessible) "bookmark" (note) them on myVidster's website. Upon receiving the bookmark myVidster automatically requests the video's "embed code" from the server that hosts (that is, stores) the video. In the present context "server" denotes a specialized computer for storing and transmitting bulky online materials, like videos. When you upload a video to the Internet, the video is stored on a server that transmits the video to other Internet users' computers on request.

The embed code contains the video's web address plus instructions for how to display the video. Armed with that code, myVidster creates a web page that makes the video appear to be on myVidster's site. When you visit the site, that video and other videos appear, each in the form of a "thumbnail," a miniature picture of a video's opening screen shot. A click on a thumbnail activates computer code that connects the visitor's computer to the server; the connection made, the visitor is now watching the video. He's watching it through a frame that myVidster has put around it, containing ads (it's by selling ads for display on its website that myVidster finances its operation). He may think, therefore, that he's seeing the video on myVidster's website. But actually the video is being transmitted directly from the server on which the video is stored to the viewer's computer. Someone had uploaded the video to that server, and later a subscriber to myVidster had come across it and decided to bookmark it. This led to the creation of a page on myVidster's website and by clicking on the page other visitors to myVidster can now view the video – but on the server that hosts the video, not on myVidster's website; the bookmarked video is not posted on myVidster's website.

Uploading a video to the Internet is commonplace and simple to do. And once uploaded it is easy to send to a friend to view and is easily found in a search of the web and viewed. Uploading is the source of the immense number of videos viewable on YouTube. But if the uploaded video is copyrighted, the uploader has (depending on the terms of use) infringed the copyright. A customer of Flava is authorized only to download the video (or if he obtained it on a DVD sold by Flava, to copy it to his computer) for his personal use. If instead he uploaded it to the Internet and so by doing so created a copy (because the downloaded video remains in his computer), he was infringing.

Is myVidster therefore a contributory infringer if a visitor to its website bookmarks the video and later someone clicks on the bookmark and views the video? myVidster is not just adding a frame around the video screen that the visitor is watching. Like a telephone exchange connecting two telephones, it is providing a connection between the server that hosts the video and the computer of myVidster's visitor. But as long as the visitor makes no copy of the copyrighted video that he is watching, he is not violating the copyright owner's exclusive right, conferred by the Copyright Act, "to reproduce the copyrighted work in copies" and "distribute copies ... of the copyrighted work to the public." 17 U.S.C. §106(1), (3). His bypassing Flava's pay wall by viewing the uploaded copy is equivalent to stealing a copyrighted book from a bookstore and reading it. That is a bad thing to do (in either case) but it is not copyright infringement. The infringer is the customer of Flava who copied Flava's copyrighted video by uploading it to the Internet.

The right to control copying is not the only exclusive right of a copyright owner. That would make life too simple for us. He also has an exclusive right "to perform the copyrighted work publicly." §106(4). But we begin our analysis with the right to prevent copying and ask whether myVidster is the copiers' accomplice.

A typical, and typically unhelpful, definition of "contributory infringer" is "one who, with knowledge of the infringing activity, induces, causes or materially contributes to the infringing conduct of another." Such a one "may be held liable as a 'contributory' infringer." But does "may be held liable" mean that a person who fits the definition of "contributory infringer" may nevertheless not be a contributory infringer after all? And what exactly does "materially contribute" mean? And how does one materially contribute to something without causing or inducing it? And how does "cause" differ from "induce"?

Brevity is the soul of wit and tediousness its limbs and outward flourishes. We therefore prefer the succinct definition of contributory infringement in Matthew Bender & Co. v. West Publishing Co., 158 F.3d 693, 706 (2d Cir. 1998): "personal conduct that encourages or assists the infringement."

Flava contends that by providing a connection to websites that contain illegal copies of its copyrighted videos, myVidster is encouraging its subscribers to circumvent Flava's pay wall, thus reducing Flava's income. No doubt. But unless those visitors copy the videos they are viewing on the infringers' websites, myVidster isn't increasing the amount of infringement. An employee of Flava who embezzled corporate funds would be doing the same thing – reducing Flava's income – but would not be infringing Flava's copyrights by doing so. myVidster displays names and addresses (that's what the thumbnails are, in effect) of videos hosted elsewhere on the Internet that may or may not be copyrighted. Someone who uses one of those addresses to bypass Flava's pay wall and watch a copyrighted video for free is no more a copyright infringer than if he had snuck into a movie theater and watched a copyrighted movie without buying a ticket. The facilitator of conduct that doesn't infringe copyright is not a contributory infringer.

A practical objection to stretching the concept of contributory infringement far enough to make a social-bookmarking service a policeman of copyright law is that the service usually won't know whether a video that a visitor bookmarks on the service's website is protected by copyright. Congress addressed this problem in the Digital Millennium Copyright Act of 1998. The Act provides a safe harbor to Internet service providers. It states that a provider isn't liable for copyright infringement by "referring or linking users to an online location containing infringing material" if it meets certain conditions – it doesn't know the material is infringing, it isn't aware of facts that would make the infringement apparent, upon learning such facts it acts expeditiously to remove or disable access to the infringing material, it doesn't receive a financial benefit directly attributable to the infringing activity, 17 U.S.C. §512(d), and it terminates repeat infringers. §512(i)(1)(A). myVidster received "takedown" notices from Flava designed to activate the duty of an Internet service provider to ban repeat infringers from its website, and Flava contends that myVidster failed to comply with the notices. But this is irrelevant unless myVidster is contributing to infringement; a noninfringer doesn't need a safe harbor. As the record stands (a vital qualification, given that the appeal is from the grant of a preliminary injunction and may therefore be incomplete), myVidster is not an infringer, at least in the form of copying or distributing copies of copyrighted work. The infringers are the uploaders of copyrighted work. There is no evidence that myVidster is encouraging them, which would make it a contributory infringer.

It might seem that the mention in the Digital Millennium Copyright Act of "referring or linking users to an online location containing infringing material" expands the concept of contributory infringement to any reference to, or linkage in the sense of facilitating access to, copyrighted material. But this is implausible, and anyway is not argued by Flava. Taken literally it would make the publication, online or otherwise, of any contact information concerning a copyrighted work a form of contributory infringement. A more plausible interpretation is that Congress wanted to make the safe harbor as capacious as possible – however broadly contributory infringement might be understood, the Internet service provider would be able to avoid liability.

Now if myVidster invited people to post copyrighted videos on the Internet without authorization or to bookmark them on its website, it would be liable for inducing infringement (...). But inducing infringement was not a ground of the preliminary injunction issued by the district judge in this case and anyway there is no proof that myVidster has issued any such invitations.

myVidster knows that some of the videos bookmarked on its site infringe copyright, but that doesn't make it a facilitator of copying. Although visitors who view those videos are viewing infringing material, they are paying nothing for it and therefore not encouraging infringement, at least in a material sense, unless perhaps the infringer gets ad revenue every time someone plays the video that he posted on the Internet – but there is no evidence of that. True, bookmarking is a way of making friends on a social network, and one needs something to bookmark, and so if you want to make friends with people who like the kind of videos that Flava produces you may be inclined to upload those videos to the Internet in the hope that someone will bookmark them on myVidster's website and someone else will watch them and be grateful to you. But this is very indirect. For will a visitor to myVidster who watches a bookmarked infringing video know whom to be grateful to – know who uploaded it, thus enabling it to be bookmarked and viewed? That is unlikely. The unauthorized copier – the uploader of the copyrighted video – is not a part of the social network unless he's a myVidster member and uploads the Flava video for the purpose of its being bookmarked on myVidster and somehow gets credit for the bookmarking and for the ensuing viewing of the bookmarked video. There is no evidence that there are any such people.

A term in the conventional definition of contributory infringement – "material contribution" – invokes common law notions of remoteness that limit efforts to impose liability for speculative imaginings of possible causal consequences. As we said in BCS Services, Inc. v. Heartwood 88, LLC, 637 F.3d 750, 755 (7th Cir. 2011), "An injury will sometimes have a cascading effect that no potential injurer could calculate in deciding how carefully to act. The effect is clear in hindsight – but only in hindsight." The absence of evidence of myVidster's effect on the amount of infringement of Flava's videos brings concern about remoteness into play.

The absence of evidence arises in part from the fact that although Flava has a specialized subject matter, myVidster does not. It's like YouTube, except that YouTube hosts the videos it provides access to and myVidster as we know does not. Another difference, however, is that YouTube refuses to provide access to pornography, and myVidster, as we also know, is not so choosy – on the contrary. It's true that its home page (...) lists videos that range from the fighting in Syria to "Obamacare" and "Ugliest Tattoos" and "Why You Should Spiral - Cut Your Wiener" (...), with nary a pornographic video among them. But this is misleading, because in the default setting on myVidster (the setting when you first click on its website) the "family filter" is turned on; if you turn it off, your visit will reveal a mixture of pornographic and nonpornographic videos, with the former predominating, and of those the majority are homosexual and many of the actors in the homosexual videos are black.

But Flava is not the only producer of such videos, and there is no information in the record concerning its market share. All we glean from the record – and it is of no help to Flava – is that of the 1.2 million bookmarks that have been made on myVidster's website, Flava has been able to identify only 300 as bookmarks of copyrighted Flava videos; and we don't know whether any visitors to myVidster's website clicked on any of them and thus actually watched an unauthorized copy of a Flava video. Flava claims that its sales have fallen by 30 to 35 percent and that as a result it probably has lost more than $100,000 in revenue. But it doesn't say over what period the decline in revenue has occurred and it acknowledges that there are at least a dozen websites besides myVidster's on which access to unauthorized copies of Flava's videos can be obtained. So the $100,000 loss in revenue can't be ascribed entirely to myVidster. Indeed, myVidster may have very little – even nothing – to do with Flava's financial troubles.

Google and Facebook in a joint amicus curiae brief friendly to myVidster manage to muddy the waters by analyzing remoteness of injury from an alleged infringement not as a matter of general tort principles but as a species of layer cake. There are the "direct" infringers, who upload copyrighted videos to the Internet without authorization. There are myVidster members who bookmark videos illegally uploaded by the "direct" infringers – the brief describes the bookmarking visitors as "secondary" infringers. And finally there is myVidster, which connects visitors to its website to the servers that host the infringing videos. The brief describes myVidster as being at worst a "tertiary" infringer, beyond the reach of copyright law because the law doesn't recognize tertiary copyright infringement. But the law doesn't recognize "secondary infringement" either. The only distinctions relevant to this case are between direct infringement (which really ought just to be called infringement – the law doesn't speak of "direct negligence" versus "contributory negligence" or "direct murder" versus "aiding and abetting murder") and contributory infringement, and between contributory infringement and noninfringement. The direct infringers in this case are the uploaders; myVidster is neither a direct nor a contributory infringer – at least of Flava's exclusive right to copy and distribute copies of its copyrighted videos.

That is an essential qualification. So far we've been discussing infringement just by copying, and we can't stop there. For remember that the Copyright Act also makes it unlawful "to perform the copyrighted work publicly," 17 U.S.C. §106(4), defined, so far as relates to this case, as "to transmit or otherwise communicate a performance ... of the work ... to the public ... whether the members of the public capable of receiving the performance ... receive it in the same place or in separate places and at the same time or at different times." §101. One possible interpretation is that uploading plus bookmarking a video is a public performance because it enables a visitor to the website to receive (watch) the performance at will, and the fact that he will be watching it at a different time or in a different place from the other viewers does not affect its "publicness," as the statute makes clear. We'll call this interpretation, for simplicity, "performance by uploading." An alternative interpretation, however – call it "performance by receiving" – is that the performance occurs only when the work (Flava's video) is transmitted to the viewer's computer (...).

On the first interpretation, performance by uploading, the performance of a movie in a movie theater might by analogy be said to begin not when the audience is seated and the movie begins but a bit earlier, when the operator of the projector loads the film and puts his finger on the start button; while on the second interpretation, performance by receiving, it begins when he presses the button and the reel begins to unwind. The second interpretation is certainly more plausible in the movie-theater setting. But in the setting of our case the viewer rather than the sender (the latter being the uploader of the copyrighted video) determines when the performance begins, and it is odd to think that every transmission of an uploaded video is a public performance. The first interpretation – public performance occurs when the video is uploaded and the public becomes capable of viewing it – is better at giving meaning to "public" in public performance but worse at giving meaning to "performance." Legislative clarification of the public-performance provision of the Copyright Act would therefore be most welcome.

The second interpretation – the performance occurs when the video is viewed – is more favorable to Flava, because myVidster plays a role there and not in up-loading. So we're surprised that Flava doesn't urge it. The first interpretation is hopeless for Flava. For there is no evidence that myVidster is contributing to the decision of someone to upload a Flava video to the Internet, where it then becomes available to be bookmarked on myVidster's website. myVidster is giving web surfers addresses where they can find entertainment. By listing plays and giving the name and address of the theaters where they are being performed, the New Yorker is not performing them. It is not "transmitting or communicating" them.

Is myVidster doing anything different? To call the provision of contact information transmission or communication and thus make myVidster a direct infringer would blur the distinction between direct and contributory infringement and by doing so make the provider of such information an infringer even if he didn't know that the work to which he was directing a visitor to his website was copyrighted. Then he would have to search for a safe harbor in the Digital Millennium Copyright Act. myVidster doesn't touch the data stream, which flows directly from one computer to another, neither being owned or operated by myVidster.

But if the public performance is the transmission of the video when the visitor to myVidster's website clicks on the video's thumbnail (the second interpretation) and viewing begins, there is an argument that even though the video uploader is responsible for the transmitting and not myVidster, myVidster is assisting the transmission by providing the link between the uploader and the viewer, and is thus facilitating public performance. There is a remote analogy to the "swap meet" operated by the defendant in Fonovisa, Inc. v. Cherry Auction, Inc., 76 F.3d 259, 262 (9th Cir. 1996). That was a flea market in which, as the defendant knew, pirated recordings of music copyrighted by the plaintiff were sold in such bulk that the subsequent performance by the buyers (when they played the recordings) may have satisfied the broad definition of public performance in the Copyright Act, although the opinion doesn't say whether the infringement consisted of unauthorized distribution of copies or unauthorized public performance and probably meant the former. Under either interpretation the swap meet operator was providing "support services" without which "it would [have been] difficult for the infringing activity to take place in the massive quantities alleged."

In contrast, Flava's pirated videos are not sold, and there isn't even admissible evidence that they're actually being accessed via myVidster, rather than via other websites, and if they are not, myVidster is not contributing to their performance. Unlike the defendant in Fonovisa, myVidster is not providing a market for pirated works, because infringers who transmit copyrighted works to myVidster's visitors are not selling them. That isn't determinative, because copyrights can be infringed without a pecuniary motive. But it is relevant to whether myVidster's bookmarking service is actually contributing significantly to the unauthorized performance of Flava's copyrighted works by visitors to myVidster's website. It's not as if myVidster were pushing the uploading of Flava videos because it had a financial incentive to encourage performance of those works, as the swap meet did.

Nor is this case like our Aimster case, cited earlier. That was a file-sharing case. Kids wanted to swap recorded music (often copyrighted) over the Internet. The swapping required special software – which Aimster provided. By doing so it created the online equivalent of a swap meet, since anyone equipped with Aimster's software could easily obtain copies of copyrighted songs in AOL chat rooms; the first three letters in "Aimster" were an acronym for "AOL instant messaging." Although it wasn't proved that all the swapped recordings were copyrighted, it was apparent that most were – and maybe all, for we noted that "Aimster has failed to produce any evidence that its service has ever been used for a noninfringing use." That can't be said about myVidster's social-bookmarking service. Unlike Aimster, it's not encouraging swapping, which in turn encourages infringement, since without infringement there is nothing to swap.

As should be clear by now, on the record compiled so far in this litigation there is no basis for the grant of a preliminary injunction. That is not to say that Flava can't establish grounds for such an injunction, consistent with the eBay standard. It seems at least entitled to an injunction against myVidster's uploading to its website videos in which Flava owns copyrights. Before it was sued by Flava, myVidster had been doing that – making copies of videos that some of its subscribers had posted, including videos copyrighted by Flava. Although myVidster doesn't charge for membership in its social network, it charges a fee for a premium membership that included the backup service. That service infringed Flava's copyrights directly – it didn't just abet others' infringements.

MyVidster has stopped offering it. But Flava would still be entitled to an injunction – cessation of an unlawful practice doesn't exonerate a defendant, since unless enjoined he might resume infringing. It's thus a surprise that the preliminary injunction doesn't enjoin the backup service, especially since the district judge considered it evidence that myVidster was contributing to the infringing activity of its members. (...) But the judge said that while the "plaintiff also referred in closing argument to its claims of direct copyright infringement and inducement of copyright infringement, ... its motion for a preliminary injunction is not based on those claims." The backup service was direct infringement – myVidster was copying videos, including some of Flava's, without authorization. Yet as the judge said, Flava didn't make a claim for direct infringement a basis for its motion for preliminary relief. It doesn't seem to be interested in such an injunction. At oral argument, however, myVidster's lawyer said his client wouldn't oppose such an injunction, and maybe this will awaken Flava's interest. This is something for consideration on remand.

Flava may be entitled to additional preliminary injunctive relief as well, if it can show, as it has not shown yet, that myVidster's service really does contribute significantly to infringement of Flava's copyrights. The preliminary injunction that the district court entered must, however, be

Vacated.

THINK IT OVER!

1. Judge Posner used an analogy to categorize embedding of videos. He differentiated between "performance by uploading" ("begin[s] not when the audience is seated and the movie begins but a bit earlier, when the operator of the projector loads the film and puts his finger on the start button") and "performance by receiving" ("begins when [the operator of the projector] presses the button and the reel begins to unwind"). He refused to accept linking as "performance by uploading" ("the first interpretation is hopeless for Flava"). *Is this argument acceptable in the light of the accession of the United States to the WIPO's Copyright Treaty (WCT) and Performances and Phonograms Treaty (WPPT)? Under the "umbrella solution", both treaties required signatories to protect* (in a freely selected way and form) *the making available to the public right of authors and related right holders?*

2. Judge Posner put less emphasis on the fact that users circumvented the paywall of Flava Works when they bookmarked the videos. *Would the EU copyright law lead to a similar or a different result?* Compare to the *Svensson* and the *C More Entertainment* rulings. There the CJEU confirmed that the circumvention of technical measures would make linking illegal due to the communication of the protected subject matter to a new public.

3. Embedding audiovisual and framing visual contents serve the *same function* as surface and deep linking of textual contents, however they lead to *direct representation* of the relevant data. (When an audiovisual content is embedded from YouTube a simple click on the start button leads to the communication of the video without any visible notice of "linking". Technically, YouTube's servers host the content rather than the linking website. The click on the start button initiates a virtual transfer of the content on the screen of the end-user.) The Supreme Court of Canada stressed in *Crookes v. Newton* that it has direct relevance with respect to liability "whether the link was user-activated or automatic". *Should direct visualization of protected subject matter have any relevance from the perspective of copyright law?*

4. The applicability of the "server test" in cases of framing and embedding is not settled yet under US copyright law. In Justin Goldman v. Breitbart News Network, LLC, et al., 302 *F.Supp.3d* 585 (2018), the district court did not view "the Server Test as the correct application of the law with regard to the facts here. (...) It is clear (...) that each and every defendant itself took active steps to put a process in place that resulted in a transmission of the photos so that they could be visibly shown. Most directly this was accomplished by the act of including the code in the overall design of their webpage; that is, embedding." Most recently, however, in Sinclair v. Ziff Davis, LLC, 18-CV-790 (KMW), the Southern District of New York confirmed the validity of the server test, although on a different legal ground. As Judge Kimba M. Wood noted, "Here, Plaintiff granted Instagram the right to sublicense the Photograph, and Instagram validly exercised that right by granting Mashable a sublicense to display the Photograph."

Further Case Law

Universal City Studios v. Shawn C. Reimerdes, 111 *F.Supp.2d* 294 (2000)

Lesley A. Kelly v. Arriba Soft, 336 *F.3d* 811 (2003)

Perfect 10, Inc. v. Amazon.com, Inc., 487 *F.3d* 701 (2007)

Wayne Crookes and West Coast Title Search Ltd. v. Jon Newton, 2011 SCC 47, [2011] 3 *S.C.R.* 269

Case C-466/12 - Nils Svensson and Others v. Retriever Sverige AB, Judgment of the Court (Fourth Chamber), 13 February 2014 [ECLI:EU:C:2014:76]

Case C-279/13 - C More Entertainment AB v. Linus Sandberg, Judgment of the Court (Ninth Chamber), 26 March 2015 [ECLI:EU:C:2015:199]

Justin Goldman v. Breitbart News Network, LLC, et al., 302 *F.Supp.3d* 585 (2018)

Sinclair v. Ziff Davis, LLC, 18-CV-790 (KMW), April 13, 2020, U.S. District Court for the Southern District of New York

Recommended readings

In English

Alain Strowel - Nicholas Ide: Liability with Regard to Hyperlinks, *Columbia Journal of Law and the Arts*, 2001: p. 403-448.

Jessica Galaif: Flava Works, Inc. v. Gunter 689 F.3d 754 (7th Cir. 2012), *Intellectual Property Law Bulletin*, Fall 2012, p. 93-97.

Jane C. Ginsburg: Hyperlinking and "making available", *European Intellectual Property Review*, Issue 3/2014: p. 147-148.

Péter Mezei: Enter the matrix: the effects of the CJEU's case law on linking and beyond, *Journal of Intellectual Property Law & Practice*, Issue 10/2016, p. 778-794.

Jane Ginsburg - Alain Strowel: *Copyright Liability for Hyperlinking*. In: Tanya Aplin (Ed.): *Research Handbook on Intellectual Property and Digital Technologies*, Edward Elgar, Cheltenham, 2020, p. 217-245.

In Spanish

Juan Pablo Aparicio Vaquero: Propiedad intelectual y suministro de contenidos digitales (Copyright and supply of digital content), *InDret*, vol. 3, 2016 (https://ssrn.com/abstract=2832177)

In Hungarian
Mezei Péter: A linkelés szerzői jogi vonatkozásai - négyszögletes dugó a hatszögletű lyukba?, *Infokommunikáció és Jog*, 2015. március (61. szám), p. 30-39.

AMERICAN BROADCASTING COMPANIES, INC., ET AL. V. AEREO, INC.

134 *S.Ct.* 2498 (2014)

Justice BREYER,

(...) I

A

For a monthly fee, Aereo offers subscribers broadcast television programming over the Internet, virtually as the programming is being broadcast. Much of this programming is made up of copyrighted works. Aereo neither owns the copyright in those works nor holds a license from the copyright owners to perform those works publicly.

Aereo's system is made up of servers, transcoders, and thousands of dime-sized antennas housed in a central warehouse. It works roughly as follows: First, when a subscriber wants to watch a show that is currently being broadcast, he visits Aereo's website and selects, from a list of the local programming, the show he wishes to see.

Second, one of Aereo's servers selects an antenna, which it dedicates to the use of that subscriber (and that subscriber alone) for the duration of the selected show. A server then tunes the antenna to the over-the-air broadcast carrying the show. The antenna begins to receive the broadcast, and an Aereo transcoder translates the signals received into data that can be transmitted over the Internet.

Third, rather than directly send the data to the subscriber, a server saves the data in a subscriber-specific folder on Aereo's hard drive. In other words, Aereo's system creates a subscriber-specific copy – that is, a "personal" copy – of the subscriber's program of choice.

Fourth, once several seconds of programming have been saved, Aereo's server begins to stream the saved copy of the show to the subscriber over the Internet. (The subscriber may instead direct Aereo to stream the program at a later time, but that aspect of Aereo's service is not before us.) The subscriber can watch the streamed program on the screen of his personal computer, tablet, smart phone, Internet-connected television, or other Internet-connected device. The streaming continues, a mere few seconds behind the over-the-air broadcast, until the subscriber has received the entire show.

Aereo emphasizes that the data that its system streams to each subscriber are the data from his own personal copy, made from the broadcast signals received by the particular antenna allotted to him. Its system does not transmit data saved in one subscriber's folder to any other subscriber. When two subscribers wish to watch the same program, Aereo's system activates two separate antennas and saves two separate copies of the program in two separate folders. It then streams the show to the subscribers through two separate transmissions – each from the subscriber's personal copy.

B

Petitioners are television producers, marketers, distributors, and broadcasters who own the copyrights in many of the programs that Aereo's system streams to its subscribers. They brought suit against Aereo for copyright infringement in Federal District Court. They sought a preliminary injunction, arguing that Aereo was infringing their right to "perform" their works "publicly," as the Transmit Clause defines those terms.

The District Court denied the preliminary injunction. Relying on prior Circuit precedent, a divided panel of the Second Circuit affirmed. In the Second Circuit's view, Aereo does not perform publicly within the meaning of the Transmit Clause because it does not transmit "to the public." Rather, each time Aereo streams a program to a subscriber, it sends a *private* transmission that is available only to that subscriber. The Second Circuit denied rehearing en banc, over the dissent of two judges. We granted certiorari.

II

This case requires us to answer two questions: First, in operating in the manner described above, does Aereo "perform" at all? And second, if so, does Aereo do so "publicly"? We address these distinct questions in turn.

Does Aereo "perform"? Phrased another way, does Aereo "transmit ... a performance" when a subscriber watches a show using Aereo's system, or is it only the subscriber who transmits? In Aereo's view, it does not perform. It does no more than supply equipment that "emulate[s] the operation of a home antenna and [digital video recorder (DVR)]." Like a home antenna and DVR, Aereo's equipment simply responds to its subscribers' directives. So it is only the subscribers who "perform" when they use Aereo's equipment to stream television programs to themselves.

Considered alone, the language of the Act does not clearly indicate when an entity "perform[s]" (or "transmit[s]") and when it merely supplies equipment that allows others to do so. But when read in light of its purpose, the Act is unmistakable: An entity that engages in activities like Aereo's performs.

A

History makes plain that one of Congress' primary purposes in amending the Copyright Act in 1976 was to overturn this Court's determination that community antenna television (CATV) systems (the precursors of modern cable systems) fell outside the Act's scope. In Fortnightly Corp. v. United Artists Television, Inc., 392 U.S. 390 (1968), the Court considered a CATV system that carried local television broadcasting, much of which was copyrighted, to its subscribers in two cities. The CATV provider placed antennas on hills above the cities and used coaxial cables to carry the signals received by the antennas to the home television sets of its subscribers. The system amplified and modulated the signals in order to improve their strength and efficiently transmit them to subscribers. A subscriber "could choose any of the ... programs he wished to view by simply turning the knob on his own television set." The CATV provider "neither edited the programs received nor originated any programs of its own."

Asked to decide whether the CATV provider infringed copyright holders' exclusive right to perform their works publicly, the Court held that the provider did not "perform" at all. The Court drew a line: "Broadcasters perform. Viewers do not perform." And a CATV provider "falls on the viewer's side of the line."

The Court reasoned that CATV providers were unlike broadcasters:

> *"Broadcasters select the programs to be viewed; CATV systems simply carry, without editing, whatever programs they receive. Broadcasters procure programs and propagate them to the public; CATV systems receive programs that have been released to the public and carry them by private channels to additional viewers."*

Instead, CATV providers were more like viewers, for "the basic function [their] equipment serves is little different from that served by the equipment generally furnished by" viewers. "Essentially," the Court said, "a CATV system no more than enhances the viewer's capacity to receive the broadcaster's signals [by] provid[ing] a well-located antenna with an efficient connection to the viewer's television set." Viewers do not become performers by using "amplifying equipment," and a CATV provider should not be treated differently for providing viewers the same equipment.

In Teleprompter, the Court considered the copyright liability of a CATV provider that carried broadcast television programming into subscribers' homes from hundreds of miles away. Although the Court recognized that a viewer might not be able to afford amplifying equipment that would provide access to those distant signals, it nonetheless found that the CATV provider was more like a viewer than a broadcaster. It explained: "The reception and rechanneling of [broadcast television signals] for simultaneous viewing is essentially a viewer function, irrespective of the distance between the broadcasting station and the ultimate viewer."

The Court also recognized that the CATV system exercised some measure of choice over what to transmit. But that fact did not transform the CATV system into a broadcaster. A broadcaster exercises significant creativity in choosing what to air, the Court reasoned. In contrast, the CATV provider makes an initial choice about which broadcast stations to retransmit, but then "'simply carr[ies], without editing, whatever programs [it] receive[s].'"

B

In 1976 Congress amended the Copyright Act in large part to reject the Court's holdings in Fortnightly and Teleprompter. Congress enacted new language that erased the Court's line between broadcaster and viewer, in respect to "perform [ing]" a work. The amended statute clarifies that to "perform" an audiovisual work means "to show its images in any sequence or to make the sounds accompanying it audible." § 101. Under this new language, *both* the broadcaster *and* the viewer of a television program "perform," because they both show the program's images and make audible the program's sounds.

Congress also enacted the Transmit Clause, which specifies that an entity performs publicly when it "transmit[s] ... a performance ... to the public." § 101. Cable system activities, like those of the CATV systems in Fortnightly and Teleprompter, lie at the heart of the activities that Congress intended this language to cover. The Clause thus makes clear that an entity that acts like a CATV system itself performs, even if when doing so, it simply enhances viewers' ability to receive broadcast television signals.

Congress further created a new section of the Act to regulate cable companies' public performances of copyrighted works. Section 111 creates a complex, highly detailed compulsory licensing scheme that sets out the conditions, including the payment of compulsory fees, under which cable systems may retransmit broadcasts.

Congress made these three changes to achieve a similar end: to bring the activities of cable systems within the scope of the Copyright Act.

C

This history makes clear that Aereo is not simply an equipment provider. Rather, Aereo, and not just its subscribers, "perform[s]" (or "transmit[s]"). Aereo's activities are substantially similar to those of the CATV companies that Congress amended the Act to reach. Aereo sells a service that allows subscribers to watch television programs, many of which are copyrighted, almost as they are being broadcast. In providing this service, Aereo uses its own equipment, housed in a centralized warehouse, outside of its users' homes. By means of its technology (antennas, transcoders, and servers), Aereo's system "receive[s] programs that have been released to the public and carr[ies] them by private channels to additional viewers." It "carr[ies]

… whatever programs [it] receive[s]," and it offers "all the programming" of each over-the-air station it carries.

Aereo's equipment may serve a "viewer function"; it may enhance the viewer's ability to receive a broadcaster's programs. It may even emulate equipment a viewer could use at home. But the same was true of the equipment that was before the Court, and ultimately before Congress, in Fortnightly and Teleprompter.

We recognize, and Aereo and the dissent emphasize, one particular difference between Aereo's system and the cable systems at issue in Fortnightly and Teleprompter. The systems in those cases transmitted constantly; they sent continuous programming to each subscriber's television set. In contrast, Aereo's system remains inert until a subscriber indicates that she wants to watch a program. Only at that moment, in automatic response to the subscriber's request, does Aereo's system activate an antenna and begin to transmit the requested program.

This is a critical difference, says the dissent. It means that Aereo's subscribers, not Aereo, "selec[t] the copyrighted content" that is "perform[ed]", and for that reason they, not Aereo, "transmit" the performance. Aereo is thus like "a copy shop that provides its patrons with a library card." A copy shop is not directly liable whenever a patron uses the shop's machines to "reproduce" copyrighted materials found in that library. And by the same token, Aereo should not be directly liable whenever its patrons use its equipment to "transmit" copyrighted television programs to their screens.

In our view, however, the dissent's copy shop argument, in whatever form, makes too much out of too little. Given Aereo's overwhelming likeness to the cable companies targeted by the 1976 amendments, this sole technological difference between Aereo and traditional cable companies does not make a critical difference here. The subscribers of the Fortnightly and Teleprompter cable systems also selected what programs to display on their receiving sets. Indeed, as we explained in Fortnightly, such a subscriber "could choose any of the … programs he wished to view by simply turning the knob on his own television set." The same is true of an Aereo subscriber. Of course, in Fortnightly the television signals, in a sense, lurked behind the screen, ready to emerge when the subscriber turned the knob. Here the signals pursue their ordinary course of travel through the universe until today's "turn of the knob" – a click on a website – activates machinery that intercepts and reroutes them to Aereo's subscribers over the Internet. But this difference means nothing to the subscriber. It means nothing to the broadcaster. We do not see how this single difference, invisible to subscriber and broadcaster alike, could transform a system that is for all practical purposes a traditional cable system into "a copy shop that provides its patrons with a library card."

In other cases involving different kinds of service or technology providers, a user's involvement in the operation of the provider's equipment and selection of the content transmitted may well bear on whether the provider performs within the meaning of the Act. But the many similarities between Aereo and cable companies, considered in light of Congress' basic purposes in amending the Copyright Act, convince us that this difference is not critical here. We conclude that Aereo is not just an equipment supplier and that Aereo "perform[s]."

III

Next, we must consider whether Aereo performs petitioners' works "publicly," within the meaning of the Transmit Clause. Under the Clause, an entity performs a work publicly when it "transmit[s] ... a performance ... of the work ... to the public." Aereo denies that it satisfies this definition. It reasons as follows: First, the "performance" it "transmit[s]" is the performance created by its act of transmitting. And second, because each of these performances is capable of being received by one and only one subscriber, Aereo transmits privately, not publicly. Even assuming Aereo's first argument is correct, its second does not follow.

We begin with Aereo's first argument. What performance does Aereo transmit? Under the Act, "[t]o 'transmit' a performance ... is to communicate it by any device or process whereby images or sounds are received beyond the place from which they are sent." And "[t]o 'perform' " an audiovisual work means "to show its images in any sequence or to make the sounds accompanying it audible."

Petitioners say Aereo transmits a *prior* performance of their works. Thus when Aereo retransmits a network's prior broadcast, the underlying broadcast (itself a performance) is the performance that Aereo transmits. Aereo, as discussed above, says the performance it transmits is the *new* performance created by its act of transmitting. That performance comes into existence when Aereo streams the sounds and images of a broadcast program to a subscriber's screen.

We assume *arguendo* that Aereo's first argument is correct. Thus, for present purposes, to transmit a performance of (at least) an audiovisual work means to communicate contemporaneously visible images and contemporaneously audible sounds of the work. When an Aereo subscriber selects a program to watch, Aereo streams the program over the Internet to that subscriber. Aereo thereby "communicate[s]" to the subscriber, by means of a "device or process," the work's images and sounds. And those images and sounds are contemporaneously visible and audible on the subscriber's computer (or other Internet-connected device). So under our assumed definition, Aereo transmits a performance whenever its subscribers watch a program.

But what about the Clause's further requirement that Aereo transmit a performance "to the public"? As we have said, an Aereo subscriber receives broadcast television signals with an antenna dedicated to him alone. Aereo's system makes from those signals a personal copy of the selected program. It streams the content of the copy to the same subscriber and to no one else. One and only one subscriber has the ability to see and hear each Aereo transmission. The fact that each transmission is to only one subscriber, in Aereo's view, means that it does not transmit a performance "to the public."

In terms of the Act's purposes, these differences do not distinguish Aereo's system from cable systems, which do perform "publicly." Viewed in terms of Congress' regulatory objectives, why should any of these technological differences matter? They concern the behind-the-scenes way in which Aereo delivers television programming to its viewers' screens. They do not render Aereo's commercial objective any different from that of cable companies. Nor do they significantly alter the viewing experience of Aereo's subscribers. Why would a subscriber who wishes to watch a television show care much whether images and sounds are delivered to his screen via a large multisubscriber antenna or one small dedicated antenna, whether they arrive instantaneously or after a few seconds' delay, or whether they are transmitted directly or after a personal copy is made? And why, if Aereo is right, could not modern CATV systems simply continue the same commercial and consumer-oriented activities, free of copyright restrictions, provided they substitute such new technologies for old? Congress would as much have intended to protect a copyright holder from the unlicensed activities of Aereo as from those of cable companies.

The text of the Clause effectuates Congress' intent. Aereo's argument to the contrary relies on the premise that "to transmit ... a performance" means to make a single transmission. But the Clause suggests that an entity may transmit a performance through multiple, discrete transmissions. That is because one can "transmit" or "communicate" something through a *set* of actions. Thus one can transmit a message to one's friends, irrespective of whether one sends separate identical e-mails to each friend or a single e-mail to all at once. So can an elected official communicate an idea, slogan, or speech to her constituents, regardless of whether she communicates that idea, slogan, or speech during individual phone calls to each constituent or in a public square.

The fact that a singular noun ("a performance") follows the words "to transmit" does not suggest the contrary. One can sing a song to his family, whether he sings the same song one-on-one or in front of all together. Similarly, one's colleagues may watch a performance of a particular play – say, this season's modern-dress version of "Measure for Measure" – whether they do so at separate or at the same showings. By the same principle, an entity may transmit a performance through one or several transmissions, where the performance is of the same work.

The Transmit Clause must permit this interpretation, for it provides that one may transmit a performance to the public "whether the members of the public capable of receiving the performance ... receive it ... at the same time or at different times." Were the words "to transmit ... a performance" limited to a single act of communication, members of the public could not receive the performance communicated "at different times." Therefore, in light of the purpose and text of the Clause, we conclude that when an entity communicates the same contemporaneously perceptible images and sounds to multiple people, it transmits a performance to them regardless of the number of discrete communications it makes.

We do not see how the fact that Aereo transmits via personal copies of programs could make a difference. The Act applies to transmissions "by means of any device or process." And retransmitting a television program using user-specific copies is a "process" of transmitting a performance. A "cop[y]" of a work is simply a "material objec[t] … in which a work is fixed … and from which the work can be perceived, reproduced, or otherwise communicated." So whether Aereo transmits from the same or separate copies, it performs the same work; it shows the same images and makes audible the same sounds. Therefore, when Aereo streams the same television program to multiple subscribers, it "transmit[s] … a performance" to all of them.

Moreover, the subscribers to whom Aereo transmits television programs constitute "the public." Aereo communicates the same contemporaneously perceptible images and sounds to a large number of people who are unrelated and unknown to each other. This matters because, although the Act does not define "the public," it specifies that an entity performs publicly when it performs at "any place where a substantial number of persons outside of a normal circle of a family and its social acquaintances is gathered." The Act thereby suggests that "the public" consists of a large group of people outside of a family and friends.

Neither the record nor Aereo suggests that Aereo's subscribers receive performances in their capacities as owners or possessors of the underlying works. This is relevant because when an entity performs to a set of people, whether they constitute "the public" often depends upon their relationship to the underlying work. When, for example, a valet parking attendant returns cars to their drivers, we would not say that the parking service provides cars "to the public." We would say that it provides the cars to their owners. We would say that a car dealership, on the other hand, does provide cars to the public, for it sells cars to individuals who lack a pre-existing relationship to the cars. Similarly, an entity that transmits a performance to individuals in their capacities as owners or possessors does not perform to "the public," whereas an entity like Aereo that transmits to large numbers of paying subscribers who lack any prior relationship to the works does so perform.

Finally, we note that Aereo's subscribers may receive the same programs at different times and locations. This fact does not help Aereo, however, for the Transmit Clause expressly provides that an entity may perform publicly "whether the members of the public capable of receiving the performance … receive it in the same place or in separate places and at the same time or at different times." In other words, "the public" need not be situated together, spatially or temporally. For these reasons, we conclude that Aereo transmits a performance of petitioners' copyrighted works to the public, within the meaning of the Transmit Clause.

IV

Aereo and many of its supporting *amici* argue that to apply the Transmit Clause to Aereo's conduct will impose copyright liability on other technologies, including new technologies, that Congress could not possibly have wanted to reach. We agree that Congress, while intending the Transmit Clause to apply broadly to cable companies and their equivalents, did not intend to discourage or to control the emergence or use of different kinds of technologies. But we do not believe that our limited holding today will have that effect.

For one thing, the history of cable broadcast transmissions that led to the enactment of the Transmit Clause informs our conclusion that Aereo "perform [s]," but it does not determine whether different kinds of providers in different contexts also "perform." For another, an entity only transmits a performance when it communicates contemporaneously perceptible images and sounds of a work.

Further, we have interpreted the term "the public" to apply to a group of individuals acting as ordinary members of the public who pay primarily to watch broadcast television programs, many of which are copyrighted. We have said that it does not extend to those who act as owners or possessors of the relevant product. And we have not considered whether the public performance right is infringed when the user of a service pays primarily for something other than the transmission of copyrighted works, such as the remote storage of content. In addition, an entity does not transmit to the public if it does not transmit to a substantial number of people outside of a family and its social circle.

We also note that courts often apply a statute's highly general language in light of the statute's basic purposes. Finally, the doctrine of "fair use" can help to prevent inappropriate or inequitable applications of the Clause.

We cannot now answer more precisely how the Transmit Clause or other provisions of the Copyright Act will apply to technologies not before us. We agree with the Solicitor General that "[q]uestions involving cloud computing, [remote storage] DVRs, and other novel issues not before the Court, as to which 'Congress has not plainly marked [the] course,' should await a case in which they are squarely presented." And we note that, to the extent commercial actors or other interested entities may be concerned with the relationship between the development and use of such technologies and the Copyright Act, they are of course free to seek action from Congress.

In sum, having considered the details of Aereo's practices, we find them highly similar to those of the CATV systems in Fortnightly and Teleprompter. And those are activities that the 1976 amendments sought to bring within the scope of the Copyright Act. Insofar as there are differences, those differences concern not the nature of the service that Aereo provides so much as the technological manner in which it provides the service. We conclude that those differences are not adequate to place Aereo's activities outside the scope of the Act.

For these reasons, we conclude that Aereo "perform[s]" petitioners' copyrighted works "publicly," as those terms are defined by the Transmit Clause. We therefore reverse the contrary judgment of the Court of Appeals, and we remand the case for further proceedings consistent with this opinion.

IT IS SO ORDERED. (...)

THINK IT OVER!

1. One of the reasons why the Aereo dispute arose is that the economic rights in the U.S. Copyright Act stem from the pre-Internet age. The right of public performance historically means a form of presenting works to the audience *in situ.* Since the 1990s, U.S. federal courts had to rule on the dissemination of works via the Internet, and they have reached a consensus that these acts fit into the concept of public performance. This interpretation did not necessarily run against the WCT, as under the "umbrella solution" signatories of the WCT are free to select any economic right (performance, distribution or communication to the public) to cover making available to the public of protected subject matters via the Internet. It is undeniable, however, that *the U.S. Copyright Act's terminology is slightly misleading.* This is clearly visible from Aereo's (mis)understanding of the right of performance and the concept of public. *Do you think that the case would have been solved differently under the European Union's copyright law?* Compare to the CJEU's ruling in *ITV v. TVCatchup.*

2. While Aereo provided access to live streams, plenty of other services allow end-users convenient digital alternatives to watching television. In *Fox Broadcasting v. Dish Network,* the plaintiff sued Dish for allowing its subscribers to set a single timer on Dish's Hopper set-top box to record and store primetime programming on the four major broadcast networks. Indeed, AutoHop feature enabled end-users to skip commercials while watching the recordings. The Ninth Circuit concluded that Dish's end-users were engaging in non commercial fair use by time-shifting the programming. Jane Ginsburg opined that "while licensed on-demand transmissions may in general be displacing private copying, entrepreneurs can, in effect, structure the enabling of end-user time-shifting to afford most of the convenience of video-ondemand (the selection of programming will not be infinite; it will be limited to whatever is broadcast over the four networks in the course of a week) without the pesky commercials (and, of course, without paying the copyright owners). The operation is technically time-shifting; in 'feel' to the consumer, however, it is essentially video-on-demand, but better." (Ginsburg, 2014, p. 1407.)

Further Case Law

Rogers Communications Inc. v. Society of Composers, Authors and Music Publishers of Canada, 2012 *SCC* 35, [2012] 2 R.C.S. 283.

Case C-607/11 - ITV Broadcasting Ltd. and Others v. TVCatchup Ltd., Judgment of the Court (Fourth Chamber), 7 March 2013 [ECLI:EU:C:2013:147]

Fox Broadcasting Corporation v. Dish Network LLC, 723 F.3d 1067 (2013)

Perfect 10, Inc., v. Giganews, Inc., et al., 847 *F.3d* 657 (2017)

BWP Media USA Inc., et al. v. Polyvore, Inc., 922 *F.3d* 42 (2019)

Recommended readings

In English

Jane C. Ginsburg: Fair Use for Free, or Permitted-but-Paid?, *Berkeley Technology Law Journal*, Issue 3/2014, p. 1383-1446.

Dallas T. Bullard: The Revolution was not Televised: Examining Copyright Doctrine after Aereo, *Berkeley Technology Law Journal*, Annual Review 2015, p. 899-931.

Ruchir Patel: The Legal Lag Behind Emerging Technology: Aereo - Innovation or Exploit?, *Boston College Intellectual Property & Technology Forum*, 2015, p. 1-5.

William E. Sterling: ABC, Inc. v. Aereo, Inc., *Boston University Journal of Science and Technology Law*, Summer 2015, p. 439-446.

Annemarie Bridy: Aereo: From Working Around Copyright to Thinking Inside the (Cable) Box, *Michigan State Law Review*, 2015, p. 465-483.

Makeen Fouad Makeen: *Video Streaming and the Communication to the Public Right in the United States and European Union.* In: Tanya Aplin (Ed.): *Research Handbook on Intellectual Property and Digital Technologies*, Edward Elgar, Cheltenham, 2020, p. 246-275.

VCAST LIMITED V. RTI SPA

Case C-265/16 - Judgment of the Court (Third Chamber), 29 November 2017 [ECLI:EU:C:2017:913]

(...) Legal context

EU law

Directive 2000/31

3 Article 3(2) of Directive 2000/31 reads as follows:
'Member States may not, for reasons falling within the coordinated field, restrict the freedom to provide information society services from another Member State.'

4 Article 3(3) of Directive 2000/31 provides that, inter alia, Article 3(2) of that directive does not apply to the fields referred to the annex to that directive, that annex concerning, inter alia, copyright and related rights.

Directive 2001/29

5 According to recital 1 of Directive 2001/29:

'The Treaty provides for the establishment of an internal market and the institution of a system ensuring that competition in the internal market is not distorted. Harmonisation of the laws of the Member States on copyright and related rights contributes to the achievement of these objectives.'

6 Recital 23 of that directive states:

'This Directive should harmonise further the author's right of communication to the public. This right should be understood in a broad sense covering all communication to the public not present at the place where the communication originates. This right should cover any such transmission or retransmission of a work to the public by wire or wireless means, including broadcasting. This right should not cover any other acts.'

7 Article 2 of that directive provides:

'Member States shall provide for the exclusive right to authorise or prohibit direct or indirect, temporary or permanent reproduction by any means and in any form, in whole or in part:

(a) for authors, of their works;

(b) for performers, of fixations of their performances;

(c) for phonogram producers, of their phonograms;

(d) for the producers of the first fixations of films, in respect of the original and copies of their films;

(e) for broadcasting organisations, of fixations of their broadcasts, whether these broadcasts are transmitted by wire or over the air, including by cable or satellite.'

8 Article 3(1) of Directive 2001/29 reads as follows:

'Member States shall provide authors with the exclusive right to authorise or prohibit any communication to the public of their works, by wire or wireless means, including the making available to the public of their works in such a way that members of the public may access them from a place and at a time individually chosen by them.'

9 Article 5(2)(b) of that directive provides:

'Member States may provide for exceptions or limitations to the reproduction right provided for in Article 2 in the following cases:

...

(b) in respect of reproductions on any medium made by a natural person for private use and for ends that are neither directly nor indirectly commercial, on condition that the rightholders

receive fair compensation which takes account of the application or non-application of technological measures referred to in Article 6 to the work or subject-matter concerned'.

10 According to Article 5(5) of that directive:

'The exceptions and limitations provided for in paragraphs 1, 2, 3 and 4 shall only be applied in certain special cases which do not conflict with a normal exploitation of the work or other subject-matter and do not unreasonably prejudice the legitimate interests of the rightholder.'

Italian law

11 Article 5(2)(b) of Directive 2001/29 was transposed into Italian law in Article 71 sexies of Legge n. 633 — Protezione del diritto d'autore e di altri diritti connessi al suo esercizio (Law No 633 on the protection of copyright and other rights relating to its exercise) of 22 April 1941 in the version in force on the date of the facts at issue in the main proceedings ('the Law on copyright'). That Article 71 sexies, which is contained in Section II of that law, entitled 'Private reproduction for personal use', provides:

'1. The private reproduction of phonograms and videograms on any media made by natural persons for personal use only shall be permitted, provided that it is not for profit or ends that are directly or indirectly commercial, in compliance with the technical measures referred to in Article 102 quater.

2. The reproduction referred to in paragraph 1 may not be carried out by a third party. The provision of services for the reproduction of phonograms and videograms by a natural person for personal use shall constitute a reproduction activity covered by the provisions in Articles 13, 72, 78 bis, 79 and 80.

…'

12 Article 71 septies of the Law on copyright provides:

'1. The authors and producers of phonograms, and the original producers of audiovisual works, the performers and producers of videograms, and their successors in title, shall be entitled to compensation for the private copying of phonograms and videograms referred to in Article 71 sexies. In respect of devices designed solely for the analogue or digital recording of phonograms or videograms, that compensation shall consist of a percentage of the price paid by the final purchaser to the retailer which, in respect of multipurpose devices, shall be calculated on the basis of the price of a device with characteristics equivalent to those of the internal component designed to record or, where that is not possible, of a fixed amount for each device. In respect of audio and video recording media, such as analogue media, digital media and internal or removable memory designed for recording phonograms or videograms, the compensation shall consist of a sum corresponding to the recording capacity provided by those media. In respect of remote video recording systems, the

compensation referred to in this paragraph shall be due from the person who provides the service and correspond to the remuneration obtained for providing that service.
2. The compensation referred to in paragraph 1 shall be set, in accordance with Community law and having regard, in any event, to the reproduction rights, by a decree of the Minister for Cultural Heritage and Activities to be adopted by 31 December 2009, after consultation with the trade associations which represent the majority of the manufacturers of the devices and media and media referred to in paragraph 1. In setting the compensation, account shall be taken of the application or non-application of the technological measures referred to in Article 102 quater and the different effect of digital copying in comparison with analogue copying. The decree shall be updated every three years.

…'

13 Article 102 quater of the Law on copyright provides:
'*1. Rightholders of any copyright or of any related right as well as of the right under paragraph 3 of Article 102 bis may apply to protected works or objects effective technological protection measures, including any technology, device or component that, in the normal course of its operation, is designed to prevent or restrict acts which are not authorised by the rightholders.*
2. Technological protection measures shall be deemed effective where the use of the protected work or object is controlled by the rightholders through the application of an access control or protection process, such as encryption, scrambling or other transformation of the work or the protected work, or if that use is limited by a copy control mechanism which achieves the objective of protection.
3. The present article shall not affect the application of the provisions concerning computer programs referred to in Title 1, Chapter IV, Part VI.'

The dispute in the main proceedings and the questions referred for a preliminary ruling

14 VCAST is a company incorporated under UK law which makes available to its customers via the Internet a video recording system, in storage space within the cloud, for terrestrial programmes of Italian television organisations, among which are those of RTI.

15 It is apparent from the order for reference that, in practice, the user selects a programme on the VCAST website, which includes all the programming from the television channels covered by the service provided by that company. The user can specify either a certain programme or a time slot. The system operated by VCAST then picks up the television signal using its own antennas and records the time slot for the selected programme in the cloud data storage space indicated by the user. That storage space is purchased by the user from another provider.

16 VCAST brought proceedings against RTI before the specialised chamber for company law of the Tribunale di Torino (District Court, Turin, Italy), seeking a declaration of the lawfulness of its activity.

17 In the course of proceedings, by an order for reference of 30 October 2015, that court upheld in part the application for interim measures submitted by RTI and prohibited VCAST, in essence, from pursuing its activity.

18 Taking the view that the resolution of the case in the main proceedings depended in part on the interpretation of EU law, in particular on Article 5(2)(b) of Directive 2001/29, the Tribunale di Torino (District Court, Turin) decided to stay the proceedings and to refer the following questions to the Court for a preliminary ruling:

'*(1) Are national rules prohibiting a commercial undertaking from providing private individuals with so-called cloud computing services for the remote video recording of private copies of works protected by copyright, by means of that commercial undertaking's active involvement in the recording, without the rightholder's consent, compatible with EU law, in particular with Article 5(2)(b) of Directive 2001/29 (as well as Directive 2000/31 and the founding Treaty)?*

(2) Are national rules which allow a commercial undertaking to provide private individuals with so-called cloud computing services for the remote video recording of private copies of works protected by copyright, even where the active involvement of that commercial undertaking in the recording is entailed, and even without the rightholder's consent, against a flat-rate compensation in favour of the rightholder, in essence subjecting the services to a compulsory licensing system, compatible with EU law, in particular with Article 5(2)(b) of Directive 2001/29 (as well as Directive 2000/31 and the founding Treaty)?'

Consideration of the questions referred

(...)

The Court's reply

30 Under Article 5(2)(b) of Directive 2001/29, Member States may provide for exceptions or limitations to the reproduction right in respect of reproductions on any medium made by a natural person for private use and for ends that are neither directly nor indirectly commercial.

31 Moreover, Article 5(5) of that directive states that the exceptions and limitations provided for, inter alia, in Article 5(2) of that directive will only be applied in certain special cases

which do not conflict with a normal exploitation of the work or other subject matter and do not unreasonably prejudice the legitimate interests of the rightholder.

32 Concerning Article 5(2)(b) of Directive 2001/29, it must be pointed out that, according to the settled case-law of the Court, the provisions of a directive which derogate from a general principle established by that directive must be interpreted strictly. It follows that Article 5(2)(b) must be given such an interpretation.

33 The Court has also held that copying by natural persons acting in a private capacity must be regarded as an act likely to cause harm to the rightholder concerned, where it is done without seeking prior authorisation from that rightholder.

34 In addition, the Court has held that, while Article 5(2)(b) of Directive 2001/29 must be understood as meaning that the private copying exception prohibits the rightholder from relying on his exclusive right to authorise or prohibit reproductions with regard to persons who make private copies of his works, that provision must not be understood as requiring, beyond that express limitation, the copyright holder to tolerate infringements of his rights which may accompany the making of private copies.

35 Last, it follows from the case-law that, in order to rely on Article 5(2)(b), it is not necessary that the natural persons concerned possess reproduction equipment, devices or media. They may also have copying services provided by a third party, which is the factual precondition for those natural persons to obtain private copies.

36 The question whether a service such as that at issue in the main proceedings, the relevant elements of which are set out in paragraphs 14 and 15 of the present judgment, is covered by Article 5(2)(b) of Directive 2001/29 should be considered in the light of the case-law cited above.

37 In that regard, it should be pointed out that the provider of that service does not merely organise the reproduction, but also provides access to the programmes of certain television channels that can be recorded remotely, with a view to reproducing them. Thus, it is the individual customers who choose which programmes are to be recorded.

38 In that regard, the service at issue in the main proceedings has a dual functionality, consisting in ensuring both the reproduction and the making available of the works and subject matter concerned.

39 However, although the private copy exception means that the rightholder must abstain from exercising his exclusive right to authorise or prohibit private copies made by natural persons under the conditions provided for in Article 5(2)(b) of Directive 2001/29, the requirement for a strict interpretation of that exception implies that that rightholder is not deprived of his right to prohibit or authorise access to the works or the subject matter of which those same natural persons wish to make private copies.

40 It follows from Article 3 of Directive 2001/29 that any communication to the public, including the making available of a protected work or subject matter, requires the rightholder's consent, given that, as is apparent from recital 23 of that directive, the right of communication of works to the public should be understood in a broad sense covering any transmission or retransmission of a work to the public by wire or wireless means, including broadcasting.

41 In that respect, the Court has already held that the concept of 'communication to the public' includes two cumulative criteria, namely an 'act of communication' of a work and the communication of that work to a 'public'.

42 That said, it must be stated, first, that the concept of an 'act of communication' refers to any transmission of the protected works, irrespective of the technical means or process used.

43 Moreover, every transmission or retransmission of a work which uses a specific technical means must, as a rule, be individually authorised by the author of the work in question.

44 Second, in order to fall within the concept of 'communication to the public', within the meaning of Article 3(1) of Directive 2001/29, it is also necessary, as noted in paragraph 41 of the present judgment, that the protected works actually be communicated to a 'public'.

45 In that connection, it follows from the Court's case-law that the term 'public' refers to an indeterminate number of potential recipients and implies, moreover, a fairly large number of persons.

46 In the present case, the service provider at issue in the main proceedings records programmes broadcast and makes them available to its customers via the Internet.

47 In the first place, it is evident that the sum of the persons targeted by that provider constitutes a 'public' within the meaning of the case-law cited in paragraph 45 of the present judgment.

48 In the second place, the original transmission made by the broadcasting organisation, on the one hand, and that made by the service provider at issue in the main proceedings, on the other, are made under specific technical conditions, using a different means of transmission for the protected works, and each is intended for its public.

49 The transmissions referred to thus constitute communications to different publics, and each of them must therefore receive the consent of the rightholders concerned.

50 In those circumstances, it is no longer necessary to examine whether the publics targeted by those communications are identical or whether the public targeted by the service provider at issue in the main proceedings constitutes a new public.

51 It follows that, without the rightholder's consent, the making of copies of works by means of a service such as that at issue in the main proceedings could undermine the rights of that rightholder.

52 Accordingly, such a remote recording service cannot fall within the scope of Article 5(2)(b) of Directive 2001/29.

53 In those circumstances, there is no longer any need to verify whether the conditions imposed by Article 5(5) of that directive have been complied with.

54 In view of all the foregoing considerations, the answer to the questions asked is that Directive 2001/29, in particular Article 5(2)(b) thereof, precludes national legislation which permits a commercial undertaking to provide private individuals with a cloud service for the remote recording of private copies of works protected by copyright, by means of a computer system, by actively involving itself in the recording, without the rightholder's consent.

THINK IT OVER!

1. The tensions around the home recording of television programs were relatively easy to solve as long as end-users relied on video tape recorders. In 1984, the U.S. Supreme Court declared such activity as fair use in the *Betamax* (*Sony v. Universal*) decision. Since the 1980s, European legislators (first in Germany, Austria and Hungary) introduced private copying levy to compensate for the losses of rights holders suffered due to private copying. Concerns arose around the legality of such recordings as soon as end-users relied on the services that provided storage on and accessing possibilities from remote servers. The Hungarian Copyright Expert Board concluded in *Expert opinion No. 31/07/1* that the recording of television signal via an IPTV service is lawful as long as the end-user fully controls the recording. In *National Rugby League Investments v Singtel Optus* (Optus TV Now), the Federal Court of Australia also found that the setting up of an automated cloud-based service that fetches and stores copies of copyrighted subject matter at the user's command makes the service provider a maker of the copy. Further, the Court added that "the contractual allocation of functions and responsibilities in making a copy of copyright material may, but does not necessarily, identify the person (or persons) who 'make(s)' the copy for copyright infringement purposes. The making of the copy may be the product of the concerted action of both parties to the contract such that they together are the 'makers' of the copy" (para. 74.). The CJEU has also confirmed in *VCAST* that the mere provision of facilities capable to create copies of protected subject matter at remote servers is not illegal *per se*. At the same time, the CJEU correctly noted that "the service at issue in the main proceedings has a dual functionality, consisting in ensuring both the reproduction and the making available of the works and subject matter concerned" (para. 38.). *What are the doctrinal prerequisites of creating private copies in the cloud?*

2. Following *VCAST*, what types of copying in the cloud fits into Article 5(2)(b) of Directive 2001/29? *Where is the dividing line between providing active services for end-users and the provision of mere technical facilities?* Compare to para. 38 et seq, especially para. 39. Compare further to the concept of "communication to the new public" developed by the CJEU.

Further Case Law

Sony Corp. of America v. Universal City Studios, Inc., 464 U.S. 417 (1984)

SzJSzT 31/07/1 - "IPTV szolgáltatás szerzői jogi megítélése". In: *Iparjogvédelmi és Szerzői Jogi Szemle*, 2008/1. szám, p. 166-178.

National Rugby League Investments Pty Limited v Singtel Optus Pty Ltd [2012] FCAFC 59 (27 April 2012)

Recommended readings

In English

Mariliana Rico: *Cloud Computing and Copyright: New Challenges in Legal Protection?* In: John N. Gathegi - Yaşar Tonta - Serap Kurbanoğlu - Umut Al - Zehra Taşkın (Ed.): Challenges of Information Management Beyond the Cloud, Springer, Heidelberg, 2013: p. 54-63.

Tito Rendas: Cloud Computing and Copyright Law: Cloud-Based Video Recording Reaches the CJEU, *Journal of Intellectual Property Law & Practice*, Issue 11/2016, p. 808.

Jan Bernd Nordemann: Recent CJEU case law on communication to the public and its application in Germany: A new EU concept of liability, *Journal of Intellectual Property Law and Practice*, Issue 9/2018, p. 744-756.

In French

Lionel Costes: La proprieté littéraire et artistique, *Droit de l'immatériel: informatique, médias, communication*, 2017, n° 143, p. 14-17.

Philippe Mouron: Les services d'enregistrement numérique, entre le droit de communication au public et l'exception de copie privée, *Droit de l'immatériel: informatique, médias, communication*, 2018, n° 148, p. 9-13.

In German

Matthias Leistner: Internet-Videorecorder und Cloud-Speicheranbieter: Warum eine Betreibervergütung die richtige Lösung für die Zukunft ist, *Computer und Recht*, Heft 7/2018, p. 436-444.

In Hungarian

Faludi Gábor - Grad-Gyenge Anikó: A cloud computing-alapú szolgáltatások szerzői jogi megítéléséről, *Infokommunikáció és jog*, 2012/3. szám, p. 105-108.

Mezei Péter: Az Európai Bíróság VCAST döntésének hatásai a felhőmegoldások jövőjére, *Gazdaság és Jog*, 2018/4. szám, p. 9-14.

WARNER MUSIC UK LTD., ET AL. V. TUNEIN INC.

[2019] *EWHC* 2923 (Ch)

(...) Targeting - the law

16. The legal principles are:

i) The mere existence of a website and its accessibility by local consumers is never enough to establish a territorial link (...).

ii) The issue of targeting is to be considered from the perspective of the public in the relevant state (i.e. the UK) (...). The trade mark cases refer to consumers or average consumers because that is the relevant person in trade mark law. For cases about communication to the public, the question focusses on the public (...).

iii) The test is objective in the sense that a party's subjective intention cannot turn a website or page which is objectively not targeted at the UK into one which is (...). However that does not mean evidence of intention is irrelevant. On the contrary such evidence is relevant and possibly determinative in an appropriate case (...).

iv) The court must carry out an evaluation of all the relevant circumstances (...).

v) It may be appropriate to treat a website as a whole, but in another case it may be appropriate to conduct a more fine grained analysis. Depending on how a website is organised, not all pages are necessarily targeted at the same place(s) (...).

17. The following is a non-exhaustive summary of factors which may be considered, the weight they bear necessarily varying from case to case:

i) The appearance of the web pages themselves, which can include explicit statements of an intention to provide goods or services to the public in the UK and the highlighting of the UK in lists or maps.

ii) Other aspects of the web pages such as language(s), currency(ies), telephone numbers, and the use of national top level domain names.

iii) The nature and size of the service provider's business, the characteristics of the goods or services offered and provided, and the number of visits made by the public from the UK.

18. Where the apps provide services akin to those provided by a website, as they do in this case, the considerations must be the same.

Targeting – the facts

19. TuneIn's website (tunein.com) had well over 1 million unique UK visitors per month in 2017 and 2018. In January 2019, it had over 5 million UK users of its free service. Figures for the service do not distinguish between the website and the apps. UK users represent about 10% of TuneIn's user base and they stream 9.8 million hours of audio content per month. The UK accounts for more than 10% of its annual indirect advertising revenue.

20. The user experiences advertisements in the TuneIn service in two ways – visual and audio. The visual advertisements appear as part of the TuneIn screens. The audio advertisement is the pre-roll which plays when a user clicks on the relevant icon to indicate they wish to start listening to a particular internet radio station. The pre-roll plays for about 15 seconds before the internet radio station audio stream starts. Both sets of advertisements are plainly targeted at the UK. Much of it is denominated in pounds sterling.

21. TuneIn also has a system for playing its own "in-stream" advertisements. Using this technique when an internet radio station starts playing its own advertisements, TuneIn's system recognises this and instead of the user hearing the advertisement which the internet radio station plays, the user hears a different advertisement put there by TuneIn. However apart from a glitch, which I accept was a one-off error, the in-stream function does not occur for users in the UK listening to music stations.

22. Also relevant is the way the audio stream from the internet radio station is presented to the user. Once it starts playing, the underlying stream URL is not obviously visible to the user. I find that the user is unlikely to appreciate that the audio content is coming directly from the third party station's website (which is what is in fact happening), rather than from TuneIn.

23. TuneIn provides local radio categorisations and search options specifically by reference to the UK and to towns and cities within the UK.

24. TuneIn argued that the targeting of the visual advertising was the result of the effect of automated advertising platforms and that TuneIn did not select the individual advertisements. In my judgment that is irrelevant because from the point of view of the user – the public in the UK – it would still appear that they were being targeted. I doubt that the relevant UK public understand how advertisement targeting works (a point was made with a view to suggesting that people knew that it was not TuneIn itself which makes the choice) but nor do I accept that that would make a difference even if they did. The objective presence of UK targeted advertisements is what matters for targeting.

25. In any event the TuneIn service carries bespoke advertising aimed at the UK such as the pre-roll advertising. There was also clear evidence that TuneIn engages the services of advertising sellers specifically for the UK and that it assists in the targeting of advertising campaigns to particular demographics within the UK. It has a UK-based employee who is responsible for contributing ideas on promotional activity arising out of events taking place in the UK and Europe. TuneIn enters into partner agreements with UK-based radio stations such as Jazz FM, Bauer, and Global Radio. There is evidence that it has procured at least some partner broadcasters in the UK to promote the TuneIn service. TuneIn has entered into an agreement with the BBC which provides that its stations will only be made available in the UK and the Republic of Ireland. This is called "geo-restriction". TuneIn can and does geo-restrict other stations so that they too are only available in the UK as well.

26. TuneIn also offers paid for ad-free services. These are the Premium services on the website and the Pro app. They are priced in sterling to UK based customers. The factors mentioned above which do not involve advertising, i.e. the user being unlikely to appreciate that the stream comes directly from the internet radio station, the UK specific categorisations and search options, and relationships with some UK based stations, are also relevant.

27. Overall, it is manifest that TuneIn's service – as a whole – provided by the website or the apps, is targeted at the UK. The UK is not the only country targeted by TuneIn but it is plainly one of them. In fact, by closing, TuneIn conceded that the TuneIn platform targeted the UK (*inter alia*) but contended that while this applied to the platform as a whole, it did not apply to the individual alleged acts of communication to the public. I do not accept that, for the reasons explained below.

28. From the user's point of view, the purpose of using the TuneIn platform is to be provided with access to the internet radio station streams. The service provides that access by serving up icons of possible stations to select. Up to that point, to UK based users, the service is and has been targeted at the UK. If it was necessary to do so I would hold that even if nothing relevant happened after that, this would be sufficient to mean that any act of communication to the public, which was not complete until later in the process, was targeted at the UK anyway. However, at least for the services with advertising, that is not the end of the matter.

29. When the user then selects a particular stream the TuneIn pages remain on the user's screen and display the visual advertisements targeted at the UK. Also the pre-roll advertisement which then plays to UK users is targeted at the UK. It is true that, at the moment a user selects a particular internet radio station, the audio stream will probably be in the middle of something – speech or a piece of music – but that is irrelevant. At the time the stream

itself starts playing, the stream – and everything which follows within it – has, for a UK based user, been targeted by TuneIn at the UK. That is true whether the stream is a UK based internet radio station or a stream from an internet radio station which had not hitherto been targeted at the UK.

30. While the stream itself is playing, again the advertisements on screen for a UK user are targeting the UK.

31. In many cases the first time that a recording of a song which is actually in the claimants' repertoire is played in the stream selected by a user will be many minutes or even longer after they have started listening. In my judgment it is not necessary to analyse targeting by focussing on individual recordings in this way, but even if it were, then I would hold that such a recording is targeted at the UK in the relevant circumstances. The targeting which occurred up to the selection of the stream is still relevant. The targeting of the service and the stream by TuneIn does not change during the time the stream is played. Also the visual advertisements on the TuneIn page which accompany the playing of the stream are UK targeted.

32. The fact that when an internet radio station is indexed by TuneIn and added to its database there is no decision by TuneIn to target the UK with such a stream is irrelevant. Even if the internet radio station actually provided to a UK user was an obscure station from a country on the other side of the world in a language the user did not understand, in which one would not *a priori* think a UK user would be interested, that is irrelevant. When it is presented to a UK user by TuneIn, from the UK user's perspective it is targeted at them.

33. Overall, I find that for all relevant purposes the acts of TuneIn radio complained of are targeted at the UK.

(...)

113. Four categories of Sample Station were agreed upon. These categories were intended to reflect points of distinction which it appeared from the pleadings might be relevant to the disputed issues. The claimants, and TuneIn, were directed to nominate 5 stations on each side in each category. The categories are:

i) music radio stations which are licensed in the UK (Category 1);

ii) music radio stations which are not licensed in the UK or elsewhere (Category 2);

iii) music radio stations which are licensed for a territory other than the UK (Category 3); and

iv) Premium music radio stations (Category 4).

(...)

Communication to the public - assessment

The TuneIn service

120. I start by considering the nature of the alleged act of communication undertaken by TuneIn. TuneIn submits that TuneIn Radio provides nothing more than a directory or search engine which links users to websites containing relevant content, akin to Google or similar internet search engines. Its position is that TuneIn Radio is simply a more specialised search engine: instead of indexing and linking to websites generally, it indexes and links to radio station streams.

121. In argument neither party put it this way but it seems to me that when making a comparison with internet search engines it is necessary to identify the appropriate comparator. The relevance of the comparison is to illuminate where the balance lies between the functioning of the internet and the freedoms associated with that on the one hand, and the high protection to be afforded to intellectual property rights on the other. The issue is whether TuneIn does something different from the kind of search engine service which is a necessary part of the normal functioning of the internet. I call that a conventional search engine. A conventional search engine provides a service which the functioning of the internet depends on. It has a database with a search facility. It will no doubt have a prominent box for search on its home page. It will (internally) have structured indices of what is on the database. It may use fuzzy logic and automatic completion of text strings. When a search term is entered, the engine simply provides links to other websites in response to search terms. If a user selects the link then, at least from their point of view, the user is taken to that other website and the involvement of the search engine ceases. The search function is optimised in all sorts of ways to try and offer users what the search engine provider thinks the user really wants, nevertheless the search results provided are essentially neutral. Sponsored links (i.e. advertisements) may also be provided, reflecting a direct relationship between the search engine and particular websites or advertisers, but that sort of material is provided alongside the search results, not instead of them.

122. The comparison is with this sort of conventional search engine. The question is not necessarily answered by looking at particular services which may be offered by major internet search providers (such as Google or anyone else).

123. Significant features of TuneIn Radio are the following:

i) Aggregation: TuneIn collates and provides access to a vast array of international radio station streams. It essentially acts as a 'one-stop shop' for users, who are easily able to browse, search for and listen to stations in one place. The alternative for users is to use a standard internet search engine to locate a webcast / simulcast station by using tailored search terms, and then click-through to their websites to listen to the specific stream. One aspect of the difference there is that in the latter case the advertising targeted to the user once they access the stream will be entirely distinct in the two cases.
ii) Categorisation: TuneIn Radio enables users to browse by categories of music, such as location, genre and language, including sub-categories within those categories. This is the most commonly used method for users to find audio content. Music stations are placed in categories based on information provided by the stations and factors such as geographical location.
iii) Curation of station lists: In addition to categorising stations, TuneIn curates lists of radio stations and programmes to present them to users as part of the browsing experience on its website and via the apps. These stations are collated by factors such as location and language or themed around current events. For example, TuneIn promotes lists of stations to users, such as "Spin the Globe" (comprising international music stations) and "Editor's Choice – Music" (a hand-curated list of music stations). Certain stations are also listed in a "Featured" section, which is frequently updated by TuneIn to keep content relevant and non-repetitive.
iv) Personalisation of content: TuneIn Radio provides a personalised service to users, which facilitates their ability to find and listen to radio stations. TuneIn recommends stations to users based on their location, the reliability of audio streams and (in respect of registered users) the user's listening history. Registered users are also able to view their listening history and tag their 'favourite' stations and/or artists, which enables them to quickly access radio stations they have previously listened to via TuneIn Radio or their favourite stations and artists.
v) Search functionality: Users are able to search TuneIn Radio for specific radio stations and artists by name. The search functionality prioritises *inter alia* reliable station streams and stations which are popular at that time.
vi) Station information: TuneIn collates information about music stations, which is presented on individual station pages. This includes the genre of the station and, where available, the artist and track currently playing, the station's show timetable and related podcasts or featured shows.
vii) Artist information: TuneIn also collates information about artists on dedicated artist pages, which can be accessed by searching for the particular artist. The artist pages include a list of stations which play the particular artist (based on metadata provided by the stations) and a list of the artist's albums. Users are also able to click-through to each album page, which displays the individual tracks on each album.

124. Before going any further, I will address a comparison between TuneIn's service and hyperlinking more generally. One of the submissions of Counsel for TuneIn is that a conclusion

in favour of the claimants interferes with the freedom of those publishing materials on other websites, such as bloggers, to use hyperlinks at all. This is a different point from the issue about search engines but the same logic applies. The comparison ought to be with a conventional sort of linking, which is the sort of linking seen in *Svensson* or *GS Media*. These links tend to appear as cross-references embedded in other information published on a website. In any event what these websites do not do however is operate as aggregators of links on the scale of TuneIn. In my judgment aggregation provides a sufficient distinction between what TuneIn does as compared to the more conventional sort of linking all over the internet. Based on this difference I do not need to be concerned any further about conventional linking. On the other hand aggregation is exactly what search engines do and I will consider that next.

125. At a technical level, like any search engine, TuneIn's service operates by providing and indexing hyperlinks to users. Mr Godsay produced diagrams to show how TuneIn's process of linking a user to a station stream worked. (...)

126. However while its technical accuracy is not in doubt, in my judgment this characterisation over-simplifies the service actually provided to users via TuneIn Radio.

127. TuneIn advertises the platform as being widely available, on any device, and emphasises that: "TuneIn empowers people to hear exactly what they love the moment they want it, and discover a universe of audio, all in one place". A fair description of TuneIn Radio is that it provides users with a user-friendly, browseable and searchable platform of radio stations and other audio content, which enables users to easily select and listen to music radio stations. While I accept many of the features of TuneIn Radio are provided by conventional search engines, and I accept that at its heart what TuneIn Radio provides is a link to a stream such that the stream, when played, comes from the internet radio station website rather than from TuneIn, nevertheless in my judgment it is not accurate to characterise TuneIn as providing a conventional search engine service. It is much more than that.

128. The most important features which, cumulatively, support this distinction are as follows:
i) The fact that TuneIn aggregates links to audio streams as opposed to links to some other form(s) of content is relevant. The audio streams carry music and as a result they engage various intellectual property rights, as TuneIn is well aware.
ii) The data collected and curated by TuneIn allows for searches of stations to be carried out by artist. Such a search returns internet radio stations which are playing music by the artist at that moment. As I understand it this is only possible as a result of TuneIn's own monitoring stream

or not target that station to UK customers. I conclude that in terms of *GS Media*, a presumption of knowledge arises.

149. TuneIn's general case that it can rebut the presumption is based on the submission that it requires all internet radio stations to give a warranty to TuneIn that they have the necessary licences and that no further licences or payments are necessary for the internet radio station to be added to TuneIn's directory. I do not accept this for a number of reasons.

150. First, there was a dispute about how internet radio stations came to be added to TuneIn's directory. In the early days of TuneIn's operation, internet radio stations were found by TuneIn's web crawler software and added to the directory without any intervention by those internet radio stations. However TuneIn's position is that since 14 February 2014 all new stations were required to fill in a "New Station Form" and more generally since 2013/14 all other stations have been required to accept "Broadcaster Terms". The only exceptions are certain stations with bespoke agreements with TuneIn but those are in substantially equivalent form. This was the evidence of Ms Robinson and also to some extent Mr Straley. The significance of this from TuneIn's point of view is the presence of warranties in the terms.

151. The claimants submitted that this evidence did not reflect what had really happened for a number of reasons. First, save for the bespoke agreements, the manner in which the internet radio stations were to indicate their acceptance of the relevant terms was by ticking a box on a website form. However there was a dispute about when that was introduced. The claimants contended it was in September 2016 and did not apply beforehand. Ms Robinson said in cross-examination that it applied to the Station Update Form since 2011. The claimants contended that this must be doubted and was inconsistent with the pleadings. I am not satisfied it was introduced earlier than 2016. The claimants submitted this means tens of thousands of stations never ticked the box. I accept that.

152. Second, in cross-examination it was put to Ms Robinson that TuneIn indexes and makes stations available regardless of whether they have accepted the terms. Although she emphasised that in her view the majority of stations had accepted the terms and she maintained TuneIn relied on them, she accepted that the point put was true. I find that there are in fact stations indexed and available on TuneIn's service for which TuneIn knows there has been no acceptance of any relevant terms.

153. Therefore I find that a substantial number of stations indexed by TuneIn have no warranty associated with them and that TuneIn is aware of this. That will include some sample stations. For example Shout FM was marked by Mr Straley as a Category 3 station which had

submitted a station update form but for which the relevant date is 8 March 2013. Radio Dudelange in Category 2 is in the same position (update form provided but relevant date before 2016).

154. Turning to the stations for which, on TuneIn's case, it has the benefit of a warranty, the claimants contended there were other problems. An important one was that for a number of stations, the terms were not in fact a warranty that appropriate licences had been obtained at all, but rather were statements that sole responsibility for obtaining licences relating to public performance in the relevant territory rested with the station. These included the agreement with Global Radio Services (which includes Heart, Classic FM, Smooth) and the Jazz FM agreement, both in the UK; the agreement with SBS Radio AB (Mix Megapol) in Sweden (Category 3); the agreement with Radio 538 BV (Sky Radio) in the Netherlands (Category 3); the agreement with Corus (Country 104) in Canada (Category 2); and the agreement with Deutschlandradio (Deutschlandfunk) in Germany (Category 3). Furthermore TuneIn's agreement with the BBC contains an express clause excluding any warranties.

155. For the stations for which it can be said a warranty has been given, even assuming everything else in TuneIn's favour, the most that can be said is that the warranty amounts to a representation that the internet radio station is operating lawfully in its home state. It is not a representation at all about the position in the UK.

156. The evidence about the warranties as a whole sheds light on TuneIn's attitude to them. I find that from TuneIn's point of view, they are not important. There is no systematic attempt to ensure the internet radio stations indexed by TuneIn are covered by such a warranty. Even if a warranty by the internet radio station that they operate lawfully in their home state was capable of being relevant to the legal analysis, I am not satisfied that on the facts of this case that TuneIn takes them sufficiently seriously for them to be relevant to the analysis of the state of TuneIn's knowledge under *GS Media.* This applies to TuneIn's activities as a whole. It is not concerned with any particular category of station.

157. Finally I will mention the effect of the warranties. Given my conclusion on Category 3, a warranty that an internet radio station operates lawfully in its home state cannot help. However I recognise that if I am wrong about Category 3 then such a warranty could be relevant if the giving of it was a true precondition to being indexed. Whether a tickbox on a webpage by reference to legal terms which had not even been read amounts to good notice to TuneIn that the internet radio station was making a considered representation, is not a matter I have to decide.

158. Therefore I conclude that TuneIn is not able to rebut the *GS Media* presumption and therefore, for those stations in Category 2 which are made available without any consent, TuneIn should be taken to know that.

159. Of course irrespective of the questions considered in this section of the judgment, no infringement will take place unless the internet radio station actually plays relevant sound recordings. There is no evidence that the Kazakhstan station Gakku FM has ever played any relevant sound recordings.

160. Therefore, assuming the stations actually broadcast relevant content, then TuneIn infringes s20 of the 1988 Act in relation to Category 2 stations by the application of the *GS Media* test.

Category 4

161. The internet radio station streams in Category 4 were created exclusively for TuneIn. For these streams, there is no prior act of making them available to the public. That means the provision of those streams by TuneIn amounts to an act of communication to the public and, since it is targeted at the UK but unlicensed, it is an act of infringement.

162. The most that can be said is that, in some cases, a provider of a Category 4 stream to TuneIn, which is ad-free, also makes other streams directly available to the public. At most that would make Category 4 the same as Category 3 if they were compliant with the regime in their home state, but I am not satisfied that the argument about Category 4 stations gets that far. That is because the streams made available to the public, to the extent they are, are not the same streams as the ones in Category 4. I hold that the fact that the same work may appear on one public stream at one moment and then on a different Category 4 stream to which TuneIn links at a different moment, does not turn the act of making the work available on the first public stream into a relevant act of communication to the public vis a vis the linking to the second stream in Category 4. The context in which the work appears the first time is materially different from the context in the second case.

163. There was some suggestion that providers created two versions of an otherwise identical stream, one with advertisements and one without. I am not certain that was the evidence but even if it were, I would not accept that the making available of a stream which included advertisements could be said to amount to a relevant first act of communication to the public vis a vis the linking to the second stream in Category 4. The contexts in which the works appear in these two streams is still materially different.

Category 1

164. The internet radio stations in Category 1 are all licensed under the relevant UK copyright. As I have already found, all are in fact available to the public without access restrictions, and, at the risk of repetition, that is something to which the rights holder for the UK has consented. That means that for each stream in Category 1 an act of communication to the public takes place logically prior to any link by TuneIn. Nevertheless the claimants contend that the intervention of TuneIn makes these stations available to a new public.

165. The question therefore is the same as for Category 3: were the public to whom TuneIn's act of communication complained of is addressed, taken into account in the deemed consent to the first act of communication?

166. The difference between Category 3 and Category 1 is that for Category 3 the answer to that question involves both the nature of TuneIn's act of communication and the territorial element whereas for Category 1 the territorial aspect does not apply.

167. I can see that there is scope for a different view but I have decided that the territorial difference is enough to mean that for Category 1 there is no new public whereas for Category 3 there is. The reason I reach that result is by considering where the overall balance ought to lie between giving high protection to intellectual property rights on the one hand and the freedoms of expression and information available via the internet on the other. To hold otherwise would be an unwarranted restriction on those freedoms in circumstances in which the copyright owners have the ability to exercise their rights in relation to the original internet radio station.

168. Contrasting the position in Category 3, it is obvious that the arrangements between the operator of the Category 1 internet radio station and the UK rights holder have taken into account the territorial feature of the public to whom TuneIn's system is targeted, since it is targeted at users in the UK. Although TuneIn's act of communication is a different kind of activity from that of the station operator, it is directed to the users in the very same territory. Moreover although I have characterised TuneIn's act as being different from the conventional linking, it is at its root a form of linking. The stream provided (subject to the pre-roll) is whatever is published by the original internet radio station. That aspect, allied with the targeting to the same territory, is enough to distinguish between Category 3 and Category 1 on these facts.

169. The claimants point out that the various licences contain detailed terms. The terms fall into two classes. One class of terms related to the programming of the content on the stream. These are unaffected by this analysis and are irrelevant, since the stream remains as it is. The other set of terms consist of various restrictions and exceptions, the most significant being terms in the PPL Traditional Radio Licence (clause 3.4), which relate to streaming of the licensee's transmission via "third party websites", which are defined as websites without a licence. TuneIn's service would be a third party website. The clause provides:

"However: ...
(a) this shall not prevent Internet Simulcast Services from being accessed via a third party website by means of a hyperlink (or "click through") to a Licensed Website; and ...
(b) this shall not oblige the Licensee to prevent Internet Simulcast Services from being accessed via a third party website by means of so-called "deep linking" (i.e., where an Internet Simulcast Service is accessed from its server without recourse to a Licensed Website)".

170. TuneIn's service would fall within (b) above however in my judgment this is irrelevant. As already explained, I am not persuaded that the answer to the questions posed by the communication right are to be found in these detailed contract terms between the claimants and the individual Category 1 internet radio station providers. To take such an approach would create real practical problems for the functioning of the internet. The critical thing in my judgment is that the act which makes the stream to which TuneIn links publicly accessible, is itself a licensed act.

171. Accordingly TuneIn's act of communication in relation to Category 1 is not an infringement under s20 of the 1988 Act.

The recording function in the TuneIn Radio Pro app

172. Until April 2017, when it was disabled for UK users, TuneIn's Radio Pro app allowed users to record content and, as a result, to replay, pause and fast forward it as the users saw fit. If sufficient metadata was provided by the stations, users could also use an 'intelligent-skip' function, which allowed users to skip to the start or end of specific audio tracks and/or skip in-stream advertisements. The claimants contend that making the sound recordings available via this app when it had that function enabled was an act of communication to the public even if, when that function was not enabled, there was no communication to the public.

173. TuneIn made a point that the ability to record sound which is playing on the radio has existed for years, which is undoubtedly true. It also relied on the fact that a record function exists on mobile devices such as the Apple iPhone. I do not believe any of this is relevant since the function under consideration is an integrated part of TuneIn's paid for app. The proper way to view the recording function in the app is as part of the overall service offered by TuneIn through the app. One aspect which bears that out is that TuneIn has the technical ability to disable its app based recording function at the level of individual internet radio stations. TuneIn also says that the interface presented to the user is essentially the same and so, from the point of view of a user not interested in using it, there will be no difference from the case when it is disabled. I accept that the function is only part of the app's interface but this argument does not help decide what the overall effect is of the app when the function is not disabled.

174. The line taken by the claimants is on the basis that the Pro app including the record function is a new technical means. The claimants cited the CJEU's decision in *VCast.* That case did involve recording technology however I do not read it as supporting the claimants. The recording function was not the new technical means, the new technical means in question was the internet itself which was used to make the works available (the first act of communication being a television broadcast). I do not believe the claimants' point is assisted by *VCast.*

175. I find that the inclusion of this feature makes a material difference to the nature of TuneIn's act of communication via the app, at least when one considers users contemplating its use (and there are a substantial number of those). When that sort of user selects and listens to an internet radio station using the app which includes the recording function it seems to me that one cannot describe TuneIn's service as nothing more than a form of linking, conventional or unconventional. A user who wants to create a library of music by a particular artist can use TuneIn's Pro app to search for internet radio stations playing that artist, listen to the streams and make recordings of the claimants' works on their device. It is TuneIn's intervention which makes feasible something which would be wholly impractical for a user otherwise.

176. TuneIn argued that the claimants case muddled up two rights, the right of communication to the public and the reproduction right. I do not accept that. Making the recording relies on the act of communication undertaken by TuneIn. In providing a user with an integrated means of finding internet radio stations, playing them through the TuneIn app and then recording and playing back individual works the subject of the claimant's rights, TuneIn

has converted the internet radio station's streaming service into a permanent download on demand service.

177. Although of course it is true that the internet is the medium by which the stream is conveyed to the user's device, I find that the Pro app itself, containing the integrated function, running on the user's device is a new and different technical means from that by which the original internet radio station was provided. That finding applies to all three of Categories 1, 2 and 3.

178. Therefore in all three of those Categories TuneIn has infringed under s20 and would do so in future if the recording function was enabled. Also if, which I have rejected, Category involved a prior act of communication then the same would apply. (...)

THINK IT OVER!

Both parties claimed victory after the ruling. TuneIn was declared lawful with respect to linking to streams that originate from the United Kingdom. The ruling confirmed the applicability of the "new public theory" in linking to live streams that are property licensed in the UK as well. [The earlier CJEU rulings were either connected to static data, e.g. news articles (in *Svensson*), still images (in *GS Media*), or static videos (in *BestWater*).] At the same time, plaintiffs scored a victory with respect to linking to the streams of other radio signals. TuneIn should have licensed anything that originated from another jurisdiction (and were not properly licensed in the UK). This conclusion is heavily based on the concept of targeting. As Jeremy Blum and Sara Sefton noted, "[t]he case law on targeting is clear – merely having an accessible site or platform online does not mean your acts are infringing acts in a territory – there needs to be targeting. In this case, it was solely the acts of TuneIn that turned some streams (targeted solely at the domestic market for the origin of the stream) into streams targeting UK consumers. It is the act of the targeting that turns the act into an infringing one, so in circumstances where a party has not done any act solely or jointly to target, it seems very rigid to find them liable too." (Blum - Sefton, 2019.) *Do you think the ruling offers for a balanced solution? Can it break the Internet?* Although this book focuses much less on jurisdictional questions, *do you think it is a practically realistic (and financially sound) approach to sue foreign entities for activities that are "targeted" to nationals of other countries? Can plaintiffs gain damages from the defendant with respect to such international infringements?* Please note that Judge Birss' ruling is subject to appeals.

Further Case Law

Case C-466/12 - Nils Svensson and Others v. Retriever Sverige AB, Judgment of the Court (Fourth Chamber), 13 February 2014 [ECLI:EU:C:2014:76]

Case C-160/15 - GS Media BV v Sanoma Media Netherlands BV and Others, Judgment of the Court (Second Chamber), 8 September 2016 [ECLI:EU:C:2016:644]

BGH 21.9.2017 (I ZR 11/16) - Vorschaubilder III. In: *Gewerblicher Rechtsschutz und Urheberrecht*, Heft 2/2018, p. 178-189.

Recommended readings

In English

Jeremy Blum - Sara Sefton: Stay tuned for insight into the CJEU's approach to 'communication to the public' - When does an internet radio service infringe copyright?, *Kluwer Copyright Blog*, 9 December 2019 (http://copyrightblog.kluweriplaw.com/2019/12/09/stay-tuned-for-insight-into-the-cjeus-approach-to-communication-to-the-public-when-does-an-internet-radio-service-infringe-copyright/)

Bernhard Heinzl: Radio Stream Aggregator TuneIn Held to Infringe Rightholders' Copyrights, *Journal of Intellectual Property Law & Practice*, Issue 2/2020, p. 84-85.

Yin Harn Lee: United Kingdom Copyright Decisions 2019, *IIC - International Review of Intellectual Property and Competition Law*, Issue 3/2020, p. 364-366.

BEIJING WEIBO SHIJIE TECHNOLOGY CO., LTD. V. BAIDU ONLINE NETWORK TECHNOLOGY (BEIJING) CO., LTD. AND BAIDU WANGXUN TECHNOLOGY CO., LTD.

(2018) Beijing No. 491 People's Court No. 1 Civil First Judgment

The plaintiff Beijing Weibo Shijie Technology Co., Ltd. (hereinafter Weibo Shijie) is the operator of the famous online video-sharing platform called "Douyin" (as known as Tik-Tok, hereinafter Tik-Tok). The defendants Baidu Online Network Technology (Beijing) Co., Ltd. and Baidu Wangxun Technology Co., Ltd. (hereinafter collectively Baidu) are the operators of another video-sharing platform known as "Huopai". On May 12, 2018, the tenth memorial day of Wenchuan Earthquake, an internet influencer with more than 25 million followers named "Blackface V", produced a 13-second video entitled "May 12, I want to tell you" by using the materials given by Medias for Party Affairs and released it on Tik-Tok. The plaintiff owned the exclusive right to communicate such work to the public over information networks worldwide with the authorization of "Blackface V", while a user of Huopai uploaded the same "I want to tell you" video without watermarks of Tik-Tok and User ID embedded. The user allowed all other users of Huopai to download this short video free of charge.

The plaintiff filed a lawsuit on the ground that the "I want to tell you" short video constitutes a work created by virtue of an analogous method of film production, and the aforementioned acts of unauthorized distribution and watermarks removal by Baidu infringed Weibo Shijie's right of communication through information network. Tik Tok sought an injunction and damages of 1,000,000 RMB, and an additional reasonable cost of 50,000 RMB. Baidu claimed that the disputed video uploaded to TikTok were too short to be considered as a work created by virtue of an analogous method of film production, and could not enjoy copyright protection due to its lack of originality. Baidu further held that its behavior did not constitutes a copyright infringement based on that facts that it was the user who provided the disputed video rather than Baidu, and Baidu immediately complied with the requirements of the notice-and-take-down procedure.

Rules

Copyright Law (2010 Revision)

Article 3 For the purposes of this Law, the term "works" includes works of literature, art, natural science, social science, engineering technology and the like which are expressed in the following forms:

(6) cinematographic works and works created by virtue of an analogous method of film production;

Article 10 The term "copyright" shall include the following personality rights and property rights:

(12) the right of communication of information on networks, that is, the right to communicate to the public a work, by wire or wireless means in such a way that members of the public may access these works from a place and at a time individually chosen by them;

Article 48 Anyone who commits any of the following acts of infringement shall bear civil liability for such remedies as ceasing the infringing act, eliminating the effects of the act, making an apology or paying damages, depending on the circumstances and may, in addition, be subjected by a copyright administration department to such administrative penalties as ceasing the infringing act, confiscating unlawful income from the act, confiscating and destroying infringing reproductions and imposing a fine; where the circumstances are serious, the copyright administration department may also confiscate the materials, tools, and equipment mainly used for making the infringing reproductions; and if the act constitutes a crime, the infringer shall be prosecuted for his criminal liability:

(1) reproducing, distributing, performing, showing, broadcasting, compiling or communicating to the public on an information network a work created by another person, without the permission of the copyright owner, unless otherwise provided in this Law.

Regulation on the Protection of the Right to Communicate Works to the Public over Information Networks (2013 Revision)

Article 22 A network service provider which provides an information storage space to a service recipient, thus enabling the service recipient to make available to the public through information network a work, performance, or sound or video recording, and which meets the following conditions, bears no liability for compensation:

(1) it clearly indicates that such information storage space is provided for the service recipient, and it makes known to the public its name, the person to be contacted and network address of the network service provider;

(2) it does not make any modification to the work, performance, or sound or video recording made available by the service recipient;

(3) it does not know or has no reasonable grounds to know that the work, performance, or sound or video recording made available by the service recipient is an infringement;

(4) it does not gain any direct financial benefit from the service recipient making available the work, performance, or sound or video recording; and

(5) upon receiving a written notification of the right owner, it removes, in accordance with the provisions of these Regulations, the work, performance, or sound or video recording which the right owner believes to be an infringement.

Article 26 For the purposes of these Regulations:

Right of dissemination via information network shall mean the right to make a work, performance, or sound or visual recording available to the public by wire or wireless means, through which the public may access the work, performance, or sound or visual recording at times and places of their respective choices.

Technical measure shall mean any effective technology, device or component used to prevent or restrict the browsing or enjoyment of a work, performance, or sound or visual recording that is not authorized by the right owner or the making available to the public via an information network of a work, performance, or sound or visual recording.

Electronic information shall mean the information indicating works and their authors, performances and their performers, or sound or visual recordings and their producers, the information on the right owners of the works, performances, or sound or visual recordings and on the conditions for use thereof, as well as the digits or codes representing the abovementioned information.

Regulation for the Implementation of the Copyright Law of the People's Republic of China (2013 Revision)

Article 2 The term "works" as referred to in the Copyright Law means intellectual creations with originality in the literary, artistic or scientific domain, insofar as they can be reproduced in a tangible form.

Article 4 For the purposes of the Copyright Law and these Regulations:

(11) "Cinematographic works and works created by means similar to cinematography" refer to works filmed on a certain medium, consisting of images with or without accompanying sounds, and disseminated with the aid of certain appropriate devices or other methods.

Interpretation of the Supreme People's Court Concerning the Application of Laws in the Trial of Civil Disputes over Copyright (2002)

Article 15 With regards to a work created by different authors on the basis of a same topic, the authors shall enjoy independent copyright if the expression of the work is completed independently and is creative.

Analysis

1. Is the disputed short video a work created by the virtue of an analogous method of film production?

In this case, the disputed video obviously meets the requirements of "filmed on a certain medium, consisting of images with or without accompanying sounds, and disseminated with the aid of certain appropriate devices or other methods". The plaintiff argued that the disputed video constitutes a work created by means similar to cinematography, while the defendant believed that the 13-seconds short video lacks originality as required by Article 4(11) of the Chinese Copyright Act. Hence, "originality" is the key point to determine whether the disputed video constitutes a work created by means similar to cinematography. According to the Article 15 of the Interpretation of the Supreme People's Court Concerning the Application of Laws in the Trial of Civil Disputes over Copyright, Article 2 and Article 4(11) of Regulation for the Implementation of the Copyright Law of the People's Republic of China, there are two fundamental requirements for "originality" of a work: "completed independently by the author" and "creativity".

(1) Independent creation

In this case, "Blackface V" responded to the initiative of Media of Party Affairs and People's Daily to produce a 13-second video entitled "May 12, I want to tell you" by using the gesture dance, soundtrack, and other elements from a demonstration video provided by the Media of Party Affairs and People's Daily, and some pictures from Internet. The Court found that the demonstration videos and online pictures are independent and separate elements. "Blackface V" combined the above elements to make a short video, which is different from the former materials and such difference could be identified objectively and obviously. Furthermore, the disputed video is quite different from other short videos produced by other users with the same topic on Tik-Tok, and there is no evidence to prove that any same or similar short video existed before the disputed video was released on Tik-Tok. Therefore, the Court held that the disputed video was created by the producer independently.

(2) Creativity

The standard of creativity is connected to the social environment and the industry characteristics of its process of formation and evolution, improved and consummated according to the social environment and the characteristics of various types of works. With the popularization of mobile intelligent terminals and the development of software technology, a large number of short video platforms have appeared since 2016 in China. Entrepreneurs of short video contents have exploded, leading to a prosperous economic boom in the short video industry. Short video works are a combination and mixture of various types of works, such as text, pictures, voice, and video, which intuitively meets users' diverse needs related to self-expression as well as communication. Defining the standard of creativity of short video works could be of great practical significance for ensuring the normal and orderly distribution of short videos, promoting cultural prosperity and creating wealth for the whole society. Judicial trials should take a cautious and positive attitude, and make proper use of the standard of "creativity" in order to facilitate the development and growth of emerging industries. Short video works have distinctive characteristics: relatively low threshold of creation, short recording time, clear and simple theme, strong sociality and interactivity, and easy facilitation of dissemination. The process of production of the short video works is simple, and the producers are mostly individuals or small teams. Based on the fact that creation and dissemination of short videos contribute to the diversified expression of the public and cultural prosperity, the court shall not set a strict and high standard of creativity for short videos. These works might be creative as long as they reflect the producer's personalized expression.

When determining the creativity of the disputed video, the Court considered the following factors. First, the length of the video is not necessarily related to the determination of creativity.

Generally speaking, it might be difficult to form an original expression if the video is too short. However, some short videos could also be works as they could fully express the thoughts, ideas and feelings of the producer. In this case, the court concluded that the shorter the video, the more difficult it is to create, and the more likely it is creative. Secondly, the disputed video shows creativity. The Court held that, even though there is a relatively limited and narrow space to show creativity, "Blackface V" produced the disputed video with given theme and materials in order to respond to the initiative of the Media of Party Affairs. The producer combined such materials into an organic and unified audiovisual work, which contains the producer's intellectual labor and creative ideas. The disputed video was created on the basis of existing materials, while the arrangement, selection, and presentation of materials, compared to other users' short videos, left a completely different impression to the audiences and reflected the personal expression of the producer. Third, the disputed video resonates with the audience. Self-improvement and the courage to face great calamities and disasters have always been the outstanding spiritual connotation of the Chinese nation. As the tenth anniversary of the Wenchuan earthquake, the disputed video delivered a warm and comforting blessing as well as a relief of self-motivation in a form that the public was willing to accept. Such spiritual value of the disputed video is a concrete embodiment of creativity, and the massive distribution of the disputed video by users of Tik-Tok could also serve as a solid proof for its creativity. Therefore, the Court determined that the disputed video meets the basic requirements of creativity.

2. Did Baidu commit a copyright infringement?

In this case, plaintiff evidenced that the disputed video was available on Huopai. Thus, plaintiff claimed that the defendant provided the disputed video and committed copyright infringement. Baidu argued that it only provided the information storage service rather than the disputed video. The Court noted that the main issues are (1) whether Baidu provided the disputed video or merely provided information storage service; and (2) if Baidu acted as an Internet Service Provider, whether defendants' behavior constituted copyright infringement.

(1) Whether Baidu provided the disputed video or merely provided information storage service

1) In cases involving infringement of the right to communicate works to the public over information networks, the defendant should bear the burden of proof that it only provided information storage service. Court should take into consideration when judging the evidences submitted by the defendant, whether the defendant's website was equipped with the function of providing information storage service for users; whether the defendant's website clearly indicated the provision of information storage service for users; and whether the defendant was

capable to provide the user name, the registered IP address, the registration time, the upload IP address, the time of upload and the contact information of the uploader.

In this case, Baidu made available to the public its end-user license agreement. The agreement defined that users could publish information through this application, and provided a notification that uploaded contents by users must not infringe the intellectual property rights of others, as well as the contact information of Baidu. Baidu also submitted back-end records containing the user name, registered IP address, registration time, upload IP address, upload time, and contact information of the uploader of the disputed video. This clearly indicated that the disputed video was uploaded by third parties, and Baidu merely acted as an information storage service provider. The Court denied plaintiff's claim that Baidu directly provided the disputed work and committed a direct infringement.

2) Plaintiff argued that defendant deleted the watermark on the disputed video, which undermined the technical measures taken by plaintiff. According to the industry practices and technologies recognized by both parties, the Court found that the disputed video downloaded from Tik-Tok should be embedded with watermarks of Tik-Tok and the user's ID, while the above-mentioned watermarks were not displayed on the disputed video distributed on Huopai. The court held that it can be presumed that the above-mentioned watermarks had been eliminated.

The above-mentioned watermarks are not technical measures under Chinese law. Technical measures stipulated in Article 26 of the Regulation on the Protection of the Right to Communicate Works to the Public over Information Networks refers to "any effective technology, device or component used to prevent or restrict the browsing or enjoyment of a work, performance, or sound or visual recording that is not authorized by the right owner or the making available to the public via an information network of a work, performance, or sound or visual recording." Technical measures are divided into access control measures and copyright protection measures. Both measures aim to prevent unauthorized access to the works and the use of them. However, there are two main differences between "technical measures" in the sense of copyright law and in the sense of technology. Firstly, "technical measures" in the view of copyright law are used on specific subject matters of copyright law such as works, performances and sound recordings; secondly, "technical measures" in the sense of copyright law prevent specific actions over the specific subject matters. Only those technical measures that prevent others from performing certain actions, are in line with legislative purpose of copyright law. The watermarks in this case cannot achieve the same functions as "technical measures" stipulated by copyright law. From the perspective of the public, watermarks indicate certain identities. Electronic information refers to the "information indicating works and their authors, performances and their performers, or sound or visual recordings and their producers, the information on the right owners of the works, performances, or sound or visual recordings and on the conditions for use thereof, as well as the digits or codes representing the abovementioned information." The watermarks contain the ID of the producer of the disputed video, and it is more suitable to be recognized as rights management information. In addition, the words "Tik-Tok" marked in the watermarks indicate the platform's information. What is more, the disputed video was uploaded by users instead of Baidu, and the defendant Baidu was not the one who removed the watermarks.

Based on these facts, the Court held that the watermarks are not technical measures in the sense of copyright law, and Baidu was not the one who eliminated the watermarks. The court denied the plaintiff's claim that Baidu undermined its technical measures and infringed its the right to communicate works to the public over information networks.

(2) Did Baidu act as an Internet Service Provider, and did it infringe the copyrights of others?

Baidu made it clear in its end-user license agreement that Huopai was provided for their clients, and disclosed its name, contact person, as well as address. Plaintiff failed to prove that defendant did not comply with Article 22(2) to (4) of the Regulation on the Protection of the Right to Communicate Works to the Public over Information Networks. Therefore, Baidu's liability depends upon whether Baidu complied with the requirements of the notice-and-take-down procedure.

Plaintiff proved in the form of two emails that it notified the defendant to remove the disputed video on August 24, 2018. Defendant deleted such contents as late as September 10, 2018. Plaintiff argued that defendant did not comply with the notice-and-take-down procedure in a reasonable period of time, and it is therefore not eligible for the "safe harbor" defense. Plaintiff was, however, unable to prove that above-mentioned e-mails arrived to Baidu's e-mail address.

Baidu submitted back-end records of the deletion, and claimed that it deleted the disputed video on September 10, 2018 after receiving the paper complaint from plaintiff on September 7, 2018. Plaintiff objected these evidences but could not submit any evidence to the contrary. In sum, the court accepted Baidu's evidences. Considering that Baidu took down the disputed video in 4 days, including a two-days long weekend, the Court held that Baidu deleted the disputed video in a reasonable period of time after receiving plaintiff's written complaint. Regardless of whether the involved Huopai users committed copyright infringement, Baidu, as an Internet Service Provider, did not commit any copyright infringement.

THINK IT OVER!

1. This ruling was included in the "Top Ten Media Law Cases in China" by the Supreme Court of the PRC in 2018. The case dealt with a series of new types of legal issues, e.g. whether and under what conditions short video works could receive protection under copyright law, how to strike a balance on interests of the public, rights holders and ISPs. Indeed, the Court also emphasized that the notice-and-take-down mechanism aims to balance the interests of copyright owners and ISPs, and to promote the healthy development of internet platforms. Therefore, judges should be in line with the principle of good faith when applying notice-and-take-down mechanism, and try to maximize the goodness of such rules.

2. In this case, parties shared diverse opinions on whether short videos comply with the requirements of originality under copyright law. The Beijing Internet Court had fully implemented the judicial policies that the scope and intensity of protection over different kinds of IPRs should be reasonably defined. The length of the video is not necessarily related to the determination of creativity. The creative space of the short video is limited to a certain extent especially when the theme and materials are given. According to the characteristics and creative space of literary and artistic works, the court took into full account the features and needs of innovation in the context of "Internet Plus", and held that the short video complies with the originality requirement as long as it was created independently and it reflects the producer's individual expression. The threshold of creativity should not be high. It is worth noting that the Court argued that the spiritual enjoyment that short videos bring to viewers could be recognized as an important factor to support that the short videos comply with requirements of creativity.

3. The Court carefully distinguished the connotations of technical measures in the sense of copyright law and technology, and held that watermarks embedded on the short video are not technical measures in the sense of copyright law. The latter requires that the measure is capable to prevent others from performing certain actions over the specific subject matter. To the contrary, watermarks merely indicate the identity of the producer and the distributor of the video, and therefore it works like a rights management information rather than a technical protection measure. After the trial, the Beijing Internet Court issued judicial suggestions to relevant departments on the application of short video watermarking technology, recommending the use of such technology and encouraging them further clarifying and standardizing such use.

Further Case Law

Shanghai Xuanting Entertainment Information and Technology Co. Ltd., v. Beijing Baidu Netcom Science and Technology Co. Ltd., (2011) Shanghai No.1 Intermediate People's Court Civil 5 (IP tribunal) Final No. 141 Civil Judgement

Shenzhen Xunlei Network Technology Co. Ltd., v. Beijing Zhuoyixunchang Technology Co. Ltd., (2016) Beijing IP Court Civil Final No. 201 Civil Judgement

LETV (Tianjin) Information Technology Co. Ltd., v. Xiaomi Technology Co. Ltd., (2017) Tianjin Binhai New District Court Civil First No. 1148 Civil Judgement

Beijing Zhongqingwen Cultural Media Co., Ltd. v. Beijing Baidu Netcom Science and Technology Co. Ltd., (2018) Supreme People's Court Civil Retrial No. 386 Civil Judgement

Recommended readings

In English

Andrea Frey: To Sue or Not to Sue: Video-Sharing Web Sites, Copyright Infringement, and the Inevitability of Corporate Control, *Brooklyn Journal of Corporate, Financial & Commercial Law,* Issue 1/2007, p. 167-195.

Liu Wenqi: A Critical Review of China's Approach to Limitation of the Internet Service Provider's Liability: A Comparative Perspective, *Journal of Intellectual Property Rights,* May 2011, p. 235-245.

Huaiwen He: Storm Brewing in 'Safe Harbor': Defective Notification and Knowledge Imputed to Service Providers Under Chinese Laws, *Journal of the Copyright Society of the U.S.A.,* 2012, p. 201-221.

Jennifer M. Urban - Joe Karaganis - Brianna Schofield: Notice and takedown in everyday practice, *UC Berkeley Public Law Research Paper* No. 2755628, 2017

Daniel J. Gervais: Feist Goes Global: A Comparative Analysis of the Notion of Originality in Copyright Law, *Journal of the Copyright Society of the U.S.A.,* Summer 2002, p. 949-981.

In Chinese (bibliographic data translated to English)

Yu Tingting: Correction of the Concept in Determining the Fault of ISPs: Oriented on Intellectual Property Monitoring Obligation, *Political Science and Law,* Issue 10/2019, p. 123-133.

Guo Rengui: Copyright Protection for Short Videos from the Perspective of Duty of Care, *Electronics Intellectual Property,* Issue 10/2016, p. 88-96.

Cui Guobin: Reshaping of the Joint Infringement Rules of Internet Service Providers, *Chinese Journal of Law,* Issue 4/2013, p. 138-159.

Wang Qian: Restudy on Copyright Infringement of Video Sharing Websites, *Studies in Law and Business,* Issue 1/2010, p. 85-94,
Shi Xueqing, Wang Yong: Safe Harbor or Storm Cape: Interpretation of Article 23 of Regulation on the Protection of the Right to Communicate Works to the Public over Information Networks, *Intellectual Property,* Issue 2/2009, p. 23-29.
Hu Kaizhong: Applying the Safe Harbor Rule in Determining Copyright Infringement of Video Sharing Websites, *Legal Science,* Issue 12/2009, p. 70-81.

BEIJING YILIANWEIDA TECHNOLOGY CO., LTD. V. SHENZHEN TENCENT COMPUTER SYSTEM CO., LTD.

(2016) Beijing IP Court No. 143 Civil Final Judgment

Defendant operates the Kuaikan application, which aggregates film and television programs. "Gong Suo Lian Cheng" (Palace 3: The Last Daughter, hereinafter referred to as Palace 3) is a TV series lawfully provided via the Letv application. YLWD provides the work at issue to Internet users on its website via deep linking by avoiding the technical measures taken by Letv. YLWD indicated the source of the work at issue and displayed the URL of Letv programs on the location bar of the webpage when it played the work at issue. Advertisements before the program and during pause time were removed, and the watermark of Letv was also deleted. In addition, the two applications edited and arranged the contents differently.

Rules

Copyright Law of the People's Republic of China (2010 Amendment)

Art. 10 The term "copyright" shall include the following personality rights and property rights:

(...)

(12) the right of communication of information on networks, that is, the right to communicate to the public a work, by wire or wireless means in such a way that members of the public may access these works from a place and at a time individually chosen by them;

Art. 48. Anyone who commits any of the following acts of infringement shall bear civil liability for such remedies as ceasing the infringing act, eliminating the effects of the act, making an apology or paying damages, depending on the circumstances' and may, in addition, be subjected by a copyright administration department to such administrative penalties as ceasing the infringing act, confiscating unlawful income from the act, confiscating and destroying infringing reproductions and imposing a fine; where the circumstances are serious, the copyright administration department may also confiscate the materials, tools, and equipment mainly used for making the infringing reproductions; and if the act constitutes a crime, the infringer shall be prosecuted for his criminal liability:

(...)

(6) intentionally circumventing or destroying the technological measures taken by a right holder for protecting the copyright or copyright-related rights in his work, sound recording or video recording, without the permission of the copyright owner, or the owner of the copyright-related rights, unless otherwise provided in law or in administrative regulations;

(7) intentionally deleting or altering the electronic right management information of a work, sound recording or video recording, without the permission of the copyright owner or the owner of a copyright-related right, unless otherwise provided in law or in administrative regulations;

Regulation on the Protection of the Right to Communicate Works to the Public over Information Networks (2013 Revision) (Regulation of Information Networks in short)

Art. 4. For the purpose of protecting the right to communicate works to the public over information networks, the owner can take technical measures.

No organization or person shall intentionally avoid or destroy the technical measures, shall intentionally manufacture, import, or provide the public with devices or components mainly used to avoid or destroy the technical measures, and shall intentionally provide technical services to others to avoid or destroy the technical measures, unless it is provided for by any law or administrative regulation that the technical measures may be avoided.

Art. 18. Anyone who violates the provisions of this Regulation and commits any of the following acts of infringement shall, depending on the circumstances, bear civil liability for such remedies as ceasing the infringements, eliminating the effects of the acts, making a public apology or paying compensation for damages;

When he or she at the same time damages the public interest, the copyright administrative departments shall order that he or she cease the act of infringement, shall confiscate the illegal earnings, where the illegal proceeds are more than 50,000 Yuan, a fine of more than one time but less than five times the illegal proceeds may be imposed thereupon; where there are no illegal proceeds or the illegal proceeds are less than 50,000 Yuan, a fine of less than 250,000 Yuan may be imposed thereupon according to the seriousness of circumstances;

If the case is serious, the copyright administrative department may also confiscate such equipment as computer that is mainly used to provide network services; when his or her act has constituted a crime, he or she shall be investigated for criminal liability in accordance with the law:

(...)

(2) intentionally avoiding or destroying technical measures;

(3) intentionally deleting or altering electronic information on the management right of works, performances, or audio-visual recordings provided to the public through the information network, or providing the public with the works, performances, or audio-visual recordings through the information network while knowing or supposed to have known the above information.

Provisions of the Supreme People's Court on Several Issues concerning the Application of Law in Hearing Civil Dispute Cases Involving Infringement of the Right of Dissemination of Information Networks (in force since January 1, 2013)

Art. 1 The people's courts shall take into account the interests of right holders, network service providers and the public when exercising their discretionary power in accordance with law during the hearing of civil dispute cases involving infringement of the right of dissemination of information networks.

Art. 3 Where a network user or network service provider provides, on an information network, any work, performance, or audio or video recording which a right holder enjoys the right to disseminate on information networks without the permission of the copyright holder, the people's court shall determine that the network user or network service provider has infringed upon the right of dissemination of information networks, except as otherwise provided for by laws and administrative regulations;

If the work, performance, audio or video recording is placed on an information network by means such as uploading to a network server, file-sharing settings or using file-sharing software, allowing the general public to download, browse or otherwise obtain the work, performance, audio or video recording at the time and place chosen individually, the people's court shall determine that the network user or network service provider has committed the act of provision as mentioned in the preceding paragraph;

Art. 5 Where a network service provider provides the alleged work for the public by means such as Web cache or thumbnail, substantively in place of another network service provider, the people's court shall determine that the network service provider has committed the act of provision;

If the act of provision as mentioned in the preceding paragraph neither affects the normal use of the alleged work nor unreasonably damages the right holder's lawful rights and interests in the work, the people's court shall support a claim of the network service provider that it has not infringed upon the right of dissemination of information networks;

Art. 6 Where the plaintiff has provided preliminary evidence that a network service provider has provided the alleged work, performance, audio or video recording but the network service provider is able to prove that it only provides network services and is not at fault, the people's court shall not determine that the network service provider has committed an infringement.

Art 7 Where a network service provider abets or aids any network user in infringing upon the right of dissemination of information networks when providing network services, the people's court shall hold the network service provider liable for the infringement;

Where a network service provider induces or encourages any network user to infringe upon the right of dissemination of information networks by means such as language, technical support promotion or bonus points, the people's court shall determine that the network service provider has abetted the infringement;

Where a network service provider which knows or should have known that a network user is using its network services to infringe upon the right of network dissemination of information fails to take necessary measures such as deletion, screening and breaking the link or provides aid such as technical support for the user, the people's court shall determine that the network service provider has aided in the infringement.

Art. 9 The people's court shall determine whether a network service provider should have known an infringement based on a clear fact that a network user has infringed upon the right of dissemination of information networks and by taking into account the following factors:

(...)

(3) Whether the network service provider has, on its own initiative, chosen, edited, modified, recommended or otherwise dealt with the work, performance, or audio or video recording.

Art. 10 Where a network service provider recommends popular movies and TV plays by means such as ranking, catalogue, index, descriptive paragraphs or brief introductions when providing network services, allowing the public to access such works directly by means such as downloading from or browsing the network service provider's Web pages, the people's court may determine that the provider should have known a network user's infringement of the right of dissemination of information networks.

Anti-Unfair Competition Law of the People's Republic of China (1993)

Article 2 Managers shall abide by the principle of voluntariness, equality, impartiality, honesty and good faith, and also adhere to public commercial moral in their business transactions.

"Unfair competition", in this Law, means activities made by managers who damage the others' legal rights and interests, disturb the order of social economy and violate the provisions of this Law.

"Manager", in this Law, means the legal person, or other economic organizations or individuals who deal with commercial business or profitable service (commodities in this Law in hereafter as to commodity which includes service).

Analysis

Tencent brought a court action against YLWD for infringing its right of dissemination of information networks. Haidian District People's Court of Beijing Municipality decided the case according to the "substantial substitute standard". Haidian Court held that the selection, arrangement, organization and other acts of YLWD with respect to "Palace 3" built a strong connection between the work at issue and the linking website. The court found that the unauthorized linking to a website is a direct dissemination of information networks. Indeed, YLWD disseminated the work at issue at an even larger scale by avoiding technical measures. In sum, the trial court concluded that defendant infringed the right of dissemination of information networks.

However, the Beijing Intellectual Property Court, acting as the court of second instance, argued that the selection, arrangement, organization of data, as well as the avoidance of technical measures should not be taken into account to determine whether the linking constitutes the dissemination of information networks. The court confirmed by virtue of the "server test" that YLWD did not put the work at issue on the server available to the public. Therefore, its linking did not infringe the right of dissemination of information networks.

1. Whether the act of YLWD is a dissemination of information networks?

Pursuant to the "substantial substitute standard", the aggregation of motion pictures and television programs by deep linking allows users to access diverse contents conveniently, and hence the scope of the dissemination of works expands, while lawful service providers shall share their profits with freeriders. The Beijing Intellectual Property Court concluded that the "server test" shall apply as the standard to examine whether the conduct in question constituted dissemination of information networks or not. Under the "server test", only the initial transmission constitutes dissemination of information networks.

The Beijing Intellectual Property Court reasoned, first, that the "server test" is based on the provisions of the relevant laws. Article 10(12) of the Copyright Act provides that the the dissemination of information networks shall reach the public. The second paragraph of Article 3 in the Provisions Involving Infringement of the Right of Dissemination of Information Networks construes "making available to the public" as "providing [protected subject matter] through an information network". The dissemination of subject matters through information networks cannot succeed without an initial transmission of the said contents from a tangible host server (including network servers, file-sharing software or sharing tools of any other kind). This interpretation is also applicable to the case where wrongdoers do not control network servers. Under this circumstance, wrongdoers have to control network servers illegally before making the work available to the public. Article 5 of the Provisions Involving Infringement of the Right of

Dissemination of Information Networks shall not be viewed as the legal source of "substantial substitute standard" either. Finally, the phrase "substantively in place of" from this provision refers to the reproduction of the subject matter instead of any dissemination of it.

Second, although competition law uses the "substantial substitute standard", the analysis of the dissemination of information networks shall follow traditional approaches. The "substantial substitute standard" focuses on the consequences of conducts rather than the conduct itself, which runs against the concept of causality. The logic of any copyright proceedings is to ascertain the scope of a given right and to investigate whether that right covers the relevant conduct. The nature of deep linking will not change due to the selection, arrangement and organization of data. Accordingly, it is inappropriate to determine the act of dissemination of information networks under its consequences. In addition, only interests protected by the Copyright Act can be taken into consideration. Advertising interests and the use of technical measures are categorized as business and contractual interests, respectively. These interests are not protected by the right of dissemination of information networks, and therefore they cannot be taken into consideration with respect to the legality of the given conduct. However, the selection, arrangement, organization and other similar conducts of any kind are likely to have an influence on the identification of the infringements. It follows from Article 7(1) of Provisions Involving Infringement of the Right of Dissemination of Information Networks that link providers may assume joint liability provided the websites being linked involve the direct infringement of the right of dissemination of information networks. As regards to the case in the main proceedings, since Letv obtained permission lawfully to disseminate the work at issue, YLWD will not assume joint liability.

Finally, the "substantial substitute standard" runs against the purpose of balancing interests as well. In this regard the preamble and Article 1 of the Provisions Involving Infringement of the Right of Dissemination on Information Networks declares that the right of dissemination of information networks, the innovation and development of information network industry and the freedom of access to information should be taken into account in hearing relevant cases. The "substantial substitute standard" would necessitate the authorization of too many works before the dissemination. Such authorization would be overly expensive for network service providers.

2. Did the circumvention/avoidance of technical measures by YLWD infringe the right of dissemination of information networks?

Linking and the avoidance of technical measures serve distinct purposes and so it is reasonable to examine them separately. As YLWD did not place the work at issue on the network server available to public, it did not infringe the right of dissemination of information networks. However, under Article 48(6) of Copyright Act and Article 18(2) of Regulation of Information Networks actors are liable for avoiding technical measures to make works available to the public. In short, deep linking might be prohibited in case it is provided by the avoidance of technical measures.

THINK IT OVER!

1. *What are the advantages and disadvantages of the "substantial substitute standard" and the "server test"? Are there any other standards that can be applied to determine whether any dissemination of information networks has occurred?*

2. The question of legality of linked sources has been address by another Chinese ruling on hyperlinks. As Professor Long has noted, "[i]n 2015, the Beijing Intellectual Property Court (Beijing IP Court) in *Beijing Shengshi Jiaoyang Culture Ltd. v. Beijing Dongyi Shiguang Net Ltd.* clearly stated that despite objectively widening the scope of distribution of the works in question, the linking itself is outside the control of the right of communication to the public via information networks; only if the operator of the linked-to website was infringing would the linker be liable for its facilitating service." (Long 2018, p. 419.) Similarly, the legality of add-ons was discussed by Chinese courts. As Professor Long informed us, in *Hunan Kuaile Yangguang Entertainment Ltd. v. Tongfang Corp.*, "the plaintiff claimed that the defendant made the copyright content available to the public by incorporating the Rabbit Video app in the set-top box that the defendant manufactured. The lower court affirmed the plaintiff's argument that users of the set-top box would perceive that the alleged content was made available by the Rabbit Video app on the ground that, from the user's visual experience, they would not have been taken to another website during the whole process of the service. This argument is called the 'user's perception test' according to which the appearance of hyperlinks shown on the screen of the user's computer is the decisive factor when the courts determine whether the linking constitutes an act of communication to the public via information networks or not. The courts must consider what impression the appearance of the viewed website creates for end users. For example, when a user clicks the link, would a specific address of a linked-to website or the source of the linked-to content show on the subsequent page on the screen of the user's computer? Could the user recognise that the viewed webpage is hosted by another website instead of the linking website? An act of hosting a link would constitute communication to the public via information networks when the answers to the above questions regarding the appearance of a webpage are negative, and so, at first glance, the linked-to website can easily appear to be material created by or hosted on the linking website. Therefore, the visual experience of the users, which might lead to confusion on their part in regard to the real source of the viewed content, instead of technical features, determines whether the linking constitutes an act of communication to the public via information networks." (Long 2018, p. 420-421.)

3. The *Yilianweida* ruling mirrors the logic of the American "server test". Interestingly enough, the applicability of the "server test" has been recently questioned. In Justin Goldman v. Breitbart News Network, LLC, et al., 302 *F.Supp.3d* 585 (2018), the district court has followed a logic that is called "substantial substitute standard" in the *Yilianweida* case. It might be interesting to see which standard prevails in both countries.

4. The final ruling in *Yilianweida* regarding the circumvention of technical protection measures comply with the CJEU's *Svensson* and *C More Entertainment* rulings. To the contrary, Judge Posner put less emphasis on the fact that users circumvented the paywall of Flava Works when they bookmarked the videos.

Further Case Law

IFPI v. Baidu (2005), Beijing Haidian District People's Court, No. 14665 Civil Final judgment

Cinepoly Records Ltd. v. Baidu (2005), Beijing No. 1 Intermediate People's Court No. 8478 Civil Final judgment

Universal Music Ltd. v. Baidu (2010), Beijing No. 1 Intermediate People's Court No. 2435 Civil Final judgment

Flava Works, Inc., v. Marques Rondale Gunter, 689 *F.3d* 754 (2012)

CCTV International Network Co., Ltd. v. Beijing WoAiLiao Network Technology Co., Ltd., (2014) Beijing No. 1 Intermediate People's Court No. 3199 Civil Final judgment

Case C-466/12 - Nils Svensson and Others v. Retriever Sverige AB, Judgment of the Court (Fourth Chamber), 13 February 2014 [ECLI:EU:C:2014:76]

Beijing Shengshi Jiaoyang Culture Ltd. v. Beijing Dongyi Shiguang Net Ltd., (2015) Beijing IP Court No. 796 Civil Final judgment

Hunan Kuaile Yangguang Entertainment Ltd. v. Tongfang Co., (2015) Beijing IP Court No. 559 Civil Final judgment

Case C-279/13 - C More Entertainment AB v. Linus Sandberg, Judgment of the Court (Ninth Chamber), 26 March 2015 [ECLI:EU:C:2015:199]

Justin Goldman v. Breitbart News Network, LLC, et al., 302 *F.Supp.3d* 585 (2018)

Sinclair v. Ziff Davis, LLC, 18-CV-790 (KMW), April 13, 2020, U.S. District Court for the Southern District of New York

Recommended readings

In English

Guan H. Tang: *Copyright and the Public Interest in China*, Edward Elgar, Cheltenham, 2011, p. 32-34.

Jingrong Long: Different Solutions for Similar Questions: Hyperlinks and the Right of Communication to the Public in China and the EU, *IIC - International Review of Intellectual Property and Competition Law*, Issue 4/2018, p. 413-435.

Ling Yu: Duty of Care of the Link Service Provider: Judicial Experiences in China, *Queen Mary Journal of Intellectual Property*, Issue 4/2019, p. 471-483.

In Chinese (bibliographic data translated to English)

Wu Handong: On the Copyright Tort Liability of Network Service Providers, *China Legal Science*, Issue 2/2011, p. 38-47.

Li Ying - Song Yushui: Reasonable Duty of Care for Network Storage Service Providers: Han Han v. Baidu Case, *Intellectual Property*, Issue 6/2013, p. 37-46.

Feng Shujie: On the Fault Form of Indirect Tort Liability of Network Service Providers, *China Legal Science*, Issue 4/2016, p. 179-197.

CCTV INTERNATIONAL NETWORK CO., LTD. V. BEIJING WOAILIAO NETWORK TECHNOLOGY CO., LTD.

(2014) Beijing No. 1 Intermediate People's Court No. 3199 Civil Final judgment

The International Olympic Committee was the exclusive owner of the sports programs of the "London Olympics 2012". It was entitled to both of the right to broadcast and exhibition worldwide. The plaintiff was exclusively authorized to broadcast and exhibit the sports programs in Mainland China. However, the defendant, an Internet company, set up the "2012 London Olympic Zone" application and provided links to make simultaneously available to the public the TV programs of London Olympic Games. The plaintiff claimed that the defendant's acts have seriously violated its right to broadcast under the Copyright Act of the People's Republic of China. The plaintiff further argued that the acts of the defendant violated the principle of fairness and the principle of good faith, resulting in large economic losses to the plaintiff. The defendant argued that the definition of "broadcasting organization" under the Copyright Act refers to TV or radio stations, and the plaintiff did not fall under the scope of this definition. Consequently, the defendant argued that the plaintiff should not enjoy the rights of broadcasting organizations. Also, the right of broadcasting organization shall not be extended to the Internet environment.

Rules

Copyright Law of the People's Republic of China (2010 Amendment)

Article 10 The term "copyright" shall include the following personality rights and property rights:

(...) (11) the right of broadcast, that is, the right to publicly broadcast or communicate to the public a work by wireless means, to communicate to the public a broadcast work by wire or wireless means, and to communicate to the public a broadcast work by a loudspeaker or by any other analogous tool used to transmit symbols, sounds or pictures;

(12) the right of communication of information on networks, that is, the right to communicate to the public a work, by wire or wireless means in such a way that members of the public may access these works from a place and at a time individually chosen by them."

Article 45 A radio station or television station shall have the right to prohibit the following acts without authorization therefrom:

(1) to rebroadcast its broadcast radio or television program; and

(2) to fix its broadcast radio or television program on a sound recording or video recording carrier and to reproduce the sound recording or video recording carrier.

Agreement on Trade-Related Aspects of Intellectual Property Rights (1994)

Article 14 Broadcasting organizations shall have the right to prohibit the following acts when undertaken without their authorization: the fixation, the reproduction of fixations, and the rebroadcasting by wireless means of broadcasts, as well as the communication to the public of television broadcasts of the same. Where Members do not grant such rights to broadcasting organizations, they shall provide owners of copyright in the subject matter of broadcasts with the possibility of preventing the above acts, subject to the provisions of the Berne Convention (1971).

Anti-unfair Competition Law of the People's Republic of China [Revised by Anti-Unfair Competition Law of the People's Republic of China (2019 Revision) (Issued on 04-23-2019 Effective on 04-23-2019)]

Article 2 Businesses shall adhere to the principles of free will, equality, fairness, and good faith, as well as generally accepted business ethics, in their market transactions.

For the purposes of this Law, "unfair competition" means a business's conduct that damages the lawful rights and interests of the other businesses and disturbs the order of social economy in violation of the provisions of this Law.

For the purposes of this Law, "businesses" means legal persons, other economic organizations, and individuals that trade in commodities or provide for-profit services (commodities and services are hereinafter collectively referred to as "commodities").

Analysis

The Beijing No. 1 Intermediate People's Court indicated that the core issue in this case was whether the defendant's acts to broadcast CCTV programs through its application via the Internet infringed plaintiff's rights and whether the acts of the defendant constituted unfair competition.

1. Did the defendant's act violate the plaintiff's right to broadcast?

The court relied on the following logic to decide whether the defendant infringed the plaintiff's right to broadcast. First, the court identified whether the plaintiff had sound reason and basis to claim the copyright infringement. Second, it determined whether the defendant's behavior infringed copyrights enjoyed by the plaintiff under the Chinese Copyright Act.

The available evidences indicated that sports programs broadcasted by CCTV5 and other CCTV channels were not aimed at presenting expressions of literature, art or science. Therefore, these sports programs did not constitute works under the Chinese Copyright Act.

According to Article 10.11 of the Chinese Copyright Act, a copyright holder enjoys the right to publicly broadcast or communicate to the public a work by wireless means, to communicate to the public a broadcasted work by wire or wireless means, and to communicate to the public a broadcasted work by a loudspeaker or by any other analogous device. As, however, the premise of applying Article 10.11 is that the sports programs disputed in the case constitute works, the plaintiff could not claim any infringement of its broadcasting rights.

2. Did the defendant violate the rebroadcasting right of the plaintiff?

The Chinese Copyright Act does not specify whether the rebroadcasting of television programs over the Internet runs against the copyrights of the respective rightsholders. It is therefore crucial to properly understand and interpret the meaning or "rebroadcasting".

First, there is no clear legal definition of rebroadcasting either in the Chinese Copyright Act or in the regulations on the implementation of the Act or any other related judicial interpretations.

Second, it is necessary to understand the legislative background of the Chinese Copyright Act as well as the relevant international treaties in order to interpret the concept of rebroadcasting comprehensively. As China is a member/signatory of the leading international copyright treaties, the Chinese Copyright Act should be consistent with the standards set out in those international treaties. According to Article 14 of TRIPs, broadcasting organizations shall enjoy the right to prohibit the following acts when undertaken without their authorization: the fixation, the reproduction of fixations, and the rebroadcasting by wireless means of broadcasts, as well as the communication to the public of television broadcasts of the same. Where members do not grant such rights to broadcasting organizations, they shall provide owners of copyright in the subject matter of broadcasts with the possibility of preventing the above acts, subject to the provisions of the Berne Convention. The protection of the right of broadcasting organization under TRIPs is not extended to the network environment. At the time of the enactment of the Chinese Copyright Act in the 1990s, the Internet environment in China was still in its very early stage. Consequently, the law had not originally prohibited broadcasting TV programs over the Internet.

Internet rebroadcasting has later become a major issue in China. Radio and television are important sources of information, and they play an important role in public education as well. As radio and television organizations effectively support access to information via the Internet, and significantly reduce the costs of transmission, any protection granted to broadcasting organization will have direct economic as well as cultural/social consequences. Moreover, if judicial interpretations allow the expansion of the scope of protection, such legal changes will also have a direct impact on the development of the Internet industry and the model of cultural innovation. Due to the complexity of making information available to the public through the Internet, courts are not allowed to interpret the right of broadcasting organization broadly, and expand those rights beyond the scope of the statutes.

In sum, the court found that the defendant did not violate the right of rebroadcasting.

3. Did the defendant's acts constitute unfair competition?

The key for determining an act of unfair competition is whether the plaintiff and the defendant enjoy a competitive relationship in the market.

First, as the defendant has provided essentially the same content of sports programs on the Internet as the plaintiff did, the two parties shared the same market, and their relationship was competitive. The content and targeted object of the service provided by the defendant is the same.

Second, the Beijing No. 1 Intermediate People's Court held that the plaintiff enjoyed legitimate interests in authorizing the sports programs. Competition law should prohibit any improper free riding of the legal interests of others. Moreover, the defendant's conduct has objectively reduced the number of visits to the plaintiff's website. The public does not need to log on to plaintiff's website or use plaintiff's application to watch the Olympic programs as they are replaced by the defendant's network services. Therefore, the defendant's conduct failed to follow the principles of voluntariness, equality, fairness, honesty and credibility and failed to observe the generally recognized business ethics. Defendant's activities therefore constituted unfair competition.

THINK IT OVER!

1. Chinese case law is consistent in concluding that *sporting events as such are not works under the Chinese Copyright Act, and they do not deserve copyright protection.* (In *Guangzhou Betta Network Technology*, the Shanghai Intellectual Property Court reached the same conclusion.) This holding is in full compliance with the US and EU case law. In *Baltimore Orioles v. MLB*, the Seventh Circuit held in dictum that "the Players' performances possess the modest creativity required for copyrightability. (...) That the [baseball] Players' performances possess great commercial value indicates that the works embody the modicum of creativity required for copyrightability". (Baltimore Orioles v. MLB, p. 669., note 7.) In the *FAPL* case, the CJEU has similarly excluded the protectability of sporting events. As the Grand Chamber noted "sporting events cannot be regarded as intellectual creations classifiable as works within the meaning of the Copyright Directive. That applies in particular to football matches, which are subject to rules of the game, leaving no room for creative freedom for the purposes of copyright." (FAPL v. QC Leisure, para. 98.)

2. *In the lack of copyright protection for the sporting events, is there any other model that might be available to protect live broadcasting of sporting events?* Under the *CCTV* ruling, broadcasters have no other chance to claim protection against unauthorized uses via the Internet than unfair competition law. This seems to indicate a significant loophole in Chinese copyright law. Both under the US and the EU law, broadcasters are protected through either copyright (in the USA) or related rights (in the EU).

3. *Can producers/organisers of sporting events contractually protect their investments against (non-contracting) third parties?*

Further Case Law

Baltimore Orioles, Inc., v. Major League Baseball Players Association, 805 *F.2d* 663 (1986)

Joined Cases C-403/08 and C-429/08 - Football Association Premier League Ltd and Others v QC Leisure and Others, and Karen Murphy v Media Protection Services Ltd., Judgment of the Court (Grand Chamber), 4 October 2011 [ECLI:EU:C:2011:631]

Case C-279/13 - C More Entertainment AB v Linus Sandberg, Judgment of the Court (Ninth Chamber), 26 March 2015 [ECLI:EU:C:2015:199]

Guangzhou Betta Network Technology Co., Ltd. v. Shanghai Yaoyu Culture Media Co., Ltd., (2015) Shanghai Intellectual Property Court No. 81 Civil Final Judgement

Beijing Yilianweida technology Co., Ltd. v. Shenzhen Tencent Computer System Co., Ltd., (2016) Beijing IP Court No. 143 Civil Final Judgment

Warner Music UK Ltd., et al. v. TuneIn Inc. [2019] EWHC 2923 (Ch), 1 November 2019

Recommended readings

In English

Liu Wenjie: System Improvement of the Broadcasting Organization Right in the Internet Era, *Global Law Review*, Issue 3/2017, p. 106-120.

In Chinese (bibliographic data translated to English)

Wang Qian: The Copyright Protection of Moving Images in Live Broadcast of Sport Event: Commenting on "Phoenix New Media Broadcast" Case, *Science of Law (Journal of Northwest University of Political Science and Law)*, Issue 1/2016, p. 182-191.

Cong Lixian: Copyright Issues Related to Sports Events Live Broadcast, *China Copyright*, Issue 4/2015, p. 9-12.

HANHAN V. BEIJING BAIDU NETCOM TECHNOLOGY CO., LTD.

(2012) Haidian People's Court Civil First No. 5558 Civil Judgement

Hanhan, a Chinese writer, found that multiple end-users have uploaded his work "Go Like the Wind" (hereinafter referred to as "Wind") to Baidu Library. On this platform, users were capable to browse and download the "Wind" for free. Hanhan has kept sending letters to Baidu requesting to cease offering the "Wind". Following Baidu's negative responses, he sued Baidu and requested Baidu to stop immediately the infringement, to take effective measures to stop any future infringements, to close Baidu Library, to publishe an apology to him, and to compensate for the economic losses of RMB 254,000 Yuan and the other relevant expenses occurred.

Rules

Tort Law of the People's Republic of China

Article 36 Internet users and Internet service providers shall bear tort liability if they utilize the Internet to infringe upon civil rights of others.

If an Internet user commits tort through Internet services, the infringed shall be entitled to inform the Internet service provider to take necessary measures, including, inter alia, deletion, blocking and disconnection. If the Internet service provider fails to take necessary measures in a timely manner upon notification, it shall be jointly and severally liable with the said Internet user for the extended damage.

If an Internet service provider is aware that an Internet user is infringing on the civil rights and interests of others through its Internet services and fails to take necessary measures, it shall be jointly and severally liable with the said Internet user for such infringement.

Copyright Law of the People's Republic of China (2010 Amendment)

Article 48 Anyone who commits any of the following acts of infringement shall bear civil liability for such remedies as ceasing the infringing act, eliminating the effects of the act, making an apology or paying damages, depending on the circumstances' and may, in addition, be subjected by a copyright administration department to such administrative penalties as ceasing the infringing act, confiscating unlawful income from the act, confiscating and destroying infringing reproductions and imposing a fine; where the circumstances are serious, the copyright administration department may also confiscate the materials, tools, and equipment mainly used for making the infringing reproductions; and if the act constitutes a crime, the infringer shall be prosecuted for his criminal liability:

(1) reproducing, distributing, performing, showing, broadcasting, compiling or communicating to the public on an information network a work created by another person, without the permission of the copyright owner, unless otherwise provided in this Law (...).

Analysis

Defendant Baidu provided information storage space to upload the "Wind" by end-users, but it did not upload any protected subject matter. Plaintiff believed that Baidu shall be liable for the unauthorized dissemination of the "Wind". According to Chinese laws, the following conditions shall be satisfied to find Baidu liable: first, Baidu's act violates the right of communication through Internet enjoyed by Hanhan; second, there is connection between Baidu's act and the damage; third, Baidu is at subjective fault.

The Haidian People's Court argued that, on the one hand, there is a causal relationship between Baidu's behavior and the damage suffered by Hanhan. Baidu manages Baidu Library, which assisted end-users to upload, store and share the "Wind". The Court found that Baidu, as the operator of Baidu Library encouraged users in various forms to upload documents with quite lenient requirements of e.g. format, size and quantity. Baidu's service provided feasibility and convenience for the widespread dissemination of the "Wind".

Baidu was also found to be at subjective fault. Upon the existing evidence, the Court could not determine whether Baidu actually knew about the illegal use of the "Wind". The court, however, believed that both the popularity of Hanhan and his book, and the extensive nature of the negotiations that Hanhan and Baidu conducted on the infringement of the "Wind" should have necessitated a higher duty of care on Baidu's side. Baidu should have taken measures to prevent the infringements. Since Baidu failed to take any steps it was found to be at subjective fault.

Baidu argued that it has taken a number of preventive technical measures to stop the spread of infringing documents in Baidu Library and Hanhan has approved these measures. However, the Haidian People's Court found that these measures have not played an effective role in stopping the infringements.

In sum, Baidu was order to compensate Hanhan for his economic losses of RMB 39,800 and reasonable expenses of RMB 4,000.

THINK IT OVER!

1. Similarly to the recent US and EU case law on subjective liability (volitional conduct) of online service providers, Chinese law imposes a subjective liability on information storage service providers (hosting service providers). While service providers are not obliged to proactively monitor and filter illegal contents, *they face liability if they do encourage users to upload materials to the host servers, and the relevant protected subject matter has a significant popularity in China.* Such argumentation is confirmed later in *Beijing Shuoshuochangchang Cultural Media Co., Ltd. v. Shanghai Quan Tudou Cultural Communication Co., Ltd.* (See at page 249.)

2. Under the US law, "safe harbor" provisions might only apply if the service providers adopt standard technical measures to protect copyright works. There is no similar provision in Chinese laws. In this case, Baidu has actively adopted technical measures other than those prescribed by laws. Because of technical loopholes, these technical measures could not function properly due to technical defects. The court held that Baidu's technical measures were therefore inadequate to prevent the infringements. *Can the court's restrictive approach discourage other service providers from investing into preventive (but not fully effective) technical measures? As a result, can the proliferation of infringements hinder technological progress?*

Further Case Law

Beijing Yilianweida technology Co., Ltd. v. Shenzhen Tencent Computer System Co., Ltd., (2016) Beijing IP Court No. 143 Civil Final Judgment

Beijing Shuoshuochangchang Cultural Media Co., Ltd. v. Shanghai Quan Tudou Cultural Communication Co., Ltd., (2017) Shanghai Intellectual Property Court No. 224 Civil Final Judgment

Columbia Pictures Industries, Inc., et al. v. Gary Fung, et al., 710 *F.3d* 1020 (2013)

BWP Media USA Inc., et al. v. Polyvore, Inc., 922 *F.3d* 42 (2019)

Case C-160/15 - GS Media BV v. Sanoma Media Netherlands BV and Others, Judgment of the Court (Second Chamber), 8 September 2016 [ECLI:EU:C:2016:644]

Case C-610/15 - Stichting Brein v. Ziggo BV and XS4All Internet BV, Judgment of the Court (Second Chamber), 14 June 2017 [ECLI:EU:C:2017:456]

Recommended readings

In English

Shi Xu: A Study on the Safe Harbor Rules for Online File Hosting Service Providers Under Copyright Law in China, *Theses and Dissertations. 2014,* Paper 1. (https://www.repository.law.indiana.edu/etd/1/)

In Chinese (bibliographic data translated to English)

Wu Handong: On the Copyright Tort Liability of Network Service Providers, *China Legal Science,* Issue 2/2011, p. 38-47.

Li Ying - Song Yushui: Reasonable Duty of Care for Network Storage Service Providers: Han Han v. Baidu Case, *Intellectual Property,* Issue 6/2013, p. 37-46.

Feng Shujie: On the Fault Form of Indirect Tort Liability of Network Service Providers, *China Legal Science,* Issue 4/2016, p. 179-197.

BEIJING SHUOSHUOCHANGCHANG CULTURAL MEDIA CO., LTD. V. SHANGHAI QUAN TUDOU CULTURAL COMMUNICATION CO., LTD.

(2017) Shanghai Intellectual Property Court No. 224 Civil Final Judgment

The plaintiff, Beijing Shuoshuochangchang Cultural Media Co., Ltd. (hereinafter referred to as "Shuochang"), has enjoyed the right to communicate through information network the film called "Hidden Marriage". The defendant, Shanghai Quan Tudou Cultural Communication Co., Ltd. (hereinafter referred to as "Tudou"), played the film on its website. Shuochang believed that Tudou's actions violated its copyright on "Hidden Marriage". The plaintiff sued the defendant before Shanghai Minhang People's Court to compensate for its economic losses and other reasonable damages worth of RMB 50,000 Yuan.

Rules

Regulation on the Protection of the Right to Communicate Works to the Public over Information Networks

Article 22 The ISP provides the information storage space for the service object to make the work, performance, audio and video products available to the public through the information network, shall not be liable for compensation under conditions provided herein below:

(i) clearly indicates that the information storage space is provided for the service object and exposes the name, contact, and network address of the ISP;

(ii) has not changed the works, performances, audio and video products provided by the clients;

(iii) it is not known and there is no reason to know that the works, performances, audio and video products provided by the clients are infringing;

(iv) failure to derive direct financial benefits from the provision of works, performances, audio and video recordings from clients;

(v) upon receipt of a notice from the right holder, the works, performances and audio and video products which the right holder considers to be infringing have been deleted in accordance with the provisions of this Ordinance.

<u>Provisions of the Supreme People's Court on Several Issues Concerning the Application of Law in the Trial of Civil Disputes over Information Communication Rights</u>

Article 8 The court shall determine whether it undertakes to instigate or assist tort liability on the basis of the fault of the ISP. The fault of the ISP includes the knowledge or knowledge of the network user's infringement of the right of information network dissemination.

If the ISP does not take the initiative to review the infringement of the right of information network dissemination by the network user, the court shall not determine that it is at fault.

If the ISP can prove that it has taken reasonable and effective technical measures, but it is still difficult to detect the behavior of network users infringing the right of information network dissemination, the court should find that it is not at fault.

Article 11 If the ISP obtains the financial benefit directly from the works, performances and audio and video products provided by the network users, the court shall determine that it has a higher duty of care for the network users to infringe the right of information network dissemination.

If the ISP earns the proceeds for the advertising of specific works, performances, audio and video products, or obtains the economic benefits of other specific links with the works, performances and audio and video products it disseminates, it shall conclude that this situation constitutes a direct gain of economic benefits. The general advertising fee, service fee, etc., charged by the ISP for the provision of network services does not fall within the circumstances provided for in this paragraph.

Article 12 In one of the following circumstances, the court may, on the basis of the circumstances of the case, determine that the ISP providing the information storage service should know that the network user violates the right of Information network dissemination:

(i) Placing the popular film and television works, etc., on the home page or other main pages can be clearly perceived by the ISP position;

(ii) Actively select, edit, collate, recommend, or set up a special leader board for the subject and content of the popular film and television works, etc.;

(iii) Other cases in which the relevant works, performances and audio and video products can be clearly perceived as unauthorized and have not yet taken reasonable measures.

Analysis

The court of first instance held that Tudou is a professional and large-scale network service provider. It should know that according to the general business rules, it is impossible for the rights holders of films to allow others to disseminate the films on an unrestricted and open network without legal authorization. End-users uploaded "Hidden Marriage" to Tudou's website. If Tudou uses expertise and skills to monitor the uploaded files, it will be able to identify that the user who uploaded the film is not the rights holder. Tudou did not only fail to take its duty of care but also activated advertisements next to the frame of the film. Therefore, Tudou was at subjective fault and objectively played a role in helping the uploader infringing others' rights. Thus, the court of the first instance ruled that Tudou should compensate Shuochang for economic losses and reasonable expenses of RMB 13,335. Tudou filed an appeal against the first instance judgment before the Shanghai Intellectual Property Court.

The Shanghai Intellectual Property Court reversed the ruling of the trial court. The Shanghai Intellectual Property Court concluded that Tudou provided network information storage space to the said film and there is a need of careful scrutiny. Before judging Tudou's indirect infringement of contributing to end-users' uploading activities, it is necessary to ascertain whether or not the defendant was subjectively at fault. First, Hidden Marriage is not a popular film, nor was it placed on Tudou's start page or other prominent location. Second, Tudou did not actively select, edit, organize, recommend, or set up leader boards for the film. Third, Tudou did not aim to directly obtain economic benefits from the end-users' uploading activities. Fourth, even though the name of the service provider, the network address and the specific contact information of the infringement notice have been specified on Tudou's website, Shuochang has not sent the infringement notice to Tudou before filing the lawsuit. This in turn shows that Tudou did not have the "knowledge" about its network users' infringements, and therefore Tudou did not need to take a higher level of duty of care.

Shuochang claimed that the film was a commercial film, and Tudou should have felt that the film was provided without permission. The Shanghai Intellectual Property Court held that the commercial nature of the film is not a necessary condition for judging the subjective fault of the service provider. What matters is the popularity, legal authorization, naming of the film, tidbits and reviews, etc., that might hinder the service provider to clearly perceive information on the infringing nature of the contents. If the service provider is required to conduct a comprehensive review of the video content, it is tantamount to require it to review all possible infringements, which is, however, not in line with the legislative intent.

In addition, the Shanghai Intellectual Property Court went on reasoning that in the case of the low-profile commercial film, the rights holder could well first seek protection through a notice-and-take-down procedure rather than turning to courts. The plaintiff failed to do so. In sum, the Shanghai Intellectual Property Court held that Tudou is not contributorily liable for the communication of the films over the Internet.

THINK IT OVER!

This ruling of the Shanghai Intellectual Property Court is a logical follow-up to the *Hanhan* ruling with respect to subjective liability. It, however, provided for a more detailed analysis regarding the service provider's duty of care. It found that in assessing a service provider's liability, it is necessary to consider not only the nature of the work involved and the network service provider's service *per se*, but also the visibility of the work involved, and the ability of the service provider to manage the work involved. *The ruling called for a more balanced analysis of the interests of rights holders and the service providers.*

Further Case Law

Hanhan v. Beijing Baidu Netcom Technology Co., Ltd., (2012) Haidian People's Court Civil First No. 5558 Civil Judgement

Columbia Pictures Industries, Inc., et al. v. Gary Fung, et al., 710 *F.3d* 1020 (2013)

BWP Media USA Inc., et al. v. Polyvore, Inc., 922 *F.3d* 42 (2019)

Case C-160/15 - GS Media BV v. Sanoma Media Netherlands BV and Others, Judgment of the Court (Second Chamber), 8 September 2016 [ECLI:EU:C:2016:644]

Case C-610/15 - Stichting Brein v. Ziggo BV and XS4All Internet BV, Judgment of the Court (Second Chamber), 14 June 2017 [ECLI:EU:C:2017:456]

Recommended readings

In Chinese (bibliographic data translated to English)

Wu Handong: On the Copyright Tort Liability of Network Service Providers, *China Legal Science*, Issue 2/2011, p. 38-47.

Feng Shujie: On the Fault Form of Indirect Tort Liability of Network Service Providers, *China Legal Science*, Issue 4/2016, p. 179-197.

Cui Guobin: On the Network Service Provider's Copyright Content Filtering Obligation, *China Legal Science*, Issue 2/2017, p. 215-237.

Chapter III
P2P File-sharing

COLUMBIA PICTURES INDUSTRIES, INC., ET AL. V. GARY FUNG, ET AL.

710 *F.3d* 1020 (2013)

BERZON, Circuit Judge

(...) TECHNOLOGICAL BACKGROUND

This case concerns a peer-to-peer file sharing protocol known as BitTorrent. We begin by providing basic background information useful to understanding the role the Fung sites play in copyright infringement.

I. Client-server vs. peer-to-peer networks

The traditional method of sharing content over a network is the relatively straightforward client-server model. In a client-server network, one or more central computers (called "servers") store the information; upon request from a user (or "client"), the server sends the requested information to the client. In other words, the server supplies information resources to clients, but the clients do not share any of their resources with the server. Client-server networks tend to be relatively secure, but they have a few drawbacks: if the server goes down, the entire network fails; and if many clients make requests at the same time, the server can become overwhelmed, increasing the time it takes the server to fulfill requests from clients. Client-server systems, moreover, tend to be more expensive to set up and operate than other systems. Websites work on a client-server model, with the server storing the website's content and delivering it to users upon demand.

"Peer-to-peer" (P2P) networking is a generic term used to refer to several different types of technology that have one thing in common: a decentralized infrastructure whereby each participant in the network (typically called a "peer," but sometimes called a "node") acts as both a supplier and consumer of information resources. Although less secure, P2P networks are generally more reliable than client-server networks and do not suffer from the same bottleneck problems. These strengths make P2P networks ideally suited for sharing large files, a feature that has led to their adoption by, among others, those wanting access to pirated media, including music, movies, and television shows. But there also are a great number of non-infringing uses for peer-to-peer networks; copyright infringement is in no sense intrinsic to the technology, any more than making unauthorized copies of television shows was to the video tape recorder.

II. Architecture of P2P networks

In a client-server network, clients can easily learn what files the server has available for download, because the files are all in one central place. In a P2P network, in contrast, there is no centralized file repository, so figuring out what information other peers have available is more challenging. The various P2P protocols permit indexing in different ways.

A. "Pure" P2P networks

In "pure" P2P networks, a user wanting to find out which peers have particular content available for download will send out a search query to several of his neighbor peers. As those neighbor peers receive the query, they send a response back to the requesting user reporting whether they have any content matching the search terms, and then pass the query on to some of their neighbors, who repeat the same two steps; this process is known as "flooding." In large P2P networks, the query does not get to every peer on the network, because permitting that amount of signaling traffic would either overwhelm the resources of the peers or use up all of the network's bandwidth (or both). Therefore, the P2P protocol will usually specify that queries should no longer be passed on after a certain amount of time (the so-called "time to live") or after they have already been passed on a certain number of times (the "hop count"). Once the querying user has the search results, he can go directly to a peer that has the content desired to download it.

This search method is an inefficient one for finding content (especially rare content that only a few peers have), and it causes a lot of signaling traffic on the network. The most popular pure P2P protocol was Gnutella. StreamCast, a Grokster defendant, used Gnutella to power its software application, Morpheus.

B. "Centralized" P2P networks

"Centralized" P2P networks, by contrast, use a centralized server to index the content available on all the peers: the user sends the query to the indexing server, which tells the user which peers have the content available for download. At the same time the user tells the indexing server what files he has available for others to download. Once the user makes contact with the indexing server, he knows which specific peers to contact for the content sought, which reduces search time and signaling traffic as compared to a "pure" P2P protocol.

Although a centralized P2P network has similarities with a client-server network, the key difference is that the indexing server does not store or transfer the content. It just tells users which other peers have the content they seek. In other words, searching is centralized, but file transfers are peer-to-peer. One consequent disadvantage of a centralized P2P network is that it has a single point of potential failure: the indexing server. If it fails, the entire system fails. Napster was a centralized P2P network, as, in part, is eDonkey, the technology upon which one of the Fung sites, ed2k-it.com, is based.

C. Hybrid P2P networks

Finally, there are a number of hybrid protocols. The most common type of hybrid systems use what are called "supernodes." In these systems, each peer is called a "node," and each node is assigned to one "supernode." A supernode is a regular node that has been "promoted," usually because it has more bandwith available, to perform certain tasks. Each supernode indexes the content available on each of the nodes attached to it, called its "descendants." When a node sends out a search query, it goes just to the supernode to which it is attached. The supernode responds to the query by telling the node which of its descendant nodes has the desired content. The supernode may also forward the query on to other supernodes, which may or may not forward the query on further, depending on the protocol.

The use of supernodes is meant to broaden the search pool as much as possible while limiting redundancy in the search. As with centralized P2P systems, supernodes only handle search queries, telling the nodes the addresses of the other nodes that have the content sought; they are not ordinarily involved in the actual file transfers themselves. Grokster's software application was based on a P2P protocol, FastTrack, that uses supernodes.

III. BitTorrent protocol

The BitTorrent protocol, first released in 2001, is a further variant on the P2P theme. BitTorrent is a hybrid protocol with some key differences from "supernode" systems. We discuss those differences after first describing BitTorrent's distinguishing feature: how it facilitates file transfers.

A. BitTorrent file transfers

Traditionally, if a user wanted to download a file on a P2P network, he would locate another peer with the desired file and download the entire file from that peer. Alternatively, if the download was interrupted - if, for example, the peer sending the file signed off - the user would find another peer that had the file and resume the download from that peer. The reliability and duration of the download depended on the strength of the connection between those two peers. Additionally, the number of peers sharing a particular file was limited by the fact that a user could only begin sharing his copy of the file with other peers once he had completed the download.

With the BitTorrent protocol, however, the file is broken up into lots of smaller "pieces," each of which is usually around 256 kilobytes (one-fourth of one megabyte) in size. Whereas under the older protocols the user would download the entire file in one large chunk from a single peer at a time, BitTorrent permits users to download lots of different pieces at the same time from different peers. Once a user has downloaded all the pieces, the file is automatically reassembled into its original form.

BitTorrent has several advantages over the traditional downloading method. Becausea user can download different pieces of the file from many different peers at the same time, downloading is much faster. Additionally, even before the entire download is complete, a user can begin sharing the pieces he has already downloaded with other peers, making the process faster for others. Generally, at any given time, each user is both downloading and uploading several different pieces of a file from and to multiple other users; the collection of peers swapping pieces with each other is known as a "swarm."

B. BitTorrent architecture

To describe the structure of BitTorrent further, an example is helpful. Let us suppose that an individual (the "publisher") decides to share via BitTorrent her copy of a particular movie. The movie file, we shall assume, is quite large, and is already on the publisher's computer; the publisher has also already downloaded and installed a BitTorrent "client" program on her computer.

To share her copy of the movie file, the publisher first creates a very small file called a "torrent" or "dot-torrent" file, which has the file extension ".torrent." The torrent file is quite small, as it contains none of the actual content that may be copyrighted but, instead, a minimal amount of vital information: the size of the (separate) movie file being shared; the number of "pieces" the movie file is broken into; a cryptographic "hash" that peers will use to authenticate the downloaded file as a true and complete copy of the original; and the address of one or more "trackers." Trackers, discussed more below, serve many of the functions of an indexing server; there are many different trackers, and they typically are not connected or related to each other.

Second, the publisher makes the torrent file available by uploading it to one or more websites ("torrent sites") that collect, organize, index, and host torrent files. Whereas Napster and Grokster had search functionality built into their client programs, the standard BitTorrent client program has no such capability. BitTorrent users thus rely on torrent sites to find and share torrent files. There is no central repository of torrent files, but torrent sites strive to have the most comprehensive torrent collection possible.

The Fung sites have two primary methods of acquiring torrent files: soliciting them from users, who then upload the files; and using several automated processes (called "bots," "crawlers," or "spiders") that collect torrent files from *other* torrent sites. Because of this latter route, which other torrent sites also routinely use, torrent sites tend to have largely overlapping collections of torrents. According to a declaration Fung signed in April 2008, there were then over 400 torrent sites. Because the torrent sites typically contain only torrent files, no copyrighted material resides on these sites.

Lastly, the publisher leaves her computer on and connected to the Internet, with her BitTorrent program running. The publisher's job is essentially done; her computer will continue to communicate with the tracker assigned to the torrent file she uploaded, standing ready to distribute the movie file (or, more accurately, parts thereof) to others upon request.

A user seeking the uploaded movie now goes to the torrent site to which the torrent file was uploaded and runs a search for the movie. The search results then provide the torrent file for the user to download. Once the user downloads the torrent file and opens it with his BitTorrent program, the program reads the torrent file, learns the address of the tracker, and contacts it. The program then informs the tracker that it is looking for the movie associated with the downloaded torrent file and asks if there are any peers online that have the movie available for download. Assuming that publishers of that movie are online, the tracker will communicate their address to the user's BitTorrent program. The user's BitTorrent program will then contact the publishers' computers directly and begin downloading the pieces of the movie. At this point, the various publishers are known as "seeders," and the downloading user a "leecher." Once the leecher has downloaded one or more pieces of the movie, he, too, can be a seeder by sending other leechers the pieces that he has downloaded.

A final few words on trackers. Although no content is stored on or passes through trackers, they serve as a central hub of sorts, managing traffic for their associated torrents. The tracker's primary purpose is to provide a list of peers that have files available for download. Fung avers that this function is the only one provided by his two trackers, discussed below.

Because trackers are periodically unavailable - they can go offline for routine maintenance, reach capacity, be shuttered by law enforcement, and so on - torrent files will often list addresses for more than one tracker. That way, if the first (or "primary") tracker is down, the user's client program can proceed to contact the backup tracker(s).

IV. Fung's role

Three of Fung's websites - isohunt.com ("isoHunt"); torrentbox.com ("Torrentbox"), and podtropolis.com ("Podtropolis") - are torrent sites. As described above, they collect and organize torrent files and permit users to browse in and search their collections. Searching is done via keyword; users can also browse by category (movies, television shows, music, etc.).

IsoHunt, however, which appears to be Fung's "flagship" site, goes a step beyond merely collecting and organizing torrent files. Each time a torrent file is added to isoHunt, the website automatically modifies the torrent file by adding additional backup trackers to it. That way, if the primary tracker is down, the users' BitTorrent client program will contact the backup trackers, making it more likely that the user will be successful in downloading the content sought. In other words, isoHunt alters the torrent files it hosts, making them more reliable than when they are uploaded to the site.

Torrentbox and Podtropolis, in addition to being torrent sites, run associated trackers. Their collections of torrent files appear to be fairly small. Every torrent file available on Torrentbox and Podtropolis is tracked by the Torrentbox and Podtropolis trackers, respectively, but the Torrentbox and Podtropolis trackers are *much* busier than the Torrentbox and Podtropolis websites. For example, a torrent file for the movie "Casino Royale" was downloaded from Torrentbox.com 50,000 times, but the Torrentbox tracker registered approximately 1.5 million downloads of the movie. This disparity indicates that users obtain the torrent files tracked by Torrentbox and Podtropolis from torrent sites other than Torrentbox.com and Podtropolis.com. The Torrentbox and Podtropolis websites both have continually-updated lists of, *inter alia,* the "Top 20 TV Shows," the "Top 20 Movies," and the "Top 20 Most Active Torrents." These rankings are based on the number of seeders and leechers for each particular torrent file, as measured by the Torrentbox and Podtropolis trackers. IsoHunt does not run a tracker, so it cannot measure how frequently the content associated with each torrent file is downloaded; instead, it keeps a continually updated list of the "Top Searches."

IsoHunt also hosts an electronic message board, or "forum," where users can post comments, queries, and the like. In addition to posting to the forum himself, Fung also had some role in moderating posts to the forum. (...)

DISCUSSION

As always, we review the district court's grant of summary judgment de novo, and "may affirm the district court's holding on any ground raised below and fairly supported by the record," As to the permanent injunction, we review the legal conclusions de novo, the factual findings for clear error, and the decision to grant a permanent injunction, as well as its scope, for an abuse of discretion. To review for abuse of discretion, "we first look to whether the trial court identified and applied the correct legal rule ... [then] to whether the trial court's resolution of the motion resulted from a factual finding that was illogical, implausible, or without support in inferences that may be drawn from the facts in the record."

I. Liability

A. Inducement liability under Grokster III

The "inducement" theory, on which the district court's liability holding was grounded, was spelled out in the Internet technology context by the Supreme Court in Grokster III Considering how to apply copyright law to file sharing over P2P networks, Grokster III addressed the circumstances in which individuals and companies are secondarily liable for the copyright infringement of others using the Internet to download protected material.

Grokster III 's inducement holding is best understood by first backtracking to Sony Corp. of America v. Universal City Studios, Inc., the seminal Supreme Court case concerning the use of new technologies to reproduce copyrighted material. *Sony* considered whether secondary liability for infringement could arise solely from the distribution of a commercial product capable of copying copyrighted material - there, the Betamax video tape recorder, made by Sony. Owners of copyrights to television programs maintained that Sony could be liable for copyright infringement when its customers used the Betamax to unlawfully tape television shows. There was no evidence that Sony sought to encourage copyright infringement through use of the Betamax or had taken steps to profit from unlawful taping. Instead, the only conceivable basis for secondary liability was distribution of the product "with constructive knowledge of the fact that [Sony's] customers may use that equipment to make unauthorized copies of copyrighted material."

Finding "no precedent in the law of copyright for the imposition of vicarious liability on such a theory," the Court borrowed from the "closest analogy" it could find, patent law's "staple article of commerce doctrine." Under that doctrine, distribution of a component part of a patented device will not violate the patent if the component is suitable for substantial non-infringing uses. As *Sony* explained, the staple article of commerce doctrine balances competing interests, a copyright holder's legitimate demand for effective – not merely symbolic – protection of the statutory monopoly, and the rights of others freely to engage in substantially unrelated areas of commerce. Accordingly, the sale of copying equipment, like the sale of other articles of commerce, does not constitute contributory infringement if the product is widely used for legitimate, unobjectionable purposes. Indeed, it need merely be capable of substantial noninfringing uses. As the Betamax was "capable of commercially significant noninfringing uses," the Court held Sony not liable for contributory copyright infringement.

The other major Supreme Court case addressing the mass copying of copyrighted material – there, music and films – through technological means, Grokster III, concerned the use of software applications based on "pure" and "hybrid" P2P network protocols. The defendants, the providers of the copying software to the public, argued for a contributory liability approach similar to that adopted in *Sony:* as their products were indisputably *capable* of substantial non-infringing uses, they maintained, they could not be secondarily liable based on their knowledge that their products could be used to infringe copyrights. Instead, the *Grokster* defendants suggested, they could be liable for contributory infringement only if they had actual knowledge of a *specific* infringement at a time when they were capable of preventing it. Accepting this theory and recognizing that there was no evidence regarding timely knowledge of specific acts of infringement, the district court granted summary judgment to the defendants.

The Supreme Court did not see Sony as providing such broad insulation from copyright liability. Rather, said the Court, Sony limits imputing culpable intent as a matter of law from the characteristics or uses of a distributed product. But nothing in Sony requires courts to ignore evidence of intent if there is such evidence, and the case was never meant to foreclose rules of *fault-based* liability derived from the common law.

The "staple article of commerce doctrine" adopted in Sony, Grokster III explained, "absolves the equivocal conduct of selling an item with substantial lawful as well as unlawful uses, and limits liability to instances of more acute fault than the mere understanding that some of one's products will be misused." "Thus, where evidence goes beyond a product's characteristics or the knowledge that it may be put to infringing uses, and shows statements or actions directed to promoting infringement, Sony 's staple-article rule will not preclude liability."

Grokster III went on to enunciate the "inducement rule," also borrowed from patent law, providing that "one who distributes a device with the object of promoting its use to infringe copyright, as shown by clear expression or other affirmative steps taken to foster infringement, is liable for the resulting acts of infringement by third parties." This inducement principle, as enunciated in Grokster III, has four elements: (1) the distribution of a device or product, (2) acts of infringement, (3) an object of promoting its use to infringe copyright, and (4) causation.

i. Distribution of a "device" or "product"

In describing the inducement liability standard, Grokster III phrased it as applying to one who distributes a "device," although it also used the word "product," seemingly interchangeably. The "device" or "product" was the software developed and distributed by the defendants - for Grokster, its eponymous software, based on FastTrack technology; and for StreamCast, also a defendant in Grokster, its software application, Morpheus, based on Gnutella.

The analogy between Grokster III and this case is not perfect. Here, Fung did not develop and does not provide the client programs used to download media products, nor did he develop the BitTorrent protocol (which is maintained by nonparty BitTorrent, Inc., a privately-held company founded by the creators of the protocol). Fung argues that because he did not develop or distribute any "device" - that is, the software or technology used for downloading - he is not liable under the inducement rule enunciated in Grokster III.

We cannot agree. Unlike patents, copyrights protect expression, not products or devices. Inducement liability is not limited, either logically or as articulated in Grokster III, to those who distribute a "device." As a result, one can infringe a copyright through culpable actions resulting in the impermissible reproduction of copyrighted expression, whether those actions involve making available a device or product or providing some service used in accomplishing the infringement. For example, a retail copying service that accepts and copies copyrighted material for customers after broadly promoting its willingness to do so may be liable for the resulting infringement although it does not produce any copying machines or sell them; all it provides is the "service" of copying. Whether the service makes copies using machines of its own manufacture, machines it owns, or machines in someone else's shop would not matter, as copyright liability depends on one's purposeful involvement in the process of reproducing copyrighted material, not the precise nature of that involvement.

Grokster III did phrase the rule it applied principally in terms of a "device." But that was because it was responding to the main argument made by the defendants in that case - that they were entitled to protection for commercial products capable of significant non-infringing uses, just as Sony was insulated from liability for infringing use of the Betamax. When explaining the *rationale* for permitting secondary infringement liability, Grokster III used more general language.

When a widely shared *service or product* is used to commit infringement, it may be impossible to enforce rights in the protected work effectively against all direct infringers, the only practical alternative being to go against the distributor of *the copying device* for secondary liability on a theory of contributory or vicarious infringement.

Since Grokster III, we have not considered a claim of inducement liability on facts closely comparable to those here. But we have, in two cases, considered claims of inducement liability against parties providing services as opposed to products, without suggesting that the difference matters. The two Perfect 10 cases confirm that, as one would expect, the inducement copyright doctrine explicated in Grokster III applies to services available on the Internet as well as to devices or products.

We hold that Columbia has carried its burden on summary judgment as to the first element of the Grokster III test for inducement liability.

ii. Acts of infringement

To prove copyright infringement on an inducement theory, Columbia also had to adduce "evidence of actual infringement by" users of Fung's services. This they have done.

Both uploading and downloading copyrighted material are infringing acts. The former violates the copyright holder's right to distribution, the latter the right to reproduction. Based on statistical sampling, Columbia's expert averred that between 90 and 96% of the content associated with the torrent files available on Fung's websites are for "confirmed or highly likely copyright infringing" material. Although Fung takes issue with certain aspects of the expert's methodology, he does not attempt to rebut the factual assertion that his services were widely used to infringe copyrights. Indeed, even giving Fung the benefit of all doubts by tripling the margins of error in the expert's reports, Columbia would still have such overwhelming evidence that any reasonable jury would have to conclude that the vastly predominant use of Fung's services has been to infringe copyrights.

In sum, as in Grokster III, "[a]lthough an exact calculation of infringing use, as a basis for a claim of damages, is subject to dispute, there is no question" that Plaintiffs have met their burden on summary judgment to warrant equitable relief.

iii. With the object of promoting its use to infringe copyright

The third, usually dispositive, requirement for inducement liability is that the "device" or service be distributed "with the object of promoting its use to infringe copyright, as shown by clear expression or other affirmative steps taken to foster infringement."

As an initial matter, Fung argues that this factor includes two separate elements - the improper object *and* "clear expression or other affirmative steps taken to foster infringement." Not so. "[C]lear expression or other affirmative steps" is not a separate requirement, but, rather, an explanation of how the improper object must be proven. In other words, Grokster III requires a high degree of proof of the improper object. Confirming that understanding of the "clear expression" phrase, Grokster III emphasized, right after articulating the inducement factor, that the improper object must be plain and must be affirmatively communicated through words or actions:

We are, of course, mindful of the need to keep from trenching on regular commerce or discouraging the development of technologies with lawful and unlawful potential. Accordingly, just as Sony did not find intentional inducement despite the knowledge of the [Betamax] manufacturer that its device could be used to infringe, mere knowledge of infringing potential or of actual infringing uses would not be enough here to subject a distributor to liability. Nor would ordinary acts incident to product distribution, such as offering customers technical support or product updates, support liability in themselves. The inducement rule, instead, premises liability on purposeful, culpable expression and conduct, and thus does nothing to compromise legitimate commerce or discourage innovation having a lawful promise.

In Grokster III itself, the Court found ample evidence, of several types, to support inducement liability. First, Grokster III relied in part on advertisements as proof of an impermissible, infringing purpose, noting that "[t]he classic instance of inducement is by advertisement or solicitation that broadcasts a message designed to stimulate others to commit violations." Both Grokster III defendants had engaged in such affirmative solicitation, advertising their software as an alternative to Napster - which notoriously facilitated wide-scale copyright infringement - at a time when Napster's unlawful activities were about to be shuttered.

Second, Grokster III relied for proof of Grokster's infringing purpose on communications that, while not in haec verba promoting infringing uses, provided information affirmatively supporting such uses. "[B]oth companies," moreover, "communicated a clear message by responding affirmatively to requests for help in locating and playing copyrighted materials." Thus, Grokster included as evidence of an infringing purpose an electronic newsletter distributed by Grokster that linked to articles promoting Grokster's ability to access copyrighted music.

A third category of "clear expression" recognized in Grokster III as pertinent to proof of improper purpose was explicit internal communication to that effect. As to one of the defendants, StreamCast, "internal communications," including proposed advertising designs, provided "unequivocal indications of unlawful purpose." The Court explained that "[w]hether the messages were communicated [to potential customers] is not ... the point. The function of the message in the theory of inducement is to prove by a defendant's own statements that his unlawful purpose disqualifies him from claiming protection." Thus, the Court went on, "[p]roving that a message was sent out ... is the preeminent but not exclusive way of showing that active steps were taken with the purpose of bringing about infringing acts."

Grokster III also mentioned two sorts of "other affirmative steps" as permissible evidence that support an inference of an intent to induce infringement, while cautioning that such sorts of circumstantial evidence would not be independently sufficient. The first was that "neither company attempted to develop filtering tools or other mechanisms to diminish the infringing activity using their software," which the Court said "underscore[d]" the defendants' "intentional facilitation of their users' infringement." The Court was careful to caution that "in the absence of other evidence of intent, a court would be unable to find contributory infringement liability merely based on a failure to take affirmative steps to prevent infringement."

Similarly, Grokster III pointed to the fact that the defendants "make money by selling advertising space, by directing ads to the screens of computers employing their software." Because "the extent of the software's use determines the gain to the distributors, the commercial sense of their enterprise turns on high-volume use, which the record shows is infringing." Here again, however, "[t]his evidence alone would not justify an inference of unlawful intent."

Using these Grokster III evidentiary categories and cautions as templates, we conclude that there is more than enough unrebutted evidence in the summary judgment record to prove that Fung offered his services with the object of promoting their use to infringe copyrighted material. No reasonable jury could find otherwise.

As for the necessary "clear expression or other affirmative steps" evidence indicative of unlawful intent, the most important is Fung's active encouragement of the uploading of torrent files concerning copyrighted content. For a time, for example, isoHunt prominently featured a list of "Box Office Movies," containing the 20 highest-grossing movies then playing in U.S. theaters. When a user clicked on a listed title, she would be invited to "upload [a] torrent" file for that movie. In other words, she would be asked to upload a file that, once downloaded by other users, would lead directly to their obtaining infringing content. Fung also posted numerous messages to the isoHunt forum requesting that users upload torrents for specific copyrighted films; in other posts, he provided links to torrent files for copyrighted movies, urging users to download them. Though not the exclusive means of proving inducement, we have characterized a distributor's communication of an inducing message to its users as "crucial" to establishing inducement liability. That crucial requirement was met here. Like Grokster's advertisements - indeed, even more so - Fung's posts were explicitly "designed to stimulate others to commit [copyright] violations," and so are highly probative of an unlawful intent.

As in Grokster, moreover, Fung "communicated a clear message by responding affirmatively to requests for help in locating and playing copyrighted materials." The record is replete with instances of Fung responding personally to queries for assistance in: uploading torrent files corresponding to obviously copyrighted material, finding particular copyrighted movies and television shows, getting pirated material to play properly, and burning the infringing content onto DVDs for playback on televisions.

Two types of supporting evidence, insufficient in themselves – like the similar evidence in Grokster III – corroborate the conclusion that Fung "acted with a purpose to cause copyright violations by use of" their services. First, Fung took no steps "to develop filtering tools or other mechanisms to diminish the infringing activity" by those using his services. Second, Fung generates revenue almost exclusively by selling advertising space on his websites. The more users who visit Fung's websites and view the advertisements supplied by Fung's business partners, the greater the revenues to Fung. Because "the extent of the [services'] use determines the gain to [Fung], the commercial sense of [his] enterprise turns on high-volume use, which the record shows is infringing." Given both the clear expression and other affirmative steps and the supporting evidence, Fung's "unlawful objective is unmistakable."

iv. Causation

Grokster III mentions causation only indirectly, by speaking of "resulting acts of infringement by third parties." The parties here advance competing interpretations of the causation requirement adopted through that locution: Fung and amicus curiae Google argue that the acts of infringement must be caused by the manifestations of the distributor's improper object - that is, by the inducing messages themselves. Columbia, on the other hand, maintains that it need only prove that the "acts of infringement by third parties" were caused by the product distributed or services provided.

We think Columbia's interpretation of Grokster III is the better one. On that view, if one provides a service that could be used to infringe copyrights, with the manifested intent that the service actually be used in that manner, that person is liable for the infringement that occurs through the use of the service. As Grokster III explained:

> *"It is not only that encouraging a particular consumer to infringe a copyright can give rise to secondary liability for the infringement that results. Inducement liability goes beyond that, and the distribution of a product can itself give rise to liability where evidence shows that the distributor intended and encouraged the product to be used to infringe. In such a case, the culpable act is not merely the encouragement of infringement but also the distribution of the tool intended for infringing use."*

We are mindful, however, of the potential severity of a loose causation theory for inducement liability. Under this theory of liability, the only causation requirement is that the product or service at issue was used to infringe the plaintiff's copyrights. The possible reach of liability is enormous, particularly in the digital age.

Copyright law attempts to strike a balance amongst three competing interests: those of the copyright holders in benefitting from their labor; those of entrepreneurs in having the latitude to invent new technologies without fear of being held liable if their innovations are used by others in unintended infringing ways; and those of the public in having access both to entertainment options protected by copyright and to new technologies that enhance productivity and quality of life. Because copyright law's "ultimate aim is (...) to stimulate artistic creativity for the general public good," 464 U.S. at 432, it is important that we not permit inducement liability's relatively lax causation requirement to "enlarge the scope of [copyright's] statutory monopolies to encompass control over an article of commerce" - such as technology capable of substantial non-infringing uses - "that is not the subject of copyright protection."

We emphasize a few points in this regard. First, as previously discussed, proper proof of the defendant's intent that its product or service be used to infringe copyrights is paramount. "[M] ere knowledge of infringing potential or of actual infringing uses" does not subject a product distributor or service provider to liability. When dealing with corporate or entity defendants, moreover, the relevant intent must be that of the entity itself, as defined by traditional agency law principles; liability cannot be premised on stray or unauthorized statements that cannot fairly be imputed to the entity.

Moreover, proving that an entity had an unlawful purpose at a particular time in providing a product or service does not infinitely expand its liability in either temporal direction. If an entity begins providing a service with infringing potential at time *A*, but does not appreciate that potential until later and so does not develop and exhibit the requisite intent to support inducement liability until time *B*, it would not be held liable for the infringement that occurred between time *A* and *B*. Relatedly, an individual or entity's unlawful objective at time *B* is not a virus that infects all future actions. People, companies, and technologies must be allowed to rehabilitate, so to speak, through actions actively discouraging the infringing use of their product, lest the public be deprived of the useful good or service they are still capable of producing.

We also note, as Fung points out, that Grokster III seemingly presupposes a condition that is absent in this case: that there is but a single producer of the "device" in question. Only Sony sold the Betamax, and only Grokster and StreamCast distributed their respective software applications. Assessing causation was thus a straightforward task. In Sony, for example, there was no question that some customers would purchase and use the Betamax in ways that infringed copyright. Thus, in a "but-for" sense, there was no question that Sony caused whatever infringement resulted from the use of Betamax sets; the Court nonetheless held Sony not liable on the ground that even if Sony caused the infringement, it was not at fault, with fault measured by Sony's intent. But as Grokster III explained, "nothing in Sony requires courts to ignore evidence of intent if there is such evidence, and the case was never meant to foreclose rules of fault-based liability." Grokster III thus held that where there is sufficient evidence of fault - that is, an unlawful objective - distributors are liable for causing the infringement that resulted from use of their products. In other words, *Grokster III* and *Sony* were able to assume causation and assess liability (or not) based on fault. In the present case, however, where other individuals and entities provide services identical to those offered by Fung, causation, even in the relatively loose sense we have delineated, cannot be assumed, even though fault is unquestionably present.

Fung argues, on this basis, that some of the acts of infringement by third parties relied upon by the district court may not have involved his websites at all. He points out, for example, that by far the largest number of torrents tracked by the Torrentbox tracker are obtained from somewhere *other* than Torrentbox.com. If a user obtained a torrent from a source other than his websites, Fung maintains, he cannot be held liable for the infringement that resulted.

On the other hand, Fung's services encompass more than the provision of torrent files. Fung's trackers manage traffic for torrent files, obtained from Torrentbox and Podtropolis as well as other torrent sites, which enables users to download copyrighted content. If Plaintiffs can show a sufficient casual connection between users' infringing activity and the use of Fung's trackers, the fact that torrent files were obtained from elsewhere may not relieve Fung of liability.

We do not decide the degree to which Fung can be held liable for having caused infringements by users of his sites or trackers. The only issue presently before us is the permanent injunction, which, as in Grokster III, does not in this case depend on the "exact calculation of infringing use as a basis for a claim of damages." We therefore need not further entertain Fung's causation arguments at this time, but leave it to the district court to consider them, in light of the observations we have made, when it calculates damages.

In sum, we affirm the district court's holding that Columbia has carried its burden of proving, on the basis of undisputed facts, Fung's liability for inducing others to infringe Columbia's copyrights.

B. DMCA Safe Harbors

Fung asserts affirmative defenses under three of the DMCA's safe harbor provisions, 17 U.S.C. §512(a), (c), and (d). Because the DMCA safe harbors are affirmative defenses, Fung has the burden of establishing that he meets the statutory requirements.

Columbia argues, and the district court agreed, that inducement liability is inherently incompatible with protection under the DMCA safe harbors. This court has already rejected the notion that there can *never* be a DMCA safe harbor defense to contributory copyright liability, holding "that ... potential liability for contributory and vicarious infringement [does not] render the [DMCA] inapplicable per se." We note, in this connection, that the DMCA does not in terms exempt from protection any mode of copyright liability, including liability under the doctrine of inducement. Moreover, the DMCA's legislative history confirms that Congress intended to provide protection for at least some vicarious and contributory infringement.

Nor is there any inherent incompatibility between inducement liability and the requirements that apply to all of the DMCA safe harbors. For example, a prerequisite for the safe harbors is that the service provider implement a policy of removing repeat infringers. Although at first glance that requirement that might seem impossible to establish where the requisites for inducing infringement are met, on closer examination the appearance of *inherent* incompatibility dissipates. In some instances, for example, the Grokster standard for inducement might be met even where a service provider has a policy of removing proven repeat infringers. It is therefore *conceivable* that a service provider liable for inducement could be entitled to protection under the safe harbors.

In light of these considerations, we are not clairvoyant enough to be sure that there are no instances in which a defendant otherwise liable for contributory copyright infringement could meet the prerequisites for one or more of the DMCA safe harbors. We therefore think it best to conduct the two inquiries independently - although, as will appear, aspects of the inducing behavior that give rise to liability are relevant to the operation of some of the DMCA safe harbors and can, in some circumstances, preclude their application.

i. "Transitory digital network communications" (17 U.S.C. §512(a))

The first safe harbor at issue, which Fung asserts only as to his trackers, provides as follows:

A service provider shall not be liable for monetary relief, or, except as provided in subsection (j), for injunctive or other equitable relief, for infringement of copyright by reason of the provider's transmitting, routing, or providing connections for, material through a system or network controlled or operated by or for the service provider, or by reason of the intermediate and transient storage of that material in the course of such transmitting, routing, or providing connections, if -

(1) the transmission of the material was initiated by or at the direction of a person other than the service provider;

(2) the transmission, routing, provision of connections, or storage is carried out through an automatic technical process without selection of the material by the service provider;

(3) the service provider does not select the recipients of the material except as an automatic response to the request of another person;

(4) no copy of the material made by the service provider in the course of such intermediate or transient storage is maintained on the system or network in a manner ordinarily accessible to anyone other than anticipated recipients, and no such copy is maintained on the system or network in a manner ordinarily accessible to such anticipated recipients for a longer period than is reasonably necessary for the transmission, routing, or provision of connections; and

(5) the material is transmitted through the system or network without modification of its content.

For purposes of this safe harbor only, "the term 'service provider' means an entity offering the transmission, routing, or providing of connections for digital online communications, between or among points specified by a user, of material of the user's choosing, without modification to the content of the material as sent or received." 17 U.S.C. §512(k)(1)(A). The district court dismissed the application of this safe harbor in a footnote, stating that it did not apply to Fung "[b] ecause infringing materials do not pass through or reside on [Fung's] system."

The district court should not have rejected this safe harbor on the ground it did. Perfect 10, Inc. v. CCBill LLC, 488 F.3d 1102 (9th Cir. 2007), held that the §512(a) safe harbor does not require that the service provider transmit or route infringing material, explaining that "[t]here is no requirement in the statute that the communications must themselves be infringing, and we see no reason to import such a requirement."

We could, perhaps, end our analysis of the §512(a) safe harbor there. The district court seemingly held Fung liable for inducement based not on Fung's trackers' routing services, but, instead, on the dot-torrent files Fung collects and indexes. And it is not clear that Columbia is seeking to establish liability based directly on the tracking functions of Fung's trackers.

It appears, however, that Fung's trackers generate information concerning the torrent files transmitted that Fung then compiles and uses to induce further infringing use of his websites and trackers. In that sense, the tracking function is connected to the basis on which liability was sought and found. Without determining whether that information-generating use would itself affect the availability of the §512(a) safe harbor, we hold that safe harbor not available for Fung's trackers on other grounds.

Unlike a P2P network like Napster, in which users select particular files to download from particular users, Fung's trackers manage a "swarm" of connections that source tiny pieces of each file from numerous users; the user seeking to download a file chooses only the file, not the particular users who will provide it, and the tracker identifies the source computers to the user seeking to download a work.

Given these characteristics, Fung's trackers do not fit the definition of "service provider" that applies to this safe harbor. The definition provides that a "service provider" provides "connections ... between or among points specified by a user." 17 U.S.C. §512(k)(1)(A). Here, it is Fung's tracker that selects the "points" to which a user's client will connect in order to download a file. The tracker, not the requesting user, selects the publishers from which chunks of data will be transmitted.

We have held that §512(a) applies to service provides who act only as "conduits" for the transmission of information. Because they select which users will communicate with each other, Fung's trackers serve as more than "conduits" between computer users. Fung's trackers therefore are not "service providers" for purposes of §512(a), and are not eligible for the §512(a) safe harbor.

Fung asserts that these functions are "automatic technical processes" that proceed "without selection of any material by us." Even so, for the tracker to be a "service provider" for purposes of the § 512(a) safe harbor, the tracker, whether its functions are automatic or not, must meet the special definition of "service provider" applicable to this "conduit" safe harbor. If those functions go beyond those covered by that definition, then it does not matter whether they are automatic or humanly controlled.

ii. "Information residing on systems or networks at direction of users" (17 U.S.C. §512(c))

This safe harbor provides:

(1) In general. A service provider shall not be liable for monetary relief, or, except as provided in subsection (j), for injunctive or other equitable relief, for infringement of copyright by reason of the storage at the direction of a user of material that resides on a system or network controlled or operated by or for the service provider, if the service provider-

(A)(i) does not have actual knowledge that the material or an activity using the material on the system or network is infringing;

(ii) in the absence of such actual knowledge, is not aware of facts or circumstances from which infringing activity is apparent; or

(iii) upon obtaining such knowledge or awareness, acts expeditiously to remove, or disable access to, the material;

(B) does not receive a financial benefit directly attributable to the infringing activity, in a case in which the service provider has the right and ability to control such activity; and

(C) upon notification of claimed infringement as described in paragraph (3), responds expeditiously to remove, or disable access to, the material that is claimed to be infringing or to be the subject of infringing activity.

The district court held that Fung is ineligible for this safe harbor for the same reason it rejected the §512(a) safe harbor - that is, because the infringing material does not actually reside on Fung's servers. As with §512(a), this holding was in error. As CCBill emphasized, we will not read requirements into the safe harbors that are not contained in the text of the statute. Moreover, §512(c) explicitly covers not just the storage of infringing material, but also infringing "activit[ies]" that "us[e] the material [stored] on the system or network." 17 U.S.C. §512(c)(1)(A)(i). Here, as we have explained, the infringing activity associated with Fung - the peer-to-peer transfer of pirated content - relies upon torrents stored on Fung's websites. According to the record, sometimes those torrents are uploaded by users of the sites, while other torrents are collected for storage by Fung's websites themselves. The former situation would be at least facially eligible for the safe harbor, assuming the other criteria are met.

a. Actual and "Red Flag" Knowledge (§512(c)(1)(A)(i)–(ii))

We nonetheless hold that Fung is not eligible for the §512(c) safe harbor, on different grounds. The §512(c) safe harbor is available only if the service provider "does not have actual knowledge that the material or an activity using the material on the system or network is infringing," 17 U.S.C. §512(c)(1)(A)(i), or "is not aware of facts or circumstances from which infringing activity is apparent," §512(c)(1)(A)(ii). In UMG Recordings, this court endorsed the Second Circuit's interpretation of § 512(c)(1)(A), that "the actual knowledge provision turns on whether the provider actually or 'subjectively' knew of specific infringement, while the red flag provision turns on whether the provider was subjectively aware of facts that would have made the specific infringement 'objectively' obvious to a reasonable person."

Fung maintains that he lacked either type of knowledge, because Columbia failed to provide statutorily compliant notification of infringement. Under §512(c)(3)(B), notification of infringement that fails to comply with the requirements set forth in §512(c)(3)(A) "shall not be considered (...) in determining whether a service provider has actual knowledge or is aware of facts or circumstances from which infringing activity is apparent." 17 U.S.C. §512(c)(3)(B)(i). And, as Fung points out, the district court noted that there was at least a "triable issue of fact as to the adequacy of the statutory notice that Plaintiffs provided to [Fung]."

We need not determine the adequacy of Columbia's notification of claimed infringement - indeed, as the district court held, it would not be appropriate to do so at this stage. Fung had "red flag" knowledge of a broad range of infringing activity for reasons independent of any notifications from Columbia, and therefore is ineligible for the §512(c) safe harbor.

As noted, the record is replete with instances of Fung actively encouraging infringement, by urging his users to both upload and download particular copyrighted works, providing assistance to those seeking to watch copyrighted films, and helping his users burn copyrighted material onto DVDs. The material in question was sufficiently current and well-known that it would have been objectively obvious to a reasonable person that the material solicited and assisted was both copyrighted and not licensed to random members of the public, and that the induced use was therefore infringing. Moreover, Fung does not dispute that he personally used the isoHunt website to download infringing material. Thus, while Fung's inducing actions do not necessarily render him per se ineligible for protection under §512(c), they are relevant to our determination that Fung had "red flag" knowledge of infringement.

Fung introduced no contrary facts with regard to identified torrents involved in these documented activities, responding only with the generalized assertion that he "ha[s] a robust copyright compliance system." But "conclusory allegations, standing alone, are insufficient to prevent summary judgment."

As Fung has not carried his burden as the non-moving party of demonstrating a genuine dispute as to the material facts regarding his eligibility for the §512(c) safe harbor, Columbia is entitled to summary judgment as to this issue.

b. "Financial benefit" & "the right and ability to control" (§512(c)(1)(B))

Under §512(c)(1)(B), a service provider loses protection under the safe harbor if two conditions are met: (1) the provider "receive[s] a financial benefit directly attributable to the infringing activity"; and (2) the "service provider has the right and ability to control such activity." 17 U.S.C. §512(c)(1)(B). Fung meets both requirements and is therefore ineligible for protection under the §512(c) safe harbor.

As to the first prong of §512(c)(1)(B), we have held, in the context of service providers who charge for their services, that a service provider receives a direct financial benefit from infringing activity where "there is a causal relationship between the infringing activity and any financial benefit a defendant reaps, regardless of *how substantial* the benefit is in proportion to a defendant's overall profits." Thus, where a service provider obtains revenue from "subscribers," the relevant inquiry is "'whether the infringing activity constitutes a draw for subscribers, not just an added benefit.'"

At the same time, our opinions have not suggested that the "financial benefit" prong of §512(c)(1)(B) is peripheral or lacks teeth. Ellison ultimately concluded that the financial benefit standard was not met, because there was inadequate proof that "customers either subscribed because of the available infringing material or cancelled subscriptions because it was no longer available." And CCBill similarly found that evidence that the service provider hosted, for a fee, websites that contain infringing material inadequate to establish the requisite financial benefit. In so holding, CCBill cited to DMCA legislative history stating that a direct financial benefit cannot be established showing that a service provider "receive[d] a one-time set-up fee and flat, periodic payments for service from a person engaging in infringing activities."

Moreover, the structure of §512(c)(1)(B) indicates that the lack of direct financial benefit prong of the safe harbor requirement is central, rather than peripheral. The statute sets out as the requirement that the service provider "not receive a financial benefit directly attributable to the infringing activity." It then states the "right and ability to control" in a dependent clause, describing a limitation on the financial benefit requirement to certain circumstances. The grammatical emphasis, then, is on the lack of direct financial benefit requirement, with the right to control prong secondary.

Against this background, we note that we have never specified what constitutes a "financial benefit *directly* attributable to the infringing activity," 17 U.S.C. §512(c)(1)(B) (emphasis added), where, as here, the service provider's revenue is derived from advertising, and not from users. We do so now.

Here, the record shows that Fung generated revenue by selling advertising space on his websites. The advertising revenue depended on the number of users who viewed and then clicked on the advertisements. Fung marketed advertising to one advertiser by pointing to the "TV and movies (...) at the top of the most frequently searched by our viewers," and provided another with a list of typical user search queries, including popular movies and television shows. In addition, there was a vast amount of infringing material on his websites – whether 90-96% or somewhat less – supporting an inference that Fung's revenue stream is predicated on the broad availability of infringing materials for his users, thereby attracting advertisers. And, as we have seen, Fung actively induced infringing activity on his sites.

Under these circumstances, we hold the connection between the infringing activity and Fung's income stream derived from advertising is sufficiently direct to meet the direct "financial benefit" prong of §512(c)(1)(B). Fung promoted advertising by pointing to infringing activity; obtained advertising revenue that depended on the number of visitors to his sites; attracted primarily visitors who were seeking to engage in infringing activity, as that is mostly what occurred on his sites; and encouraged that infringing activity. Given this confluence of circumstances, Fung's revenue stream was tied directly to the infringing activity involving his websites, both as to his ability to attract advertisers and as to the amount of revenue he received.

With respect to the second prong of §512(c)(1)(B), we recently explained in *UMG* that the "right and ability to control" infringing activity involves "something more" than "merely having the general ability to locate infringing material and terminate users' access." Adopting the

Second Circuit's interpretation of §512(c)(1)(B), we held that "in order to have the 'right and ability to control,' the service provider must [also] 'exert[ ] substantial influence on the activities of users.'" Id. In doing so, we noted that "'[s]ubstantial influence' may include ... purposeful conduct, as in Grokster." In the absence of any evidence of inducement or any other reason to suggest the defendant exerted substantial influence over its users' activities, we concluded the defendant was not ineligible for protection under this provision.

Here, we are confronted with the opposite situation. Fung unquestionably had the ability to locate infringing material and terminate users' access. In addition to being able to locate material identified in valid DMCA notices, Fung organized torrent files on his sites using a program that matches file names and content with specific search terms describing material likely to be infringing, such as "screener" or "PPV." And when users could not find certain material likely to be infringing on his sites, Fung personally assisted them in locating the files. Fung also personally removed "fake, infected, or otherwise bad or abusive torrents" in order to "protect the integrity of [his websites'] search index[es]."

Crucially, Fung's ability to control infringing activity on his websites went well beyond merely locating and terminating users' access to infringing material. As noted, there is overwhelming evidence that Fung engaged in culpable, inducing activity like that in Grokster III. Although Fung's inducement actions do not categorically remove him from protection under §512(c), they demonstrate the substantial influence Fung exerted over his users' infringing activities, and thereby supply one essential component of the financial benefit/right to control exception to the §512(c) safe harbor.

Because he meets both prongs of §512(c)(1)(B), Fung is not eligible for protection under the §512(c) safe harbor.

We have no difficulty concluding that where the §512(c)(1)(B) safe harbor requirements are not met, the service provider loses protection with regard to any infringing activity using the service. As we held in UMG, the §512(c)(1)(B) "right and ability to control" requirement does not depend only upon the ability to remove known or apparent infringing material. Instead, there must also be substantial influence on the infringing activities of users, indicating that it is the overall relationship between the service provider and infringing users that matters. Also, to the degree this DMCA provision had its origin in vicarious liability concepts, those concepts rest on the overall relationship between the defendant and the infringers, rather than on specific instances of infringement. The term "right and ability to control such activity" so reflects, as it emphasizes a general, structural relationship and speaks of "such activity," not any particular activity.

We therefore hold that because Fung does not meet the requirements of §512(c)(1)(B), he is outside of the §512(c) safe harbor with respect to all infringement activity on the sites that are the subject of this suit.

iii. "Information location tools" (17 U.S.C. §512(d))

The last safe harbor Fung invokes provides:

> *A service provider shall not be liable for monetary relief, or, except as provided in subsection (j), for injunctive or other equitable relief, for infringement of copyright by reason of the provider referring or linking users to an online location containing infringing material or infringing activity, by using information location tools, including a directory, index, reference, pointer, or hypertext link, if the service provider -*
>
> *(1)(A) does not have actual knowledge that the material or activity is infringing;*
>
> *(B) in the absence of such actual knowledge, is not aware of facts or circumstances from which infringing activity is apparent; or*
>
> *(C) upon obtaining such knowledge or awareness, acts expeditiously to remove, or disable access to, the material;*
>
> *(2) does not receive a financial benefit directly attributable to the infringing activity, in a case in which the service provider has the right and ability to control such activity; and*
>
> *(3) upon notification of claimed infringement as described in subsection (c)(3), responds expeditiously to remove, or disable access to, the material that is claimed to be infringing or to be the subject of infringing activity, except that, for purposes of this paragraph, the information described in subsection (c)(3)(A)(iii) shall be identification of the reference or link, to material or activity claimed to be infringing, that is to be removed or access to which is to be disabled, and information reasonably sufficient to permit the service provider to locate that reference or link.*

We affirm the grant of summary judgment to Columbia on Fung's claim to the §512(d) safe harbor for the reasons just discussed with regard to §512(c): Fung was broadly "aware of facts or circumstances from which infringing activity [wa]s apparent." 17 U.S.C. §512(d)(1)(B). Moreover, he received a direct financial benefit from that infringing activity, and had the "right and ability to control such activity." §512(d)(2). (...)

AFFIRMED IN PART, VACATED IN PART, INJUNCTION MODIFIED IN PART.

THINK IT OVER

1. In the first ever proceedings against a P2P service provider, Napster was found liable under the concepts of contributory and vicarious liability in 2001. Napster, a first generation P2P platform, provided a system that satisfied all requirements for indirect liability: it had objective knowledge of the direct infringements of end-users and induced/materially contributed to such infringements under contributory liability; and it had the right and ability to control infringements and received direct or indirect financial benefits from such infringements under vicarious liability. (See *A&M v. Napster.*) In the most notable case against a second generation P2P service provider, Grokster was found liable under the concept of contributory liability (especially its "inducement" prong) by the U.S. Supreme Court in 2005. (See *MGM v. Grokster.*) BitTorrent represents the third generation of P2P file-sharing, and the *Fung* decision is a leading precedent against such platforms.

2. *Under what circumstances, if any, could isoHunt and Fung have relied on the shield of the "staple article of commerce" doctrine? Is this doctrine applicable to the producer of the BitTorrent protocol, namely BitTorrent, Inc.? What, if any, would have made it possible for isoHunt and Fung to be protected under the "safe harbor" provisions [especially §512(c)] of the DMCA? What are the consequences of the the application of in rem jurisdiction for services that are running entirely from outside of the United States?*

3. Criminal law has also been used in many notable cases against P2P file-sharing system operators. In one of the earliest file-sharing cases, Daniel Dove, the administrator of EliteTorrents.org was found guilty by a jury for criminal copyright infringement and conspiracy to commit criminal copyright infringement in 2005. He was sentenced to 18 months imprisonment on each count, to be served concurrently. At the same time, two victims (the Recording Industry Association of America and Lionsgate Entertainment, Inc.) submitted requests for restitution. In 2008, the District Court for the Western District of Virginia concluded that there is no special rule for a mandatory restitution in copyright infringement cases. The Court also ruled that the Mandatory Victims Restitution Act of 1996 (MVRA) does not apply to criminal copyright infringements, since the statute applies to offenses against "property", under title 18 of the U.S. Code, while copyright is covered by title 17 of the Code. Dove was, however, convicted of conspiracy to engage in criminal copyright infringement under the general conspiracy statute as well, which fells under title 18 of the Code. This claim satisfied the prerequisites of the MVRA. Nevertheless, the MVRA allows for restitution, among other factors, if the government is able to prove the actual losses of the victims. The District Court found that victims' estimate on their losses (the "diverted profits theory of loss") is insufficient. *While criminal law might serve as a tool to fight against copyright offenses, U.S. federal law does not provide a solid ground for restitution.*

From the many other criminal procedures, the one against – among others – the founder of the MegaUpload cyberlocker, Kim Dotcom, has gained significant popularity. Kim Dotcom was arrested in New Zealand in 2012 upon the request of the United States, but he is not yet extradited by the New Zealand authorities (as of the end of March 2020). If extradition would ever happen, the criminal proceedings on US soil would easily last for some further years. *Criminal trials might work well if personal jurisdiction is given, but they seem to be burdensome and time consuming (if not impossible), if only in rem jurisdiction is present.*

Further Case Law

A&M Technology, Inc., et al., v. Napster, Inc., et al., 239 *F.3d* 1004 (2001)

In re: Aimster Copyright Litigation, 334 *F.3d* 643 (2003)

Metro-Goldwyn-Mayer Studios, Inc., et al., v. Grokster, Ltd., et al., 545 *U.S.* 913 (2005)

United States of America v. Daniel Dove, 585 *F.Supp.2d* 865 (2008)

Arista Records LLC, et al., v. Lime Group LLC, et al., 784 *F.Supp.2d* 313 (2011)

Recommended readings

In English

Robyn Axberg: File-Sharing Tools and Copyright Law: A Study of In Re Aimster Copyright Litigation and MGM Studios, Inc. v. Grokster, Ltd., *Loyola University Chicago Law Review*, 2003: p. 389-456.

William S. Coats - Heather D. Rafter - Vickie L. Feeman - John G. Given: Blows against the Empire: Napster, Aimster, Grokster and the War against P2P File Sharing, *Practising Law Institute*, 2003: p. 445-488.

Raymond Shih Ray Ku: Grokking Grokster, *Wisconsin Law Review*, 2005: p. 1217-1282.

John Blevins: Uncertainty as Enforcement Mechanism: the New Expansion of Secondary Copyright Liability to Internet Platforms, *Cardozo Law Review*, June 2013, p. 1821-1887.

Benton Martin - Jeremiah Newhall: Criminal Copyright Enforcement Against Filesharing Services, *North Carolina Journal of Law and Technology*, October 2013, p. 101-151.

Kimberlee Weatherall: *Criminal Sanctions as a Tool against Online Infringement: National Law, International Treaties, Transnational Cooperation.* In: Tanya Aplin (Ed.): *Research Handbook on Intellectual Property and Digital Technologies*, Edward Elgar, Cheltenham, 2020, p. 531-552.

In Hungarian
Mezei Péter: *A fájlcsere dilemma - A perek lassúak, az internet gyors*, HVG-Orac, Budapest, 2012: p. 112-131.

STICHTING BREIN V. ZIGGO BV AND XS4ALL INTERNET BV

Case C-610/15 - Judgment of the Court (Second Chamber), 14 June 2017 [ECLI:EU:C:2017:456]

(...) Legal context

3 Recitals 9, 10, 23 and 27 of Directive 2001/29 state:
'(9) Any harmonisation of copyright and related rights must take as a basis a high level of protection, since such rights are crucial to intellectual creation. Their protection helps to ensure the maintenance and development of creativity in the interests of authors, performers, producers, consumers, culture, industry and the public at large. Intellectual property has therefore been recognised as an integral part of property.
(10) If authors or performers are to continue their creative and artistic work, they have to receive an appropriate reward for the use of their work, as must producers in order to be able to finance this work. The investment required to produce products such as phonograms, films or multimedia products, and services such as "on-demand" services, is considerable. Adequate legal protection of intellectual property rights is necessary in order to guarantee the availability of such a reward and provide the opportunity for satisfactory returns on this investment.

...

(23) This Directive should harmonise further the author's right of communication to the public. This right should be understood in a broad sense covering all communication to the public not present at the place where the communication originates. This right should cover any such transmission or retransmission of a work to the public by wire or wireless means, including broadcasting. This right should not cover any other acts.

...

(27) The mere provision of physical facilities for enabling or making a communication does not in itself amount to communication within the meaning of this Directive.'

4 Article 3 of that directive, entitled 'Right of communication to the public of works and right of making available to the public other subject matter', provides in paragraph 1:
'Member States shall provide authors with the exclusive right to authorise or prohibit any communication to the public of their works, by wire or wireless means, including the making available

to the public of their works in such a way that members of the public may access them from a place and at a time individually chosen by them.'

5 Article 8 of that directive, entitled 'Sanctions and remedies', provides in paragraph 3:
'Member States shall ensure that rightholders are in a position to apply for an injunction against intermediaries whose services are used by a third party to infringe a copyright or related right.'

6 Recital 23 of Directive 2004/48 is worded as follows:
'Without prejudice to any other measures, procedures and remedies available, rightholders should have the possibility of applying for an injunction against an intermediary whose services are being used by a third party to infringe the rightholder's industrial property right. The conditions and procedures relating to such injunctions should be left to the national law of the Member States. As far as infringements of copyright and related rights are concerned, a comprehensive level of harmonisation is already provided for in Directive 2001/29/EC. Article 8(3) of Directive 2001/29/EC should therefore not be affected by this Directive.'

7 Article 11 of Directive 2004/48, entitled 'Injunctions', provides:
'Member States shall ensure that, where a judicial decision is taken finding an infringement of an intellectual property right, the judicial authorities may issue against the infringer an injunction aimed at prohibiting the continuation of the infringement. Where provided for by national law, non-compliance with an injunction shall, where appropriate, be subject to a recurring penalty payment, with a view to ensuring compliance. Member States shall also ensure that rightholders are in a position to apply for an injunction against intermediaries whose services are used by a third party to infringe an intellectual property right, without prejudice to Article 8(3) of Directive 2001/29/EC.'

The dispute in the main proceedings and the questions referred for a preliminary ruling

8 Stichting Brein is a Netherlands foundation which safeguards the interests of copyright holders.

9 Ziggo and XS4ALL are internet access providers. A significant number of their subscribers use the online sharing platform TPB, an indexer of BitTorrent files. BitTorrent is a protocol through which users (known as 'peers') can share files. The essential characteristic of BitTorrent is that it divides files for sharing into segments, thus removing the need to rely on a central server to store those files, which lessens the burden on individual servers during the sharing process. In order to be able to share files, users must first download specific

software called 'BitTorrent Client', which is not provided by the online sharing platform TPB. 'BitTorrent Client' is software which allows the creation of torrent files.

10 Users (called 'seeders') who wish to make a file on their computer available to other users (called 'leechers') have to create a torrent file through their BitTorrent Client. Torrent files refer to a central server (called a 'tracker') which identifies the users available to share a particular torrent file as well as the underlying media file. These torrent files are uploaded by the seeders to an online sharing platform, such as TPB, which then proceeds to index them so that they can be found by the users of the online sharing platform and the works to which those torrent files refer can be downloaded onto the users' computers in several segments through their BitTorrent Client.

11 "Magnet links" are often used in place of torrent files. These links identify the content of a torrent file and refer to it through a digital fingerprint.

12 The torrent files offered on the online sharing platform TPB relate mainly to copyright-protected works, without the rightholders having given their consent to the operators or users of that platform to carry out the sharing acts in question.

13 In the context of the main proceedings, Stichting Brein's principal request is that Ziggo and XS4ALL be ordered to block the domain names and IP addresses of the online sharing platform TPB in order to prevent the services of those internet access providers from being used to infringe the copyright and related rights of the rightholders, whose interests Stichting Brein protects.

14 The court of first instance upheld Stichting Brein's requests. However, these were rejected on appeal.

15 The Hoge Raad der Nederlanden (Supreme Court of the Netherlands) notes that, in the present case, it has been established that the actions of the online sharing platform TPB make protected works available to the public without the rightholders' consent. It has also been established that subscribers to Ziggo and XS4ALL, through this platform, make protected works available without the rightholders' consent and thus infringe the copyright and related rights of those rightholders.

16 The Hoge Raad der Nederlanden (Supreme Court of the Netherlands) notes, however, that the Court's case-law does not allow it to reply with any certainty to the question as to

whether the online sharing platform TPB also communicates works to the public within the meaning of Article 3(1) of Directive 2001/29, in particular:

– by creating and maintaining a system in which internet users connect with each other in order to be able to share, in segments, works present on their own computers;

– by operating a website from which users can download torrent files which refer to segments of those works; and

– by indexing the torrent files placed online on this website and by categorising them in such a way that the segments of those underlying works can be located and the users can download those works (as a whole) onto their computers.

17 Under those circumstances, the Hoge Raad der Nederlanden (Supreme Court of the Netherlands) decided to stay the proceedings before it and to refer the following questions to the Court for a preliminary ruling:

'(1) Is there a communication to the public within the meaning of Article 3(1) of Directive 2001/29 by the operator of a website, if no protected works are available on that website, but a system exists … by means of which metadata on protected works which are present on the users' computers are indexed and categorised for users, so that the users can trace and upload and download the protected works on the basis thereof? (…)

Consideration of the questions referred

The first question

18 By its first question, the referring court asks, in essence, whether the concept of 'communication to the public', within the meaning of Article 3(1) of Directive 2001/29, should be interpreted as covering, in circumstances such as those at issue in the main proceedings, the making available and management, on the internet, of a sharing platform which, by means of indexation of metadata relating to protected works and the provision of a search engine, allows users of that platform to locate those works and to share them in the context of a peer-to-peer network.

19 It follows from Article 3(1) of Directive 2001/29 that Member States are required to ensure that authors have the exclusive right to authorise or prohibit any communication to the public of their works, by wire or wireless means, including the making available to the public of their works in such a way that members of the public may access them from a place and at a time individually chosen by them.

20 Under that provision, authors thus have a right which is preventive in nature and allows them to intervene between possible users of their work and the communication to the public which such users might contemplate making, in order to prohibit such communication.

21 As Article 3(1) of Directive 2001/29 does not define the concept of 'communication to the public', the meaning and scope of that concept must be determined in light of the objectives pursued by that directive and the context in which the provision being interpreted is set.

22 In that regard, it should be borne in mind that it follows from recitals 9 and 10 of Directive 2001/29 that the latter's principal objective is to establish a high level of protection for authors, allowing them to obtain an appropriate reward for the use of their works, including on the occasion of communication to the public. It follows that the concept of 'communication to the public' must be interpreted broadly, as recital 23 of the directive indeed expressly states.

23 The Court has also specified that the concept of 'communication to the public', within the meaning of Article 3(1) of Directive 2001/29, requires an individual assessment.

24 It is clear from Article 3(1) of Directive 2001/29 that the concept of 'communication to the public' involves two cumulative criteria, namely an 'act of communication' of a work and the communication of that work to a 'public'.

25 In order to determine whether a user is making a 'communication to the public' within the meaning of Article 3(1) of Directive 2001/29, it is necessary to take into account several complementary criteria, which are not autonomous and are interdependent. Consequently, those criteria must be applied both individually and in their interaction with one another, since they may, in different situations, be present to widely varying degrees.

26 Amongst those criteria, the Court has emphasised, firstly, the indispensable role played by the user and the deliberate nature of his intervention. That user makes an act of communication when he intervenes, in full knowledge of the consequences of his action, to give his customers access to a protected work, particularly where, in the absence of that intervention, those customers would not be able to enjoy the broadcast work, or would be able to do so only with difficulty.

27 Secondly, it has specified that the concept of the 'public' refers to an indeterminate number of potential viewers and implies, moreover, a fairly large number of people.

28 The Court has also noted that, according to a settled line of case-law, in order to be categorised as a 'communication to the public', a protected work must be communicated using specific technical means, different from those previously used or, failing that, to a 'new public', that is to say, to a public that was not already taken into account by the copyright holders when they authorised the initial communication of their work to the public.

29 Finally, the Court has underlined, on numerous occasions, that the profit-making nature of a communication, within the meaning of Article 3(1) of Directive 2001/29, is not irrelevant.

30 As regards, in the first place, the question of whether making available and managing an online sharing platform, such as that at issue in the main proceedings, is an 'act of communication' for the purposes of Article 3(1) of Directive 2001/29, it must be noted, as recital 23 of Directive 2001/29 states, that the author's right of communication to the public, provided for in Article 3(1), covers any transmission or retransmission of a work to the public by wire or wireless means, including broadcasting.

31 Furthermore, as is apparent from Article 3(1) of Directive 2001/29, in order for there to be an 'act of communication', it is sufficient, in particular, that a work is made available to a public in such a way that the persons comprising that public may access it, from wherever and whenever they individually choose, irrespective of whether they avail themselves of that opportunity.

32 The Court has already held, in this regard, that the provision, on a website, of clickable links to protected works published without any access restrictions on another site, affords users of the first site direct access to those works.

33 The Court has also held the same to be the case for the sale of a multimedia player on which there are pre-installed add-ons, available on the internet, containing hyperlinks to websites – that are freely accessible to the public – on which copyright-protected works have been made available without the consent of the rightholders.

34 It can therefore be inferred from this case-law that, as a rule, any act by which a user, with full knowledge of the relevant facts, provides its clients with access to protected works is liable to constitute an 'act of communication' for the purposes of Article 3(1) of Directive 2001/29.

35 In the present case it must be found, first, as the Advocate General has noted, in essence, in point 45 of his Opinion, that it is not disputed that copyright-protected works are, by

means of the online sharing platform TPB, made available to the users of that platform in such a way that they may access those works from wherever and whenever they individually choose.

36 Second, it is true, as noted by the referring court, that the works thus made available to the users of the online sharing platform TPB have been placed online on that platform not by the platform operators but by its users. However, the fact remains that those operators, by making available and managing an online sharing platform such as that at issue in the main proceedings, intervene, with full knowledge of the consequences of their conduct, to provide access to protected works, by indexing on that platform torrent files which allow users of the platform to locate those works and to share them within the context of a peer-to-peer network. In this respect, as the Advocate General stated, in essence, in point 50 of his Opinion, without the aforementioned operators making such a platform available and managing it, the works could not be shared by the users or, at the very least, sharing them on the internet would prove to be more complex.

37 The view must therefore be taken that the operators of the online sharing platform TPB, by making that platform available and managing it, provide their users with access to the works concerned. They can therefore be regarded as playing an essential role in making the works in question available.

38 Finally, the operators of the online sharing platform TPB cannot be considered to be making a 'mere provision' of physical facilities for enabling or making a communication, within the meaning of recital 27 of Directive 2001/29. It is clear from the order for reference that that platform indexes torrent files in such a way that the works to which the torrent files refer may be easily located and downloaded by the users of that sharing platform. Moreover, it is clear from the observations submitted to the Court that, in addition to a search engine, the online sharing platform TPB offers an index classifying the works under different categories, based on the type of the works, their genre or their popularity, within which the works made available are divided, with the platform's operators checking to ensure that a work has been placed in the appropriate category. In addition, those operators delete obsolete or faulty torrent files and actively filter some content.

39 In the light of the foregoing, the making available and management of an online sharing platform, such as that at issue in the main proceedings, must be considered to be an act of communication for the purposes of Article 3(1) of Directive 2001/29.

40 In the second place, in order to be categorised as a 'communication to the public', within the meaning of Article 3(1) of Directive 2001/29, the protected works must also in fact be communicated to a 'public'.

41 In that regard, the Court has stated, first, that the concept of 'public' involves a certain *de minimis* threshold, which excludes from that concept groups of persons concerned which are too small, or insignificant. Second, in order to determine that number, the cumulative effect of making the works available to potential recipients should be taken into account. Thus, it is necessary to know not only how many persons have access to the same work at the same time, but also how many of them have access to it in succession.

42 In the present case, it is apparent from the order for reference that a large number of subscribers to Ziggo and XS4ALL have downloaded media files using the online sharing platform TPB. It is also clear from the observations submitted to the Court that this platform is used by a considerable number of persons, the operators of TPB claiming, on their online sharing platform, to have several dozens of millions of 'peers'. In this respect, the communication at issue in the main proceedings covers, at the very least, all of the platform's users. These users can access, at any time and simultaneously, the protected works which are shared by means of the platform. Thus, that communication is aimed at an indeterminate number of potential recipients and involves a large number of persons.

43 It follows that, by a communication such as that at issue in the main proceedings, protected works are indeed communicated to a 'public' within the meaning of Article 3(1) of Directive 2001/29.

44 Furthermore, with regard to the question whether those works have been communicated to a 'new' public within the meaning of the case-law cited in paragraph 28 of the present judgment, the Court, in its [*Svensson*] judgment (...) as well as in its [*Bestwater*] order (...), has held that such a public is a public that was not taken into account by the copyright holders when they authorised the initial communication.

45 In the present case, it is apparent from the observations submitted to the Court, first, that the operators of the online sharing platform TPB were informed that this platform, which they make available to users and manage, provides access to works published without authorisation of the rightholders and, second, that the same operators expressly display, on blogs and forums available on that platform, their purpose to make protected works available to the users, and encourage the latter to make copies of those works. In any event, it is clear from the order for reference that the operators of the online sharing platform TPB

could not be unaware that this platform provides access to works published without the consent of the rightholders, given that, as expressly highlighted by the referring court, a very large number of torrent files on the online sharing platform TPB relate to works published without the consent of the rightholders. In those circumstances, it must be held that there is communication to a 'new public'.

46 Furthermore, there can be no dispute that the making available and management of an online sharing platform, such as that at issue in the main proceedings, is carried out with the purpose of obtaining profit therefrom, it being clear from the observations submitted to the Court that that platform generates considerable advertising revenues.

47 Therefore, it must be held that the making available and management of an online sharing platform, such as that at issue in the main proceedings, constitutes a 'communication to the public', within the meaning of Article 3(1) of Directive 2001/29.

48 In the light of all the foregoing considerations, the answer to the first question is that the concept of 'communication to the public', within the meaning of Article 3(1) of Directive 2001/29, must be interpreted as covering, in circumstances such as those at issue in the main proceedings, the making available and management, on the internet, of a sharing platform which, by means of indexation of metadata referring to protected works and the provision of a search engine, allows users of that platform to locate those works and to share them in the context of a peer-to-peer network. (...)

THINK IT OVER

1. The final decision of the Stockholm Court of Appeals in 2010 against The Pirate Bay confirmed the operators' liability for incitement of criminal activities. (The four defendants were sentenced to prison, and they were ordered to pay massive damages as well.) Nevertheless, The Pirate Bay was taken over by new owners and the site is still running (as of the end of March 2020). The *Ziggo* case originated from the Netherlands, and it also addressed The Pirate Bay's service. The CJEU found that the service of The Pirate Bay allows for the communication of protected subject matter to "new public". Under the case law of the CJEU, such activitiy is illegal in the lack of authorization. The importance of the decision lies in the fact that secondary copyright liability doctrines are generally unknown in Europe (compare to the Dutch *KaZaa* decision from 2003), and P2P platforms practically remained immune against indirect copyright claims. Instead of indirect copyright liability, criminal law (e.g. in the Swedish *The Pirate Bay* case) or e-commerce law (e.g. in the Dutch *Mininova* case) was used against system operators in various European countries. *What are the advantages and disadvantages of relying on criminal and e-commerce law in the fight against unauthorized file-sharing?* In *Ziggo*, the CJEU concluded that The Pirate Bay's contribution to end-users' illegal activities was directly illegal. This way the CJEU sidestepped the issue of indirect liability, and allowed for a much broader enforcement of copyrights against P2P (and other) platforms. *Is there any other method of law enforcement? Are website blockings, three-strike regimes or domain seizures such options?*

2. The severe enforcement of copyrights due to massive online copyright infringements might lead to an imbalance between rights holders' interests and fundamental rights of other members of the society. The freedom of expression is called to be under attack by broad enforcement practices. Such arguments were raised after the introduction of France's HADOPI law (on the graduated response system) in 2009, and in the *Fredrik Neij and Peter Sunde Kolmisoppi v Sweden* case tried by the European Court of Human Rights. There the ECtHR has concluded that the final decision in the Swedish *The Pirate Bay* case was not against the right to freedom of expression of the applicants (two of the founders of The Pirate Bay). Viewed from the perspective of freedom of expression, *is there any difference between participation in the discussion on political issues, or topics having general/public interest and sharing copyright-protected contents via the Internet without the rightholders permission?* Another fundamental right that shall be balanced against copyrights is the freedom to run a business. The CJEU has a significant case law on this matter. Compare to the *UPC Telekabel Wien* decision of the CJEU on page 344.

3. In its ruling, the CJEU claimed that the administrators of The Pirate Bay have used the capability of the platform to allow others sharing protected subject matter by the BitTorrent protocol. *What if the staff of a similar platform is not dedicated to piracy, but the platform is used for purposes like education and research?*

4. The idea of direct liability of platform operators remained a hot topic after the *Ziggo* ruling. Indeed, Article 17 (formerly known as Article 13) of the Copyright in the Digital Single Market Directive [Directive (EU) 2019/790] aims to close the "value gap" (the significant imbalance between various platforms' economic benefits and rights-holders incomes lost due to the unlicensed offering of user generated/uploaded contents by those platforms) by obliging online content sharing service providers (e.g. YouTube) to authorize the use of protected subject matters by the end-users on the said platforms. If the service provider fails to license user generated contents, it becomes obliged to filter out the infringing materials. If the service provider fails to eliminate the illegal contents, it bears direct liability for the materials uploaded to its servers. *Is this norm in compliance with Article 15 of the E-Commerce Directive (Directive 2000/31/EC) that prohibits general monitoring by e-commerce service providers?* (While academia is divided on this matter, the answer to this question is most probably negative.) *What other concerns do you have regarding "private ordering", that is, against the "private policing" of the (unlicensed) use by the platforms?*

Further Case Law

Vereinigung Buma / Stichting Stemra v. Kazaa B.V., Nr. C02/186HR, Supreme Court of the Netherlands, 19 December 2003

Supreme Court of Norway 27.1.2005 - Napster.no, *IIC - International Review of Intellectual Property and Competition Law*, Issue 1/2006, p. 120-123.

LJN: BJ6008 - *Mininova*, Rechtbank Utrecht, 250077 / HA ZA 08-1124, 26 August 2009

Mål B 4041-09 - *The Pirate Bay*, Svea Hovrätt, Stockholm, 26 November 2011

ECtHR (Section V), 19 February 2013, no. 40397/12, *Fredrik Neij and Peter Sunde Kolmisoppi v Sweden*

Case C-314/12 - UPC Telekabel Wien GmbH v Constantin Film Verleih GmbH and Wega Filmproduktionsgesellschaft mbH, Judgment of the Court (Fourth Chamber), 27 March 2014 [ECLI:EU:C:2014:192]

Case C-527/15 - Stichting Brein v Jack Frederik Wullems, Judgment of the Court (Second Chamber), 26 April 2017 [ECLI:EU:C:2017:300]

Recommended readings

In English

Gerald Spindler - Matthias Leistner: Secondary Copyright Infringement - New Perspectives in Germany and Europe, *IIC - International Review of Intellectual Property and Competition Law*, Issue 7/2006, p. 788-822.

Giuseppe Mazziotti: *EU Digital Copyright Law and the End-User*, Springer, Berlin, 2010

Enrico Bonadio: File sharing, copyright and freedom of speech, *European Intellectual Property Review*, Issue 10/2011, p. 619-631.

Giancarlo F. Frosio: From horizontal to vertical: an intermediary liability earthquake in Europe, *Journal of Intellectual Property Law & Practice*, Issue 7/2016, p. 565-575.

Cliona Kelly: Facilitation of Peer-to-Peer File Sharing by The Pirate Bay and Copyright Infringement: Stichting Brein v Ziggo BV, *Commercial Law Practitioner*, Issue 7/2017, p. 152-154.

Sophie Stalla-Bourdillon - Eleonora Rosati - Karmen Turk - Christina Angelopoulos -Aleksandra Kuczerawy - Miquel Peguera - Martin Husovec: An academic perspective on the copyright reform, *Computer Law & Security Review*, 2017, p. 3-13.

Irini Stamatoudi: *'Linking' and 'Browsing' in the Light of the EU Court of Justice's Case Law.* In: Tana Pistorius (Ed.): Intellectual Property Perspectives on the Regulation of New Technologies, Edward Elgar, Cheltenham, 2018, p. 179-207.

Ben Allgrove - John Groom: *Enforcement in a Digital Context: Intermediary Liability.* In: Tanya Aplin (Ed.): *Research Handbook on Intellectual Property and Digital Technologies*, Edward Elgar, Cheltenham, 2020, p. 506-530.

In French

Olivia Roche - Étienne Drouard: Pour la CJUE, les plateformes «peer-to-peer» réalisent des «actes de communication au public», *Droit de l'immatériel: informatique, médias, communication*, 2017, n° 140, p. 9-12.

Vincent Cassiers: Arrêt «Ziggo»: la plate-forme Youtube sera-t-elle bientôt hors-la-loi?, *Journal de droit européen*, 2017, n° 243, p. 359-360.

In German

Matthias Leistner: Die „The Pirate Bay"-Entscheidung des EuGH: ein Gerichtshof als Ersatzgesetzgeber, *Gewerblicher Rechtsschutz und Urheberrecht*, Heft 8/2017, p. 755-760.

Paul Fischer: Öffentliche Wiedergabe durch Peer-to-Peer Filesharing-Plattformen, *Medien und Recht*, Heft 4/2017, p. 191-193.

Franz Hofmann: Öffentliche Wiedergabe durch Bereitstellung und Betrieb einer Filesharing-Plattform, *Zeitschrift für Urheber- und Medienrecht*, Heft 10/2017, p. 750-752.

Franz Hofmann: Fünfzehn Thesen zur Plattformhaftung nach Art. 17 DSM-RL, *Gewerblicher Rechtsschutz und Urheberrecht*, Heft 12/2019, p. 1219-1229.

In Spanish

J. F. Alcaine Sánchez: *Propiedad Intelectual y Redes P2P*, 2015 (http://hdl.handle.net/10251/56040)
Carlos Aguilar-Paredes, et al.: El ecosistema para acceder a series de television y peliculas en España: un esbozo de la situación a raíz de la Ley de propiedad intelectual 2015, *El Profesional de la Informacion*, vol. 25, no. 6, 2016, p. 870+.

In Hungarian

Szabó Imre: A „The Pirate Bay" ügy elsőfokú ítélete a magyar büntetőjog tükrében, *Infokommunikáció és Jog*, 2010. augusztus, p. 141-146.
Hajdú Dóra: A fájlcserélés elleni küzdelem egy lehetséges útja. Három a francia igazság?, *Infokommunikáció és Jog*, 2011. június, p. 95-103.
Faludi Gábor - Gyenge Anikó: A fájlmegosztás - hazai és uniós szemmel, *Iparjogvédelmi és Szerzői Jogi Szemle*, 2011. december, p. 77-90.
Mezei Péter: *A fájlcsere dilemma - A perek lassúak, az internet gyors*, HVG-Orac, Budapest, 2012: p. 112-131.
Ferge Zsigmond: Médialejátszók és online megosztóplatformok, avagy hogyan értelmezte az Európai Bíróság a nyilvánossághoz közvetítés fogalmát a Stichting Brein, szerzői jogok jogosultjainak érdekeit védő alapítvány kontra Jack Frederik Wullems-, valamint a Ziggo BV és XS4ALL Internet BV-ügyben hozott ítéletében, *Iparjogvédelmi és Szerzői Jogi Szemle*, 2017/5. szám, p. 15-46.

BMG MUSIC, ET AL., V. CECILIA GONZALEZ

430 *F.3d* 888 (2005)

EASTERBROOK, Circuit Judge.

Last June the Supreme Court held in MGM Studios, Inc. v. Grokster, Ltd., 545 U.S. 913 (2005), that a distributed file-sharing system is engaged in contributory copyright infringement when its principal object is the dissemination of copyrighted material. The foundation of this holding is a belief that people who post or download music files are primary infringers. In re Aimster Copyright Litigation, 334 F.3d 643, 645 (7th Cir. 2003), which anticipated *Grokster*, made the same assumption. In this appeal Cecilia Gonzalez, who downloaded copyrighted music through the KaZaA file-sharing network, denies the premise of *Grokster* and *Aimster*. She contends that her activities were fair use rather than infringement. The district court disagreed and granted summary judgment for the copyright proprietors. The court enjoined Gonzalez from further infringement and awarded $22,500 in damages under 17 U.S.C. §504(c).

A "fair use" of copyrighted material is not infringement. Gonzalez insists that she was engaged in fair use under the terms of 17 U.S.C. §107 - or at least that a material dispute entitles her to a trial. It is undisputed, however, that she downloaded more than 1,370 copyrighted songs during a few weeks and kept them on her computer until she was caught. Her position is that she was just sampling music to determine what she liked enough to buy at retail. Because this suit was resolved on summary judgment, we must assume that Gonzalez is telling the truth when she says that she owned compact discs containing some of the songs before she downloaded them and that she purchased others later. She concedes, however, that she has never owned legitimate copies of 30 songs that she downloaded. (How many of the remainder she owned is disputed.)

Instead of erasing songs that she decided not to buy, she retained them. It is these 30 songs about which there is no dispute concerning ownership that formed the basis of the damages award. This is not a form of time-shifting, along the lines of Sony Corp. of America v. Universal City Studios, Inc., 464 U.S. 417 (1984). A copy downloaded, played, and retained on one's hard drive for future use is a direct substitute for a purchased copy-and without the benefit of the license fee paid to the broadcaster. The premise of *Betamax* is that the broadcast was licensed for one transmission and thus one viewing. *Betamax* held that shifting the time of this single viewing is fair use. The files that Gonzalez obtained, by contrast, were posted in violation of copyright law; there was no license covering a single transmission or hearing-and, to repeat, Gonzalez kept the copies. Time-shifting by an authorized recipient this is not.

Section 107 provides that when considering a defense of fair use the court must take into account "(1) the purpose and character of the use, including whether such use is of a commercial nature or is for nonprofit educational purposes; (2) the nature of the copyrighted work; (3) the amount and substantiality of the portion used in relation to the copyrighted work as a whole; and (4) the effect of the use upon the potential market for or value of the copyrighted work." Gonzalez was not engaged in a nonprofit use; she downloaded (and kept) whole copyrighted songs (for which, as with poetry, copying of more than a couplet or two is deemed excessive); and she did this despite the fact that these works often are sold per song as well as per album. This leads her to concentrate on the fourth consideration: "the effect of the use upon the potential market for or value of the copyrighted work."

As she tells the tale, downloading on a try-before-you-buy basis is good advertising for copyright proprietors, expanding the value of their inventory. The Supreme Court thought otherwise in *Grokster,* with considerable empirical support. As file sharing has increased over the last four years, the sales of recorded music have dropped by approximately 30%. Perhaps other economic factors contributed, but the events likely are related. Music downloaded for free from the Internet is a close substitute for purchased music; many people are bound to keep the downloaded files without buying originals. That is exactly what Gonzalez did for at least 30 songs. It is no surprise, therefore, that the only appellate decision on point has held that downloading copyrighted songs cannot be defended as fair use, whether or not the recipient plans to buy songs she likes well enough to spring for.

Although BMG Music sought damages for only the 30 songs that Gonzalez concedes she has never purchased, all 1,000+ of her downloads violated the statute. All created copies of an entire work. All undermined the means by which authors seek to profit. Gonzalez proceeds as if the authors' only interest were in selling compact discs containing collections of works. Not so; there is also a market in ways to introduce potential consumers to music.

Think of radio. Authors and publishers collect royalties on the broadcast of recorded music, even though these broadcasts may boost sales. Downloads from peer-to-peer networks such as KaZaA compete with licensed broadcasts and hence undermine the income available to authors. This is true even if a particular person never buys recorded media. Many radio stations stream their content over the Internet, paying a fee for the right to do so. Gonzalez could have listened to this streaming music to sample songs for purchase; had she done so, the authors would have received royalties from the broadcasters (and reduced the risk that files saved to disk would diminish the urge to pay for the music in the end).

Licensed Internet sellers, such as the iTunes Music Store, offer samples-but again they pay authors a fee for the right to do so, and the teasers are just a portion of the original. Other intermediaries (not only Yahoo! Music Unlimited and Real Rhapsody but also the revived Napster, with a new business model) offer licensed access to large collections of music; customers may rent the whole library by the month or year, sample them all, and purchase any songs they want to keep. New technologies, such as SNOCAP, enable authorized trials over peer-to-peer systems.

Authorized previews share the feature of evanescence: if a listener decides not to buy (or stops paying the rental fee), no copy remains behind. With all of these means available to consumers who want to choose where to spend their money, downloading full copies of copyrighted material without compensation to authors cannot be deemed "fair use." Copyright law lets authors make their own decisions about how best to promote their works; copiers such as Gonzalez cannot ask courts (and juries) to second-guess the market and call wholesale copying "fair use" if they think that authors err in understanding their own economic interests or that Congress erred in granting authors the rights in the copyright statute. Nor can she defend by observing that other persons were greater offenders; Gonzalez's theme that she obtained "only 30" (or "only 1,300") copyrighted songs is no more relevant than a thief's contention that he shoplifted "only 30" compact discs, planning to listen to them at home and pay later for any he liked.

BMG Music elected to seek statutory damages under 17 U.S.C. §504(c)(1) instead of proving actual injury. This section provides that the author's entitlement, per infringed work, is "a sum of not less than $750 or more than $30,000 as the court considers just." But if an "infringer sustains the burden of proving, and the court finds, that such infringer was not aware and had no reason to believe that his or her acts constituted an infringement of copyright, the court in its discretion may reduce the award of statutory damages to a sum of not less than $200." 17 U.S.C. §504(c)(2). Gonzalez asked the district court to reduce the award under this proviso, but the judge concluded that §402(d) bars any reduction in the minimum award. This subsection provides: "If a notice of copyright in the form and position specified by this section appears on the published phonorecord or phonorecords to which a defendant in a copyright infringement suit had access, then no weight shall be given to such a defendant's interposition of a defense based on innocent infringement in mitigation of actual or statutory damages". It is undisputed that BMG Music gave copyright notice as required-"on the surface of the phonorecord, or on the phonorecord label or container" (§402(c)). It is likewise undisputed that Gonzalez had "access" to records and compact disks bearing the proper notice. She downloaded data rather than discs, and the data lacked copyright notices, but the statutory question is whether "access" to legitimate works was available rather than whether infringers earlier in the chain attached copyright notices to the pirated works. Gonzalez readily could have learned, had she inquired, that the music was under copyright.

If BMG Music had requested more than $750 per work, then Gonzalez would have been entitled to a trial. What number between $750 and $30,000 is "just" recompense is a question for the jury, unless both sides agree to decision by the court. But BMG Music was content with $750 per song, which the district judge awarded on summary judgment. Gonzalez contends that this was improper: *Feltner,* she contends, holds that a jury must decide whether even the statutory minimum award will be allowed.

Feltner holds that a claim for statutory damages under § 504(c) is a suit at law to which the seventh amendment applies. This does not mean, however, that a jury must resolve every dispute. When there are no disputes of material fact, the court may enter summary judgment without transgressing the Constitution. While acknowledging this proposition, Gonzalez insists that copyright cases are different. She relies entirely on a single passage from *Feltner*: "The right to a jury trial includes the right to have a jury determine the *amount* of statutory damages, if any, awarded to the copyright owner." 523 U.S. at 353. Gonzalez maintains that by adding "if any" the Court allowed a jury to send an author home empty handed, even if the statute makes $750 the minimum. In other words, she contends that *Feltner* creates a system of jury nullification unique to copyright litigation.

The Justices did not purport to give defendants in copyright cases the right to ask jurors to return verdicts in the teeth of the law. The sentence we have quoted is a general description of the jury's role, which the Court drew from seventeenth-century English jurisprudence. That's hardly a plausible source for a rule unique to American copyright law. In *Feltner* neither side had sought summary judgment. We read *Feltner* as establishing no more (and no less) than that cases under §504(c) are normal civil actions subject to the normal allocation of functions between judge and jury. When there is a material dispute of fact to be resolved or discretion to be exercised in selecting a financial award, then either side is entitled to a jury; if there is no material dispute and a rule of law eliminates discretion in selecting the remedy, then summary judgment is permissible.

Gonzalez says that the ninth circuit understood Feltner differently on remand, but that's mistaken. A jury trial was held-for there were material factual disputes-and the jury returned a verdict of $31.68 million in statutory damages (or $72,000 per infringed work, an award made possible by the jury's conclusion that infringement had been wilful). The defendant, ruing its Pyrrhic victory in the Supreme Court (the judge's original award, which the Court vacated, had been $8.8 million), maintained that §504(c) is unconstitutional, and that only actual damages may be awarded, because §504(c) does not provide for a jury trial. The court of appeals rejected that contention, noting that after the Supreme Court's decision a jury trial had been held. Whether a jury resolves the dispute because of statutory language or because of the seventh amendment is all the same to the litigants. It is not possible to find, in a decision affirming a jury's verdict, a rule of law that a jury is required even when there are no factual disputes to resolve and no discretion to exercise.

As for the injunction: Gonzalez contends that this should be vacated because she has learned her lesson, has dropped her broadband access to the Internet, and is unlikely to download copyrighted material again. A private party's discontinuation of unlawful conduct does not make the dispute moot, however. An injunction remains appropriate to ensure that the wrongdoer does not recur as soon as the case ends. The district court did not abuse its discretion in awarding prospective relief.

AFFIRMED.

THINK IT OVER

1. Imagine that a law professor downloads multiple sound recording via a P2P file-sharing application in order to insert the downloaded sound recordings into his/her presentation on copyright law. *Is it possible that the professor relies on the fair use doctrine to excuse himself/herself from liability?*

2. The *USCA* allows the copyright owner to elect to recover statutory damages instead of the actual damages. An award of statutory damages shall not be less than $750 and more than $30,000 per infringement. The minimum amount can be reduced to $200 in case the infringer was not aware and had no reason to believe that her act constituted an infringement of copyright, and the maximum amount might be increased to $150,000 in case the infringement was committed willfully. See: *USCA* §504. After multiple rounds of jury trials and appeals, Jammie Thomas-Rasset was ordered to pay $222.000 as damages ($9.250 in damages for the downloaded 24 songs each). Joel Tenenbaum was ordered to pay $675.000 for the downloading of 30 individual tracks. Some have argued "[w]hen a minimum statutory damage award has a large punitive component, the danger arises that the award's punitive effect, when aggregated across many similar acts, will become so tremendous that it imposes a penalty grossly excessive in relation to any legitimate interest in punishment or deterrence. (...) The recent copyright infringement lawsuits targeting illegal file-sharing create the context in which these factual predicates exist: a statutory damage award with a substantial punitive component, a large number of like-kind violations, and fairly low reprehensibility as assessed under the relevant Gore guidepost. Thus, massively aggregated awards of even the minimum statutory damages for illegal file-sharing will impose huge penalties, like the constitutionally infirm punitive damage award of Gore. Congress needs to act now and modify the minimum statutory damage provision of U.S. copyright law to remove the possibility of grossly excessive punishment." [Barker (2004), p. 559.] *Barker ultimately argued that extensive statutory damages run against the procedural due process clause of the US Constitution, Amendment XIV? Do you agree with this opinion?*

3. *Is an IP-Address a reasonable evidence to find the account holder liable for a copyright infringement?* The U.S. Dictrict Court for the Western District of Washington held in *Elf-Man v. Cariveau* that "simply identifying the account holder associated with an IP address tells us very little about who actually downloaded 'Elf-Man' using that IP address. While it is possible that the subscriber is the one who participated in the BitTorrent swarm, it is also possible that a family member, guest, or freeloader engaged in the infringing conduct".

(*Elf-Man v. Cariveau*, p. 2.) In *Malibu Media*, another US district court held that "defendant also claims that the complaint does not plausibly allege copyright infringement by him because the only facts alleged are that he had an internet account and that some computer associated with that account held some bits of Plaintiff's works. Defendant relies on Elf-Man, which held that similar allegations failed to state a claim. The Court disagrees with Defendant and the Elf-Man court. The allegations that Defendant is the internet subscriber whose internet address was being used to distribute bits of Plaintiff's movies make it plausible that he was the infringer. These allegations are not so sketchy or implausible that they fail to give Defendant sufficient notice of Plaintiff's claim." (*Malibu Media v. Gilvin*, p. 3.) In *Cobbler Nevada*, the Ninth Circuit had to answer whether a registered internet subscriber is directly and contributorily liable for P2P file-sharing activities. The Court found that "allegations are not 'enough to raise a right to relief above a speculative level'". (*Cobbler Nevada v. Gonzales*, p. 1147.) Thus, instead of submitting the IP-Address of the alleged infringer, the plantiff is obliged to properly evidence that a given end-user is the exact infringer of copyrights. The Court has further refused to apply contributory liability against the defendant. The Court found that the failure of the subscriber to take affirmative steps to secure internet connection was insufficient to state a claim of contributory copyright infringement. Neither did Gonzales induce others to commit copyright infringements. Indeed, as the Ninth Circuit noted, "[p]roviding internet access can hardly be said to be distributing a product or service that is not 'capable of substantial' or 'commercially significant noninfringing uses'". (*Cobbler Nevada v. Gonzales*, p. 1149.) *The above rulings indicate that any proceedings against individual file-sharers in the United States shall lay on solid factual grounds. This is a serious limitation of "John Doe" claims; however, it works as a guarantee to limit "copyright trolls" to sue end-users on a massive scale without any reliable evidences.*

Further Case Law

Atlantic Recording Corporation, et al., v. Pamela and Jeffrey Howell, 554 *F.Supp.2d* 976 (2008)

London-Sire Records, Inc., et al., v. Doe 1, et al., 542 *F.Supp.2d* 153 (2008)

Sony BMG Music Entertainment, et al., v. Joel Tenenbaum, 660 *F.3d* 487 (2011)

Capitol Records, Inc., et al. v. Jammie Thomas-Rasset, 692 *F.3d* 899 (2012)

Elf-Man, LLC, v. Eric Cariveau, et al., 2014 *WL* 202096 (2014)

Malibu Media LLC v. Kaleb Gilvin, 2014 *WL* 1260110 (2014)

Cobbler Nevada, LLC v. Thomas Gonzales, 901 *F.3d* 1142 (2018)

Recommended readings

In English

J. Cam Barker: Grossly Excessive Penalties in the Battle Against Illegal File-sharing: The Trouble Effects of Aggregating Minimum Statutory Damages for Copyright Infringement, *Texas Law Review*, 2004: p. 525-559.

Ken Nicholds: The Free Jammie Movement: Is Making a File Available To Other Users Over a Peer-to-Peer Computer Network Sufficient to Infringe The Copyright Owner's 17 U.S.C. § 106(3) Distribution Right?, *Fordham Law Review*, 2009: p. 983-1028.

Lydia Pallas Loren - R. Anthony Reese: Proving Infringement: Burdens of Proof in Copyright Infringement Litigation, *Lewis & Clark Law Review*, 2019, p. 621-680.

Kerry E. Kleiman - Andrew P. Dunning: Two Wrongs Don't Make a Copyright - Mass-Defendant Copyright Infringement Litigation: The Plaintiffs, the Pirates & the People Who Pay, *Nevada Lawyer*, January 2019, p. 14-17.

In Hungarian

Mezei Péter: *A fájlcsere dilemma - A perek lassúak, az internet gyors*, HVG-Orac, Budapest, 2012: p. 158-166.

PRODUCTORES DE MÚSICA DE ESPAÑA (PROMUSICAE) V. TELEFÓNICA DE ESPAÑA SAU

Case C-275/06 - Judgment of the Court (Grand Chamber), 29 January 2008 [ECLI:EU:C:2008:54]

(...) Legal context

International law

3 Part III of the Agreement on Trade-Related Aspects of Intellectual Property Rights ('the TRIPs Agreement'), which constitutes Annex 1C to the Agreement establishing the World Trade Organisation ('the WTO'), signed at Marrakesh on 15 April 1994 and approved by Council Decision 94/800/EC of 22 December 1994 concerning the conclusion on behalf of the European Community, as regards matters within its competence, of the agreements reached in the Uruguay Round multilateral negotiations (1986-1994), is headed 'Enforcement of intellectual property rights'. That part includes Article 41(1) and (2), according to which:

'1. Members shall ensure that enforcement procedures as specified in this Part are available under their law so as to permit effective action against any act of infringement of intellectual property

rights covered by this Agreement, including expeditious remedies to prevent infringements and remedies which constitute a deterrent to further infringements. These procedures shall be applied in such a manner as to avoid the creation of barriers to legitimate trade and to provide for safeguards against their abuse.
2. Procedures concerning the enforcement of intellectual property rights shall be fair and equitable. They shall not be unnecessarily complicated or costly, or entail unreasonable time-limits or unwarranted delays.'

4 In Section 2 of Part III, 'Civil and administrative procedures and remedies', Article 42, headed 'Fair and Equitable Procedures', provides: 'Members shall make available to right holders civil judicial procedures concerning the enforcement of any intellectual property right covered by this Agreement'

5 Article 47 of the TRIPs Agreement, headed 'Right of Information', provides: 'Members may provide that the judicial authorities shall have the authority, unless this would be out of proportion to the seriousness of the infringement, to order the infringer to inform the right holder of the identity of third persons involved in the production and distribution of the infringing goods or services and of their channels of distribution.'

Community law

Provisions relating to the information society and the protection of intellectual property, especially copyright:

<u>Directive 2000/31</u>

6 Article 1 of Directive 2000/31 states:
'1. This Directive seeks to contribute to the proper functioning of the internal market by ensuring the free movement of information society services between the Member States.
2. This Directive approximates, to the extent necessary for the achievement of the objective set out in paragraph 1, certain national provisions on information society services relating to the internal market, the establishment of service providers, commercial communications, electronic contracts, the liability of intermediaries, codes of conduct, out-of-court dispute settlements, court actions and cooperation between Member States.
3. This Directive complements Community law applicable to information society services without prejudice to the level of protection for, in particular, public health and consumer interests, as established by Community acts and national legislation implementing them in so far as this does not restrict the freedom to provide information society services.

5. This Directive shall not apply to:

(b) questions relating to information society services covered by Directives 95/46/EC and 97/66/ EC;'

7 According to Article 15 of Directive 2000/31:

'1. Member States shall not impose a general obligation on providers, when providing the services covered by Articles 12, 13 and 14, to monitor the information which they transmit or store, nor a general obligation actively to seek facts or circumstances indicating illegal activity.

2. Member States may establish obligations for information society service providers promptly to inform the competent public authorities of alleged illegal activities undertaken or information provided by recipients of their service or obligations to communicate to the competent authorities, at their request, information enabling the identification of recipients of their service with whom they have storage agreements.'

8 Article 18 of Directive 2000/31 provides:

'1. Member States shall ensure that court actions available under national law concerning information society services' activities allow for the rapid adoption of measures, including interim measures, designed to terminate any alleged infringement and to prevent any further impairment of the interests involved.'

Directive 2001/29

9 According to Article 1(1) of Directive 2001/29, the directive concerns the legal protection of copyright and related rights in the framework of the internal market, with particular emphasis on the information society.

10 Under Article 8 of Directive 2001/29:

'1. Member States shall provide appropriate sanctions and remedies in respect of infringements of the rights and obligations set out in this Directive and shall take all the measures necessary to ensure that those sanctions and remedies are applied. The sanctions thus provided for shall be effective, proportionate and dissuasive.

2. Each Member State shall take the measures necessary to ensure that rightholders whose interests are affected by an infringing activity carried out on its territory can bring an action for damages and/or apply for an injunction and, where appropriate, for the seizure of infringing material as well as of devices, products or components referred to in Article 6(2).

3. Member States shall ensure that rightholders are in a position to apply for an injunction against intermediaries whose services are used by a third party to infringe a copyright or related right.'

11 Article 9 of Directive 2001/29 reads:

'This Directive shall be without prejudice to provisions concerning in particular patent rights, trade marks, design rights, utility models, topographies of semi-conductor products, type faces, conditional access, access to cable of broadcasting services, protection of national treasures, legal deposit requirements, laws on restrictive practices and unfair competition, trade secrets, security, confidentiality, data protection and privacy, access to public documents, the law of contract.'

Directive 2004/48

12 Article 1 of Directive 2004/48 states:

'This Directive concerns the measures, procedures and remedies necessary to ensure the enforcement of intellectual property rights'.

13 According to Article 2(3) of Directive 2004/48:

'3. This Directive shall not affect:

(a) the Community provisions governing the substantive law on intellectual property, Directive 95/46/EC, Directive 1999/93/EC or Directive 2000/31/EC, in general, and Articles 12 to 15 of Directive 2000/31/EC in particular;

(b) Member States' international obligations and notably the TRIPS Agreement, including those relating to criminal procedures and penalties;

(c) any national provisions in Member States relating to criminal procedures or penalties in respect of infringement of intellectual property rights.'

14 Article 3 of Directive 2004/48 provides:

'1. Member States shall provide for the measures, procedures and remedies necessary to ensure the enforcement of the intellectual property rights covered by this Directive. Those measures, procedures and remedies shall be fair and equitable and shall not be unnecessarily complicated or costly, or entail unreasonable time-limits or unwarranted delays.

2. Those measures, procedures and remedies shall also be effective, proportionate and dissuasive and shall be applied in such a manner as to avoid the creation of barriers to legitimate trade and to provide for safeguards against their abuse.'

15 Article 8 of Directive 2004/48 provides:

'1. Member States shall ensure that, in the context of proceedings concerning an infringement of an intellectual property right and in response to a justified and proportionate request of the claimant, the competent judicial authorities may order that information on the origin and distribution networks of the goods or services which infringe an intellectual property right be provided by the infringer and/or any other person who:

(a) was found in possession of the infringing goods on a commercial scale;

(b) was found to be using the infringing services on a commercial scale;

(c) was found to be providing on a commercial scale services used in infringing activities; or

(d) was indicated by the person referred to in point (a), (b) or (c) as being involved in the production, manufacture or distribution of the goods or the provision of the services.

2. The information referred to in paragraph 1 shall, as appropriate, comprise:

(a) the names and addresses of the producers, manufacturers, distributors, suppliers and other previous holders of the goods or services, as well as the intended wholesalers and retailers;

(b) information on the quantities produced, manufactured, delivered, received or ordered, as well as the price obtained for the goods or services in question.

3. Paragraphs 1 and 2 shall apply without prejudice to other statutory provisions which:

(a) grant the rightholder rights to receive fuller information;

(b) govern the use in civil or criminal proceedings of the information communicated pursuant to this Article;

(c) govern responsibility for misuse of the right of information; or

(d) afford an opportunity for refusing to provide information which would force the person referred to in paragraph 1 to admit to his/her own participation or that of his/her close relatives in an infringement of an intellectual property right; or

(e) govern the protection of confidentiality of information sources or the processing of personal data.'

Provisions on the protection of personal data:

Directive 95/46/EC

16 Article 2 of Directive 95/46/EC of the European Parliament and of the Council of 24 October 1995 on the protection of individuals with regard to the processing of personal data and on the free movement of such data states:

'For the purposes of this Directive:

(a) "personal data" shall mean any information relating to an identified or identifiable natural person ("data subject"); an identifiable person is one who can be identified, directly or indirectly, in particular by reference to an identification number or to one or more factors specific to his physical, physiological, mental, economic, cultural or social identity;

(b) "processing of personal data" ("processing") shall mean any operation or set of operations which is performed upon personal data, whether or not by automatic means, such as collection, recording, organisation, storage, adaptation or alteration, retrieval, consultation, use, disclosure by transmission, dissemination or otherwise making available, alignment or combination, blocking, erasure or destruction;'

17 According to Article 3 of Directive 95/46:

'1. This Directive shall apply to the processing of personal data wholly or partly by automatic means, and to the processing otherwise than by automatic means of personal data which form part of a filing system or are intended to form part of a filing system.'

18 Article 7 of Directive 95/46 reads as follows:

'Member States shall provide that personal data may be processed only if:

(f) processing is necessary for the purposes of the legitimate interests pursued by the controller or by the third party or parties to whom the data are disclosed, except where such interests are overridden by the interests or fundamental rights and freedoms of the data subject which require protection under Article 1(1).'

19 Article 8 of Directive 95/46 provides:

'1. Member States shall prohibit the processing of personal data revealing racial or ethnic origin, political opinions, religious or philosophical beliefs, trade-union membership, and the processing of data concerning health or sex life.

2. Paragraph 1 shall not apply where:

(c) processing is necessary to protect the vital interests of the data subject or of another person where the data subject is physically or legally incapable of giving his consent.'

20 According to Article 13 of Directive 95/46:

'1. Member States may adopt legislative measures to restrict the scope of the obligations and rights provided for in Articles 6(1), 10, 11(1), 12 and 21 when such a restriction constitutes a necessary measure to safeguard:

(a) national security;

(b) defence;

(c) public security;

(d) the prevention, investigation, detection and prosecution of criminal offences, or of breaches of ethics for regulated professions;

(e) an important economic or financial interest of a Member State or of the European Union, including monetary, budgetary and taxation matters;

(f) a monitoring, inspection or regulatory function connected, even occasionally, with the exercise of official authority in cases referred to in (c), (d) and (e);

(g) the protection of the data subject or of the rights and freedoms of others.'

Directive 2002/58/EC

21 Article 1 of Directive 2002/58/EC of the European Parliament and of the Council of 12 July 2002 concerning the processing of personal data and the protection of privacy in the electronic communications sector (Directive on privacy and electronic communications) states:
'1. This Directive harmonises the provisions of the Member States required to ensure an equivalent level of protection of fundamental rights and freedoms, and in particular the right to privacy, with respect to the processing of personal data in the electronic communication sector and to ensure the free movement of such data and of electronic communication equipment and services in the Community.
2. The provisions of this Directive particularise and complement Directive 95/46/EC for the purposes mentioned in paragraph 1.
3. This Directive shall not apply to activities which fall outside the scope of the Treaty establishing the European Community, such as those covered by Titles V and VI of the Treaty on European Union, and in any case to activities concerning public security, defence, State security (including the economic well-being of the State when the activities relate to State security matters) and the activities of the State in areas of criminal law.'

22 Under Article 2 of Directive 2002/58:
'Save as otherwise provided, the definitions in Directive 95/46/EC and in Directive 2002/21/EC of the European Parliament and of the Council of 7 March 2002 on a common regulatory framework for electronic communications networks and services (Framework Directive) shall apply.
The following definitions shall also apply:
(b) "traffic data" means any data processed for the purpose of the conveyance of a communication on an electronic communications network or for the billing thereof;
(d) "communication" means any information exchanged or conveyed between a finite number of parties by means of a publicly available electronic communications service. This does not include any information conveyed as part of a broadcasting service to the public over an electronic communications network except to the extent that the information can be related to the identifiable subscriber or user receiving the information;'

23 Article 3 of Directive 2002/58 provides:
'1. This Directive shall apply to the processing of personal data in connection with the provision of publicly available electronic communications services in public communications networks in the Community.'

24 Article 5 of Directive 2002/58 provides:

'1. Member States shall ensure the confidentiality of communications and the related traffic data by means of a public communications network and publicly available electronic communications services, through national legislation. In particular, they shall prohibit listening, tapping, storage or other kinds of interception or surveillance of communications and the related traffic data by persons other than users, without the consent of the users concerned, except when legally authorised to do so in accordance with Article 15(1). This paragraph shall not prevent technical storage which is necessary for the conveyance of a communication without prejudice to the principle of confidentiality.'

25 Article 6 of Directive 2002/58 provides:

'1. Traffic data relating to subscribers and users processed and stored by the provider of a public communications network or publicly available electronic communications service must be erased or made anonymous when it is no longer needed for the purpose of the transmission of a communication without prejudice to paragraphs 2, 3 and 5 of this Article and Article 15(1).

2. Traffic data necessary for the purposes of subscriber billing and interconnection payments may be processed. Such processing is permissible only up to the end of the period during which the bill may lawfully be challenged or payment pursued.

3. For the purpose of marketing electronic communications services or for the provision of value added services, the provider of a publicly available electronic communications service may process the data referred to in paragraph 1 to the extent and for the duration necessary for such services or marketing, if the subscriber or user to whom the data relate has given his/her consent. Users or subscribers shall be given the possibility to withdraw their consent for the processing of traffic data at any time.

5. Processing of traffic data, in accordance with paragraphs 1, 2, 3 and 4, must be restricted to persons acting under the authority of providers of the public communications networks and publicly available electronic communications services handling billing or traffic management, customer enquiries, fraud detection, marketing electronic communications services or providing a value added service, and must be restricted to what is necessary for the purposes of such activities.

6. Paragraphs 1, 2, 3 and 5 shall apply without prejudice to the possibility for competent bodies to be informed of traffic data in conformity with applicable legislation with a view to settling disputes, in particular interconnection or billing disputes.'

26 Under Article 15 of Directive 2002/58:

'1. Member States may adopt legislative measures to restrict the scope of the rights and obligations provided for in Article 5, Article 6, Article 8(1), (2), (3) and (4), and Article 9 of this Directive when such restriction constitutes a necessary, appropriate and proportionate measure within a democratic society to safeguard national security (i.e. State security), defence, public security, and

the prevention, investigation, detection and prosecution of criminal offences or of unauthorised use of the electronic communication system, as referred to in Article 13(1) of Directive 95/46/EC. To this end, Member States may, inter alia, adopt legislative measures providing for the retention of data for a limited period justified on the grounds laid down in this paragraph. All the measures referred to in this paragraph shall be in accordance with the general principles of Community law, including those referred to in Article 6(1) and (2) of the Treaty on European Union.'

27 Article 19 of Directive 2002/58 provides:
'Directive 97/66/EC is hereby repealed with effect from the date referred to in Article 17(1). References made to the repealed Directive shall be construed as being made to this Directive.'

National law

28 Under Article 12 of Law 34/2002 on information society services and electronic commerce of 11 July 2002, headed 'Duty to retain traffic data relating to electronic communications':
'1. Operators of electronic communications networks and services, providers of access to telecommunications networks and providers of data storage services must retain for a maximum of 12 months the connection and traffic data generated by the communications established during the supply of an information society service, under the conditions established in this article and the regulations implementing it.
2. The operators of electronic communications networks and services and the service providers to which this article refers may not use the data retained for purposes other than those indicated in the paragraph below or other purposes permitted by the Law and must adopt appropriate security measures to avoid the loss or alteration of the data and unauthorised access to the data.
3. The data shall be retained for use in the context of a criminal investigation or to safeguard public security and national defence, and shall be made available to the courts or the public prosecutor at their request. Communication of the data to the forces of order shall be effected in accordance with the provisions of the rules on personal data protection.'

The main proceedings and the order for reference

29 Promusicae is a non-profit-making organisation of producers and publishers of musical and audiovisual recordings. By letter of 28 November 2005 it made an application to the Juzgado de lo Mercantil N° 5 de Madrid (Commercial Court No 5, Madrid) for preliminary measures against Telefónica, a commercial company whose activities include the provision of internet access services.

30 Promusicae asked for Telefónica to be ordered to disclose the identities and physical addresses of certain persons whom it provided with internet access services, whose IP address and date and time of connection were known. According to Promusicae, those persons used the KaZaA file exchange program (peer-to-peer or P2P) and provided access in shared files of personal computers to phonograms in which the members of Promusicae held the exploitation rights.

31 Promusicae claimed before the national court that the users of KaZaA were engaging in unfair competition and infringing intellectual property rights. It therefore sought disclosure of the above information in order to be able to bring civil proceedings against the persons concerned.

32 By order of 21 December 2005 the Juzgado de lo Mercantil N° 5 de Madrid ordered the preliminary measures requested by Promusicae.

33 Telefónica appealed against that order, contending that under the LSSI the communication of the data sought by Promusicae is authorised only in a criminal investigation or for the purpose of safeguarding public security and national defence, not in civil proceedings or as a preliminary measure relating to civil proceedings. Promusicae submitted for its part that Article 12 of the LSSI must be interpreted in accordance with various provisions of Directives 2000/31, 2001/29 and 2004/48 and with Articles 17(2) and 47 of the Charter, provisions which do not allow Member States to limit solely to the purposes expressly mentioned in that law the obligation to communicate the data in question.

34 In those circumstances the Juzgado de lo Mercantil N° 5 de Madrid decided to stay the proceedings and refer the following question to the Court for a preliminary ruling:

'Does Community law, specifically Articles 15(2) and 18 of Directive [2000/31], Article 8(1) and (2) of Directive [2001/29], Article 8 of Directive [2004/48] and Articles 17(2) and 47 of the Charter ... permit Member States to limit to the context of a criminal investigation or to safeguard public security and national defence, thus excluding civil proceedings, the duty of operators of electronic communications networks and services, providers of access to telecommunications networks and providers of data storage services to retain and make available connection and traffic data generated by the communications established during the supply of an information society service?'

(...) The question referred for a preliminary ruling

41 By its question the national court asks essentially whether Community law, in particular Directives 2000/31, 2001/29 and 2004/48, read also in the light of Articles 17 and 47 of the

Charter, must be interpreted as requiring Member States to lay down, in order to ensure effective protection of copyright, an obligation to communicate personal data in the context of civil proceedings.

Preliminary observations

42 Even if, formally, the national court has limited its question to the interpretation of Directives 2000/31, 2001/29 and 2004/48 and the Charter, that circumstance does not prevent the Court from providing the national court with all the elements of interpretation of Community law which may be of use for deciding the case before it, whether or not that court has referred to them in the wording of its question.

43 It should be observed to begin with that the intention of the provisions of Community law thus referred to in the question is that the Member States should ensure, especially in the information society, effective protection of industrial property, in particular copyright, which Promusicae claims in the main proceedings. The national court proceeds, however, from the premiss that the Community law obligations required by that protection may be blocked, in national law, by the provisions of Article 12 of the LSSI.

44 While that law, in 2002, transposed the provisions of Directive 2000/31 into domestic law, it is common ground that Article 12 of the law is intended to implement the rules for the protection of private life, which is also required by Community law under Directives 95/46 and 2002/58, the latter of which concerns the processing of personal data and the protection of privacy in the electronic communications sector, which is the sector at issue in the main proceedings.

45 It is not disputed that the communication sought by Promusicae of the names and addresses of certain users of KaZaA involves the making available of personal data, that is, information relating to identified or identifiable natural persons, in accordance with the definition in Article 2(a) of Directive 95/46. That communication of information which, as Promusicae submits and Telefónica does not contest, is stored by Telefónica constitutes the processing of personal data within the meaning of the first paragraph of Article 2 of Directive 2002/58, read in conjunction with Article 2(b) of Directive 95/46. It must therefore be accepted that that communication falls within the scope of Directive 2002/58, although the compliance of the data storage itself with the requirements of that directive is not at issue in the main proceedings.

46 In those circumstances, it should first be ascertained whether Directive 2002/58 precludes the Member States from laying down, with a view to ensuring effective protection of copyright, an obligation to communicate personal data which will enable the copyright holder to bring civil proceedings based on the existence of that right. If that is not the case, it will then have to be ascertained whether it follows directly from the three directives expressly mentioned by the national court that the Member States are required to lay down such an obligation. Finally, if that is not the case either, in order to provide the national court with an answer of use to it, it will have to be examined, starting from the national court's reference to the Charter, whether in a situation such as that at issue in the main proceedings other rules of Community law might require a different reading of those three directives.

Directive 2002/58

47 Article 5(1) of Directive 2002/58 provides that Member States must ensure the confidentiality of communications by means of a public communications network and publicly available electronic communications services, and of the related traffic data, and must inter alia prohibit, in principle, the storage of that data by persons other than users, without the consent of the users concerned. The only exceptions relate to persons lawfully authorised in accordance with Article 15(1) of that directive and the technical storage necessary for conveyance of a communication. In addition, as regards traffic data, Article 6(1) of Directive 2002/58 provides that stored traffic data must be erased or made anonymous when it is no longer needed for the purpose of the transmission of a communication without prejudice to paragraphs 2, 3 and 5 of that article and Article 15(1) of the directive.

48 With respect, first, to paragraphs 2, 3 and 5 of Article 6, which relate to the processing of traffic data in accordance with the requirements of billing and marketing services and the provision of value added services, those provisions do not concern the communication of that data to persons other than those acting under the authority of the providers of public communications networks and publicly available electronic communications services. As to the provisions of Article 6(6) of Directive 2002/58, they do not relate to disputes other than those between suppliers and users concerning the grounds for storing data in connection with the activities referred to in the other provisions of that article. Since Article 6(6) thus clearly does not concern a situation such as that of Promusicae in the main proceedings, it cannot be taken into account in assessing that situation.

49 With respect, second, to Article 15(1) of Directive 2002/58, it should be recalled that under that provision the Member States may adopt legislative measures to restrict the scope inter alia of the obligation to ensure the confidentiality of traffic data, where such a restriction

constitutes a necessary, appropriate and proportionate measure within a democratic society to safeguard national security (i.e. State security), defence, public security, and the prevention, investigation, detection and prosecution of criminal offences or of unauthorised use of the electronic communications system, as referred to in Article 13(1) of Directive 95/46.

50 Article 15(1) of Directive 2002/58 thus gives Member States the possibility of providing for exceptions to the obligation of principle, imposed on them by Article 5 of that directive, to ensure the confidentiality of personal data.

51 However, none of these exceptions appears to relate to situations that call for the bringing of civil proceedings. They concern, first, national security, defence and public security, which constitute activities of the State or of State authorities unrelated to the fields of activity of individuals, and, second, the prosecution of criminal offences.

52 As regards the exception relating to unauthorised use of the electronic communications system, this appears to concern use which calls into question the actual integrity or security of the system, such as the cases referred to in Article 5(1) of Directive 2002/58 of the interception or surveillance of communications without the consent of the users concerned. Such use, which, under that article, makes it necessary for the Member States to intervene, also does not relate to situations that may give rise to civil proceedings.

53 It is clear, however, that Article 15(1) of Directive 2002/58 ends the list of the above exceptions with an express reference to Article 13(1) of Directive 95/46. That provision also authorises the Member States to adopt legislative measures to restrict the obligation of confidentiality of personal data where that restriction is necessary inter alia for the protection of the rights and freedoms of others. As they do not specify the rights and freedoms concerned, those provisions of Article 15(1) of Directive 2002/58 must be interpreted as expressing the Community legislature's intention not to exclude from their scope the protection of the right to property or situations in which authors seek to obtain that protection in civil proceedings.

54 The conclusion must therefore be that Directive 2002/58 does not preclude the possibility for the Member States of laying down an obligation to disclose personal data in the context of civil proceedings.

55 However, the wording of Article 15(1) of that directive cannot be interpreted as compelling the Member States, in the situations it sets out, to lay down such an obligation.

56 It must therefore be ascertained whether the three directives mentioned by the national court require those States to lay down that obligation in order to ensure the effective protection of copyright.

The three directives mentioned by the national court

57 It should first be noted that, as pointed out in paragraph 43 above, the purpose of the directives mentioned by the national court is that the Member States should ensure, especially in the information society, effective protection of industrial property, in particular copyright. However, it follows from Article 1(5)(b) of Directive 2000/31, Article 9 of Directive 2001/29 and Article 8(3)(e) of Directive 2004/48 that such protection cannot affect the requirements of the protection of personal data.

58 Article 8(1) of Directive 2004/48 admittedly requires Member States to ensure that, in the context of proceedings concerning an infringement of an intellectual property right and in response to a justified and proportionate request of the claimant, the competent judicial authorities may order that information on the origin and distribution networks of the goods or services which infringe an intellectual property right be provided. However, it does not follow from those provisions, which must be read in conjunction with those of paragraph 3(e) of that article, that they require the Member States to lay down, in order to ensure effective protection of copyright, an obligation to communicate personal data in the context of civil proceedings.

59 Nor does the wording of Articles 15(2) and 18 of Directive 2000/31 or that of Article 8(1) and (2) of Directive 2001/29 require the Member States to lay down such an obligation.

60 As to Articles 41, 42 and 47 of the TRIPs Agreement, relied on by Promusicae, in the light of which Community law must as far as possible be interpreted where – as in the case of the provisions relied on in the context of the present reference for a preliminary ruling – it regulates a field to which that agreement applies, while they require the effective protection of intellectual property rights and the institution of judicial remedies for their enforcement, they do not contain provisions which require those directives to be interpreted as compelling the Member States to lay down an obligation to communicate personal data in the context of civil proceedings.

Fundamental rights

61 The national court refers in its order for reference to Articles 17 and 47 of the Charter, the first of which concerns the protection of the right to property, including intellectual property, and the second of which concerns the right to an effective remedy. By so doing, that court must be regarded as seeking to know whether an interpretation of those directives to the effect that the Member States are not obliged to lay down, in order to ensure the effective protection of copyright, an obligation to communicate personal data in the context of civil proceedings leads to an infringement of the fundamental right to property and the fundamental right to effective judicial protection.

62 It should be recalled that the fundamental right to property, which includes intellectual property rights such as copyright, and the fundamental right to effective judicial protection constitute general principles of Community law.

63 However, the situation in respect of which the national court puts that question involves, in addition to those two rights, a further fundamental right, namely the right that guarantees protection of personal data and hence of private life.

64 According to recital 2 in the preamble to Directive 2002/58, the directive seeks to respect the fundamental rights and observes the principles recognised in particular by the Charter. In particular, the directive seeks to ensure full respect for the rights set out in Articles 7 and 8 of that Charter. Article 7 substantially reproduces Article 8 of the European Convention for the Protection of Human Rights and Fundamental Freedoms signed at Rome on 4 November 1950, which guarantees the right to respect for private life, and Article 8 of the Charter expressly proclaims the right to protection of personal data.

65 The present reference for a preliminary ruling thus raises the question of the need to reconcile the requirements of the protection of different fundamental rights, namely the right to respect for private life on the one hand and the rights to protection of property and to an effective remedy on the other.

66 The mechanisms allowing those different rights and interests to be balanced are contained, first, in Directive 2002/58 itself, in that it provides for rules which determine in what circumstances and to what extent the processing of personal data is lawful and what safeguards must be provided for, and in the three directives mentioned by the national court, which reserve the cases in which the measures adopted to protect the rights they regulate affect the protection of personal data. Second, they result from the adoption by the

Member States of national provisions transposing those directives and their application by the national authorities.

67 As to those directives, their provisions are relatively general, since they have to be applied to a large number of different situations which may arise in any of the Member States. They therefore logically include rules which leave the Member States with the necessary discretion to define transposition measures which may be adapted to the various situations possible.

68 That being so, the Member States must, when transposing the directives mentioned above, take care to rely on an interpretation of the directives which allows a fair balance to be struck between the various fundamental rights protected by the Community legal order. Further, when implementing the measures transposing those directives, the authorities and courts of the Member States must not only interpret their national law in a manner consistent with those directives but also make sure that they do not rely on an interpretation of them which would be in conflict with those fundamental rights or with the other general principles of Community law, such as the principle of proportionality.

69 Moreover, it should be recalled here that the Community legislature expressly required, in accordance with Article 15(1) of Directive 2002/58, that the measures referred to in that paragraph be adopted by the Member States in compliance with the general principles of Community law, including those mentioned in Article 6(1) and (2) EU.

70 In the light of all the foregoing, the answer to the national court's question must be that Directives 2000/31, 2001/29, 2004/48 and 2002/58 do not require the Member States to lay down, in a situation such as that in the main proceedings, an obligation to communicate personal data in order to ensure effective protection of copyright in the context of civil proceedings. However, Community law requires that, when transposing those directives, the Member States take care to rely on an interpretation of them which allows a fair balance to be struck between the various fundamental rights protected by the Community legal order. Further, when implementing the measures transposing those directives, the authorities and courts of the Member States must not only interpret their national law in a manner consistent with those directives but also make sure that they do not rely on an interpretation of them which would be in conflict with those fundamental rights or with the other general principles of Community law, such as the principle of proportionality.

THINK IT OVER

1. Following the *Promusicae* decision, the CJEU further cristallized its practice in balancing copyright law and data protection. In order to bring a civil action against alleged copyright infringers, LSG (the collective rights management organisation of Austrian phonogram producers) requested Tele2 to disclose the data (e.g. the IP addresses and access date and time) of certain persons to whom it provided Internet access. Tele2 rejected the request, arguing that Tele2 is not an intermediary and has no right to collect login data. The CJEU ruled that *Community law does not prevent Member States from establishing an obligation to transmit personal data to third parties in order to bring a civil action for copyright infringement.* However, Community law requires that Member States must ensure a fair balance between the different fundamental rights as well as complying with the general principle of proportionality. Later, the CJEU confirmed in *Bonnier* that national legislators might regulate the disclosure of personal data by Internet access providers in civil cases as well. (Only Austria and Sweden have introduced such laws in the European Union so far.)

2. *Is an IP-Address a reasonable evidence to find the account holder liable for a copyright infringement?* In *Bastei Lübbe*, the CJEU concluded that the subscriber can be liable for the infringements committed through file-sharing platforms even if he can name a family member who might have had access to the Internet, however, he fails to prove any further details as to when and how Internet was used by the family member. In this case, the defendant was living with his parents, who have not used the Internet at all (or at least the defendant was unable/unwilling to prove that). The CJEU has accepted the referring court's position that "Mr Strotzer [was] therefore seriously likely to have committed the copyright infringement". (*Bastei Lübbe*, para. 18.)

3. *Is an IP Address personal data?* (Consequently, is an IP Address subject to strict data protection even if it is a necessary tool to commit copyright infringements over the Internet?) In *Scarlet Extended*, the CJEU stressed that "[i]t is common ground, first, that the injunction requiring installation of the contested filtering system would involve a systematic analysis of all content and the collection and identification of users' IP addresses from which unlawful content on the network is sent. *Those addresses are protected personal data because they allow those users to be precisely identified.*" (See para. 51.) Later, the German Federal Supreme Court requested a preliminary ruling on the interpretation of the EU Data Protection Directive concerning the definition of the term "personal data" therein and on the logging of data related to the dynamic IP Addresses by ISPs.

In *Breyer*, the CJEU concluded that "[t]he fact that the additional data necessary to identify the user of a website are held not by the online media services provider, but by that user's internet service provider does not appear to be such as to exclude that dynamic IP addresses registered by the online media services provider constitute personal data within the meaning of Article 2(a) of Directive 95/46. (...) [I]t appears that the online media services provider has the means which may likely reasonably be used in order to identify the data subject, with the assistance of other persons, namely the competent authority and the internet service provider, on the basis of the IP addresses stored." (*Breyer*, para. 44 and 48.)

Further Case Law

Case C-557/07 - LSG-Gesellschaft zur Wahrnehmung von Leistungsschutzrechten GmbH v. Tele2 Telecommunication GmbH, Order of the Court (Eighth Chamber), February 19, 2009 [ECLI:EU:C:2009:107]

SGAE v. Indice-web.com, Barcelona Appellation Court (15th Section), Judgement 301 / 2011, 7 July 2011 (ROJ: SAP B 4207/2011 - ECLI:ES:APB:2011:4207)

Case C-70/10 - Scarlet Extended SA v Société belge des auteurs, compositeurs et éditeurs SCRL (SABAM), Judgment of the Court (Third Chamber), 24 November 2011 [ECLI:EU:C:2011:771]

Case C-461/10 - Bonnier Audio AB, Earbooks AB, Norstedts Förlagsgrupp AB, Piratförlaget AB, Storyside AB v. Perfect Communication Sweden AB, Judgement of the Court (Third Chamber), 19 April 2012 [ECLI:EU:C:2012:219]

Case C-582/14 - Patrick Breyer v. Bundesrepublik Deutschland, Judgment of the Court (Second Chamber), 19 October 2016 [ECLI:EU:C:2016:779]

Case C-149/17 - Bastei Lübbe GmbH & Co. KG v Michael Strotzer, Judgment of the Court (Third Chamber), 18 October 2018 [ECLI:EU:C:2018:841]

Recommended readings

In English

Christopher Kuner: Data Protection and Rights Protection on the Internet: The Promusicae Judgment of the European Court of Justice, *European Intellectual Property Review*, Issue 5/2008, p. 199-202.

Isabel Davies - Stuart Helmer: Productores de Música de España ("Promusicae") v Telefónica de España SAU ("Telefónica") (C-275/06), *European Intellectual Property Review*, Issue 8/2008, p. 307-308.
Tuomas Mylly: The Constitutionalization of the European Legal Order: Impact of Human Rights on Intellectual Property in the EU. In: Christophe Geiger: *Research Handbook on Human Rights and Intellectual Property*, Edgar Elgar, 2015: p. 103-131.

In French
Christophe Caron: Appréciation de l'obligation de communiquer des données à caractère personnel dans le cadre d'une procédure civile, *La Semaine juridique - entreprise et affaires* 2008 n° 1270, p. 19-20.
Laurent Szuskin - Maxime De Guillenschmidt: L'arrêt «Promusicae» beaucoup de bruit pour rien?, *Droit de l'immatériel: informatique, médias, communication* 2008 n° 37, p. 6-8.
Frédéric Pollaud-Dulian: Propriétés incorporelles. Propriété littéraire et artistique, *Revue trimestrielle de droit commercial et de droit économique* 2008, p. 302-306.
Alexandra Bensamoun: Responsabilité du titulaire d'un accès à internet en cas de contrefaçon: „Si ce n'est toi, c'est donc ton ..."?, *Dalloz IP / IT*, 2019 n° 01, p. 40-43.

In German
Gerald Spindler: „Die Tür ist auf" - Europarechtliche Zulässigkeit von Auskunftsansprüchen gegenüber Providern, *Gewerblicher Rechtsschutz und Urheberrecht*, Heft 7/2008, p. 574-577.
Christian Czychowski - Jan Bernd Nordemann: Vorratsdaten und Urheberrecht - Zulässige Nutzung gespeicherter Daten, Neue juristische Wochenschrift, Heft 43/2008, p. 3095-3099.
Reto Mantz: Haftung für Filesharing bei Familienanschluss - Bastei Lübbe, *Multimedia und Recht*, Heft 12/2018, p. 805-808.
Michel M. Walter: Filesharing - Haftung des Inhabers einer IP-Adresse, *MR-Int: Internationale Rundschau zum Medienrecht, IP- & IT-Recht*, Heft 1/2019, p. 19-24.

In Spanish
Luis González Vaqué: El TJCE se pronuncia sobre la obligación de comunicar datos personales a fin de garantizar la protección de los derechos de autor en un procedimiento civil: la sentencia 'Promusicae', *Unión Europea Aranzadi*, n°5, 2008 (http://works.bepress.com/luis_gonzalez_vaque/82/)
Julia Montes Heras: El contencioso entre Promusicae y Telefónica o la batalla por las direcciones IP, *Cineinforme*, 46 (810), octubre, 2007, p. 26-27.
Raquel Xalabander Plantada: La responsabilidad de los prestadores de servicios en Internet (ISP) por infracciones de propiedad intellectual cometidas por sus usuarios, *IDP. Revista de Internet, Derecho y Política*, n° 2, 2006 (http://www.redalyc.org/html/788/78800204/)

In Hungarian

Békés Gergely: Internetszolgáltatók a fájlcsere ellen?, *Infokommunikáció és Jog*, 2009. október, p. 194-200.

Faludi Gábor - Gyenge Anikó: A fájlmegosztás - hazai és uniós szemmel, *Iparjogvédelmi és Szerzői Jogi Szemle*, 2011/6. szám, p. 77-90.

Mezei Péter: *A fájlcsere dilemma - A perek lassúak, az internet gyors*, HVG-Orac, Budapest, 2012: p. 185-211.

Lábody Péter: A közvetítő szolgáltatók bevonása a szerzői jogi jogérvényesítésbe - Közösségi jogi lehetőségek, *Infokommunikáció és Jog*, 2012. február, p. 3-10.

Liber Ádám: A közvetítő szolgáltatók felelőssége a szellemi tulajdon megsértéséért az Európai Unióban, *Iparjogvédelmi és Szerzői Jogi Szemle*, 2013/3. szám, p. 5-42.

ACI ADAM BV AND OTHERS V. STICHTING DE THUISKOPIE

Case C-435/12 - Judgment of the Court (Fourth Chamber), 10 April 2014 [ECLI:EU:C:2014:254]

(...) Legal context

EU law

Directive 2001/29

3 Recitals 22, 31, 32, 35, 38 and 44 in the preamble to Directive 2001/29 state the following:

'(22) The objective of proper support for the dissemination of culture must not be achieved by sacrificing strict protection of rights or by tolerating illegal forms of distribution of counterfeited or pirated works.

(31) A fair balance of rights and interests between the different categories of rightholders, as well as between the different categories of rightholders and users of protected subject-matter must be safeguarded.

(32) This Directive provides for an exhaustive enumeration of exceptions and limitations to the reproduction right and the right of communication to the public. Some exceptions or limitations only apply to the reproduction right, where appropriate. This list takes due account of the different legal traditions in Member States, while, at the same time, aiming to ensure a functioning internal market. Member States should arrive at a coherent application of these exceptions and limitations, which will be assessed when reviewing implementing legislation in the future.

(35) In certain cases of exceptions or limitations, rightholders should receive fair compensation to compensate them adequately for the use made of their protected works or other subject-matter.

When determining the form, detailed arrangements and possible level of such fair compensation, account should be taken of the particular circumstances of each case. When evaluating these circumstances, a valuable criterion would be the possible harm to the rightholders resulting from the act in question. In cases where rightholders have already received payment in some other form, for instance as part of a licence fee, no specific or separate payment may be due. The level of fair compensation should take full account of the degree of use of technological protection measures referred to in this Directive. In certain situations where the prejudice to the rightholder would be minimal, no obligation for payment may arise.
(38) Member States should be allowed to provide for an exception or limitation to the reproduction right for certain types of reproduction of audio, visual and audio-visual material for private use, accompanied by fair compensation. This may include the introduction or continuation of remuneration schemes to compensate for the prejudice to rightholders. Although differences between those remuneration schemes affect the functioning of the internal market, those differences, with respect to analogue private reproduction, should not have a significant impact on the development of the information society. Digital private copying is likely to be more widespread and have a greater economic impact. Due account should therefore be taken of the differences between digital and analogue private copying and a distinction should be made in certain respects between them.
(44) When applying the exceptions and limitations provided for in this Directive, they should be exercised in accordance with international obligations. Such exceptions and limitations may not be applied in a way which prejudices the legitimate interests of the rightholder or which conflicts with the normal exploitation of his work or other subject-matter. The provision of such exceptions or limitations by Member States should, in particular, duly reflect the increased economic impact that such exceptions or limitations may have in the context of the new electronic environment. Therefore, the scope of certain exceptions or limitations may have to be even more limited when it comes to certain new uses of copyright works and other subject-matter.'

4 Article 2(a) of Directive 2001/29 provides:
'Member States shall provide for the exclusive right to authorise or prohibit direct or indirect, temporary or permanent reproduction by any means and in any form, in whole or in part:
(a) for authors, of their works'.

5 Article 5(2) and (5) of that directive provides:
'2. Member States may provide for exceptions or limitations to the reproduction right provided for in Article 2 in the following cases:
(b) in respect of reproductions on any medium made by a natural person for private use and for ends that are neither directly nor indirectly commercial, on condition that the rightholders receive fair compensation which takes account of the application or non-application of technological measures referred to in Article 6 to the work or subject-matter concerned;

5. The exceptions and limitations provided for in paragraphs 1, 2, 3 and 4 shall only be applied in certain special cases which do not conflict with a normal exploitation of the work or other subject-matter and do not unreasonably prejudice the legitimate interests of the rightholder.'

6 Article 6 of Directive 2001/29 provides:

'1. Member States shall provide adequate legal protection against the circumvention of any effective technological measures, which the person concerned carries out in the knowledge, or with reasonable grounds to know, that he or she is pursuing that objective.

3. For the purposes of this Directive, the expression "technological measures" means any technology, device or component that, in the normal course of its operation, is designed to prevent or restrict acts, in respect of works or other subject-matter, which are not authorised by the rightholder of any copyright or any right related to copyright as provided for by law or the sui generis right provided for in Chapter III of [Directive 96/9/EC of the European Parliament and of the Council of 11 March 1996 on the legal protection of databases (OJ 1996 L 77, p. 20)]. Technological measures shall be deemed "effective" where the use of a protected work or other subject-matter is controlled by the rightholders through application of an access control or protection process, such as encryption, scrambling or other transformation of the work or other subject-matter or a copy control mechanism, which achieves the protection objective.

4. Notwithstanding the legal protection provided for in paragraph 1, in the absence of voluntary measures taken by rightholders, including agreements between rightholders and other parties concerned, Member States shall take appropriate measures to ensure that rightholders make available to the beneficiary of an exception or limitation provided for in national law in accordance with Article 5(2)(a), (2)(c), (2)(d), (2)(e), (3)(a), (3)(b) or (3)(e) the means of benefiting from that exception or limitation, to the extent necessary to benefit from that exception or limitation and where that beneficiary has legal access to the protected work or subject-matter concerned.'

Directive 2004/48

7 Article 1 of Directive 2004/48 defines its subject-matter as follows:

'This Directive concerns the measures, procedures and remedies necessary to ensure the enforcement of intellectual property rights. For the purposes of this Directive, the term "intellectual property rights" includes industrial property rights.'

8 Article 2 of Directive 2004/48, which relates to the scope of that directive, provides in paragraph 1:

'Without prejudice to the means which are or may be provided for in Community or national legislation, in so far as those means may be more favourable for rightholders, the measures, procedures and remedies provided for by this Directive shall apply, in accordance with Article 3, to

any infringement of intellectual property rights as provided for by Community law and/or by the national law of the Member State concerned.'

Netherlands law

9 Article 1 of the Law on copyright ('the AW') confers on the creator of a literary, scientific or artistic work, or his legal successors, inter alia the exclusive right to reproduce that work subject to the limitations provided for by law.

10 Article 16c(1) and (2) of the AW establishes the principle of the private copying levy. That provision is worded as follows:
'1. The reproduction of a work or a part thereof on an item designed for the performance, representation or reproduction of a work shall not be regarded as an infringement of the copyright in that work if the reproduction is made for ends that are neither directly nor indirectly commercial and serves exclusively for the own practice, study or use of the natural person making the reproduction.
2. Payment of a fair remuneration in respect of the reproduction referred to in paragraph 1 shall be due to the creator of the work or his legal successors. The manufacturer or importer of the items referred to in paragraph 1 shall be liable for payment of the remuneration.'

11 Article 1019h of the Code of Civil Procedure, which constitutes the transposition of Article 14 of Directive 2004/48, is worded as follows:
'In so far as is necessary, by way of derogation from Book I, Title II, Section 12, Paragraph 2 and Article 843a(1), the unsuccessful party shall be ordered to pay the reasonable and proportionate legal costs and other expenses incurred by the successful party, unless equity does not allow this.'

The dispute in the main proceedings and the questions referred for a preliminary ruling

12 ACI Adam and Others are importers and/or manufacturers of blank data media such as CDs and CD-Rs.

13 Under Article 16c of the AW, ACI Adam and Others are required to pay the private copying levy, the amount of which is determined by SONT, to Thuiskopie.

14 ACI Adam and Others submit that that amount incorrectly takes into account the harm suffered, as the case may be, by copyright holders as a result of copies made from unlawful sources.

15 Consequently, ACI Adam and Others brought proceedings against Thuiskopie and SONT before the Rechtbank te 's-Gravenhage (District Court, The Hague) claiming, in essence, that the private copying levy provided for in Article 16c(2) of the AW is intended exclusively to remunerate copyright holders for acts of reproduction falling within the scope of paragraph 1 of that article, with the result that the amount of that fee should not take into account compensation for harm suffered as a result of copies of works made from unlawful sources.

16 The Rechtbank te 's-Gravenhage dismissed the application of ACI Adam and Others by judgment of 25 June 2008.

17 ACI Adam and Others appealed against that judgment before the Gerechtshof te 's-Gravenhage (Regional Court of Appeal, The Hague). By judgment of 15 November 2010, that court upheld the judgment delivered by the Rechtbank te 's-Gravenhage.

18 The referring court, before which ACI Adam and Others appealed in cassation against the judgment of the Gerechtshof te 's-Gravenhage, takes the view that Directive 2001/29 does not specify whether reproductions made from an unlawful source must be taken into account in determining the fair compensation referred to in Article 5(2)(b) of that directive.

19 In those circumstances, the Hoge Raad der Nederlanden (Supreme Court of the Netherlands) decided to stay the proceedings and to refer the following questions to the Court of Justice for a preliminary ruling:

'(1) Should Article 5(2)(b) – whether or not in conjunction with Article 5(5) – of Directive [2001/29] be interpreted as meaning that the limitation on copyright referred to therein applies to reproductions which satisfy the requirements set out in that provision, regardless of whether the copies of the works from which the reproductions were taken became available to the natural person concerned lawfully – that is to say: without infringing the copyright of the rightholders – or does that limitation apply only to reproductions taken from works which have become available to the person concerned without infringement of copyright?

(2) a. If the answer to question 1 is that expressed at the end of the question, can the application of the "three-stage test" referred to in Article 5(5) of Directive [2001/29] form the basis for the expansion of the scope of the exception of Article 5(2), or can its application only lead to the reduction of the scope of the limitation?

b. If the answer to question 1 is that expressed at the end of the question, is a rule of national law which provides that in the case of reproductions made by a natural person for private use and without any direct or indirect commercial objective, fair compensation is payable, regardless of whether the making of those reproductions is authorised under Article 5(2) of Directive

[2001/29] – and without there being any infringement by that rule of the prohibition right of the rightholder and his entitlement to damages – contrary to Article 5 of [that] Directive, or to any other rule of EU law?

In the light of the "three-stage test" of Article 5(5) of Directive [2001/29], is it important when answering that question that technological measures to combat the making of unauthorised private copies are not (yet) available?

(3) Is Directive [2004/48] applicable to proceedings such as these where – after a Member State, on the basis of Article 5(2)(b) of Directive [2001/29], has imposed the obligation to pay the fair compensation referred to in that provision on producers and importers of media which are suitable and intended for the reproduction of works, and has determined that that fair compensation should be paid to an organisation designated by that Member State which has been charged with collecting and distributing the fair compensation – those liable to pay the compensation bring an action for a declaration by the courts, in respect of certain contested circumstances which have a bearing on the determination of the fair compensation, against the organisation concerned, which defends the action?'

Consideration of the questions referred

The first and second questions

20 By its first and second questions, which it is appropriate to examine together, the referring court asks, in essence, whether EU law, in particular Article 5(2)(b) of Directive 2001/29, read in conjunction with paragraph 5 of that article, is to be interpreted as precluding national legislation, such as that at issue in the main proceedings, which does not distinguish the situation in which the source from which a reproduction for private use is made is lawful from that in which that source is unlawful.

21 It should be noted at the outset that Article 2 of Directive 2001/29 provides that Member States are to grant authors the exclusive right to authorise or prohibit direct or indirect, temporary or permanent reproduction by any means and in any form, in whole or in part of their works, while reserving to those Member States the option, under Article 5(2) of that directive, of providing for exceptions and limitations to that right.

22 As regards the scope of those exceptions and limitations, it must be pointed out that, according to the settled case-law of the Court, the provisions of a directive which derogate from a general principle established by that directive must be interpreted strictly.

23 It follows that the different exceptions and limitations provided for in Article 5(2) of Directive 2001/29 must be interpreted strictly.

24 Furthermore, it must be pointed out that Article 5(5) of Directive 2001/29 requires that the exceptions and limitations to the reproduction right are to be applied only in certain special cases which do not conflict with a normal exploitation of the work or other subject-matter and do not unreasonably prejudice the legitimate interests of the rightholder.

25 As is apparent from its wording, that provision of Directive 2001/29 simply specifies the conditions for the application of the exceptions and limitations to the reproduction right which are authorised by Article 5(2) of that directive, namely that those exceptions and limitations are to be applied only in certain special cases, which do not conflict with a normal exploitation of the work or other subject-matter and do not unreasonably prejudice the legitimate interests of the rightholder. Article 5(5) of that directive does not therefore define the substantive content of the different exceptions and limitations set out in Article 5(2) of that directive, but takes effect only at the time when they are applied by the Member States.

26 Consequently, Article 5(5) of Directive 2001/29 is not intended either to affect the substantive content of provisions falling within the scope of Article 5(2) of that directive or, inter alia, to extend the scope of the different exceptions and limitations provided for therein.

27 Furthermore, it is apparent from recital 44 in the preamble to Directive 2001/29 that the EU legislature meant to envisage, when Member States provide for the exceptions or limitations referred to by that directive, that the scope of those exceptions or limitations could be limited even more when it comes to certain new uses of copyright works and other subject-matter. By contrast, neither that recital nor any other provision of that directive envisages the possibility of the scope of such exceptions or limitations being extended by the Member States.

28 In particular, under Article 5(2)(b) of Directive 2001/29, Member States may provide for an exception to the author's exclusive reproduction right in his work in respect of reproductions on any medium made by a natural person for private use and for ends that are neither directly nor indirectly commercial ('the private copying exception').

29 That provision does not address expressly the lawful or unlawful nature of the source from which a reproduction of the work may be made.

30 The wording of that provision must therefore be interpreted by applying the principle of strict interpretation, as referred to in paragraph 23 of the present judgment.

31 Such an interpretation requires Article 5(2)(b) of Directive 2001/29 to be understood as meaning that the private copying exception admittedly prohibits copyright holders from relying on their exclusive right to authorise or prohibit reproductions with regard to persons who make private copies of their works; however, it precludes that provision from being understood as requiring, beyond that limitation which is provided for expressly, copyright holders to tolerate infringements of their rights which may accompany the making of private copies.

32 Such a finding is, moreover, borne out by the context of which Article 5(2)(b) of Directive 2001/29 forms part and by its underlying objectives.

33 In that regard, first, it is apparent from recital 32 in the preamble to Directive 2001/29 that the list of exceptions provided for in Article 5 thereof has to ensure a balance between the different legal traditions in Member States and the proper functioning of the internal market.

34 It follows that the Member States have the option of introducing the different exceptions provided for in Article 5 of that directive, in accordance with their legal traditions, but that, once they have made the choice of introducing a certain exception, it must be applied coherently, so that it cannot undermine the objectives which Directive 2001/29 pursues with the aim of ensuring the proper functioning of the internal market.

35 If the Member States had the option of adopting legislation which also allowed reproductions for private use to be made from an unlawful source, the result of that would clearly be detrimental to the proper functioning of the internal market.

36 Secondly, it is apparent from recital 22 in the preamble to Directive 2001/29, that the objective of proper support for the dissemination of culture must not be achieved by sacrificing strict protection of rights or by tolerating illegal forms of distribution of counterfeited or pirated works.

37 Consequently, national legislation which makes no distinction between private copies made from lawful sources and those made from counterfeited or pirated sources cannot be tolerated.

38 Furthermore, when it is applied, national legislation, such as that at issue in the main proceedings, which does not draw a distinction according to whether the source from which a reproduction for private use is made is lawful or unlawful, may infringe certain conditions laid down by Article 5(5) of Directive 2001/29.

39 First, to accept that such reproductions may be made from an unlawful source would encourage the circulation of counterfeited or pirated works, thus inevitably reducing the volume of sales or of other lawful transactions relating to the protected works, with the result that a normal exploitation of those works would be adversely affected.

40 Secondly, the application of such national legislation may, having regard to the finding made in paragraph 31 of the present judgment, unreasonably prejudice copyright holders.

41 It is apparent from the foregoing considerations that Article 5(2)(b) of Directive 2001/29 must be interpreted as not covering the case of private copies made from an unlawful source.

42 Against the same background of Article 5(5) of Directive 2001/29, the referring court also inquires whether, in assessing whether national legislation, such as that at issue in the main proceedings, is in conformity with EU law, regard must be had to the fact that technological measures, within the meaning of Article 6 of that directive, and to which Article 5(2)(b) of that directive refers, do not, or not yet, exist at the time when that legislation is implemented.

43 In that regard, the Court has already held that the technological measures to which Article 5(2)(b) of Directive 2001/29 refers are intended to restrict acts which are not authorised by the rightholders, that is to say to ensure the proper application of that provision and thus to prevent acts which do not comply with the strict conditions imposed by that provision.

44 Furthermore, inasmuch as it is the Member States and not the rightholders which establish the private copying exception and which authorise, for the purposes of the making of such a copy, such use of protected works or other subject-matter, it is, consequently, for the Member State which, by the establishment of that exception, has authorised the making of the private copy to ensure the proper application of that exception, and thus to restrict acts which are not authorised by the rightholders.

45 It is apparent from paragraphs 39 and 40 of the present judgment that national legislation, such as that at issue in the main proceedings, which does not distinguish the situation in which the source from which a reproduction for private use is made is lawful from that in which that source is unlawful, is not capable of ensuring the proper application of the private copying exception. The fact that no applicable technological measures to combat the making of unlawful private copies exist is not capable of calling that finding into question.

46 It follows that, in assessing whether national legislation, such as that at issue in the main proceedings, is in conformity with EU law, there is no need to take into account the fact that technological measures, within the meaning of Article 6 of Directive 2001/29, and to which Article 5(2)(b) of that directive refers, do not, or do not yet, exist.

47 Lastly, the finding which the Court reached in paragraph 41 of the present judgment is not called into question in the light of the condition of 'fair compensation' referred to in Article 5(2)(b) of Directive 2001/29.

48 In that regard, it must, first, be pointed out that, under that provision, Member States which decide to introduce the private copying exception into their national law are required to provide for the payment of 'fair compensation' to rightholders.

49 It is also important to bear in mind that an interpretation of that provision according to which Member States which have introduced the private copying exception, provided for by EU law and including, as set out in recitals 35 and 38 in the preamble to that directive, the concept of 'fair compensation' as an essential element, are free to determine the limits in an inconsistent and unharmonised manner which may vary from one Member State to another, would be incompatible with the objective of that directive of harmonising certain aspects of the Law on copyright and related rights in the information society and ensuring competition in the internal market is not distorted as a result of Member States' different legislation.

50 The purpose of such compensation is, according to the case-law of the Court, to compensate authors for private copies made of their protected works without their authorisation, with the result that it must be regarded as recompense for the harm suffered by authors as a result of such unauthorised copies.

51 Accordingly, it is, in principle, for the person who has caused such harm, namely the person who has made the copy of the protected work without seeking prior authorisation from the

rightholder, to make good the harm suffered by financing the compensation which will be paid to that rightholder.

52 The Court has, however, accepted that, given the practical difficulties connected with such a system of fair compensation, it is open to the Member States to establish a levy for the purposes of financing fair compensation chargeable not directly to the private persons concerned, but to those who may pass on the amount of that levy in the price charged for making reproduction equipment, devices and media available or in the price for the copying service supplied, the burden of that levy thus ultimately being borne by the private user who pays that price.

53 Secondly, it is apparent from recital 31 in the preamble to Directive 2001/29 that the levy system introduced by the Member State concerned must safeguard a fair balance between the rights and interests of authors, who are the recipients of the fair compensation, on the one hand, and those of users of protected subject-matter, on the other.

54 A private copying levy system, such as that at issue in the main proceedings, which does not, as regards the calculation of the fair compensation payable to its recipients, distinguish the situation in which the source from which a reproduction for private use has been made is lawful from that in which that source is unlawful, does not respect the fair balance referred to in the preceding paragraph.

55 Under such a system, the harm caused, and therefore the amount of the fair compensation payable to the recipients, is calculated on the basis of the criterion of the harm caused to authors both by reproductions for private use which are made from a lawful source and by reproductions made from an unlawful source. The sum thus calculated is then, ultimately, passed on in the price paid by users of protected subject-matter at the time when equipment, devices and media which enable private copies to be made are made available to them.

56 Consequently, all the users who purchase such equipment, devices and media are indirectly penalised since, by bearing the burden of the levy which is determined regardless of the lawful or unlawful nature of the source from which such reproductions are made, they inevitably contribute towards the compensation for the harm caused by reproductions for private use made from an unlawful source, which are not permitted by Directive 2001/29, and are thus led to assume an additional, non-negligible cost in order to be able to make the private copies covered by the exception provided for by Article 5(2)(b) of that directive.

57 Such a situation cannot be regarded as satisfying the condition of the fair balance to be found between, on the one hand, the rights and interests of the recipients of the fair compensation and, on the other, those of those users.

58 In the light of all of the foregoing considerations, the answer to the first and second questions is that EU law, in particular Article 5(2)(b) of Directive 2001/29, read in conjunction with paragraph 5 of that article, must be interpreted as precluding national legislation, such as that at issue in the main proceedings, which does not distinguish the situation in which the source from which a reproduction for private use is made is lawful from that in which that source is unlawful.

The third question

59 By its third question, the referring court asks, in essence, whether Directive 2004/48 is to be interpreted as meaning that it may apply to proceedings, such as those in the main proceedings, in which those liable for payment of the fair compensation bring an action before that court for a ruling against the body responsible for collecting that remuneration and distributing it to copyright holders, which defends that action.

60 It must be borne in mind that Directive 2004/48 seeks, as is apparent from Article 1 thereof, to ensure the enforcement of intellectual property rights by means of the introduction, for that purpose, of various measures, procedures and remedies within the Member States.

61 The Court has held that the provisions of Directive 2004/48 are intended to govern only the aspects of intellectual property rights related to, first, the enforcement of those rights and, secondly, to infringement of them, by requiring that there must be effective legal remedies designed to prevent, terminate or rectify any infringement of an existing intellectual property right.

62 Furthermore, it is apparent from Article 2(1) of Directive 2004/48 that the provisions thereof simply ensure the enforcement of the various rights enjoyed by persons who have acquired intellectual property rights, namely the proprietors of such rights, and cannot be interpreted as being intended to govern the various measures and procedures available to persons who are not themselves the proprietors of such rights, and which do not relate solely to an infringement of those rights.

63 Proceedings, such as those in the main proceedings, which relate to the scope of the private copying exception scheme and to its impact on the collection and distribution of the fair

compensation which has to be paid by importers and/or manufacturers of blank media, in accordance with Article 5(2)(b) of Directive 2001/29, do not derive from an action brought by rightholders which seeks to prevent, terminate or rectify any infringement of an existing intellectual property right, but from an action brought by economic operators regarding the fair compensation which it is for them to pay.

64 Accordingly, Directive 2004/48 cannot apply.

65 In the light of the foregoing considerations, the answer to the third question is that Directive 2004/48 must be interpreted as not applying to proceedings, such as those in the main proceedings, in which those liable for payment of the fair compensation bring an action before the referring court for a ruling against the body responsible for collecting that remuneration and distributing it to copyright holders, which defends that action. (...)

THINK IT OVER

1. *ACI Adam* originated from the Netherlands. Other countries have taken pro-active steps to exclude private copies made of illegal sources from the scope of the private copying exception. Under Article 53(1) of the German Copyright Act, only copies that were lawfully created or – since 2008 – were made available to the public might serve as a source for any private copying. *Which concept is more acceptable from a dogmatic point of view? The Dutch or the German model?*

2. *ACI Adam* represents a pure dogmatic interpretation of the InfoSoc Directive, as well as a modern application of the ancient Roman doctrine of "*nemo plus iuris*". The ruling serves as a logical follow-up to the CJEU's case law related to the private copying levies. A partially similar and at the same time different conclusion was drawn by the Hungarian Copyright Expert Board in its Expert opinions no. 17/2006 and 07/08/1. The Copyright Expert Board found that the reproduction of unlawful sources runs against the law, but – at the same time – the panel believed that the private copying levy is still due. The latter interpretation seems to solve the practical difficulties that arise under *ACI Adam* (and the former case law, especially *Padawan*), according to which the reproduction of unauthorized materials leads to an infringement, and does not fit into the concept of private copying, therefore end-users are not obliged to pay the levies.

3. Interestingly enough, the CJEU sidestepped its own logic in *BestWater*, where the Court declared the embedding of unauthorized YouTube videos legal. *Which interpretation/ruling is more acceptable?*

Further Case Law

SzJSzT 17/2006 - "A jogellenes forrásból történő másolás kérdése", *Iparjogvédelmi és Szerzői Jogi Szemle*, 2006/4. szám, p. 228-248.

SzJSzT 07/08/01 - "Szerzői művek online fájlcserélő rendszerek segítségével megvalósuló felhasználása", *Iparjogvédelmi és Szerzői Jogi Szemle*, 2008/4. szám, p. 109-129.

Case C-467/08 - Padawan SL v. Sociedad General de Autores y Editores de España (SGAE), Judgment of the Court (Third Chamber), 21 October 2010 [ECLI:EU:C:2010:620]

Case C-348/13 - BestWater International GmbH v. Michael Mebes and Stefan Potsch, Judgment of the Court (Third Chamber), 21 October 2014 [ECLI:EU:C:2014:2315]

Recommended readings

In English

Kateryna Frolova: Auteurswhat? Dutch Copyright Law not Tolerated by the CJEU: ACI Adam BV and Others v Stichting de Thuiskopie and Stichting Onderhandelingen Thuiskopie vergoeding (C-435/12), *European Intellectual Property Review*, Issue 11/2014, p. 738-743.

Eleonora Rosati: Copyright: Private copying exception may only apply to reproductions from licensed sources, *Journal of Intellectual Property Law and Practice*, Issue 9/2014, p. 710-711.

In French

Denys Simon: Droits d'auteurs et droits voisins, *Europe*, 2014 Juin, n° 6, p. 37-38.

In German

Angela Hildebrand: Die Bedeutung der EuGH-Urteile »ACI Adam« und »GS Media« für die deutsche Privatkopieschranke, *Zeitschrift für Urheber- und Medienrecht*, Heft 1/2017, p. 16-23.

In Hungarian

Mezei Péter: *A fájlcsere dilemma - A perek lassúak, az internet gyors*, HVG-Orac, Budapest, 2012: p. 166-170.

Mezei Péter - Hajdú Dóra: Az Európai Unió Bíróságának ACI Adam döntése a jogellenes forrásból történő másolatkészítés után fizetendő jogdíjak egyes kérdéseiről, *Európai jog*, 2014/5. szám, p. 33-47.

THE FOOTBALL ASSOCIATION PREMIER LEAGUE LTD. V. BRITISH SKY BROADCASTING LTD., ET AL.

[2013] *EWHC* 2058 (Ch)

MR JUSTICE ARNOLD

Introduction

1. The Claimant ("FAPL") is the governing body of the football competition known as the Barclays Premier League ("the Premier League"). As explained in more detail below, FAPL owns the copyright in recordings of television footage of all Premier League matches, and in artistic works which appear within that footage. The Defendants are the six main retail internet service providers ("ISPs") in the United Kingdom. Between them they have a fixed line market share of some 94% of UK internet users. By this claim FAPL seeks an injunction against the Defendants pursuant to section 97A of the Copyright, Designs and Patents Act 1988 ("the 1988 Act"), which implements Article 8(3) of European Parliament and Council Directive 2001/29/EC of 22 May 2001 on the harmonisation of certain aspects of copyright and related rights in the information society ("the Information Society Directive"), requiring the Defendants to take measures to block or at least impede access by their customers to a website known as FirstRow Sports ("FirstRow"). (...)

The present application

6. The present application differs from the applications considered in the judgments referred to above in a number of respects. First, the applicant and its supporters constitute a different class of rightholder. Secondly, unlike the websites the subject of the previous applications, FirstRow is not a peer-to-peer ("P2P") file-sharing website. Rather, it is a website which facilitates access to streams of television broadcasts of sporting events. Thirdly, as a result, the issues on infringement are somewhat different.

7. As in the *Dramatico v Sky* and *EMI v Sky* cases, FAPL seeks orders in terms which have been agreed with the Defendants and the Defendants do not oppose the making of those orders. That does not absolve the Court of the responsibility of determining whether the orders sought are justified. I have considered the matter on paper.

FAPL and its rights

8. FAPL is authorised by its member clubs to license broadcasters throughout the world to provide coverage of Premier League matches. A high proportion of the revenue generated by FAPL derives from the sale of such rights. The rights are offered to broadcasters by open competitive tender for a specified territory or groups of territories and term. The rights for the United Kingdom and the Republic of Ireland are sold separately from the rest of the world. The broadcast rights for the UK alone were last auctioned for some £3.018 billion, which is by a very considerable margin the largest amount paid for sporting broadcast rights in the UK.

9. The broadcasting of Premier League matches for viewing in the UK during the "Closed Period" is restricted by Article 48 of the Statutes of UEFA. This empowers each national football association to designate a period of two and half hours in each week during which the broadcasting of football matches in that territory is prohibited. The purpose of this is to encourage attendance at football matches, and in that way to support the sport of football. The Football Association has designated 2.45 pm to 5.15 pm on Saturdays as the Closed Period in England.

10. Each Premier League match is filmed by one of three broadcasters (referred to as the "Host Broadcasters"), using between 8 and 25 cameras with built-in microphones. The live pictures and ambient sound from the stadium are referred as the "Clean Live Feed". The Clean Live Feed also includes action replays added by the Host Broadcaster's production team. These consist of recordings of pictures of incidents of particular interest ("the Action Replay Films"). The Clean Live Feed is transmitted directly to some broadcasters who have been licensed by FAPL, notably those in the UK, Republic of Ireland, United States of America and India.

11. The Clean Live Feed is also transmitted to IMG Media Ltd, which incorporates certain onscreen graphics and logos into it to produce the "World Feed". Prior to the 2012/2013 season, the World Feed was transmitted live to broadcasters who had been licensed by FAPL other than those who receive the Clean Live Feed. Since the beginning of the 2012/2013 season, the World Feed has been recorded ("the Recorded World Feed") before it is transmitted to the broadcasters.

12. For the purposes of the present application, FAPL claims copyright in the following works:
   i) the films comprising the Action Replay Films included in the Clean Live Feed (and hence the Recorded World Feed);
   ii) the films comprising the Recorded World Feed;

iii) the artistic works comprising the Premier League and Barclays logos which are incorporated in the Recorded World Feed; and

iv) the artistic works comprising two sets of on-screen graphics (referred to as the "AEL Onscreen Graphics" and the "IMG Onscreen Graphics") which are incorporated in the Recorded World Feed.

13. I am satisfied by the evidence filed by FAPL that copyright subsists in these works and that FAPL owns those copyrights.

FirstRow

14. FirstRow is a website which has been operating for some time as an indexing and aggregation portal to streamed broadcasts of sporting events. The site is currently located at www.firstrow1.eu, although a number of other domain names have been used, some of which have been seized by the US Department of Homeland Security. A visitor to the FirstRow website is presented with lists of links, organised by sport and time of the day, to streams containing live coverage of a wide range of sporting events, including in particular Premier League matches and events organised by the other supporting rightholders. Upon clicking on one of those links, the user is taken to a new page which features a "frame" or window in which that live coverage then appears, accompanied by advertising. As an alternative, the user can download a free app from the website to their computer which will enable them to access links.

15. The streams that are indexed on FirstRow are provided by third party streamers using one of a number of User Generated Content ("UGC") websites. There are around six or seven such UGC sites which are commonly used for this purpose, one of the most popular of which is called 04stream.com. There are a number of stages to the process. First, the third party streamer digitally captures a broadcast of a live sports event on his or her computer. The captured broadcast may be one that the streamer is watching on his television or computer legally (e.g. via a legitimate subscription) or it may be an illegal stream. Secondly, the streamer sends the captured images in real time to the server of a UGC site. Thirdly, the streamer uses the UGC site to create an "embed code" which enables the stream player to be embedded into a website like FirstRow. Fourthly, the streamer submits the embed code to FirstRow. If it is accepted, it will be listed as a link on FirstRow. It appears that FirstRow has moderators who vet and index these submissions. It is common for multiple links to be listed for each event. These may comprise multiple versions of the same broadcast and/or different broadcasts. Fifthly, the user clicks on the link, thereby enabling the user to watch the stream.

16. Three points should be noted about this process. First, whilst FirstRow gives the impression - by way of a "Submit your video" link - that it is open to the submission of streams by any member of the public, this does not in fact appear to be the case. FAPL's evidence is that it is likely that it works with a number of existing, trusted streamers (and, perhaps, new streamers introduced by existing streamers). Secondly, FAPL's evidence is that none of the streams links to which are provided by FirstRow comes directly from an official source (such as a broadcaster licensed by FAPL). Thirdly, FirstRow itself does not itself transmit any of the streams. Rather, the streams emanate from the UGC sites.

17. The scale of FirstRow's activities is very large. There are a large number of links listed on the site at any one time. FirstRow was ranked by Alexa as the 268th most popular website in the UK in January 2013 and the 239th most popular in April 2013. To put that in perspective, FirstRow was on that basis more popular, in January 2013, than both www.lastminute.com and www.ft.com. In April 2013 alone, FirstRow received 9.98 million unique user hits worldwide.

18. The generation of traffic at these levels enables FirstRow to make considerable sums in advertising and affiliation revenues. Using his expertise acquired from over twelve years of researching and analysing digital piracy, and on the basis of a detailed analysis of the website and the adverts which appear there, FAPL's expert witness Dr David Price estimates that FirstRow is likely to be generating between £5,360,680 and £9,505,564 in annual revenue. Many of the UGC streamers are also motivated by financial reward, since they are able to add their own adverts to the streams.

19. FirstRow does not have permission from FAPL to engage in this activity. Nor, as the witnesses make clear, does FirstRow have permission from the other supporting rightholders, all of whose content has also been streamed via FirstRow.

20. FirstRow is not merely used to watch coverage of sporting events in users' homes. On the contrary, FAPL's agents have discovered that FirstRow is being used by some public houses in the UK so as to show their customers broadcasts of Premier League matches, including during the Closed Period on a Saturday afternoon.

21. FAPL has been unable to establish who the operators of FirstRow are and where they can be contacted. FirstRow has been registered under many different domain names, using a mixture of what appear to be false name and address details and registrations via proxy registration firms. The current host of the site is Portlane in Sweden, which FAPL's witness Tim Cooper, Chief Technology Officer of NetResult Solutions Ltd ("NetResult"), a company

specialising in internet investigation, monitoring and enforcement, describes as "a well-known haven for pirate sites".

22. NetResult has sent a number of cease and desist letters on behalf of FAPL to FirstRow, but these have not been responded to. Furthermore, although FirstRow states that it will accept takedown notices, the address given turns out to be fictitious. (...)

Are the Defendants service providers?

25. As I stated in *Dramatico v Sky (No 2)* at [5], I am in no doubt that the Defendants are service providers within the meaning of regulation 2 of the Electronic Commerce (EC Directive) Regulations 2002, SI 2002/2013, and hence within the meaning of section 97A of the 1988 Act. None of the Defendants has suggested otherwise.

Do the operators and users of FirstRow infringe FAPL copyrights?

26. FAPL contends that the operators of FirstRow infringe their copyrights in two ways. First, by communicating the copyright works to the public within section 20 of the 1988 Act, alternatively by acting as joint tortfeasors with the operators of the UGC websites. Secondly, by authorising infringements by users. FAPL contends that some UK users of FirstRow, namely the publicans who use FirstRow to show Premier League matches in their public houses, infringe their copyrights by communicating the copyright works to the public.

27. In view of the Supreme Court's decision and reference to the Court of Justice of the European Union in *Public Relations Consultants Association Ltd v The Newspaper Licensing Agency Ltd* [2013] UKSC 18, [2013] ECDR 10, FAPL does not advance any claim based on copying, whilst reserving its right to do so in later proceedings.

Communication to the public

28. Section 20 of the 1988 Act provides:

(a) a literary, dramatic, musical or artistic work,

(b) a sound recording or film, or

(c) a broadcast.

(2) References in this part to communication to the public are to communications to the public by electronic transmission, and in relation to a work includes-

(a) the broadcasting of the work;

(b) the making available to the public of the work by electronic transmission in such a way that members of the public may access it from a place and at a time individually chosen by them."

29. Section 20 implements Article 3 of the Information Society Directive, which provides as follows:

"Right of communication to the public of works and right of making available to the public other subject-matter

1. Member States shall provide authors with the exclusive right to authorise or prohibit any communication to the public of their works, by wire or wireless means, including the making available to the public of their works in such a way that members of the public may access them from a place and at a time individually chosen by them.

2. Member States shall provide for the exclusive right to authorise or prohibit the making available to the public, by wire or wireless means, in such a way that members of the public may access them from a place and at a time individually chosen by them:

(a) for performers, of fixations of their performances;

(b) for phonogram producers, of their phonograms;

(c) for the producers of the first fixations of films, of the original and copies of their films;

(d) for broadcasting organisations, of fixations of their broadcasts, whether these broadcasts are transmitted by wire or over the air, including by cable or satellite.

3. The rights referred to in paragraphs 1 and 2 shall not be exhausted by any act of communication to the public or making available to the public as set out in this Article."

30. I reviewed the law with regard to communication to the public under Article 3 of the Information Society Directive and section 20 of the 1988 Act in *Dramatico v Sky* at [45]-[70] (...).

31. I concluded in *EMI v Sky* that whether there is a communication to the public depends on the answers to three questions:

i) Is there a communication of copyright works by way of electronic transmission?

ii) Is there a communication to a new public, that is to say, to a public which was not taken into account by the authors of the protected works when they authorised their communication to the original public?

iii) Does the act of communication to the public take place in the UK? If the communication originates from outside the UK, that depends on whether it is targeted at the public in the UK.

32. The CJEU has since given judgment in Case C-607/11 *ITV Broadcasting Ltd v TVCatchup Ltd* [2013] ECR-0000, [2013] ECDR 9. That case concerned a website which re-transmitted live

television broadcasts, via the internet, to persons who already held a licence to watch such broadcasts on a television. As to whether there was a "communication" under Article 3, the Court of Justice held:

"22. Directive 2001/29 does not define the concept of 'communication' exhaustively. Thus, the meaning and scope of that concept must be defined in the light of the context in which it occurs and also in the light of the objective referred to in paragraph 20 above.

23. It follows, in particular, from recital 23 in the preamble to Directive 2001/29 that the author's right of communication to the public covers any transmission or retransmission of a work to the public not present at the place where the communication originates, by wire or wireless means, including broadcasting. In addition, it is apparent from Article 3(3) of that directive that authorising the inclusion of protected works in a communication to the public does not exhaust the right to authorise or prohibit other communications of those works to the public.

24. If follows that, by regulating the situations in which a given work is put to multiple use, the European Union legislature intended that each transmission or retransmission of a work which uses a specific technical means must, as a rule, be individually authorised by the author of the work in question.

25. Those findings are, moreover, supported by Articles 2 and 8 of Directive 93/83, which require fresh authorisation for a simultaneous, unaltered and unabridged retransmission by satellite or cable of an initial transmission of television or radio programmes containing protected works, even though those programmes may already be received in their catchment area by other technical means, such as by wireless means or terrestrial networks.

26. Given that the making of works available through the retransmission of a terrestrial television broadcast over the internet uses a specific technical means different from that of the original communication, that retransmission must be considered to be a 'communication' within the meaning of Article 3(1) of Directive 2001/29. Consequently, such a retransmission cannot be exempt from authorisation by the authors of the retransmitted works when these are communicated to the public.

27. That conclusion cannot be undermined by TVC's objection that the making of the works available over the internet, as was done in the case in the main proceedings, is merely a technical means to ensure or improve reception of the terrestrial television broadcast in its catchment area.

28. Admittedly, it follows from the case-law of the Court that a mere technical means to ensure or improve reception of the original transmission in its catchment area does not constitute a 'communication' within the meaning of Article 3(1) of Directive 2001/29 (see, to that effect, Football Association Premier League and Others, paragraph 194, and Airfield and Canal Digitaal, paragraphs 74 and 79).

29. Thus, the intervention of such a technical means must be limited to maintaining or improving the quality of the reception of a pre-existing transmission and cannot be used for any other transmission.

30. In the present case, however, the intervention by TVC consists in a transmission of the protected works at issue which is different from that of the broadcasting organisation concerned. TVC's intervention is in no way intended to maintain or improve the quality of the transmission by that other broadcasting organisation. In those circumstances, that intervention cannot be considered to be a mere technical means within the meaning specified in paragraph 28 above."

33. Thus the Court has confirmed that any retransmission of a terrestrial television broadcast via the internet will constitute a communication because it involves "...a specific technical means different from that of the original communication" and an "...intervention ... which is different from that of the broadcasting organisation concerned". This reasoning is equally applicable to re-transmission of satellite and cable television broadcasts via the internet.

34. The Court then went on to consider the issue of whether there was communication to the "public":

"32. In that connection, it follows from the case-law of the Court that the term 'public' in Article 3(1) of Directive 2001/29 refers to an indeterminate number of potential recipients and implies, moreover, a fairly large number of persons (see, to that effect, SGAE, paragraphs 37 and 38 and the case law cited).

33. As regards that last criterion specifically, the cumulative effect of making the works available to potential recipients should be taken into account. In that connection, it is in particular relevant to ascertain the number of persons who have access to the same work at the same time and successively (SGAE, paragraph 39).

34. In that context, it is irrelevant whether the potential recipients access the communicated works through a one-to-one connection. That technique does not prevent a large number of persons having access to the same work at the same time.

35. In the present case, it should be noted that the retransmission of the works over the internet at issue in the main proceedings is aimed at all persons resident in the United Kingdom who have an internet connection and who claim to hold a television licence in that State. Those people may access the protected works at the same time, in the context of the 'live streaming' of television programmes on the internet.

36. Thus, the retransmission in question is aimed at an indeterminate number of potential recipients and implies a large number of persons. Consequently, it must be held that, by the retransmission in question, the protected works are indeed communicated to a 'public' within the meaning of Article 3(1) of Directive 2001/29."

35. Finally, the Court considered whether there was a "new public" in that particular case, because of the pre-existence of a television licence:

"37 TVC contends that the retransmission at issue in the main proceedings does not satisfy the requirement that there must be a new public, which is none the less necessary within the meaning of the judgments in SGAE (paragraph 40), Football Association Premier League and Others (paragraph 197), and Airfield and Canal Digitaal (paragraph 72). The recipients of the retransmission effected by TVC are, it submits, entitled to follow the televised broadcast, identical in content, using their own television sets.

38. In that connection, it should be noted that the situations examined in the cases which gave rise to the abovementioned judgments differ clearly from the situation at issue in the case in the main proceedings. In those cases, the Court examined situations in which an operator had made accessible, by its deliberate intervention, a broadcast containing protected works to a new public which was not considered by the authors concerned when they authorised the broadcast in question.

39. By contrast, the main proceedings in the present case concern the transmission of works included in a terrestrial broadcast and the making available of those works over the internet. As is apparent from paragraphs 24 to 26 above, each of those two transmissions must be authorised individually and separately by the authors concerned given that each is made under specific technical conditions, using a different means of transmission for the protected works, and each is intended for a public. In those circumstances, it is no longer necessary to examine below the requirement that there must be a new public, which is relevant only in the situations on which the Court of Justice had to rule in the cases giving rise to the judgments in SGAE, Football Association Premier League and Others and Airfield and Canal Digitaal."

36. The Court thus held that, where a television broadcast is re-transmitted via the internet, there is no need to show that the "public" to which the re-transmission is communicated is any different from the public to which the original transmission was addressed. The fact that it is a separate communication to the public by a different technical means suffices.

Communication to the public by the operators of FirstRow

37. Although some of the copyright works relied on by FAPL are "films" within the meaning of the 1988 Act and some are artistic works, it is not necessary to differentiate between them for the purposes of considering FAPL's claims of infringement by communication to the public for the reasons explained in *Dramatico v Sky* at [61]-[65].

38. *Is there a communication by FirstRow?* FAPL contends that FirstRow communicates FAPL's copyright works by electronic transmission. In my judgment it is clear from the CJEU's reasoning in *ITV v TVCatchup* at [26] and [30] that there is a communication of the works. More specifically, the works are made available by electronic transmission in such a way

that members of the public may access the recordings from a place and at a time individually chosen by them within section 20(2)(b).

39. The more difficult question is whether FirstRow is responsible for the communication. FAPL accepts that, in technical terms, the streams emanate from the UGC sites and not from FirstRow itself. FAPL nevertheless contends that both the UGC sites and FirstRow communicate the works.

40. In support of this contention, FAPL relies upon the reasoning of Kitchin J (as he then was) in *Twentieth Century Fox Film Corp v Newzbin Ltd* [2010] EWHC 608 (Ch), [2010] FSR 21 at [125]:

"The defendant has provided a service which, upon payment of a weekly subscription, enables its premium members to identify films of their choice using the Newzbin cataloguing and indexing system and then to download those films using the NZB facility, all in the way I have described in detail earlier in this judgment. This service is not remotely passive. Nor does it simply provide a link to a film of interest which is made available by a third party. To the contrary, the defendant has intervened in a highly material way to make the claimants' films available to a new audience, that is to say its premium members. Furthermore it has done so by providing a sophisticated technical and editorial system which allows its premium members to download all the component messages of the film of their choice upon pressing a button, and so avoid days of (potentially futile) effort in seeking to gather those messages together for themselves. As a result, I have no doubt that the defendant's premium members consider that Newzbin is making available to them the films in the Newzbin index. Moreover, the defendant has provided its service in full knowledge of the consequences of its actions."

41. FAPL also relies on what I said in *EMI v Sky* at [46]:

"I would add that I see nothing in Football Dataco v Sportradar to exclude the possibility that more than one person may be involved in an act of communication to the public. In the present situation, the communication to the public involves both the operators of Websites, who provide a mechanism specifically designed to achieve this, and the users, who provide the actual recordings. (Even if I am wrong about this, the operators may still be liable on the grounds of authorisation and joint tortfeasance.)"

42. In the present case the operators of FirstRow have intervened in a manner which, although technically different, is analogous to that of the websites under consideration in those cases. FirstRow aggregates together a large number of streams from a variety of streamers, indexes them for the convenience of the user and provides a simple link for the user to click on in order to access a specific stream. It is true that the technical effect of clicking on the link

is to direct the stream from the UCG site to the user's computer, but even so the stream is presented in a frame provided by FirstRow. In all the circumstances, I consider that FirstRow is responsible for the communication.

43. Even if I am wrong about that, I consider that FirstRow is jointly liable for the communication by the UGC sites: compare *EMI v Sky* at [71]-[74].

44. *Is the communication to the public?* FAPL contends that the communication is to the public, relying on the reasoning of the CJEU in *ITV v TVCatchup* at [35]-[36]. I agree that this reasoning is equally applicable to the present case. Furthermore, FAPL contends that it is not necessary for it to show that the communication is to a new public, relying on *ITV v TVCatchup* at [39]. I accept this. In any event, even if FAPL had to show that the communication was to a new public, I consider that it is clear that that requirement is satisfied, since the effect of FirstRow's activities is to make the broadcasts available to persons who are not legitimately entitled to view them either because those persons have not subscribed to the broadcaster's service or because the broadcaster has only been licensed by FAPL for a different territory.

45. *Is the communication in the UK?* FAPL accepts that it must show an intention on the part of the operators of FirstRow to target the public in the UK. FAPL relies upon the following matters as evidencing such an intention:
i) The website is an English language website.
ii) The advertising on FirstRow includes adverts for companies located in the UK and products consumed in the UK.
iii) FirstRow provides access to a large number of competitions which are extremely popular with UK audiences. In particular, the amount of Premier League content on the website is up to 11% whilst a Premier League match is being played.
iv) As noted above, FirstRow is a very popular site in the UK.
v) Between 12 and 13.7% of the worldwide traffic to the site comes from the UK.
vi) FirstRow is discussed on internet blogs and forums, where a significant proportion of the internet traffic to those blogs and forums comes from the UK.

46. I accept that these matters evidence an intention to target the public in the UK. Accordingly, there is communication to the public in the UK.

47. *Conclusion.* I am satisfied that FirstRow communicates FAPL's copyright works to the public in the UK and thereby infringes FAPL's copyrights in those works.

Communication to the public by users of FirstRow who are publicans

48. FAPL contends that publicans who use FirstRow to screen Premier League matches in their public houses are thereby communicating FAPL's copyright works to the public. In support of this, FAPL relies upon the decision of the CJEU in *FAPL v QC*, where the Court held at [207] that:
"... *'communication to the public' within the meaning of Article 3(1) of the Copyright Directive must be interpreted as covering transmission of the broadcast works, via a television screen and speakers, to the customers present in a public house.*"

49. Clearly, the same reasoning must apply where the technical means used is a computer rather than a television. Accordingly, I conclude that the publicans communicate FAPL's copyright works to the public.

Authorisation by the operators of FirstRow

50. FAPL contends that the operators of FirstRow authorise the infringements by the users and thus also infringe in that way. I have to say that I have doubts as to whether it can be said that the operators of FirstRow authorise the screening of Premier League matches using FirstRow in public houses. It is not necessary for me to reach a conclusion on this point, however, given that I have already concluded that the operators of FirstRow infringe FAPL's copyrights by communication to the public.

Do the users and/or operators use the Defendants' services to infringe?

51. I held in *20CFox v BT* at [99]-[113], *Dramatico v Sky (No 2)* at [6] and *EMI v Sky* at [76]-[88] that both users and the operators of the websites in issue used the Defendants' services to infringe the claimants' copyrights. In my judgment that reasoning is equally applicable to the present case.

Do the Defendants have actual knowledge?

52. On 7 June 2013 FAPL's solicitors sent detailed letters before action to the Defendants which attached the evidence relied upon by FAPL in the present application. I am satisfied that, as a result, the Defendants do have actual knowledge that users and the operators of the Websites use the Defendants' services to infringe copyright. Indeed, I note that none of the Defendants denies this.

Proportionality and discretion

53. FAPL contends that I should exercise my discretion to make the orders sought. Unlike in *20C Fox v BT*, the Defendants do not advance any reasons as to why I should exercise my discretion to refuse to make the orders sought. Even so, as FAPL rightly accepts, the onus remains on FAPL to satisfy the Court that it is appropriate to make such orders, and in particular that the orders are proportionate.

54. I reviewed the correct approach to the assessment of proportionality in *EMI v Sky* at [91]-[106]. I shall adopt the same approach here.

55. FAPL contends that the orders are proportionate for the following reasons:
i) As between FAPL and the Defendants, the Defendants do not oppose the making of the orders and the terms of the orders have been agreed between FAPL and the Defendants. The costs to the Defendants of implementation are modest and proportionate.
ii) The orders are necessary to protect the copyrights of FAPL and the supporting rightholders, which are being infringed on a large scale. Given the difficulty of identifying, let alone bringing proceedings against, the operators of FirstRow, no other effective remedy is open to FAPL in this jurisdiction.
iii) The orders are also necessary, or at least desirable, in order to protect the sporting objectives which lie behind the Closed Period, and in that sense are in the public interest. This is a legitimate factor to take into account.
iv) While FirstRow features international content some of which may not be protected by copyright or may be licensed, the vast bulk of the content which is likely to be of interest to UK users infringes the rights of FAPL and the supporting rightholders.
v) The orders are narrow and targeted ones, and they contain safeguards in the event of any change of circumstances. While they are unlikely to be completely efficacious, since some users will be able to circumvent the technical measures which the orders require the Defendants to adopt, it is likely that they will be reasonably effective.

56. So far as sub-paragraph (v) is concerned, two points should be noted. First, the orders require IP address blocking of the IP address for FirstRow's domain name firstrow1.eu. FAPL's evidence is that this will not result in over-blocking since that IP address is not shared. The orders also require IP address re-routing and URL blocking for URLs at any shared IP addresses.

57. Secondly, on 25 June 2013 Mann J granted orders under section 97A concerning a website known as EZTV. He required the orders to contain an additional liberty to apply in the following terms:

"The operator(s) of the Target Website (as defined in the Schedule to this order) and the operators of any other website who claim to be affected by this Order, are to have permission to apply to vary or discharge this Order insofar as it affects such an applicant, any such application to be on notice to all the parties and to be supported by materials setting out and justifying the grounds of the application. Any such application shall clearly indicate the status of the applicant and indicate clearly (supported by evidence) that it is the operator of the website which is the subject of the application."

58. I agree that this is a beneficial provision to include in orders of this nature. In the present case, the parties have agreed to the inclusion of a similar provision.

59. Having considered the proportionality of the orders sought by the present applications as between FAPL (and the supporting rightholders) and the Defendants and as between FAPL and the operators and users of FirstRow, I am satisfied that the orders sought are proportionate for the reasons advanced by FAPL. The interests of FAPL and the supporting rightholders in enforcing their copyrights clearly outweigh the Article 11 EU Charter rights of the users of the Websites, who can obtain the copyright works from lawful sources. They even more clearly outweigh the Article 11 rights of the operators of the Websites, who are profiting from infringement on a large scale. They also outweigh the Defendants' Article 11 rights to the extent that they are engaged.

Conclusion

60. I will make the orders requested by FAPL.

THINK IT OVER

1. In the last ten to fifteen years, rights holders have succeeded in several cases to force ISPs to block different torrent indexing sites. Dutch, Belgian, Italian, Finnish, Danish and most importantly British ISPs were forced to block access to e.g. The Pirate Bay, btjunkie, Newzbin, Newzbin 2, H33T or Fenopy. In the United Kingdom, the number of blocked torrent and of streaming sites has crossed over 1000 by 2015. [See: Arif (2019).] Rights holders have also suffered major losses in several cases. In Sweden, the Stockholm District Court denied to issue a blocking order against B2 ISP in 2016. Similarly, in January 2014, the Dutch Supreme Court ordered the cease of blockade of The Pirate Bay by Ziggo and XS4ALL due to the inefficiency of the blockade. Nevertheless, the CJEU has later confirmed in *Ziggo* that ISPs can be ordered by the domestic courts to block accessing The Pirate Bay. Website blocking is present in non-European countries as well. The Federal Court of Canada ordered the blocking of the website GoldTV in 2019.

2. A research paper concluded that "blocking The Pirate Bay had little impact on UK users' consumption through legal channels. Instead blocked users switched to other piracy sites or circumvented the block by using Virtual Private Networks. However, unlike the May 2012 Pirate Bay block, our results showed that when 19 sites were blocked simultaneously, former users of these sites increased their usage of paid legal streaming sites by 12% on average, relative to the control group. The blocks caused the lightest users of the blocked sites (and thus the users who were least affected by the blocks, other than the control group) to increase their use of paid streaming sites by 3.5% while they caused the heaviest users of the blocked sites to increase paid streaming visits by 23.6%, strengthening the causal inference in our result. As we discuss in our paper, the most likely explanation for this result – and one supported by other observations in the data – is that when only one site is blocked, most pirates have an easy time finding and switching to other piracy sites. But, blocking many sites can increase the cost of finding alternate sources of piracy enough that a significant number of former pirates will switch their behavior toward legal sources" [Danaher - Smith - Telang (2015)]. *Do you think that blocking of illicit websites is a practical and effective method of fights against file-sharing?*

Further Case Law

Twentieth Century Fox Film Corp v British Telecommunications plc [2011] *EWHC* 1981 (Ch)

Twentieth Century Fox Film Corp v British Telecommunications plc (No 2) [2011] *EWHC* 2714 (Ch)

Dramatico Entertainment Ltd v British Sky Broadcasting Ltd [2012] *EWHC* 268 (Ch), [2012]

Dramatico Entertainment Ltd v British Sky Broadcasting Ltd (No 2) [2012] *EWHC* 1152 (Ch)

EMI Records Ltd v British Sky Broadcasting Ltd [2013] *EWHC* 379 (Ch)

The Football Association Premier League Ltd v British Sky Broadcasting Ltd & Ors [2013] *EWHC* 2058 (Ch)

Paramount Home Entertainment International Ltd & Ors v British Sky Broadcasting Ltd & Ors [2013] *EWHC* 3479 (Ch)

Paramount Home Entertainment & Anor v British Sky Broadcasting & Ors [2014] *EWHC* 937 (Ch)

1967 Limited v British Sky Broadcasting [2014] *EWHC* 3444 (Ch)

Twentieth Century Fox Film Corporation & Ors v Sky UK Ltd & Ors [2015] *EWHC* 1082 (Ch)

Cartier International AG v British Sky Broadcasting Ltd [2014] *EWHC* 3354 (Ch)

Cartier International AG v British Sky Broadcasting [2016] *EWCA* Civ 658

Cartier International Limited v British Telecommunications [2016] *EWHC* 339 (Ch)

Football Association Premier League and Others v British Telecommunications and Others [2017] *EWHC* 480 (Ch)

Football Association Premier League Ltd v British Telecommunications PLC [2017] *EWHC* 1877 (Ch)

Union Des Associations Européennes De Football v British Telecommunications PLC [2017] *EWHC* 3414 (Ch)

Nintendo Co Ltd v. Sky UK Ltd. [2019] *EWHC* 2376 (Ch)

Case C-610/15 - Stichting Brein v Ziggo BV and XS4All Internet BV, Judgment of the Court (Second Chamber), 14 June 2017 [ECLI:EU:C:2017:456]

Bell Media Inc. v. GoldTV.Biz [2019] *FC* 1432. In: *Computer Law Review International*, Issue 6/2019, p. 181-186.

Recommended readings

In English

Rachel Alexander: FirstRow - Access Denied, *Entertainment Law Review*, Issue 8/2013, p. 280-283.

Pekka Savola: Blocking Injunctions and Website Operators' Liability for Copyright Infringement for User-Generated Links, *European Intellectual Property Review*, Issue 5/2014, p. 279-288.

Pekka Savola: The Ultimate Copyright Shopping Opportunity - Jurisdiction and Choice of Law in Website Blocking Injunctions, *IIC - International Review of Intellectual Property and Competition Law*, Issue 3/2014, p. 287-315.

Brett Danaher - Michael D. Smith - Rahul Telang: The Effect of Piracy Website Blocking on Consumer Behaviour, 2019 (manuscript) (http://ssrn.com/abstract=2612063)

Shabana Arif: The Number of Requests for Piracy Sites to Be Blocked in the UK Has Been Dropping, *Gizmodo*, 17 July 2019 (https://www.gizmodo.co.uk/2019/07/the-number-of-requests-for-piracy-sites-to-be-blocked-in-the-uk-has-been-dropping/)

Emir Crowne: All that Glitters: Federal Court of Canada Issues Canada's First Website Blocking Order Against GoldTV, *Journal of Intellectual Property Law & Practice*, Issue 2/2020, p. 83-84.

Yin Harn Lee: United Kingdom Copyright Decisions 2019, *IIC - International Review of Intellectual Property and Competition Law*, Issue 3/2020, p. 366-367.

Ben Allgrove - John Groom: *Enforcement in a Digital Context: Intermediary Liability*. In: Tanya Aplin (Ed.): *Research Handbook on Intellectual Property and Digital Technologies*, Edward Elgar, Cheltenham, 2020, p. 506-530.

Mark Hyland: A Critical Evaluation of the Effectiveness and Legitimacy of Webblocking Injunctions, *Law, Innovation and Technology*, Issue 1/2020, p. 30-59.

In Hungarian

Harkai István: Hozzáférés megtagadva - a weboldalak blokkolása, mint a jogérvényesítés lehetséges eszköze I. rész, *Iparjogvédelmi és Szerzői Jogi Szemle*, 2016/2. szám, p. 23-51.

Harkai István: Hozzáférés megtagadva - a weboldalak blokkolása, mint a jogérvényesítés lehetséges eszköze II. rész, *Iparjogvédelmi és Szerzői Jogi Szemle*, 2016/3. szám, p. 71-99.

UPC TELEKABEL WIEN GMBH V. CONSTANTIN FILM VERLEIH GMBH, WEGA FILMPRODUKTIONSGESELLSCHAFT MBH

Case C-314/12 - Judgment of the Court (Fourth Chamber), 27 March 2014 [ECLI:EU:C:2014:192]

(...) Legal context

EU law

3 Recitals 9 and 59 in the preamble to Directive 2001/29 state:
'(9) Any harmonisation of copyright and related rights must take as a basis a high level of protection, since such rights are crucial to intellectual creation. ... Intellectual property has therefore been recognised as an integral part of property.

...

(59) In the digital environment, in particular, the services of intermediaries may increasingly be used by third parties for infringing activities. In many cases such intermediaries are best placed to bring such infringing activities to an end. Therefore, without prejudice to any other sanctions and remedies available, rightholders should have the possibility of applying for an injunction against an intermediary who carries a third party's infringement of a protected work or other subject-matter in a network. ... The conditions and modalities relating to such injunctions should be left to the national law of the Member States.'

4 Article 1 of that directive, headed 'Scope', provides in paragraph 1:
'This Directive concerns the legal protection of copyright and related rights in the framework of the internal market, with particular emphasis on the information society.'

5 Article 3 of the same directive, headed 'Right of communication to the public of works and right of making available to the public other subject-matter', provides in paragraph 2:
'Member States shall provide for the exclusive right to authorise or prohibit the making available to the public, by wire or wireless means, in such a way that members of the public may access them from a place and at a time individually chosen by them:

...

(c) for the producers of the first fixations of films, of the original and copies of their films;

...'

6 Article 8 of Directive 2001/29, headed 'Sanctions and remedies', states in paragraph 3:
'Member States shall ensure that rightholders are in a position to apply for an injunction against intermediaries whose services are used by a third party to infringe a copyright or related right.'

Austrian law

7 Paragraph 18a(1) of the Law on copyright (Urheberrechtsgesetz) of 9 April 1936 (BGBl. 111/1936), as amended by the new law of 2003 on copyright (Urheberrechtsgesetz-Novelle 2003, BGBl. I, 32/2003, 'the UrhG'), reads:

'The author has the exclusive right to make the work available to the public, by wire or wireless means, in such a way which allows members of the public to access it from a place and at a time chosen by them.'

8 Paragraph 81(1) and (1a) of the UrhG state:

'(1) A person who has suffered an infringement of any exclusive rights conferred by this Law, or who fears such an infringement, shall be entitled to bring proceedings for a restraining injunction. Legal proceedings may also be brought against the proprietor of a business if the infringement is committed in the course of the activities of his business by one of his employees or by a person acting under his control, or if there is a danger that such an infringement will be committed; Paragraph 81(1a) shall apply mutatis mutandis.

(1a) If the person who has committed such an infringement, or by whom there is a danger of such an infringement being committed, uses the services of an intermediary for that purpose, the intermediary shall also be liable to an injunction under subparagraph (1). ...'

9 Paragraph 355(1) of the Code of Enforcement (Executionsordnung) states:

'Enforcement against the person obligated to desist from an activity or to tolerate the carrying out of an activity shall take place, at the time of consent to enforcement, by the imposition by the enforcement court, upon application, of a fine for any non-compliance after the obligation became executory. In the event of further non-compliance, the enforcement court shall, upon application, impose a further fine or a period of imprisonment of up to one year in total. ...'

10 It is apparent from the explanations given by the referring court in its request for a preliminary ruling that, at the stage of the enforcement procedure, the addressee of the prohibition can argue, in order to avoid liability, that he has taken all of the measures that could be expected of him in order to prevent the result prohibited.

The dispute in the main proceedings and the questions referred for a preliminary ruling

11 Having established that a website was offering, without their agreement, either a download or 'streaming' of some of the films which they had produced, Constantin Film and Wega, two film production companies, referred the matter to the court responsible for hearing

applications for interim measures with a view to obtaining, on the basis of Article 81(1a) of the UrhG, an order enjoining UPC Telekabel, an internet service provider, to block the access of its customers to the website at issue, inasmuch as that site makes available to the public, without their consent, cinematographic works over which they hold a right related to copyright.

12 By order of 13 May 2011, the Handelsgericht Wien (Commercial Court, Vienna) (Austria) prohibited UPC Telekabel from providing its customers with access to the website at issue; that prohibition was to be carried out in particular by blocking that site's domain name and current IP ('Internet Protocol') address and any other IP address of that site of which UPC Telekabel might be aware.

13 In June 2011, the website at issue ceased its activity following an action of the German police forces against its operators.

14 By order of 27 October 2011, the Oberlandesgericht Wien (Higher Regional Court, Vienna) (Austria), as an appeal court, partially reversed the order of the court of first instance in so far as it had wrongly specified the means that UPC Telekabel had to introduce in order to block the website at issue and thus execute the injunction. In order to reach that conclusion, the Oberlandesgericht Wien first of all held that Article 81(1a) of the UrhG must be interpreted in the light of Article 8(3) of Directive 2001/29. It then held that, by giving its customers access to content illegally placed online, UPC Telekabel had to be regarded as an intermediary whose services were used to infringe a right related to copyright, with the result that Constantin Film and Wega were entitled to request that an injunction be issued against UPC Telekabel. However, as regards the protection of copyright, the Oberlandesgericht Wien held that UPC Telekabel could only be required, in the form of an obligation to achieve a particular result, to forbid its customers access to the website at issue, but that it had to remain free to decide the means to be used.

15 UPC Telekabel appealed on a point of law to the Oberster Gerichtshof (Supreme Court) (Austria).

16 In support of its appeal, UPC Telekabel submits inter alia that its services could not be considered to be used to infringe a copyright or related right within the meaning of Article 8(3) of Directive 2001/29 because it did not have any business relationship with the operators of the website at issue and it was not established that its own customers acted unlawfully. In any event, UPC Telekabel claims that the various blocking measures which may be introduced can all be technically circumvented and that some of them are excessively costly.

17 In those circumstances, the Oberster Gerichtshof decided to stay the proceedings and to refer the following questions to the Court of Justice for a preliminary ruling:

'(1) Is Article 8(3) of Directive 2001/29 ... to be interpreted as meaning that a person who makes protected subject-matter available on the internet without the rightholder's consent [for the purpose of Article 3(2) of Directive 2001/29] is using the services of the [internet] access providers of persons seeking access to that protected subject-matter? (...)

(3) Is it compatible with Union law, in particular with the necessary balance between the parties' fundamental rights, to prohibit in general terms an [internet] access provider from allowing its customers access to a certain website (thus without ordering specific measures) as long as the material available on that website is provided exclusively or predominantly without the rightholder's consent, if the access provider can avoid incurring coercive penalties for breach of the prohibition by showing that it had nevertheless taken all reasonable measures? (...)'

Consideration of the questions referred

(...)

The first question

23 By its first question, the referring court asks, essentially, whether Article 8(3) of Directive 2001/29 must be interpreted as meaning that a person who makes protected subject-matter available to the public on a website without the agreement of the rightholder, for the purpose of Article 3(2) of that directive, is using the services of the internet service provider of the persons accessing that subject-matter, which is to be regarded as an intermediary within the meaning of Article 8(3) of Directive 2001/29.

24 As a preliminary point, it should be noted that, in the case in the main proceedings, it is common ground that the protected subject-matter was made available to users of a website without the consent of the rightholders mentioned in Article 3(2) of Directive 2001/29.

25 Given that, according to that provision, rightholders have the exclusive right to authorise or prohibit any act of making available to the public, it must be stated that an act of making protected subject-matter available to the public on a website without the rightholders' consent infringes copyright and related rights.

26 In order to remedy such a situation of infringement of the rights at issue, Article 8(3) of Directive 2001/29 provides for the possibility for rightholders to apply for an injunction against intermediaries whose services are used by a third party to infringe one of their rights.

27 As Recital 59 in the preamble to Directive 2001/29 states, since the services of intermediaries are increasingly used for infringing copyright or related rights, such intermediaries are, in many cases, best placed to bring such infringing activities to an end.

28 In the present case, the Handelsgericht Wien and then the Oberlandesgericht Wien ordered UPC Telekabel, the internet service provider addressed by the injunction at issue in the main proceedings, to bring the infringement of the rights of Constantin Film and of Wega to an end.

29 However, UPC Telekabel disputes that it may be considered, for the purposes of Article 8(3) of Directive 2001/29, to be an intermediary whose services are used to infringe a copyright or related right.

30 In this respect, it follows from Recital 59 in the preamble to Directive 2001/29 that the term 'intermediary' used in Article 8(3) of that directive covers any person who carries a third party's infringement of a protected work or other subject-matter in a network.

31 Having regard to the objective pursued by Directive 2001/29, as shown in particular by Recital 9 thereof, which is to guarantee rightholders a high level of protection, the concept of infringement thus used must be understood as including the case of protected subject-matter placed on the internet and made available to the public without the agreement of the rightholders at issue.

32 Accordingly, given that the internet service provider is an inevitable actor in any transmission of an infringement over the internet between one of its customers and a third party, since, in granting access to the network, it makes that transmission possible, it must be held that an internet service provider, such as that at issue in the main proceedings, which allows its customers to access protected subject-matter made available to the public on the internet by a third party is an intermediary whose services are used to infringe a copyright or related right within the meaning of Article 8(3) of Directive 2001/29.

33 Such a conclusion is borne out by the objective pursued by Directive 2001/29. To exclude internet service providers from the scope of Article 8(3) of Directive 2001/29 would substantially diminish the protection of rightholders sought by that directive.

34 That conclusion cannot be called into question by the argument that, for Article 8(3) of Directive 2001/29 to be applicable, there has to be a contractual link between the internet service provider and the person who infringed a copyright or related right.

35 Neither the wording of Article 8(3) nor any other provision of Directive 2001/29 indicates that a specific relationship between the person infringing copyright or a related right and the intermediary is required. Furthermore, that requirement cannot be inferred from the objectives pursued by that directive, given that to admit such a requirement would reduce the legal protection afforded to the rightholders at issue, whereas the objective of that directive, as is apparent inter alia from Recital 9 in its preamble, is precisely to guarantee them a high level of protection.

36 Nor is the conclusion reached by the Court in paragraph 30 of this judgment invalidated by the assertion that, in order to obtain the issue of an injunction against an internet service provider, the holders of a copyright or of a related right must show that some of the customers of that provider actually access, on the website at issue, the protected subject-matter made available to the public without the agreement of the rightholders.

37 Directive 2001/29 requires that the measures which the Member States must take in order to conform to that directive are aimed not only at bringing to an end infringements of copyright and of related rights, but also at preventing them.

38 Such a preventive effect presupposes that the holders of a copyright or of a related right may act without having to prove that the customers of an internet service provider actually access the protected subject-matter made available to the public without their agreement.

39 That is all the more so since the existence of an act of making a work available to the public presupposes only that the work was made available to the public; it is not decisive that persons who make up that public have actually had access to that work or not.

40 In view of the above, the answer to the first question is that Article 8(3) of Directive 2001/29 must be interpreted as meaning that a person who makes protected subject-matter available to the public on a website without the agreement of the rightholder, for the purpose of Article 3(2) of that directive, is using the services of the internet service provider of the persons accessing that subject-matter, which must be regarded as an intermediary within the meaning of Article 8(3) of Directive 2001/29. (...)

The third question

42 By its third question, the referring court asks, essentially, whether the fundamental rights recognised by EU law must be interpreted as precluding a court injunction prohibiting an internet service provider from allowing its customers access to a website placing protected

subject-matter online without the agreement of the rightholders when that injunction does not specify the measures which that access provider must take and when that access provider can avoid incurring coercive penalties for breach of that injunction by showing that it has taken all reasonable measures.

43 In this respect, as is apparent from Recital 59 in the preamble to Directive 2001/29, the rules for the injunctions which the Member States must lay down pursuant to Article 8(3) of the directive, such as those relating to the conditions to be met and the procedure to be followed, are a matter for national law.

44 That said, those national rules, and likewise their application by the national courts, must observe the limitations arising from Directive 2001/29 and from the sources of law to which Recital 3 in its preamble refers.

45 In order to assess whether an injunction such as that at issue in the main proceedings, taken on the basis of Article 8(3) of Directive 2001/29, is consistent with EU law, it is therefore necessary to take account in particular of the requirements that stem from the protection of the applicable fundamental rights, and to do so in accordance with Article 51 of the Charter of Fundamental Rights of the European Union ('the Charter').

46 The Court has already ruled that, where several fundamental rights are at issue, the Member States must, when transposing a directive, ensure that they rely on an interpretation of the directive which allows a fair balance to be struck between the applicable fundamental rights protected by the European Union legal order. Then, when implementing the measures transposing that directive, the authorities and courts of the Member States must not only interpret their national law in a manner consistent with that directive but also ensure that they do not rely on an interpretation of it which would be in conflict with those fundamental rights or with the other general principles of EU law, such as the principle of proportionality.

47 In the present case, it must be observed that an injunction such as that at issue in the main proceedings, taken on the basis of Article 8(3) of Directive 2001/29, makes it necessary to strike a balance, primarily, between (i) copyrights and related rights, which are intellectual property and are therefore protected under Article 17(2) of the Charter, (ii) the freedom to conduct a business, which economic agents such as internet service providers enjoy under Article 16 of the Charter, and (iii) the freedom of information of internet users, whose protection is ensured by Article 11 of the Charter.

48 As regards the freedom to conduct a business, the adoption of an injunction such as that at issue in the main proceedings restricts that freedom.

49 The freedom to conduct a business includes, inter alia, the right for any business to be able to freely use, within the limits of its liability for its own acts, the economic, technical and financial resources available to it.

50 An injunction such as that at issue in the main proceedings constrains its addressee in a manner which restricts the free use of the resources at his disposal because it obliges him to take measures which may represent a significant cost for him, have a considerable impact on the organisation of his activities or require difficult and complex technical solutions.

51 However, such an injunction does not seem to infringe the very substance of the freedom of an internet service provider such as that at issue in the main proceedings to conduct a business.

52 First, an injunction such as that at issue in the main proceedings leaves its addressee to determine the specific measures to be taken in order to achieve the result sought, with the result that he can choose to put in place measures which are best adapted to the resources and abilities available to him and which are compatible with the other obligations and challenges which he will encounter in the exercise of his activity.

53 Secondly, such an injunction allows its addressee to avoid liability by proving that he has taken all reasonable measures. That possibility of exoneration clearly has the effect that the addressee of the injunction will not be required to make unbearable sacrifices, which seems justified in particular in the light of the fact that he is not the author of the infringement of the fundamental right of intellectual property which has led to the adoption of the injunction.

54 In that regard, in accordance with the principle of legal certainty, it must be possible for the addressee of an injunction such as that at issue in the main proceedings to maintain before the court, once the implementing measures which he has taken are known and before any decision imposing a penalty on him is adopted, that the measures taken were indeed those which could be expected of him in order to prevent the proscribed result.

55 None the less, when the addressee of an injunction such as that at issue in the main proceedings chooses the measures to be adopted in order to comply with that injunction,

he must ensure compliance with the fundamental right of internet users to freedom of information.

56 In this respect, the measures adopted by the internet service provider must be strictly targeted, in the sense that they must serve to bring an end to a third party's infringement of copyright or of a related right but without thereby affecting internet users who are using the provider's services in order to lawfully access information. Failing that, the provider's interference in the freedom of information of those users would be unjustified in the light of the objective pursued.

57 It must be possible for national courts to check that that is the case. In the case of an injunction such as that at issue in the main proceedings, the Court notes that, if the internet service provider adopts measures which enable it to achieve the required prohibition, the national courts will not be able to carry out such a review at the stage of the enforcement proceedings if there is no challenge in that regard. Accordingly, in order to prevent the fundamental rights recognised by EU law from precluding the adoption of an injunction such as that at issue in the main proceedings, the national procedural rules must provide a possibility for internet users to assert their rights before the court once the implementing measures taken by the internet service provider are known.

58 As regards intellectual property, it should be pointed out at the outset that it is possible that the enforcement of an injunction such as that in the main proceedings will not lead to a complete cessation of the infringements of the intellectual property right of the persons concerned.

59 First, as has been stated, the addressee of such an injunction has the possibility of avoiding liability, and thus of not adopting some measures that may be achievable, if those measures are not capable of being considered reasonable.

60 Secondly, it is possible that a means of putting a complete end to the infringements of the intellectual property right does not exist or is not in practice achievable, as a result of which some measures taken might be capable of being circumvented in one way or another.

61 The Court notes that there is nothing whatsoever in the wording of Article 17(2) of the Charter to suggest that the right to intellectual property is inviolable and must for that reason be absolutely protected.

62 None the less, the measures which are taken by the addressee of an injunction, such as that at issue in the main proceedings, when implementing that injunction must be sufficiently effective to ensure genuine protection of the fundamental right at issue, that is to say that they must have the effect of preventing unauthorised access to the protected subject-matter or, at least, of making it difficult to achieve and of seriously discouraging internet users who are using the services of the addressee of that injunction from accessing the subject-matter made available to them in breach of that fundamental right.

63 Consequently, even though the measures taken when implementing an injunction such as that at issue in the main proceedings are not capable of leading, in some circumstances, to a complete cessation of the infringements of the intellectual property right, they cannot however be considered to be incompatible with the requirement that a fair balance be found, in accordance with Article 52(1), in fine, of the Charter, between all applicable fundamental rights, provided that (i) they do not unnecessarily deprive internet users of the possibility of lawfully accessing the information available and (ii) that they have the effect of preventing unauthorised access to protected subject-matter or, at least, of making it difficult to achieve and of seriously discouraging internet users who are using the services of the addressee of that injunction from accessing the subject-matter that has been made available to them in breach of the intellectual property right.

64 In the light of the foregoing considerations, the answer to the third question is that the fundamental rights recognised by EU law must be interpreted as not precluding a court injunction prohibiting an internet service provider from allowing its customers access to a website placing protected subject-matter online without the agreement of the rightholders when that injunction does not specify the measures which that access provider must take and when that access provider can avoid incurring coercive penalties for breach of that injunction by showing that it has taken all reasonable measures, provided that (i) the measures taken do not unnecessarily deprive internet users of the possibility of lawfully accessing the information available and (ii) that those measures have the effect of preventing unauthorised access to the protected subject-matter or, at least, of making it difficult to achieve and of seriously discouraging internet users who are using the services of the addressee of that injunction from accessing the subject-matter that has been made available to them in breach of the intellectual property right, that being a matter for the national authorities and courts to establish. (...)

THINK IT OVER!

1. In its two earlier preliminary rulings (the two *Sabam* cases) the CJEU concluded that any obligation against ISPs and hosting service providers to filter out all electronic communication passed via their services or information stored on their servers as a preventive measure, exclusively at their expense, for an unlimited period, and where such measures apply indiscriminately to all their customers runs afoul of the prohibition of general monitoring obligation under Article 15 of the E-Commerce Directive. According to the concept of "Erfolgsverbot" a given result must be reached or at least reasonable steps need to be taken to succeed, but the obliged service provider is flexible in selecting the necessary measures to reach this goal, too. *Is this concept specific enough to remain outside of the scope of Article 15? Does the filtering of allegedly infringing materials by ISPs or hosting providers have any deterring effects on end-users? What kind of measures can have the "effect of preventing unauthorized access to the protected subject-matter"? Is a continuous, pro-active/ preventive filtering still in compliance wth Article 15?* In *Alone in the Dark*, the German Federal Supreme Court concluded that the file-hosting service provider (cyberlocker) RapidShare is obliged to take steps to *prevent any further similar infringements* after being noticed, including manually controlling indexing sites. Furthermore, in *File-Hosting Dienst*, the same court held that RapidShare is similarly obliged to manually monitor Google's search engine, Twitter and Facebook, and filter out links to infringing materials.

2. The protection of intellectual property rights, including copyrights, is guaranteed as a fundamental right under the Charter of Fundament Rights of the European Union [see Article 17(2)], as well as the freedom to conduct a business (see Article 16) and the freedom of expression and information (see Article 11). *How is it possible to balance these different, but equally protected fundamental rights in the digital environment, especially in a P2P file-sharing context?*

Further Case Law

Case C-70/10 - Scarlet Extended SA v Société belge des auteurs, compositeurs et éditeurs SCRL (SABAM), Judgment of the Court (Third Chamber), 24 November 2011 [ECLI:EU:C:2011:771]

Case C-360/10 - Belgische Vereniging van Auteurs, Componisten en Uitgevers CVBA (SABAM) v Netlog NV, Judgment of the Court (Third Chamber), 16 February 2012 [ECLI:EU:C:2012:85]

The Football Association Premier League Ltd. v. British Sky Broadcasting Ltd., et al. [2013] *EWHC* 2058 (Ch)

BGH 12.7.2012 (I ZR 18/11) - Voraussetzungen für Störerhaftung von File-Hosting-Diensten - Alone in the Dark, *Gewerblicher Rechtsschutz und Urheberrecht*, Heft 4/2013, p. 370-375.

BGH 15.8.2013 (I ZR 80/12) - Konkretisierung der Störerhaftung von RapidShare - File-Hosting-Dienst, *Gewerblicher Rechtsschutz und Urheberrecht*, Heft 10/2013, p. 1030-1035.

Recommended readings

In English

Marianna Rantou: The growing tension between copyright and personal data protection on an online environment: The position of Internet Service Providers according to the European Court of Justice, *European Journal of Law and Technology*, Issue 2/2012, p. 1-24.

Evangelia Psychogiopoulou: Copyright Enforcement, Human Rights Protection and the Responsibilities of Internet Service Providers after Scarlet, *European Intellectual Property Review*, Issue 8/2012, p. 552-555.

Daniel Nagel: Network Blocking in the EU: A Slippery Slope to (Third Party) Censorship?, *Computer und Recht*, Issue 4/2014, p. 113-116.

Christina Angelopoulos: Are blocking injunctions against ISPs allowed in Europe? Copyright enforcement in the post-Telekabel EU legal landscape, *Journal of Intellectual Property Law and Practice*, Issue 10/2014, p. 812-821.

Tuomas Mylly: The Constitutionalization of the European Legal Order: Impact of Human Rights on Intellectual Property in the EU. In: Christophe Geiger: *Research Handbook on Human Rights and Intellectual Property*, Edgar Elgar, 2015: p. 103-131.

Karlijn Van den Heuvel: Next chapter in ISP's blocking battle: Dutch Supreme Court refers questions about indirect infringement by operators of the Pirate Bay to the CJEU, *European Intellectual Property Review*, Issue 9/2016, p. 577-580.

In French

Antonino Troianiello: La CJUE s'oppose au filtrage généralisé de l'internet, *Droit de l'immatériel: informatique, médias, communication*, 2012, n° 78, p. 71-75.

Lionel Costes: Mise en ligne sur des sites d'objets protégés sans l'accord des titulaires de droits: les précisions de la CJUE, *Droit de l'immatériel: informatique, médias, communication*, 2014, n° 103, p. 23-24.

Céline Castets-Renard: La coopération des fournisseurs d'accès à l'internet dans la lutte contre la contrefaçon: quelques précisions d'envergure, *Recueil Le Dalloz*, 2014, p. 1246-1249.

Guillaume Busseuil: La libre circulation des contenus numériques entre accès et consentement: les précisions de la CJUE en matière de respect des droits de propriété intellectuelle, *Droit de l'immatériel: informatique, médias, communication*, 2014, n° 105, p. 12-19.

Olivier Roux: Le FAI seul juge des mesures techniques «raisonnables» qu'il doit mettre en place pour exécuter une injonction de bloquer un site, *Droit de l'immatériel: informatique, médias, communication*, 2014, n° 105, p. 74-78.

Olivier Pignatari: Blocage de sites par un FAI: la CJUE débloque la situation en faveur du droit d'auteur?, *Droit de l'immatériel: informatique, médias, communication*, 2014, n° 105, p. 79-82.

In German

Nikolaus Kraft: Zugangssperren zu Webseiten als Mittel der Rechtsdurchsetzung - Anmerkungen zu den kino.to-Entscheidungen des EuGH und des OGH, *Medien und Recht*, Heft 4/2014, p. 171-174.

Jan Bernd Nordemann: Anmerkung zu EuGH, Urteil vom 27. März 2014 – C-314/12 – UPC Telekabel Wien GmbH/Constantin Film Verleih GmbH, Wega Filmproduktionsgesellschaft mbH (»Kino.to«), *Zeitschrift für Urheber- und Medienrecht*, Heft 6/2014, p. 499-501.

Gerald Spindler: Zivilrechtliche Sperrverfügungen gegen Access Provider nach dem EuGH-Urteil „UPC Telekabel“, *Gewerblicher Rechtsschutz und Urheberrecht*, Heft 9/2014, p. 826-834.

Guido Brinkel - Wolf Osthaus: Netzsperren - rote Linie der Verantwortlichkeit von Internet Zugangsvermittlern, *Computer und Recht*, Heft 10/2014, p. 642-650.

In Spanish

Sergio Salinas Alcega: Orden judicial a un proveedor de Internet para que bloquee el acceso de sus clientes a sitios que ponen a disposición del público producciones protegidas sin el consentimiento de los titulares de los derechos de autor - Sentencia del Tribunal de Justicia de 27 de marzo de 2014 (As. C-314/12) UPC Telekabel Wien, *Revista Aranzadi Unión Europea* 2014 n° 6, p. 53-56.

In Hungarian

Mezei Péter: *A fájlcsere dilemma - A perek lassúak, az internet gyors*, HVG-Orac, Budapest, 2012: p. 185-211.

Mezei Péter: Az Európai Bíróság ítélete a jogellenes tartalmakat szolgáltató streaming oldalak blokkolásának egyes kérdéseiről, *Jogesetek Magyarázata*, 2014/4. szám, p. 63-72.

BMG RIGHTS MANAGEMENT (US) LLC, ET AL. V. COX COMMUNICATIONS, INC., ET AL.

881 *F.3d* 293 (2018)

Motz, Circuit Judge

(...) Cox is a conduit Internet service provider ("ISP"), providing approximately 4.5 million subscribers with high-speed Internet access for a monthly fee. Some of Cox's subscribers shared and received copyrighted files, including music files, using a technology known as BitTorrent. BitTorrent is not a software program, but rather describes a protocol – a set of rules governing the communication between computers – that allows individual computers on the Internet to transfer files directly to other computers. This method of file sharing is commonly known as "peer-to-peer" file sharing, and contrasts with the traditional method of downloading a file from a central server using a Web browser.

Although peer-to-peer file sharing is not new, what makes BitTorrent unique is that it allows a user to download a file from multiple peers at the same time – even peers who only have a piece of the file, rather than the complete file. In other words, as soon as a user has downloaded a piece of the file, he or she can begin sharing that piece with others (while continuing to download the rest of the file). This innovation makes sharing via BitTorrent particularly fast and efficient. Although BitTorrent can be used to share any type of digital file, many use it to share copyrighted music and video files without authorization.

As a conduit ISP, Cox only provides Internet access to its subscribers. Cox does not create or sell software that operates using the BitTorrent protocol, store copyright-infringing material on its own computer servers, or control what its subscribers store on their personal computers.

Cox's agreement with its subscribers reserves the right to suspend or terminate subscribers who use Cox's service "to post, copy, transmit, or disseminate any content that infringes the patents, copyrights ... or proprietary rights of any party." To enforce that agreement and protect itself from liability, however, Cox created only a very limited automated system to process notifications of alleged infringement received from copyright owners. Cox's automated system rests on a thirteen-strike policy that determines the action to be taken based on how many notices

Cox has previously received regarding infringement by a particular subscriber. The first notice alleging a subscriber's infringement produces no action from Cox. The second through seventh notices result in warning emails from Cox to the subscriber. After the eighth and ninth notices, Cox limits the subscriber's Internet access to a single webpage that contains a warning, but the subscriber can reactivate complete service by clicking an acknowledgement. After the tenth and eleventh notices, Cox suspends services, requiring the subscriber to call a technician, who, after explaining the reason for suspension and advising removal of infringing content, reactivates service. After the twelfth notice, the subscriber is suspended and directed to a specialized technician, who, after another warning to cease infringing conduct, reactivates service. After the thirteenth notice, the subscriber is again suspended, and, for the first time, considered for termination. Cox never automatically terminates a subscriber.

The effectiveness of Cox's thirteen-strike policy as a deterrent to copyright infringement has several additional limitations. Cox restricts the number of notices it will process from any copyright holder or agent in one day; any notice received after this limit has been met does not count in Cox's graduated response escalation. Cox also counts only one notice per subscriber per day. And Cox resets a subscriber's thirteen-strike counter every six months.

BMG, a music publishing company, owns copyrights in musical compositions. To protect this copyrighted material, BMG hired Rightscorp, Inc., which monitors BitTorrent activity to determine when infringers share its clients' copyrighted works. When Rightscorp identifies such sharing, it emails an infringement notice to the alleged infringer's ISP (here, Cox). The notice contains the name of the copyright owner (here, BMG), the title of the copyrighted work, the alleged infringer's IP address, a time stamp, and a statement under penalty of perjury that Rightscorp is an authorized agent and the notice is accurate.

Rightscorp also asks the ISP to forward the notice to the allegedly infringing subscriber, since only the ISP can match the IP address to the subscriber's identity. For that purpose, the notice contains a settlement offer, allowing the alleged infringer to pay twenty or thirty dollars for a release from liability for the instance of infringement alleged in the notice. Cox has determined to refuse to forward or process notices that contain such settlement language. When Cox began receiving Rightscorp notices in the spring of 2011 (before Rightscorp had signed BMG as a client), Cox notified Rightscorp that it would process the notices only if Rightscorp removed the settlement language. Rightscorp did not do so. Cox never considered removing the settlement language itself or using other means to inform its subscribers of the allegedly infringing activity observed by Rightscorp.

Rightscorp continued to send Cox large numbers of settlement notices. In the fall of 2011, Cox decided to "blacklist" Rightscorp, meaning Cox would delete notices received from Rightscorp without acting on them or even viewing them. BMG hired Rightscorp in December 2011 – *after* Cox blacklisted Rightscorp. Thus, Cox did not ever view a single one of the millions of notices that Rightscorp sent to Cox on BMG's behalf.

On November 26, 2014, BMG initiated this action against Cox. BMG alleged that Cox was vicariously and contributorily liable for acts of copyright infringement by its subscribers.

At the conclusion of discovery, the parties filed multi-issue cross-motions for summary judgment, which the district court resolved in a careful written opinion. Among these issues, BMG asserted that Cox had not established a policy entitling it to the safe harbor defense contained in the Digital Millennium Copyright Act ("DMCA"), 17 U.S.C. § 512(a). To qualify for that safe harbor, an ISP, like Cox, must have "adopted and reasonably implemented ... a policy that provides for the termination in appropriate circumstances of subscribers ... who are repeat infringers." § 512(i)(1)(A). The district court agreed with BMG and held that no reasonable jury could find that Cox implemented a policy that entitled it to that DMCA safe harbor. The court explained that BMG had offered evidence that "Cox knew accounts were being used repeatedly for infringing activity yet failed to terminate" those accounts and that Cox did "not come forward with any evidence" to the contrary. Accordingly, the court granted summary judgment to BMG on Cox's safe harbor defense.

The case proceeded to a jury trial that involved the testimony of more than a dozen witnesses and admission of numerous documents. At the conclusion of the trial, the district court instructed the jury that to prove contributory infringement, BMG had to show "direct infringement of BMG's copyrighted works" by Cox subscribers, that "Cox knew or should have known of such infringing activity," and that "Cox induced, caused, or materially contributed to such infringing activity." The court further instructed the jury that BMG could prove Cox's knowledge of infringing activity by showing willful blindness, if Cox "was aware of a high probability that Cox users were infringing BMG's copyrights but consciously avoided confirming that fact."

The jury found Cox liable for willful contributory infringement and awarded BMG $25 million in statutory damages. The jury also found that Cox was not liable for vicarious infringement. The district court denied all post-trial motions and entered judgment in accordance with the verdict. Cox appeals, arguing that BMG should not have been granted summary judgment as to the DMCA safe harbor and that erroneous jury instructions entitle it to a new trial.

We first address Cox's contention that the district court erred in denying it the § 512(a) DMCA safe harbor defense. We review de novo the grant of summary judgment.

The DMCA provides a series of safe harbors that limit the copyright infringement liability of an ISP and related entities. As a conduit ISP, Cox seeks the benefit of the safe harbor contained in 17 U.S.C. § 512(a). To fall within that safe harbor, Cox must show that it meets the threshold requirement, common to all § 512 safe harbors, that it has "adopted and reasonably implemented ... a policy that provides for the termination in appropriate circumstances of subscribers ... who are repeat infringers."

Cox's principal contention is that "repeat infringers" means *adjudicated* repeat infringers: people who have been held liable by a court for multiple instances of copyright infringement. Cox asserts that it complied with § 512(i)(1)(A)'s requirement and is therefore entitled to the §

512(a) DMCA safe harbor because BMG did not show that Cox failed to terminate any adjudicated infringers. BMG responds that Cox's interpretation of "repeat infringers" is contrary to "the DMCA's plain terms."

Because the statute does not define the term "repeat infringers," to resolve that question, we turn first to the term's ordinary meaning. The ordinary meaning of an infringer is "[s]omeone who interferes with one of the exclusive rights of a ... copyright" holder – in short, one who infringes a copyright. A repeat infringer, then, is one who infringes a copyright more than once.

Cox contends that because the repeat infringer provision uses the term "infringer" without modifiers such as "alleged" or "claimed" that appear elsewhere in the DMCA, "infringer" must mean "adjudicated infringer." But the DMCA's use of phrases like "alleged infringer" in other portions of the statute indicates only that the term "infringer" alone must mean something different than "alleged infringer," otherwise, the word "alleged" would be superfluous. Using the ordinary meaning of "infringer," however, fully accords with this principle: someone who *actually* infringes a copyright differs from someone who has merely *allegedly* infringed a copyright, because an allegation could be false. The need to differentiate the terms "infringer" and "alleged infringer" thus does not mandate Cox's proposed definition.

Moreover, other provisions of the Copyright Act use the term "infringer" (and similar terms) to refer to all who engage in infringing activity, not just the narrow subset of those who have been so adjudicated by a court. For example, § 501(a), which creates a civil cause of action for copyright owners, states that "[a]nyone who violates any of the exclusive rights of the copyright owner" provided for in the statute "is an *infringer* of the copyright or right of the author."

Similarly, the DMCA itself provides that ISPs who store copyrighted material are generally not liable for removing "material or activity *claimed to be infringing or* based on facts or circumstances from which *infringing activity is apparent*, regardless of whether the material or activity is *ultimately determined to be infringing*." § 512(g)(1) (emphases added). This provision expressly distinguishes among three categories of activity: activity merely "claimed to be infringing," actual "infringing activity" (as is apparent from "facts or circumstances"), and activity "ultimately determined to be infringing." The distinction between "infringing activity" and activity "ultimately determined to be infringing" in § 512(g) shelters ISPs from being liable for taking down material that *is* "infringing," even if no court "ultimately determine[s]" that it is infringing – because, for example, the copyright holder simply does not file a lawsuit against the person who uploaded the infringing material. As this provision illustrates, Congress knew how to expressly refer to adjudicated infringement, but did not do so in the repeat infringer provision. That suggests the term "infringer" in § 512(i) is not limited to adjudicated infringers.

The legislative history of the repeat infringer provision supports this conclusion. Both the House Commerce and Senate Judiciary Committee Reports explained that "those who repeatedly or flagrantly abuse their access to the Internet through disrespect for the intellectual property rights of others should know that there is a realistic threat of losing that access." H.R. Rep. No. 105-551, pt. 2, at 61 (1998); S. Rep. No. 105-190, at 52 (1998). This passage makes clear that if persons "abuse their access to the Internet through disrespect for the intellectual property rights of others" – that is, if they infringe copyrights – they should face a "realistic threat of losing" their Internet access. The passage does not suggest that they should risk losing Internet access only once they have been sued in court and found liable for multiple instances of infringement. Indeed, the risk of losing one's Internet access would hardly constitute a "realistic threat" capable of deterring infringement if that punishment applied only to those *already* subject to civil penalties and legal fees as adjudicated infringers.

The only circuit to expressly consider the definition of a "repeat infringer" in the DMCA has defined it to mean "someone who interferes with one of the exclusive rights of a copyright" "again or repeatedly." Cox does not cite a single case adopting its contrary view that only adjudicated infringers can be "repeat infringers" for purposes of the DMCA.

Accordingly, we reject Cox's argument that the term "repeat infringers" in § 512(i) is limited to adjudicated infringers.

Section 512(i) thus requires that, to obtain the benefit of the DMCA safe harbor, Cox must have reasonably implemented "a policy that provides for the termination in appropriate circumstances" of its subscribers who repeatedly infringe copyrights. We are mindful of the need to afford ISPs flexibility in crafting repeat infringer policies, and of the difficulty of determining when it is "appropriate" to terminate a person's access to the Internet. At a minimum, however, an ISP has not "reasonably implemented" a repeat infringer policy if the ISP fails to enforce the terms of its policy in any meaningful fashion. Here, Cox formally adopted a repeat infringer "policy," but, both before and after September 2012, made every effort to avoid reasonably implementing that policy. Indeed, in carrying out its thirteen-strike process, Cox very clearly determined *not* to terminate subscribers who in fact repeatedly violated the policy.

The words of Cox's own employees confirm this conclusion. In a 2009 email, Jason Zabek, the executive managing the Abuse Group, a team tasked with addressing subscribers' violations of Cox's policies, explained to his team that "if a customer is terminated for DMCA, you are able to reactivate them," and that "[a]fter you reactivate them the DMCA 'counter' restarts." The email continued, "This is to be an unwritten semi-policy." Zabek also advised a customer service representative asking whether she could reactivate a terminated subscriber that "[i]f it is for DMCA you can go ahead and reactivate." Zabek explained to another representative: "Once the customer has been terminated for DMCA, we have fulfilled the obligation of the DMCA safe harbor and can start over." He elaborated that this would allow Cox to "collect a few extra weeks of payments for their account. ;-)." Another email summarized Cox's practice more succinctly: "DMCA = reactivate." As a result of this practice, from the beginning of the litigated time period until September 2012, Cox *never* terminated a subscriber for infringement without reactivating them.

Cox nonetheless contends that it lacked "actual knowledge" of its subscribers' infringement and therefore did not have to terminate them. That argument misses the mark. The evidence shows that Cox *always* reactivated subscribers after termination, regardless of its knowledge of the subscriber's infringement. Cox did not, for example, advise employees *not* to reactivate a subscriber if the employees had reliable information regarding the subscriber's repeat infringement. An ISP cannot claim the protections of the DMCA safe harbor provisions merely by terminating customers as a symbolic gesture before indiscriminately reactivating them within a short timeframe.

In September 2012, Cox abandoned its practice of routine reactivation. An internal email advised a new customer service representative that "we now terminate, for real." BMG argues, however, that this was a change in form rather than substance, because instead of terminating and then reactivating subscribers, Cox simply stopped terminating them in the first place. The record evidence supports this view. Before September 2012, Cox was terminating (and reactivating) 15.5 subscribers per month on average; after September 2012, Cox abruptly began terminating *less than one* subscriber per month on average. From September 2012 until the end of October 2014, the month before BMG filed suit, Cox issued only 21 terminations in total. Moreover, at least 17 of those 21 terminations concerned subscribers who had either failed to pay their bills on time or used excessive bandwidth (something that Cox subjected to a strict three-strike termination policy). Cox did not provide evidence that the remaining four terminations were for repeat copyright infringement. But even assuming they were, they stand in stark contrast to the over 500,000 email warnings and temporary suspensions Cox issued to alleged infringers during the same time period.

Moreover, Cox dispensed with terminating subscribers who repeatedly infringed BMG's copyrights in particular when it decided to delete automatically all infringement notices received from BMG's agent, Rightscorp. As a result, Cox received none of the millions of infringement notices that Rightscorp sent to Cox on BMG's behalf during the relevant period. Although our inquiry concerns Cox's policy toward all of its repeatedly infringing subscribers, not just those who infringed BMG's copyrights, Cox's decision to categorically disregard all notices from Rightscorp provides further evidence that Cox did not reasonably implement a repeat infringer policy.

BMG also provided evidence of particular instances in which Cox failed to terminate subscribers whom Cox employees regarded as repeat infringers. For example, one subscriber "was advised to stop sharing ... and remove his PTP programs," and a Cox employee noted that the subscriber was "well aware of his actions" and was "upset that 'after years of doing this' he is now getting caught." Nonetheless, Cox did not terminate the subscriber. Another customer was advised that "further complaints would result in termination" and that it was the customer's "absolute last chance to ... remove ALL" file-sharing software. But when Cox received another complaint, a manager directed the employee *not* to terminate, but rather to "suspend this Customer, one LAST time," noting that "[t]his customer pays us over $400/month" and that "[e]very terminated Customer becomes lost revenue."

Cox responds that these post-September 2012 emails do not necessarily "*prove* actual knowledge of repeat infringement." Again, that argument is misplaced. Cox bears the burden of proof on the DMCA safe harbor defense; thus, Cox had to point to evidence showing that it reasonably implemented a repeat infringer policy. The emails show that Cox internally concluded that a subscriber should be terminated after the next strike, but then declined to do so because it did not want to lose revenue. In other words, Cox failed to follow through on its own policy. Cox argues that these emails only concerned "four cases," and that "occasional lapses" are forgivable. But even four cases are significant when measured against Cox's equally small total number of relevant terminations in this period – also four. More importantly, Cox did not produce any evidence of instances in which it *did* follow through on its policy and terminate subscribers after giving them a final warning to stop infringing.

In addition, Cox suggests that because the DMCA merely requires termination of repeat infringers in "appropriate circumstances," Cox decided not to terminate certain subscribers only when "appropriate circumstances" were lacking. But Cox failed to provide evidence that a determination of "appropriate circumstances" played *any* role in its decisions to terminate (or not to terminate). Cox did not, for example, point to any criteria that its employees used to determine whether "appropriate circumstances" for termination existed. Instead, the evidence shows that Cox's decisions not to terminate had nothing to do with "appropriate circumstances" but instead were based on one goal: not losing revenue from paying subscribers.

Cox failed to qualify for the DMCA safe harbor because it failed to implement its policy in any consistent or meaningful way – leaving it essentially with no policy. Accordingly, the district court did not err in holding that Cox failed to offer evidence supporting its entitlement to the § 512(a) safe harbor defense and therefore granting summary judgment on this issue to BMG.

We turn to Cox's other principal challenge to the judgment: that the district court erred in instructing the jury as to contributory infringement. (...)

Cox's initial jury instruction argument rests on its contention that it cannot be held liable for contributory copyright infringement because its technology is "capable of substantial noninfringing use." According to Cox, the district court erred in refusing "to instruct the jury on this principle."

This argument is meritless. Of course, the mere sale of a product that has both lawful and unlawful uses does not in and of itself establish an intent to infringe. That is the holding of *Sony Corp. of Am. v. Universal City Studios, Inc.* In *Sony*, copyright holders sought to hold Sony contributorily liable for selling video cassette recorders (VCRs) that customers used to tape copyrighted programs. The Supreme Court rejected that claim, holding that because a VCR was "capable of commercially significant noninfringing uses," its manufacturer, Sony, could not be held contributory liable for distribution of the VCR.

A few courts initially interpreted *Sony*'s limitation, as Cox does, to mean that if a product can be substantially used lawfully, its producer *cannot* be contributorily liable for copyright infringement. But in *Grokster*, the Supreme Court rejected this broad reading. The Court clarified that "*Sony* barred secondary liability based on *presuming or imputing intent* to cause infringement solely from the design or distribution of a product capable of substantial lawful use, which the distributor knows is in fact used for infringement." The *Grokster* Court explained that under *Sony*, intent to infringe will not be presumed from "the equivocal conduct of selling an item with substantial lawful as well as unlawful uses," even when the seller has the "understanding that some of [his or her] products will be misused." More is needed. But the fact that a product is "capable of substantial lawful use" does not mean the "producer can never be held contributorily liable."

Exactly the same flaw infects Cox's related argument that the district court erred in refusing to instruct the jury that "[i]t is not a material contribution to provide a product or service that is capable of substantial non-infringing uses." As the Supreme Court explained, reversal was required in *Grokster* because the Ninth Circuit had "read *Sony*'s limitation to mean that whenever a product is capable of substantial lawful use, the producer can never be held contributorily liable for third parties' infringing use of it .... [t]his view of *Sony*, however, was error".

Because the instruction Cox requested misstates the law, the district court did not err in refusing to give it. In fact, providing a product with "substantial non-infringing uses" *can* constitute a material contribution to copyright infringement. *Grokster* makes clear that what matters is not simply whether the product has some or even many non-infringing uses, but whether the product is distributed with the *intent* to cause copyright infringement.

Thus, contrary to Cox's argument, the fact that its technology can be substantially employed for a noninfringing use does not immunize it from liability for contributory copyright infringement. The district court did not err in refusing to instruct the jury to the contrary.

Alternatively, Cox offers a more nuanced attack on the contributory infringement instructions. Cox contends that the court erred in charging the jury as to the intent necessary to prove contributory infringement. Specifically, Cox challenges the district court's instructions that the jury could impose liability for contributory infringement if the jury found "Cox knew or should have known of such infringing activity." We agree that in so instructing the jury, the court erred.

Grokster teaches that "[o]ne infringes contributorily by *intentionally* inducing or encouraging direct infringement." The requisite intent may, however, be presumed according to the "rules of fault-based liability derived from the common law." The most relevant of these common law rules is that if a person "knows that the consequences are certain, or substantially certain, to result from his act, and still goes ahead, he is treated by the law as if he had in fact desired to produce the result." Under this principle, "when an article is good for nothing else but infringement ... there is no injustice in presuming or imputing an intent to infringe" based on its sale. Assuming the seller is aware of the nature of his product – that its only use is infringing – he knows that infringement is substantially certain to result from his sale of that product and he may therefore be presumed to intend that result.

A similar result follows when a person sells a product that has lawful uses, but with the *knowledge* that the buyer *will in fact* use the product to infringe copyrights. In that circumstance, the seller knows that infringement is substantially certain to result from the sale; consequently, the seller intends to cause infringement just as much as a seller who provides a product that has exclusively unlawful uses. Indeed, *Henry*, a hundred-year-old Supreme Court case involving contributory patent infringement that the Supreme Court cited in *Grokster* and *Sony*, rests on this very reasoning. There, the Court affirmed a judgment for contributory infringement based on the defendants' sale to a specific person with knowledge that the product would be used to infringe, even though the product – ink – also had noninfringing uses. The Court reasoned that because the defendants sold the ink "with the expectation that it would be used" to infringe, "the purpose and intent that it would be so used" could be presumed.

These principles apply equally in cases, like this one, that involve subscription services or rentals rather than one-time sales. Consider a company that leases VCRs, learns that specific customers use their VCRs to infringe, but nonetheless renews the lease to those infringing customers. Given those facts, the company knows that its action – renewing the lease of the VCR to these specific customers – is substantially certain to result in infringement, and so an intent to cause infringement may be presumed.

It is well-established that one mental state slightly less demanding than actual knowledge – willful blindness – can establish the requisite intent for contributory copyright infringement. This is so because the law recognizes willful blindness as *equivalent* to actual knowledge.

Whether other mental states – such as negligence (where a defendant "should have known" of infringement) – can suffice to prove contributory copyright infringement presents a more difficult question. The notion that contributory liability could be imposed based on something less than actual knowledge, or its equivalent, willful blindness, is not entirely without support. Nonetheless, we believe for several reasons, that, as Cox contends, negligence does not suffice to prove contributory infringement; rather, at least willful blindness is required.

First, *Grokster*'s recitation of the standard – that "[o]ne infringes contributorily by *intentionally* inducing or encouraging direct infringement" – is on its face difficult to reconcile with a negligence standard. In addition, it would have been unnecessary for the Court to discuss in detail the situations in which intent may be presumed, and those situations, like *Sony*, in which it may not, if liability did not require intent at all, but merely required negligence.

Looking to patent law, as the Supreme Court did in *Sony* and *Grokster*, further counsels against a negligence standard. The Supreme Court has long held that contributory patent infringement requires knowledge of direct infringement. And in 2011, the Court held that willful blindness satisfies this knowledge requirement, but recklessness ("one who merely knows of a substantial and unjustified risk of ... wrongdoing") and negligence ("one who should have known of a similar risk but, in fact, did not") do not. The Court reaffirmed this holding in 2015, stating that contributory patent infringement "requires proof the defendant knew the acts were infringing," and that *Global–Tech* "was clear in rejecting any lesser mental state as the standard." The Court expressly rejected the possibility "that a person, or entity, could be liable even though he did not know the acts were infringing." Thus, in the patent context, it is clear that contributory infringement cannot be based on a finding that a defendant "should have known" of infringement.

In both *Grokster* and *Sony*, the Supreme Court adopted now-codified patent law doctrines – the staple article doctrine and the inducement rule. The Court did so because of "the historic kinship between patent law and copyright law," and the similar need in both contexts to impose liability on "culpable expression and conduct" without "discouraging the development of technologies with lawful and unlawful potential". We are persuaded that the *Global–Tech* rule developed in the patent law context, which held that contributory liability can be based on willful blindness but not on recklessness or negligence, is a sensible one in the copyright context. It appropriately targets culpable conduct without unduly burdening technological development.

The law of aiding and abetting, "the criminal counterpart to contributory infringement," similarly militates against adoption of a negligence standard. A person "aids and abets a crime when ... he intends to facilitate that offense's commission." The necessary intent can be presumed only "when a person actively participates in a criminal venture with full *knowledge* of the circumstances constituting the charged offense."

Furthermore, "[t]he Restatement of Torts, under a concert of action principle, accepts a doctrine with rough similarity to criminal aiding and abetting," and therefore provides another analog to contributory infringement. "An actor is liable for harm resulting to a third person from the tortious conduct of another 'if he *knows* that the other's conduct constitutes a breach of duty and gives substantial assistance or encouragement to the other.'" Because the Restatement here uses only the word "knows," where in other places it uses phrases like "knows or should know," it is clear that "knows" here refers to actual knowledge, not any lesser mental state. And the Second Circuit's widely-cited *Gershwin* decision on contributory infringement expressly drew on precisely this "common law doctrine that one who *knowingly* participates or furthers a tortious act is jointly and severally liable with the prime tortfeasor."

We therefore hold that proving contributory infringement requires proof of at least willful blindness; negligence is insufficient.

In arguing to the contrary, BMG relies on a pre-*Grokster* decision, *Ellison v. Robertson*, in which the Ninth Circuit stated that some of its precedents had "interpreted the knowledge requirement for contributory copyright infringement to include both those with *actual knowledge* and those who *have reason to know* of direct infringement." But the Ninth Circuit has since clarified, consistent with our holding today, that contributory infringement requires "actual knowledge of specific acts of infringement" or "[w]illful blindness of specific facts."

BMG also argues that "*Sony* itself described a case where the defendant 'knew *or should have known*' of the infringement as a "situation[ ] in which the imposition of [contributory] liability is manifestly just." BMG misreads *Sony*. The quoted sentence refers to *vicarious* liability, stating that imposing liability is "manifestly just" where the defendant can "control the use of copyrighted works by others" – which is an element of vicarious liability, but not of contributory infringement.

In a footnote to that sentence, *Sony* cited numerous lower court cases, including one in which the district court held that an infringer's advertising agency and similar defendants could be held contributorily liable if they "knew or should have known that they were dealing in illegal goods." Although that district court used the phrase "knew or should have known," the allegation in that case was that the defendants were dealing with counterfeit musical records priced "so suspiciously below the usual market price" that the defendants must have known or "deliberately closed [their] eyes" to the fact that the records were infringing. In such circumstances, liability could be imposed based on a theory of willful blindness, making it unnecessary to permit the imposition of liability based on a lesser negligence standard.

In sum, the district court erred in charging the jury that Cox could be found liable for contributory infringement if it "knew or should have known of such infringing activity." The formulation "should have known" reflects negligence and is therefore too low a standard. And because there is a reasonable probability that this erroneous instruction affected the jury's verdict, we remand for a new trial.

Cox asserts two further errors in the district court's contributory infringement instructions. Although Cox may not have adequately preserved these errors for review, we address them in the interest of judicial economy to ensure the correctness of the contributory infringement instructions on remand.

First, Cox contends that the district court erred in instructing the jury that Cox could be held liable for contributory copyright infringement on the basis of proof of "direct infringement of BMG's copyrighted works by users of Cox's Internet services" and that Cox knew "of such activity." Cox maintains that such "generalized knowledge – that infringement was occurring somewhere on its network – is exactly what falls short under *Sony*." We must agree.

Selling a product with both lawful and unlawful uses suggests an intent to cause infringement only if the seller knows of *specific* instances of infringement, but not if the seller only *generally* knows of infringement. A seller who only generally knows of infringement is aware that "some of [his] products will be misused" – but critically, not *which* products will be misused. Thus, when that seller makes a sale to a specific customer, the seller knows only that the customer *may* infringe, not that the customer is substantially certain to do so.

BMG does not dispute that the requisite mental state must be tied to specific infringements; it contends, however, that the court's instructions in fact "tied knowledge to specific acts of direct infringement." BMG rests on the fact that the instruction required that Cox knew "of *such* infringing activity," and that *such* infringing activity referred back to "direct infringement of BMG's copyrighted works by users of Cox's Internet service."

It does not follow, however, that a jury so instructed found that Cox had knowledge of specific infringements. For example, the jury could have found that Cox knew of "direct infringement of BMG's copyrighted works" by its subscribers if Cox had data showing that *some number of its subscribers* were infringing BMG's copyrights, even if the data did not show *which ones* were infringing. That level of generalized knowledge does not reflect an intent to cause infringement, because it is not knowledge that infringement is substantially certain to result from Cox's continued provision of Internet access to particular subscribers. Put another way, the proper standard requires a defendant to have specific enough knowledge of infringement that the defendant could *do* something about it. On remand, therefore, the contributory infringement instruction should require that Cox knew of specific instances of infringement or was willfully blind to such instances.

Relatedly, Cox challenges the district court's willful blindness instruction. The court instructed the jury that Cox "acted with willful blindness if it was aware of a high probability that Cox users were infringing BMG's copyrights but consciously avoided confirming that fact." Since we have held that contributory infringement requires knowledge of, or willful blindness to, *specific instances* of infringement, the court's willful blindness instruction should similarly require a conclusion that Cox consciously avoided learning about specific instances of infringement, not merely that Cox avoided confirming the fact that "Cox users were infringing BMG's copyrights" in general.

Although we have concluded that the district court incorrectly instructed the jury in some instances, we reject Cox's argument that with proper instructions, it is entitled to judgment as a matter of law. The district court's thoroughness and sure grasp of numerous complex issues provide a model of fair administration of justice. At trial, BMG offered powerful evidence from which a reasonable jury could find that Cox willfully blinded itself to specific instances of infringement by its subscribers, such as evidence that Cox prevented itself from receiving any of the more than one million notices Rightscorp sent on BMG's behalf. Indeed, that appears to be the primary theory for liability advanced by BMG. That determination, of course, must be made by a jury properly instructed as to the law. But the trial record provides no basis for judgment as a matter of law in Cox's favor.

Cox advances several other claims of error. None have merit.

Cox challenges the district court's willfulness instruction, arguing that it incorrectly required "the jury to analyze Cox's knowledge of its *subscribers'* actions," rather than Cox's knowledge that "*its actions* constitute an infringement." BMG contends that Cox failed to preserve this objection. We need not address whether Cox waived the objection because we reject it on the merits. Cox does not dispute that willfulness in copyright law is satisfied by recklessness, and the case law defines recklessness broadly. For example, we have explained that copyright infringement is willful if the defendant "recklessly disregards a copyright holder's rights." The Second Circuit has similarly held that a finding of willfulness is appropriate if "the defendant's actions were the result of 'reckless disregard' for … the copyright holder's rights." Contributorily (or vicariously) infringing with knowledge that one's subscribers are infringing is consistent with at least reckless disregard for the copyright holder's rights.

Cox next argues that the court erred by declining to give an innocent infringer instruction. Again, we disagree. Innocent infringer status (which may reduce damages) is only available if the infringer can prove that he or she "had no reason to believe that his or her acts constituted an infringement." 17 U.S.C. § 504(c)(2). For example, the Second Circuit upheld a district court's conclusion as to innocent infringement where an infringing music wholesaler reasonably believed that it had received the right to make copies of copyrighted albums under an agreement with the copyright holder. Cox does not suggest such circumstances were present here. The district court therefore correctly concluded that an innocent infringer instruction was not available to Cox.

Cox also challenges the district court's DMCA instruction. At trial, witnesses and documents often referred to the DMCA and its safe harbor provisions. Because the court held Cox not entitled to any DMCA safe harbor defense at summary judgment, it instructed the jury that "the DMCA is not a defense in this case and must be disregarded." Cox fails to show that this instruction – which is not a misstatement of the law – constitutes an abuse of discretion. Cox's theory is that the instruction "suggested that Cox's alleged failure to qualify for the DMCA defense made it liable for infringement." But the district court clearly instructed the jury that it alone would determine the facts and weigh the evidence. And indeed, the jury found Cox not liable for vicarious infringement, suggesting it was not so easily confused.

We also reject Cox's assertions that the district court erred in its evidentiary rulings, which we review for abuse of discretion.

Cox unpersuasively argues that the court abused its discretion by admitting Rightscorp's notices because the notices were hearsay. The district court correctly concluded that the information contained in the notices was not hearsay because it was generated by a computer and thus was not a "statement." Contrary to Cox's argument, the fact that the machine-generated notices also contained the signature of Rightscorp's CEO and an oath under penalty of perjury does not transform them into statements, since the information itself was not prepared or created by a human.

Nor were the notices excludable as more prejudicial than probative under Federal Rule of Evidence 403. The notices were certainly probative, and although they disfavored Cox's position, Cox fails to demonstrate that they were "*unfairly* prejudicial." "The 'mere fact that the evidence will damage the defendant's case is not enough' " to establish unfair prejudice.

Cox next faults the district court for admitting two studies examining how much of the content shared using BitTorrent is infringing. Cox argues that the court erred by admitting these studies under Federal Rule of Evidence 803(17), the hearsay exception for "compilations that are generally relied on ... by persons in particular occupations." Given that BMG's expert, Dr. William Lehr, testified that the two studies "were widely cited in the industry" and were "the most substantial published publicly available studies" on the issue, the court did not abuse its discretion.

Finally, Cox contends that the district court erroneously "allowed BMG's witnesses and attorneys to use the term 'infringement' pervasively when referring to Rightscorp's automated observations." But as we have explained above, the court clearly and carefully instructed the jurors that they alone could determine infringement. The court even interrupted BMG's expert testimony to instruct the jury that BMG's expert was using the word infringement to describe "the contents in the notices," but that the jury would "be making the ultimate decision" on infringement. Accordingly, the court did not abuse its discretion.

For the reasons stated above, we affirm the district court's grant of summary judgment to BMG on the § 512(a) DMCA safe harbor defense, but reverse and remand for a new trial. We also vacate the district court's grant of attorney's fees and costs to BMG and its denial of fees and costs to Cox.

AFFIRMED IN PART, REVERSED IN PART, VACATED IN PART, AND REMANDED.

THINK IT OVER!

1. The Court concluded that Cox's repeat infringer policy wasn't effectively executed, and that it was generally loose, too. *What can be an effective repeat infringer policy under the DMCA? Would the elimination of "rolling-up" the daily complaints make Cox's system reasonable enough? Are the 14 notices too many?* For your consideration: the E-Commerce Directive of the European Union does not include any word on repeat infringer policies. *Would it be reasonable to introduce such a new obligation on the service providers' side in the EU?* You might take a look at the European Union's Directive (EU) 2019/790 on copyright and related rights in the Digital Single Market. Under the heavily contested Article 17 (or Article 13 in the drafts) of the directive, online content-sharing service providers shall be obliged to authorize all uses via their platforms. In case the service provider misses to authorize the uses, it "shall be liable for unauthorised acts of communication to the public, including making available to the public, of copyright-protected works and other subject matter, unless the service providers demonstrate that they have:

(a) made best efforts to obtain an authorisation, and

(b) made, in accordance with high industry standards of professional diligence, best efforts to ensure the unavailability of specific works and other subject matter for which the rightholders have provided the service providers with the relevant and necessary information; and in any event

(c) acted expeditiously, upon receiving a sufficiently substantiated notice from the rightholders, to disable access to, or to remove from their websites, the notified works or other subject matter, and made best efforts to prevent their future uploads in accordance with point (b)."

Is this a more effective method to tackle infringements rather than the termination of repeat infringers' subscriptions?

2. The Circuit Court spent considerable time with the discussion of what standard (level of knowledge) is required for finding Cox liable. The Court refused the low standard of negligence, but referred to "factual knowledge" ["(...) the knowledge that the buyer will in fact use the product (...)"], "actual knowledge", "willful blindness", and "intentional inducement". *Please discuss what these standards might mean, and which is the most relevant to use in a platform economy.*

Further Case Law

Hotaling v. Church of Jesus Christ of Latter-Day Saints, 118 *F.3d* 199 (1997)

Capitol Records, Inc. v. MP3Tunes, LLC, 821 *F.Supp.2d* 627 (2011)

Viacom International Inc., et al., v. YouTube Inc., et al., 940 *F.Supp.2d* 110 (2013)

UMG Recordings, Inc., et al. v. Grande Communications Networks LLC, 384 F.Supp.3d 743 (2019)

Recommended readings

In English
Erik Estrada - Caitlin Cronin - Bill Gillespie: How Much Can Dumb Pipes Know? BMG v. Cox and Why a Knowledge Bar to DMCA Safe Harbor for Internet Service Providers is Inappropriate, *Denver Law Review Online*, 2016: p. 1-5.
Amanda Reid: Considerin Fair Use: DMCA's Take Down & Repeat Infringers Policies, *Communication Law and Policy*, Winter, 2019: p. 101-141.

ZHUANG ZEDONG, SASAKI MIKI V. SHANGHAI YINZHI NETWORK TECHNOLOGY CO., LTD.

(2010) Shanghai No. 1. Intermediate People's Court Civil (IP tribunal) Final No.33 Civil Judgement

The plaintiffs, Zhuang Zedong and Sasaki Miki, are the authors of the book "Deng Xiaoping's Approval of Our Marriage". The defendant, Yinzhi Company, is the operator of the VeryCD website. The website provides a P2P file-sharing platform. In March 2010, the plaintiffs found that the defendant's website provided access to an audio book version of "Deng Xiaoping's Approval of Our Marriage". The username of the releaser of the audio book was "nobodyvs-somebody". The plaintiffs believed that the defendant spread the audio book without authorization, and so infringed their copyright. The plaintiffs filed a suit and claimed that the defendant should stop the infringement and compensate for their economic losses of RMB 530,000. The defendant argued that the website did not provide the work on its own initiative, and the audio book was uploaded by an end-user. The defendand argued that it is neither directly, nor contributorily liable for end-users' acts. The defendant further argued that it took timely measures to block the keywords of the book, fulfilling its management responsibility with duty of care, and thus it should not take the corresponding legal responsibility.

Rules

Regulation on the Protection of the Right to Communicate Works to the Public over Information Networks (2006)

Article 23 Where a network service provider provides any searching or linking service to its service objects or cuts off the link to any infringing works, performance, or audio-visual product after receiving a notice from the right owner according to the provisions of this Regulation, it is not required to assume the liabilities of compensation. However, when anyone is fully aware or should know that any of the works, performance or audio-visual products it has linked to constitutes any infringement, it shall be subject to the liabilities of joint infringement.

Analysis

The court of first instance held that audio books differ from film and television works, as readers might easily share their audio books via the Internet. It can be assumed that the defendant knows or should know that the works involved are infringing in nature, and thus the defendant shall refrain from providing the link without the authorization of the rights holders. At the same time, the defendant took technical measures to block the keyword link after receiving plaintiffs' complaint. It has fulfilled its responsibility as a network service provider under the relevant Regulation. Therefore, the court of the first instance dismissed the plaintiff's claim.

The Shanghai No. 1. Intermediate People's Court held that the user "nobodyvssomebody" infringed plaintiffs' copyright. This user posted a large number of content on the VeryCD website, and many of these works were from famous writers. Ordinary end-users could be aware that the posted contents are illegal in nature. As a professional network service provider, Yinzhi Company is negligent in fulfilling its corresponding duty of care. The defendant had subjective fault to let "nobodyvssomebody" publish the work on the website, and so plaintiff's right to communicate works to the public over information networks was infringed. In sum, the defendant was found to be contributorily liable.

1. Standards for determining the liability of network service providers providing P2P services

P2P technology does not only serve malicious purposes. When an end-user shares works via P2P platforms without authorization, the network service provider shall jointly take responsibility for the infringement. The P2P service provider does not directly transmit the infringing works or store the infringing works for the purpose of downloading, and therefore it does not directly infringe the right to communicate works to the public over information networks. At the same time, joint or contributory liability might stand, if (1) there is at least one direct infringement; (2) the service provider participates in or assists the direct infringer; (3) and the the service provider is at subjective fault. In this case, "nobodyvssomebody" illegally disseminated the works involved, and the Yinzhi Company provided P2P technological support. The defendant's behavior in this case met the first two components indicated above. The remaining question is whether the third component is met.

2. Standards of determining whether the P2P platform service provider is of subjective fault

The P2P service provider might be at subjective fault, if it knows or should know about the use of its platform for illegal purposes. "Know" shall mean that the P2P service provider clearly knows that the P2P user infringes the copyright of others through the platform, but does not take any measures to eliminate the infringement. "Should know" refers to the predictable capacity and scope of the P2P service provider, namely, where the service provider should have foreseen that the end-user infringes the copyright of others and causes damages to them, but it has not fulfilled the duty of care to prevent such infringements.

In this case, the defendant Yinzhi Company denied that it knew about the posting of illegal copies of the relevant works, and argued that the plaintiffs did not prove that the defendant has a subjective knowledge of users' activities. The Shanghai No. 1. Intermediate People's Court viewed it differently. According to the court, the defendant should have been aware that "nobodyvssomebody" committed copyright infringements. First, the specific user has infringed other copyrights earlier as well. Second, the user uploaded a large number of contents involving popular works written by famous writers. The defendant, as a P2P service provider shall be able to recognize the user's activities. Third, the user uploaded a large amount of materials with high quality (better resources attract more audiences), which brought considerable advertising revenue to the defendant. According to the principle of equality between rights and duties, the defendant obtained considerable income (advertising revenue) from contents uploaded by the end-users. Therefore, the defendant was required to undertake a reasonable duty of care.

Based on the above factors, the defendant should have been aware of the infringements, and therefore it was jointly liable for the infringements occured.

THINK IT OVER!

1. Under the ruling, joint or contributory liability might be applied under Chinese copyright law, if (1) there is a direct infringement; (2) the contributor participates in or provides help to the direct infringement; and (3) the contributor has subjective fault. Compare this standard with the U.S. concept of contributory liability (see e.g. the *Fung* case), as well as with the CJEU's recent *The Pirate Bay/Ziggo* ruling.

2. China is in the process of amending its Copyright Act (for the third time since 1990). Based on the European or American statutory norms or case law, *do you feel any need to amend the "right to communicate works to the public over information networks"? Should this right be included in the right of communication to the public, or shall it be regulated as a separate right?*

Further Case Law

Hanhan v. Beijing Baidu Netcom Technology Co., Ltd., (2012) Haidian People's Court Civil First No. 5558 Civil Judgement

Beijing Shuoshuochangchang Cultural Media Co., Ltd. v. Shanghai Quan Tudou Cultural Communication Co., Ltd., (2017) Shanghai Intellectual Property Court No. 224 Civil Final Judgment

Columbia Pictures Industries, Inc., et al. v. Gary Fung, et al., 710 *F.3d* 1020 (2013)

BWP Media USA Inc., et al. v. Polyvore, Inc., 922 *F.3d* 42 (2019)

Case C-160/15 - GS Media BV v. Sanoma Media Netherlands BV and Others, Judgment of the Court (Second Chamber), 8 September 2016 [ECLI:EU:C:2016:644]

Case C-610/15 - Stichting Brein v. Ziggo BV and XS4All Internet BV, Judgment of the Court (Second Chamber), 14 June 2017 [ECLI:EU:C:2017:456]

Recommended readings

In English

Weixiao Wei: Filtering Mandate: a Cure for Peer-to-Peer File-Sharing Copyright Infringement in China?, *Queen Mary Journal of Intellectual Property*, Issue 2/2012, p. 182-194.
Xiao Ma: Regulating Peer-to-Peer Technology in China: Inspiration from the United Kingdom, *Queen Mary Journal of Intellectual Property*, Issue 4/2018, p. 290-312.

In Chinese (bibliographic data translated to English)
Liu Yingliang: Information network communication right and its boundary with broadcasting rights, *Chinese Journal of Law*, Issue 6/2017, p. 97-114.
Liu Yingliang: The Legal Nature of Deep Links under the Framework of Information Network Communication Right, *Global Law Review*, Issue 6/2017, p. 84-104.
Zhang Jinping: The connotation of "providing to the public" in the right of communication, *Tsinghua University Law Journal*, Issue 2/2018, p. 125-143.

Chapter IV
Preservation of and Access to Cultural Heritage

THE AUTHORS GUILD, ET AL. V. GOOGLE, INC.

804 *F.3d* 202 (2015)
LEVAL, Circuit Judge

(...) BACKGROUND

I. Plaintiffs

The author-plaintiffs are Jim Bouton, author of *Ball Four;* Betty Miles, author of *The Trouble with Thirteen;* and Joseph Goulden, author of *The Superlawyers: The Small and Powerful World of the Great Washington Law Firms.* Each of them has a legal or beneficial ownership in the copyright for his or her book. Their books have been scanned without their permission by Google, which made them available to Internet users for search and snippet view on Google's website.

II. Google Books and the Google Library Project

Google's Library Project, which began in 2004, involves bi-lateral agreements between Google and a number of the world's major research libraries. Under these agreements, the participating libraries select books from their collections to submit to Google for inclusion in the project. Google makes a digital scan of each book, extracts a machine-readable text, and creates an index of the machine-readable text of each book. Google retains the original scanned image of each book, in part so as to improve the accuracy of the machine-readable texts and indices as image-to-text conversion technologies improve.

Since 2004, Google has scanned, rendered machine-readable, and indexed more than 20 million books, including both copyrighted works and works in the public domain. The vast majority of the books are non-fiction, and most are out of print. All of the digital information created by

Google in the process is stored on servers protected by the same security systems Google uses to shield its own confidential information.

The digital corpus created by the scanning of these millions of books enables the Google Books search engine. Members of the public who access the Google Books website can enter search words or terms of their own choice, receiving in response a list of all books in the database in which those terms appear, as well as the number of times the term appears in each book. A brief description of each book, entitled "About the Book," gives some rudimentary additional information, including a list of the words and terms that appear with most frequency in the book. It sometimes provides links to buy the book online and identifies libraries where the book can be found. The search tool permits a researcher to identify those books, out of millions, that do, as well as those that do not, use the terms selected by the researcher. Google notes that this identifying information instantaneously supplied would otherwise not be obtainable in lifetimes of searching.

No advertising is displayed to a user of the search function. Nor does Google receive payment by reason of the searcher's use of Google's link to purchase the book.

The search engine also makes possible new forms of research, known as "text mining" and "data mining." Google's "ngrams" research tool draws on the Google Library Project corpus to furnish statistical information to Internet users about the frequency of word and phrase usage over centuries. This tool permits users to discern fluctuations of interest in a particular subject over time and space by showing increases and decreases in the frequency of reference and usage in different periods and different linguistic regions. It also allows researchers to comb over the tens of millions of books Google has scanned in order to examine "word frequencies, syntactic patterns, and thematic markers" and to derive information on how nomenclature, linguistic usage, and literary style have changed over time. The district court gave as an example "track[ing] the frequency of references to the United States as a single entity ('the United States is') versus references to the United States in the plural ('the United States are') and how that usage has changed over time."

The Google Books search function also allows the user a limited viewing of text. In addition to telling the number of times the word or term selected by the searcher appears in the book, the search function will display a maximum of three "snippets" containing it. A snippet is a horizontal segment comprising ordinarily an eighth of a page. Each page of a conventionally formatted book[7] in the Google Books database is divided into eight non-overlapping horizontal segments, each such horizontal segment being a snippet. (Thus, for such a book with 24 lines to a page, each snippet is comprised of three lines of text.) Each search for a particular word or term within a book will reveal the same three snippets, regardless of the number of computers from which the search is launched. Only the first usage of the term on a given page is displayed. Thus, if the top snippet of a page contains two (or more) words for which the user searches, and Google's program is fixed to reveal that particular snippet in response to a search for either term, the second search will duplicate the snippet already revealed by the first search, rather than moving to reveal a different snippet containing the word because the first snippet was already revealed. Google's program does not allow a searcher to increase the number of snippets revealed by repeated entry of the same search term or by entering searches from different computers. A searcher can view more than three snippets of a book by entering additional searches for different terms. However, Google makes permanently unavailable for snippet view one snippet on each page and one complete page out of every ten—a process Google calls "blacklisting."

Google also disables snippet view entirely for types of books for which a single snippet is likely to satisfy the searcher's present need for the book, such as dictionaries, cookbooks, and books of short poems. Finally, since 2005, Google will exclude any book altogether from snippet view at the request of the rights holder by the submission of an online form.

Under its contracts with the participating libraries, Google allows each library to download copies—of both the digital image and machine-readable versions—of the books that library submitted to Google for scanning (but not of books submitted by other libraries). This is done by giving each participating library access to the Google Return Interface ("GRIN"). The agreements between Google and the libraries, although not in all respects uniform, require the libraries to abide by copyright law in utilizing the digital copies they download and to take precautions to prevent dissemination of their digital copies to the public at large. Through the GRIN facility, participant libraries have downloaded at least 2.7 million digital copies of their own volumes.

III. Procedural History

Plaintiffs brought this suit on September 20, 2005, as a putative class action on behalf of similarly situated, rights-owning authors. After several years of negotiation, the parties reached a proposed settlement that would have resolved the claims on a class-wide basis. The proposed settlement allowed Google to make substantially more extensive use of its scans of copyrighted books than contemplated under the present judgment, and provided that Google would make payments to the rights holders in return. On March 22, 2011, however, the district court rejected the proposed settlement as unfair to the class members who relied on the named plaintiffs to represent their interests.

On October 14, 2011, Plaintiffs filed a fourth amended class action complaint, which is the operative complaint for this appeal. The district court certified a class on May 31, 2012. Google appealed from the certification, and moved in the district court for summary judgment on its fair use defense. Plaintiffs cross-moved in the district court for summary judgment. On the appeal from the class certification, our court – questioning whether it was reasonable to infer that the putative class of authors favored the relief sought by the named plaintiffs – provisionally vacated that class certification without addressing the merits of the issue, concluding instead that "resolution of Google's fair use defense in the first instance will necessarily inform and perhaps moot our analysis of many class certification issues."

On November 14, 2013, the district court granted Google's motion for summary judgment, concluding that the uses made by Google of copyrighted books were fair uses, protected by §107. Upon consideration of the four statutory factors of §107, the district court found that Google's uses were transformative, that its display of copyrighted material was properly limited, and that the Google Books program did not impermissibly serve as a market substitute for the original works. The court entered judgment initially on November 27, 2013, followed by an amended judgment on December 10, 2013, dismissing Plaintiffs' claims with prejudice. Plaintiffs filed timely notice of appeal.

DISCUSSION

I. The Law of Fair Use

The ultimate goal of copyright is to expand public knowledge and understanding, which copyright seeks to achieve by giving potential creators exclusive control over copying of their works, thus giving them a financial incentive to create informative, intellectually enriching works for public consumption. This objective is clearly reflected in the Constitution's empowerment of Congress "*To promote the Progress of Science* ... by securing for limited Times to Authors ... the exclusive Right to their respective Writings." Thus, while authors are undoubtedly important intended beneficiaries of copyright, the ultimate, primary intended beneficiary is the public, whose access to knowledge copyright seeks to advance by providing rewards for authorship.

For nearly three hundred years, since shortly after the birth of copyright in England in 1710, courts have recognized that, in certain circumstances, giving authors *absolute* control over all copying from their works would tend in some circumstances to limit, rather than expand, public knowledge. In the words of Lord Ellenborough, "[W]hile I shall think myself bound to secure every man in the enjoyment of his copy-right, one must not put manacles upon science." Courts thus developed the doctrine, eventually named fair use, which permits unauthorized copying in some circumstances, so as to further "copyright's very purpose, '[t]o promote the Progress of Science and useful Arts.'"Although well established in the common law development of copyright, fair use was not recognized in the terms of our statute until the adoption of §107 in the Copyright Act of 1976.

§107, in its present form, provides:

[T]he fair use of a copyrighted work ... for purposes such as criticism, comment, news reporting, teaching (including multiple copies for classroom use), scholarship, or research, is not an infringement of copyright. In determining whether the use made of a work in any particular case is a fair use the factors to be considered shall include –

(1) the purpose and character of the use, including whether such use is of a commercial nature or is for nonprofit educational purposes;

(2) the nature of the copyrighted work;

(3) the amount and substantiality of the portion used in relation to the copyrighted work as a whole; and

(4) the effect of the use upon the potential market for or value of the copyrighted work.

The fact that a work is unpublished shall not itself bar a finding of fair use if such finding is made upon consideration of all the above factors.

As the Supreme Court has designated fair use an affirmative defense, the party asserting fair use bears the burden of proof.

The statute's wording, derived from a brief observation of Justice Joseph Story in *Folsom v. Marsh,* does not furnish standards for recognition of fair use. Its instruction to consider the "purpose and character" of the secondary use and the "nature" of the copyrighted work does not explain what types of "purpose and character" or "nature" favor a finding of fair use and which do not. In fact, as the Supreme Court observed in *Campbell,* the House Report makes clear that, in passing the statute, Congress had no intention of normatively dictating fair use policy. The purpose of the enactment was to give recognition in the statute itself to such an important part of copyright law developed by the courts through the common law process. "Congress meant §107 'to restate the present judicial doctrine of fair use, not to change, narrow, or enlarge it an any way,' and intended that courts continue the common-law tradition of fair use adjudication." Furthermore, notwithstanding fair use's long common-law history, not until the *Campbell* ruling in 1994 did courts undertake to explain the standards for finding fair use.

The *Campbell* Court undertook a comprehensive analysis of fair use's requirements, discussing every segment of §107. Beginning with the examples of purposes set forth in the statute's preamble, the Court made clear that they are "illustrative and not limitative" and "provide only general guidance about the sorts of copying that courts and Congress most commonly ha [ve] found to be fair uses." The statute "calls for case-by-case analysis" and "is not to be simplified with bright-line rules." §107's four factors are not to "be treated in isolation, one from another. All are to be explored, and the results weighed together, in light of the purposes of copyright." Each factor thus stands as part of a multifaceted assessment of the crucial question: how to define the boundary limit of the original author's exclusive rights in order to best serve the overall objectives of the copyright law to expand public learning while protecting the incentives of authors to create for the public good.

At the same time, the Supreme Court has made clear that some of the statute's four listed factors are more significant than others. The Court observed in *Harper & Row Publishers, Inc. v. Nation Enterprises* that the fourth factor, which assesses the harm the secondary use can cause to the market for, or the value of, the copyright for the original, "is undoubtedly the single most important element of fair use." This is consistent with the fact that the copyright is a commercial right, intended to protect the ability of authors to profit from the exclusive right to merchandise their own work.

In *Campbell,* the Court stressed also the importance of the first factor, the "purpose and character of the secondary use." The more the appropriator is using the copied material for new, transformative purposes, the more it serves copyright's goal of enriching public knowledge and the less likely it is that the appropriation will serve as a substitute for the original or its plausible derivatives, shrinking the protected market opportunities of the copyrighted work.

With this background, we proceed to discuss each of the statutory factors, as illuminated by *Campbell* and subsequent case law, in relation to the issues here in dispute.

II. The Search and Snippet View Functions

A. Factor One

(1) Transformative purpose. Campbell's explanation of the first factor's inquiry into the "purpose and character" of the secondary use focuses on whether the new work, "in Justice Story's words, ... merely 'supersede[s] the objects' of the original creation, ... or instead adds something new, with a further purpose.... [I]t asks, in other words, whether and to what extent the new work is 'transformative.'" While recognizing that a transformative use is "not absolutely necessary for a finding of fair use," the opinion further explains that the "goal of copyright, to promote science and the arts, is generally furthered by the creation of transformative works" and that "[s]uch works thus lie at the heart of the fair use doctrine's guarantee of breathing space within the confines of copyright." In other words, transformative uses tend to favor a fair use finding because a transformative use is one that communicates something new and different from the original or expands its utility, thus serving copyright's overall objective of contributing to public knowledge.

The word "transformative" cannot be taken too literally as a sufficient key to understanding the elements of fair use. It is rather a suggestive symbol for a complex thought, and does not mean that any and all changes made to an author's original text will necessarily support a finding of fair use. The Supreme Court's discussion in *Campbell* gave important guidance on assessing when a transformative use tends to support a conclusion of fair use. The defendant in that case defended on the ground that its work was a parody of the original and that parody is a time-honored category of fair use. Explaining why parody makes a stronger, or in any event more obvious, claim of fair use than satire, the Court stated,

> *[T]he heart of any parodist's claim to quote from existing material ... is the use of ... a prior author's composition to ... comment[ ] on that author's works.... If, on the contrary, the commentary has no critical bearing on the substance or style of the original composition, which the*

alleged infringer merely uses to get attention or to avoid the drudgery in working up something fresh, the claim to fairness in borrowing from another's work diminishes accordingly (if it does not vanish).... Parody needs to mimic an original to make its point, and so has some claim to use the creation of its victim's ... imagination, whereas satire can stand on its own two feet and so requires justification for the very act of borrowing.

In other words, the would-be fair user of another's work must have justification for the taking. A secondary author is not necessarily at liberty to make wholesale takings of the original author's expression merely because of how well the original author's expression would convey the secondary author's different message. Among the best recognized justifications for copying from another's work is to provide comment on it or criticism of it. A taking from another author's work for the purpose of making points that have no bearing on the original may well be fair use, but the taker would need to show a justification. This part of the Supreme Court's discussion is significant in assessing Google's claim of fair use because, as discussed extensively below, Google's claim of transformative purpose for copying from the works of others is to provide otherwise unavailable information about the originals.

A further complication that can result from oversimplified reliance on whether the copying involves transformation is that the word "transform" also plays a role in defining "derivative works," over which the original rights holder retains exclusive control. Section 106 of the Act specifies the "exclusive right[ ]" of the copyright owner "(2) to prepare derivative works based upon the copyrighted work." The statute defines derivative works largely by example, rather than explanation. The examples include "translation, musical arrangement, dramatization, fictionalization, motion picture version, sound recording, art reproduction, abridgement, condensation," to which list the statute adds "any other form in which a work may be ... *transformed.*" As we noted in *Authors Guild, Inc. v. HathiTrust,* "[p]aradigmatic examples of derivative works include the translation of a novel into another language, the adaptation of a novel into a movie or play, or the recasting of a novel as an e-book or an audiobook." While such changes can be described as transformations, they do not involve the kind of transformative purpose that favors a fair use finding. The statutory definition suggests that derivative works generally involve transformations in the nature of *changes of form.* By contrast, copying from an original for the purpose of criticism or commentary on the original or provision of information about it, tends most clearly to satisfy *Campbell*'s notion of the "transformative" purpose involved in the analysis of Factor One.

With these considerations in mind, we first consider whether Google's search and snippet views functions satisfy the first fair use factor with respect to Plaintiffs' rights in their books. (The question whether these functions might infringe upon Plaintiffs' derivative rights is discussed in the next Part.)

(2) Search Function. We have no difficulty concluding that Google's making of a digital copy of Plaintiffs' books for the purpose of enabling a search for identification of books containing a term of interest to the searcher involves a highly transformative purpose, in the sense intended by *Campbell.* Our court's exemplary discussion in *HathiTrust* informs our ruling. That case involved a dispute that is closely related, although not identical, to this one. Authors brought claims of copyright infringement against HathiTrust, an entity formed by libraries participating in the Google Library Project to pool the digital copies of their books created for them by Google. The suit challenged various usages HathiTrust made of the digital copies. Among the challenged uses was HathiTrust's offer to its patrons of "full-text searches," which, very much like the search offered by Google Books to Internet users, permitted patrons of the libraries to locate in which of the digitized books specific words or phrases appeared. We concluded that both the making of the digital copies and the use of those copies to offer the search tool were fair uses.

Notwithstanding that the libraries had downloaded and stored complete digital copies of entire books, we noted that such copying was essential to permit searchers to identify and locate the books in which words or phrases of interest to them appeared. We concluded "that the creation of a full-text searchable database is a quintessentially transformative use ... [as] the result of a word search is different in purpose, character, expression, meaning, and message from the page (and the book) from which it is drawn." (...)

As with *HathiTrust* (and *iParadigms*), the purpose of Google's copying of the original copyrighted books is to make available significant information *about those books,* permitting a searcher to identify those that contain a word or term of interest, as well as those that do not include reference to it. In addition, through the ngrams tool, Google allows readers to learn the frequency of usage of selected words in the aggregate corpus of published books in different historical periods. We have no doubt that the purpose of this copying is the sort of transformative purpose described in *Campbell* as strongly favoring satisfaction of the first factor.

We recognize that our case differs from *HathiTrust* in two potentially significant respects. First, HathiTrust did not "display to the user any text from the underlying copyrighted work," whereas Google Books provides the searcher with snippets containing the word that is the subject of the search. Second, HathiTrust was a nonprofit educational entity, while Google is a profit-motivated commercial corporation. We discuss those differences below.

(3) Snippet View. Plaintiffs correctly point out that this case is significantly different from *HathiTrust* in that the Google Books search function allows searchers to read snippets from the book searched, whereas HathiTrust did not allow searchers to view any part of the book. Snippet view adds important value to the basic transformative search function, which tells only whether and how often the searched term appears in the book. Merely knowing that a term of interest appears in a book does not necessarily tell the searcher whether she needs to obtain the

book, because it does not reveal whether the term is discussed in a manner or context falling within the scope of the searcher's interest. (...)

Google's division of the page into tiny snippets is designed to show the searcher just enough context surrounding the searched term to help her evaluate whether the book falls within the scope of her interest (without revealing so much as to threaten the author's copyright interests). Snippet view thus adds importantly to the highly transformative purpose of identifying books of interest to the searcher. With respect to the first factor test, it favors a finding of fair use (unless the value of its transformative purpose is overcome by its providing text in a manner that offers a competing substitute for Plaintiffs' books, which we discuss under factors three and four below).

(4) Google's Commercial Motivation. Plaintiffs also contend that Google's commercial motivation weighs in their favor under the first factor. Google's commercial motivation distinguishes this case from *HathiTrust,* as the defendant in that case was a non-profit entity founded by, and acting as the representative of, libraries. Although Google has no revenues flowing directly from its operation of the Google Books functions, Plaintiffs stress that Google is profit-motivated and seeks to use its dominance of book search to fortify its overall dominance of the Internet search market, and that thereby Google indirectly reaps profits from the Google Books functions.

For these arguments Plaintiffs rely primarily on two sources. First is Congress's specification in spelling out the first fair use factor in the text of §107 that consideration of the "purpose and character of the [secondary] use" should "include[e] whether such use is of a commercial nature or is for nonprofit educational purposes." Second is the Supreme Court's assertion in dictum in *Sony Corporation of America v. Universal City Studios, Inc,* that "every commercial use of copyrighted material is presumptively ... unfair." If that were the extent of precedential authority on the relevance of commercial motivation, Plaintiffs' arguments would muster impressive support. However, while the commercial motivation of the secondary use can undoubtedly weigh against a finding of fair use in some circumstances, the Supreme Court, our court, and others have eventually recognized that the *Sony* dictum was enormously overstated. (...)

Our court has since repeatedly rejected the contention that commercial motivation should outweigh a convincing transformative purpose and absence of significant substitutive competition with the original. (...)

While we recognize that in some circumstances, a commercial motivation on the part of the secondary user will weigh against her, especially, as the Supreme Court suggested, when a persuasive transformative purpose is lacking, we see no reason in this case why Google's overall profit motivation should prevail as a reason for denying fair use over its highly convincing transformative purpose, together with the absence of significant substitutive competition, as reasons for granting fair use. Many of the most universally accepted forms of fair use, such as news reporting and commentary, quotation in historical or analytic books, reviews of books, and performances, as well as parody, are all normally done commercially for profit.

B. Factor Two

The second fair use factor directs consideration of the "nature of the copyrighted work." While the "transformative purpose" inquiry discussed above is conventionally treated as a part of first factor analysis, it inevitably involves the second factor as well. One cannot assess whether the copying work has an objective that differs from the original without considering both works, and their respective objectives.

The second factor has rarely played a significant role in the determination of a fair use dispute. The Supreme Court in *Harper & Row* made a passing observation in dictum that, "[t]he law generally recognizes a greater need to disseminate factual works than works of fiction or fantasy." Courts have sometimes speculated that this might mean that a finding of fair use is more favored when the copying is of factual works than when copying is from works of fiction. However, while the copyright does not protect facts or ideas set forth in a work, it does protect that author's manner of expressing those facts and ideas. At least unless a persuasive fair use justification is involved, authors of factual works, like authors of fiction, should be entitled to copyright protection of their protected expression. The mere fact that the original is a factual work therefore should not imply that others may freely copy it. Those who report the news undoubtedly create factual works. It cannot seriously be argued that, for that reason, others may freely copy and re-disseminate news reports.

In considering the second factor in *HathiTrust,* we concluded that it was "not dispositive," commenting that courts have hardly ever found that the second factor in isolation played a large role in explaining a fair use decision. The same is true here. While each of the three Plaintiffs' books in this case is factual, we do not consider that as a boost to Google's claim of fair use. If one (or all) of the plaintiff works were fiction, we do not think that would change in any way our appraisal. Nothing in this case influences us one way or the other with respect to the second factor considered in isolation. To the extent that the "nature" of the original copyrighted work necessarily combines with the "purpose and character" of the secondary work to permit assessment of whether the secondary work uses the original in a "transformative" manner, as the term is used in *Campbell,* the second factor favors fair use not because Plaintiffs' works are factual, but because the secondary use transformatively provides valuable information about the original, rather than replicating protected expression in a manner that provides a meaningful substitute for the original.

C. Factor Three

The third statutory factor instructs us to consider "the amount and substantiality of the portion used in relation to the copyrighted work as a whole." The clear implication of the third factor is that a finding of fair use is more likely when small amounts, or less important passages, are copied than when the copying is extensive, or encompasses the most important parts of the original. The obvious reason for this lies in the relationship between the third and the fourth factors. The larger the amount, or the more important the part, of the original that is copied, the greater the likelihood that the secondary work might serve as an effectively competing substitute for the original, and might therefore diminish the original rights holder's sales and profits.

(1) Search Function. The Google Books program has made a digital copy of the entirety of each of Plaintiffs' books. Notwithstanding the reasonable implication of Factor Three that fair use is more likely to be favored by the copying of smaller, rather than larger, portions of the original, courts have rejected any categorical rule that a copying of the entirety cannot be a fair use. Complete unchanged copying has repeatedly been found justified as fair use when the copying was reasonably appropriate to achieve the copier's transformative purpose and was done in such a manner that it did not offer a competing substitute for the original. The Supreme Court said in *Campbell* that "the extent of permissible copying varies with the purpose and character of the use" and characterized the relevant questions as whether "the amount and substantiality of the portion used ... are reasonable in relation to the purpose of the copying," noting that the answer to that question will be affected by "the degree to which the [copying work] may serve as a market substitute for the original or potentially licensed derivatives".

In *HathiTrust,* our court concluded in its discussion of the third factor that "[b]ecause it was reasonably necessary for the [HathiTrust Digital Library] to make use of the entirety of the works in order to enable the full-text search function, we do not believe the copying was excessive." As with *HathiTrust,* not only is the copying of the totality of the original reasonably appropriate to Google's transformative purpose, it is literally necessary to achieve that purpose. If Google copied less than the totality of the originals, its search function could not advise searchers reliably whether their searched term appears in a book (or how many times).

While Google *makes* an unauthorized digital copy of the entire book, it does not reveal that digital copy to the public. The copy is made to enable the search functions to reveal limited, important information about the books. With respect to the search function, Google satisfies the third factor test, as illuminated by the Supreme Court in *Campbell.*

(2) Snippet View. Google's provision of snippet view makes our third factor inquiry different from that inquiry in *HathiTrust.* What matters in such cases is not so much "the amount and substantiality of the portion used" *in making a copy,* but rather the amount and substantiality

of *what is thereby made accessible* to a public for which it may serve as a competing substitute. In *HathiTrust,* notwithstanding the defendant's full-text copying, the search function revealed virtually nothing of the text of the originals to the public. Here, through the snippet view, more is revealed to searchers than in *HathiTrust.*

Without doubt, enabling searchers to see portions of the copied texts could have determinative effect on the fair use analysis. The larger the quantity of the copyrighted text the searcher can see and the more control the searcher can exercise over what part of the text she sees, the greater the likelihood that those revelations could serve her as an effective, free substitute for the purchase of the plaintiff's book. We nonetheless conclude that, at least as presently structured by Google, the snippet view does not reveal matter that offers the marketplace a significantly competing substitute for the copyrighted work.

Google has constructed the snippet feature in a manner that substantially protects against its serving as an effectively competing substitute for Plaintiffs' books. In the Background section of this opinion, we describe a variety of limitations Google imposes on the snippet function. These include the small size of the snippets (normally one eighth of a page), the blacklisting of one snippet per page and of one page in every ten, the fact that no more than three snippets are shown – and no more than one per page – for each term searched, and the fact that the same snippets are shown for a searched term no matter how many times, or from how many different computers, the term is searched. In addition, Google does not provide snippet view for types of books, such as dictionaries and cookbooks, for which viewing a small segment is likely to satisfy the searcher's need. The result of these restrictions is, so far as the record demonstrates, that a searcher cannot succeed, even after long extended effort to multiply what can be revealed, in revealing through a snippet search what could usefully serve as a competing substitute for the original.

The blacklisting, which permanently blocks about 22% of a book's text from snippet view, is by no means the most important of the obstacles Google has designed. While it is true that the blacklisting of 22% leaves 78% of a book *theoretically* accessible to a searcher, it does not follow that any large part of that 78% is in fact accessible. The other restrictions built into the program work together to ensure that, even after protracted effort over a substantial period of time, only small and randomly scattered portions of a book will be accessible. In an effort to show what large portions of text searchers can read through persistently augmented snippet searches, Plaintiffs' counsel employed researchers over a period of weeks to do multiple word searches on Plaintiffs' books. In no case were they able to access as much as 16% of the text, and the snippets collected were usually not sequential but scattered randomly throughout the book. Because Google's snippets are arbitrarily and uniformly divided by lines of text, and not by complete sentences, paragraphs, or any measure dictated by content, a searcher would have great difficulty constructing a search so as to provide any extensive information about the book's use of that term. As snippet view never reveals more than one snippet per page in response to repeated searches for the same term, it is at least difficult, and often impossible, for a searcher to gain access to more than a single snippet's worth of an extended, continuous discussion of the term.

The fact that Plaintiffs' searchers managed to reveal nearly 16% of the text of Plaintiffs' books overstates the degree to which snippet view can provide a meaningful substitute. At least as important as the percentage of words of a book that are revealed is the manner and order in which they are revealed. Even if the search function revealed 100% of the words of the copyrighted book, this would be of little substitutive value if the words were revealed in alphabetical order, or any order other than the order they follow in the original book. It cannot be said that a revelation is "substantial" in the sense intended by the statute's third factor if the revelation is in a form that communicates little of the sense of the original. The fragmentary and scattered nature of the snippets revealed, even after a determined, assiduous, time-consuming search, results in a revelation that is not "substantial," even if it includes an aggregate 16% of the text of the book. If snippet view could be used to reveal a coherent block amounting to 16% of a book, that would raise a very different question beyond the scope of our inquiry.

D. Factor Four

The fourth fair use factor, "the effect of the [copying] use upon the potential market for or value of the copyrighted work," focuses on whether the copy brings to the marketplace a competing substitute for the original, or its derivative, so as to deprive the rights holder of significant revenues because of the likelihood that potential purchasers may opt to acquire the copy in preference to the original. Because copyright is a commercial doctrine whose objective is to stimulate creativity among potential authors by enabling them to earn money from their creations, the fourth factor is of great importance in making a fair use assessment.

Campbell stressed the close linkage between the first and fourth factors, in that the more the copying is done to achieve a purpose that differs from the purpose of the original, the less likely it is that the copy will serve as a satisfactory substitute for the original. Consistent with that observation, the *HathiTrust* court found that the fourth factor favored the defendant and supported a finding of fair use because the ability to search the text of the book to determine whether it includes selected words "does not serve as a substitute for the books that are being searched."

However, *Campbell*'s observation as to the likelihood of a secondary use serving as an effective substitute goes only so far. Even if the *purpose* of the copying is for a valuably transformative purpose, such copying might nonetheless harm the value of the copyrighted original if done in a manner that results in widespread revelation of sufficiently significant portions of the original as to make available a significantly competing substitute. The question for us is whether snippet view, notwithstanding its transformative purpose, does that. We conclude that, at least as snippet view is presently constructed, it does not.

Especially in view of the fact that the normal purchase price of a book is relatively low in relation to the cost of manpower needed to secure an arbitrary assortment of randomly scattered snippets, we conclude that the snippet function does not give searchers access to effectively competing substitutes. Snippet view, at best and after a large commitment of manpower, produces discontinuous, tiny fragments, amounting in the aggregate to no more than 16% of a book. This does not threaten the rights holders with any significant harm to the value of their copyrights or diminish their harvest of copyright revenue.

We recognize that the snippet function can cause *some* loss of sales. There are surely instances in which a searcher's need for access to a text will be satisfied by the snippet view, resulting in either the loss of a sale to that searcher, or reduction of demand on libraries for that title, which might have resulted in libraries purchasing additional copies. But the possibility, or even the probability or certainty, of some loss of sales does not suffice to make the copy an effectively competing substitute that would tilt the weighty fourth factor in favor of the rights holder in the original. There must be a meaningful or significant effect "upon the potential market for or value of the copyrighted work." (...)

Even if the snippet reveals some authorial expression, because of the brevity of a single snippet and the cumbersome, disjointed, and incomplete nature of the aggregation of snippets made available through snippet view, we think it would be a rare case in which the searcher's interest *in the protected aspect* of the author's work would be satisfied by what is available from snippet view, and rarer still – because of the cumbersome, disjointed, and incomplete nature of the aggregation of snippets made available through snippet view – that snippet view could provide a significant substitute for the purchase of the author's book.

Accordingly, considering the four fair use factors in light of the goals of copyright, we conclude that Google's making of a complete digital copy of Plaintiffs' works for the purpose of providing the public with its search and snippet view functions (at least as snippet view is presently designed) is a fair use and does not infringe Plaintiffs' copyrights in their books. (...)

CONCLUSION

The judgment of the district court is **AFFIRMED.**

THINK IT OVER!

What are the consequences of the Second Circuit's decision on an international level? Article 5(2)(c) of the InfoSoc-Directive allows Member States to introduce limitations or exceptions to the *reproduction right* for the benefit of publicly accessible libraries, educational establishments or museums, or by archives, if they do not reproduce works for direct or indirect economic or commercial advantages. Article 5(3)(n) further allows Member States to introduce limitations or exceptions with regards „communication or making available, for the purpose of research or private study, to individual members of the public by dedicated terminals on the premises of establishments referred to in paragraph 2(c) of works and other subject-matter not subject to purchase or licensing terms which are contained in their collections". *Would Google Books fall under any limitation or exception of the EU copyright law?* Compare to the preliminary ruling of the CJEU in *TUD v. Ulmer.* (See at page 394.) *Would HathiTrust's service be compatible with the EU copyright law?*

Further Case Law

Lesley A. Kelly v. Arriba Soft, 336 *F.3d* 811 (2003)

The Authors Guild, Inc., et al., v. HathiTrust, et al., 755 *F.3d* 87 (2014)

Case C-117/13 - Technische Universität Darmstadt v. Eugen Ulmer KG, Judgment of the Court (Fourth Chamber), 11 September 2014 [ECLI:EU:C:2014:2196]

Recommended readings

In English

Jonathan Band: The Long and Winding Road to the Google Books Settlement, *John Marshall Review of Intellectual Property Law*, 2010: p. 227-329.

Matthew Sag: The Google Book Settlement and the Fair Use Counterfactual, *New York Law School Law Review*, 2010-2011: p. 19-75.

Maurizio Borghi - Stavroula Karapapa: Non-display uses of digital works: Google Books and beyond, *Queen Mary Journal of Intellectual Property*, Issue 1/2011, p. 21-52.

Priya Hari: Is Scanning Books Really Fair Use?: The Next Chapter in the Google Books Litigation, *Charlotte Law Review*, Fall 2015, p. 111-133.

Lance Koonce: Anothet Page in the Google Books Saga: Appeals Court Blesses Mass Digitization Project as Fair Use, *Intellectual Property & Technology Law Journal*, February 2016, p. 20-23.

In French

Jane C. Ginsburg – Pierre Sirinelli: Google Book Search. Les enjeux internationaux pour le droit d'auteur, *La Semaine Juridique Edition Générale*, n° 17, 26 Avril 2010, doctr. 486.

In German

Manuel Kleinemenke: Google Books und Fair Use – Lehren für eine flexiblere Ausgestaltung und Anwendung urheberrechtlicher Schrankenbestimmungen (auch) im deutschen und europäischen Recht, *Gewerblicher Rechtsschutz und Urheberrecht Internationaler Teil*, Heft 10/2014, p. 892-901.

In Spanish

Torres Ripa - Javier y Gómez Hernández - José Antonio (coords.): *El copyright en cuestión. Diálogos sobre propiedad intelectual*, Deusto Digital, Universidad de Deusto, 2011

In Hungarian

Mezei Péter: A szerzői jog jövője (is) a tét - Gondolatok a Google Books könyvdigitalizálási projektről, *Iparjogvédelmi és Szerzői Jogi Szemle*, 2011/5. szám, p. 5-47.

Mezei Péter: *Jogerős döntés a Google Books ügyben: fair use!* In: Gál Andor - Karsai Krisztina (Szerk.): Ad Valorem - Ünnepi tanulmányok Vida Mihály 80. születésnapjára, Iurisperitus Kiadó, Szeged, 2016: p. 273-282.

TECHNISCHE UNIVERSITÄT DARMSTADT V. EUGEN ULMER

Case C-117/13 - Judgment of the Court (Fourth Chamber), 11 September 2014 [ECLI:EU:C:2014:2196]

(...) Legal context

European Union law

3 Recitals (...) 34, 36 (...) in the preamble to Directive 2001/29 are worded as follows:

(...) (34) Member States should be given the option of providing for certain exceptions or limitations for cases such as educational and scientific purposes, for the benefit of public institutions such as libraries and archives, for purposes of news reporting, for quotations, for use by people with disabilities, for public security uses and for uses in administrative and judicial proceedings.

(...)

(36) The Member States may provide for fair compensation for rightholders also when applying the optional provisions on exceptions or limitations which do not require such compensation.

(...) 6 Article 5 of the same directive, entitled 'Exceptions and limitations', provides in paragraph 2:

'Member States may provide for exceptions or limitations to the reproduction right provided for in Article 2 in the following cases:

(a) in respect of reproductions on paper or any similar medium, effected by the use of any kind of photographic technique or by some other process having similar effects, with the exception of sheet music, provided that the rightholders receive fair compensation;

(b) in respect of reproductions on any medium made by a natural person for private use and for ends that are neither directly nor indirectly commercial, on condition that the rightholders receive fair compensation which takes account of the application or non-application of technological measures referred to in Article 6 to the work or subject-matter concerned;

(c) in respect of specific acts of reproduction made by publicly accessible libraries, educational establishments or museums, or by archives, which are not for direct or indirect economic or commercial advantage; (...)'

7 Article 5(3) of that directive provides:

'Member States may provide for exceptions or limitations to the rights provided for in Articles 2 and 3 in the following cases:

(...)

(n) use by communication or making available, for the purpose of research or private study, to individual members of the public by dedicated terminals on the premises of establishments referred to in paragraph 2(c) of works and other subject-matter not subject to purchase or licensing terms which are contained in their collections; (...)'

8 According to Article 5(5) of the same directive:

'The exceptions and limitations provided for in paragraphs 1, 2, 3 and 4 shall only be applied in certain special cases which do not conflict with a normal exploitation of the work or other subject-matter and do not unreasonably prejudice the legitimate interests of the rightholder.'

German law

9 Paragraph 52b of the German Law on copyright (Urheberrechtsgesetz, 'UrhG') of 9 September 1965 (BGBl. I, p. 1273), in the version applicable at the date of the facts in the main proceedings, is worded as follows:

'Reproduction of works at electronic reading points in public libraries, museums and archives

So far as there are no contractual provisions to the contrary, it shall be permissible to make published works available from the holdings of publicly accessible libraries, museums or archives, which neither directly nor indirectly serve economic or commercial purposes, exclusively on the premises of the relevant establishment at electronic reading points dedicated to the purpose of research and for private study. The number of copies of a work made available at electronic reading points shall not, in principle, be higher than the number held by the establishment. Equitable remuneration shall be paid in consideration of their being made available. The claim may be asserted only by a collecting society.'

The dispute in the main proceedings and the questions referred for a preliminary ruling

10 TU Darmstadt operates a regional and academic library in which it installed electronic reading points that allow the public to consult works contained in the collection of that library.

11 Since January or February 2009, those works have included the textbook of Schulze W., Einführung in die neuere Geschichte ('the textbook at issue'), published by Ulmer, a scientific publishing house established in Stuttgart (Germany).

12 TU Darmstadt did not take up Ulmer's offer of 29 January 2009 of an opportunity to purchase and use the textbooks it publishes as electronic books ('e-books'), including the textbook at issue.

13 TU Darmstadt digitised that textbook so as to make it available to users on electronic reading points installed in its library. Those points did not allow for a greater number of copies of that work to be consulted at any one time than the number owned by the library. Users of the reading points could print out the work on paper or store it on a USB stick, in part or in full, and take it out of the library in that form.

14 In an action brought by Ulmer, the Landgericht (Regional Court) Frankfurt am Main held, by judgment of 6 March 2011, that the rightholder and establishment must have reached prior agreement on the digital use of the work concerned for Paragraph 52b of the UrhG not to apply. That court also rejected Ulmer's application seeking to prohibit TU Darmstadt from digitising the textbook at issue or having it digitised. However, it granted that company's request to prohibit users of the TU Darmstadt library from being able, at electronic reading points installed therein, to print out that work and/or store it on a USB stick and/or take such reproductions out of the library.

15 Hearing an appeal by TU Darmstadt on a point of law, the Bundesgerichtshof (Federal Court of Justice) considers, in the first place, that the question arises whether works and other protected objects are 'subject to purchase or licensing terms', within the meaning of

Article 5(3)(n) of Directive 2001/29, where the rightholder offers to conclude with an establishment referred to in that provision appropriately worded licensing agreements in respect of those works or whether a different interpretation of that provision must be adopted, in terms of which only cases where the owner and the establishment have entered into an agreement on that matter are covered.

16 That court takes the view that, unlike the German language version of the provision, the English and French language versions are consistent with the first of the above interpretations. That interpretation could also be justified on the basis of the purpose and general scheme of Directive 2001/29. However, if only the entering into an agreement would allow for the application of that provision to be ruled out, it would be open to the establishment to refuse an appropriate offer from the rightholder so as to benefit from the limiting provision in question, which would also mean that the owner would not receive appropriate remuneration, which nevertheless is one of the objectives of that directive.

17 In the second place, the referring court is uncertain whether Article 5(3)(n) of Directive 2001/29 must be interpreted to mean that it allows Member States to confer on the establishments referred to in that provision the right to digitise the works contained in their collections to the extent that the communication or making available of those works on their terminals requires such reproduction. The referring court takes the view that Member States should have an ancillary competence in order to provide for such an exception to the reproduction right referred to in Article 2 of that directive or such a limitation of that right; otherwise the effectiveness of Article 5(3)(n) would not be guaranteed. That competence could, in any event, be inferred from Article 5(2)(c) of the directive.

18 In the third place, the referring court takes the view that the dispute in the main proceedings raises the question whether, pursuant to Article 5(3)(n) of Directive 2001/29, Member States may provide for a limiting provision permitting the users of an establishment referred to in that provision to print out on paper or store on a USB stick, in part or in full, the works reproduced or made available by the establishment on its terminals.

19 In that regard, that court considers, first of all, that while those printouts, stored copies or downloads, being related to the reproduction of a work, are not, in principle, covered by the limitation provided for in Article 5(3)(n) of Directive 2001/29, they could nevertheless be permitted, as an extension of the communication or of the making available of a work by the establishment in question, under another limitation, in particular, pursuant to the so-called 'private copying' exception provided for in Article 5(2)(b) of that directive.

20 Next, the court finds that the objective referred to in Article 5(3)(n) of Directive 2001/29, which entails permitting the efficient use, for the purpose of research or private study, of texts communicated or made available on the terminals of an establishment such as a library, is consistent with an interpretation of that provision to the effect that the printing out on paper of a work from a terminal should be permitted, whereas storage on a USB stick should not be.

21 Lastly, the referring court considers that such an interpretation of Article 5(3)(n) of Directive 2001/29 would also ensure that the scope of the limitation provided for in that provision respects the threefold condition provided for in Article 5(5) of that directive. In its view, storage of a work on a USB stick encroaches upon the rights of the author of that work more than printing it out on paper.

22 In those circumstances, the Bundesgerichtshof decided to stay the proceedings and refer the following questions to the Court for a preliminary ruling:

'(1) Is a work subject to purchase or licensing terms, within the meaning of Article 5(3)(n) of Directive 2001/29, where the rightholder offers to conclude with the establishments referred to therein licensing agreements for the use of that work on appropriate terms?

(2) Does Article 5(3)(n) of Directive 2001/29 entitle the Member States to confer on those establishments the right to digitise the works contained in their collections, if that is necessary in order to make those works available on terminals?

(3) May the rights which the Member States lay down pursuant to Article 5(3)(n) of Directive 2001/29 go so far as to enable users of the terminals to print out on paper or store on a USB stick the works made available there?'

Consideration of the questions referred for a preliminary ruling

The first question

23 By its first question, the referring court is essentially asking whether a work is subject to 'purchase or licensing terms', within the meaning of Article 5(3)(n) of Directive 2001/29, where the rightholder has offered to conclude with an establishment referred to in that provision, such as a publicly accessible library, on appropriately worded terms a licensing agreement in respect of that work.

24 All of the interested parties that have presented written observations, with the exception of Ulmer, propose that the first question be answered in the negative and essentially support an interpretation to the effect that the concept of 'purchase or licensing terms', mentioned

in Article 5(3)(n) of Directive 2001/29, must be understood to mean that the rightholder and establishment concerned must have concluded a licensing agreement in respect of the work in question that sets out the conditions in which that establishment may use the work.

25 Ulmer argues that the mere fact that the rightholder offers to conclude a licensing agreement with a publicly accessible library is sufficient for ruling out the application of Article 5(3)(n) of Directive 2001/29, provided always that such offer is 'appropriate'.

26 In that regard, first of all, a comparison of the language versions of Article 5(3)(n) of Directive 2001/29, particularly the English, French, German and Spanish versions – which use the words 'terms', 'conditions', 'Regelung' and 'condiciones', respectively – shows that, in that provision, the EU legislature used the concepts 'terms' or 'provisions', which refer to contractual terms actually agreed as opposed to mere contractual offers.

27 Next, it should be recalled that the limitation under Article 5(3)(n) of Directive 2001/29 aims to promote the public interest in promoting research and private study, through the dissemination of knowledge, which constitutes, moreover, the core mission of publicly accessible libraries.

28 The interpretation favoured by Ulmer implies that the rightholder could, by means of a unilateral and essentially discretionary action, deny the establishment concerned the right to benefit from that limitation and thereby prevent it from realising its core mission and promoting the public interest.

29 Moreover, recital 40 in the preamble to Directive 2001/29 states that specific contracts or licences should be promoted which, without creating imbalances, favour such establishments and the disseminative purposes they serve.

30 As noted by the Advocate General in points 21 and 22 of his Opinion, recitals 45 and 51 in the preamble to Directive 2001/29 confirm (including in their German version) that, in the context, inter alia, of the exceptions and limitations listed in Article 5(3) of Directive 2001/29, it is existing contractual relations and the conclusion and implementation of existing contractual agreements that are at issue, and not mere prospects of contracts or licences.

31 Furthermore, the interpretation proposed by Ulmer is difficult to reconcile with the aim pursued by Article 5(3)(n) of Directive 2001/29, which is to maintain a fair balance between the rights and interests of rightholders, on the one hand, and, on the other hand, users of

protected works who wish to communicate them to the public for the purpose of research or private study undertaken by individual members of the public.

32 In addition, if the mere act of offering to conclude a licensing agreement were sufficient to rule out the application of Article 5(3)(n) of Directive 2001/29, such an interpretation would be liable to negate much of the substance of the limitation provided for in that provision, or indeed its effectiveness, since, were it to be accepted, the limitation would apply, as Ulmer has maintained, only to those increasingly rare works of which an electronic version, primarily in the form of an e-book, is not yet offered on the market.

33 Lastly, the interpretation to the effect that there must be contractual terms actually agreed also cannot be ruled out – contrary to what is maintained by Ulmer – by reason of the fact that it would conflict with the threefold condition provided for in Article 5(5) of Directive 2001/29.

34 In that regard, it is sufficient to state that the limitation provided for in Article 5(3)(n) of Directive 2001/29 is accompanied by a number of restrictions that guarantee – even though the application of that provision is ruled out only in the event that contractual terms have actually been concluded – the continuing applicability of such a limitation in special cases which do not conflict with a normal exploitation of the works and do not unreasonably prejudice the legitimate interests of the rightholder.

35 In the light of the foregoing considerations, the answer to the first question is that the concept of 'purchase or licensing terms' provided for in Article 5(3)(n) of Directive 2001/29 must be understood as requiring that the rightholder and an establishment, such as a publicly accessible library, referred to in that provision must have concluded a licensing agreement in respect of the work in question that sets out the conditions in which that establishment may use that work.

The second question

36 By its second question, the referring court is essentially asking whether Article 5(3)(n) of Directive 2001/29 must be interpreted to mean that it precludes Member States from granting to publicly accessible libraries covered by that provision the right to digitise the works contained in their collections, if such act of reproduction is necessary for the purpose of making those works available to users, by means of dedicated terminals, within those establishments.

37 The first point to be noted is that the digitisation of a work, which essentially involves the conversion of the work from an analogue format into a digital one, constitutes an act of reproduction of the work.

38 The question therefore arises whether Article 5(3)(n) of Directive 2001/29 permits Member States to grant that reproduction right to publicly accessible libraries, since, under Article 2 of that directive, it is the authors that have the exclusive right to authorise or prohibit the reproduction of their works.

39 In that regard, it should first be stated that, according to the first sentence of Article 5(3) of Directive 2001/29, the exceptions and limitations set out in that paragraph relate to the rights provided for in Articles 2 and 3 of that directive and thus both the exclusive reproduction right enjoyed by the rightholder and the right of communication to the public of works.

40 However, Article 5(3)(n) of the directive limits the use of works, within the meaning of that provision, to the 'communication or making available' of those works and thus to acts which fall under the sole exclusive right of communication to the public of works referred to in Article 3 of that directive.

41 Next, it should be recalled that for there to be an 'act of communication' for the purposes of Article 3(1) of Directive 2001/29, it is sufficient, in particular, that those works are made available to a public in such a way that the persons forming that public may access them, irrespective of whether they avail themselves of that opportunity.

42 It follows that, in circumstances such as those of the case in the main proceedings, where an establishment, such as a publicly accessible library, which falls within Article 5(3)(n) of Directive 2001/29, gives access to a work contained in its collection to a 'public', namely all of the individual members of the public using the dedicated terminals installed on its premises for the purpose of research or private study, that must be considered to be 'making [that work] available' and, therefore, an 'act of communication' for the purposes of Article 3(1) of that directive.

43 Such a right of communication of works enjoyed by establishments such as publicly accessible libraries covered by Article 5(3)(n) of Directive 2001/29, within the limits of the conditions provided for by that provision, would risk being rendered largely meaningless, or indeed ineffective, if those establishments did not have an ancillary right to digitise the works in question.

44 Those establishments are recognised as having such a right pursuant to Article 5(2)(c) of Directive 2001/29, provided that 'specific acts of reproduction' are involved.

45 That condition of specificity must be understood as meaning that, as a general rule, the establishments in question may not digitise their entire collections.

46 However, that condition is, in principle, observed where the digitisation of some of the works of a collection is necessary for the purpose of the 'use by communication or making available, for the purpose of research or private study, to individual members of the public by dedicated terminals', as provided in Article 5(3)(n) of Directive 2001/29.

47 Furthermore, the scope of that ancillary right of digitisation must be determined by interpreting Article 5(2)(c) of Directive 2001/29 in the light of Article 5(5) of that directive, under which that limitation is applicable only in certain special cases which do not prejudice the normal exploitation of the work or other protected object or cause unjustified harm to the legitimate interests of the rightholder, the latter provision, however, not being intended to extend the scope of the exceptions and limitations provided for in Article 5(2) of the directive.

48 In the present case, it must be stated that the applicable national legislation takes due account of the conditions provided for in Article 5(5) of the directive, since it follows, first, from Article 52b of the UrhG, that the digitisation of works by publicly accessible libraries cannot have the result of the number of copies of each work made available to users by dedicated terminals being greater than that which those libraries have acquired in analogue format. Secondly, although, by virtue of that provision of national law, the digitisation of the work is not, as such, coupled with an obligation to provide compensation, the subsequent making available of that work in digital format, on dedicated terminals, gives rise to a duty to make payment of adequate remuneration.

49 Having regard to the foregoing considerations, the answer to the second question is that Article 5(3)(n) of Directive 2001/29, read in conjunction with Article 5(2)(c) of that directive, must be interpreted to mean that it does not preclude Member States from granting to publicly accessible libraries covered by those provisions the right to digitise the works contained in their collections, if such act of reproduction is necessary for the purpose of making those works available to users, by means of dedicated terminals, within those establishments.

The third question

50 By its third question, the referring court is essentially asking whether Article 5(3)(n) of Directive 2001/29 must be interpreted to mean that it precludes Member States from granting to publicly accessible libraries covered by that provision the right to make works available to users by dedicated terminals which permit the printing out of those works on paper or their storage on a USB stick.

51 As is clear from paragraphs 40 and 42 of the present judgment, the limitation laid down in Article 5(3)(n) of Directive 2001/29 covers, in principle, only certain acts of communication normally falling under the exclusive right of the author provided for in Article 3 of that directive, namely those by which the establishments in question make a work available to individual members of the public, for the purpose of research or private study, by dedicated terminals installed on their premises.

52 It is undisputed that acts such as the printing out of a work on paper or its storage on a USB stick, even if made possible by the specific features of the dedicated terminals on which that work can be consulted, are not acts of 'communication', within the meaning of Article 3 of Directive 2001/29, but rather of 'reproduction', within the meaning of Article 2 of that directive.

53 What is involved is the creation of a new analogue or digital copy of the work that an establishment makes available to users by means of dedicated terminals.

54 Such acts of reproduction, unlike some operations involving the digitisation of a work, also cannot be permitted under an ancillary right stemming from the combined provisions of Articles 5(2)(c) and 5(3)(n) of Directive 2001/29, since they are not necessary for the purpose of making the work available to the users of that work, by dedicated terminals, in accordance with the conditions laid down by those provisions. Moreover, since those acts are carried out not by the establishments referred to in Article 5(3)(n) of Directive 2001/29, but rather by the users of the dedicated terminals installed within those establishments, they cannot be authorised under that provision.

55 By contrast, such acts of reproduction on analogue or digital media may, if appropriate, be authorised under the national legislation transposing the exceptions or limitations provided for in Article 5(2)(a) or (b) of Directive 2001/29 since, in each individual case, the conditions laid down by those provisions, in particular as regards the fair compensation which the rightholder must receive, are met.

56 Furthermore, such acts of reproduction must observe the conditions set out in Article 5(5) of Directive 2001/29. Consequently, the extent of the texts reproduced may not, in particular, unreasonably prejudice the legitimate interests of the rightholder.

57 Having regard to the foregoing considerations, the answer to the third question is that Article 5(3)(n) of Directive 2001/29 must be interpreted to mean that it does not extend to acts such as the printing out of works on paper or their storage on a USB stick, carried out by users from dedicated terminals installed in publicly accessible libraries covered by that provision. However, such acts may, if appropriate, be authorised under national legislation transposing the exceptions or limitations provided for in Article 5(2)(a) or (b) of that directive provided that, in each individual case, the conditions laid down by those provisions are met. (...)

THINK IT OVER!

1. The CJEU employed a new language to describe the action taken by the public library when it mentioned "*ancillary right of digitization*" instead of "*limitation and exception to the reproduction right*". Similarly to classic limitations or exceptions, the CJEU applied the three-step test to this ancillary right, the Court declare libraries' privilege a "user right". *What kind of future consequences can such categorization have?* The concept of "user rights" has been confirmed by the CJEU in various other preliminary rulings: in *Deckmyn* regarding parodies/freedom of expression (Case C-201/13, para. 34.); in *UPC Telekabel* regarding online law enforcement/freedom of information (Case C-314/12, para. 56-57.); and in *Spiegel Online* regarding reporting on current events/freedom of press (Case C-516/17, para. 54.).

2. The CJEU specified that the ancillary right of digitization does not allow publicly accessible libraries to digitize their entire collection (paragraph 45). In principle, digitization might only cover a limited amount of the works held in the institution's collection, and only if the digitization is necessary for the purpose laid down in Article 5(3)(n). It remains unclear how to interpret the condition of "some of the works". *Would it be lawful to digitize a substantial volume of the collection?*

3. The European Union's Directive (EU) 2019/790 on copyright and related rights in the Digital Single Market (CDSM Directive) now opens a new perspective regarding uses of works by cultural heritage institutions. Since digital technologies offer new ways of preserving works or other subject matters included in the collections of such institutions, the EU legislator decided to adapt the legal framework in order to allow reproduction of these works and subject matters. Article 6 of the CDSM Directive provides for an exception to the exclusive right of reproduction in order to allow cultural heritage institutions to make copies of any works or other subject matter that are permanently in their collections, in any format or medium, for purposes of preservation of such works or other subject matter and to the extent necessary for such preservation. Cultural heritage institution means a publicly accessible library or museum, an archive or a film or audio heritage institution. *Could those cultural heritage institutions be allowed to rely on third party services while benefiting from the exception? Could Member States implement this Article to grant fair remuneration to rights holders?*

Further Case Law

Case C-201/13 - Johan Deckmyn and Others v. Helena Vandersteen and Others, Judgment of the Court (Grand Chamber), 3 September 2014 [ECLI:EU:C:2014:2132]

Case C-314/12 - UPC Telekabel Wien GmbH v Constantin Film Verleih GmbH and Wega Filmproduktionsgesellschaft mbH, Judgment of the Court (Fourth Chamber), 27 March 2014 [ECLI:EU:C:2014:192]

Case C-516/17 - Spiegel Online GmbH v. Volker Beck, Judgment of the Court (Grand Chamber), 29 July 2019 [ECLI:EU:C:2019:625]

Recommended readings

In English

Emma Linklater: Make me an offer I won't regret: Offers to license works on acceptable terms cannot block libraries' "right" to digitize for access on dedicated terminals: Technische Universität Darmstadt, *Common Market Law Review*, Issue 3/2015, p. 813-823.
Eleonora Rosati: Copyright: CJEU says that Member States may grant public libraries the right to digitize works in their collections, *Journal of Intellectual Property Law and Practice*, Issue 1/2015, p. 6-8.
Ulrich Loewenheim: Boundaries of use of electronic terminals, *Journal of Intellectual Property Law and Practice*, Issue 5/2015 p. 384-387.

Péter Mezei: *The Painter, the One Horn Cow, and Ole Hank Wilson's Back Lot: The Future of Library Digitization in Hungary and the European Union.* In: Mira T. Sundara Rajan (Ed.): Cambridge Handbook on Intellectual Property in Central and Eastern Europe, Cambridge University Press, 2019: p. 284-309.

In French

Christophe Caron: A propos de la consultation d'œuvres numérisées dans les bibliothèques, *Communication, commerce électronique*, 2014/11. comm. 83.

Lionel Costes: Numérisation de livres par les bibliothèques: l'analyse de la CJUE, *Droit de l'immatériel: informatique, médias, communication*, 2014, n° 108, p. 21-22.

Emmanuel Derieux: Numérisation et mise à disposition des ouvrages des bibliothèques publiques, *Droit de l'immatériel: informatique, médias, communication*, 2014, n° 108, p. 50-54.

Guillaume Busseuil: À propos de la numérisation des oeuvres par les bibliothèques: effet utile ou déconstruction des exceptions au droit d'auteur?, *Droit de l'immatériel: informatique, médias, communication*, 2014, n° 108, p. 55-60.

In German

Ulrich Löwenheim: Grenzen der Nutzung elektronischer Leseplätze, *Gewerblicher Rechtsschutz und Urheberrecht*, Heft 11/2014, p. 1057-1060.

Michel M. Walter: Digitale Nutzung von Werken in Bibliotheken - „Terminalausnahme", *MR-Int: Internationale Rundschau zum Medienrecht, IP- & IT-Recht*, Heft 3/2014, p. 82-84.

Andreas Wiebe - Daniel Bernhard Müller: Die Zulässigkeit elektronischer Leseplätze in Bibliotheken, *Neue juristische Wochenschrift*, Heft 11/2015, p. 741-744.

MARC SOULIER, SARA DOKE V. PREMIER MINISTER, MINISTRE DE LA CULTURE ET DE LA COMMUNICATION

Case C-301/15 - Judgment of the Court (Third Chamber), 16 November 2016 [ECLI:EU:C:2016:878]

(...) Legal context

International law

Berne Convention (...)

5 Article 5 of that Convention provides, inter alia, in paragraphs 1 and 2 thereof:
'1. Authors shall enjoy, in respect of works for which they are protected under this Convention, in countries of the Union other than the country of origin, the rights which their respective laws do now or may hereafter grant to their nationals, as well as the rights specially granted by this Convention.
2. The enjoyment and the exercise of those rights shall not be subject to any formality; such enjoyment and such exercise shall be independent of the existence of protection in the country of origin of the work. Consequently, apart from the provisions of this Convention, the extent of protection, as well as the means of redress afforded to the author to protect his rights, shall be governed exclusively by the laws of the country where protection is claimed.'

(...) EU law

10 Recitals 9, 15 and 32 of Directive 2001/29 state:
(32) This Directive provides for an exhaustive enumeration of exceptions and limitations to the reproduction right and the right of communication to the public. Some exceptions or limitations only apply to the reproduction right, where appropriate. This list takes due account of the different legal traditions in Member States, while, at the same time, aiming to ensure a functioning internal market. Member States should arrive at a coherent application of these exceptions and limitations, which will be assessed when reviewing implementing legislation in the future.'

(...) 13 Article 5 of that directive, entitled 'Exceptions and limitations', states, inter alia, in paragraphs 2 and 3 thereof, that the Member States may, in the cases listed therein, provide for various exceptions and limitations to the reproduction right and the right of communication to the public provided for in Articles 2 and 3 of that directive.

French law

14 The Loi No 2012-287, du 1er mars 2012, relative à l'exploitation numérique des livres indisponibles du XXème siècle (Law No 2012-287 of 1 March 2012 on the digital exploitation of out-of-print 20th century books) (JORF No 53 of 2 March 2012, p. 3986) added to Title III of Book One of the first part of the Intellectual Property Code, which deals with the exploitation of rights related to copyright, a Chapter IV, entitled 'Special provisions relating to the digital exploitation of out-of-print books', comprising Articles L. 134-1 to L. 134-9 of that code. Some of those articles were subsequently amended or repealed by the Loi No 2015-195, du 20 février 2015, portant diverses dispositions d'adaptation au droit de l'Union européenne dans les domaines de la propriété littéraire et artistique et du patrimoine culturel (Law No 2015-195 of 20 February 2015 containing various provisions implementing EU law in the fields of literary and artistic property and cultural heritage) (JORF No 45 of 22 February 2015, p. 3294).

15 Articles L. 134-1 to L. 134-9 of the Intellectual Property Code, as drafted following those two laws, read as follows:

'Article L. 134-1

For the purposes of this Chapter, an out-of-print book means a book published in France before 1 January 2001 which is no longer commercially distributed by a publisher and is not currently published in print or in a digital format.

Article L. 134-2

A public database indexing out-of-print books shall be created and made openly available, free of charge, through an online, public communication service. The Bibliothèque nationale de France (National Library of France) shall be responsible for implementing and updating it and for recording the information provided for in Articles L. 134-4, L. 134-5 and L. 134-6.

(...)

Article L. 134-3

I. When a book has been registered in the database referred to in Article L. 134-2 for more than six months, the right to authorise its reproduction and performance in digital format shall be exercised by a collecting society governed by Title II of Book III of this Part and approved for that purpose by the Minister responsible for culture.

With the exception of the case provided for in the third subparagraph of Article L. 134-5, the reproduction and performance of the book in digital format shall be authorised, in return for remuneration, on a non-exclusive basis and for a renewable period of five years.

II. Approved societies shall have standing to bring legal proceedings with a view to protecting the rights that they administer.
III. The approval provided for in I shall be issued having regard to:

(...)

2° equal representation of authors and publishers among the members and within the executive bodies;

(...)

5° the fairness of the rules governing the distribution of collected income among successors in title, whether or not they are parties to the publishing contract. The amount of the sums received by the author or authors of the book may not be less than the amount of the sums received by the publisher;

6° the evidentiary measures which the society intends to apply in order to identify and locate rightholders, for the purposes of distributing the collected income;

(...)

Article L. 134-4
I. The author of an out-of-print book or a publisher with the right to reproduce printed copies of that book may oppose the exercise by an approved collecting society of the right of authorisation referred to in the first subparagraph of Article L. 134-3(I). Notification of that opposition shall be submitted in writing to the body referred to in the first subparagraph of Article L. 134-2 no later than six months after the book in question has been registered in the database referred to in the same subparagraph.

(...)

Article L. 134-5

If, upon expiration of the period laid down in Article L. 134-4(I), the author or publisher has not given notice of opposition, the collecting society shall offer authorisation to reproduce and perform an out-of-print book in digital format to the publisher having the right to reproduce that book in print.

(...)

The exploitation authorisation referred to in the first subparagraph shall be issued by the collecting society on an exclusive basis for a 10-year period which is tacitly renewable.

(...)

If the offer referred to in the first subparagraph is not accepted ..., the reproduction and performance of the book in digital format shall be authorised by the collecting society as provided for in the second subparagraph of Article L. 134-3(I).

(...)

Article L. 134-6

The author and publisher having the right of reproduction in print of an out-of-print book shall at any time jointly notify the collecting society referred to in Article L. 134-3 of their decision to withdraw the latter's right to authorise the reproduction and performance of that book in digital format.

The author of an out-of-print book may decide at any time to withdraw from the collecting society referred to in Article L. 134-3 the right to authorise the reproduction and performance of a book in digital format if he provides evidence that he alone holds the rights laid down in L. 134-3. He shall notify it of his decision.

(...)

Article L. 134-7

The detailed rules for the application of this Chapter, in particular the arrangements for access to the database provided for in Article L. 134-2, the nature and format of the data collected and the most appropriate publicity measures to ensure that successors in title are as well informed as possible, the conditions for issuing and withdrawing the approval of collecting societies provided for in Article L. 134-3, shall be laid down in a decree of the Conseil d'État (Council of State).

Article L. 134-9

By derogation from the provisions in the first three subparagraphs of Article L. 321-9, income collected through the exploitation of out-of-print books which it has not been possible to distribute because the recipients could not be identified or located before expiry of the period provided for in the last subparagraph of L. 321-1 shall be used by the approved societies referred to in Article L. 134-3 for initiatives to support creative activities, initiatives to develop writers and initiatives by libraries to promote reading amongst the public.'

16 The detailed rules for the application of Articles L. 134-1 to L. 134-9 of the Intellectual Property Code were subsequently laid down, pursuant to Article L. 134-7 of that code, by Decree No 2013-182, which inserted, inter alia, Article R. 134-11 into that code (...).

The dispute in the main proceedings and the question referred for a preliminary ruling

17 Within the meaning of the Intellectual Property Code, an 'out-of-print book' means a book published in France before 1 January 2001 which is no longer commercially distributed by a publisher and is not currently published in print or in digital form. Articles L. 134-1 to L. 134-9 of that code established a legal framework intended to make those books accessible

once again by organising their commercial exploitation in digital form. The detailed rules for the application of those provisions were laid down by Decree No 2013-182.

18 By application registered on 2 May 2013, Mr Soulier and Ms Doke, who are both authors of literary works, requested the Conseil d'État (Council of State, France) to annul Decree No 2013-182.

19 In support of their claim, they submit, in particular, that Articles L. 134-1 to L. 134-9 of the Intellectual Property Code establish an exception or a limitation to the exclusive reproduction right laid down in Article 2(a) of Directive 2001/29 and that that exception or limitation is not included among those listed exhaustively in Article 5 thereof.

20 The Syndicat des écrivains de langue française (SELF), the Autour des auteurs association and 35 natural persons subsequently intervened in the proceedings in support of the claim brought by Mr Soulier and Ms Doke.

21 In their respective defences, the Prime Minister and the Minister for Culture and Communication both contested that the claim should be dismissed.

22 SOFIA subsequently intervened in the proceedings, also seeking to have those claims dismissed. SOFIA presents itself as a society made up equally of authors and publishers, mandated to manage the right to authorise the reproduction and representation of out-of-print books in digital form, the public lending right and the remuneration for digital private copying in the field of writing.

23 After dismissing all the pleas of Mr Soulier and Ms Doke that rested on legal bases other than Articles 2 and 5 of Directive 2001/29, the referring court started the examination of the pleas relating to those articles by holding, immediately, that the treatment of that aspect of the case depends on the interpretation to be given of those articles.

24 In those circumstances, the Conseil d'État (Council of State) decided to stay the proceedings and to refer the following question to the Court of Justice for a preliminary ruling:
'Do [Articles 2 and 5] of Directive 2001/29 preclude legislation, such as that [established in Articles L. 134-1 to L. 134-9 of the Intellectual Property Code], that gives approved collecting societies the right to authorise the reproduction and the representation in digital form of "out-of-print books", while allowing the authors of those books, or their successors in title, to oppose or put an end to that practice, on the conditions that it lays down?'

The question referred for a preliminary ruling

Preliminary observations

25 It is common ground, on the one hand, that the national legislation at issue in the main proceedings concerns not only the right to authorise the reproduction of out-of-print books in digital form, within the meaning of Article 2(a) of Directive 2001/29, but also the right to authorise the representation under that form and that such a representation constitutes a 'communication to the public' within the meaning of Article 3(1) of that directive.

26 On the other hand, that legislation does not fall within the scope of any of the exceptions and limitations that the Member States have the option of placing, on the basis of Article 5 of Directive 2001/29, on the rights of reproduction and communication to the public laid down in Article 2(a) and Article 3(1) of that directive. The list of exceptions and limitations authorised by that directive is exhaustive in nature, as is apparent from recital 32 thereof.

27 It therefore follows that Article 5 of Directive 2001/29 appears to be irrelevant for the purposes of the main proceedings.

28 In those circumstances, it must be considered that, by its question, the referring court asks, in essence, whether Article 2(a) and Article 3(1) of Directive 2001/29 must be interpreted as precluding national legislation, such as that at issue in the main proceedings, that gives an approved collecting society the right to authorise the reproduction and communication to the public, in digital form, of out-of-print books, while allowing the authors of those books or their successors in title to oppose or put an end to that practice on the conditions that that legislation lays down.

The Court's reply

29 Article 2(a) and Article 3(1) of Directive 2001/29 provide, respectively, that the Member States are to grant authors the exclusive right to authorise or prohibit direct or indirect reproduction of their works by any means and in any form and the exclusive right to authorise or prohibit any communication to the public of their works.

30 In that regard, it must be observed, first of all, that the protection conferred by those provisions on authors must be given a broad interpretation.

31 Therefore, that protection must be understood, in particular, as not being limited to the enjoyment of the rights guaranteed by Article 2(a) and Article 3(1) of Directive 2001/29, but as also extending to the exercise of those rights.

32 Such an interpretation is supported by the Berne Convention, Articles 1 to 21 of which the European Union is required to comply with under Article 1(4) of the WIPO Copyright Treaty, to which the European Union is a party and which Directive 2001/29 is intended, in particular, to implement, as stated in recital 15 thereof. It is apparent from Article 5(2) of that convention that the protection which it guarantees to authors extends both to the enjoyment and to the exercise of the rights of reproduction and communication to the public referred to in Article 9(1) and Article 11a(1) thereof, which correspond to those protected by Directive 2001/29.

33 Next, it is important to emphasise that the rights guaranteed to authors by Article 2(a) and Article 3(1) of Directive 2001/29 are preventive in nature, in the sense that any reproduction or communication to the public of a work by a third party requires the prior consent of its author.

34 It follows that, subject to the exceptions and limitations laid down exhaustively in Article 5 of Directive 2001/29, any use of a work carried out by a third party without such prior consent must be regarded as infringing the copyright in that work.

35 Nevertheless, Article 2(a) and Article 3(1) of Directive 2001/29 do not specify the way in which the prior consent of the author must be expressed, so that those provisions cannot be interpreted as requiring that such consent must necessarily be expressed explicitly. It must be held, on the contrary, that those provisions also allow that consent to be expressed implicitly.

36 Thus, in a case in which it was questioned about the concept of a 'new public', the Court held that, in a situation in which an author had given prior, explicit and unreserved authorisation to the publication of his articles on the website of a newspaper publisher, without making use of technological measures restricting access to those works from other websites, that author could be regarded, in essence, as having authorised the communication of those works to the general internet public.

37 However, the objective of increased protection of authors to which recital 9 of Directive 2001/29 refers implies that the circumstances in which implicit consent can be admitted

must be strictly defined in order not to deprive of effect the very principle of the author's prior consent.

38 In particular, every author must actually be informed of the future use of his work by a third party and the means at his disposal to prohibit it if he so wishes.

39 Failing any actual prior information relating to that future use, the author is unable to adopt a position on it and, therefore, to prohibit it, if necessary, so that the very existence of his implicit consent appears purely hypothetical in that regard.

40 Consequently, without guarantees ensuring that authors are actually informed as to the envisaged use of their works and the means at their disposal to prohibit it, it is de facto impossible for them to adopt any position whatsoever as to such use.

41 Concerning national legislation such as that at issue in the main proceedings, it must be stated that it gives an approved society the right to authorise the digital exploitation of out-of-print books, while allowing the authors of those books to oppose that practice in advance, within a time limit of six months after their registration in a database established to that effect.

42 Exercise of the right of opposition established by such legislation for the benefit of all the holders of rights in the books concerned, and in particular the authors, thus has the effect of prohibiting the use of those works, whereas the lack of opposition of a given author within the prescribed period can be construed, with regard to Article 2(a) and Article 3(1) of Directive 2001/29, as the expression of his implicit consent to that use.

43 It does not follow from the decision to refer that that legislation offers a mechanism ensuring authors are actually and individually informed. Therefore, it is not inconceivable that some of the authors concerned are not, in reality, even aware of the envisaged use of their works and, therefore, that they are not able to adopt a position, one way or the other, on it. In those circumstances, a mere lack of opposition on their part cannot be regarded as the expression of their implicit consent to that use.

44 This is all the more true considering that such legislation is aimed at books which, while having been published and commercially distributed in the past, are so no longer. That particular context precludes the conclusion that it can reasonably be presumed that, without opposition on their part, every author of these 'forgotten' books is, however, in favour of the 'resurrection' of their works, in view of their commercial use in a digital format.

45 Admittedly, Directive 2001/29 does not preclude national legislation, such as that at issue in the main proceedings, from pursuing an objective such as the digital exploitation of out-of-print books in the cultural interest of consumers and of society as a whole. However, the pursuit of that objective and of that interest cannot justify a derogation not provided for by the EU legislature to the protection that authors are ensured by that directive.

46 Lastly, it must be stated that legislation such as that at issue in the main proceedings enables, in particular, authors to put an end to the commercial exploitation of their works in digital format, either by mutual agreement with the publishers of those works in printed format or alone, on condition, however, in that second case, that they provide evidence that they alone hold the rights in their works.

47 In that regard, it is important to point out, first, that it follows from the exclusive nature of the rights of reproduction and communication to the public laid down in Article 2(a) and Article 3(1) of Directive 2001/29 that the authors are the only persons to whom that directive gives, by way of original grant, the right to exploit their works.

48 It follows that, if Directive 2001/29 does not prohibit Member States from granting certain rights or certain benefits to third parties, such as publishers, it is provided that those rights and benefits do not harm the rights which that directive gives exclusively to authors.

49 Consequently, it must be considered that, when the author of a work decides, in the context of the implementation of legislation such as that at issue in the main proceedings, to put an end to the future exploitation of that work in a digital format, that right must be capable of being exercised without having to depend, in certain cases, on the concurrent will of persons other than those to whom that author had given prior authorisation to proceed with such a digital exploitation and, thus, on the agreement of the publisher holding only the rights of exploitation of that work in a printed format.

50 Secondly, it follows from Article 5(2) of the Berne Convention, which is binding on the Union for the reasons set out in paragraph 32 of the present judgment, that the enjoyment and the exercise of the rights of reproduction and communication to the public given to authors by that convention and corresponding to those laid down in Article 2(a) and 3(1) of Directive 2001/29 may not be subject to any formality.

51 It follows, in particular, that, in the context of legislation such as that at issue in the main proceedings, the author of a work must be able to put an end to the exercise, by a third party, of rights of exploitation in digital format that he holds on that work, and in so doing

prohibit him from any future use in such a format, without having to submit beforehand, in certain circumstances, to a formality consisting of proving that other persons are not, otherwise, holders of other rights in that work, such as those concerning its exploitation in printed format.

52 Having regard to all of the foregoing considerations, the answer to the question is that Article 2(a) and Article 3(1) of Directive 2001/29 must be interpreted as precluding national legislation, such as that at issue in the main proceedings, that gives an approved collecting society the right to authorise the reproduction and communication to the public in digital form of 'out-of-print' books, namely, books published in France before 1 January 2001 which are no longer commercially distributed by a publisher and are not currently published in print or in digital form, while allowing the authors of those books, or their successors in title, to oppose or put an end to that practice, on the conditions that that legislation lays down. (...)

THINK IT OVER!

1. The relevance of this preliminary ruling goes well beyond the compliance of the French regulation with the InfoSoc-Directive. This is the first judicial revision of a non-voluntary collective licensing on a general basis. Some arguments of the CJEU might be valid to similar regimes (especially to compulsory and extended collective licensing). In accordance with the previous case law regarding the distinction between enjoyment and exercise of exclusive rights (see paragraphs 31-32), the CJEU also stated that the French collective licensing regime shall not be considered as a copyright exception or limitation. *Do you think this clarification will have an immediate effect on national copyright legislation as it was the case with the Padawan decision?*

2. Another key finding of the CJEU involved the consent of the author to the collective exercise of his rights. The Court acknowledged that an implicit consent might be sufficient, however, several prerequisites need to be met: "[i]n particular, every author must actually be informed of the future use of his work by a third party and the means at his disposal to prohibit it if he so wishes. Failing any actual prior information relating to that future use, the author is unable to adopt a position on it and, therefore, to prohibit it, if necessary, so that the very existence of his implicit consent appears purely hypothetical in that regard" (paragraphs 38-39). It seems uncertain how collective management organizations can satisfy their obligation to individually inform each and every author of the future uses of their work. *Can this condition justify non-voluntary collective licensing of certain exclusive rights in the case of mass-uses of the protected works?*

3. The EU's Directive (EU) 2019/790 on copyright and related rights in the Digital Single Market (CDSM Directive) now regulates the question of out of commerce works. Paragraph 30 acknowledges that prior authorization from right holders may be very difficult regarding the nature and amount of out of commerce works involved in mass digitization projects. Under the CDSM Directive a work or other subject matter is deemed out of commerce when it can be presumed in good faith that the whole work or other subject matter is not available to the public through customary channels of commerce, after a reasonable effort has been made to determine whether it is available to the public. Article 8 of the directive provides for a way to facilitate the use of these works by cultural heritage institutions inspired by non-voluntary collective licensing systems. Three conditions are imposed to such collective licensing: (i) the CMO should be sufficiently representative of right holders in the relevant type of works or other subject matter and of the rights that are the subject of the license, (ii) all right holders are guaranteed equal treatment in relation to the terms of the license, and (iii) all right holders may, at any time, easily and effectively, exclude their works or other subject matter from the collective licensing mechanism. *Are those criteria aligned with the Court's finding in the Soulier and Doke case? If you were the EU legislator, how would you deal with a situation where there is no sufficiently representative CMO in some of the Member States? Would you allow Member States to clarify further the definition of out of commerce works, and on what condition? How would you guarantee that right holders may effectively opt out from the collective licensing mechanism?*

Further Case Law

In French

Décision du Conseil constitutionnel n° 2013-370 QPC du 28 février 2014

Conseil d'État du 7 juin 2017 n° 368208

Recommended readings

In English

Jane C. Ginsburg: Fair Use for Free, or Permitted-bud-Paid? *Berkeley Technology Law Journal*, Issue 3/2015, p. 1383-1446.

Oleksandr Bulayenko: Permissibility of Non-Voluntary Collective Management of Copyright under EU-Law - The Case of the French Law on Out-of-Commerce Books, *JIPITEC*, Issue 1/2016, p. 51-68.

Caterina Sganga: The Eloquent Silence of Soulier and Doke and its Critical Implications for EU Copyright Law, *Journal of Intellectual Property Law & Practice*, Issue 4/2017, p. 321-330.

Franck Macrez: *The French Case: From Orphan Books to Out-of-Print Works (and Vice-Versa)* (June 23, 2017), Center for International Intellectual Property Studies (CEIPI) Research Paper No. 2017-14 (https://ssrn.com/abstract=3116783)

Eleonora Rosati: *Ebooks and Mass Digitization Projects: the Role of Licensing.* In: Tanya Aplin (Ed.): *Research Handbook on Intellectual Property and Digital Technologies*, Edward Elgar, Cheltenham, 2020, p. 204-208.

In French

Emmanuel Derieux: Sanction européenne du régime français des livres indisponibles, *Revue Lamy Droit de l'Immatériel*, 2016/132

Lamia El Badawi: La necessaire revision du régime français d'exploitation numérique des livres indisponibles, *Revue de l'Union européenne*, 2017, p. 78.

Valérie-Laure Benabou: Pourquoi l'arrêt Soulier et Doke dépasse le cas ReLire: le contrôle par la CJUE des modalités de l'autorisation préalable de l'auteur, *Dalloz IP/IT*, 2017, p. 108.

Franck Macrez: "Soulier" et la résurgence de l'auteur, *Recueil Dalloz*, 2017, p. 84.

Florence-Marie Piriou: Nouvelle règlementation européenne sur les œuvres indisponibles et la gestion collective étendue (Commentaire des articles 8 à 11 de la directive), *Communication Commerce électronique*, n° 10, Octobre 2019, dossier 4.

Maïté Guillemain: Le consentement de l'auteur dans l'exploitation numérique des livres indisponibles, *La Semaine Juridique Entreprise et Affaires*, n° 9, 2 Mars 2017, 1128.

In German

Michel M. Walter: Die digitale Verbreitung vergriffener Werke, *Medien und Recht*, Heft 1/2017, p. 31-39.

In Hungarian

Hajdú Dóra: A kereskedelmi forgalomban nem kapható könyvek digitalizálása Franciaországban, *Infokommunikáció és Jog*, 2013/55. szám, p. 53-59

Tarr Péter: Beszerezhetetlenné vált, ismét kapható könyvek. Digitálisan pótolt „hiánycikk-könyvek" a XX. századból, *Iparjogvédelmi és Szerzői Jogi Szemle*, 2013/6. szám, p. 108-134.

Pogácsás Anett: Az Európai Bíróság ítélete az out-of-commerce művekre vonatkozó francia nemzeti szabályozásról, *Jogesetek Magyarázata*, 2017/1-2. szám, p. 59-66.

Chapter V
Digital Exhaustion

USEDSOFT GMBH V. ORACLE INTERNATIONAL CORP.

Case C-128/11 - Judgment of the Court (Grand Chamber), 3 July 2012 [ECLI:EU:C:2012:407]

(...) Legal context

International law

3 The World Intellectual Property Organisation (WIPO) adopted the WIPO Copyright Treaty ('the Copyright Treaty') in Geneva on 20 December 1996. That treaty was approved on behalf of the European Community by Council Decision 2000/278/EC of 16 March 2000 (OJ 2000 L 89, p. 6).

4 Article 4 of the Copyright Treaty, 'Computer programs', reads as follows:
'Computer programs are protected as literary works within the meaning of Article 2 of the Berne Convention. Such protection applies to computer programs, whatever may be the mode or form of their expression.'

5 Article 6 of the Copyright Treaty, 'Right of distribution', provides:
'1. Authors of literary and artistic works shall enjoy the exclusive right of authorising the making available to the public of the original and copies of their works through sale or other transfer of ownership.
2. Nothing in this Treaty shall affect the freedom of Contracting Parties to determine the conditions, if any, under which the exhaustion of the right in paragraph 1 applies after the first sale or other transfer of ownership of the original or a copy of the work with the authorisation of the author.'

6 Article 8 of the Copyright Treaty provides:

'... authors of literary and artistic works shall enjoy the exclusive right of authorising any communication to the public of their works, by wire or wireless means, including the making available to the public of their works in such a way that members of the public may access these works from a place and at a time individually chosen by them'.

7 In the agreed statements concerning Articles 6 and 7 of the Copyright Treaty, it is declared that:

'As used in these Articles, the expressions "copies" and "original and copies" being subject to the right of distribution and the right of rental under the said Articles, refer exclusively to fixed copies that can be put into circulation as tangible objects.'

European Union law

Directive 2001/29

8 Recitals 28 and 29 in the preamble to Directive 2001/29/EC of the European Parliament and of the Council of 22 May 2001 on the harmonisation of certain aspects of copyright and related rights in the information society (OJ 2001 L 167, p. 10) state:

'(28) Copyright protection under this Directive includes the exclusive right to control distribution of the work incorporated in a tangible article. The first sale in the Community of the original of a work or copies thereof by the rightholder or with his consent exhausts the right to control resale of that object in the Community. This right should not be exhausted in respect of the original or of copies thereof sold by the rightholder or with his consent outside the Community. Rental and lending rights for authors have been established in Directive 92/100/EEC. The distribution right provided for in this Directive is without prejudice to the provisions relating to the rental and lending rights contained in Chapter I of that Directive.

(29) The question of exhaustion does not arise in the case of services and on-line services in particular. This also applies with regard to a material copy of a work or other subject-matter made by a user of such a service with the consent of the rightholder. Therefore, the same applies to rental and lending of the original and copies of works or other subject-matter which are services by nature. Unlike CD-ROM or CD-I, where the intellectual property is incorporated in a material medium, namely an item of goods, every on-line service is in fact an act which should be subject to authorisation where the copyright or related right so provides.'

9 In accordance with Article 1(2)(a) of Directive 2001/29, the directive 'shall leave intact and shall in no way affect existing Community provisions relating to ... the legal protection of computer programs'.

10 Article 3 of Directive 2001/29 provides:

'1. Member States shall provide authors with the exclusive right to authorise or prohibit any communication to the public of their works, by wire or wireless means, including the making available to the public of their works in such a way that members of the public may access them from a place and at a time individually chosen by them.

3. The rights referred to in paragraphs 1 and 2 shall not be exhausted by any act of communication to the public or making available to the public as set out in this Article.'

11 Article 4 of Directive 2001/29, 'Distribution right', provides:

'1. Member States shall provide for authors, in respect of the original of their works or of copies thereof, the exclusive right to authorise or prohibit any form of distribution to the public by sale or otherwise.

2. The distribution right shall not be exhausted within the Community in respect of the original or copies of the work, except where the first sale or other transfer of ownership in the Community of that object is made by the rightholder or with his consent.'

Directive 2009/24

12 According to recital 1 in the preamble to Directive 2009/24, that directive codifies Council Directive 91/250/EEC of 14 May 1991 on the legal protection of computer programs (OJ 1991 L 122, p. 42).

13 According to recital 7 in that preamble, '[f]or the purpose of this Directive, the term "computer program" shall include programs in any form, including those which are incorporated into hardware.'

14 According to recital 13 in that preamble, 'the acts of loading and running necessary for the use of a copy of a program which has been lawfully acquired, and the act of correction of its errors, may not be prohibited by contract'.

15 Article 1(1) of Directive 2009/24 provides that 'Member States shall protect computer programs, by copyright, as literary works within the meaning of the Berne Convention for the Protection of Literary and Artistic Works'.

16 Under Article 1(2) of that directive, '[p]rotection in accordance with this Directive shall apply to the expression in any form of a computer program'.

17 Article 4 of the directive, 'Restricted acts', provides:

'1. Subject to the provisions of Articles 5 and 6, the exclusive rights of the rightholder within the meaning of Article 2 shall include the right to do or to authorise:

(a) the permanent or temporary reproduction of a computer program by any means and in any form, in part or in whole; in so far as loading, displaying, running, transmission or storage of the computer program necessitate such reproduction, such acts shall be subject to authorisation by the rightholder;

(b) the translation, adaptation, arrangement and any other alteration of a computer program and the reproduction of the results thereof, without prejudice to the rights of the person who alters the program;

(c) any form of distribution to the public, including the rental, of the original computer program or of copies thereof.

2. The first sale in the Community of a copy of a program by the rightholder or with his consent shall exhaust the distribution right within the Community of that copy, with the exception of the right to control further rental of the program or a copy thereof.'

18 Article 5 of the directive, 'Exceptions to the restricted acts', provides in paragraph 1:
'In the absence of specific contractual provisions, the acts referred to in points (a) and (b) of Article 4(1) shall not require authorisation by the rightholder where they are necessary for the use of the computer program by the lawful acquirer in accordance with its intended purpose, including for error correction.'

German law

19 Paragraphs 69c and 69d of the Law on copyright and related rights (Gesetz über Urheberrecht und verwandte Schutzrechte (Urheberrechtsgesetz)) of 9 September 1965, as amended ('the UrhG'), transpose Articles 4 and 5 of Directive 2009/24 into national law.

Facts of the main proceedings and questions referred for a preliminary ruling

20 Oracle develops and markets computer software. It is the proprietor of the exclusive user rights under copyright law in those programs. It is also the proprietor of the German and Community word marks Oracle, which are registered inter alia for computer software.

21 Oracle distributes the software at issue in the main proceedings, namely databank software, in 85% of cases by downloading from the internet. The customer downloads a copy of the software directly to his computer from Oracle's website. The software is what is known as 'client-server-software'. The user right for such a program, which is granted by a licence agreement, includes the right to store a copy of the program permanently on a server and to

allow a certain number of users to access it by downloading it to the main memory of their work-station computers. On the basis of a maintenance agreement, updated versions of the software ('updates') and programs for correcting faults ('patches') can be downloaded from Oracle's website. At the customer's request, the programs are also supplied on CD-ROM or DVD.

22 Oracle offers group licences for the software at issue in the main proceedings for a minimum of 25 users each. An undertaking requiring licences for 27 users thus has to acquire two licences.

23 Oracle's licence agreements for the software at issue in the main proceedings contain the following term, under the heading 'Grant of rights':

'With the payment for services you receive, exclusively for your internal business purposes, for an unlimited period a non-exclusive non-transferable user right free of charge for everything that Oracle develops and makes available to you on the basis of this agreement.'

24 UsedSoft markets used software licences, including user licences for the Oracle computer programs at issue in the main proceedings. For that purpose UsedSoft acquires from customers of Oracle such user licences, or parts of them, where the original licences relate to a greater number of users than required by the first acquirer.

25 In October 2005 UsedSoft promoted an 'Oracle Special Offer' in which it offered for sale 'already used' licences for the Oracle programs at issue in the main proceedings. In doing so it pointed out that the licences were all 'current' in the sense that the maintenance agreement concluded between the original licence holder and Oracle was still in force, and that the lawfulness of the original sale was confirmed by a notarial certificate.

26 Customers of UsedSoft who are not yet in possession of the Oracle software in question download a copy of the program directly from Oracle's website, after acquiring such a used licence. Customers who already have that software and then purchase further licences for additional users are induced by UsedSoft to copy the program to the work stations of those users.

27 Oracle brought proceedings in the Landgericht München I (Regional Court, Munich I) seeking an order that UsedSoft cease the practices described in paragraphs 24 to 26 above. That court allowed Oracle's application. UsedSoft's appeal against the decision was dismissed. UsedSoft thereupon appealed on a point of law to the Bundesgerichtshof (Federal Court of Justice).

28 According to the Bundesgerichtshof, the actions of UsedSoft and its customers infringe Oracle's exclusive right of permanent or temporary reproduction of computer programs within the meaning of Article 4(1)(a) of Directive 2009/24. UsedSoft's customers cannot, in that court's view, rely on a right validly transferred to them by Oracle to reproduce the computer programs. Oracle's licence agreements state that the right to use the programs is 'non-transferable'. Oracle's customers are not therefore entitled to transfer to third parties the right of reproduction of those programs.

29 The outcome of the dispute depends, according to that court, on whether the customers of UsedSoft can successfully rely on Paragraph 69d(1) of the UrhG, which transposes Article 5(1) of Directive 2009/24 into German law.

30 The question arises, first, whether a person who, like UsedSoft's customers, does not hold a user right in the computer program granted by the rightholder, but relies on the exhaustion of the right to distribute a copy of the computer program, is a 'lawful acquirer' of that copy within the meaning of Article 5(1) of Directive 2009/24. The referring court considers that that is the case. It explains that the marketability of a copy of the computer program which arises from the exhaustion of the distribution right would be largely meaningless if the acquirer of such a copy did not have the right to reproduce the program. The use of a computer program, unlike the use of other works protected by copyright, generally requires its reproduction. Article 5(1) of Directive 2009/24 thus serves to safeguard the exhaustion of the distribution right under Article 4(2) of Directive 2009/24.

31 Next, the referring court considers whether, in a case such as that in the main proceedings, the right to distribute a copy of a computer program is exhausted under the second sentence of Paragraph 69c(3) of the UrhG, which transposes Article 4(2) of Directive 2009/24.

32 There are several possible interpretations. First, Article 4(2) of Directive 2009/24 could be applicable if the rightholder allows a customer, after the conclusion of a licence agreement, to make a copy of a computer program by downloading that program from the internet and storing it on a computer. That provision attaches the legal consequence of exhaustion of the distribution right to the first sale of a copy of the program and does not necessarily presuppose the putting into circulation of a physical copy of the program. Secondly, Article 4(2) of Directive 2009/24 could be applicable by analogy in the case of the sale of a computer program by means of on-line transmission. According to the supporters of that view, there is an unintended lacuna in the law ('planwidrige Regelungslücke') because the authors of the directive did not regulate or contemplate on-line transmission of computer programs. Thirdly, Article 4(2) of Directive 2009/24 is inapplicable because the exhaustion

of the distribution right under that provision always presupposes the putting into circulation of a physical copy of the program by the rightholder or with his consent. The authors of the directive deliberately refrained from extending the rule on exhaustion to the on-line transmission of computer programs.

33 Finally, the referring court raises the question whether a person who has acquired a used licence may, for making a copy of the program (as UsedSoft's customers do in the dispute in the main proceedings by downloading a copy of Oracle's program onto a computer from Oracle's website or uploading it to the main memory of other work stations), rely on exhaustion of the right of distribution of the copy of the program made by the first acquirer, with the consent of the rightholder, by downloading it from the internet, if the first acquirer has deleted his copy or no longer uses it. The referring court considers that the application by analogy of Articles 5(1) and 4(2) of Directive 2009/24 can be ruled out. Exhaustion of the distribution right is intended solely to guarantee the marketability of a copy of a program which is incorporated in a particular data carrier and sold by the rightholder or with his consent. The effect of exhaustion should not therefore be extended to the non-physical data transmitted on-line.

34 In those circumstances the Bundesgerichtshof decided to stay the proceedings and to refer the following questions to the Court for a preliminary ruling:

'*1. Is the person who can rely on exhaustion of the right to distribute a copy of a computer program a "lawful acquirer" within the meaning of Article 5(1) of Directive 2009/24?*

2. If the reply to the first question is in the affirmative: is the right to distribute a copy of a computer program exhausted in accordance with the first half-sentence of Article 4(2) of Directive 2009/24 when the acquirer has made the copy with the rightholder's consent by downloading the program from the internet onto a data carrier?

3. If the reply to the second question is also in the affirmative: can a person who has acquired a "used" software licence for generating a program copy as "lawful acquirer" under Article 5(1) and the first half-sentence of Article 4(2) of Directive 2009/24 also rely on exhaustion of the right to distribute the copy of the computer program made by the first acquirer with the rightholder's consent by downloading the program from the internet onto a data carrier if the first acquirer has erased his program copy or no longer uses it?'

Consideration of the questions referred

Question 2

35 By its second question, which should be addressed first, the referring court essentially seeks to know whether and under what conditions the downloading from the internet of a copy of a computer program, authorised by the copyright holder, can give rise to exhaustion of the right of distribution of that copy in the European Union within the meaning of Article 4(2) of Directive 2009/24.

36 It should be recalled that under Article 4(2) of Directive 2009/24 the first sale in the European Union of a copy of a computer program by the rightholder or with his consent exhausts the distribution right within the European Union of that copy.

37 According to the order for reference, the copyright holder itself, in this case Oracle, makes available to its customers in the European Union who wish to use its computer program a copy of that program which can be downloaded from its website.

38 To determine whether, in a situation such as that at issue in the main proceedings, the copyright holder's distribution right is exhausted, it must be ascertained, first, whether the contractual relationship between the rightholder and its customer, within which the downloading of a copy of the program in question has taken place, may be regarded as a 'first sale ... of a copy of a program' within the meaning of Article 4(2) of Directive 2009/24.

39 According to settled case-law, the need for a uniform application of European Union law and the principle of equality require that the terms of a provision of European Union law which makes no express reference to the law of the Member States for the purpose of determining its meaning and scope must normally be given an independent and uniform interpretation throughout the European Union.

40 The wording of Directive 2009/24 does not make any reference to national laws as regards the meaning to be given to the term 'sale' in Article 4(2) of the directive. It follows that that term must be regarded, for the purposes of applying the directive, as designating an autonomous concept of European Union law, which must be interpreted in a uniform manner throughout the territory of the European Union.

41 That conclusion is supported by the subject-matter and purpose of Directive 2009/24. Recitals 4 and 5 in the preamble to that directive, which is based on Article 95 EC, to which

Article 114 TFEU corresponds, state that its objective is to remove differences between the laws of the Member States which have adverse effects on the functioning of the internal market and concern computer programs. A uniform interpretation of the term 'sale' is necessary in order to avoid the protection offered to copyright holders by that directive varying according to the national law applicable.

42 According to a commonly accepted definition, a 'sale' is an agreement by which a person, in return for payment, transfers to another person his rights of ownership in an item of tangible or intangible property belonging to him. It follows that the commercial transaction giving rise, in accordance with Article 4(2) of Directive 2009/24, to exhaustion of the right of distribution of a copy of a computer program must involve a transfer of the right of ownership in that copy.

43 Oracle submits that it does not sell copies of its computer programs at issue in the main proceedings. It says that it makes available to its customers, free of charge, on its website a copy of the program concerned, and they can download that copy. The copy thus downloaded may not, however, be used by the customers unless they have concluded a user licence agreement with Oracle. Such a licence gives Oracle's customers a non-exclusive and non-transferable user right for an unlimited period for that program. Oracle submits that neither the making available of a copy free of charge nor the conclusion of the user licence agreement involves a transfer of the right of ownership of that copy.

44 In this respect, it must be observed that the downloading of a copy of a computer program and the conclusion of a user licence agreement for that copy form an indivisible whole. Downloading a copy of a computer program is pointless if the copy cannot be used by its possessor. Those two operations must therefore be examined as a whole for the purposes of their legal classification.

45 As regards the question whether, in a situation such as that at issue in the main proceedings, the commercial transactions concerned involve a transfer of the right of ownership of the copy of the computer program, it must be stated that, according to the order for reference, a customer of Oracle who downloads the copy of the program and concludes with that company a user licence agreement relating to that copy receives, in return for payment of a fee, a right to use that copy for an unlimited period. The making available by Oracle of a copy of its computer program and the conclusion of a user licence agreement for that copy are thus intended to make the copy usable by the customer, permanently, in return for payment of a fee designed to enable the copyright holder to obtain a remuneration corresponding to the economic value of the copy of the work of which it is the proprietor.

46 In those circumstances, the operations mentioned in paragraph 44 above, examined as a whole, involve the transfer of the right of ownership of the copy of the computer program in question.

47 It makes no difference, in a situation such as that at issue in the main proceedings, whether the copy of the computer program was made available to the customer by the rightholder concerned by means of a download from the rightholder's website or by means of a material medium such as a CD-ROM or DVD. Even if, in the latter case too, the rightholder formally separates the customer's right to use the copy of the program supplied from the operation of transferring the copy of the program to the customer on a material medium, the operation of downloading from that medium a copy of the computer program and that of concluding a licence agreement remain inseparable from the point of view of the acquirer, for the reasons set out in paragraph 44 above. Since an acquirer who downloads a copy of the program concerned by means of a material medium such as a CD-ROM or DVD and concludes a licence agreement for that copy receives the right to use the copy for an unlimited period in return for payment of a fee, it must be considered that those two operations likewise involve, in the case of the making available of a copy of the computer program concerned by means of a material medium such as a CD-ROM or DVD, the transfer of the right of ownership of that copy.

48 Consequently, in a situation such as that at issue in the main proceedings, the transfer by the copyright holder to a customer of a copy of a computer program, accompanied by the conclusion between the same parties of a user licence agreement, constitutes a 'first sale ... of a copy of a program' within the meaning of Article 4(2) of Directive 2009/24.

49 As the Advocate General observes in point 59 of his Opinion, if the term 'sale' within the meaning of Article 4(2) of Directive 2009/24 were not given a broad interpretation as encompassing all forms of product marketing characterised by the grant of a right to use a copy of a computer program, for an unlimited period, in return for payment of a fee designed to enable the copyright holder to obtain a remuneration corresponding to the economic value of the copy of the work of which he is the proprietor, the effectiveness of that provision would be undermined, since suppliers would merely have to call the contract a 'licence' rather than a 'sale' in order to circumvent the rule of exhaustion and divest it of all scope.

50 Secondly, the argument put forward by Oracle and the European Commission that the making available of a copy of a computer program on the copyright holder's website constitutes a 'making available to the public' within the meaning of Article 3(1) of Directive

2001/29, which, in accordance with Article 3(3) of that directive, cannot give rise to exhaustion of the right of distribution of the copy, cannot be accepted.

51 It is apparent from Article 1(2)(a) of Directive 2001/29 that the directive 'leave[s] intact and ... in no way affect[s] existing ... provisions [of European Union law] relating to ... the legal protection of computer programs' conferred by Directive 91/250, which was subsequently codified by Directive 2009/24. The provisions of Directive 2009/24, in particular Article 4(2), thus constitute a *lex specialis* in relation to the provisions of Directive 2001/29, so that even if the contractual relationship at issue in the main proceedings or an aspect of it might also be covered by the concept of 'communication to the public' within the meaning of Article 3(1) of the latter directive, the 'first sale ... of a copy of a program' within the meaning of Article 4(2) of Directive 2009/24 would still give rise, in accordance with that provision, to exhaustion of the right of distribution of that copy.

52 Moreover, as stated in paragraph 46 above, in a situation such as that at issue in the main proceedings, the copyright holder transfers the right of ownership of the copy of the computer program to his customer. As the Advocate General observes in point 73 of his Opinion, it follows from Article 6(1) of the Copyright Treaty, in the light of which Articles 3 and 4 of Directive 2001/29 must, so far as possible, be interpreted (...), that the existence of a transfer of ownership changes an 'act of communication to the public' provided for in Article 3 of that directive into an act of distribution referred to in Article 4 of the directive which, if the conditions in Article 4(2) of the directive are satisfied, can, like a 'first sale ... of a copy of a program' referred to in Article 4(2) of Directive 2009/24, give rise to exhaustion of the distribution right.

53 Thirdly, it must also be examined whether, as argued by Oracle, the governments which have submitted observations to the Court, and the Commission, the exhaustion of the distribution right referred to in Article 4(2) of Directive 2009/24 relates only to tangible property and not to intangible copies of computer programs downloaded from the internet. They refer in this respect to the wording of Article 4(2) of Directive 2009/24, recitals 28 and 29 in the preamble to Directive 2001/29, Article 4 of Directive 2001/29 read in conjunction with Article 8 of the Copyright Treaty, and the agreed statement concerning Articles 6 and 7 of the Copyright Treaty, whose transposition is one of the aims of Directive 2001/29.

54 Furthermore, according to the Commission, recital 29 in the preamble to Directive 2001/29 confirms that '[t]he question of exhaustion does not arise in the case of services and on-line services in particular'.

55 On this point, it must be stated, first, that it does not appear from Article 4(2) of Directive 2009/24 that the exhaustion of the right of distribution of copies of computer programs mentioned in that provision is limited to copies of programmes on a material medium such as a CD-ROM or DVD. On the contrary, that provision, by referring without further specification to the 'sale ... of a copy of a program', makes no distinction according to the tangible or intangible form of the copy in question.

56 Next, it must be recalled that Directive 2009/24, which concerns specifically the legal protection of computer programs, constitutes a *lex specialis* in relation to Directive 2001/29.

57 Article 1(2) of Directive 2009/24 states that '[p]rotection in accordance with this Directive shall apply to the expression in any form of a computer program'. Recital 7 in the preamble to that directive specifies that the 'computer programs' it aims to protect 'include programs in any form, including those which are incorporated into hardware'.

58 Those provisions thus make abundantly clear the intention of the European Union legislature to assimilate, for the purposes of the protection laid down by Directive 2009/24, tangible and intangible copies of computer programs.

59 In those circumstances, it must be considered that the exhaustion of the distribution right under Article 4(2) of Directive 2009/24 concerns both tangible and intangible copies of a computer program, and hence also copies of programs which, on the occasion of their first sale, have been downloaded from the internet onto the first acquirer's computer.

60 It is true that the concepts used in Directives 2001/29 and 2009/24 must in principle have the same meaning. However, even supposing that Article 4(2) of Directive 2001/29, interpreted in the light of recitals 28 and 29 in its preamble and in the light of the Copyright Treaty, which Directive 2001/29 aims to implement, indicated that, for the works covered by that directive, the exhaustion of the distribution right concerned only tangible objects, that would not be capable of affecting the interpretation of Article 4(2) of Directive 2009/24, having regard to the different intention expressed by the European Union legislature in the specific context of that directive.

61 It should be added that, from an economic point of view, the sale of a computer program on CD-ROM or DVD and the sale of a program by downloading from the internet are similar. The on-line transmission method is the functional equivalent of the supply of a material medium. Interpreting Article 4(2) of Directive 2009/24 in the light of the principle of equal treatment confirms that the exhaustion of the distribution right under that provision takes

effect after the first sale in the European Union of a copy of a computer program by the copyright holder or with his consent, regardless of whether the sale relates to a tangible or an intangible copy of the program.

62 As to the Commission's argument that European Union law does not provide for the exhaustion of the distribution right in the case of services, it must be recalled that the objective of the principle of the exhaustion of the right of distribution of works protected by copyright is, in order to avoid partitioning of markets, to limit restrictions of the distribution of those works to what is necessary to safeguard the specific subject-matter of the intellectual property concerned.

63 To limit the application, in circumstances such as those at issue in the main proceedings, of the principle of the exhaustion of the distribution right under Article 4(2) of Directive 2009/24 solely to copies of computer programs that are sold on a material medium would allow the copyright holder to control the resale of copies downloaded from the internet and to demand further remuneration on the occasion of each new sale, even though the first sale of the copy had already enabled the rightholder to obtain an appropriate remuneration. Such a restriction of the resale of copies of computer programs downloaded from the internet would go beyond what is necessary to safeguard the specific subject-matter of the intellectual property concerned.

64 Fourthly, it must also be examined whether, as Oracle claims, the maintenance agreement concluded by the first acquirer prevents in any event the exhaustion of the right provided for in Article 4(2) of Directive 2009/24, since the copy of the computer program which the first acquirer may transfer to a second acquirer no longer corresponds to the copy he downloaded but to a new copy of the program.

65 According to the order for reference, the used licences offered by UsedSoft are 'current', in that the sale of the copy of the program by Oracle to its customer was accompanied by the conclusion of a maintenance agreement for that copy.

66 It must be observed that the exhaustion of the right of distribution of a copy of a computer program under Article 4(2) of Directive 2009/24 only concerns copies which have been the subject of a first sale in the European Union by the copyright holder or with his consent. It does not relate to contracts for services, such as maintenance agreements, which are separable from such a sale and were concluded, possibly for an unlimited period, on the occasion of the sale.

67 None the less, the conclusion of a maintenance agreement, such as those at issue in the main proceedings, on the occasion of the sale of an intangible copy of a computer program has the effect that the copy originally purchased is patched and updated. Even if the maintenance agreement is for a limited period, the functionalities corrected, altered or added on the basis of such an agreement form an integral part of the copy originally downloaded and can be used by the acquirer of the copy for an unlimited period, even in the event that the acquirer subsequently decides not to renew the maintenance agreement.

68 In such circumstances, the exhaustion of the distribution right under Article 4(2) of Directive 2009/24 extends to the copy of the computer program sold as corrected and updated by the copyright holder.

69 It should be pointed out, however, that if the licence acquired by the first acquirer relates to a greater number of users than he needs, as stated in paragraphs 22 and 24 above, the acquirer is not authorised by the effect of the exhaustion of the distribution right under Article 4(2) of Directive 2009/24 to divide the licence and resell only the user right for the computer program concerned corresponding to a number of users determined by him.

70 An original acquirer who resells a tangible or intangible copy of a computer program for which the copyright holder's right of distribution is exhausted in accordance with Article 4(2) of Directive 2009/24 must, in order to avoid infringing the exclusive right of reproduction of a computer program which belongs to its author, laid down in Article 4(1)(a) of Directive 2009/24, make his own copy unusable at the time of its resale. In a situation such as that mentioned in the preceding paragraph, the customer of the copyright holder will continue to use the copy of the program installed on his server and will not thus make it unusable.

71 Moreover, even if an acquirer of additional user rights for the computer program concerned did not carry out a new installation – and hence a new reproduction – of the program on a server belonging to him, the effect of the exhaustion of the distribution right under Article 4(2) of Directive 2009/24 would in any event not extend to such user rights. In such a case the acquisition of additional user rights does not relate to the copy for which the distribution right was exhausted at the time of that transaction. On the contrary, it is intended solely to make it possible to extend the number of users of the copy which the acquirer of additional rights has himself already installed on his server.

72 On the basis of all the foregoing, the answer to Question 2 is that Article 4(2) of Directive 2009/24 must be interpreted as meaning that the right of distribution of a copy of a computer

program is exhausted if the copyright holder who has authorised, even free of charge, the downloading of that copy from the internet onto a data carrier has also conferred, in return for payment of a fee intended to enable him to obtain a remuneration corresponding to the economic value of the copy of the work of which he is the proprietor, a right to use that copy for an unlimited period.

Questions 1 and 3

73 By its first and third questions the referring court seeks essentially to know whether, and under what conditions, an acquirer of used licences for computer programs, such as those sold by UsedSoft, may, as a result of the exhaustion of the distribution right under Article 4(2) of Directive 2009/24, be regarded as a 'lawful acquirer' within the meaning of Article 5(1) of Directive 2009/24 who, in accordance with that provision, enjoys the right of reproduction of the program concerned in order to enable him to use the program in accordance with its intended purpose.

74 Article 5(1) of Directive 2009/24 provides that, in the absence of specific contractual provisions, the reproduction of a computer program does not require authorisation by the author of the program where that reproduction is necessary for the use of the computer program by the lawful acquirer in accordance with its intended purpose, including for error correction.

75 When the customer of the copyright holder purchases a copy of a computer program that is on the rightholder's website, he performs, by downloading the copy onto his computer, a reproduction of the copy which is authorised under Article 5(1) of Directive 2009/24. This is a reproduction that is necessary for the use of the program by the lawful acquirer in accordance with its intended purpose.

76 Moreover, recital 13 in the preamble to Directive 2009/24 states that 'the acts of loading and running necessary for the use of a copy of a program which has been lawfully acquired ... may not be prohibited by contract'.

77 It must be recalled, next, that the copyright holder's distribution right is exhausted, in accordance with Article 4(2) of Directive 2009/24, on the occasion of the first sale in the European Union by that rightholder, or with his consent, of any copy, tangible or intangible, of his computer program. It follows that, by virtue of that provision and notwithstanding the existence of contractual terms prohibiting a further transfer, the rightholder in question can no longer oppose the resale of that copy.

78 Admittedly, as stated in paragraph 70 above, the original acquirer of a tangible or intangible copy of a computer program for which the copyright holder's distribution right is exhausted in accordance with Article 4(2) of Directive 2009/24 who resells that copy must, in order to avoid infringing that rightholder's exclusive right of reproduction of his computer program under Article 4(1)(a) of Directive 2009/24, make the copy downloaded onto his computer unusable at the time of its resale.

79 As Oracle rightly observes, ascertaining whether such a copy has been made unusable may prove difficult. However, a copyright holder who distributes copies of a computer program on a material medium such as a CD-ROM or DVD is faced with the same problem, since it is only with great difficulty that he can make sure that the original acquirer has not made copies of the program which he will continue to use after selling his material medium. To solve that problem, it is permissible for the distributor – whether 'classic' or 'digital' – to make use of technical protective measures such as product keys.

80 Since the copyright holder cannot object to the resale of a copy of a computer program for which that rightholder's distribution right is exhausted under Article 4(2) of Directive 2009/24, it must be concluded that a second acquirer of that copy and any subsequent acquirer are 'lawful acquirers' of it within the meaning of Article 5(1) of Directive 2009/24.

81 Consequently, in the event of a resale of the copy of the computer program by the first acquirer, the new acquirer will be able, in accordance with Article 5(1) of Directive 2009/24, to download onto his computer the copy sold to him by the first acquirer. Such a download must be regarded as a reproduction of a computer program that is necessary to enable the new acquirer to use the program in accordance with its intended purpose.

82 The argument put forward by Oracle, Ireland and the French and Italian Governments that the concept of 'lawful acquirer' in Article 5(1) of Directive 2009/24 relates only to an acquirer who is authorised, under a licence agreement concluded directly with the copyright holder, to use the computer programme cannot be accepted.

83 That argument would have the effect of allowing the copyright holder to prevent the effective use of any used copy in respect of which his distribution right has been exhausted under Article 4(2) of Directive 2009/24, by relying on his exclusive right of reproduction laid down in Article 4(1)(a) of that directive, and would thus render ineffective the exhaustion of the distribution right under Article 4(2).

84 In the case of a situation such as that at issue in the main proceedings, it must be recalled that in paragraphs 44 and 48 above it was found that the downloading onto the customer's server of a copy of the computer program on the rightholder's website and the conclusion of a user licence agreement for that copy form an indivisible whole which, as a whole, must be classified as a sale. Having regard to that indivisible link between the copy on the rightholder's website, as subsequently corrected and updated, on the one hand, and the user licence relating to the copy, on the other, the resale of the user licence entails the resale of 'that copy' within the meaning of Article 4(2) of Directive 2009/24, and thus benefits from the exhaustion of the distribution right under that provision, notwithstanding the term in the licence agreement set out in paragraph 23 above.

85 As may be seen from paragraph 81 above, it follows that a new acquirer of the user licence, such as a customer of UsedSoft, will be able, as a 'lawful acquirer' within the meaning of Article 5(1) of Directive 2009/24 of the corrected and updated copy of the computer program concerned, to download that copy from the copyright holder's website, with that downloading constituting a reproduction of a computer program that is necessary to enable the new acquirer to use the program in accordance with its intended purpose.

86 It should be recalled, however, that, if the licence acquired by the first acquirer relates to a greater number of users than he needs, that acquirer is not authorised by the effect of the exhaustion of the distribution right under Article 4(2) of Directive 2009/24 to divide the licence and resell only the user right for the computer program concerned corresponding to a number of users determined by him, as explained in paragraphs 69 to 71 above.

87 Moreover, a copyright holder such as Oracle is entitled, in the event of the resale of a user licence entailing the resale of a copy of a computer program downloaded from his website, to ensure by all technical means at his disposal that the copy still in the hands of the reseller is made unusable.

88 It follows from the foregoing that the answer to Questions 1 and 3 is that Articles 4(2) and 5(1) of Directive 2009/24 must be interpreted as meaning that, in the event of the resale of a user licence entailing the resale of a copy of a computer program downloaded from the copyright holder's website, that licence having originally been granted by that rightholder to the first acquirer for an unlimited period in return for payment of a fee intended to enable the rightholder to obtain a remuneration corresponding to the economic value of that copy of his work, the second acquirer of the licence, as well as any subsequent acquirer of it, will be able to rely on the exhaustion of the distribution right under Article 4(2) of that directive, and hence be regarded as lawful acquirers of a copy of a computer program

within the meaning of Article 5(1) of that directive and benefit from the right of reproduction provided for in that provision. (...)

THINK IT OVER

1. In its preliminary ruling the CJEU concluded that a licence might be characterized as a sale if the right to use a computer program (1) lasts for an indefinite period, and (2) "in return for payment of a fee designed to enable the copyright holder to obtain a remuneration corresponding to the economic value of the copy of the work of which he is the proprietor". Furthermore, (3) merely calling a contract a licence is not enough "to circumvent the rule of exhaustion and divest it of all scope". *Are these feathures enough to treat an agreement sale rather than licence? What about Oracle's prohibiton of the transfer of computer programs? Is the right to use an intangible software an equivalent of property ownership over physical goods?*

2. The CJEU differentiated between two types of Internet uses. In the first scenario, uses that do not lead to the permanent reproduction or sale of any copy of a protected subject matter governed by the making available to the public right. Such an example might be the posting of content on a website, on-demand streaming or dissemination of files via P2P file-sharing applications. Under the second scenario, a permanent copy is received by the end-user in exchange of consideration and is retained on a permanent basis. The best example might be the purchase of a track from iTunes. The *UsedSoft* case serves as another great example. The CJEU declared this second category as sale and distribution of copies of works. *Is the CJEU's syllogism correct?*

3. *Is the theory of functional equivalence applicable to copyrightable subject matter other than computer programs?* Referring back to the CJEU's point according to which the online transmission of computer program is from an economic (and at the same time from a technological) perspective functionally the same as selling a data carrier in a tangible format, the answer shall be a clear "no". Sound recordings, audiovisual contents or audio books have multiple ways of exploitation, including the distribution of copies on tangible data carriers, making available to the public or selling a digital copy via the Internet, communication to the public by wire or wireless means, public performance/display etc. *Is it correct, if we paraphrase the CJEU's logic in the following way: "from an economic point of view, the sale of a sound recording/audio-book on a physical data carrier and the sale of the said content by downloading from the Internet are not similar. The on-line transmission method is not the functional equivalent of the supply of a material medium"? Is the outcome the same from the technological point of view?* Compare to the *Tom Kabinet* ruling at page 462.

Further Case Law

OLG Stuttgart 03.11.2011 (2 U 49/11) - Keine Erschöpfung bei Online-Vertrieb von Hörbüchern, *Computer und Recht*, Heft 5/2012, p. 301-302. (Anm. Schmidt)

OLG Hamm 15.05.2014 (22 U 60/13) - Keine Erschöpfung bei Audiodateien - Hörbuch-AGB, *Gewerblicher Rechtsschutz und Urheberrecht*, Heft 9/2014, p. 853-863.

Case C-355/12 - Nintendo Co. Ltd and Others v PC Box Srl and 9Net Srl, Judgment of the Court (Fourth Chamber), 23 January 2014 [ECLI:EU:C:2014:25]

Case C-166/15 - Aleksandrs Ranks and Jurijs Vasiļevičs v Finanšu un ekonomisko noziegumu izmeklēšanas prokoratūra and Microsoft Corp., Judgment of the Court (Third Chamber), 12 October 2016 [ECLI:EU:C:2016:762]

BGH 19.3.2015 (I ZR 4/14) - Voraussetzungen zur Zulässigkeit der Weiterveräußerung gebrauchter Software - Green-IT, *Gewerblicher Rechtsschutz und Urheberrecht*, Heft 11/2015, p. 1108–1114.

Union Fédérale des Consommateurs - Que Choisir v. S.A.R.L. Valve, Tribunal de Grande Instance de Paris, N° RG 16/01008

Case C-263/18 - Nederlands Uitgeversverbond, Groep Algemene Uitgevers v. Tom Kabinet Internet BV and Others, Judgment of the Court (Grand Chamber), 19 December 2019 [ECLI:EU:C:2019:1111]

Recommended readings

In English

Alexander Göbel: The principle of exhaustion and the resale of downloaded software – the UsedSoft v. Oracle case [UsedSoft GmbH v. Oracle International Corporation, ECJ (Grand Chamber), Judgment of 3 July 2012, C-128/11], *European Law Reporter*, Issue 9/2012, p. 226-234.

Lukas Feiler: Birth of the First-Download Doctrine: the Application of the First-Sale Doctrine to Internet Downloads under EU and U.S. Copyright Law, *Journal of Internet Law*, October 2012, p. 16-17.

Ellen Franziska Schulze: Resale of digital content such as music, films or eBooks under European law, *European Intellectual Property Review*, Issue 1/2014, p. 9-13.

Giorgio Spedicato: *Online Exhaustion and the Boundaries of Interpretation.* In: Roberto Caso - Federica Giovanella (Eds.): *Balancing Copyright Law in the Digital Age - Comparative Perspectives*, Springer Verlag, Berlin - Heidelberg, 2015: p. 27-64.

Péter Mezei: *Copyright Exhaustion - Law and Policy in the United States and the European Union*, Cambridge University Press, Cambridge, 2018, p. 93-98.
Caterina Sganga: A Plea for Digital Exhaustion in EU Copyright Law, *JIPITEC*, Issue 3/2018, p. 211-2390.

In French

André Lucas: Droit d'auteur et droits voisins - Droit de distribution - Logiciel - Téléchargement - Épuisement (oui), *Propriétés intellectuelles*, n° 44, 2012, p. 333-337.
Audrey Lefèvre: La mise à disposition de copies de logiciels par téléchargement sur internet épuise le droit exclusif de distribution de l'éditeur sur ces copies, *Droit de l'immatériel: informatique, médias, communication*, n° 85, 2012, p. 21-26.
Lionel Costes: Protection juridique de programmes d'ordinateur: les importantes précisions de la CJUE, *Droit de l'immatériel: informatique, médias, communication*, n° 85, 2012, p. 32-34.
Mathieu Coulaud: CJUE, 3 juillet 2012, Usedsoft GmbH c/ Oracle International Corp. (affaire C-128/11): une décision surprenante retreint, dans certains cas, le droit des éditeurs de logiciels, *Droit de l'immatériel: informatique, médias, communication*, n° 85, 2012, p. 129-130.
Christophe Caron: La revente de la copie de sauvegarde est interdite, *Communication Commerce électronique*, n° 12, Décembre 2016, comm. 99.
Thibaud Guillebon: La portée de la jurisprudence Usedsoft sur la revente de copies de sauvegarde de logiciels, *La Semaine Juridique Entreprise et Affaires*, n° 13-14, 30 Mars 2017, 1189.
Yves Bismuth: L'influence de la jurisprudence de la Cour de justice de l'Union européenne sur le droit d'auteur français des logiciels et des bases de données, *Communication Commerce électronique*, n° 1, Janvier 2019, étude 2

In German

Michel M. Walter: Handel mit Gebrauchtsoftware, *MR-Int: Internationale Rundschau zum Medienrecht, IP- & IT-Recht*, Heft 1-2/2012, p. 40-42.
Jochen Schneider - Gerald Spindler: Der Kampf um die gebrauchte Software - Revolution im Urheberrecht?, *Computer und Recht*, Heft 8/2012, p. 489-498.
Helmut Haberstumpf: Der Handel mit gebrauchter Software im harmonisierten Urheberrecht, *Computer und Recht*, Heft 9/2012, p. 561-572.
Martin Senftleben: Die Fortschreibung des urheberrechtlichen Erschöpfungsgrundsatzes im digitalen Umfeld, *Neue juristische Wochenschrift*, Heft 40/2012, p. 2924-2927.
Thomas Rainer Schmitt: Der Online-Vertrieb von Software nach dem EuGH-Urteil „UsedSoft", *Medien und Recht*, Heft 5/2012, p. 256-260.
Nikita Malevanny: Die UsedSoft-Kontroverse: Auslegung und Auswirkungen des EuGH-Urteils, *Computer und Recht*, Heft 7/2013, p. 422-427.

In Spanish

Gemma Minero Alejandre: Reventa de software de segunda mano. Estado de la cuestión en la Unión Europea tras la sentencia *Usedsoft c. Oracle International*, Revista Jurídica de la Universidad Autónoma de Madrid, nº 26, 2012 (https://revistas.uam.es/revistajuridica/article/view/210/192)

In Hungarian

Farkas Henrietta Regina: A „használt" szoftverek értékesítésének jogi megítélése az Európai Unióban: a UsedSoft kontra Oracle ügy, *Infokommunikáció és Jog*, 2013. december (56. szám), p. 126-130.

Jaczó Dániel: A használt szoftverekkel való kereskedés szerzői jogi értékelése és bírsági gyakorlata az Európai Unió irányelveinek és esetjogának tükrében, *Infokommunikáció és Jog*, 2014. szeptember (59. szám), p. 142-150.

Mezei Péter: *Jogkimerülés a szerzői jogban*, Médiatudományi Intézet, Budapest, 2016, p. 114-118.

TIMOTHY S. VERNOR V. AUTODESK, INC.

621 *F.3d* 1102 (2010)

OPINION

CALLAHAN, Circuit Judge:

(...) I. A. Autodesk's Release 14 software and licensing practices

The material facts are not in dispute. Autodesk makes computer-aided design software used by architects, engineers, and manufacturers. It has more than nine million customers. It first released its AutoCAD software in 1982. It holds registered copyrights in all versions of the software including the discontinued Release 14 version, which is at issue in this case. It provided Release 14 to customers on CD-ROMs.

Since at least 1986, Autodesk has offered AutoCAD to customers pursuant to an accompanying software license agreement ("SLA"), which customers must accept before installing the software. A customer who does not accept the SLA can return the software for a full refund. Autodesk offers SLAs with different terms for commercial, educational institution, and student users. The commercial license, which is the most expensive, imposes the fewest restrictions on users and allows them software upgrades at discounted prices.

The SLA for Release 14 first recites that Autodesk retains title to all copies. Second, it states that the customer has a nonexclusive and nontransferable license to use Release 14. Third, it imposes transfer restrictions, prohibiting customers from renting, leasing, or transferring the software without Autodesk's prior consent and from electronically or physically transferring the software out of the Western Hemisphere. Fourth, it imposes significant use restrictions:

"YOU MAY NOT: (1) modify, translate, reverse-engineer, decompile, or disassemble the Software ... (3) remove any proprietary notices, labels, or marks from the Software or Documentation; (4) use ... the Software outside of the Western Hemisphere; (5) utilize any computer software or hardware designed to defeat any hardware copy-protection device, should the software you have licensed be equipped with such protection; or (6) use the Software for commercial or other revenue-generating purposes if the Software has been licensed or labeled for educational use only."

Fifth, the SLA provides for license termination if the user copies the software without authorization or does not comply with the SLA's restrictions. Finally, the SLA provides that if the software is an upgrade of a previous version:

> "[Y]ou must destroy the software previously licensed to you, including any copies resident on your hard disk drive ... within sixty (60) days of the purchase of the license to use the upgrade or update.... Autodesk reserves the right to require you to show satisfactory proof that previous copies of the software have been destroyed."

Autodesk takes measures to enforce these license requirements. It assigns a serial number to each copy of AutoCAD and tracks registered licensees. It requires customers to input "activation codes" within one month after installation to continue using the software. The customer obtains the code by providing the product's serial number to Autodesk. Autodesk issues the activation code after confirming that the serial number is authentic, the copy is not registered to a different customer, and the product has not been upgraded. Once a customer has an activation code, he or she may use it to activate the software on additional computers without notifying Autodesk.

B. Autodesk's provision of Release 14 software to CTA

In March 1999, Autodesk reached a settlement agreement with its customer Cardwell/Thomas & Associates, Inc. ("CTA"), which Autodesk had accused of unauthorized use of its software. As part of the settlement, Autodesk licensed ten copies of Release 14 to CTA. CTA agreed to the SLA, which appeared (1) on each Release 14 package that Autodesk provided to CTA; (2) in the settlement agreement; and (3) on-screen, while the software is being installed.

CTA later upgraded to the newer, fifteenth version of the AutoCAD program, AutoCAD 2000. It paid $495 per upgrade license, compared to $3,750 for each new license. The SLA for AutoCAD 2000, like the SLA for Release 14, required destruction of copies of previous versions of the software, with proof to be furnished to Autodesk on request. However, rather than destroying its Release 14 copies, CTA sold them to Vernor at an office sale with the handwritten activation codes necessary to use the software.

C. Vernor's eBay business and sales of Release 14

Vernor has sold more than 10,000 items on eBay. In May 2005, he purchased an authentic used copy of Release 14 at a garage sale from an unspecified seller. He never agreed to the SLA's terms, opened a sealed software packet, or installed the Release 14 software. Though he was aware of the SLA's existence, he believed that he was not bound by its terms. He posted the software copy for sale on eBay.

Autodesk filed a Digital Millennium Copyright Act ("DMCA") take-down notice with eBay claiming that Vernor's sale infringed its copyright, and eBay terminated Vernor's auction. Autodesk advised Vernor that it conveyed its software copies pursuant to non-transferable licenses, and resale of its software was copyright infringement. Vernor filed a DMCA counter-notice with eBay contesting the validity of Autodesk's copyright claim. Autodesk did not respond to the counter-notice. eBay reinstated the auction, and Vernor sold the software to another eBay user.

In April 2007, Vernor purchased four authentic used copies of Release 14 at CTA's office sale. The authorization codes were handwritten on the outside of the box. He listed the four copies on eBay sequentially, representing, "This software is not currently installed on any computer." On each of the first three occasions, the same DMCA process ensued. Autodesk filed a DMCA take-down notice with eBay, and eBay removed Vernor's auction. Vernor submitted a counter-notice to which Autodesk did not respond, and eBay reinstated the auction.

When Vernor listed his fourth, final copy of Release 14, Autodesk again filed a DMCA take-down notice with eBay. This time, eBay suspended Vernor's account because of Autodesk's repeated charges of infringement. Vernor also wrote to Autodesk, claiming that he was entitled to sell his Release 14 copies pursuant to the first sale doctrine, because he never installed the software or agreed to the SLA. In response, Autodesk's counsel directed Vernor to stop selling the software. Vernor filed a final counter-notice with eBay. When Autodesk again did not respond to Vernor's counter-notice, eBay reinstated Vernor's account. At that point, Vernor's eBay account had been suspended for one month, during which he was unable to earn income on eBay.

Vernor currently has two additional copies of Release 14 that he wishes to sell on eBay. Although the record is not clear, it appears that Vernor sold two of the software packages that he purchased from CTA, for roughly $600 each, but did not sell the final two to avoid risking further suspension of his eBay account. (...)

III.

Copyright is a federal law protection provided to the authors of "original works of authorship," including software programs. The Copyright Act confers several exclusive rights on copyright owners, including the exclusive rights to reproduce their works and to distribute their works by sale or rental. The exclusive distribution right is limited by the first sale doctrine, an affirmative defense to copyright infringement that allows owners of copies of copyrighted works to resell those copies. The exclusive reproduction right is limited within the software context by the essential step defense, another affirmative defense to copyright infringement that is discussed further *infra*. Both of these affirmative defenses are unavailable to those who are only licensed to use their copies of copyrighted works.

This case requires us to decide whether Autodesk sold Release 14 copies to its customers or licensed the copies to its customers. If CTA owned its copies of Release 14, then both its sales to Vernor and Vernor's subsequent sales were non-infringing under the first sale doctrine. However, if Autodesk only licensed CTA to use copies of Release 14, then CTA's and Vernor's sales of those copies are not protected by the first sale doctrine and would therefore infringe Autodesk's exclusive distribution right.

A. The first sale doctrine

The Supreme Court articulated the first sale doctrine in 1908, holding that a copyright owner's exclusive distribution right is exhausted after the owner's first sale of a particular copy of the copyrighted work. In Bobbs–Merrill Co. v. Straus, 210 U.S. 339 (1908), the plaintiff-copyright owner sold its book with a printed notice announcing that any retailer who sold the book for less than one dollar was responsible for copyright infringement. Plaintiff sought injunctive relief against defendants-booksellers who failed to comply with the price restriction. The Supreme Court rejected the plaintiff's claim, holding that its exclusive distribution right applied only to first sales of copies of the work. The distribution right did not permit plaintiff to dictate that subsequent sales of the work below a particular price were infringing. The Court noted that its decision solely applied to the rights of a copyright owner that distributed its work without a license agreement.

Congress codified the first sale doctrine the following year. In its current form, it allows the "owner of a particular copy" of a copyrighted work to sell or dispose of his copy without the copyright owner's authorization. The first sale doctrine does not apply to a person who possesses a copy of the copyrighted work without owning it, such as a licensee.

B. Owners vs. licensees

We turn to our precedents governing whether a transferee of a copy of a copyrighted work is an owner or licensee of that copy. We then apply those precedents to CTA's and Vernor's possession of Release 14 copies.

1. *United States v. Wise*

In *Wise*, a criminal copyright infringement case, we considered whether copyright owners who transferred copies of their motion pictures pursuant to written distribution agreements had executed first sales. The defendant was found guilty of copyright infringement based on his for-profit sales of motion picture prints. The copyright owners distributed their films to third parties pursuant to written agreements that restricted their use and transfer. On appeal, the defendant argued that the government failed to prove the absence of a first sale for each film. If the copyright owners' initial transfers of the films were first sales, then the defendant's resales were protected by the first sale doctrine and thus were not copyright infringement.

To determine whether a first sale occurred, we considered multiple factors pertaining to each film distribution agreement. Specifically, we considered whether the agreement (a) was labeled a license, (b) provided that the copyright owner retained title to the prints, (c) required the return or destruction of the prints, (d) forbade duplication of prints, or (e) required the transferee to maintain possession of the prints for the agreement's duration. Our use of these several considerations, none dispositive, may be seen in our treatment of each film print.

For example, we reversed the defendant's conviction with respect to *Camelot*. It was unclear whether the *Camelot* print sold by the defendant had been subject to a first sale. Copyright owner Warner Brothers distributed *Camelot* prints pursuant to multiple agreements, and the government did not prove the absence of a first sale with respect to each agreement. We noted that, in one agreement, Warner Brothers had retained title to the prints, required possessor National Broadcasting Company ("NBC") to return the prints if the parties could select a mutual agreeable price, and if not, required NBC's certification that the prints were destroyed. We held that these factors created a license rather than a first sale.

We further noted, however, that Warner Brothers had also furnished another *Camelot* print to actress Vanessa Redgrave. The print was provided to Redgrave at cost, and her use of the print was subject to several restrictions. She had to retain possession of the print and was not allowed to sell, license, reproduce, or publicly exhibit the print. She had no obligation to return the print to Warner Brothers. We concluded, "While the provision for payment for the cost of the film, standing alone, does not establish a sale, when taken with the rest of the language of the agreement, it reveals a transaction strongly resembling a sale with restrictions on the use of the print." There was no evidence of the print's whereabouts, and we held that "[i]n the absence of such proof," the government failed to prove the absence of a first sale with respect to this Redgrave print. Since it was unclear which copy the defendant had obtained and resold, his conviction for sale of *Camelot* had to be reversed.

Thus, under *Wise*, where a transferee receives a particular copy of a copyrighted work pursuant to a written agreement, we consider all of the provisions of the agreement to determine whether the transferee became an owner of the copy or received a license. We may consider (1) whether the agreement was labeled a license and (2) whether the copyright owner retained title to the copy, required its return or destruction, forbade its duplication, or required the transferee to maintain possession of the copy for the agreement's duration. We did not find any one factor dispositive in Wise: we did not hold that the copyright owner's retention of title itself established the absence of a first sale or that a transferee's right to indefinite possession itself established a first sale.

2. The "MAI trio" of cases

Over fifteen years after *Wise*, we again considered the distinction between owners and licensees of copies of copyrighted works in three software copyright cases, the "*MAI* trio". In the *MAI* trio, we considered which software purchasers were owners of copies of copyrighted works for purposes of a second affirmative defense to infringement, the essential step defense.

The enforcement of copyright owners' exclusive right to reproduce their work under the Copyright Act, has posed special challenges in the software context. In order to use a software program, a user's computer will automatically copy the software into the computer's random access memory ("RAM"), which is a form of computer data storage. Congress enacted the essential step defense to codify that a software user who is the "owner of a copy" of a copyrighted software program does not infringe by making a copy of the computer program, if the new copy is "created as an essential step in the utilization of the computer program in conjunction with a machine and ... is used in no other manner."

The Copyright Act provides that an "owner of a copy" of copyrighted software may claim the essential step defense, and the "owner of a particular copy" of copyrighted software may claim the first sale doctrine. The *MAI* trio construed the phrase "owner of a copy" for essential step defense purposes. Neither Vernor nor Autodesk contends that the first sale doctrine's inclusion of the word "particular" alters the phrase's meaning, and we "presume that words used more than once in the same statute have the same meaning throughout." Accordingly, we consider the *MAI* trio's construction of "owner of a copy" controlling in our analysis of whether CTA and Vernor became "owner[s] of a particular copy" of Release 14 software.

In *MAI* and *Triad*, the defendants maintained computers that ran the plaintiffs' operating system software. When the defendants ran the computers, the computers automatically loaded plaintiffs' software into RAM. The plaintiffs in both cases sold their software pursuant to restrictive license agreements, and we held that their customers were licensees who were therefore not entitled to claim the essential step defense. We found that the defendants infringed plaintiffs' software copyrights by their unauthorized loading of copyrighted software into RAM. In *Triad*, the plaintiff had earlier sold software outright to some customers. We noted that these customers were owners who were entitled to the essential step defense, and the defendant did not infringe by making RAM copies in servicing their computers.

In *Wall Data*, plaintiff sold 3,663 software licenses to the defendant. The licenses (1) were non-exclusive; (2) permitted use of the software on a single computer; and (3) permitted transfer of the software once per month, if the software was removed from the original computer. The defendant installed the software onto 6,007 computers via hard drive imaging, which saved it from installing the software manually on each computer. It made an unverified claim that only 3,663 users could simultaneously access the software.

The plaintiff sued for copyright infringement, contending that the defendant violated the license by "over-installing" the software. The defendant raised an essential step defense, contending that its hard drive imaging was a necessary step of installation. On appeal, we held that the district court did not abuse its discretion in denying the defendant's request for a jury instruction on the essential step defense. Citing *MAI*, we held that the essential step defense does not apply where the copyright owner grants the user a license and significantly restricts the user's ability to transfer the software. Since the plaintiff's license imposed "significant restrictions" on the defendant's software rights, the defendant was a licensee and was not entitled to the essential step defense.

In *Wall Data*, we acknowledged that *MAI* had been criticized in a Federal Circuit decision, but declined to revisit its holding, noting that the facts of *Wall Data* led to the conclusion that any error in the district court's failure to instruct was harmless. Even if the defendant owned its copies of the software, its installation of the software on a number of computers in excess of its license was not an essential step in the software's use.

We read *Wise* and the *MAI* trio to prescribe three considerations that we may use to determine whether a software user is a licensee, rather than an owner of a copy. First, we consider whether the copyright owner specifies that a user is granted a license. Second, we consider whether the copyright owner significantly restricts the user's ability to transfer the software. Finally, we consider whether the copyright owner imposes notable use restrictions. Our holding reconciles the *MAI* trio and *Wise*, even though the *MAI* trio did not cite *Wise*.

In response to *MAI*, Congress amended §117 to permit a *computer owner* to copy software for maintenance or repair purposes. However, Congress did not disturb *MAI*'s holding that licensees are not entitled to the essential step defense.

IV. A. The district court's decision

The district court interpreted *Wise* to hold that a first sale occurs whenever the transferee is entitled to keep the copy of the work. Since Autodesk does not require its customers to return their copies of Release 14, the district court found that Autodesk had sold Release 14 to CTA. It reasoned that thus, CTA and Vernor were successive "owner[s] of a copy" of the software and were entitled to resell it under the first sale doctrine. The district court also found that Vernor's customers' copying of software during installation was protected by the essential step defense.

The district court acknowledged that were it to follow the *MAI* trio, it would conclude that Autodesk had licensed Release 14 copies to CTA, rather than sold them. However, it viewed *Wise* and the *MAI* trio as irreconcilable, and it followed *Wise* as the first-decided case.

B. Analysis

We hold today that a software user is a licensee rather than an owner of a copy where the copyright owner (1) specifies that the user is granted a license; (2) significantly restricts the user's ability to transfer the software; and (3) imposes notable use restrictions. Applying our holding to Autodesk's SLA, we conclude that CTA was a licensee rather than an owner of copies of Release 14 and thus was not entitled to invoke the first sale doctrine or the essential step defense.

Autodesk retained title to the software and imposed significant transfer restrictions: it stated that the license is nontransferable, the software could not be transferred or leased without Autodesk's written consent, and the software could not be transferred outside the Western Hemisphere. The SLA also imposed use restrictions against the use of the software outside the Western Hemisphere and against modifying, translating, or reverse-engineering the software, removing any proprietary marks from the software or documentation, or defeating any copy protection device. Furthermore, the SLA provided for termination of the license upon the licensee's unauthorized copying or failure to comply with other license restrictions. Thus, because Autodesk reserved title to Release 14 copies and imposed significant transfer and use restrictions, we conclude that its customers are licensees of their copies of Release 14 rather than owners.

CTA was a licensee rather than an "owner of a particular copy" of Release 14, and it was not entitled to resell its Release 14 copies to Vernor under the first sale doctrine. Therefore, Vernor did not receive title to the copies from CTA and accordingly could not pass ownership on to others. Both CTA's and Vernor's sales infringed Autodesk's exclusive right to distribute copies of its work.

Because Vernor was not an owner, his customers are also not owners of Release 14 copies. Therefore, when they install Release 14 on their computers, the copies of the software that they make during installation infringe Autodesk's exclusive reproduction right because they too are not entitled to the benefit of the essential step defense.

Although unnecessary to our resolution of the case, we address the legislative history in order to address the arguments raised by the parties and amici. That legislative history supports our conclusion that licensees such as CTA are not entitled to claim the first sale doctrine. The House Report for §109 underscores Congress' view that the first sale doctrine is available only to a person who has acquired a copy via an "outright sale". The report also asserts that the first sale doctrine does not "apply to someone who merely possesses a copy or phonorecord without having acquired ownership of it."

Our conclusion that those who rightfully possess, but do not own, a copy of copyrighted software are not entitled to claim the essential step defense is also supported by the legislative history. Congress enacted §117 following a report from the National Commission on New Technological Uses of Copyrighted Works ("CONTU") proposing Copyright Act amendments. CONTU's proposed version of §117 was identical to the version that Congress enacted with one exception. CONTU's version provided, "[I]t is not an infringement for the rightful possessor of a copy of a computer program to make or authorize the making of another copy or adaptation of that program...." Without explanation, Congress substituted "owner" for "rightful possessor." This modification suggests that more than rightful possession is required for §117 to apply – i.e., that Congress did not intend licensees subject to significant transfer and use restrictions to receive the benefit of the essential step defense. (...)

VACATED AND REMANDED.

THINK IT OVER!

1. In an amicus curiae brief the Software & Information Industry Association (SIAA) "argue[d] that a license can exist even where a customer (1) receives his copy of the work after making a single payment and (2) can indefinitely possess a software copy, because it is the software code and associated rights that are valuable rather than the inexpensive discs on which the code may be stored." (*Vernor v. Autodesk*, p. 1115.) To the contrary, eBay contended that "a broad view of the first sale doctrine is necessary to facilitate the creation of secondary markets for copyrighted works, which contributes to the public good by (1) giving consumers additional opportunities to purchase and sell copyrighted works, often at below-retail prices; (2) allowing consumers to obtain copies of works after a copyright owner has ceased distribution; and (3) allowing the proliferation of businesses." (Ibid.) *Which policy argument do you agree with?*

2. *Vernor* and *UsedSoft* are distinguishable on the ground that *UsedSoft* focused on the resale of licence keys of computer programs, and *Vernor* ruled on the resale of tangible data carriers. The CJEU and the Ninth Circuit discussed the "license versus sale" dichotomy significantly differently (where the CJEU favoured the lawful acquirer and the Ninth Circuit ruled in favour of the copyright holder). *Please read note 1 on page 436 again, and discuss which solution is more convincing to you.*

3. Other courts reached a different conclusion than the Ninth Circuit in *Vernor*. In *Softman v. Adobe*, a district court concluded that "the circumstances surrounding the transaction strongly suggests (sic!) that the transaction is in fact a sale rather than a license. For example, the purchaser commonly obtains a single copy of the software, with documentation, for a single price, which the purchaser pays at the time of the transaction, and which constitutes the entire payment for the 'license.' The license runs for an indefinite term without provisions for renewal. In light of these indicia, many courts and commentators conclude that a 'shrinkwrap license' transaction is a sale of goods rather than a license." (*SoftMan v. Adobe*, p. 1085.) C.f. *Krause v. Titleserv.* To the contrary, in *ProCD v. Zeidenberg*, the Seventh Circuit concluded that the end user accepted the computer programs under §2-204(1) and §2-606 of the Uniform Commercial Code when he read the license terms on his computer screen. (*ProCD v. Zeidenberg, p.* 1452-1453.) Aaron Perzanowski and Jason Schultz noted that "according to Judge Easterbrook, the fact that Zeidenberg was put on notice that the licence terms were forthcoming, even if he had No. idea what they were at the time of purchase, was enough to make them part of a binding legal argument." (Perzanowski and Schultz, 2016, p. 68.)

Further Case Law

United States v. Wise, 550 *F.2d* 1180 (1977)

MAI Systems Corp. v. Peak Computer, Inc., 991 *F.2d* 511 (1993)

Triad Systems Corp. v. Southeastern Express Co., 64 *F.3d* 1330 (1995)

SoftMan Products Co. v. Adobe Sys. Inc., 171 *F.Supp.2d* 1075 (2001)

William Krause v. Titleserv, Inc., 402 *F.3d* 119 (2005)

Wall Data, Inc. v. Los Angeles County Sheriff's Department, 447 *F.3d* 769 (2006)

Recommended readings

In English

Andrew Degner: Wise-ing Up about the First Sale Doctrine: A Look at the Ninth Circuit's Approach to Vernor v. Autodesk, *Columbia Journal of Law & the Arts*, 2012, p. 581-606.

Gary Donatello: Killing the Secondary Market: How the Ninth Circuit Interpreted Vernor and Aftermath to Destroy the First Sale Doctrine, *Seton Hall Journal of Sports and Entertainment Law*, 2012, p. 59-92.

Rachel Ann Geist: A "Licence to Read": The Effect of E-books on Publishers, Libraries and the First Sale Doctrine, *IDEA*, 2012, p. 63-100.

Donald Frank Jankowski II: The End of Ownership?, *Marquette Intellectual Property Law Review*, 2013, p. 103-121.

Ariel Katz - Aaron Perzanowski - Guy A. Rub: The Interaction of Exhaustion and the General Law: A Reply to Duffy and Hynes, *Virginia Law Review Online*, Vol. 102/2016, p. 8-24.

Aaron Perzanowski - Jason Schultz: *The End of Ownership – Personal Property in the Digital Economy*, MIT Press, Cambridge, 2016

Péter Mezei: *Copyright Exhaustion - Law and Policy in the United States and the European Union*, Cambridge University Press, Cambridge, 2018, p. 100-105.

In Hungarian

Mezei Péter: *Jogkimerülés a szerzői jogban*, Médiatudományi Intézet, Budapest, 2016, p. 121-126.

CAPITOL RECORDS, LLC, V. REDIGI INC.

910 *F.3d* 649 (2018)

Opinion

LEVAL, Circuit Judge

BACKGROUND

I. Facts

Plaintiffs are record companies, which own copyrights or licenses in sound recordings of musical performances. Plaintiffs distribute those sound recordings in numerous forms, of which the most familiar twenty years ago was the compact disc. Today, Plaintiffs also distribute their music in the form of digital files, which are sold to the public by authorized agent services, such as Apple iTunes, under license from Plaintiffs. Purchasers from the Apple iTunes online store download the files onto their personal computers or other devices.

ReDigi was founded by Defendants Ossenmacher and Rudolph in 2009 with the goal of creating enabling technology and providing a marketplace for the lawful resale of lawfully purchased digital music files. Ossenmacher served as ReDigi's Chief Executive Officer and Rudolph, who spent twelve years as a Principal Research Scientist at the Massachusetts Institute of Technology, served as ReDigi's Chief Technical Officer. During the period addressed by the operative complaint, ReDigi, through its system version 1.0, hosted resales of digital music files containing the Plaintiffs' music by persons who had lawfully purchased the files from iTunes.

Considering the evidence in the light most favorable to ReDigi, ReDigi's system version 1.0 operates as follows.

1. Music Manager: A person who owns a digital music file lawfully purchased from iTunes and intends to employ ReDigi's system to resell it (the "user") must first download and install onto her computer ReDigi's "Music Manager" software program ("Music Manager"). Once Music Manager has been installed, it analyzes the digital file intended for resale, verifies that the file was originally lawfully purchased from iTunes, and scans it for indications of tampering. If the file was lawfully purchased, Music Manager deems it an "Eligible File" that may be resold.

2. Data Migration: The ReDigi user must then cause the file to be transferred to ReDigi's remote server, known as the "Cloud Locker." To effectuate this transfer, ReDigi developed a new method that functions differently from the conventional file transfer. The conventional process is to reproduce the digital file at the receiving destination so that, upon completion of the transfer, the file exists simultaneously on both the receiving device and on the device from which it was transferred. If connectivity is disrupted during such a standard transfer, the process can be repeated because the file remains intact on the sender's device.

Under ReDigi's method – which it calls "data migration" – ReDigi's software "begins by breaking the [digital] music file into small 'blocks' [of data] of roughly four thousand bytes in length." Once the file has been broken into blocks of data ("packets"), ReDigi's system creates a "transitory copy" of each packet in the initial purchaser's computer buffer. Upon copying (or "reading") a packet into the initial purchaser's computer buffer, ReDigi's software sends a command to delete that packet of the digital file from permanent storage on the initial purchaser's device. ReDigi's software then sends the packet to the ReDigi software to be copied into the buffer and deleted from the user's device. During the data migration process, the digital file cannot be accessed, played, or perceived. If connectivity is disrupted during the data migration process, the remnants of the digital file on the user's device are unusable, and the transfer cannot be re-initiated. In such circumstances, ReDigi (according to its brief) bears the cost of the user's loss.

Once all the packets of the source file have been transferred to ReDigi's server, the Eligible File has been entirely removed from the user's device. The packets are then re-assembled into a complete, accessible, and playable file on ReDigi's server.

ReDigi describes its primary technological innovation using the metaphor of a train (the digital file) leaving from one station (the original purchaser's device) and arriving at its destination (in the first instance, ReDigi's server). Under either the typical method or ReDigi's method, packets are sent sequentially, such that, conceptually, "each packet is a car" moving from the source to the destination device. Once all the packets arrive at the destination device, they are reassembled into a usable file. At that moment, in a typical transfer, the entire digital file in usable form exists on both devices. ReDigi's system differs in that it effectuates a deletion of each packet from the user's device immediately after the "transitory copy" of that packet arrives in the computer's buffer (before the packet is forwarded to ReDigi's server). In other words, as each packet "leaves the station," ReDigi deletes it from the original purchaser's device such that it "no longer exists" on that device. As a result, the entire file never exists in two places at once.

After the file has reached ReDigi's server but before it has been resold, the user may continue to listen to it by streaming audio from the user's Cloud Locker on ReDigi's server. If the user later re-downloads the file from her Cloud Locker to her computer, ReDigi will delete the file from its own server.

3. *Resale:* Once an Eligible File has "migrated" to ReDigi's server, it can be resold by the user utilizing ReDigi's market function. If it is resold, ReDigi gives the new purchaser exclusive access to the file. ReDigi will (at the new purchaser's option) either download the file to the new

purchaser's computer or other device (simultaneously deleting the file from its own server) or will retain the file in the new purchaser's Cloud Locker on ReDigi's server, from which the new purchaser can stream the music. ReDigi's terms of service state that digital media purchases may be streamed or downloaded only for personal use.

4. *Duplicates:* ReDigi purports to guard against a user's retention of duplicates of her digital music files after she sells the files through ReDigi. To that end, Music Manager continuously monitors the user's computer hard drive and connected devices to detect duplicates. When a user attempts to upload an Eligible File to ReDigi's server, ReDigi "prompt[s]" her to delete any pre-existing duplicates that Music Manager has detected. If ReDigi detects that the user has not deleted the duplicates, ReDigi blocks the upload of the Eligible File. After an upload is complete, Music Manager continues to search the user's connected devices for duplicates. If it detects a duplicate of a previously uploaded Eligible File, ReDigi will prompt the user to authorize ReDigi to delete that duplicate from her personal device and, if authorization is not granted, it will suspend her account.

Plaintiffs point out, and ReDigi does not dispute, that these precautions do not *prevent* the retention of duplicates after resale through ReDigi. Suspension of the original purchaser's ReDigi account does not negate the fact that the original purchaser has both sold and retained the digital music file after she sold it. So long as the user retains previously-made duplicates on devices not linked to the computer that hosts Music Manager, Music Manager will not detect them. This means that a user could, prior to resale through ReDigi, store a duplicate on a compact disc, thumb drive, or third-party cloud service unconnected to the computer that hosts Music Manager and access that duplicate post-resale. While ReDigi's suspension of the original purchaser's ReDigi account may be a disincentive to the retention of sold files, it does not prevent the user from retaining sold files. (...)

DISCUSSION

I. The First Sale Doctrine

The primary issue on appeal is whether ReDigi's system version 1.0 lawfully enables resales of its users' digital files. Sections 106(1) and (3) of the Copyright Act respectively grant the owner of a copyright the exclusive right to control the reproduction and the distribution of the copyrighted work. Under the first sale doctrine, codified in § 109(a), the rights holder's control *over the distribution* of any particular copy or phonorecord that was lawfully made effectively terminates when that copy or phonorecord is distributed to its first recipient. Section 109(a) provides:

> "Notwithstanding the provisions of section 106(3), the owner of a particular copy or phonorecord lawfully made under this title, or any person authorized by such owner, is entitled, without the authority of the copyright owner, to sell or otherwise dispose of the possession of that copy or phonorecord."

Under this provision, it is well established that the lawful purchaser of a copy of a book is free to resell, lend, give, or otherwise transfer that copy without violating the copyright holder's exclusive right of distribution. The copy so resold or re-transferred may be re-transferred again and again without violating the exclusive distribution right. It is undisputed that one who owns a digital file from iTunes of music that is fixed in a material object qualifies as "the owner of a particular ... phonorecord lawfully made", and is thus entitled under § 109(a) "to sell or otherwise dispose of the possession of *that* ... phonorecord", without violating § 106(3). On the other hand, § 109(a) says nothing about the rights holder's control under § 106(1) over *reproduction* of a copy or phonorecord.

The district court found that resales through ReDigi were infringing for two reasons. The first reason was that, in the course of ReDigi's transfer, the phonorecord has been reproduced in a manner that violates the Plaintiffs' exclusive control of *reproduction* under § 106(1); the second was that the digital files sold through ReDigi, being unlawful reproductions, are not subject to the resale right established by § 109(a), which applies solely to a "particular ... phonorecord ... lawfully made." We agree with the first reason underlying the district court's finding of infringement. As that is a sufficient reason for affirmance of the judgment, we make no ruling on the district court's second reason.

ReDigi argues on appeal that its system effectuates transfer of the *particular* digital file that the user lawfully purchased from iTunes, that it should not be deemed to have reproduced that file, and that it should therefore come within the protection of § 109(a). ReDigi makes two primary contentions in support of these arguments.

First, ReDigi asserts – as it must for its first sale argument to succeed – that the digital files should be considered "material objects" and therefore, under § 101's definition of "phonorecords" as "material objects," should qualify as "phonorecords" eligible for the protection of § 109(a).

Second, ReDigi argues that from a technical standpoint, its process should not be seen as making a reproduction. ReDigi emphasizes that its system simultaneously "causes [packets] to be removed from the ... file remaining in the consumer's computer" as those packets are copied into the computer buffer and then transferred to the ReDigi server, so that the complete file never exists in more than one place at the same time, and the "file on the user's machine continually shrinks in size while the file on the server grows in size." ReDigi points out that the "sum of the size of the data" stored in the original purchaser's computer and in ReDigi's server never exceeds the "size of the original file," which, according to ReDigi, "confirms that no reproductions are made during the transfer process."

As for ReDigi's first argument, that the digital file it transfers is a phonorecord protected by § 109(a), we do not decide this issue because we find that ReDigi effectuates an unlawful reproduction even if the digital file itself qualifies as a phonorecord.

As for ReDigi's second argument, we reject it for the following reasons. The Copyright Act defines phonorecords as "material objects in which sounds ... are fixed by any method now known or later developed, and from which the sounds can be perceived, reproduced, or otherwise communicated, either directly or with the aid of a machine or device." Accordingly, when the purchaser of a digital music file from iTunes possesses that file, embodied "for a period of more than transitory duration" in a computer or other physical storage device, that device – or at least the portion of it in which the digital music file is fixed (*e.g.*, the location on the hard drive) – becomes a phonorecord. In the course of transferring a digital music file from an original purchaser's computer, through ReDigi, to a new purchaser, the digital file is first received and stored on ReDigi's server and then, at the new purchaser's option, may also be subsequently received and stored on the new purchaser's device. At each of these steps, the digital file is fixed in a new material object "for a period of more than transitory duration." The fixing of the digital file in ReDigi's server, as well as in the new purchaser's device, creates a new phonorecord, which is a reproduction. ReDigi version 1.0's process for enabling the resale of digital files thus inevitably involves the creation of new phonorecords by reproduction, even if the standalone digital file is deemed to be a phonorecord.

As for the argument that, as ReDigi copies a packet of data, it deletes the equivalent packet in the user's device so that the amount of data extant in the transfer process remains constant, this does not rebut or nullify the fact that the eventual receipt and storage of that file in ReDigi's server, as well as in the new purchaser's device (at his option), does involve the making of new phonorecords. Unless the creation of those new phonorecords is justified by the doctrine of fair use, which we discuss and reject in a later portion of this opinion, the creation of such new phonorecords involves unauthorized reproduction, which is not protected, or even addressed, by § 109(a).

ReDigi makes several additional arguments designed to characterize its process as involving the transfer of its users' lawfully made phonorecords, rather than the creation of new phonorecords. None of these arguments negates the crucial fact that each transfer of a digital music file to ReDigi's server and each new purchaser's download of a digital music file to his device creates new phonorecords. ReDigi argues, for example, that during a transfer through ReDigi's data migration technology, each packet of data from the original source file resides in a buffer "for less than a second" before being overwritten, and thus fails to satisfy the requirement that a sound recording must be embodied "for a period of more than transitory duration" to qualify as a phonorecord. Even if, during transfer, ReDigi's system retains each digital file *in a computer buffer* for a period of no more than transitory duration, those files subsequently become embodied in ReDigi's server and in the new purchaser's device, where they remain for periods "of more than transitory duration." ReDigi's server and the resale purchaser's device on which the digital music files are fixed constitute or contain new phonorecords under the statute.

ReDigi next argues that, in the course of transferring a user's file to ReDigi's own server, and to the resale purchaser's device, ReDigi sees to it that all of the original purchaser's preexisting duplicates are destroyed. As an initial matter, as noted above, ReDigi here overclaims. It does not ensure against retention of duplicate phonorecords created by the original owner. ReDigi's assertion that "there is never an instance when [an] Eligible File could exist in more than one place or be accessed by more than one user" is simply not supported by ReDigi's own evidence. In addition, even if ReDigi effectively compensated (by offsetting deletions) for the making of unauthorized reproductions in violation of the rights holder's exclusive reproduction right under §106(1), nonetheless ReDigi's process itself involves the making of unauthorized reproductions that infringe the exclusive reproduction right unless justified under fair use. We are not free to disregard the terms of the statute merely because the entity performing an unauthorized reproduction makes efforts to nullify its consequences by the counterbalancing destruction of the preexisting phonorecords.

ReDigi further argues that the computer hard drive into which the original purchaser's digital file is embedded cannot be her lawfully made phonorecord. A computer hard drive, ReDigi argues, cannot qualify as a phonorecord under § 101 because it contains more than a sound recording. This argument misinterprets *ABKCO*. We held in *ABKCO* that a license to publish a phonorecord did not authorize the publication of compact discs for use in karaoke that contained both sound recordings and visual depictions of song lyrics. The *ABKCO* opinion undertook to construe the breadth of a compulsory license. The opinion does not support the conclusion that a compact disc that stores visual depictions of words as well as recorded music does not *contain* a phonorecord. To be sure, a license to distribute phonorecords of a particular song would not by its terms authorize the distribution of whatever other copyrighted content is contained in a computer hard drive that also contains the recording of the song. But it does not follow that a device or other "material object[ ] in which sounds ... are fixed ... and from which the sounds can be perceived, reproduced, or otherwise communicated," is not a phonorecord, merely because it contains other matter as well. We reject ReDigi's argument.

Finally, ReDigi argues that the district court's conclusion makes no sense because it would "require a customer to sell her [valuable] computer in order to be able to sell a[n] ... iTunes music file" that was lawfully purchased for under $1.00. Of course it would make no economic sense for a customer to sell her computer or even a $5.00 thumb drive in order to sell "a[n] ... iTunes music file" purchased for $1.00. But ReDigi far overstates its economic argument when it asserts that the "district court's ruling ... eliminat[es] any meaningful competition from resellers" as "no secondary market ... can ever develop if consumers are required to give away their computer hard disks as part of any resale." A secondary market can readily be imagined for first purchasers who cost-effectively place 50 or 100 (or more) songs on an inexpensive device such as a thumb drive and sell it. Furthermore, other technology may exist or be developed that could lawfully effectuate a digital first sale.

We conclude that the operation of ReDigi version 1.0 in effectuating a resale results in the making of at least one unauthorized reproduction. Unauthorized reproduction is not protected by § 109(a). It violates the rights holder's exclusive reproduction rights under § 106(1) unless excused as fair use. For reasons explained below, we conclude that the making of such reproductions is not a fair use.

Our conclusion is supported by the fact that the Copyright Office also concluded that the resale of digital files is infringing. In 1998, Congress mandated that the Register of Copyrights evaluate "the relationship between existing and emergent technology and the operation of section[ ] 109 ...". The Copyright Office conducted a multi-year evaluation, including review of comments and testimony from the public, academia, libraries, copyright organizations and copyright owners. The Register concluded that §109 does not apply to otherwise unauthorized digital transmissions of a copyrighted work, reasoning that such transmissions cause the recipient to obtain a new copy of the work. The Register reasoned that the creation of a new copy of the work would constitute an unauthorized reproduction falling outside the authorization of § 109(a).

ReDigi argues that the Register's 2001 report is obsolete because it presumed that the only way to transfer digital files over the Internet was by the traditional "copy and delete" method, whereas new technologies either have been or might be developed that transfer digital files over the Internet using a non-infringing method. Plaintiffs counter that, in 2016, the Register again asserted that "a digital file transfer creates a new copy or phonorecord on the transferee's computer" and thus does not qualify for first sale protection. We need not pronounce upon the ongoing relevance of the Register's 2001 report, or decide whether *all* digital file transmissions over the Internet make reproductions, to determine that ReDigi's system version 1.0 does so.

II. Fair Use

ReDigi argues that, regardless of whether what it does is protected by § 109(a), its actions are protected under the doctrine of fair use. We evaluate ReDigi's claim in accordance with the fair use statute. Section 107 of the Copyright Act provides:

> *"[T]he fair use of a copyrighted work ... for purposes such as criticism, comment, news reporting, teaching (including multiple copies for classroom use), scholarship, or research, is not an infringement of copyright. In determining whether the use made of a work in any particular case is a fair use the factors to be considered shall include*
>
> *(1) the purpose and character of the use, including whether such use is of a commercial nature or is for nonprofit educational purposes;*

(2) the nature of the copyrighted work;

(3) the amount and substantiality of the portion used in relation to the copyrighted work as a whole; and

(4) the effect of the use upon the potential market for or value of the copyrighted work.

The fact that a work is unpublished shall not itself bar a finding of fair use if such finding is made upon consideration of all the above factors."

ReDigi's argument for fair use in its opening brief did not address the statutory factors. Nonetheless, we consider each in turn.

A. Factor One

Factor One considers "the purpose and character of the use, including whether such use is of a commercial nature or is for nonprofit educational purposes." The Supreme Court has observed that this factor favors secondary uses that are transformative, meaning that the use "adds something new, with a further purpose or different character, altering the first with new expression, meaning, or message[,]" rather than merely superseding the original work. Uses that criticize, comment on, provide information about, or provide new uses for the copyrighted work are those likely to be deemed transformative. Similarly, a secondary use may be transformative if it provides information about the original, "or expands its utility." Examples of such utility-expanding transformative fair uses have included scanning books to create a full-text searchable database and public search function (in a manner that did not allow users to read the texts); copying works into a database used to detect plagiarism; displaying tiny, low-resolution "thumbnail" reproductions of art works to provide links serving as Internet pathways to the appropriate websites containing the originals; and copying by one who has acquired the right to view the content of a telecast to enable a single, non-commercial home viewing at a more convenient time. In *Sony*, the "apparent reasoning was that a secondary use may be a fair use if it utilizes technology to achieve the transformative purpose of improving the efficiency of delivering content without unreasonably encroaching on the commercial entitlements of the rights holder" because the improved delivery was to one entitled to receive the content.

ReDigi makes no change in the copyrighted work. It provides neither criticism, commentary, nor information about it. Nor does it deliver the content in more convenient and usable form to one who has acquired an entitlement to receive the content. What ReDigi does is essentially to provide a market for the resale of digital music files, which resales compete with sales of the same recorded music by the rights holder. These characteristics of ReDigi's use favor Plaintiffs under Factor One.

In addition, while the mere fact of a commercial motivation rarely pushes the first factor determination against fair use (as so many of the canonical fair uses, such as book reviews; quotation of prominent figures in news reports, news commentary, and history books; the performance of parodic plays; and the sale of parodic books, are all commercial, in some circumstances a commercial motive will weigh against a finding of fair use under Factor One. As noted in Campbell, the less a use provides transformative value, the more its commercialism will weigh against a finding of fair use. Here, ReDigi hosts a remunerative marketplace that enables resale by purchasers of digital music files, which is a commercial purpose. Especially in view of the total absence (or at least very low degree) of transformative purpose, the commercial motivation here argues against ReDigi with respect to Factor One.

B. Factor Two

The second fair use factor concerns "the nature of the copyrighted work." Except to the extent that the nature of the copyrighted work is necessarily considered alongside the character and purpose of the secondary use in deciding whether the secondary use has a transformative purpose, it rarely, by itself, furnishes any substantial reasoning for favoring or disfavoring fair use. This case is no exception.

C. Factor Three

The third factor considers "the amount and substantiality of the portion [of the original] used in relation to the copyrighted work as a whole." ReDigi's system makes identical copies of the whole of Plaintiffs' copyrighted sound recordings. Although use of the entirety of a digital file is not necessarily inconsistent with a finding of fair use, it tends to disfavor a finding of fair use.

D. Factor Four

The fourth statutory factor is "the effect of the [copying] use upon the potential market for or value of the copyrighted work." When a secondary use competes in the rightsholder's market as an effective substitute for the original, it impedes the purpose of copyright to incentivize new creative works by enabling their creators to profit from them. For this reason, the Supreme Court in *Harper & Row* described the fourth factor as "undoubtedly the single most important element of fair use." Factor Four "focuses on whether the copy brings to the marketplace a competing substitute for the original, or its derivative, so as to deprive the rights holder of significant revenues because of the likelihood that potential purchasers may opt to acquire the copy in preference to the original." Factor Four is necessarily intertwined with Factor One; the more the objective of secondary use differs from that of the original, the less likely it will supplant the commercial market for the original.

As Plaintiffs argue, ReDigi made reproductions of Plaintiffs' works for the purpose of resale in competition with the Plaintiffs' market for the sale of their sound recordings. ReDigi's replicas were sold to the same consumers whose objective in purchasing was to acquire Plaintiffs' music. It is also of possible relevance that there is a distinction between ReDigi's resales and resales of physical books and records. The digital files resold by ReDigi, although used, do not deteriorate the way printed books and physical records deteriorate. As the district court observed, the principal difference between the "product sold in ReDigi's secondary market" and that sold by Plaintiffs or their licensees in the primary market was its lower price.

Factor Four weighs powerfully against fair use.

E. Four Factors Weighed Together

The Supreme Court has instructed that, to ascertain whether there is fair use, all four of the statutory factors must be weighed together. Our consideration is informed by our recent holding in TVEyes. TVEyes copied all televised video programming throughout the nation, together with its accompanying closed-captioned text, into a database. It offered a commercial subscription service through which business and professional clients could search the transcripts, receive a list of video segments that mentioned the searched terms, and then view up to ten minutes of each video segment. Fox News Network, a producer of televised content, sued, claiming that TVEyes's distribution of Fox's programming to TVEyes's subscribers infringed Fox's copyright. We found that TVEyes's secondary use deployed modestly transformative technology (akin to the time shifting technology of *Sony*) in that "it enable[d] nearly instant access to a subset of material – and to information about the material – that would otherwise be irretrievable, or else retrievable only through prohibitively inconvenient or inefficient means." As in *Sony*, it enabled its customers to view "programming they want at a time and place that is convenient to them, rather than at the time and place of broadcast." Nonetheless, we held that TVEyes's use was not a fair use because it substantially competed with the rights holders' legitimate market. By providing Fox's copyrighted programming to its clients "*without* payment to [the rights holder], TVEyes ... usurped a market that properly belong[ed] to the copyright-holder."

TVEyes is a substantial precedent for our holding here. The transformative purpose and character of TVEyes's use, while modest, was far more transformative than what ReDigi has shown here. TVEyes's transformative uses were nonetheless easily outweighed by the harm to the rights holders' market considered under Factor Four. Even if ReDigi is credited with some faint showing of a transformative purpose, that purpose is overwhelmed by the substantial harm ReDigi inflicts on the value of Plaintiffs' copyrights through its direct competition in the rights holders' legitimate market, offering consumers a substitute for purchasing from the rights holders. We find no fair use justification.

* * *

We conclude by addressing policy-based arguments raised by ReDigi and its amici. They contend that ReDigi's version 1.0 ought to be validated as in compliance with § 109(a) because it allows for realization of an economically beneficial practice, originally authorized by the courts in the common law development of copyright, and later endorsed by Congress. They also contend that the Copyright Act must be read to vindicate purchasers' ability to alienate digital copyrighted works under the first sale doctrine – emphasizing that § 109(a) is styled as an entitlement rather than a defense to infringement – without regard to technological medium. On this score, they rely heavily on the breadth of the common law first sale doctrine, and on a purported imperative, described as the "principle of technological neutrality" by amici and the "equal treatment principle" by ReDigi, not to disadvantage purchasers of digital copyrighted works, as compared with purchasers of physical copyrighted works.

As for whether the economic consequences of ReDigi's program are beneficial and further the objectives of copyright, we take no position. Courts are poorly equipped to assess the inevitably multifarious economic consequences that would result from such changes of law. So far as we can see, the establishment of ReDigi's resale marketplace would benefit some, especially purchasers of digital music, at the expense of others, especially rightsholders, who, in the sale of their merchandise, would have to compete with resellers of the same merchandise in digital form, which, although second hand, would, unlike second hand books and records, be as good as new.

Furthermore, as to the argument that we should read § 109(a) to accommodate digital resales because the first sale doctrine protects a fundamental entitlement, without regard to the terms of § 109(a) (and incorporated definitions), we think such a ruling would exceed the proper exercise of the court's authority. The copyright statute is a patchwork, sometimes varying from clause to clause, as between provisions for which Congress has taken control, dictating both policy and the details of its execution, and provisions in which Congress approximatively summarized common law developments, implicitly leaving further such development to the courts. The paradigm of the latter category is § 107 on fair use. In the provisions here relevant, Congress dictated the terms of the statutory entitlements. Notwithstanding the purported breadth of the first sale doctrine as originally articulated by the courts, Congress, in promulgating § 109(a), adopted a narrower conception, which negates a claim of unauthorized *distribution* in violation of the author's exclusive right under § 106(3), but not a claim of unauthorized *reproduction* in violation of the exclusive right provided by § 106(1). If ReDigi and its champions have persuasive arguments in support of the change of law they advocate, it is Congress they should persuade. We reject the invitation to substitute our judgment for that of Congress.

CONCLUSION

We have considered ReDigi's remaining arguments against the district court's ruling and find them to be without merit. The judgment of the district court is **AFFIRMED**.

THINK IT OVER

1. The ruling accepted the direct liability of ReDigi for the reproduction and distribution of Capitol Records' sound recordings. More precisely, ReDigi's extensive contribution to the users' activities of uploading, migrating, selling, purchasing, and, finally, downloading musical files was found to be illegal. *Is such broad interpretation of direct liability reasonable? Cartoon Network* highlighted that users create copies in the "cloud", rather than service providers. *Isn't ReDigi only secondarily/indirectly liable for these acts (under the doctrines of contributory or vicarious liability)? Is the Court of Appeals' fair use analysis correct?* The fair use doctrine applies to direct infringements. If ReDigi would face indirect liability, the fair use doctrine would only be relevant with respect to the lawfulness of end-users' activities. The Second Circuit confirmed in *RIAA v. Diamond* that "space-shifting" – that is, reproduction of sound recordings from computers to portable devices and *vice versa* – of digital contents is fair use.

2. The Ninth Circuit balanced several factors in *Wise* when it analysed several contracts for the use of film reels. These factors included the designation of an agreement as a license; the reservation of title in the copyright holder; a single, upfront payment by the transferee for a particular copy; the requirement to destroy the transferred copies; significant restrictions on the terms of use; and the inability of the right holder to regain possession. The Ninth Circuit held that especially those contracts led to a sale rather than a licence, where the transferee paid a single, upfront payment for the film reels; where it was impossible to return the said reels to the right holders, or it was not required to do so; and the transferee's possession over the copy was, consequently, for an indefinite period. Later, the Ninth Circuit held in *Vernor v. Autodesk* that "we considered [in the Wise decision] whether the agreement (a) was labeled a license, (b) provided that the copyright owner retained title to the prints, (c) required the return or destruction of the prints, (d) forbade duplication of prints, or (e) required the transferee to maintain possession of the prints for the agreement's duration. (...) We read Wise (...) to prescribe three considerations that we may use to determine whether a software user is a licensee, rather than an owner of a copy. First, we consider whether the copyright owner specifies that a user is granted a license. Second, we consider whether the copyright owner significantly restricts the user's ability to transfer the software. Finally, we consider whether the copyright owner imposes notable use restrictions." *Which decision is more convincing?*

Further Case Law

United States v. Wise, 550 *F.2d* 1180 (1977)

Recording Industry Association of America v. Diamond Multimedia Systems, Inc., 180 *F.3d* 1072 (1999)

The Cartoon Network, LLLP v. CSC Holdings, Inc., 536 *F.3d* 121 (2008)

Timothy S. Vernor v. Autodesk, Inc., 621 *F.3d* 1102 (2010)

Disney Enterprises, Inc., v. VidAngel, Inc., 869 *F.3d* 848 (2017)

Recommended readings

In English

Mathias Lejeune: Remarks to USA: No Second Hand Digital Music (Yet), *Computer Law Review International*, Issue 3/2013, p. 88-90.
John T. Soma - Michael K. Kugler: Why Rent When You Can Own? How ReDigi, Apple, and Amazon Will Use the Cloud and the Digital First Sale Doctrine to Resell Music, E-books, Games, and Movies, *North Carolina Journal of Law & Technology*, March 2014, p. 436-449.
B. Makoa Kawabata: Unresolved Textual Tension: Capitol Records v. ReDigi and a Digital First Sale Doctrine, *UCLA Entertainment Law Review*, Winter 2014, p. 55-71.
Péter Mezei: *Copyright Exhaustion - Law and Policy in the United States and the European Union*, Cambridge University Press, Cambridge, 2018, p. 105-111.

NEDERLANDS UITGEVERSVERBOND, GROEP ALGEMENE UITGEVERS V. TOM KABINET INTERNET BV AND OTHERS

Case C-263/18 - Judgment of the Court (Grand Chamber), 19 December 2019 [ECLI:EU:C:2019:1111]

(...) Legal context

International law

3 The World Intellectual Property Organisation (WIPO) adopted the WIPO Copyright Treaty ('the WCT') in Geneva on 20 December 1996, a treaty which was approved on behalf of the European Community by Council Decision 2000/278/EC of 16 March 2000 (OJ 2000 L 89,

p. 6) and which entered into force with respect to the European Union on 14 March 2010 (OJ 2010 L 32, p. 1).

4 Article 6 of the WCT, entitled 'Right of distribution', provides in paragraph 1:
'Authors of literary and artistic works shall enjoy the exclusive right of authorising the making available to the public of the original and copies of their works through sale or other transfer of ownership.'

5 Article 8 of the WCT, entitled 'Right of communication to the public', provides:
'Without prejudice to the provisions of Articles 11(1)(ii), 11bis(1)(i) and (ii), 11ter(1)(ii), 14(1)(ii) and 14bis(1) of the Berne Convention, authors of literary and artistic works shall enjoy the exclusive right of authorising any communication to the public of their works, by wire or wireless means, including the making available to the public of their works in such a way that members of the public may access these works from a place and at a time individually chosen by them.'

6 Agreed statements concerning the WCT ('the Agreed Statements') were adopted by the Diplomatic Conference on 20 December 1996.

7 The Agreed Statements concerning Articles 6 and 7 of the WCT are worded as follows:
'As used in these Articles, the expressions "copies" and "original and copies", being subject to the right of distribution and the right of rental under the said Articles, refer exclusively to fixed copies that can be put into circulation as tangible objects.'

European Union law

Directive 2001/29

8 Recitals 2, 4, 5, 9, 10, 15, 23 to 25, 28 and 29 of Directive 2001/29 state:
'(2) The European Council, meeting at Corfu on 24 and 25 June 1994, stressed the need to create a general and flexible legal framework at Community level in order to foster the development of the information society in Europe. This requires, inter alia, the existence of an internal market for new products and services. Important Community legislation to ensure such a regulatory framework is already in place or its adoption is well under way. Copyright and related rights play an important role in this context as they protect and stimulate the development and marketing of new products and services and the creation and exploitation of their creative content. (...)
(4) A harmonised legal framework on copyright and related rights, through increased legal certainty and while providing for a high level of protection of intellectual property, will foster substantial investment in creativity and innovation, including network infrastructure, and lead in

turn to growth and increased competitiveness of European industry, both in the area of content provision and information technology and more generally across a wide range of industrial and cultural sectors. This will safeguard employment and encourage new job creation.
(5) Technological development has multiplied and diversified the vectors for creation, production and exploitation. While no new concepts for the protection of intellectual property are needed, the current law on copyright and related rights should be adapted and supplemented to respond adequately to economic realities such as new forms of exploitation. (...)
(9) Any harmonisation of copyright and related rights must take as a basis a high level of protection, since such rights are crucial to intellectual creation. Their protection helps to ensure the maintenance and development of creativity in the interests of authors, performers, producers, consumers, culture, industry and the public at large. Intellectual property has therefore been recognised as an integral part of property.
(10) If authors or performers are to continue their creative and artistic work, they have to receive an appropriate reward for the use of their work, as must producers in order to be able to finance this work. The investment required to produce products such as phonograms, films or multimedia products, and services such as "on-demand" services, is considerable. Adequate legal protection of intellectual property rights is necessary in order to guarantee the availability of such a reward and provide the opportunity for satisfactory returns on this investment. (...)
(15) The Diplomatic Conference held under the auspices of the World Intellectual Property Organisation (WIPO) in December 1996 led to the adoption of two new Treaties, the "WIPO Copyright Treaty" and the "WIPO Performances and Phonograms Treaty", dealing respectively with the protection of authors and the protection of performers and phonogram producers. (...) This Directive also serves to implement a number of the new international obligations. (...)
(23) This Directive should harmonise further the author's right of communication to the public. This right should be understood in a broad sense covering all communication to the public not present at the place where the communication originates. This right should cover any such transmission or retransmission of a work to the public by wire or wireless means, including broadcasting. This right should not cover any other acts.
(24) The right to make available to the public subject matter referred to in Article 3(2) should be understood as covering all acts of making available such subject matter to members of the public not present at the place where the act of making available originates, and as not covering any other acts.
(25) The legal uncertainty regarding the nature and the level of protection of acts of on-demand transmission of copyright works and subject matter protected by related rights over networks should be overcome by providing for harmonised protection at Community level. It should be made clear that all rightholders recognised by this Directive should have an exclusive right to make available to the public copyright works or any other subject matter by way of interactive on-demand transmissions. Such interactive on-demand transmissions are characterised by the fact

that members of the public may access them from a place and at a time individually chosen by them. (...)

(28) Copyright protection under this Directive includes the exclusive right to control distribution of the work incorporated in a tangible article. The first sale in the Community of the original of a work or copies thereof by the rightholder or with his consent exhausts the right to control resale of that object in the Community. This right should not be exhausted in respect of the original or of copies thereof sold by the rightholder or with his consent outside the Community. Rental and lending rights for authors have been established in [Council] Directive 92/100/EEC [of 19 November 1992 on rental right and lending right and on certain rights related to copyright in the field of intellectual property (OJ 1992 L 346, p. 61)]. The distribution right provided for in this Directive is without prejudice to the provisions relating to the rental and lending rights contained in Chapter I of that Directive.

(29) The question of exhaustion does not arise in the case of services and online services in particular. This also applies with regard to a material copy of a work or other subject matter made by a user of such a service with the consent of the rightholder. Therefore, the same applies to rental and lending of the original and copies of works or other subject matter which are services by nature. Unlike CD-ROM or CD-I, where the intellectual property is incorporated in a material medium, namely an item of goods, every online service is in fact an act which should be subject to authorisation where the copyright or related right so provides.'

9 Article 2 of Directive 2001/29, entitled 'Reproduction right', provides:

'Member States shall provide for the exclusive right to authorise or prohibit direct or indirect, temporary or permanent reproduction by any means and in any form, in whole or in part:

(a) for authors, of their works;'

10 Article 3 of Directive 2001/29, entitled 'Right of communication to the public of works and right of making available to the public other subject matter', provides, in paragraphs 1 and 3:

'1. Member States shall provide authors with the exclusive right to authorise or prohibit any communication to the public of their works, by wire or wireless means, including the making available to the public of their works in such a way that members of the public may access them from a place and at a time individually chosen by them.

(...)

3. The rights referred to in paragraphs 1 and 2 shall not be exhausted by any act of communication to the public or making available to the public as set out in this Article.'

11 Article 4 of Directive 2001/29, entitled 'Distribution right', reads as follows:

'1. Member States shall provide for authors, in respect of the original of their works or of copies thereof, the exclusive right to authorise or prohibit any form of distribution to the public by sale or otherwise.
2. The distribution right shall not be exhausted within the Community in respect of the original or copies of the work, except where the first sale or other transfer of ownership in the Community of that object is made by the rightholder or with his consent.'

12 Article 5 of Directive 2001/29, entitled 'Exceptions and limitations', states, in paragraph 1:
'Temporary acts of reproduction referred to in Article 2, which are transient or incidental, which are an integral and essential part of a technological process and the sole purpose of which is to enable:

(a) a transmission in a network between third parties by an intermediary, or

(b) a lawful use

of a work or other subject matter to be made, and which have no independent economic significance, shall be exempted from the reproduction right provided for in Article 2.'

Directive 2009/24/EC

13 Article 4 of Directive 2009/24/EC of the European Parliament and of the Council of 23 April 2009 on the legal protection of computer programs (OJ 2009 L 111, p. 16), entitled 'Restricted acts', provides:
'1. Subject to the provisions of Articles 5 and 6, the exclusive rights of the rightholder within the meaning of Article 2 shall include the right to do or to authorise:

(...)

(c) any form of distribution to the public, including the rental, of the original computer program or of copies thereof.

2. The first sale in the Community of a copy of a program by the rightholder or with his consent shall exhaust the distribution right within the Community of that copy, with the exception of the right to control further rental of the program or a copy thereof.'

Netherlands law

14 According to Article 1 of the Auteurswet (Law on copyright) of 23 September 1912, in the version applicable to the dispute in the main proceedings ('the Law on copyright'):
'Copyright is the exclusive right of the author of a literary, scientific or artistic work or those entitled under him to publish that work and to reproduce it, subject to the restrictions laid down by law.'

15 Article 12(1) of the Law on copyright provides:

'Publication of a literary, scientific or artistic work means:

1°. the publication of a reproduction of the whole or a part of the work;'

16 Article 12b of the Law on copyright reads as follows:

'If a copy of a literary, scientific or artistic work has been put into circulation by transfer of ownership for the first time in one of the Member States of the European Union or in a State Party to the Agreement on the European Economic Area by or with the consent of its author or a person entitled under him, the putting into circulation of that copy in another fashion, apart from by rental or loan, shall not constitute a breach of copyright.'

17 Article 13 of that law provides:

'Reproduction of a literary, scientific or artistic work means the translation, musical arrangement, cinematographic adaptation or dramatisation and generally any partial or total adaptation or reproduction in a modified form, which cannot be regarded as a new, original work.'

18 Article 13a of the Law on copyright states:

'The reproduction of a literary, scientific or artistic work does not include temporary acts of reproduction which are transient or incidental, which are an integral and essential part of a technological process and the sole purpose of which is to enable

(a) a transmission in a network between third parties by an intermediary, or

(b) a lawful use

and which have no independent economic value.'

19 Article 16b(1) of the Law on copyright provides:

'Reproduction shall not be regarded as an infringement of the copyright in a literary, scientific or artistic work if it is restricted to a few copies intended exclusively for personal practice, study or use by the natural person who, without any direct or indirect commercial objective, made the reproduction or caused it to be made exclusively for his own benefit.'

The dispute in the main proceedings and the questions referred for a preliminary ruling

20 NUV and GAU, associations whose purpose it is to defend the interests of Netherlands publishers, were mandated by several publishers to ensure that the copyright granted to them by copyright holders by means of exclusive licences is protected and observed.

21 Tom Kabinet Holding is the sole shareholder of Tom Kabinet Uitgeverij, a publisher of books, e-books and databases, and also of Tom Kabinet. Tom Kabinet operates a website on which, on 24 June 2014, it launched an online service consisting in a virtual market for 'second-hand' e-books.

22 On 1 July 2014, NUV and GAU brought an action under the Law on copyright against Tom Kabinet, Tom Kabinet Holding and Tom Kabinet Uitgeverij before the urgent applications judge at the rechtbank Amsterdam (District Court, Amsterdam, Netherlands) in respect of that online service. The rechtbank Amsterdam (District Court, Amsterdam) dismissed their application on the ground that, according to that court, there was no prima facie breach of copyright.

23 NUV and GAU appealed against that decision before the Gerechtshof te Amsterdam (Court of Appeal, Amsterdam, Netherlands), which, by judgment of 20 January 2015, upheld the decision but prohibited Tom Kabinet from offering an online service that allowed the sale of unlawfully downloaded e-books. No appeal on a point of law was lodged against that judgment.

24 From 8 June 2015 onwards, Tom Kabinet modified the services offered up to that point and replaced them with the '*Tom Leesclub*' (Tom reading club, 'the reading club'), within which Tom Kabinet is an e-book trader. In return for payment of a sum of money, the reading club offers its members 'second-hand' e-books which have been either purchased by Tom Kabinet or donated to Tom Kabinet free of charge by members of the club. In the latter case, those members must provide the download link in respect of the book in question and declare that they have not kept a copy of the book. Tom Kabinet then uploads the e-book from the retailer's website and places its own digital watermark on it, which serves as confirmation that it is a legally acquired copy.

25 Initially, e-books available through the reading club could be purchased for a fixed price of EUR 1.75 per e-book. Once payment had been made, the member could download the e-book from Tom Kabinet's website and subsequently resell it to Tom Kabinet. Membership of the reading club was subject to payment by members of a monthly subscription of EUR 3.99. Any e-book provided free of charge by a member resulted in that member being entitled to a discount of EUR 0.99 on the following month's subscription.

26 Since 18 November 2015, payment of a monthly subscription has ceased to be a requirement of membership of the reading club. On the one hand, the price of every e-book is now set at EUR 2. On the other hand, the members of the reading club also need 'credits' in order to

be able to acquire an e-book through the reading club; credits can be obtained by providing the club with an e-book, either for consideration or free of charge. Such credits can also be purchased when making an order.

27 NUV and GAU applied to the rechtbank Den Haag (District Court, The Hague, Netherlands) for an injunction prohibiting Tom Kabinet, Tom Kabinet Holding and Tom Kabinet Uitgeverij, on pain of a periodic penalty payment, from infringing the copyright of NUV's and GAU's affiliates by the making available or the reproduction of e-books. In particular, in their view Tom Kabinet is, in the context of the reading club, making an unauthorised communication of e-books to the public.

28 In an interim judgment of 12 July 2017, the referring court found that the e-books at issue were to be classified as works, within the meaning of Directive 2001/29, and that Tom Kabinet's offer, in circumstances such as those at issue in the main proceedings, did not constitute a communication to the public of those works, within the meaning of Article 3(1) of that directive.

29 The referring court observes, however, that the answers to the questions as to whether the making available remotely by the downloading, for payment, of an e-book for use for an unlimited period may constitute an act of distribution for the purposes of Article 4(1) of Directive 2001/29, and as to whether the right of distribution may thus be exhausted, within the meaning of Article 4(2) of that directive, are unclear. It also wonders whether the copyright holder may, in the event of a resale, object, on the basis of Article 2 of that directive, to the acts of reproduction necessary for the lawful transmission between subsequent purchasers of the copy for which the distribution right is, if such be the case, exhausted. Nor is the answer to be given to that question apparent from the case-law of the Court of Justice, according to the referring court.

30 In those circumstances, the rechtbank Den Haag (District Court, The Hague) decided to stay the proceedings and to refer the following questions to the Court of Justice for a preliminary ruling:

'(1) Is Article 4(1) of [Directive 2001/29] to be interpreted as meaning that "any form of distribution to the public by sale or otherwise of the original of their works or copies thereof" as referred to therein includes the making available remotely by downloading, for use for an unlimited period, of e-books (being digital copies of books protected by copyright) at a price by means of which the copyright holder receives remuneration equivalent to the economic value of the work belonging to him?

(2) If question 1 is to be answered in the affirmative, is the distribution right with regard to the original or copies of a work as referred to in Article 4(2) of [Directive 2001/29] exhausted in the European Union, when the first sale or other transfer of that material, which includes the making available remotely by downloading, for use for an unlimited period, of e-books (being digital copies of books protected by copyright) at a price by means of which the copyright holder receives remuneration equivalent to the economic value of the work belonging to him, takes place in the European Union through the rightholder or with his consent?
(3) Is Article 2 of [Directive 2001/29] to be interpreted as meaning that a transfer between successive acquirers of a lawfully acquired copy in respect of which the distribution right has been exhausted constitutes consent to the acts of reproduction referred to therein, in so far as those acts of reproduction are necessary for the lawful use of that copy and, if so, which conditions apply?
(4) Is Article 5 of [Directive 2001/29] to be interpreted as meaning that the copyright holder may no longer oppose the acts of reproduction necessary for a transfer between successive acquirers of the lawfully acquired copy in respect of which the distribution right has been exhausted and, if so, which conditions apply?'

Consideration of the questions referred

The first question

31 It should be noted as a preliminary point that, in the procedure laid down by Article 267 TFEU providing for cooperation between national courts and the Court of Justice, it is for the latter to provide the national court with an answer which will be of use to it and enable it to determine the case before it. To that end, the Court may have to reformulate the questions referred to it. The Court has a duty to interpret all provisions of EU law which national courts require in order to decide on the actions pending before them, even if those provisions are not expressly indicated in the questions referred to the Court by those courts.

32 To that end, the Court can extract from all the information provided by the national court, in particular from the grounds of the order for reference, the points of EU law which require interpretation in view of the subject matter of the dispute in the main proceedings.

33 In the present case, although by its first question the referring court is asking the Court of Justice, in essence, whether the expression 'any form of distribution to the public by sale or otherwise [of the original of authors' works or of copies thereof]', in Article 4(1) of Directive 2001/29, covers 'the making available remotely by downloading, for use for an unlimited period, of e-books [...] at a price', it is apparent from the grounds of the order for reference that the question arises as to whether, in the dispute that is pending before that

court, the supply by downloading, for permanent use, of an e-book constitutes an act of distribution for the purposes of Article 4(1) of that directive, or whether such supply is covered by the concept of 'communication to the public' within the meaning of Article 3(1) of that directive. The crux of that question in the dispute in the main proceedings is whether such supply is subject to the rule on exhaustion of the distribution right provided for in Article 4(2) of that directive or whether, on the contrary, it falls outside such a rule, as expressly provided for in Article 3(3) of the directive in the case of the right of communication to the public.

34 In the light of these considerations, the first question put by the referring court must be reformulated to the effect that the referring court thereby asks, in essence, whether the supply by downloading, for permanent use, of an e-book is covered by the concept of 'communication to the public' within the meaning of Article 3(1) of Directive 2001/29, or by that of 'distribution to the public', as referred to in Article 4(1) of that directive.

35 As is apparent from Article 3(1) of Directive 2001/29, authors have the exclusive right to authorise or prohibit any communication to the public of their works, by wire or wireless means, including the making available to the public of their works in such a way that members of the public may access them from a place and at a time individually chosen by them.

36 Article 4(1) of that directive, on the other hand, provides that authors have, in respect of the original of their works or of copies thereof, the exclusive right to authorise or prohibit any form of distribution to the public by sale or otherwise, that right being, under Article 4(2) of that directive, exhausted where the first sale or other transfer of ownership in the European Union of the original or of a copy of the work is made by the rightholder or with his or her consent.

37 It cannot be determined, either on the basis of those provisions or of any other provision of Directive 2001/29, having regard to the wording alone, whether the supply by downloading, for permanent use, of an e-book constitutes a communication to the public, in particular a making available to the public of a work in such a way that members of the public may access it from a place and at a time individually chosen by them, or an act of distribution for the purposes of that directive.

38 According to settled case-law, the interpretation of a provision of EU law requires that account be taken not only of its wording, but also of its context, the objectives pursued by the rules of which it is part and, where appropriate, its origins. EU legislation must, moreover, so far as possible, be interpreted in a manner that is consistent with international law,

in particular where its provisions are intended specifically to give effect to an international agreement concluded by the European Union.

39 In the first place, it must be noted that, as is apparent from recital 15 of Directive 2001/29, the directive serves, inter alia, to implement a number of the European Union's obligations under the WCT. It follows that the concepts of 'communication to the public' and 'distribution to the public' referred to in Article 3(1) and in Article 4(1) of that directive must, so far as possible, be interpreted in accordance with the definitions contained, respectively, in Article 8 and in Article 6(1) of the WCT.

40 Article 6(1) of the WCT defines the right of distribution as the exclusive right of authors to authorise the making available to the public of the original and copies of their works through sale or other transfer of ownership. It is apparent from the wording of the Agreed Statements concerning Articles 6 and 7 of the WCT that 'the expressions "copies" and "original and copies", being subject to the right of distribution and the right of rental under the said Articles, refer exclusively to fixed copies that can be put into circulation as tangible objects', and therefore that Article 6(1) cannot cover the distribution of intangible works such as e-books.

41 The explanatory memorandum in the proposal for a European Parliament and Council Directive on the harmonisation of certain aspects of copyright and related rights in the Information Society of 10 December 1997 (COM(97) 628 final, 'the proposal for the directive'), which led to Directive 2001/29, is in line with that statement. It is noted there that the words 'including the making available to the public of [authors'] works in such a way that members of the public may access these works from a place and at a time individually chosen by them', which appear in Article 8 of the WCT and were essentially reproduced in Article 3(1) of Directive 2001/29, reflect the proposal that had been made in that respect by the European Community and its Member States during the negotiations, and concern 'interactive activities'.

42 In the second place, the European Commission also stated in the explanatory memorandum in the proposal for the directive that that proposal '[gave] an opportunity to provide for a coherent level playing field for the electronic and tangible distribution of protected material and to draw a clear line between them'.

43 In that context, the Commission noted that interactive on-demand transmission was a new form of exploitation of intellectual property, in relation to which the Member States were of the view that it should be covered by the right to control communication to the public,

while stating that it was generally accepted that the distribution right, which applies exclusively to the distribution of physical copies, does not cover such transmission.

44 Still in that explanatory memorandum, the Commission added that the expression 'communication to the public' of a work covers acts of interactive on-demand transmission, thereby confirming that the right of communication to the public is also pertinent when several unrelated persons, who are members of the public, may have individual access, from different places and at different times, to a work which is on a publicly accessible website, while making clear that that right covers any communication 'other than the distribution of physical copies', since physical copies which can be put into circulation as tangible objects are covered by the distribution right.

45 It thus follows from that explanatory memorandum that the intention underlying the proposal for the directive was that any communication to the public of a work, other than the distribution of physical copies of the work, should be covered not by the concept of 'distribution to the public', referred to in Article 4(1) of Directive 2001/29, but by that of 'communication to the public' within the meaning of Article 3(1) of that directive.

46 In the third place, it should be noted that that interpretation is supported by the aim of that directive, as set out in the preamble thereto, and by the context of Article 3(1) and Article 4(1) of that directive.

47 It is clear from recitals 2 and 5 of Directive 2001/29 that that directive seeks to create a general and flexible framework at EU level in order to foster the development of the information society and to adapt and supplement the current law on copyright and related rights in order to respond to technological development, which has created new ways of exploiting protected works.

48 It is, moreover, apparent from recitals 4, 9 and 10 of that directive that its principal objective is to establish a high level of protection of authors, allowing them to obtain an appropriate reward for the use of their works, including when a communication to the public takes place.

49 In order to achieve that objective, 'communication to the public' should, as is underlined by recital 23 of Directive 2001/29, be understood in a broad sense covering all communication to the public not present at the place where the communication originates and, thus, any such transmission or retransmission of a work to the public by wire or wireless means, including broadcasting.

50 Recital 25 of that directive adds that rightholders recognised by that directive should have an exclusive right to make their works available to the public by way of interactive on-demand transmissions, such transmissions being characterised by the fact that members of the public may access them from a place and at a time individually chosen by them.

51 Furthermore, recitals 28 and 29 of Directive 2001/29, relating to the distribution right, state, respectively, that that right includes the exclusive right to control 'distribution of the work incorporated in a tangible article' and that the question of exhaustion of the right does not arise in the case of services and online services in particular, it being made clear that, unlike CD-ROM or CD-I, where the intellectual property is incorporated in a material medium, namely an item of goods, every online service is in fact an act which should be subject to authorisation where the copyright or related right so provides.

52 In the fourth place, an interpretation of the distribution right referred to in Article 4(1) of Directive 2001/29 as applying only to the distribution of works incorporated in a material medium follows equally from Article 4(2) of that directive, as interpreted by the Court in relation to exhaustion of that right, the Court having ruled that the EU legislature, by using the terms 'tangible article' and 'that object' in recital 28 of that directive, wished to give authors control over the initial marketing in the European Union of each tangible object incorporating their intellectual creation.

53 Admittedly, as the referring court notes, the Court of Justice has ruled, in relation to the exhaustion of the right of distribution of copies of computer programs mentioned in Article 4(2) of Directive 2009/24, that it does not appear from that provision that exhaustion is limited to copies of computer programs on a material medium, but that, on the contrary, that provision, by referring without further specification to the 'sale ... of a copy of a program', makes no distinction according to the tangible or intangible form of the copy in question.

54 However, as the referring court correctly points out and as the Advocate General noted in point 67 of his Opinion, an e-book is not a computer program, and it is not appropriate therefore to apply the specific provisions of Directive 2009/24.

55 In that regard, first, as the Court expressly stated in paragraphs 51 and 56 of the judgment of 3 July 2012, *UsedSoft*, Directive 2009/24, which concerns specifically the protection of computer programs, constitutes a *lex specialis* in relation to Directive 2001/29. The relevant provisions of Directive 2009/24 make abundantly clear the intention of the EU legislature to assimilate, for the purposes of the protection laid down by that directive, tangible and

intangible copies of computer programs, so that the exhaustion of the distribution right under Article 4(2) of Directive 2009/24 concerns all such copies.

56 Such assimilation of tangible and intangible copies of works protected for the purposes of the relevant provisions of Directive 2001/29 was not, however, desired by the EU legislature when it adopted that directive. As has been recalled in paragraph 42 of the present judgment, it is apparent from the *travaux préparatoires* for that directive that a clear distinction was sought between the electronic and tangible distribution of protected material.

57 Second, the Court noted in paragraph 61 of the judgment of 3 July 2012, *UsedSoft* that, from an economic point of view, the sale of a computer program on a material medium and the sale of a computer program by downloading from the internet are similar, since the online transmission method is the functional equivalent of the supply of a material medium. Accordingly, interpreting Article 4(2) of Directive 2009/24 in the light of the principle of equal treatment justifies the two methods of transmission being treated in a similar manner.

58 The supply of a book on a material medium and the supply of an e-book cannot, however, be considered equivalent from an economic and functional point of view. As the Advocate General noted in point 89 of his Opinion, dematerialised digital copies, unlike books on a material medium, do not deteriorate with use, and used copies are therefore perfect substitutes for new copies. In addition, exchanging such copies requires neither additional effort nor additional cost, so that a parallel second-hand market would be likely to affect the interests of the copyright holders in obtaining appropriate reward for their works much more than the market for second-hand tangible objects, contrary to the objective referred to in paragraph 48 of the present judgment.

59 Even if an e-book were to be considered complex matter, comprising both a protected work and a computer program eligible for protection under Directive 2009/24, it would have to be concluded that such a program is only incidental in relation to the work contained in such a book. As the Advocate General noted in point 67 of his Opinion, an e-book is protected because of its content, which must therefore be considered to be the essential element of it, and the fact that a computer program may form part of an e-book so as to enable it to be read cannot therefore result in the application of those specific provisions.

60 The referring court also states that the supply of an e-book, in circumstances such as those of the main proceedings, does not satisfy the conditions set by the Court for classification as a communication to the public, within the meaning of Article 3(1) of Directive 2001/29.

In particular, the referring court notes that, if there is no communication of the actual content of the protected work in the offer of sale of the e-book on the reading club platform, there can be no question of an act of communication. Moreover, there would be no public, the e-book being made available only to a single member of the reading club.

61 In that regard, it is clear from Article 3(1) of Directive 2001/29 that the concept of 'communication to the public' involves two cumulative criteria, namely an act of communication of a work and the communication of that work to a public.

62 As regards, in the first place, the question whether the supply of an e-book, such as that at issue in the main proceedings, constitutes an act of communication within the meaning of Article 3(1) of Directive 2001/29, it must be noted, as is recalled in paragraph 49 of the present judgment, that 'communication to the public' within the meaning of that provision covers any transmission or retransmission of a work to the public not present at the place where the communication originates, by wire or wireless means.

63 In addition, as regards the concept of 'making available to the public' within the meaning of that same provision, which forms part of the wider concept of 'communication to the public', the Court has held that, in order to be classified as an act of making available to the public, an act must meet, cumulatively, both conditions set out in the provision, namely that members of the public may access the protected work from a place and at a time individually chosen by them, irrespective of whether the persons comprising that public avail themselves of that opportunity.

64 As regards, specifically, the making available to the public of a work or a protected article in such a way that members of the public may access it from a place and at a time individually chosen by them, it is apparent from the explanatory memorandum in the proposal for the directive that 'the critical act is the "making available of the work to the public", thus the offering [of] a work on a publicly accessible site, which precedes the stage of its actual "on-demand transmission"', and that 'it is not relevant whether any person actually has retrieved it or not'.

65 In the present case, it is common ground that Tom Kabinet makes the works concerned available to anyone who is registered with the reading club's website, that person being able to access the site from a place and at a time individually chosen by him or her. Accordingly, the supply of such a service must be considered to be the communication of a work within the meaning of Article 3(1) of Directive 2001/29, irrespective of whether that person avails himself or herself of that opportunity by actually retrieving the e-book from that website.

66 In the second place, in order to be categorised as a 'communication to the public' within the meaning of that provision, the protected works must in fact be communicated to the public, that communication being directed at an indeterminate number of potential recipients.

67 It is also apparent from the explanatory memorandum in the proposal for the directive, first, as is recalled in paragraph 44 of the present judgment, that the right of communication to the public is also pertinent when several unrelated persons (members of the public) may have individual access, from different places and at different times, to a work which is on a publicly available website and, second, that the public consists of individual members of the public.

68 In that regard, the Court has previously had occasion to clarify, first, that the concept of 'public' involves a certain *de minimis* threshold, which excludes from that concept a group of persons concerned that is too small, and, second, that in order to determine that number, the cumulative effect of making a protected work available, by downloading, to potential recipients should be taken into consideration. Account should therefore be taken, in particular, of the number of persons able to access the work at the same time, but also of how many of them may access it in succession.

69 In the present case, having regard to the fact, noted in paragraph 65 of the present judgment, that any interested person can become a member of the reading club, and to the fact that there is no technical measure on that club's platform ensuring that (i) only one copy of a work may be downloaded in the period during which the user of a work actually has access to the work and (ii) after that period has expired, the downloaded copy can no longer be used by that user, it must be concluded that the number of persons who may have access, at the same time or in succession, to the same work via that platform is substantial. Consequently, subject to verification by the referring court taking into account all the relevant information, the work in question must be regarded as being communicated to a public, within the meaning of Article 3(1) of Directive 2001/29.

70 Last, the Court has held that, in order to be categorised as a communication to the public, a protected work must be communicated using specific technical means, different from those previously used or, failing that, to a new public, that is to say, to a public that was not already taken into account by the copyright holders when they authorised the initial communication of their work to the public.

71 In the present case, since the making available of an e-book is, as NUV and GAU have noted, generally accompanied by a user licence authorising the user who has downloaded

the e-book concerned only to read that e-book from his or her own equipment, it must be held that a communication such as that effected by Tom Kabinet is made to a public that was not already taken into account by the copyright holders and, therefore, to a new public within the meaning of the case-law cited in the preceding paragraph of the present judgment.

72 In the light of all the foregoing considerations, the answer to the first question is that the supply to the public by downloading, for permanent use, of an e-book is covered by the concept of 'communication to the public' and, more specifically, by that of 'making available to the public of [authors'] works in such a way that members of the public may access them from a place and at a time individually chosen by them', within the meaning of Article 3(1) of Directive 2001/29.

The second, third and fourth questions

73 In view of the answer given to the first question, there is no need to answer the second, third and fourth questions. (...)

THINK IT OVER!

1. The most important question of the referring Dutch court was related to the applicable economic right regarding Tom Kabinet's business model. The CJEU favoured the making available to the public right over the distribution right. In *Case C-479/13*, a preliminary proceedings related to the taxation aspects of e-books, a similar logic led the CJEU to rule that the online supply of e-books represents a service rather than a sale of goods. The CJEU missed to refer to this ruling, even though it would strongly support its final conclusion. In the lack of such reference, we might note that, in *Tom Kabinet*, the CJEU paid no attention to the practical reasons why Oracle's agreement was declared to be a sale. As mentioned earlier, the CJEU ruled in *UsedSoft* that a license might be "transformed" into a sale if the right to use a computer program lasts for an indefinite period "in return for payment of a fee designed to enable the copyright holder to obtain a remuneration corresponding to the economic value of the copy of the work of which he is the proprietor". (See at page 428.) As the CJEU failed to criticize or overrule this argument, and the online supply of e-books fulfills the doctrinal requirements of the CJEU'S *UsedSoft* standard, such "transformation" of contracts (and thus the economic rights) looks entirely valid and applicable to the supply e-books as well. *Which opinion do you favour? Can the distribution right cover the online supply of e-books? Or shall the making available to the public right apply to all online supply of files, irrespective of the contractual background of the transaction?*

2. The CJEU partially misconstrued the theory of functional equivalence as well. Although the CJEU correctly stressed that the material and immaterial supply of copies of software are functionally similar, as the copy shall be installed, and hence the source of the file(s) might be economically and materially irrelevant. The CJEU, however, unnecessarily extended the scope of the functional equivalence theory by the reference to the non-deterioration of digital copies. The Court treated the files perfect substitutes to the original copies, which therefore pose an economic danger to the original market of rights holders. Such arguments are true for software as well, but – more importantly – they are independent from the functional equivalence theory. Indeed, they represent serious (and plausible) policy arguments. Such a mistake by the CJEU is directly documented by the Court itself. The Grand Chamber refers to point 89 of the Advocate General's Opinion, which was located in the Advocate General's policy considerations.

3. The CJEU might completely misunderstood Tom Kabinet's business model. Point 69 of the Judgment is problematic, as the referring court briefed the facts of the case to the direct opposite. Imagine that – under the real facts of the case – the CJEU incorrectly viewed the members of the reading club as "public", and turn your eyes on the other element of the CJEU's argumentation: "having regard to the fact (…) that there is no technical measure on that club's platform". Imagine that Tom Kabinet (or any other platform) applies technical measures that guarantee the accession of a single copy of a work by one end-user at a given time. (We might call such a measure an effective forward-and-delete technology.) *Should the CJEU's syllogism mean that digital exhaustion is acceptable in the latter situation? Or – even worse – should that mean that the CJEU believes there is no "public" in the latter situation, and so the making available to the public right "quasi exhausts"?*

4. Following *Tom Kabinet*, the doctrine of exhaustion can practically lose its relevance in the online environment. *Is such castration of the doctrine really in the interests of the society? Wouldn't it be wiser to force/keep competition between the rights holders and newcomers in order to guarantee the best available services for the benefit of the whole society?* Indeed, the CJEU's ruling might render the CJEU's "liberal" view on e-lending meaningless as well (as the acceptance of e-lending in *VOB* was partially based on a *de facto* acceptance of digital exhaustion).

5. The legal distinction between the online supply of software and other subject matter necessarily leads to tensions with other legal norms, especially consumer protection law. As we have seen above, the European Union's directive on consumer protection treats the online supply of contents equally – irrespective of the copyright status of the works. Consumers can have a valid claim to treat their purchases on an equal footing – and to apply the doctrine of exhaustion to lawfully acquired copies of subject matter other than software, too. This argument is accepted by a recent trial court ruling in France.

In *Union Fédérale des Consommateurs*, an association representing consumers' interests successfully claimed that a leading computer games producer's strict limitations to the resale of lawfully acquired computer games runs against French consumer protection laws. The French court also held that such computer games (in compliance with the CJEU's *Nintendo* ruling) fall under the scope of the InfoSoc-Directive as mixed works, rather than the Software Directive. Consequently, consumers/end-users shall be allowed to dispose of the copies they downloaded against payment from the software corporation's website under the doctrine of exhaustion. If this ruling will be confirmed by the court of appeals, *it can serve as a solid ground for a "consumer law based doctrine of exhaustion" on a European level, too.*

6. As the CJEU missed to answer the remaining questions of the referring court, an important issue remained unanswered. The referring court requested clarification whether the resale of the device containing the digital files fits into the concept of exhaustion. No doubt that such resales shall not be prohibited by the EU law.

Further Case Law

Case C-128/11 - UsedSoft GmbH v. Oracle International Corp., Judgment of the Court (Grand Chamber), 3 July 2012 [ECLI:EU:C:2012:407]

Case C-355/12 - Nintendo Co. Ltd and Others v. PC Box Srl and 9Net Srl, Judgment of the Court (Fourth Chamber), 23 January 2014 [ECLI:EU:C:2014:25]

Case C-479/13 - European Commission v. France, Judgment of the Court (Fourth Chamber), 5 March 2015 [ECLI:EU:C:2015:141]

Union Fédérale des Consommateurs - Que Choisir v. S.A.R.L. Valve, Tribunal de Grande Instance de Paris, N° RG 16/01008

Recommended readings

In English

Stavroula Karapapa: *Exhaustion of Rights on Digital Content under EU Copyright: Positive and Normative Perspectives.* In: Tanya Aplin (Ed.): *Research Handbook on Intellectual Property and Digital Technologies*, Edward Elgar, Cheltenham, 2020, p. 483-505.

Alexandra Morgan - Paul Abbott - Christopher Stothers: ECJ Rules that the Sale of Second-hand E-books Infringes Copyright, *Journal of Intellectual Property Law & Practice*, 2020 (under publication)

Péter Mezei: The Doctrine of Exhaustion in Limbo - Critical Remarks on the CJEU's Tom Kabinet Ruling, *Prace z Prawa Własności Intelektualnej*, Issue 2/2020, p. 130-153.

In German

Philipp Homar: Unzulässigkeit der Weiterveräußerung von E-Books - Schlussfolgerungen aus EuGH C-263/18 - *Tom Kabinet, MR-Int: Internationale Rundschau zum Medienrecht, IP- & IT-Recht*, Heft 1/2020, p. 27-35.

Ansgar Ohly: Anmerkung zur EuGH: „Öffentliche Wiedergabe" durch Verkauf „gebrauchter" E-Books - NUV ua/Tom Kabinet, *Gewerblicher Rechtsschutz und Urheberrecht*, Heft 2/2020, p. 184-186.

Franz Hofmann: Recht der digitalen Güter: Keine digitale Erschöpfung bei der Weitergabe von E-Books - Anmerkung zu EuGH, Urteil vom 19.12.2019 - C-263/18 - NUV u. a./Tom Kabinet Internet u. a. (ZUM 2020, 129), *Zeitschrift für Urheber- und Medienrecht*, Heft 2/2020, p. 136-138.

Chapter VI
Sampling

Bridgeport Music, Inc. v. Dimension Films

410 *F.3d* 792 (2005)

AMENDED OPINION ON REHEARING

GUY, JR., Circuit Judge

(...) **I.**

The claims at issue in this appeal were originally asserted in an action filed on May 4, 2001, by the related entities Bridgeport Music, Southfield Music, Westbound Records, and Nine Records, alleging nearly 500 counts against approximately 800 defendants for copyright infringement and various state law claims relating to the use of samples without permission in new rap recordings. In August 2001, the district court severed that original complaint into 476 separate actions, this being one of them, based on the allegedly infringing work and ordered that amended complaints be filed.

The claims in this case were brought by all four plaintiffs: Bridgeport and Southfield, which are in the business of music publishing and exploiting musical composition copyrights, and Westbound Records and Nine Records, which are in the business of recording and distributing sound recordings. It was conceded at the time of summary judgment, however, that neither Southfield Music nor Nine Records had any ownership interest in the copyrights at issue in this case. As a result, the district court ordered that they be jointly and severally liable for 10% of the attorney fees and costs awarded to No Limit Films.

Bridgeport and Westbound claim to own the musical composition and sound recording copyrights in "Get Off Your Ass and Jam" by George Clinton, Jr. and the Funkadelics. We assume, as did the district court, that plaintiffs would be able to establish ownership in the copyrights they claim. There seems to be no dispute either that "Get Off" was digitally sampled or that the recording "100 Miles" was included on the sound track of *I Got the Hook Up*. Defendant No Limit Films, in conjunction with Priority Records, released the movie to theaters on May 27, 1998. The movie was apparently also released on VHS, DVD, and cable television. Fatal to Bridgeport's claims of infringement was the Release and Agreement it entered into with two of the original owners of the composition "100 Miles," Ruthless Attack Muzick (RAM) and Dollarz N Sense Music (DNSM), in December 1998, granting a sample use license to RAM, DNSM, and their licensees. Finding that No Limit Films had previously been granted an oral synchronization license to use the composition "100 Miles" in the sound track of *Hook Up*, the district court concluded Bridgeport's claims against No Limit Films were barred by the unambiguous terms of the Release and Agreement. Although Bridgeport does not appeal from this determination, it is relevant to the district court's later decision to award attorney fees to No Limit Films.

Westbound's claims are for infringement of the sound recording "Get Off." Because defendant does not deny it, we assume that the sound track of *Hook Up* used portions of "100 Miles" that included the allegedly infringing sample from "Get Off." The recording "Get Off" opens with a three-note combination solo guitar "riff" that lasts four seconds. According to one of plaintiffs' experts, Randy Kling, the recording "100 Miles" contains a sample from that guitar solo. Specifically, a two-second sample from the guitar solo was copied, the pitch was lowered, and the copied piece was "looped" and extended to 16 beats. Kling states that this sample appears in the sound recording "100 Miles" in five places; specifically, at 0:49, 1:52, 2:29, 3:20 and 3:46. By the district court's estimation, each looped segment lasted approximately 7 seconds. As for the segment copied from "Get Off," the district court described it as follows:

> "The portion of the song at issue here is an arpeggiated chord – that is, three notes that, if struck together, comprise a chord but instead are played one at a time in very quick succession – that is repeated several times at the opening of "Get Off." The arpeggiated chord is played on an unaccompanied electric guitar. The rapidity of the notes and the way they are played produce a high-pitched, whirling sound that captures the listener's attention and creates anticipation of what is to follow."

No Limit Films moved for summary judgment, arguing (1) that the sample was not protected by copyright law because it was not "original"; and (2) that the sample was legally insubstantial and therefore does not amount to actionable copying under copyright law.

Mindful of the limited number of notes and chords available to composers, the district court explained that the question turned not on the originality of the chord but, rather, on "the use of and the aural effect produced by the way the notes and the chord are played, especially here where copying of the sound recording is at issue." The district court found, after carefully listening to the recording of "Get Off," "that a jury could reasonably conclude that the way the arpeggiated chord is used and memorialized in the 'Get Off' sound recording is original and creative and therefore entitled to copyright protection." No Limit Films does not appeal from this determination.

Turning then to the question of *de minimis* copying in the context of digital sampling, the district court concluded that, whether the sampling is examined under a qualitative/quantitative *de minimis* analysis or under the so-called "fragmented literal similarity" test, the sampling in this case did not "rise to the level of a legally cognizable appropriation." Westbound argues that the district court erred both in its articulation of the applicable standards and its determination that there was no genuine issue of fact precluding summary judgment on this issue.

On October 11, 2002, the district court granted summary judgment to No Limit Films on the claims of Bridgeport and Westbound; dismissed with prejudice the claims of Southfield and Nine Records; denied as moot the motion of Bridgeport and Westbound for partial summary judgment on the issue of copyright ownership; and entered final judgment accordingly. Bridgeport and Westbound appealed. The facts relevant to the earlier denial of Bridgeport's motion to amend the complaint will be discussed below. No Limit Films filed a post-judgment motion for attorney fees and costs, which the district court granted for the reasons set forth in its memorandum opinion and order of April 24, 2003. Bridgeport, Southfield Music, and Nine Records appealed from that award.

II.

The district court's decision granting summary judgment is reviewed *de novo*. In deciding a motion for summary judgment, the court must view the evidence and reasonable inferences in the light most favorable to the nonmoving party. Summary judgment is appropriate when there are no genuine issues of material fact in dispute and the moving party is entitled to judgment as a matter of law.

In granting summary judgment to defendant, the district court looked to general *de minimis* principles and emphasized the paucity of case law on the issue of whether digital sampling amounts to copyright infringement. Drawing on both the quantitative/qualitative and "fragmented literal similarity" approaches, the district court found the *de minimis* analysis was a derivation of the substantial similarity element when a defendant claims that the literal copying of a small and insignificant portion of the copyrighted work should be allowed. After listening to the copied segment, the sample, and both songs, the district court found that no reasonable juror, even one familiar with the works of George Clinton, would recognize the source of the sample without having been told of its source. This finding, coupled with findings concerning the quantitatively small amount of copying involved and the lack of qualitative similarity between the works, led the district court to conclude that Westbound could not prevail on its claims for copyright infringement of the sound recording.

Westbound does not challenge the district court's characterization of either the segment copied from "Get Off" or the sample that appears in "100 Miles." Nor does Westbound argue that there is some genuine dispute as to any material fact concerning the nature of the protected material in the two works. The heart of Westbound's arguments is the claim that no substantial similarity or *de minimis* inquiry should be undertaken at all when the defendant has not disputed that it digitally sampled a copyrighted sound recording. We agree and accordingly must reverse the grant of summary judgment.

A. Digital Sampling of Copyrighted Sound Recordings

At the outset it is important to make clear the precise nature of our decision. Our conclusions are as follows:

1. The analysis that is appropriate for determining infringement of a musical composition copyright, is not the analysis that is to be applied to determine infringement of a sound recording. We address this issue only as it pertains to sound recording copyrights.

2. Since the district court decision essentially tracked the analysis that is made if a musical composition copyright were at issue, we depart from that analysis.

3. We agree with the district court's analysis on the question of originality. On remand, we assume that Westbound will be able to establish it has a copyright in the sound recording and that a digital sample from the copyrighted sound recording was used in this case.

4. This case involves "digital sampling" which is a term of art well understood by the parties to this litigation and the music industry in general. Accordingly, we adopt the definition commonly accepted within the industry.

5. Because of the court's limited technological knowledge in this specialized field, our opinion is limited to an instance of digital sampling of a sound recording protected by a valid copyright. If by analogy it is possible to extend our analysis to other forms of sampling, we leave it to others to do so.

6. Advances in technology[7] coupled with the advent of the popularity of hip hop or rap music have made instances of digital sampling extremely common and have spawned a plethora of copyright disputes and litigation.

7. The music industry, as well as the courts, are best served if something approximating a bright-line test can be established. Not necessarily a "one size fits all" test, but one that, at least, adds clarity to what constitutes actionable infringement with regard to the digital sampling of copyrighted sound recordings.

B. Analysis

We do not set forth the arguments made by Westbound since our analysis differs somewhat from that offered by the plaintiff. Our analysis begins and largely ends with the applicable statute. Section 114(a) of Title 17 of the United States Code provides:

> "The exclusive rights of the owner of copyright in a sound recording are limited to the rights specified by clauses (1), (2), (3) and (6) of section 106, and do not include any right of performance under section 106(4)."

Section 106 provides:

"Subject to sections 107 through 122, the owner of copyright under this title has the exclusive rights to do and to authorize any of the following:

> (1) to reproduce the copyrighted work in copies or phonorecords;
> (2) to prepare derivative works based upon the copyrighted work;
> (3) to distribute copies or phonorecords of the copyrighted work to the public by sale or other transfer of ownership, or by rental, lease, or lending;
> (4) in the case of literary, musical, dramatic, and choreographic works, pantomimes, and motion pictures and other audiovisual works to perform the copyrighted work publicly;
> (5) in the case of literary, musical, dramatic, and choreographic works, pantomimes, and pictorial, graphic, or sculptural works, including the individual images of a motion picture or other audiovisual work, to display the copyrighted work publicly; and
> (6) in the case of sound recordings, to perform the copyrighted work publicly by means of a digital audio transmission."

Section 114(b) states:

> "(b) The exclusive right of the owner of copyright in a sound recording under clause (1) of section 106 is limited to the right to duplicate the sound recording in the form of phonorecords or copies that directly or indirectly recapture the actual sounds fixed in the recording. The exclusive right of the owner of copyright in a sound recording under clause (2) of section 106 is limited to

> the right to prepare a derivative work in which the actual sounds fixed in the sound recording are rearranged, remixed, or otherwise altered in sequence or quality. The exclusive rights of the owner of copyright in a sound recording under clauses (1) and (2) of section 106 do not extend to the making or duplication of another sound recording that consists entirely of an independent fixation of other sounds, even though such sounds imitate or simulate those in the copyrighted sound recording. The exclusive rights of the owner of copyright in a sound recording under clauses (1), (2), and (3) of section 106 do not apply to sound recordings included in educational television and radio programs (as defined in section 397 of title 47) distributed or transmitted by or through public broadcasting entities (as defined by section 118(g)): *Provided,* That copies or phonorecords of said programs are not commercially distributed by or through public broadcasting entities to the general public."

Before discussing what we believe to be the import of the above quoted provisions of the statute, a little history is necessary. The copyright laws attempt to strike a balance between protecting original works and stifling further creativity. The provisions, for example, for compulsory licensing make it possible for "creators" to enjoy the fruits of their creations, but not to fence them off from the world at large. Although musical compositions have always enjoyed copyright protection, it was not until 1971 that sound recordings were subject to a separate copyright. If one were to analogize to a book, it is not the book, *i.e.,* the paper and binding, that is copyrightable, but its contents. There are probably any number of reasons why the decision was made by Congress to treat a sound recording differently from a book even though both are the medium in which an original work is fixed rather than the creation itself. None the least of them certainly were advances in technology which made the "pirating" of sound recordings an easy task. The balance that was struck was to give sound recording copyright holders the exclusive right "to duplicate the sound recording in the form of phonorecords or copies that directly or indirectly recapture the actual sounds fixed in the recording." This means that the world at large is free to imitate or simulate the creative work fixed in the recording so long as an actual copy of the sound recording itself is not made. That leads us directly to the issue in this case. If you cannot pirate the whole sound recording, can you "lift" or "sample" something less than the whole. Our answer to that question is in the negative.

Section 114(b) provides that "[t]he exclusive right of the owner of copyright in a sound recording under clause (2) of section 106 is limited to the right to prepare a derivative work in which the actual sounds fixed in the sound recording are rearranged, remixed, or otherwise altered in sequence or quality." Further, the rights of sound recording copyright holders under clauses (1) and (2) of section 106 "do not extend to the making or duplication of another sound recording that consists *entirely* of an independent fixation of other sounds, even though such sounds imitate or simulate those in the copyrighted sound recording." The significance of this provision is amplified by the fact that the Copyright Act of 1976 added the word "entirely" to this language. In other words, a sound recording owner has the exclusive right to "sample" his own recording. We find much to recommend this interpretation.

To begin with, there is ease of enforcement. Get a license or do not sample. We do not see this as stifling creativity in any significant way. It must be remembered that if an artist wants to incorporate a "riff" from another work in his or her recording, he is free to duplicate the sound of that "riff" in the studio. Second, the market will control the license price and keep it within bounds. The sound recording copyright holder cannot exact a license fee greater than what it would cost the person seeking the license to just duplicate the sample in the course of making the new recording. Third, sampling is never accidental. It is not like the case of a composer who has a melody in his head, perhaps not even realizing that the reason he hears this melody is that it is the work of another which he had heard before. When you sample a sound recording you know you are taking another's work product.

This analysis admittedly raises the question of why one should, without infringing, be able to take three notes from a musical composition, for example, but not three notes by way of sampling from a sound recording. Why is there no *de minimis* taking or why should substantial similarity not enter the equation. Our first answer to this question is what we have earlier indicated. We think this result is dictated by the applicable statute. Second, even when a small part of a sound recording is sampled, the part taken is something of value. No further proof of that is necessary than the fact that the producer of the record or the artist on the record intentionally sampled because it would (1) save costs, or (2) add something to the new recording, or (3) both. For the sound recording copyright holder, it is not the "song" but the sounds that are fixed in the medium of his choice. When those sounds are sampled they are taken directly from that fixed medium. It is a physical taking rather than an intellectual one.

This case also illustrates the kind of mental, musicological, and technological gymnastics that would have to be employed if one were to adopt a *de minimis* or substantial similarity analysis. The district judge did an excellent job of navigating these troubled waters, but not without dint of great effort. When one considers that he has hundreds of other cases all involving different samples from different songs, the value of a principled bright-line rule becomes apparent. We would want to emphasize, however, that considerations of judicial economy are not what drives this opinion. If any consideration of economy is involved it is that of the music industry. As this case and other companion cases make clear, it would appear to be cheaper to license than to litigate.

Since our holding arguably sets forth a new rule, several other observations are in order. First, although there were no existing sound recording judicial precedents to follow, we did not pull this interpretation out of thin air. Several law review and text writers, some of whom have been referenced in this opinion, have suggested that this is the proper interpretation of the copyright statute as it pertains to sound recordings. Since digital sampling has become so commonplace and rap music has become such a significant part of the record industry, it is not surprising that there are probably a hundred articles dealing with sampling and its ramifications. It is also not surprising that the viewpoint expressed in a number of these articles appears driven by whose ox is being gored. As is so often the case, where one stands depends on where one sits. For example, the sound recording copyright holders favor this interpretation as do the studio musicians and their labor organization. On the other hand, many of the hip hop artists may view this rule as stifling creativity. The record companies and performing artists are not all of one mind, however, since in many instances, today's sampler is tomorrow's samplee. The incidence of "live and let live" has been relatively high, which explains why so many instances of sampling go unprotested and why so many sampling controversies have been settled.

Second, to pursue further the subject of stifling creativity, many artists and record companies have sought licenses as a matter of course. Since there is no record of those instances of sampling that either go unnoticed or are ignored, one cannot come up with precise figures, but it is clear that a significant number of persons and companies have elected to go the licensing route. Also there is a large body of pre-1972 sound recordings that is not subject to federal copyright protection. Additionally, just as many artists and companies choose to sample and take their chances, it is likely that will continue to be the case.

Third, the record industry, including the recording artists, has the ability and know-how to work out guidelines, including a fixed schedule of license fees, if they so choose.

Fourth, we realize we are announcing a new rule and because it is new, it should not play any role in the assessment of concepts such as "willful" or "intentional" in cases that are currently before the courts or had their genesis before this decision was announced.

Finally, and unfortunately, there is no Rosetta stone for the interpretation of the copyright statute. We have taken a "literal reading" approach. The legislative history is of little help because digital sampling wasn't being done in 1971. If this is not what Congress intended or is not what they would intend now, it is easy enough for the record industry, as they have done in the past, to go back to Congress for a clarification or change in the law. This is the best place for the change to be made, rather than in the courts, because as this case demonstrates, the court is never aware of much more than the tip of the iceberg. To properly sort out this type of problem with its complex technical and business overtones, one needs the type of investigative resources as well as the ability to hold hearings that is possessed by Congress.

These conclusions require us to reverse the entry of summary judgment entered in favor of No Limit Films on Westbound's claims of copyright infringement. Since the district judge found no infringement, there was no necessity to consider the affirmative defense of "fair use." On remand, the trial judge is free to consider this defense and we express no opinion on its applicability to these facts. (...)

AFFIRMED in part, REVERSED in part, and REMANDED for further proceedings consistent with this opinion.

THINK IT OVER!

1. In *Grand Upright*, the first ever ruling on sampling, the New York district court concluded that Biz Markie's easily noticeable sample of Gilbert O'Sullivan's piano play is nothing else than theft. The district court cited from the Ten Commandments of the Holy Bible when it held that "thou shalt not steal". The Sixth Circuit's bright-line rule seems to follow this strict approach.

2. *Do you agree with the ruling of the Sixth Circuit? Bridgeport* was the first ever sampling case to be decided by a circuit court. Academia almost unanimously agree that the Sixth Circuit misinterpreted the *USCA*, as it omitted to look at the preparatory materials of the Act, as well as the historical relevance and background of the excluded doctrines. Section 114 rights might only be infringed, if "*all or any substantial*" piece of the pre-existing sound recording is reproduced. Consequently, the *de minimis* exception shall apply to sound recordings as well, otherwise sound recording producers would receive broader protection than composers – which is against the current norms of the *USCA*. No statutory basis exists for the Sixth Circuit's separation of physical and intellectual takings either. The bright-line rule equally misses the point. On the one hand, it runs against the U.S. Supreme Court's earlier rulings that have expressly embraced the *de minimis* exception. ("The law does not concern itself with trifles". See *Ringgold v. Black Entertainment Television*, p. 74.) The importance and legitimacy of the exception is further backed by its close connection to the fair use doctrine. In *Sony v. Universal*, the Supreme Court has viewed that "[i]n certain situations, the copyright owner suffers no substantial harm from the use of his work. (...) Here again, is the partial marriage between the doctrine of fair use and the legal maxim *de minimis non curat lex*." [*Sony v. Universal*, p. 451.] Similarly, the case-by-case approach had broader support in intellectual property law than bright-line rules. Furthermore, the Sixth Circuit's ruling that even the quantitatively or qualitatively smallest piece of a sound recording deserves unconditional protection runs against the Supreme Court's ruling in *Feist* where the (historic) "*sweat of the brow*" doctrine was refuted [*Feist v. Rural*, p. 352.]

Further Case Law

Sony Corp. of America v. Universal City Studios, Inc., 464 *U.S.* 417 (1984)

Feist Publications, Inc., v. Rural Telephone Company, 499 *U.S.* 340 (1991)

Grand Upright Music Ltd. v. Warner Brothers Records, Inc., et al., 780 *F.Supp.* 182 (1992)

Ringgold v. Black Entertainment Television Inc., 126 *F.3d* 70 (1997)

Newton v. Diamond, 388 *F.3d* 1189 (2004)

TufAmerica, Inc., v. WB Music Corp., et. al., 67 *F.Supp.3d* 590 (2014)

VMG Salsoul, LLC, v. Madonna Louise Ciccone, et. al., 824 *F.3d* 871 (2016)

Recommended readings

In English

Matthew R. Brodin: Bridgeport Music, Inc. v. Dimension Films: The Death of the Substantial Similarity Test in Digital Sampling Copyright Infringement Claims - The Sixth Circuit's Flawed Attempt at a Bright-line Rule, *Minnesota Journal of Law, Science & Technology*, 2005: p. 825-868.

Steven D. Kim: Taking De Minimis Out of the Mix: The Sixth Circuit Threatens to Pull the Plug on Digital Sampling in Bridgeport Music, Inc. v. Dimension Films, *Villanova Sports & Entertainment Law Journal*, 2006: p. 103-131.

M. Leah Somoano: Bridgeport Music, Inc. v. Dimension Films: Has Unlicensed Digital Sampling of Copyrighted Sound Recordings Come to an End?, *Berkeley Technology Law Journal*, 2006: p. 289-309.

Amanda Webber: Digital Sampling and the Legal Implications of its Use after Bridgeport, *Saint John's Journal of Legal Commentary*, 2007: p. 373-415.

Simon Apel: Bridgeport Music, Inc. v. Dimension Films (USA), Metall auf Metall (Germany) and Digital Sound Sampling - 'Bright Line Rules'?, *Zeitschrift für Geistiges Eigentum / Journal of Intellectual Property Law*, Issue 3/2010, p. 331-350.

In German

Simon Apel: Ein Recht auf Referenz im U.S.-amerikanischen Copyright?, *UFITA - Archiv für Medienrecht und Medienwissenschaft*, Heft 1/2019, p. 62-85.

In Hungarian

Mezei Péter: Digitális sampling az amerikai szerzői jogban - Sírba szálltok, „groove robbers"?, *Iparjogvédelmi és Szerzői Jogi Szemle*, 2008/3. szám, p. 5-24.

VMG SALSOUL, LLC, V. MADONNA LOUISE CICCONE, ET. AL.

824 *F.3d* 871 (2016)

OPINION

GRABER, Circuit Judge:

FACTUAL AND PROCEDURAL HISTORY

Because this case comes to us on appeal from a grant of summary judgment to Defendants, we recount the facts in the light most favorable to Plaintiff.

In the early 1980s, Pettibone recorded the song *Ooh I Love It (Love Break)*, which we refer to as *Love Break*. In 1990, Madonna and Pettibone recorded the song *Vogue*, which would become a mega-hit dance song after its release on Madonna's albums. Plaintiff alleges that, when recording *Vogue*, Pettibone "sampled" certain sounds from the recording of *Love Break* and added those sounds to *Vogue*. "Sampling" in this context means the actual physical copying of sounds from an existing recording for use in a new recording, even if accomplished with slight modifications such as changes to pitch or tempo.

Plaintiff asserts that it holds copyrights to the composition and to the sound recording of *Love Break*. Plaintiff argues that, because *Vogue* contains sampled material from *Love Break*, Defendants have violated both copyrights. Although Plaintiff originally asserted improper sampling of strings, vocals, congas, "vibraslap," and horns from *Love Break* as well as another song, Plaintiff now asserts a sole theory of infringement: When creating two commercial versions of *Vogue*, Pettibone sampled a "horn hit" from *Love Break*, violating Plaintiff's copyrights to both the composition and the sound recording of *Love Break*.

The horn hit appears in *Love Break* in two forms. A "single" horn hit in *Love Break* consists of a quarter-note chord comprised of four notes – E-flat, A, D, and F –in the key of B-flat. The single horn hit lasts for 0.23 seconds. A "double" horn hit in *Love Break* consists of an eighth-note chord of those same notes, followed immediately by a quarter-note chord of the same notes. Plaintiff's expert identified the instruments as "predominantly" trombones and trumpets.

The alleged source of the sampling is the "instrumental" version of *Love Break*, which lasts 7 minutes and 46 seconds. The single horn hit occurs 27 times, and the double horn hit occurs 23 times. The horn hits occur at intervals of approximately 2 to 4 seconds in two different segments: between 3:11 and 4:38, and from 7:01 to the end, at 7:46. The general pattern is single-double repeated, double-single repeated, single-single-double repeated, and double-single repeated. Many other instruments are playing at the same time as the horns.

The horn hit in *Vogue* appears in the same two forms as in *Love Break*: single and double. A "single" horn hit in *Vogue* consists of a quarter-note chord comprised of four notes – E, A-sharp, D-sharp, and F-sharp – in the key of B-natural. A double horn hit in *Vogue* consists of an eighth-note chord of those same notes, followed immediately by a quarter-note chord of the same notes.

The two commercial versions of *Vogue* that Plaintiff challenges are known as the "radio edit" version and the "compilation" version. The radio edit version of *Vogue* lasts 4 minutes and 53 seconds. The single horn hit occurs once, the double horn hit occurs three times, and a "breakdown" version of the horn hit occurs once. They occur at 0:56, 1:02, 3:41, 4:05, and 4:18. The pattern is single-double-double-double-breakdown. As with *Love Break*, many other instruments are playing at the same time as the horns.

The compilation version of *Vogue* lasts 5 minutes and 17 seconds. The single horn hit occurs once, and the double horn hit occurs five times. They occur at 1:14, 1:20, 3:59, 4:24, 4:40, and 4:57. The pattern is single-double-double-double-double-double. Again, many other instruments are playing as well.

One of Plaintiff's experts transcribed the composition of the horn hits in the two songs as follows.

Love Break's single horn hit:

Vogue's single horn hit:

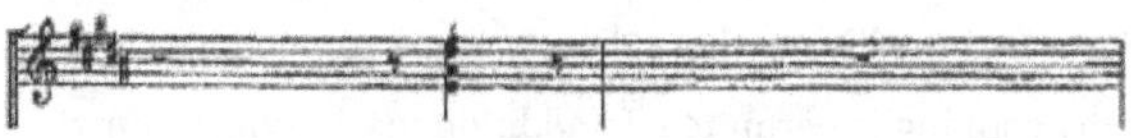

Love Break's double horn hit:

Vogue's double horn hit:

In a written order, the district court granted summary judgment to Defendants on two alternative grounds. First, neither the composition nor the sound recording of the horn hit was "original" for purposes of copyright law. Second, the court ruled that, even if the horn hit was original, any sampling of the horn hit was "de minimis or trivial." In a separate order, the district court awarded attorney's fees to Defendants under 17 U.S.C. § 505. Plaintiff timely appeals both orders.

DISCUSSION

Plaintiff has submitted evidence of actual copying. In particular, Tony Shimkin has sworn that he, as Pettibone's personal assistant, helped with the creation of *Vogue* and that, in Shimkin's presence, Pettibone directed an engineer to introduce sounds from *Love Break* into the recording of *Vogue.* Additionally, Plaintiff submitted reports from music experts who concluded that the horn hits in *Vogue* were sampled from *Love Break.* Defendants do not concede that sampling occurred, and they have introduced much evidence to the contrary. But for purposes of summary judgment, Plaintiff has introduced sufficient evidence (including direct evidence) to create a genuine issue of material fact as to whether copying in fact occurred. Taking the facts in the light most favorable to Plaintiff, Plaintiff has demonstrated actual copying. Accordingly, our analysis proceeds to the next step.

Our leading authority on actual copying is *Newton.* We explained in *Newton* that proof of actual copying is insufficient to establish copyright infringement:

> "For an unauthorized use of a copyrighted work to be actionable, the use must be significant enough to constitute infringement. This means that even where the fact of copying is conceded, no legal consequences will follow from that fact unless the copying is substantial. The principle that trivial copying does not constitute actionable infringement has long been a part of copyright law. Indeed, as [a judge] observed over 80 years ago: 'Even where there is some copying, that fact is not conclusive of infringement. Some copying is permitted. In addition to copying, it must be shown that this has been done to an unfair extent.' This principle reflects the legal maxim, *de minimis non curatlex* (often rendered as, 'the law does not concern itself with trifles')."

In other words, to establish its infringement claim, Plaintiff must show that the copying was greater than de minimis.

Plaintiff's claim encompasses two distinct alleged infringements: infringement of the copyright to the *composition* of *Love Break* and infringement of the copyright to the *sound recording* of Love Break. We squarely held in *Newton,* that the de minimis exception applies to claims of infringement of a copyrighted composition. But it is an open question in this circuit whether the exception applies to claims of infringement of a copyrighted sound recording.

Below, we address (A) whether the alleged copying of the composition or the sound recording was de minimis, (B) whether the de minimis exception applies to alleged infringement of copyrighted sound recordings, and (C) whether the district court abused its discretion in awarding attorney's fees to Defendants under 17 U.S.C. § 505.

A. Application of the De Minimis Exception

A "use is de minimis only if the average audience would not recognize the appropriation." Accordingly, we must determine whether a reasonable juror could conclude that the average audience would recognize the appropriation. We will consider the composition and the sound recording copyrights in turn.

1. Alleged Infringement of the Composition Copyright

When considering an infringement claim of a copyrighted musical composition, what matters is not how the musicians actually played the notes but, rather, a "generic rendition of the composition." That is, we must compare the written compositions of the two pieces.

Viewing the evidence in the light most favorable to Plaintiff, Defendants copied two distinct passages in the horn part of the score for *Love Break*. First, Defendants copied the quarter-note single horn hit. But no additional part of the score concerning the single horn hit is the same, because the single horn hit appears at a different place in the measure. In *Love Break*, the notes for the measure are: half-note rest, quarter-note rest, single horn hit. In *Vogue*, however, the notes for the measure are: half-note rest, eighth-note rest, single horn hit, eighth-note rest. Second, Defendants copied a full measure that contains the double horn hit. In both songs, the notes for the measure are: half-note rest, eighth-note rest, eighth-note horn hit, quarter-note horn hit. In sum, Defendants copied, at most, a quarter-note single horn hit and a full measure containing rests and a double horn hit.

After listening to the recordings, we conclude that a reasonable jury could *not* conclude that an average audience would recognize the appropriation of the composition. Our decision in *Newton* is instructive. That case involved a copyrighted composition of "a piece for flute and voice." The defendants used a six-second sample that "consist[ed] of three notes, C – D flat – C, sung over a background C note played on the flute." The composition also "require[d] overblowing the background C note that is played on the flute." The defendants repeated a six-second sample "throughout [the song], so that it appears over forty times in various renditions of the song." After listening to the recordings, we affirmed the grant of summary judgment because "an average audience would not discern [the composer's] hand as a composer."

The snippets of the composition that were (as we must assume) taken here are much smaller than the sample at issue in *Newton*. The copied elements from the *Love Break* composition are very short, much shorter than the six-second sample in *Newton*. The single horn hit lasts less than a quarter-second, and the double horn hit lasts – even counting the rests at the beginning of the measure – less than a second. Similarly, the horn hits appear only five or six times in *Vogue*, rather than the dozens of times that the sampled material in *Newton* occurred in the challenged song in that case. Moreover, unlike in *Newton*, in which the challenged song copied *the entire composition* of the original work for the given temporal segment, the sampling at issue here involves only *one instrument group* out of many. As noted above, listening to the audio recordings confirms what the foregoing analysis of the composition strongly suggests: A reasonable jury could not conclude that an average audience would recognize an appropriation of the *Love Break* composition.

2. Alleged Infringement of the Sound Recording Copyright

When considering a claimed infringement of a copyrighted sound recording, what matters is how the musicians *played* the notes, that is, how their rendition distinguishes the recording from a generic rendition of the same composition. Viewing the evidence in the light most favorable to Plaintiff, by accepting its experts' reports, Pettibone sampled one single horn hit, which occurred at 3:35 in *Love Break*. Pettibone then used that sampled single horn hit to create the double horn hit used in *Vogue*.

The horn hit itself was not copied precisely. According to Plaintiff's expert, the chord "was modified by transposing it upward, cleaning up the attack slightly in order to make it punchier [by truncating the horn hit] and overlaying it with other sounds and effects. One such effect mimicked the reverse cymbal crash.... The reverb/delay 'tail' ... was prolonged and heightened." Moreover, as with the composition, the horn hits are not isolated sounds. Many other instruments are playing at the same time in both *Love Break* and *Vogue*.

In sum, viewing the evidence in the light most favorable to Plaintiff, Pettibone copied one quarter-note of a four-note chord, lasting 0.23 seconds; he isolated the horns by filtering out the other instruments playing at the same time; he transposed it to a different key; he truncated it; and he added effects and other sounds to the chord itself. For the double horn hit, he used the same process, except that he duplicated the single horn hit and shortened one of the duplicates to create the eighth-note chord from the quarter-note chord. Finally, he overlaid the resulting horn hits with sounds from many other instruments to create the song *Vogue*.

After listening to the audio recordings submitted by the parties, we conclude that a reasonable juror could *not* conclude that an average audience would recognize the appropriation of the horn hit. That common-sense conclusion is borne out by dry analysis. The horn hit is very short – less than a second. The horn hit occurs only a few times in *Vogue*. Without careful attention, the horn hits are easy to miss. Moreover, the horn hits in *Vogue* do not sound identical to the horn hits from *Love Break*. As noted above, assuming that the sampling occurred, Pettibone truncated the horn hit, transposed it to a different key, and added other sounds and effects to the horn hit itself. The horn hit *then* was added to *Vogue* along with many other instrument tracks. Even if one grants the dubious proposition that a listener recognized some similarities between the horn hits in the two songs, it is hard to imagine that he or she would conclude that sampling had occurred.

A quirk in the procedural history of this case is illuminating on this point. Plaintiff's primary expert originally *misidentified* the source of the sampled double horn hit. In his original report, the expert concluded that both a single horn hit *and a double horn hit* were sampled from *Love Break*. The parties later discovered the original tracks to *Vogue* and were able to listen to the horn hits without interference from the many other instruments. After listening to those tracks, the expert decided that he had erred in opining that a double horn hit was sampled. He concluded instead that only a single horn hit was sampled, which was used to create the double horn hit in *Vogue*. In other words, a highly qualified and trained musician listened to the recordings with the express aim of discerning which parts of the song had been copied, and he could not do so accurately. An average audience would not do a better job.

In sum, the district court correctly held that summary judgment to Defendants was appropriate on the issue of de minimis copying.

B. The De Minimis Exception and Sound Recordings

Plaintiff argues, in the alternative, that even if the copying here is trivial, that fact is irrelevant because the de minimis exception does not apply to infringements of copyrighted sound recordings. Plaintiff urges us to follow the Sixth Circuit's decision in *Bridgeport*, which adopted a bright-line rule: For copyrighted sound recordings, any unauthorized copying – no matter how trivial – constitutes infringement.

The rule that infringement occurs only when a substantial portion is copied is firmly established in the law. The leading copyright treatise traces the rule to the mid-1800s. We recognized the rule as early as 1977: "If copying is established, then only does there arise the second issue, that of illicit copying (unlawful appropriation). On that issue the test is the response of the ordinary lay hearer...." The reason for the rule is that the "plaintiff's legally protected interest [is] the potential financial return from his compositions which derive from the lay public's approbation of his efforts." If the public does not recognize the appropriation, then the copier has not benefitted from the original artist's expressive content. Accordingly, there is no infringement.

Other than *Bridgeport* and the district courts following that decision, we are aware of no case that has held that the de minimis doctrine does not apply in a copyright infringement case. Instead, courts consistently have applied the rule in *all* cases alleging copyright infringement. Indeed, we stated in dictum in *Newton* that the rule "applies *throughout the law of copyright*, including cases of music sampling."

Plaintiff nevertheless argues that Congress intended to create a special rule for copyrighted sound recordings, eliminating the de minimis exception. We begin our analysis with the statutory text.

Title 17 U.S.C. § 102, titled "Subject matter of copyright: In general," states, in relevant part:

> "(a) Copyright protection subsists, in accordance with this title, in original works of authorship fixed in any tangible medium of expression, now known or later developed, from which they can be perceived, reproduced, or otherwise communicated, either directly or with the aid of a machine or device. Works of authorship include the following categories:
>
> (1) literary works;
> (2) musical works, including any accompanying words;
> (3) dramatic works, including any accompanying music;
> (4) pantomimes and choreographic works;
> (5) pictorial, graphic, and sculptural works;
> (6) motion pictures and other audiovisual works;
> (7) *sound recordings*; and
> (8) architectural works."

That provision treats sound recordings identically to all other types of protected works; nothing in the text suggests differential treatment, for any purpose, of sound recordings compared to, say, literary works. Similarly, nothing in the neutrally worded statutory definition of "sound recordings" suggests that Congress intended to eliminate the de minimis exception.

Title 17 U.S.C. § 106, titled "Exclusive rights in copyrighted works," states:

> "Subject to sections 107 through 122, the owner of copyright under this title has the exclusive rights to do and to authorize any of the following:
>
> (1) to reproduce the copyrighted work in copies or phonorecords;
>
> (2) to prepare derivative works based upon the copyrighted work;
>
> (3) to distribute copies or phonorecords of the copyrighted work to the public by sale or other transfer of ownership, or by rental, lease, or lending;
>
> (4) in the case of literary, musical, dramatic, and choreographic works, pantomimes, and motion pictures and other audiovisual works, to perform the copyrighted work publicly;
>
> (5) in the case of literary, musical, dramatic, and choreographic works, pantomimes, and pictorial, graphic, or sculptural works, including the individual images of a motion picture or other audiovisual work, to display the copyrighted work publicly; and
>
> (6) in the case of sound recordings, to perform the copyrighted work publicly by means of a digital audio transmission."

Again, nothing in that provision suggests differential treatment of de minimis copying of sound recordings compared to, say, sculptures. Although subsection (6) deals exclusively with sound recordings, that subsection concerns public performances; nothing in its text bears on de minimis copying.

Instead, Plaintiff's statutory argument hinges on the third sentence of 17 U.S.C. § 114(b), which states:

> "The exclusive rights of the owner of copyright in a sound recording under clauses (1) and (2) of section 106 do not extend to the making or duplication of another sound recording that consists entirely of an independent fixation of other sounds, even though such sounds imitate or simulate those in the copyrighted sound recording."

Like all the other sentences in § 114(b), the third sentence imposes an express *limitation* on the rights of a copyright holder: "The exclusive rights of the owner of a copyright in a sound recording ... *do not extend* to the making or duplication of another sound recording [with certain qualities]." We ordinarily would hesitate to read an *implicit expansion* of rights into Congress' statement of an *express limitation* on rights. Given the considerable background of consistent application of the de minimis exception across centuries of jurisprudence, we are particularly hesitant to read the statutory text as an unstated, implicit elimination of that steadfast rule.

A straightforward reading of the third sentence in § 114(b) reveals Congress' intended limitation on the rights of a sound recording copyright holder: A new recording that mimics the copyrighted recording is not an infringement, even if the mimicking is very well done, so long as there was no actual copying. That is, if a band played and recorded its own version of *Love Break* in a way that sounded very similar to the copyrighted recording of *Love Break*, then there would be no infringement so long as there was no actual copying of the recorded *Love Break*. But the quoted passage does not speak to the question that we face: whether Congress intended to eliminate the longstanding de minimis exception for sound recordings in all circumstances even where, as here, the new sound recording as a whole sounds nothing like the original.

Even if there were some ambiguity as to congressional intent with respect to § 114(b), the legislative history clearly confirms our analysis on each of the above points. Congress intended § 114 to limit, not to expand, the rights of copyright holders: "The approach of the bill is to set forth the copyright owner's exclusive rights in broad terms in section 106, and then to provide various limitations, qualifications, or exemptions in the 12 sections that follow. Thus, everything in section 106 is made 'subject to sections 107 through 118,' and must be read in conjunction with those provisions."

With respect to § 114(b) specifically, a House Report stated:

> "Subsection (b) of section 114 makes clear that statutory protection for sound recordings extends only to the particular sounds of which the recording consists, and would not prevent a separate recording of another performance in which those sounds are

imitated. Thus, infringement takes place whenever all *or any substantial portion* of the actual sounds that go to make up a copyrighted sound recording are reproduced in phonorecords by repressing, transcribing, recapturing off the air, or any other method, or by reproducing them in the soundtrack or audio portion of a motion picture or other audiovisual work. Mere imitation of a recorded performance would not constitute a copyright infringement even where one performer deliberately sets out to simulate another's performance as exactly as possible."

That passage strongly supports the natural reading of § 114(b), discussed above. Congress intended to make clear that imitation of a recorded performance cannot be infringement so long as no actual copying is done. There is no indication that Congress intended, through § 114(b), to expand the rights of a copyright holder to a sound recording.

Perhaps more importantly, the quoted passage articulates the principle that "infringement takes place whenever all *or any substantial portion* of the actual sounds ... are reproduced." That is, when enacting this specific statutory provision, Congress clearly understood that the de minimis exception applies to copyrighted sound recordings, just as it applies to all other copyrighted works. In sum, the statutory text, confirmed by the legislative history, reveals that Congress intended to maintain the de minimis exception for copyrighted sound recordings.

In coming to a different conclusion, the Sixth Circuit reasoned [in *Bridgeport*] as follows:

> "[T]he rights of sound recording copyright holders under clauses (1) and (2) of section 106 'do not extend to the making or duplication of another sound recording that consists *entirely* of an independent fixation of other sounds, even though such sounds imitate or simulate those in the copyrighted sound recording.' The significance of this provision is amplified by the fact that the Copyright Act of 1976 added the word "entirely" to this language. In other words, a sound recording owner has the exclusive right to "sample" his own recording."

We reject that interpretation of § 114(b). *Bridgeport* ignored the statutory structure and § 114(b)'s express *limitation* on the rights of a copyright holder. *Bridgeport* also declined to consider legislative history on the ground that "digital sampling wasn't being done in 1971." But the state of technology is irrelevant to interpreting Congress' intent as to statutory structure. Moreover, as Nimmer points out, *Bridgeport*'s reasoning fails on its own terms because contemporary technology plainly allowed the copying of small portions of a protected sound recording.

Close examination of *Bridgeport*'s interpretive method further exposes its illogic. In effect, *Bridgeport* inferred from the fact that "exclusive rights ... *do not extend* to the making or duplication of another sound recording that *consists* entirely of an independent fixation of other sounds", the conclusion that exclusive rights *do extend* to the making of another sound recording that *does not consist* entirely of an independent fixation of other sounds. As pointed out by Nimmer, *Bridgeport*'s interpretive method "rests on a logical fallacy." A statement that rights do not extend to a particular circumstance does not automatically mean that the rights extend to all other circumstances. In logical terms, it is a fallacy to infer the inverse of a conditional from the conditional.

For example, take as a given the proposition that "if it has rained, then the grass is not dry." It does not necessarily follow that "if it has not rained, then the grass is dry." Someone may have watered the lawn, for instance. We cannot infer the second if-then statement from the first. The first if-then statement does not tell us *anything* about the condition of the grass if it has not rained. Accordingly, even though it is true that, "if the recording consists entirely of independent sounds, then the copyright does not extend to it," that statement does not necessarily mean that "if the recording does not consist entirely of independent sounds, then the copyright does extend to it."

The Sixth Circuit also looked beyond the statutory text, to the nature of a sound recording, and reasoned:

> "[E]ven when a small part of a sound recording is sampled, the part taken is something of value. No further proof of that is necessary than the fact that the producer of the record or the artist on the record intentionally sampled because it would (1) save costs, or (2) add something to the new recording, or (3) both. For the sound recording copyright holder, it is not the "song" but the sounds that are fixed in the medium of his choice. When those sounds are sampled they are taken directly from that fixed medium. It is a physical taking rather than an intellectual one."

We disagree for three reasons. *First*, the possibility of a "physical taking" exists with respect to other kinds of artistic works as well, such as photographs, as to which the usual de minimis rule applies. A computer program can, for instance, "sample" a piece of one photograph and insert it into another photograph or work of art. We are aware of no copyright case carving out an exception to the de minimis requirement in that context, and we can think of no principled reason to differentiate one kind of "physical taking" from another. *Second*, even accepting the premise that sound recordings differ qualitatively from other copyrighted works and therefore *could warrant* a different infringement rule, that theoretical difference does not mean that Congress *actually adopted* a different rule. *Third*, the distinction between a "physical taking" and an "intellectual one," premised in part on "sav[ing] costs" by not having to hire musicians, does not advance the Sixth Circuit's view. The Supreme Court has held unequivocally that the Copyright Act protects only the expressive aspects of a copyrighted work, and *not* the "fruit of the [author's] labor." Indeed, the Supreme Court in *Feist* explained at length why, though that result may seem unfair, protecting only the expressive aspects of a copyrighted work is actually a key part of the design of the copyright laws. Accordingly, all that remains of *Bridgeport*'s argument is that the second artist has taken some expressive content from the original artist. But that is always true, regardless of the nature of the work, and the de minimis test nevertheless applies.

Because we conclude that Congress intended to maintain the "de minimis" exception for copyrights to sound recordings, we take the unusual step of creating a circuit split by disagreeing with the Sixth Circuit's contrary holding in *Bridgeport.* We do so only after careful reflection because, as we noted in *Seven Arts,* "the creation of a circuit split would be particularly troublesome in the realm of copyright. Creating inconsistent rules among the circuits would lead to different levels of protection in different areas of the country, even if the same alleged infringement is occurring nationwide." We acknowledge that our decision has consequences. But the goal of avoiding a circuit split cannot override our independent duty to determine congressional intent. Otherwise, we would have no choice but to blindly follow the rule announced by whichever circuit court decided an issue first, even if we were convinced, as we are here, that our sister circuit erred.

Moreover, other considerations suggest that the "troublesome" consequences ordinarily attendant to the creation of a circuit split are diminished here. In declining to create a circuit split in *Seven Arts,* we noted that "the leading copyright treatise," Nimmer, agreed with the view of our sister circuits. As to the issue before us, by contrast, Nimmer devotes many pages to explaining why the Sixth Circuit's opinion is, in no uncertain terms, wrong.

Additionally, as a practical matter, a deep split among the federal courts *already exists.* Since the Sixth Circuit decided *Bridgeport,* almost every district court not bound by that decision has declined to apply *Bridgeport*'s rule. Although we are the first circuit court to follow a different path than *Bridgeport*'s, we are in well-charted territory.

Plaintiff next argues that, because Congress has not amended the copyright statute in response to *Bridgeport,* we should conclude that *Bridgeport* correctly divined congressional intent. We disagree. The Supreme Court has held that congressional inaction in the face of a judicial statutory interpretation, even with respect to the Supreme Court's own decisions affecting the entire nation, carries almost no weight. Here, Congress' inaction with respect to a decision by one circuit court has even less import, especially considering that many other courts have declined to apply *Bridgeport*'s rule.

Finally, Plaintiff advances several reasons why *Bridgeport*'s rule is superior *as a matter of policy.* For example, the Sixth Circuit opined that its bright-line rule was easy to enforce; that "the market will control the license price and keep it within bounds"; and that "sampling is never accidental" and is therefore easy to avoid. Those arguments are for a legislature, not a court. They speak to what Congress *could decide*; they do not inform what Congress *actually decided.*

We hold that the "de minimis" exception applies to actions alleging infringement of a copyright to sound recordings. (...)

Judgment AFFIRMED; award of fees VACATED and REMANDED for reconsideration. (...)

THINK IT OVER!

1. Shortly before *VMG Salsoul*, a New York district court published an important ruling in *TufAmerica*. Shortly before the VMG Salsoul ruling was handed over, the plaintiff held the copyright of the composition and the recording of Eddie Bo and the Soul Finder's "*Hook & Sling Part I*". The defendant was the producer of the "*Run This Town*" recording performed by Jay-Z, Rihanna and Kanye West. The plaintiff claimed that Eddie Bo's short "oh" shouting was sampled and looped 42 times by the defendant. Although the district court had fundamental concerns regarding the protectability of that "oh" shouting, it assumed copyright protection in order to discuss the question of potential infringement. The district court declared the use lawful due to the quantitative and qualitative insignificance of the sample. The quantitative significance is foreclosed by the fact that the "oh" shouting is shorter than a second, while the source work lasts for more than two and a half minutes. As the district court noted, any argument to the contrary would render the test of quantitative significance meaningless. The district court further stressed that the qualitative significance of the segment shall never be judged according to plaintiff's view, but merely by comparing it with the source material. Thus, the district court held that "*Hook & Sling Part I*" would not lose from its quality if the "oh" shouting be omitted. Further, the sample remained in the background of "Run This Town", and an average lay listener would hardly notice it independently. Taken all these together, the district court concluded that the sample is *de minimis*, which made any further analysis unnecessary. *TufAmerica* was the first post-*Bridgeport* sampling case to apply the *de minimis* exception.

2. In *VMG Salsoul*, the Ninth Circuit refrained from the Sixth Circuit's bright-line rule, and explicitly applied the *de minimis* exception. The Ninth Circuit returned to its earlier ruling in *Newton*, where an approximately three seconds long, three note flute sample was taken. There, the Ninth Circuit found the use lawful. In *VMG Salsoul*, the panel ruled that no reasonable jury would find an even shorter sample illegal, especially as the horn was only one of the many instruments used in the more complex source work. The court similarly found the sampled recording trivial. The court also stressed that the *de minimis* exception dates back to the 19th century, and it is a quintessential piece of the federal copyright law, which applies to all subject matters on an equal basis. The Ninth Circuit further opined that the Sixth Circuit totally misunderstood *USCA* Section 114(b), which is an explicit limitation to the sound recording producers' copyrights. The implicit expansion of these rights by the Sixth Circuit was clearly erroneous. *Which approach do you favour?*

The bright-line rule of the Sixth Circuit (favouring sound-recording producers) or the fact-specific approach of the Ninth Circuit?

3. *The Ninth Circuit purposefully created a circuit split.* Circuit splits can allow for the Supreme Court to grant a *certiorari* to rule on a given case, and thus to provide for a uniform interpretation of a given legal question. Although the Supreme Court rarely addresses copyright cases, the economic relevance of and the longstanding debate around sampling can make it plausible that a *certiorari* will be granted soon. This could be accelerated by a third circuit court ruling, either by accepting one of the existing approaches or by the introduction of a third solution. The Second Circuit, having jurisdiction over the home of hip-hop (and thus sampling), New York City, has the greatest chance to become that third circuit court. Interestingly enough, no sampling cases reached the Second Circuit yet. If the Supreme Court grants a *certiorari* in the near future, it (currently) seems to be more plausible that it will follow the Ninth Circuit's approach, at least for two reasons. First, the applicability of the *de minimis* exception in musical copyright cases is historically unquestionable. Second, the Supreme Court has never supported the use of bright-line rules in intellectual property cases. Granting the *certiorari* could also open the eyes of the Congress in order to regulate sampling – most probably by the amendment of *USCA* Section §114(b).

Further Case Law

Newton v. Diamond, 388 *F.3d* 1189 (2004)

Bridgeport Music, Inc. v. Dimension Films, 410 *F.3d* 792 (2005)

Seven Arts Filmed Entertainment Ltd. v. Content Media Corporation, 733 *F.3d* 1251 (2013)

TufAmerica, Inc., v. WB Music Corp., et. al., 67 *F.Supp.3d* 590 (2014)

Recommended readings

In English

Francesco Di Cosmo: Return of the De Minimis Exception in Digital Music Sampling: the Ninth Circuit's Recent Holding in VMG Salsoul Improves upon the Sixth Circuit's Holding in Bridgeport, but Raises Questions of its Own, *Washington University Law Review*, 2017: p. 227-250.

Tyler B. Burns: And They Sayin' It's Because of the Internet: Applying the De Minimis Exception to Digital Sound Sampling in the Wake of VMG Salsoul, LLC v. Ciccione, *Drexel Law Review*, 2018: p. 445-495.

Ryan Beeck: Creativity or Copyright Infringement?: Evaluating the De Minimis Exception in Digital Sampling Through VMG Salsoul, LLC and Bridgeport Music, Inc., *Rutgers University Law Review*, Winter 2018: p. 521-556.
Stefan Caris Love: Circuit Split: De Minimis Sampling from Copyrighted Recordings After VMG Salsoul, LLC v. Ciccione, *UCLA Journal of Law and Technology*, Summer 2018, p. 521-556.
Péter Mezei: Thou Shalt (Not) Sample? New Drifts in the Ocean of Sampling, *Zeitschrift für Geistiges Eigentum / Journal of Intellectual Property Law*, Issue 2/2019, p. 170-198.
Péter Mezei: The Dimensions of the *De Minimis* Exception and Musical Sampling, *Medien und Recht International*, Issue 2/2019, p. 48-51.

In German
Sibel Kocatepe: To Sample or Not to Sample: Geben Madonna und Drake bald den Ton im US-amerikanischen Copyright Law an?, *Gewerblicher Rechtsschutz und Urheberrecht Internationaler Teil*, Heft 1/2018, p. 11-19.
Simon Apel: Ein Recht auf Referenz im U.S.-amerikanischen Copyright?, *UFITA - Archiv für Medienrecht und Medienwissenschaft*, Heft 1/2019, p. 62-85.

In Hungarian
Mezei Péter: Thou Shalt Sample! Pozitív változások a samplingelés amerikai gyakorlatában, *Infokommunikáció és Jog*, 2018/2. szám, p. 47-53.

ESTATE OF JAMES OSCAR SMITH, ET ANO., V. CASH MONEY RECORDS, INC., ET AL.

253 *F.Supp.3d* 737 (2017)

OPINION & ORDER

PAULEY III, District Judge:

BACKGROUND

In 1982, Jimmy Smith recorded an album released by Elektra/Asylum Records titled *Off the Top*. The first six tracks are purely instrumental, and the last track is a spoken-word recording titled "Jimmy Smith Rap" ("JSR"). The lyrics to JSR are:

> Good God Almighty, like back in the old days

You know, years ago they had the A & R men to tell you what to play, how to play it and you know whether it's disco rock, but we just told Bruce that we want a straight edge jazz so we got the fellas together Grady Tate, Ron Carter, George Benson, Stanley Turrentine.

Stanley was coming off a cool jazz festival, Ron was coming off a cool jazz festival. And we just went in the studio and we did it.

We had the champagne in the studio, of course, you know, compliments of the company and we just laid back and did it.

Also, Grady Tate's wife brought us down some home cooked chicken and we just laid back and we was chomping on chicken and having a ball.

Jazz is the only real music that's gonna last. All that other bullshit is here today and gone tomorrow. But jazz was, is and always will be.

We may not do this sort of recording again, I may not get with the fellas again. George, Ron, Grady Tate, Stanley Turrentine.

So we hope you enjoy listening to this album half as much as we enjoyed playing it for you. Because we had a ball.

The label on each side of the record lists each song with the composer in parentheses, except for JSR, which lists no writer. Although Raymond Janifer, Jimmy Smith's nephew and co-manager of the Estate, was not present at the recording of JSR, he recalls Jimmy Smith telling him that he "laid down a dynamite rap on them and hope they don't cut it off the album." Janifer also explained that Jimmy Smith did not write music, but instead made the music and words up in his head and then performed and recorded on tape. Additionally, the website www.discogs.com lists Jimmy Smith as the author of JSR.

In April 2013, the Estate entered into an Administration Agreement with Modern Works Music Publishing ("Modern Works"). The Agreement designated Modern Works as the "sole and exclusive Administrator" for the Estate, while noting that "[o]wnership remain[ed] with" the Estate. Modern Works agreed to register "all claims to copyright in the Compositions ... with the United States Copyright Office" in the Estate's name. In return, the Estate conferred on Modern Works "the exclusive right to administer and exploit the Compositions throughout the Territory during the Term." A contemporaneous document explained that the Estate "entered into a worldwide, full-catalog administration agreement for the Compositions."

On September 24, 2013, Cash Money Records and Universal Republic Records released an album titled *Nothing Was the Same* (the "Album") by Aubrey Drake Graham ("Drake"). The last song on the Album is "Pound Cake/Paris Morton Music 2" ("Pound Cake"). The opening to Pound Cake samples about 35 seconds of JSR. The sampled portions are:

Good God Almighty, like back in the old days.

> You know, years ago they had the A & R men to tell you what to play, how to play it and you know whether it's disco rock, but we just went in the studio and we did it.
>
> We had champagne in the studio, of course, you know, compliments of the company, and we just laid back and did it.
>
> So we hope you enjoy listening to this album half as much as we enjoyed playing it for you. Because we had a ball.
>
> Only real music is gonna last, all that other bullshit is here today and gone tomorrow.

While some words from JSR were rearranged or deleted, no words were added.

In producing the Album, Cash Money arranged for a music licensing company to ensure that parties obtained all necessary licenses. Defendants obtained a license for the JSR recording, but not for the JSR composition. The JSR composition copyright was not registered with the U.S. Copyright Office or any performing rights organization prior to the Album's release. The Estate maintains that it would not have granted a license for the composition because Jimmy Smith "wasn't a fan of hip hop." The JSR recording license stated that Defendants received "all requisite consents and permissions of ... the copyright owners of the musical composition."

Stephen Hacker is the principal of Hebrew Hustle, a music publisher that represents songwriters in negotiating the licensing of copyrights. Prior to the release of the Album, Hacker had ongoing business relationships with many of the Defendants.

Approximately one week before the Album's release, Hacker reviewed an advance copy of the credits "to look for openings in rights, sign those rights and then disclose that to the Drake representatives" <u>after</u> the release of the Album. Hacker noticed that Defendants had secured a license for the recording of JSR, but not for the composition. He reached out to Janifer to alert the Estate of Defendants' use of the JSR composition in the Album. Thereafter, the Estate entered into a co-publishing agreement with Hebrew Hustle, assigning 50% of the copyright in the JSR composition to Hebrew Hustle and granting an exclusive right to exploit it. Hebrew Hustle registered the JSR composition with the U.S. Copyright Office on October 23, 2013 in the name of Hebrew Hustle. Two months after the Album's release, the Estate's counsel sent a cease and desist letter, which was the first time Defendants learned of any alleged composition copyright interest in JSR. (...)

DISCUSSION

I. <u>COPYRIGHT INFRINGEMENT</u>

"To establish infringement, two elements must be proven: (1) ownership of a valid copyright, and (2) copying of constituent elements of the work that are original." Defendants argue that neither element is satisfied: Plaintiffs have no evidence that Jimmy Smith wrote JSR, and JSR and Pound Cake are not substantially similar.

a. Ownership of a Copyright

In a copyright infringement suit, the plaintiff bears the initial burden of coming forward with evidence that it possesses a valid copyright. "Copyright in a work ... vests initially in the author or authors of the work." The "author" is the person who translates an original and minimally creative idea into a fixed, tangible expression. The Estate derives its copyright from Jimmy Smith, who passed away in February 2005. For the Estate to hold the copyright, Jimmy Smith must have owned the copyright as the author of the work. However, the record evidence does not resolve the question of JSR's authorship.

As an initial matter, this Court affords the January 2013 registration of the composition copyright in JSR minimal weight. While copyright registration normally constitutes prima facie evidence of validity, "[t]he evidentiary weight to be accorded the certificate of a registration made [more than five years after the first publication] shall be within the discretion of the court." Here, the Estate registered the JSR composition copyright thirty-one years after initial publication, and only in response to Defendants' sampling of JSR on the Album. "Accordingly, the registration does not constitute prima facie evidence that the copyright is valid, and [Plaintiff] has the burden of proving the validity of its copyright."

The lyrics of JSR indicate that it is a behind-the-scenes recollection of the recording of *Off the Top*. Indeed, the statement on the *Off the Top* album cover explains that it was recorded with "no charts, music format or nothing ... just playing what we felt ... off the top of our heads." But this information only speaks to the process of recording *Off the Top*, and not necessarily to the authorship of JSR. Interpreting this in the light most favorable to the non-moving party creates a dispute of material fact.

Similarly, Janifer asserted that Jimmy Smith did not write music by putting pen to paper, instead making the words up in his head before performing and recording the sounds on tape. But Janifer did not witness Jimmy Smith record JSR, and that lack of firsthand knowledge makes his testimony less probative.

Janifer also claims that, prior to the release of *Off the Top*, Jimmy Smith told him "I laid down the dynamite rap on them and I hope they don't cut it from the album." Hearsay problems aside, there is no indication that Jimmy Smith was referring to JSR and not to some other song that was, in fact, cut from the album.

The song listings for *Off the Top* are similarly unhelpful, as they list the writers of each song except JSR. Although the album's original packaging contained a copyright notice that listed "Elektra/Asylum Records" as the copyright claimant for the sound recordings and any other uncredited material, such a notice must "be placed on publicly distributed copies from which the work can be visually perceived." Because the lyrics were not displayed on the album jacket, they could not be visually perceived. Plaintiffs' suggestion that there was no need to list the author of JSR because it was self-evident is circular and therefore cannot support summary judgment.

The fact that a single music-focused website recognizes Jimmy Smith as the author does not advance the inquiry. The website www.discogs.com, which Plaintiffs claim is a commonly used and relied-upon source, lists Jimmy Smith as the author of JSR. But that website is a user-built database, and anyone can contribute to it. There is no evidence that whoever entered the data had any personal knowledge of JSR's authorship.

Ultimately, a genuine issue of material fact exists as to the authorship of JSR. Accordingly, summary judgment is not appropriate on this issue.

b. Substantial Similarity

"In order to establish a claim of copyright infringement, a plaintiff with a valid copyright must demonstrate that: (1) the defendant has actually copied the plaintiff's work; and (2) the copying is illegal because a substantial similarity exists between the defendant's work and the protectible elements of plaintiff's." "In general, the question of substantial similarity is a close question of fact; therefore, summary judgment has traditionally been frowned upon in copyright litigation. Yet, summary judgment may be granted when any similarity concerns non-protectable elements or no reasonable trier of fact could find the works substantially similar."

Multiple tests exist to determine substantial similarity, including the "ordinary observer test," the "comprehensive non-literal test," and the "fragmented literal similarity test." Defendants argue for the application of the ordinary observer test, while Plaintiffs maintain that the fragmented literal similarity test is appropriate.

The ordinary observer test is the "standard test for substantial similarity." It asks "whether an ordinary observer, unless he set out to detect the disparities, would be disposed to overlook them, and regard the aesthetic appeal as the same."

By contrast, "fragmented literal similarity exists where the defendant copies a portion of the plaintiff's work exactly or nearly exactly, without appropriating the work's overall essence or structure." Under the fragmented literal similarity test, "the question of substantial similarity is determined by an analysis of 'whether the copying goes to trivial or substantial elements' of the original work."

Both tests ask "whether 'the copying is quantitatively and qualitatively sufficient' to support a finding of infringement." "It is only where the points of dissimilarity exceed those that are similar and those similar are – when compared to the original work – of small import quantitatively or qualitatively that a finding of no infringement is appropriate." But "[b]ecause they involve literal copying, in cases of 'fragmented literal similarity,' more so than under the 'ordinary observer test,' the copying of even a 'relatively small' quantitative 'portion of the pre-existing work may be substantial if it is of great qualitative importance to the [pre-existing] work as a whole.'"

Under either test, only the protectable portions of the copyrighted works are compared for substantial similarity. "To qualify for copyright protection, a work must be original to the author. Original, as the term is used in copyright, means only that the work was independently created by the author (as opposed to copied from other works), and that it possesses at least some minimal degree of creativity." Where works "have both protectible and unprotectible elements [the] analysis must be more discerning and ... [courts] must attempt to extract the unprotectible elements from ... consideration and ask whether the protectible elements, standing alone, are substantially similar."

Cliché language is not subject to copyright protection. And "[o]rdinary historical facts and events are not protectable elements under the Copyright Act.... [Only] 'thin' copyright protection ... exist[s] for an original selection or arrangement of facts, 'but the copyright is limited to the particular selection or arrangement.'"

Although Pound Cake copies much of JSR verbatim, Defendants contend that the sampled portion removes much of the factual account, is primarily cliché that is not entitled to protection, and only "goes to trivial ... elements of the original work."

But courts must not "dissect the works at issue into separate components and compare only the copyrightable elements." Instead, courts should "examine the works for their total concept and feel." And while "[an] 'ordinary' phrase may enjoy no protection as such ... its use in a sequence of expressive words does not cause the entire passage to lose protection." Thus, creative expression employing the use of clichéd words may still be protectable.

In the end, "[i]t would be a dangerous undertaking for persons trained only to the law to constitute themselves final judges of the worth of [art], outside of the narrowest and most obvious limits." Ultimately, a determination of whether the copied portions of JSR are entitled to copyright protection depends on a subjective assessment better suited for a jury than a court. Accordingly, summary judgment on the elements of infringement is not appropriate here.

II. FAIR USE

Alternatively, Defendants argue that Plaintiffs' claims are barred by the fair use doctrine. Fair use is an affirmative defense to copyright infringement, and thus the party asserting fair use bears the burden of proof.

The doctrine of fair use has its roots in the "ultimate goal" of copyright law – that is, "to expand public knowledge and understanding, [a goal] which copyright seeks to achieve by giving potential creators exclusive control over copying of their works, thus giving them a financial incentive to create informative, intellectually enriching works for public consumption."

Implied in this objective is the principle that "while authors are undoubtedly important intended beneficiaries of copyright, the ultimate, primary intended beneficiary is the public, whose access to knowledge copyright seeks to advance by providing rewards for authorship." Accordingly, courts developed the fair use doctrine to preclude a finding of infringement where "the copyright law's goal of 'promoting the Progress of Science and useful Arts' ... would be better served by allowing the use than by preventing it."

Congress codified the fair use doctrine in the Copyright Act of 1976. Section 107 of the Act provides that:

> Notwithstanding the provisions of sections 106 and 106A, the fair use of a copyrighted work ... for purposes such as criticism, comment, news reporting, teaching ..., scholarship, or research is not an infringement of copyright. In determining whether the use made of a work in any particular case is a fair use the factors to be considered shall include—
>
> (1) The purpose and character of the use, including whether such use is of a commercial nature or is for nonprofit educational purposes;
>
> (2) The nature of the copyrighted work;
>
> (3) The amount and substantiality of the portion used in relation to the copyrighted work as a whole; and
>
> (4) The effect of the use upon the potential market for or value of the copyrighted work.

Because the fair use determination is "an open-ended and context-sensitive inquiry," the examples and factors in the statute are "illustrative and not limitative ... [and] provide only general guidance about the sorts of copying that courts and Congress most commonly had found to be fair uses." Ultimately, fair use analysis asks a simple question: Is this the type of use that furthers the essential goal of copyright law and should be excused from liability for infringement?

Because copyright infringement involves highly fact-dependent analysis, courts "should be especially wary of granting summary judgment." "This is especially true in fair use cases, as the viability of the defense rests on the particular circumstances of each case and the balancing of various factual considerations." When "the likelihood that additional, non-cumulative evidence will be presented at trial is slight," however, summary judgment may be appropriate. Indeed, "[a]lthough fair use is a mixed question of law and fact, courts in the Second Circuit have 'on a number of occasions' resolved fair use determinations at the summary judgment stage where there are no genuine issues of material fact."

a. Factor #1: Purpose and Character of the Use

The first statutory factor, which courts have referred to as "[t]he heart of the fair use inquiry," focuses on the nature and purposes of the allegedly infringing use. The central question is "whether and to what extent the new work is 'transformative.'" This is a critical issue because "[t]he more the appropriator is using the copied material for new, transformative purposes, the more it serves copyright's goal of enriching public knowledge and the less likely it is that the appropriation will serve as a substitute for the original or its plausible derivatives." Accordingly, the relevant inquiry on this factor is whether the new work "merely supersedes the objects of the original creation, or instead adds something new, with a further purpose or different character, altering the first with new expression, meaning, or message."

Defendants advance three arguments for the transformative nature of their use of JSR. First, Defendants claim that Pound Cake fundamentally alters the message of the original work – that is, by editing the recording from "Jazz is the only real music that's gonna last" to "Only real music is gonna last," Drake transformed Jimmy Smith's dismissive comment into a statement on the relevance and staying power of "real music," regardless of genre. Second, Defendants note that Pound Cake omits all references to the recording of *Off the Top*, thereby making the words applicable to the process of making Drake's album rather than Jimmy Smith's. Finally, Defendants claim that the addition of background music, the rearrangement of some words, and the placement of the recording in a seven-minute hip hop track renders their use transformative.

Defendants' second and third arguments are misplaced because they conflate the nature of a fair use with that of a derivative work. The word "transform" appears in the statutory definition of derivative works, which of course require a license and are not protected by the fair use doctrine. Although derivative works typically involve transformative changes, "[t]he statutory definition suggests that derivative works generally involve transformations in the nature of changes of form." Thus, when a new work transforms a copyrighted work but uses it for "the same [ ] purpose for which the [original] is sold," the new work is a derivative work rather than fair use. Drake's use of JSR to describe his own recording process, although literally transformative in the sense that he does not appropriate JSR verbatim, would bear the same purpose that Jimmy Smith had when he first recorded JSR. Accordingly, these arguments cannot support a fair use defense.

Defendants' first argument, on the other hand, strikes on a compelling reason to find this use transformative. There can be no reasonable dispute that the key phrase of JSR – "Jazz is the only real music that's gonna last. All that other bullshit is here today and gone tomorrow. But jazz was, is and always will be." – is an unequivocal statement on the primacy of jazz over all other forms of popular music. Defendants' use of JSR, by contrast, transforms Jimmy Smith's brazen dismissal of all non-jazz music into a statement that "real music," with no qualifiers, is "the only thing that's gonna last." Thus, Defendants' "purposes in using [the original work] are sharply different from [the original artist's] goals in creating it." This is precisely the type of use that "adds something new, with a further purpose or different character, altering the first [work] with new expression, meaning, or message."

Plaintiffs contend that the use cannot be transformative because the copied portions are not readily identifiable as JSR and because the track does not identify Jimmy Smith. Thus, Plaintiffs argue, there can be no viable claim that Pound Cake is commenting on an obscure spoken-word track by a relatively unknown jazz musician (at least outside of the jazz community). This argument fails because Plaintiffs seek to apply the standard for fair use in parody to this non-parodic use. Although it is certainly true that the object of a parody must be ascertainable to the average observer – and with reason, for what good is parody if the listener cannot identify the target of derision? – this is not a universal prerequisite for finding a transformative use. For example, the court in Blanch v. Koons found that the defendant's appropriation of a small part of a magazine advertisement (specifically, a picture of a woman's legs and feet) into a larger mixed-media artwork was a transformative use even though no reasonable observer would identify the legs as being from the original advertisement. Because the defendant used the copyrighted work as "raw material ... in furtherance of distinct creative or communicative objectives," the Blanch court found that the use was a transformative one.

Similarly, Defendants' use of JSR is transformative regardless of whether the average listener would identify the source of the sample and immediately comprehend Drake's purposes. The critical question is "how the work <u>in question</u> appears to the reasonable observer," not the quality or accessibility of the commentary. The average listener of Pound Cake would understand the sampled portions of JSR as a statement that, regardless of how a song was made or how one might classify it, "only <u>real</u> music is gonna last." Because this purpose is "sharply different" from Jimmy Smith's purpose in creating the original track, Defendants' use is transformative and this factor weighs in favor of a finding of fair use.

b. Factor #2: Nature of the Copyrighted Work

The second statutory factor "calls for recognition that some works are closer to the core of intended copyright protection than others, with the consequence that fair use is more difficult to establish when the former works are copied." "Two types of distinctions as to the nature of the copyrighted work have emerged that have figured in the decisions evaluating the second factor: (1) whether the work is expressive or creative, such as a work of fiction, or more factual, with greater leeway being allowed to a claim of fair use where the work is factual or informational, and (2) whether the work is published or unpublished, with the scope for fair use involving unpublished works being considerably narrower." As the Second Circuit has noted, this factor "is rarely found to be determinative."

Because JSR is a work of creative expression, this factor weighs against a finding of fair use. Defendants' contention that JSR is only entitled to "thin" copyright because it is merely a factual account of the recording of *Off the Top* ignores the Supreme Court's instruction that facts "clothe[d] ... with an original collocation of words" are still entitled to copyright protection. This factor is of particularly "limited usefulness" in this case, however, because this Court has already determined that "the creative work of art is being used for a transformative purpose."

c. Factor #3: Amount and Substantiality of the Portion Used

The next factor asks the court to consider "the amount and substantiality of the portion used in relation to the copyrighted work as a whole." The "clear implication" of this inquiry "is that a finding of fair use is more likely when small amounts, or less important passages, are copied than when the copying is more extensive, or encompasses the most important parts of the original." Thus, the test is "whether the quantity and value of the materials used[ ] are reasonable in relation to the purpose of the copying."

Plaintiffs contend that Defendants appropriated an unreasonable portion of JSR when they used thirty-five seconds of the one-minute track, and that any statement on the staying power of "real" music would necessitate the use of only that single line. The law "does not require," however, "that the secondary artist ... take no more than is necessary," and instead permits the secondary user "to 'conjure up' <u>at least</u> enough of the original" to accomplish his transformative purpose.

Here, the Court finds the amount taken by Defendants to be reasonable in proportion to the needs of the intended transformative use. Far from being extraneous to Pound Cake's statement on the importance of "real" music, Defendants' use of the lines describing the recording of *Off the Top* serve to drive the point home. The full extent of the commentary is, in this Court's view, that <u>many</u> musicians make records in similar ways (<u>e.g.</u> with the help of A & R experts or the stimulating effects of champagne), but that only "real" music – regardless of creative process or genre – will stand the test of time. Accordingly, this factor favors a finding of fair use.

d. Factor #4: Effect on the Market for the Copyrighted Work

On the final factor, courts analyze "the effect of the [secondary] use upon the potential market for or value of the copyrighted work." As the ability to reap financial rewards from creative endeavors is a critical component of the copyright regime, the Supreme Court has noted that this factor is "undoubtedly the single most important element of fair use." At this stage, courts ask "whether the copy brings to the marketplace a competing substitute for the original, or its derivative, so as to deprive the rights holder of significant revenues because of the likelihood that potential purchasers may opt to acquire the copy in preference to the original." The fourth factor is also, however, closely linked to the first, in the sense that "the more the copying is done to achieve a purpose that differs from the purpose of the original, the less likely it is that the copy will serve as a satisfactory substitute for the original."

There is no evidence in the record to suggest that Pound Cake usurps any potential market for JSR or its derivatives. JSR, a spoken-word criticism of non-jazz music at the end of an improvisational jazz album, targets a sharply different primary market than Pound Cake, a hip-hop track. Further, Plaintiffs never attempted to establish a market for licensed derivative uses of the JSR composition copyright until Defendants used the recording on the Album. These considerations, coupled with the finding that Defendants' use is highly transformative, forestalls the conclusion that Defendants took such "sufficiently significant portions of the original as to make available a significantly competing substitute." Thus, the fourth factor favors the Defendants.

Having considered the four factors in light of the goals of copyright law and the facts in the record, this Court concludes that Defendants' inclusion of the copied portions of JSR in the recording of Pound Cake is a fair use and does not infringe Plaintiffs' composition copyright.

CONCLUSION

Because there is a genuine dispute of material fact as to ownership and copying, neither party is entitled to summary judgment on Plaintiffs' infringement claims. For the reasons discussed above, however, this Court finds that any liability for Defendants' appropriation of JSR is barred by the doctrine of fair use. Accordingly, Plaintiffs' motion for summary judgment is denied and Defendants' motion for summary judgment is granted. (...)

SO ORDERED

THINK IT OVER!

1. The district court accepted Drake's fair use defense. *This conclusion is not against the existing case law of the doctrine.* Some may say that Drake's use was not transformative, as almost nothing else but a few lines were erased from the source work. Nevertheless, the transformative nature has been broadly applied by federal courts so far. Similarly, 35 seconds seem to be quite a lot quantitatively, especially as the "Jimmy Smith Rap" was only a minute long, but courts have been flexible to fit significant quantities into the third factor of the doctrine. The concept of "*conjuring up*" has only been confirmed by the Supreme Court in parody cases so far. [See *Campbell v. Acuff-Rose*, p. 588.] In plenty of other cases, especially in *Google Books*, courts accepted more significant copying in case of transformative uses. Finally, the analysis of potential market effects fully complied with the Supreme Court's holding in *Campbell v. Acuff-Rose.* The district court's decision was affirmed by the Second Circuit's summary order on February 3, 2020. (See Estate of James Oscar Smith, et al., v. Aubrey Drake Graham, et al., 799 *Fed.Appx.* 36.) Summary orders have no precedential value in the US, and the ruling was not published in the Federal Reporter either.

2. Edward Lee analysed all musical copyright cases that were published between January 1, 1978 (the entry into force of the U.S. Copyright Act) and January 15, 2018. Lee excluded all cases from his study, where the copyrights of sound recording producers were infringed. He believed that the significant differences in court decisions, especially with respect to sampling, exclude the possibility to objectively measure whether the uses can be treated as transformative (under the first factor of the fair use test). Such a direct exclusion of cases might decrease the relevance of Lee's study for this textbook.

His findings are, however, directly relevant in understanding the significance of the fair use doctrine in musical copyright cases. During the four-decade period covered by Lee's research 177 musical copyright decisions were published in the United States, from which 127 were decided on the merits. Surprisingly, in 91% of the cases (115 times) the court refused the plaintiffs' claims, and the fair use doctrine was not even raised in 116 cases. From the latter 116 cases defendants won 105 times. In the 11 cases, where the defendant relied on the fair use doctrine, the court decided on the merits four times; defendants successfully argued parody five times; the parody defence failed once; and once a non-parody fair use defence also remained unsuccessful. This very last case was *Cash Money Records.* Lee deemed this ruling as an outlier, as Drake sampled verbal rather than musical expressions. In the vast majority of the cases defendants were not required to rely on the fair use doctrine at all. According to Lee, in 71 of the 115 cases (61.7%) the defendant prevailed as the plaintiff either failed to evidence the access to his work (in 36 times) or no substantial similarity was found between the two works (in 35 cases). In other cases, the trivial use or the public domain nature of the source material guaranteed defendant's success. No clear reason for plaintiffs' losses was found in 22 decisions. It seems so that *the fair use doctrine is not the most important defence strategy in musical copyright cases.* This is underlined by the fact that the doctrine was raised in only 9.1% of the cases; and that in 11 cases where the defendant lost its case the doctrine was not referred to at all. Lee termed this conservative approach as "*fair use avoidance*". Lee named the easiness to reach out-of-court settlements; the doctrine's history; and any clear precedent in musical copyright cases as the concurring reasons for fair use avoidance. The Supreme Court's *Campbell v. Acuff-Rose* ruling does not function as a general precedent, as it covered a parody, and only a fragment of musical cases involve parodies. It was similarly interesting that in 90% of the cases "established" musicians were sued, and in 54% of the cases "unestablished" musicians sued "established" artists. Lee argued that in such circumstances, the reliance on the fair use doctrine might impose more dangers to musicians than advantages. The doctrine could function as a "double-edged sword" that could be used by "unestablished" musicians against "established" ones, if the doctrine becomes a successful means of defence for "established" artists.

Further Case Law

Luther R. Campbell, et al., v. Acuff-Rose Music, Inc., 510 *U.S.* 569 (1994)

Castle Rock Entm't, Inc. v. Carol Pub. Grp., Inc., 150 *F.3d* 132 (1998)

Newton v. Diamond, 388 *F.3d* 1189 (2004)

Blanch v. Koons, 467 *F.3d* 244 (2006)

Cariou v. Prince, 714 *F.3d* 694 (2013)

TufAmerica, Inc. v. Diamond, 968 *F.Supp.2d* 588 (2013)

Recommended readings

In English

Sibel Kocatepe: To Sample or Not to Sample: Geben Madonna und Drake bald den Ton im US-amerikanischen Copyright Law an?, *Gewerblicher Rechtsschutz und Urheberrecht Internationaler Teil*, Heft 1/2018, p. 11-19.

Edward Lee: Fair Use Avoidance in Music Copyright Cases, *Boston College Law Review*, June 2018: p. 1873-1931.

Péter Mezei: Thou Shalt (Not) Sample? New Drifts in the Ocean of Sampling, *Zeitschrift für Geistiges Eigentum / Journal of Intellectual Property Law*, Issue 2/2019, p. 170-198.

In Hungarian

Mezei Péter: Thou Shalt Sample! Pozitív változások a samplingelés amerikai gyakorlatában, *Infokommunikáció és Jog*, 2018/2. szám, p. 47-53.

PELHAM GMBH, MOSES PELHAM, MARTIN HAAS V. RALF HÜTTER, FLORIAN SCHNEIDER-ESLEBEN

Case C-476/17 - Judgment of the Court (Grand Chamber), 29 July 2019 [ECLI:EU:C:2019:624]

(...) Legal context

International law

3 Article 1 of the Convention for the Protection of Producers of Phonograms Against Unauthorised Duplication of Their Phonograms, signed in Geneva on 29 October 1971 ('the Geneva Convention'), reads as follows:

'For the purposes of this Convention:

(a) "phonogram" means any exclusively aural fixation of sounds of a performance or of other sounds;

(b) "producer of phonograms" means the person who, or the legal entity which, first fixes the sounds of a performance or other sounds;

(c) "duplicate" means an article which contains sounds taken directly or indirectly from a phonogram and which embodies all or a substantial part of the sounds fixed in that phonogram;

(d) "distribution to the public" means any act by which duplicates of a phonogram are offered, directly or indirectly, to the general public or any section thereof.'

4 Article 2 of the Geneva Convention provides:

'Each Contracting State shall protect producers of phonograms who are nationals of other Contracting States against the making of duplicates without the consent of the producer and against the importation of such duplicates, provided that any such making or importation is for the purpose of distribution to the public, and against the distribution of such duplicates to the public.'

European Union law

Directive 2001/29

5 Recitals 3, 4, 6, 7, 9, 10, 31 and 32 of Directive 2001/29 state:

'(3) The proposed harmonisation will help to implement the four freedoms of the internal market and relates to compliance with the fundamental principles of law and especially of property, including intellectual property, and freedom of expression and the public interest.

(4) A harmonised legal framework on copyright and related rights, through increased legal certainty and while providing for a high level of protection of intellectual property, will foster substantial investment in creativity and innovation, including network infrastructure, and lead in turn to growth and increased competitiveness of European industry, both in the area of content provision and information technology and more generally across a wide range of industrial and cultural sectors. This will safeguard employment and encourage new job creation.

(...)

(6) Without harmonisation at [EU] level, legislative activities at national level which have already been initiated in a number of Member States in order to respond to the technological challenges might result in significant differences in protection and thereby in restrictions on the free movement of services and products incorporating, or based on, intellectual property, leading to a refragmentation of the internal market and legislative inconsistency. The impact of such legislative differences and uncertainties will become more significant with the further development of the information society, which has already greatly increased transborder exploitation of intellectual property. This development will and should further increase. Significant legal differences and uncertainties in protection may hinder economies of scale for new products and services containing copyright and related rights.

(7) The [EU] legal framework for the protection of copyright and related rights must, therefore, also be adapted and supplemented as far as is necessary for the smooth functioning of the internal market. To that end, those national provisions on copyright and related rights which vary considerably from one Member State to another or which cause legal uncertainties hindering the smooth functioning of the internal market and the proper development of the information society in Europe should be adjusted, and inconsistent national responses to the technological developments

should be avoided, whilst differences not adversely affecting the functioning of the internal market need not be removed or prevented.

(...)

(9) Any harmonisation of copyright and related rights must take as a basis a high level of protection, since such rights are crucial to intellectual creation. Their protection helps to ensure the maintenance and development of creativity in the interests of authors, performers, producers, consumers, culture, industry and the public at large. ...

(10) If authors or performers are to continue their creative and artistic work, they have to receive an appropriate reward for the use of their work, as must producers in order to be able to finance this work. The investment required to produce products such as phonograms, films or multimedia products, and services such as "on-demand" services, is considerable. Adequate legal protection of intellectual property rights is necessary in order to guarantee the availability of such a reward and provide the opportunity for satisfactory returns on this investment.

(...)

(31) A fair balance of rights and interests between the different categories of rightholders, as well as between the different categories of rightholders and users of protected subject-matter must be safeguarded. The existing exceptions and limitations to the rights as set out by the Member States have to be reassessed in the light of the new electronic environment. ... In order to ensure the proper functioning of the internal market, such exceptions and limitations should be defined more harmoniously. The degree of their harmonisation should be based on their impact on the smooth functioning of the internal market.

(32) This Directive provides for an exhaustive enumeration of exceptions and limitations to the reproduction right and the right of communication to the public. Some exceptions or limitations only apply to the reproduction right, where appropriate. This list takes due account of the different legal traditions in Member States, while, at the same time, aiming to ensure a functioning internal market. Member States should arrive at a coherent application of these exceptions and limitations, which will be assessed when reviewing implementing legislation in the future.'

6 Under the heading 'Reproduction right', Article 2 of Directive 2001/29 provides:

'Member States shall provide for the exclusive right to authorise or prohibit direct or indirect, temporary or permanent reproduction by any means and in any form, in whole or in part:

(...)

(c) for phonogram producers, of their phonograms;'

7 Article 5 of Directive 2001/29 sets out the exceptions and limitations to the rights referred to in Articles 2 to 4 thereof. Article 5(3) and (5) provides:

'3. Member States may provide for exceptions or limitations to the rights provided for in Articles 2 and 3 in the following cases:

(...)

(d) quotations for purposes such as criticism or review, provided that they relate to a work or other subject-matter which has already been lawfully made available to the public, that, unless this turns out to be impossible, the source, including the author's name, is indicated, and that their use is in accordance with fair practice, and to the extent required by the specific purpose;

5. The exceptions and limitations provided for in paragraphs 1, 2, 3 and 4 shall only be applied in certain special cases which do not conflict with a normal exploitation of the work or other subject-matter and do not unreasonably prejudice the legitimate interests of the rightholder.'

Directive 2006/115

8 Recitals 2, 5 and 7 of Directive 2006/115 state:

'(2) Rental and lending of copyright works and the subject matter of related rights protection is playing an increasingly important role in particular for authors, performers and producers of phonograms and films. Piracy is becoming an increasing threat.

(...)

(5) The creative and artistic work of authors and performers necessitates an adequate income as a basis for further creative and artistic work, and the investments required particularly for the production of phonograms and films are especially high and risky. The possibility of securing that income and recouping that investment can be effectively guaranteed only through adequate legal protection of the rightholders concerned.

(...)

(7) The legislation of the Member States should be approximated in such a way as not to conflict with the international conventions on which the copyright and related rights laws of many Member States are based.'

9 Under the heading 'Object of harmonisation', Article 1(1) of that directive provides:

'In accordance with the provisions of this Chapter, Member States shall provide, subject to Article 6, a right to authorise or prohibit the rental and lending of originals and copies of copyright works, and other subject matter as set out in Article 3(1).'

10 Under the heading 'Distribution right', Article 9(1) of the directive provides:

'Member States shall provide the exclusive right to make available to the public, by sale or otherwise, the objects indicated in points (a) to (d), including copies thereof, hereinafter "the distribution right":

(...)

(b) for phonogram producers, in respect of their phonograms;'

11 The first paragraph of Article 10(2) of Directive 2006/115 reads as follows:

'(...)any Member State may provide for the same kinds of limitations with regard to the protection of performers, producers of phonograms, broadcasting organisations and of producers of the first fixations of films, as it provides for in connection with the protection of copyright in literary and artistic works.'

German law

12 Paragraph 24 of the Gesetz über Urheberrecht und verwandte Schutzrechte – Urheberrechtsgesetz (Law on copyright and related rights) of 9 September 1965 (BGBl. 1965 I, p. 1273; 'the UrhG') provides:

'1. An independent work created in the free use of the work of another person may be published and exploited without the consent of the author of the work used.

2. Subparagraph 1 shall not apply to the use of a musical work in which a melody is recognisably taken from the work and used as the basis for a new work.'

13 Paragraph 85(1) of the UrhG, which transposes Article 2(c) of Directive 2001/29 and Article 9 of Directive 2006/115, provides, in its first sentence, first and second cases, that the producer of a phonogram has the exclusive right to reproduce and distribute the phonogram.

The case in the main proceedings and the questions referred for a preliminary ruling

14 Hütter and another are members of the group Kraftwerk. In 1977, that group published a phonogram featuring the song '*Metall auf Metall*'.

15 Mr Pelham and Mr Haas composed the song '*Nur mir*', which was released on phonograms recorded by Pelham GmbH in 1997.

16 Hütter and another submit that Pelham electronically copied ('sampled') approximately 2 seconds of a rhythm sequence from the song '*Metall auf Metall*' and used that sample in a continuous loop in the song '*Nur mir*', although it would have been possible for them to play the adopted rhythm sequence themselves.

17 As the phonogram producers, Hütter and another's principal claim is that Pelham infringed their copyright-related right. In the alternative, they claim that their intellectual property right as performers and Mr Hütter's copyright in the musical work were infringed. In the further alternative, they claim that Pelham infringed competition law.

18 Hütter and another brought an action before the Landgericht Hamburg (Regional Court, Hamburg, Germany) seeking a prohibitory injunction, damages, the provision of information and the surrender of the phonograms for the purposes of their destruction.

19 That court upheld the action, and Pelham's appeal before the Oberlandesgericht Hamburg (Higher Regional Court, Hamburg, Germany) was dismissed. Following an appeal on a point of law (*Revision*) brought by Pelham before the Bundesgerichtshof (Federal Court of Justice, Germany), the judgment of the Oberlandesgericht Hamburg (Higher Regional Court, Hamburg) was overturned and the case was referred back to that court for re-examination. That court dismissed Pelham's appeal a second time. In a judgment of 13 December 2012, the Bundesgerichtshof (Federal Court of Justice) once again dismissed Pelham's appeal on a point of law. That judgment was overturned by the Bundesverfassungsgericht (Federal Constitutional Court, Germany), which referred the case back to the referring court.

20 The referring court notes that the outcome of the *Revision* proceedings turns on the interpretation of Article 2(c) and Article 5(3)(d) of Directive 2001/29 and of Article 9(1)(b) and Article 10(2) of Directive 2006/115.

21 According to the referring court, it must, in the first place, be determined whether, by using Hütter and another's sound recording in the production of its own phonogram, Pelham encroached on the exclusive right of Hütter and another to reproduce and distribute the phonogram featuring the song '*Metall auf Metall*', as laid down in Paragraph 85(1) of the UrhG, which transposes Article 2(c) of Directive 2001/29 and Article 9 of Directive 2006/115. In particular, it must be determined whether such an infringement can be found where, as in the present case, 2 seconds of a rhythm sequence are taken from a phonogram then transferred to another phonogram, and whether that amounts to a copy of another phonogram within the meaning of Article 9(1)(b) of Directive 2006/115.

22 In the second place, if it is found that there has been an infringement of the phonogram producer's right, the question arises of whether Pelham may rely on the 'right to free use', laid down in Paragraph 24(1) of the UrhG, which is applicable by analogy to the phonogram producer's right, according to which an independent work created in the free use of the work of another person may be published or exploited without the consent of the author of the work used. The referring court notes, in that context, that that provision has no express equivalent in EU law and therefore asks whether that right is consistent with EU law in the light of the fact that that provision limits the scope of protection of the phonogram producer's exclusive right to reproduce and distribute his or her phonogram.

23 In the third place, the national law exceptions and limitations to the reproduction right referred to in Article 2(c) of Directive 2001/29 and to the distribution right referred to in Article 9(1)(b) of Directive 2006/115 are based on Article 5(3) of Directive 2001/29 and the first paragraph of Article 10(2) of Directive 2006/115. However, the referring court harbours doubts as to the interpretation of those provisions in circumstances such as those at issue in the main proceedings.

24 In the fourth place, the referring court notes that EU law must be interpreted and applied in the light of the fundamental rights enshrined in the Charter of Fundamental Rights of the European Union ('the Charter'). In that context, it asks whether the Member States have any discretion for the purposes of the transposition into national law of Article 2(c) and Article 5(2) and (3) of Directive 2001/29 and of Article 9(1)(b) and the first paragraph of Article 10(2) of Directive 2006/115. The referring court notes that, according to case-law of the Bundesverfassungsgericht (Federal Constitutional Court), national legislation which transposes an EU directive must be measured, as a rule, not against the fundamental rights guaranteed by the Grundgesetz für die Bundesrepublik Deutschland (Basic Law for the Federal Republic of Germany) of 23 May 1949 (BGBl. 1949 I, p. 1), but solely against the fundamental rights guaranteed by EU law, where that directive does not allow the Member States any discretion in its transposition. That court also harbours doubts as to the interpretation of those fundamental rights in circumstances such as those at issue in the main proceedings.

25 In those circumstances, the Bundesgerichtshof (Federal Court of Justice) decided to stay the proceedings and to refer the following questions to the Court of Justice for a preliminary ruling:

'(1) Is there an infringement of the phonogram producer's exclusive right under Article 2(c) of Directive 2001/29 to reproduce its phonogram if very short audio snatches are taken from its phonogram and transferred to another phonogram?

(2) Is a phonogram which contains very short audio snatches transferred from another phonogram a copy of the other phonogram within the meaning of Article 9(1)(b) of Directive 2006/115?

(3) Can the Member States enact a provision which — in the manner of Paragraph 24(1) of [the UrhG] — inherently limits the scope of protection of the phonogram producer's exclusive right to reproduce (Article 2(c) of Directive 2001/29) and to distribute (Article 9(1)(b) of Directive 2006/115) its phonogram in such a way that an independent work created in free use of its phonogram may be exploited without the phonogram producer's consent?

(4) Can it be said that a work or other subject matter is being used for quotation purposes within the meaning of Article 5(3)(d) of Directive 2001/29 if it is not evident that another person's work or another person's subject matter is being used?

(5) Do the provisions of EU law on the reproduction right and the distribution right of the phonogram producer (Article 2(c) of Directive 2001/29 and Article 9(1)(b) of Directive 2006/115) and the exceptions or limitations to those rights (Article 5(2) and (3) of Directive 2001/29 and the first paragraph of Article 10(2) of Directive 2006/115) allow any latitude in terms of implementation in national law?

(6) In what way are the fundamental rights set out in [the Charter] to be taken into account when ascertaining the scope of protection of the exclusive right of the phonogram producer to reproduce (Article 2(c) of Directive 2001/29) and to distribute (Article 9(1)(b) of Directive 2006/115) its phonogram and the scope of the exceptions or limitations to those rights (Article 5(2) and (3) of Directive 2001/29 and the first paragraph of Article 10(2) of Directive 2006/115)?'

Consideration of the questions referred

The first and sixth questions

26 By its first and sixth questions, which it is appropriate to consider together, the referring court asks, in essence, whether Article 2(c) of Directive 2001/29 must, in the light of the Charter, be interpreted as meaning that the exclusive right granted to a phonogram producer to reproduce and distribute his or her phonogram allows him to prevent another person from taking a sound sample, even if very short, of his or her phonogram for the purposes of including that sample in another phonogram.

27 Under Article 2(c) of Directive 2001/29, Member States are to provide for the exclusive right of phonogram producers 'to authorise or prohibit direct or indirect, temporary or permanent reproduction by any means and in any form, in whole or in part' of their phonograms.

28 Directive 2001/29 does not define the concept of 'reproduction ... in whole or in part' of a phonogram for the purposes of that provision. The meaning and scope of those words must, as the Court has consistently held, be determined by considering their usual meaning in everyday language, while also taking into account the context in which they occur and the purposes of the rules of which they are part.

29 It is clear from the wording of Article 2(c) of Directive 2001/29 stated in paragraph 27 above, that the reproduction by a user of a sound sample, even if very short, of a phonogram must, in principle, be regarded as a reproduction 'in part' of that phonogram within the meaning of the provision, and that such a reproduction therefore falls within the exclusive right granted to the producer of such a phonogram under that provision.

30 That literal interpretation of Article 2(c) of Directive 2001/29 is consistent, first, with the general objective of that directive which is, as follows from recitals 4, 9 and 10, to establish a high level of protection of copyright and related rights, and, second, the specific objective of the exclusive right of the phonogram producer, referred to in recital 10, which is to protect a phonogram producer's investment. As stated in that recital, the investment required to produce products such as phonograms, is considerable to such an extent that it is necessary in order to guarantee phonogram producers the opportunity of satisfactory returns.

31 However, where a user, in exercising the freedom of the arts, takes a sound sample from a phonogram in order to use it, in a modified form unrecognisable to the ear, in a new work, it must be held that such use does not constitute 'reproduction' within the meaning of Article 2(c) of Directive 2001/29.

32 It must be borne in mind, in that regard, that it follows from recitals 3 and 31 of Directive 2001/29 that the harmonisation effected by that directive aims to safeguard, in particular in the electronic environment, a fair balance between, on the one hand, the interest of the holders of copyright and related rights in the protection of their intellectual property rights now guaranteed by Article 17(2) of the Charter and, on the other hand, the protection of the interests and fundamental rights of users of protected subject matter as well as of the public interest.

33 The Court has thus previously held that there is nothing whatsoever in the wording of Article 17(2) of the Charter or in the Court's case-law to suggest that the intellectual property rights enshrined in that article are inviolable and must for that reason be protected as absolute rights.

34 A balance must be struck between that right and other fundamental rights, including freedom of the arts, enshrined in Article 13 of the Charter, which, in so far as it falls within the scope of freedom of expression, enshrined in Article 11 of the Charter and in Article 10(1) of the European Convention for the Protection of Human Rights and Fundamental Freedoms, signed at Rome on 4 November 1950, affords the opportunity to take part in the public exchange of cultural, political and social information and ideas of all kinds.

35 In that context, it should be noted that the technique of 'sampling', which consists in a user taking a sample from a phonogram, most often by means of electronic equipment, and using the sample for the purposes of creating a new work, constitutes a form of artistic expression which is covered by freedom of the arts, as protected in Article 13 of the Charter.

36 In exercising that freedom, the user of a sound sample, when creating a new work, may decide to modify the sample taken from a phonogram to such a degree that that sample is unrecognisable to the ear in that new work.

37 Thus, to regard a sample taken from a phonogram and used in a new work in a modified form unrecognisable to the ear for the purposes of a distinct artistic creation, as constituting 'reproduction' of that phonogram within the meaning of Article 2(c) of Directive 2001/29 would not only run counter to the usual meaning of that word in everyday language, within the meaning of the case-law set out in paragraph 28 above, but would also fail to meet the requirement of a fair balance set out in paragraph 32 above.

38 In particular, such an interpretation would allow the phonogram producer to prevent another person from taking a sound sample, even if very short, from his or her phonogram for the purposes of artistic creation in such a case, despite the fact that such sampling would not interfere with the opportunity which the producer has of realising satisfactory returns on his or her investment.

39 In the light of the foregoing considerations, the answer to the first and sixth questions is that Article 2(c) of Directive 2001/29 must, in the light of the Charter, be interpreted as meaning that the phonogram producer's exclusive right under that provision to reproduce and distribute his or her phonogram allows him or her to prevent another person from taking a sound sample, even if very short, of his or her phonogram for the purposes of including that sample in another phonogram, unless that sample is included in the phonogram in a modified form unrecognisable to the ear.

The second question

40 By its second question, the referring court asks, in essence, whether Article 9(1)(b) of Directive 2006/115 must be interpreted as meaning that a phonogram which contains sound samples transferred from another phonogram constitutes a 'copy', within the meaning of that provision, of that phonogram.

41 Under Article 9(1)(b) of Directive 2006/115, Member States are to provide phonogram producers with the exclusive right to make available to the public, by sale or otherwise, their phonograms, including copies thereof.

42 Neither Article 9 of Directive 2006/115 nor any other provision of that directive defines the concept of 'copy' within the meaning of that article.

43 That concept must therefore be interpreted by taking into account the legislative context of the provision in question and the purposes of the relevant legislation.

44 It must be borne in mind that the phonogram producer's exclusive distribution right provided for in Article 9(1)(b) of Directive 2006/115 is intended to afford a producer, through adequate legal protection of intellectual property rightholders, with the possibility of recouping investments made by him or her in order to produce phonograms, since those investments can prove to be especially high and risky, as stated in recitals 2 and 5 of Directive 2006/115.

45 In that regard, it is clear from recital 2 of Directive 2006/115 that the protection conferred on a phonogram producer under that directive aims, in particular, to fight piracy, that is, as the Advocate General stated in point 45 of his Opinion, the production and distribution to the public of counterfeit copies of phonograms. The distribution of such copies poses a particularly serious threat to the interests of such phonogram producers in that it is capable of significantly decreasing the revenue that they receive by making phonograms available.

46 As the Advocate General stated in point 46 of his Opinion, only an article which reproduces all or a substantial part of the sounds fixed in a phonogram is, by its nature, intended to replace lawful copies of that phonogram and, therefore, capable of constituting a copy of that phonogram within the meaning of Article 9(1) of Directive 2006/115.

47 That is not, by contrast, the case of an article which, without reproducing all or a substantial part of the sounds fixed in a phonogram, merely embodies sound samples, where relevant in a modified form, transferred from that phonogram for the purposes of creating a new and distinct work from that phonogram.

48 That interpretation of Article 9(1)(b) of Directive 2006/115 in the light of its purposes is supported by the legislative context of which that provision is part.

49 In that regard, as stated in recital 7 of Directive 2006/115, that directive aims to approximate the legislation of the Member States in such a way as not to conflict with the international conventions on which the copyright and related rights laws of many Member States are based.

50 The Geneva Convention is one of those conventions, which, according to its preamble, has, inter alia, the aim of addressing the widespread and increasing unauthorised duplication of phonograms and the damage that this is occasioning to the interests of producers.

51 Article 2 of that convention contains an analogous provision to Article 9(1)(b) of Directive 2006/115 which specifically provides that the producers of phonograms are to be protected against the making and distribution to the public of 'duplicates' of their phonograms without their consent.

52 According to Article 1(c) of the Geneva Convention, a 'duplicate' means an article which contains sounds taken directly or indirectly from a phonogram and which embodies 'all or a substantial part' of the sounds fixed in that phonogram.

53 It is true that the provisions of the Geneva Convention do not form part of the EU legal order, in that, first, the European Union is not a contracting party to that convention and, second, the European Union cannot be regarded as having taken the place of its Member States as regards its application, if only because not all of those States are parties to that convention. The fact remains, however, that it is one of the international conventions referred to in paragraph 49 above and therefore the provisions of Directive 2006/115 must be interpreted, so far as possible, in the light of that convention.

54 It follows that it should be considered, as did the Advocate General in points 46 and 47 of his Opinion, that the concept of 'copy' within the meaning of Article 9(1)(b) of Directive 2006/115 must be interpreted consistently with the same concept as it is used in Article 1(c) and Article 2 of the Geneva Convention.

55 In the light of the foregoing considerations, the answer to the second question is that Article 9(1)(b) of Directive 2006/115 must be interpreted as meaning that a phonogram which contains sound samples transferred from another phonogram does not constitute a 'copy', within the meaning of that provision, of that phonogram, since it does not reproduce all or a substantial part of that phonogram.

The third question

56 The referring court notes that, according to Paragraph 24(1) of the UrhG, applicable by analogy to a phonogram producer's right, an independent work created using the work of another person may be used and exploited without the consent of the author of the work used. It states that such a 'right to free use' does not constitute a derogation from copyright as such but rather sets out an inherent limitation to its scope of protection, based on the idea that it is not possible to conceive of a cultural creation without that creation building upon the previous work of other authors.

57 In those circumstances, since it is clear from the answer to the second question that a reproduction such as that at issue in the main proceedings does not fall within the scope of Article 9(1)(b) of Directive 2006/115, it must be held that, by its third question, the referring court asks, in essence, whether a Member State may, in its national law, lay down an exception or limitation, other than those provided for in Article 5 of Directive 2001/29, to the phonogram producer's right provided for in Article 2(c) of Directive 2001/29.

58 As is clear both from the Explanatory Memorandum to the Proposal for a European Parliament and Council Directive on the harmonisation of certain aspects of copyright and related rights in the Information Society of 10 December 1997 (COM(97) 628 final) and from recital 32 of Directive 2001/29, the list of exceptions and limitations contained in Article 5 of that directive is exhaustive, as the Court has also pointed out on several occasions.

59 In that regard, it has been recalled, in paragraph 32 above, that the harmonisation effected by Directive 2001/29 aims to safeguard, in particular in the electronic environment, a fair balance between, on the one hand, the interest of the holders of copyright and related rights in the protection of their intellectual property rights and, on the other hand, the protection of the interests and fundamental rights of users of protected subject matter as well as of the public interest.

60 The mechanisms allowing those different rights and interests to be balanced are contained in Directive 2001/29 itself, in that it provides inter alia, first, in Articles 2 to 4 thereof, rightholders with exclusive rights and, second, in Article 5 thereof, for exceptions and limitations to those rights which may, or even must, be transposed by the Member States, since those mechanisms must nevertheless find concrete expression in the national measures transposing that directive and in their application by national authorities.

61 The Court has repeatedly held that the fundamental rights now enshrined in the Charter, the observance of which the Court ensures, draw inspiration from the constitutional traditions common to the Member States and from the guidelines supplied by international instruments for the protection of human rights on which the Member States have collaborated or to which they are signatories.

62 Article 5(5) of Directive 2001/29 also contributes to the fair balance mentioned in paragraph 32 above, in that it requires that the exceptions and limitations provided for in Article 5(1) to (4) of the directive be applied only in certain special cases which do not conflict with a normal exploitation of the work or other subject matter and do not unreasonably prejudice the legitimate interests of the rightholder.

63 In that context, to allow, notwithstanding the express intention of the EU legislature, set out in paragraph 58 above, each Member State to derogate from an author's exclusive rights, referred to in Articles 2 to 4 of Directive 2001/29, beyond the exceptions and limitations exhaustively set out in Article 5 of that directive, would endanger the effectiveness of the harmonisation of copyright and related rights effected by that directive, as well as the objective of legal certainty pursued by it. It is expressly clear from recital 31 of that directive that the differences that existed in the exceptions and limitations to certain restricted acts had direct negative effects on the functioning of the internal market of copyright and related rights, since the list of the exceptions and limitations set out in Article 5 of Directive 2001/29 is aimed at ensuring such proper functioning of the internal market.

64 In addition, as is clear from recital 32 of that directive, the Member States are required to apply those exceptions and limitations consistently. The requirement of consistency in the implementation of those exceptions and limitations could not be ensured if the Member States were free to provide for such exceptions and limitations beyond those expressly set out in Directive 2001/29, since the Court has moreover previously held that no provision of Directive 2001/29 envisages the possibility for the scope of such exceptions or limitations to be extended by the Member States.

65 In the light of the foregoing considerations, the answer to the third question is that a Member State cannot, in its national law, lay down an exception or limitation other than those provided for in Article 5 of Directive 2001/29 to the phonogram producer's right provided for in Article 2(c) of that directive.

The fourth question

66 By its fourth question, which concerns a situation in which it is found that there has been an infringement of the phonogram producer's exclusive right provided for in Article 2(c) of Directive 2001/29, the referring court asks, in essence, whether Article 5(3)(d) of that directive must be interpreted as meaning that the concept of 'quotations', referred to in that provision, extends to a situation in which it is not possible to identify the work concerned by the quotation in question.

67 Under Article 5(3)(d) of Directive 2001/29, Member States may provide for exceptions or limitations to the exclusive rights of reproduction and of communication to the public referred to in Articles 2 and 3 of that directive in the case of quotations for purposes such as criticism or review, provided that they relate to a work or other subject matter which has already been lawfully made available to the public, that, unless this turns out to be

impossible, the source, including the author's name, is indicated, and that their use is in accordance with fair practice, and to the extent required by the specific purpose.

68 First of all, it must be considered, as did the Advocate General in points 62 and 63 of his Opinion, that, in the light of the wording in Article 5(3)(d) of Directive 2001/29 which refers to 'a work or other subject-matter', the exception or limitation provided for in that article may apply to the use of a protected musical work, provided that the conditions provided for in that article are satisfied.

69 In particular, for Article 5(3)(d) of Directive 2001/29 to apply, as has been stated in paragraph 67 above, the use in question must be made 'in accordance with fair practice, and to the extent required by the specific purpose', so that the use at issue for the purposes of quotation must not be extended beyond the confines of what it necessary to achieve the informatory purpose of that particular quotation.

70 Since Directive 2001/29 gives no definition of the term 'quotation', the meaning and scope of that term must, according to the Court's settled case-law set out in paragraph 28 above, be determined by considering its usual meaning in everyday language, while also taking into account the legislative context in which it occurs and the purposes of the rules of which it is part.

71 As regards the usual meaning of the word 'quotation' in everyday language, it should be noted that the essential characteristics of a quotation are the use, by a user other than the copyright holder, of a work or, more generally, of an extract from a work for the purposes of illustrating an assertion, of defending an opinion or of allowing an intellectual comparison between that work and the assertions of that user, since the user of a protected work wishing to rely on the quotation exception must therefore have the intention of entering into 'dialogue' with that work, as the Advocate General stated in point 64 of his Opinion.

72 In particular, where the creator of a new musical work uses a sound sample taken from a phonogram which is recognisable to the ear in that new work, the use of that sample may, depending on the facts of the case, amount to a 'quotation', on the basis of Article 5(3)(d) of Directive 2001/29 read in the light of Article 13 of the Charter, provided that that use has the intention of entering into dialogue with the work from which the sample was taken, within the meaning referred to in paragraph 71 above, and that the conditions set out in Article 5(3)(d) are satisfied.

73 However, as the Advocate General stated in point 65 of his Opinion, there can be no such dialogue where it is not possible to identify the work concerned by the quotation at issue.

74 In the light of the foregoing considerations, the answer to the fourth question is that Article 5(3)(d) of Directive 2001/29 must be interpreted as meaning that the concept of 'quotations', referred to in that provision, does not extend to a situation in which it is not possible to identify the work concerned by the quotation in question.

The fifth question

75 As a preliminary matter, it should be noted, as is clear from paragraph 24 above, that the fifth question relates, in particular, to the application by the referring court, for the purposes of disposing of the case in the main proceedings, of Article 2(c) and Article 5(3)(d) of Directive 2001/29, and of Article 9(1)(b) and the first paragraph of Article 10(2) of Directive 2006/115.

76 In that context, the referring court asks whether those provisions of EU law allow the Member States discretion in their transposition, since, according to the case-law of the Bundesverfassungsgericht (Federal Constitutional Court), national legislation which transposes an EU directive must be measured, as a rule, not against the fundamental rights guaranteed by the Basic Law for the Federal Republic of Germany, but solely against the fundamental rights guaranteed by EU law, where that directive does not allow the Member States any discretion in its transposition.

77 As regards the answer to the second and fourth questions, it must be held that, by its fifth question, the referring court asks, in essence, whether Article 2(c) of Directive 2001/29 must be interpreted as constituting measures of full harmonisation.

78 In that regard, it should be stated that, by virtue of the principle of primacy of EU law, which is an essential feature of the EU legal order, rules of national law, even of a constitutional order, cannot be allowed to undermine the effectiveness of EU law in the territory of that State.

79 It should be noted in that connection that, since the transposition of a directive by the Member States is covered, in any event, by the situation, referred to in Article 51 of the Charter, in which the Member States are implementing Union law, the level of protection of fundamental rights provided for in the Charter must be achieved in such a transposition, irrespective of the Member States' discretion in transposing the directive.

80 That said, where, in a situation in which action of the Member States is not entirely determined by EU law, a national provision or measure implements EU law for the purposes of Article 51(1) of the Charter, national authorities and courts remain free to apply national standards of protection of fundamental rights, provided that the level of protection provided for by the Charter, as interpreted by the Court, and the primacy, unity and effectiveness of EU law are not thereby compromised.

81 Thus, it is consistent with EU law for national courts and authorities to make that application subject to the condition, emphasised by the referring court, that the provisions of a directive 'allow [some] discretion in terms of implementation in national law', provided that that condition is understood as referring to the degree of the harmonisation effected in those provisions, since such an application is conceivable only in so far as those provisions do not effect full harmonisation.

82 In the present case, the objective of Directive 2001/29 is to harmonise only certain aspects of the law on copyright and related rights, of which a number of provisions also disclose the intention of the EU legislature to grant a degree of discretion to the Member States in the implementation of the directive.

83 As regards the exclusive right of holders, referred to in Article 2(c) of Directive 2001/29, it has been stated, in paragraph 27 above, that, according to that provision, Member States are to provide for the exclusive right of phonogram producers 'to authorise or prohibit direct or indirect, temporary or permanent reproduction by any means and in any form, in whole or in part' of their phonograms.

84 That provision therefore defines a phonogram producer's exclusive right of reproduction in the European Union in unequivocal terms. Furthermore, that provision is not qualified by any condition, nor is it subject, in its implementation or effects, to any measure being taken in any particular form.

85 It follows that Article 2(c) of Directive 2001/29 constitutes a measure of full harmonisation of the corresponding substantive law.

86 In the light of the foregoing considerations, the answer to the fifth question is that Article 2(c) of Directive 2001/29 must be interpreted as constituting a measure of full harmonisation of the corresponding substantive law.

THINK IT OVER!

1. The *BGH* ruled in favour of the plaintiffs in two distinct rulings (in 2008 and 2012), and concluded that the taking of the shortest pieces of sound recordings shall be authorized. Both rulings practically rejected the concept of *de minimis*. The rulings refused the application of the concept of "*free use*" ("*freie Benutzung*") under § 24 *UrhG*. As this rule is located in the *UrhG*'s chapter on authors, a valid question arose, whether it can be equally applied to related rights holders as well. In the *Metall auf Metall I* ruling the *BGH* still saw the rule analogically applicable to the rights holders; however, the court changed its mind in *Metall auf Metall II*, where the panel excluded the applicability of § 24 *UrhG* in cases where the recognizable melody of the source work had been taken. The *BGH* found the relevant sample of "*Metall auf Metall*" such a melody. Indeed, if the user can directly recreate the given melody without sampling it, he has no right to use the source work directly. Further, the fundamental purpose of § 24 *UrhG*, namely, the development of culture ("*Fortentwicklung des Kulturschaffens*"), is better served, if the secondary artist creates the melody individually. In conclusion, when balancing the various interests of samplers and recording studios, the *BGH* favoured the latter. Later, the German Federal Constitutional Court (hereinafter: *BVerfG*) overturned the BGH's approach to sampling. It declared sampling as a form of free artistic expression in compliance with the German Constitution (Grundgesetz). The *BVerfG* argued that the respective case stems from the clash of recording studios' economic rights (under § 85 I *UrhG* first sentence) and the freedom of users (under §24 *UrhG*). These rights are backed by constitutional norms: Art. 14 I GG on the protection of property interests, and Art. 5 III GG first sentence on artistic freedom, respectively. As both of these fundamental rights are historically important and they are also equally protected by the Constitution, they must be balanced on a case-by-case basis. The *BVerfG* accepted the primacy of artistic freedom over property rights. Following the disagreement of the two German top courts, the *Metall Auf Metall* case finally reached the CJEU.

2. Two main approaches are in conflict currently in Europe regarding the protection of sound recording producers. One approach interprets the sound recording producers' rights broadly, and argues that these rights are absolute, and they provide protection for the (trivial) parts of the recordings as well. The other approach believes that these rights shall be viewed from a competition law perspective as they are oriented to tackle massive piracy of sound recordings. [Ohly (2017), p. 965-966.] One of the strongest pro-copyright positions was taken by AG Szpunar in his Opinion to the *Pelham* case. He expressly refused the application of the *de minimis* exception to sound recordings on various grounds. First, all recorded sounds represent the achievement of the producer, irrespective of the recordings' originality. Second, the *de minimis* exception is a US case-law doctrine, which cannot be applied in a significantly different European copyright environment.

Third, the *de minimis* exception is surrounded by various practical difficulties, especially with respect to the quantitative and qualitative analysis of the samples, and such difficulties might erode the harmonizing effects of the InfoSoc-Directive. Finally, AG Szpunar doubted that the related rights of sound recording producers shall only tackle massive illegal uses, but not trivial infringements. (*Case C-476/17*, Opinion of AG Szpunar, para. 28-39.) Several counter-arguments exist, too. Subject matter and economic rights are totally independent concepts. In *Infopaq*, the CJEU held that the reproduction right is an autonomous concept of copyright law, and it must be interpreted broadly. Nonetheless, independently of the previous argument, the CJEU also discussed whether 11 words may be treated as an original work of expression. (*Case C-5/08*, para. 27 and 48, respectively.) Such logic shall similarly apply with respect to sound recordings. The fact that the reproduction right of phonogram producers is harmonized by the InfoSoc-Directive does not mean that all recordings, and even the smallest sound bites, are protectable subject matter. *Which approach is more balanced from the perspective of copyright law and competition law?*

3. One of the main purposes of copyright law is to protect artistic expressions. Sampling is such an example, where the use of source materials is not piratical, but self-expressive and artistic. It is important to know, whether the economic rights can solely be limited through internal means (norms included in the copyright act, like the exception of citation), or via external means as well. One of such external means can be the fundamental right of freedom of expression. The cat-and-dog life of copyright law and freedom of expression derives from their overlaps. Both of them are fundamental rights, but they protect different – original v. secondary – creators and their expressions. The resolution of the tensions between these rights requires careful balancing. The need for such balance is mentioned by the InfoSoc-Directive, and the Charter of Fundamental Rights of the European Union renders it obligatory, too. The CJEU – following AG Szpunar's Opinion – held that no external limitations exist in copyright law. The CJEU missed to bring its case law closer to (or into full compliance with) the case law of the European Court of Human Rights (ECtHR). The ECtHR allows for the use of external copyright limitations. Although the ECtHR refused to apply the freedom of expression to a professional photographer commercial uses in *Ashby Donald*, and to the founders of The Pirate Bay in *Neij and Sunde*, such conclusions were reached on the facts of the given cases. The ECtHR did not exclude the applicability of the freedom of expressions for the purposes of political or artistic purposes. *Which approach do you favour? The one that refuses the application of external limitations in copyright cases, or the one that accepts such idea?*

Further Case Law

Case C-5/08 - Infopaq International A/S v. Danske Dagblades Forening, Judgement of the Court (Fourth Chamber), 16 July 2009 [ECLI:EU:C:2009:465]

BGH Urt. v. 13.12.2012 (I ZR 182/11) - Metall auf Metall II, *Gewerblicher Rechtsschutz und Urheberrecht*, Heft 6/2013, p. 614-617.

BGH Urt. v. 16.04.2015 (I ZR 225/12) - Goldrapper, *Gewerblicher Rechtsschutz und Urheberrecht*, Heft 12/2015, p. 1189-1198.

BVerfG Urt. v. 31.05.2016 (1 BvR 1585/13) - Zulässige Verwendung von Samples ohne Zustimmung des Tonträgerherstellers - Metall auf Metall, *Gewerblicher Rechtsschutz und Urheberrecht*, Heft 7/2016, p. 690-696.

Case C-469/17 - Funke Medien NRW GmbH v. Federal Republic of Germany, Judgment of the Court (Grand Chamber), 29 July 2019 [ECLI:EU:C:2019:623]

Case C-516/17 - Spiegel Online GmbH v. Volker Beck, Judgment of the Court (Grand Chamber), 29 July 2019 [ECLI:EU:C:2019:625]

ECtHR (Section V), 10 January, 2013, App. No. 36769/08, *Ashby Donald v France*

ECtHR (Section V), 19 February 2013, App. No. 40397/12, *Fredrik Neij and Peter Sunde Kolmisoppi v Sweden*

Case C-476/17 - Pelham GmbH, Moses Pelham, Martin Haas v. Ralf Hütter, Florian Schneider-Esleben, Opinion of AG Szpunar, 12 December 2018 [ECLI:EU:C:2018:1002]

Recommended readings

In English

Ines Duhanic: Copy this Sound! The Cultural Importance of Sampling for Hip Hop Music in Copyright Law - A Copyright Law Analysis of the Sampling Decision of the German Federal Constitutional Court, *Gewerblicher Rechtsschutz und Urheberrecht Internationaler Teil*, Heft 11/2016, p. 1007-1017.

Bernd Justin Jütte: *Sampling of sound recordings in the United States and Germany: revival of a discussion on musical creativity.* In: Paul Torremans (Ed.): Research Handbook on Copyright Law, Second Edition, Edward Elgar, Cheltenham, 2017: p. 273-297.

Bernd Justin Jütte - Henrike Maier: A human right to sample - will the CJEU dance to the BGH-beat?, *Journal of Intellectual Property Law and Practice*, Issue 9/2017, p. 784-796.

Péter Mezei: De Minimis and Artistic Freedom: Sampling on the Right Track?, *Zeszyty Naukowe Uniwersytetu Jagiellońskiego / Jagiellonian University Intellectual Property Law Review*, Issue 1/2018, p. 56-67.

Lionel Bently - Séverine Dusollier - Christophe Geiger - Jonathan Griffiths - Axel Metzger - Alexander Peukert - Martin Senftleben: Sound Sampling, a Permitted Use Under EU Copyright Law? Opinion of the European Copyright Society in Relation to the Pending Reference before the CJEU in Case C-476/17, Pelham GmbH v. Hütter, *IIC - International Review of Intellectual Property and Competition Law*, Issue 4/2019, p. 467-490.

Péter Mezei: Thou Shalt (Not) Sample? New Drifts in the Ocean of Sampling, *Zeitschrift für Geistiges Eigentum / Journal of Intellectual Property Law*, Issue 2/2019, p. 170-198.

Péter Mezei: The Dimensions of the *De Minimis* Exception and Musical Sampling, *Medien und Recht International*, Issue 2/2019, p. 48-51.

Thom Snijders - Stijn van Deursen: The Road Not Take - the CJEU Sheds Light ont he Role of Fundamental Right sin the European Copyright Framework - a Case note ont he Pelham, Spiegel Online and Funke Medien Decisions, *IIC - International Review of Intellectual Property and Competition Law*, Issue 8/2019, p. 1176-1190.

In French

Christophe Caron: Les arrêts du 29 juillet 2019 (1/3) : à propos de l'échantillonnage, *Communication Commerce électronique*, n° 12, Décembre 2019, comm. 75.

Jean-Michel Bruguière: L'équilibre des droits en matière de droit d'auteur selon la Cour de justice: toutes les exceptions, rien que les exceptions mais pas que les exceptions, *La Semaine Juridique Edition Générale*, n° 40, 30 Septembre 2019, 992.

In German

Simon Apel: Bridgeport Music, Inc. v. Dimension Films (USA), Metall auf Metall (Germany) and Digital Sound Sampling - 'Bright Line Rules'?, *Zeitschrift für Geistiges Eigentum / Journal of Intellectual Property Law*, Issue 3/2010, p. 331–350.

Matthias Leistner: Die 'Metall auf Metall' - Entscheidung des BVerfG - Oder: Warum das Urheberrecht in Karlsruhe in guten Handen ist, *Gewerblicher Rechtsschutz und Urheberrecht*, Heft 8/2016, p. 772-777.

Alexis von Kruedener: Die Entscheidung des Bundesverfassungsgerichts zu "Metall auf Metall", *Zeitschrift für Geistiges Eigentum / Journal of Intellectual Property Law*, Heft 4/2016, p. 462-481.

Ansgar Ohly: Hip Hop und die Zukunft der "freien Benutzung" im EU-Urheberrecht Anmerkungen zum Vorlagebeschluss des BGH "Metall auf Metall III", *Gewerblicher Rechtsschutz und Urheberrecht*, Heft 10/2017, p. 964-969.

Simon Apel: Interpretenrecht (§§ 73 ff. UrhG) und Teileschutz. "Metall auf Metall" remixed?, *Zeitschrift für Geistiges Eigentum / Journal of Intellectual Property Law*, Heft 2/2018, p. 162-201.

Simon Apel: Sampling ohne Zustimmung kann Eingriff in Rechte des Tonträgerherstellers darstellen - „Metall auf Metall“, *Multimedia und Recht*, Heft 9/2019, p. 596-603.

Philipp Homar: Enge Handlungsspielräume für das Sampling Anmerkung zu EuGH, Urteil vom 29.7.2019 - C-476/17 - Pelham u. a./Hütter u. a., *Zeitschrift für Urheber- und Medienrecht*, Heft 10/2019, p. 731-737.

In Hungarian

Békés Gergely - Mezei Péter: A sampling megítélése a magyar szerzői jogban, *Iparjogvédelmi és Szerzői Jogi Szemle*, 2010/6. szám, p. 5-32.

Mezei Péter: Új utak a sampling megítélésében, *Acta Universitatis Sapientiae Legal Studies*, 2017/2. szám, p. 309-322.

Mezei Péter: Sampling az Európai Bíróság előtt - Szerzői jogok kontra művészeti szabadság, *Európai Jog*, 2019/3. szám, p. 29-35.

Paku Dorottya: Digitális sampling a magyar és a német szerzői jogban, I. rész, *Iparjogvédelmi és Szerzői Jogi Szemle*, 2019/4. szám, p. 74-108.; II. rész, *Iparjogvédelmi és Szerzői Jogi Szemle*, 2019/4. szám, p. 98-131.

Test Your Knowledge

1. Open Library, a non-profit institution, allows members of the public to become a patron of the library for a fixed yearly subscription fee. Patrons can lend books free of charge. Open Library also operates a request-based photocopy service for the patrons. The photocopy service is not free of charge; however, the library only asks for the production costs of the photocopies. Patrons may request the reproduction of copyrighted or public domain works. In case the patron cannot visit the library in person, she may ask for the delivery of the copy by mail, facsimile or via e-mail. In case the patron asks for sending the copy via mail or facsimile, she has to pay an extra flat rate for the postal or telephone service. The owner of a publishing company (Mr. Publisher) visits you in your office, and reveals that he has evidences that Open Library made 14 copies of the book titled "The history of photocopying" (hereinafter: Book). The Book was published in Turku, Finland, and subsequently in New York, US in 2000. Mr. Publisher owns the copyright of the Book. Four copies were shipped by mail, three copies were sent via e-mail and two by facsimile to the patrons, and the rest was handed over to the patron personally. Mr. Publisher seeks your advice, whether Open Library's practice is illegal or not. Please consider Mr. Publisher's question under the European Union's law.

2. *SpaceCable*, a French cable television company contracted *Throughcom*, a French TV channel owner to transmit the audiovisual contents of the television channel via cable television to its subscribers. The contract was validly formed in 2011 and it covers the transmission of television signals within the borders of France, and it requires that the transmitted signals are received within the home of the subscribers, irrespectively of the type of receiver of the signals (including, but not limited to, televisions, personal computers, portable devices). *SpaceCable* decided in 2017 to publish a new application (*SCableTV*) for tablets that subscribers of *SpaceCable* can download at no price. With the help of *SCableTV* users can stream audiovisual contents on their tablets for no extra fee. *SpaceCable* also published a second application (*SCableTV+*) with which subscribers can bookmark the television programs of *Throughcom*. SpaceCable analyses subscribers' bookmarking practices and publishes the TOP10 bookmarked contents on a daily basis. All *SCableTV+* users can stream the TOP10 contents free of charge. SpaceCable displays short (5 seconds long) advertisements before each TOP10 content is streamed by the end-users. *Throughcom* asks you to discuss whether

the copyrights on the television programs are infringed by *SpaceCable* and/or the respective subscribers.

3. *SzegedAir*, a new air company that launched its first flights between Szeged and multiple European cities within the Schengen area on January 1, 2018. Besides offering sweet Hungarian chocolate, tasty pálinka and hot szalámi on the aircrafts, *SzegedAir* offered on-board personal entertainment for the clients. The clients can register to *SzegedAir*'s website and can directly check-in to the purchased flights there. Following check-in clients are able to download SzegedAir's On-Board Entertainment App (hereinafter: App) from *SzegedAir*'s website. The App works on the SzegedAir's aircrafts between take-off and landing. Travelers might stream movies, episodes of TV-shows, sound recordings and online radio programs that are hosted on SzegedAir's website. The servers of the website are located in Szeged, Hungary. Please analyze, whether SzegedAir needs any permission for such service.

4. *ExpressYourself* (EY) is a Lyon-based P2P file-sharing platform. Its users can provide access to contents through BitTorrent technology via EY's platform. All users shall install EY's client software, place the relevant data in their Shared Folder, and generate a torrent file (a link) that directs other users to the relevant data. EY automatically browses its users' Shared Folder for torrent files. All users are allowed to search for contents via EY's search engine. EY's website provides only a search engine. No "best of" lists are offered, and no contents are directly stored on EY's servers. EY's business model is based on advertisements. EY publicly advertises its system as "a place to share your opinion", whatever opinion that is. EY claims itself as the free marketplace to exchange private music, videos, photos, and scientific papers. *ProtectCopyright* (PC) is an association dedicated to the EU-wide enforcement of copyrights of various stakeholders. PC claims that EY's system is purposefully aimed at assisting the P2P based exchange of copyright protected materials, including third-party music, videos, photos, and scientific papers.

PC seeks your guidance on the following questions:

(1) Is the CJEU's case law on the liability of P2P file-sharing applicable to the instant case?

(2) Is it relevant with respect to the right of communication to the public that "seeding" in BitTorrent means the sharing of individual pieces of the full content, and pieces are unusable on an individual basis? Is there any de minimis threshold under which the right of communication cannot be infringed?

(3) Is it relevant that end-users' computers make contents available to the public (share) automatically, that is, maybe without the actual knowledge of the given end-user?

(4) Can EY defend itself under the Charter of Fundamental Rights, more precisely under the freedom of expression and information (Art. 11.)?

PC is not seeking guidance on evidencing or data protection issues at this stage, although it believes such issues might also have direct relevance in this case.

About the Authors

Péter Mezei is an associate professor of law and the deputy head of the Institute of Comparative Law and Legal Theory, Faculty of Law and Political Sciences, University of Szeged. He is an adjunct professor (dosentti) of the University of Turku, Finland. He is a member of the Hungarian Copyright Expert Board. He is the author of over 120 publications. He has held lectures on comparative digital copyright law at universities in Finland, France, the United States of America, Germany, the United Kingdom and Italy over 60 times since 2007. He prepared the national report for the 18th International Congress of Comparative Law (2010) on the limitations and exceptions in Hungarian copyright law and he co-authored the national report for the 19th International Congress of Comparative Law (2014) on license contracts, free software and Creative Commons. He has participated in several research projects commissioned and financed by the Hungarian Copyright Forum Association, the Hungarian Intellectual Property Office, and the European Commission. He is the founder of the leading Hungarian copyright blog (www.copy21.com). Prof. Mezei may be contacted at mezei@juris.u-szeged.hu.

Dóra Hajdú defended her PhD thesis on copyright law in 2016 in a joint program between the University of Szeged (Hungary) and the Paris-Saclay University (France). She has successfully passed the French bar exam and recently started to work as an intellectual property in-house counsel at a major software development company. Author of a book analysing author's exclusive rights exercised collectively and several articles, she contributes to the Copy21 blog. Ms. Hajdú may be contacted at hajdudora.hd@gmail.com.

Luis Javier Capote-Pérez is a Lecturer in Private Law at the University of La Laguna, San Cristóbal de La Laguna, Tenerife, Spain. He holds a Ph.D. in Law from the University of La Laguna. His research interests include tourism, Land Register, family law, cultural and intellectual property and gender perspective of private law. Professor Capote-Pérez is a member of many university institutions, like Cultural Cathedra "Francisco Tomás y Valiente" or "Radio Campus" – the oldest university radio station in Spain – of the University of La Laguna. He is also a member of the Editorial Board of the "Santander Art and Culture Law Review" and of UNESCO Cultural Chair "Cultural Property Law" of the University of Opole. He has been Acting Judge at the Appellation Court of Santa Cruz de Tenerife since 2006. He works also in the area of divulgation, acting as a member of the Scientific Divulgation Cultural Chair of the University of La Laguna and creating many materials for legal divulgation. Some of these materials are available in audiovisual format in ULLMedia, the YouTube channel of the University of La Laguna. Prof. Capote-Pérez may be contacted at lcapote@ull.es.

Jie Qin is an associate professor of Intellectual Property Law of Civil & Commercial Law School, and the Vice Dean of the School of International Education, Southwest University of Political Science & Law. Her research is focused on intellectual property law, international private law and translational education. She has hosted dozens of research projects run by the Ministry of Education of China as well as the Chongqing Academy of Social Sciences and SWUPL over the past five years. She has published numerous papers and research reports. She is the co-author of the book titled *Introduction to Intellectual Property, Legal Protection of Trade Secret* and *Intellectual Property & Competition.* She is the translator of the book *Failing Law Schools, International Encyclopedia of Comparative Law.* Professor Qin was a visiting professor of the University of Antwerp Belgium, the Prince Sonkhla University Thailand, the University of Montana, the Gonzaga University, and the Case Western University of United States. Professor Qin may be contacted at qinjie@swupl.edu.cn or at 478487540@qq.com.